Perfect Places

Second Edition

Cover Photo

The Garden Court
The Sheraton Palace, San Francisco

The Sheraton Palace's Garden Court may be the most exquisite room in San Francisco, and it's undoubtedly the finest skylit dining room in the country.

Completed in 1909, its crystal chandeliers, marble columns and gold detailing reflect the opulence of France's *belle epoque*. No expense was spared in the hotel's original construction or in its recent two-year, $150 million restoration.

As part of the transformation, all 25,000 pale amber and silvery glass panes in the Garden Court's translucent dome were individually taken down, cleaned, repaired if necessary and replaced in a re-built armature under a handsome new outer skylight. The result of these painstaking efforts is a resplendent and luminous space that has few equals anywhere in the world.

Perfect Places

Northern California

Over 350 Exceptional Locations For

PARTIES, SPECIAL EVENTS
& BUSINESS FUNCTIONS

Lynn Broadwell
Jan Brenner

Hopscotch Press · Berkeley · California

Perfect Places

Library of Congress Cataloging-in-Publication Data

Broadwell, Lynn   1951—

Perfect Places ©

Second Edition
Includes Index

Library of Congress Catalog Card Number Pending
ISBN 0-9625155-3-1

Inside Illustration: Michael Tse, Lynn Broadwell

Printed in the U.S.A.

For information, write or call:

HOPSCOTCH PRESS
1563 Solano Ave., Suite 135
Berkeley, CA 94707
510/525-3379

For Matthew.
You've been a really good boy.
Uncomplaining and patient throughout.
Although you're too young to understand exactly why
Mommie has to stay at the office at night and on weekends,
you already know how to be supportive.
Thanks.
I love you.

Contents

Restaurant Private Dining Room Guide

Special Event Locations

The Picnic Directory

Service Directory

Acknowledgements

I'd like to thank my husband,
Doug Broadwell,
for his consistent support and
unwavering confidence in me.

I can only hope that
at some point, mine sweet,
I will be able to make your dream
come true.

A Personal Note

If you're like me, you love to have really good information at your fingertips—the kind that's intelligently compiled, easy to assimilate and most importantly, easy to use. *Perfect Places* is designed with this in mind, so I know you'll find it an invaluable resource.

But no matter how hard I've tried to make the information in *Perfect Places* completely accurate, it isn't. Some facilities give us incorrect data. Some go out of business. And when places change ownership or management, everything can be turned upside down overnight. If you add these factors to normal changes that occur over time, you'll understand why it's difficult to make a large body of data absolutely perfect.

So what can you do to insure you're getting correct information? The answer is simple:

CALL AND CONFIRM OUR DATA
WITH THE FACILITY COORDINATOR OR MANAGER.

Read them the text from *Perfect Places* that pertains to their location, and get them to *verify* that it's still current. If it isn't, jot down the new information directly into your book.

I can't stress enough how important is it to take this final step.

If you do your research using our guide, and confirm everything with each facility you contact, you can't go wrong.

Preface

Searching for a place to have an event is not easy and usually not much fun. Whether it's an office party, luncheon meeting or family get-together, the amount of time consumed in calling up places, asking questions and compiling information can be mind-boggling. And who has that kind of time nowadays? Certainly not people who work full time. Since most functions are planned by people who are not event professionals, this book is designed to cut your search time by over ninety percent and help you plan your event like a professional.

I certainly understand how much time it can take. My foray into location guidebooks started with the first edition of *Here Comes The Guide*, which grew out of my own frustration in trying to find a place to tie the knot. I was absolutely amazed that nobody had a comprehensive list with the kind of detailed information I needed. I discovered a patchwork quilt of information. Each Chamber of Commerce was different. Some had locations all organized and ready to mail out; others had nothing and knew nothing. Event planners and caterers had lots of information, but most were too busy to describe over the phone all the places in their respective repertoires. *Here Comes The Guide*, which is now in its third edition, was designed specifically to help couples locate wedding and reception sites in the Greater Bay Area. I knew there was a need for this kind of resource, but had no idea that my book would turn into a regional best-seller. Now, I get calls and letters every week from people who feel they've benefited tremendously from the type of information my books provide. When you start receiving emotional quotes like, "It was a godsend" and "It saved my life," you know you've hit on something big.

Since I started publishing in 1989, the event industry has undergone some changes—most resulting from a downturn in the economy. Businesses have tightened their belts, reducing both the number as well as the overall amount of funds spent on meetings and special events. At some companies, the costly annual gala has been changed to a smaller scale, budget-minded company picnic. Some companies no longer have off-site functions, eliminating the need for special event sites altogether. Family social functions, seen as an extraneous expense, have been cut back or put on hold.

As you can imagine, the service market which grew tremendously through the 80s as more and more people joined the ranks of the events industry, has had trouble with this downward spiral. As a whole, the industry is struggling with smaller pieces of a diminishing special event pie. Event planners compete for fewer corporate clients; caterers have had to be more creative with reduced budgets.

Surprisingly, the two areas that have been growing by leaps and bounds are the *wedding* and *facility-related* markets.

People continue to get married. Although some brides and grooms have tightened their reception budgets, weddings, in general, have turned out to be recession-proof. Also, we've observed a surprising proliferation of event sites. In the last five years, there has been a dramatic increase in the number of event locations because site owners and managers see events as a way to generate revenue. Bed and breakfasts, summer camps, private estates, schools and clubs and homeowners have all turned to the events market as a way to offset increased operating costs. The most interesting trend we've noted is that restaurants are moving into the event business in a big way. Private dining rooms are now being promoted for business meetings, luncheons and rehearsal dinners. Many of the restaurants we contacted are more than willing to close for a private party, as long as there is a guaranteed guest minimum.

The media has shown more interest in special event facilities because the public is asking for more and better resources. On talk shows, I always field questions from audiences interested in unique sites for birthdays, anniversaries, meetings, retreats, awards ceremonies, fund raising events and celebrations. Clearly, there is a genuine need for a comprehensive event location guide.

Perfect Places—with event sites for everybody and every pocketbook—is the essential resource for planning an event in Northern California. Would you like to rent an island? No problem. Interested in a private dining room in one of the poshest restaurants in San Francisco? How about a cocktail party in a private mansion in Pacific Heights or a corporate picnic at Marine World Africa, USA? Each new edition of this book will expand and change with trends in the event industry, and we'll continue to bring you more interesting and unusual locations in the years to come. So don't pick an ordinary place when so many extraordinary ones are available. The place *does* make all the difference.

Introduction

This is a unique guidebook.

Perfect Places is the only book in Northern California that offers practical tips and step-by-step guidance for reviewing, evaluating and selecting both event sites and services. It will save you an enormous amount of time, *and* since detailed information about fees, deposits and in-house catering costs are included, you can comparison shop and save money, too.

This book is loaded with invaluable information that has been selectively compiled with your needs in mind.

We've tried to anticipate the questions you'd ask and collect data that is important for decision-making. In this edition, we've improved some of the features and have added a lot of new information to make it more useful to you. If you find that the most popular spots are already booked (especially during the holiday season), you'll still have a long list of wonderful locations from which to choose. You'll discover delightful places that you might not have found on your own and ideas for planning events that you might never have considered. This book is intended to open your eyes to a variety of new possibilities. We give you tips to help you quickly evaluate and select dozens of sites and their services—and no matter what kind of place you finally choose, *Perfect Places* is designed to make all your planning efforts a lot easier.

We've added two new features: the *Private Dining Room Guide* and *The Picnic Directory*.

This edition has broadened its scope of special event locations. Private dining rooms in restaurants now constitute the fastest growing segment of our industry because people have less and less time to handle the details of event planning. For groups, restaurants offer enormous flexibility with the least amount of worry. Hush-hush meetings, office celebrations, social get-togethers and rehearsal dinners can be arranged speedily, with just two or three phone calls. Some restaurants have separate rooms where you can close the doors; others will let you rent the entire place with a guaranteed minimum. Menus can be customized and special amenities, such as balloons, cakes, favors or wines, can all be arranged by restaurant staff or in-house event planners.

The *Private Dining Room Guide* is our response to the many requests we've received for information about event spaces in restaurants. Because it's new, it's not as extensive as the other sections of the book. If you'd like to suggest additional restaurants that have spaces for special events, don't hesitate to call or write to us, and we'll consider them for upcoming editions.

The other special feature we've added this year is *The Picnic Directory*. As more companies respond to the economy by downsizing and reducing the cost of events, the number of business-related picnics has increased. The problem is that most of the people responsible for planning the company picnic don't know where to go. In Northern California, as urban growth encroaches into undeveloped open space, many privately owned picnic areas have disappeared. The ones that are left are few and overbooked. Public parks are often used for events, but with maintenance decreasing due to California's financial woes, it's hard to know which are best for company or association picnics, family reunions or other social events. As with the *Private Dining Room Guide*, we'd love to hear from you. If you have any suggestions for great group picnic spots, let us know.

Our service directory is different—we've screened everyone for you!

If you worry about locating top-notch services—don't. *We've done all the legwork.*

Finding a first-rate caterer, band, florist, cake maker or photographer can be difficult. How do you know they're really good at what they do? We developed a *screened* service directory at the back of this guide to bring you the best services we could find. *Screened* means that we did our homework so you don't have to. We required 10 to 30 trade references to qualify each of these service providers for our publication because we wanted to make sure that the people we recommend are not only technically competent, but professional, personable and serious about providing good service.

Unlike other publications that take ad dollars indiscriminately, we wouldn't allow a vendor to advertise with us until they'd received a great review from other professionals in the industry. When you ask 10 to 30 people in the event trade about the quality of someone's product or service, ultimately you figure out who's good and who's not. Given the enormous amount of work we did to qualify our advertisers, we feel very confident about giving a *personal endorsement* to each and every one of them. We think you'll save lots of time and aggravation if you call these folks first, before you search through the yellow pages or elsewhere. These service providers are not ordinary—they're the best in the business.

If you can't find the perfect spot in *Perfect Places*, just call us.

I can't publish the names of all the sites I've discovered, so I keep computer files that include those locations that missed our print deadlines as well as exclusive locations that want to be known strictly by word-of-mouth. I've personally inspected, screened and reviewed hundreds of places. As a consequence, I'm often sought after as a location scout, conducting searches for clients seeking particularly hard-to-find spots. Even with over 350 places in this book and over 900 in the computer, I'm still finding out about more sites because people like you call in with new leads. And I'm always impressed by the countless variations in ambiance, price and services available to those willing to explore a bit further. So if you can't find what you're looking for in this guide, call us. We'll explain how our location scouting service works and you can decide if you want more help.

Use our helpful matrix to speed up your search.

One of the greatest benefits of using *Perfect Places* is the enormous amount of time you'll save. And, you can save even more time using the find-it-fast feature. Because of the sheer number of facilities included in this book, we've designed a helpful matrix, placed conveniently in front of the main body of *Perfect Places*. It enables you to breeze through all of the entries by city, capacity and other important criteria, and preselect those sites you wish to read about in more depth.

Private dining rooms are a hot commodity.

In addition to requests for cocktail reception, rehearsal dinner and unusual party spots, we're getting phone inquiries from all over the U.S. for private dining rooms. People want to know where they can go for meeting luncheons and dinners, bachelor parties, wedding showers and family get-togethers. It's not too hard to understand why. They just don't have extra time to plan a party.

Private dining rooms in restaurants are the perfect solution for smaller celebrations. Often, one call does it all. If the standard menu isn't exactly what you want, many restaurants will customize one for you. Staff, tables, chairs, linens and silver are included at no extra charge. Corporate gifts, cakes, flowers and special wines can be arranged, too. There is hardly a faster, more efficient way of hosting an event than going through a restaurant that has a private dining room. If you need this kind of facility, we've compiled a list of Northern California restaurants that love to host special events. Turn to the *Restaurant Private Dining Room Guide* for detailed descriptions.

Perfect Places covers Northern California.

Take advantage of the fact that Northern California is home to some of the most outstanding facilities in the United States. There are so many locations that offer exceptional environments, top-notch cuisine and professional event services, you're sure to find a special place that suits your needs. So grab this guide and explore! We've covered Sacramento, Tahoe, the Gold Country, the North Coast and the Monterey Peninsula as well as the central Bay Area. When you discover the perfect spot for your event, you'll feel confident that you made the right choice because you did your homework.

How To Use This Guidebook

A Few Thoughts On Picking a Geographical Location

Your first big decision is to select a geographical location that will make sense to you and the majority of your guests or business associates. If you've planned a function close to home or the office, there's little to consider. But if you pick a spot out of town, you need to think about the logistics of getting everyone to your event site.

If there are few financial or other constraints, then it really doesn't matter how far from home base you go. If, however, you live or work in San Francisco and want to have a seminar in Carmel, it's worth considering the total driving time to and from your destination, whether people are bringing spouses and whether an overnight stay will be required. When the distance is over two hours driving time, an overnight stay may be in order. A distant location may limit you to a Saturday night event since guests may have to spend many hours traveling. And if you have guests arriving by plane, it's certainly helpful if there's an airport nearby. If you'll be serving alcohol, and you know your associates or family members enjoy drinking, try to house them close to the event site. Check out the average temperatures where you plan to hold your event—it may be sunny in Marin in June but foggy and cold in Monterey.

There's no reason why you can't contemplate a party in Napa Valley or a company retreat in the wilds of Big Sur. Just remember that the further out you go, the more time it will take—and you may end up having to delegate the details of event planning to someone else.

Selecting an Event Location

Identify What Kind of Function You Want and Establish Selection Criteria Early

Before you jump into the facility descriptions in *Perfect Places*, take stock of all your needs and wants. Here are some basics:

Your Budget

This is a big one. Throwing a party or hosting an event can be *very* expensive, and you'd be surprised how many people are unrealistic about what they can afford. Most novice planners aren't very experienced with event budgeting and don't know how to estimate what locations, products and services will ultimately cost.

To be realistic, you have to be aware of all the details involved in staging an event, know what they cost, and be able to handle some basic arithmetic. For instance, the fundraiser who has $5,000 dollars for 250 guests should realize that $20 per guest won't go very far. Tax and gratuity combined can consume an average of 25% of the food and beverage budget (the range is 22–28%). If you subtract that 25% from $20, you have $15 left. If you also serve alcohol at $6/person, you're down to $9/person for food. That's not enough for a seated meal, let alone the location rental fees, band, flowers, printed materials, etc.

Before you make any major decisions or commit any of your funds for specific items, take a serious look at your total budget and make sure it can cover *all* your anticipated expenses. If it can't, it's time to make some hard decisions. If you have a very large guest list and a small pocketbook, you may need to shorten the list or simplify some of the amenities offered. No matter who foots the bill, be advised that doing the homework here really counts. Pin down your costs at the beginning of the planning stage and get all estimates in writing.

Style

Do you know what kind of function you want? Will it be a formal or informal event, a traditional affair or a creative, innovative party? Will it be held at night by flickering candlelight or during the day, indoors or outdoors? Will guests be dressed in black tie or in Western country garb? Know what you want before you look for a location or the sheer number of options will be overwhelming.

Guest Count

How many people are anticipated? Many facilities want a guaranteed guest count 60 to 90 days in advance of your function—and they will require a deposit based on the figure you give them. It's important to know what the numbers are early on in order to plan your budget. Once you have a firm number in mind, use it to select the right spot.

Seasonal Differences

The time of year and hours of the day may be major factors in site selection, so be clear about the seasonal temperatures where your event is planned. There's a good reason why most outdoor venues in Northern California are booked spring through fall. If you're arranging an outdoor winter party, make sure you have a backup plan that includes an inside space. If your budget can cover the costs, tents are another option to insure against inclement weather.

Special Requirements

Some places have strict rules and regulations. If most of your guests smoke, then pick a location that does not restrict smoking. If alcohol is going to be consumed, make sure it's allowed and find out if bar service needs to be licensed. If dancing or a big band are critical, then limit yourself to those locations that can accommodate them and the accompanying decibels. Do you have children, seniors or disabled guests on your list? If so, you need to plan for them, too. It's essential that you identify the special factors that are important for your event before you sign a contract.

Parking

Where to put your car is usually not a critical factor if you get married outside an urban area. However, if you're planning a party in downtown Sacramento, San Francisco, Monterey or Carmel, make sure you understand what arrangements need to be made to facilitate parking.

Professional Help

If you are a busy person with limited time to plan and execute an event, pick a facility that offers complete coordination services, from catering and flowers to decorations and bar service. Or better yet, hire a professional event or meeting planner. Either way, you'll make your life considerably easier by having someone else handle the details.

Selecting a Location for Business Functions

Business Function Ambiance

If you're setting up a retreat for small groups to discuss vital issues, consider a quiet spot, conducive to contemplation, renewal or creative thinking. If you've got a large conference, note that *Perfect Places* highlights full-service hotels as well as many unusual facilities that can accommodate big groups. You *can* set the ambiance or tone of the workshop, seminar or meeting by selecting the right location.

Business Services

Many conferences require full service capability, including private phone lines, fax, audio-visual equipment and all-day coffee/food service. Make sure you know precisely what's necessary for the function to flow smoothly and submit an itemized list to the facility. Request conference materials and equipment well in advance so you don't end up competing with the group down the hall for a projector or screen. One of the most common mistakes is to bring in audio visual equipment, only to find that there are no meeting rooms which can be darkened enough for presentations. It's helpful to organize breaks and something for participants to do during relief periods. Pick a place that can provide other non-meeting amenities such as a spa, a beach or bicycles. If the business event is several days long, supplemental activities are important to revitalize meeting-weary participants.

Food Quality

Sometimes, food accounts for the greatest portion of the event budget. Consequently, menu selection is a big deal, and countless hours are spent poring over menu details. Food should also be an important consideration for business meetings, conferences and seminars—but often it's not. Given the amount of money you will spend on this item alone, you should be concerned about the type, quantity and quality of meals. If in-house catering is provided, we suggest you pay critical attention to the facility's choices and services offered prior to paying a facility deposit. Details make a big difference and might not cost much more. For instance, what does Continental Breakfast really mean—Sanka and a jelly donut or freshly brewed coffee and a flaky croissant? Try sampling different menu options in advance if you can. If you'd like to see how a facility handles setup and food presentation, work with the caterer to arrange a visit about a half an hour prior to a similar function.

Hidden Costs

This may come as a surprise, but not all business services and equipment are covered in the rental fee. Get it in writing! The cost of all extraneous elements can really add up. Watch out for those facilities that hide the true cost of renting their space by having a low rental fee. It is possible to get nickeled and dimed for all the extras: tables, chairs, linens, glassware, security, valet service and audio-visual equipment. Save yourself a big headache by understanding exactly what's included in the rental fee and what's not before you sign any contract.

The important point we're trying to make here is that if you know what kind of event you want, and are clear about the essentials, your search will be made faster and easier. If you try to pick a location before you've made basic decisions, selection will be a struggle and it will take longer to find a spot that will make you happy.

Understanding the Information in Perfect Places

Each location entry in this book follows the same format. To help you understand our thinking, what follows below is an explanation of the selection criteria, in the same order as they appear.

Reserve In Advance

What we've indicated here is only a suggested timeframe for making reservations in advance. Naturally, if a popular spot books twelve months in advance for special events and you want to have a function there next week, your choice may prove unrealistic. If the reserve in advance information is in conflict with your plans, don't despair! Find out if your particular date is available. Who knows? There are always cancellations and occasionally a popular date is not booked. If there's a location that seems just perfect for you, take a chance and call, even if it seems an unlikely possibility. For meetings, especially luncheon meetings, the suggested timeframe is much shorter. Many locations can schedule meetings with little advance notice.

Description

Once you've selected a geographical area and you're clear about your needs, then thoroughly review all the sites listed in your area of preference. If you're pressed for time, you can read through the find-it-fast matrix first to preview facilities for location, capacity and other critical factors. Then, you can forge ahead to the main body of *Perfect Places* and read the descriptions of only those sites that seem to be a good fit, based on your preliminary preview. If the facility still appeals to you after you've read the description and it fulfills your location requirements, mark it with a ✔ and then move on to capacity.

Capacity

By now you should have a rough idea of how many people will be attending. If not, you may be in trouble, since many facilities want a deposit based on an estimated guest count. Look at the capacity figures for each event location. *Seated* or *sit-down* capacity refers to guests seated at tables. *Reception* or *standing* capacity refers to a function where the majority of guests are not seated, such as a cocktail/hors d'oeuvres reception. *Theater-style* refers to auditorium row seating, with chairs arranged closely together, and *classroom-style* refers to an organized table and chair arrangement, usually in rows. Put a ✔ next to those facilities that fit your requirements. If you're planning well in advance and don't have your guest list whittled down yet, then you'll just have to estimate and refine the count as the date draws near. There's a big difference in cost and planning effort between an intimate party of 60 and a large function with over 500 guests. Pin down your numbers as soon as you can.

Meeting Rooms

We've highlighted those rooms or areas which can accommodate meetings and have listed the number of participants each space can hold.

Fees and Deposits

Look at the data regarding fees and deposits and *remember that these figures change regularly and usually in one direction—up*. It's a good idea to confirm the information we give in *Perfect Places* with the restaurant or facility you're calling, just to make sure it's still valid. If you're planning far in advance, anticipate increases by the time your function occurs. Once you're definite about your location, try to lock in your fees in a contract, protecting yourself from possible rate increases later. Make sure you ask about every service provided and are clear about all of the extras that can really add up. Don't be surprised to see taxes and gratuities (or service charges) in set amounts applied to the total bill if the facility provides restaurant or catering services. Although it may seem redundant to indicate that tax and service charges are additional in each entry, we find that most people forget (or just don't want to accept the painful reality) that 23–28% will be applied to the food and beverage total.

Sometimes deposits are non-refundable. If the deposit is a large percentage of the total bill, make sure you know whether it's refundable or not. If refundable, then read the cancellation policy thoroughly. Also make sure you understand the policies which will ensure you get your cleaning and security deposit returned in full.

Food costs vary considerably. Carefully plan your menu with the caterer, event consultant or chef. Depending on the style of service and the type of food being served, your total food bill will vary dramatically, even if provided by the same caterer. Expect a multi-course seated meal with beverages to be the most expensive part of your event.

Alcohol is expensive, too. Look closely at the alcohol restrictions. Can you bring your own wine or champagne? Does the facility charge a corkage fee? Some facilities discourage you from bringing your own (BYO) by charging exorbitant fees for removing the cork (corkage) and pouring. Other places have limited permits which do not allow them to serve alcohol or restrict them from serving certain kinds; some will let you serve alcohol, others will require someone with a license. Make sure you know what's allowed. Decide what your budget is for alcohol and determine what types you're willing to provide. *And keep in mind that the catering fees you are quoted rarely include the cost of alcohol.* A comment about trends in alcohol consumption is warranted. People are drinking less wine and hard alcohol than ever before and consumption of mineral water is on the rise. If you provide the alcohol, make sure you keep your purchase receipts so you can return any unopened bottles.

How much money can you afford to spend? Facility deposits are usually not large, but sometimes the rental fees plus food and beverage services can add up to $30,000 or more, depending on the location and number of guests. Be sure you have a sensible handle on your budget and read all the fine print before you sign any contract.

Availability

Some facilities are available 7am to 2am for special events; others offer very limited "windows." If you'd like to save some money, consider a weekday or weeknight function. For holiday parties, you should plan at least 6–12 months in advance. Even the most sought-after places have openings midweek and during non-peak months, and at reduced costs. *Facilities want your business and are more likely to negotiate terms and prices if they have nothing else scheduled.* Again, read all the fine print carefully and ✔ those facilities that have time slots that meet your needs. If you inquire about the date you have in mind, and the reply is that it's already booked, it doesn't hurt to ask if someone actually *confirmed* that date by paying a deposit or signing a contract. If they haven't, you may be in luck.

Services/Amenities

Most facilities and restaurants provide something in the way of services. We've attempted to give you a brief description of what each individual location has to offer. Because of space limitations, we have shortened words and developed a key to help you decipher our abbreviated notations. Please refer to the *Services/Amenities and Restrictions Key* for clarification and explanation. When you become familiar with our notation style, go back to Services/Amenities and put a ✔ where your requirements are met by the facility. You'll be able to quickly see what essentials on your list are covered and which ones are not.

Previewing a Facility

Once you've tallied up all your ✔ marks, you should have a handful of sites that require a personal preview. If you plan to visit a lot of locations, here are some handy tips.

Appointments

Should you attempt to drive by first or schedule an appointment? If you reviewed the description and liked what you read, then we recommend you make an appointment to see each location. Sometimes the exterior of a great building looks worse than the beautiful and secluded garden it hides from the street. And sometimes, the reverse is true—a stunning facade will attract you and upon entry you discover an interior that doesn't appeal to your taste.

When you call for appointments, don't forget to ask for cross streets. Some places are hidden and take forever to find. Try to cluster your visits so that you can easily drive from one place to another without backtracking. Get a good, detailed street map of the area, and before you go to the sites, locate each one on the map in red or another contrasting color. Schedule at least 30 minutes per facility and arrange for ample driving time in between each stop. The key here is efficiency. Don't over-schedule yourself, however. It's best to view places when you're fresh. If you've reached your saturation point after five visits and you still have several more to go, those last places might get "bad reviews" simply because you're looking at them through bleary eyes and can't absorb any more information. While you want to accomplish as much as you can in as brief a time as possible, you will ultimately do yourself a disservice if your judgment is clouded by fatigue.

Make sure when you're previewing a facility to check out the restrooms, dance floor and kitchen facilities. Sometimes it's easy to get so carried away by a great view or an extraordinary gold ceiling that you forget a major item—like a place for the band.

Be Organized

Whether you're visiting a handful of facilities or canvassing an entire region, be organized. After you've decided on your event requirements, selected the facilities you want to see and arranged a workable visiting schedule, there are still things you can do to make this process easy on yourself.

Bring a camera. Take pictures of whatever you want to recall about a place—the front exterior, the landscaped patio, etc. A Polaroid is wonderful because it gives you instant "memories." If you bring a 35mm camera, we recommend asa 200 print film which is usually fast enough to take interior shots. Also, bring plenty of film. Make sure to write the name of the facility on the back of photos—you'd be surprised how easy it is to confuse various sites when you've got a dozen of them competing for space in your mind and you can't remember which garden or dining room corresponds to which place. And, if you have a video camera, by all means, bring it along.

Bring a tape recorder. During or after each visit, record your immediate impressions. Your likes, dislikes and any other observations can be quickly recorded. You can write up your notes when you have more time. If you don't have a recorder, jot down your comments in *Perfect Places* itself or in a notebook. Observe not only the physical surroundings, but pay close attention to how you are treated by the manager, the owner or the event coordinator. No matter how you do it, thorough note-taking is crucial if you are going to be able to adequately evaluate everything you have seen and heard.

File everything. Many facilities will provide you with pamphlets, menus, rate charts and other materials. One good way to handle the deluge is to put each facility's paperwork in a 9" x 12" manila envelope with its name on it. A binder with plastic pocket inserts is also handy. The idea is to avoid having to sort through a pile of things later. You want to keep your notes, photos and handouts clearly identified and easily accessible.

Bring snacks. Driving from place to place can make you hungry and thirsty. If you take a little something to eat you can munch en route and keep your energy level up.

Working with a Facility
Confirm All the Details

We can't over emphasize the importance of accurate information. *When you make the initial phone call, confirm that the information presented here is still valid.*

We have asked each site to give us current information, but we know from long experience that *facilities change prices and policies overnight.* Show or read to the site's representative the information that refers to his/her facility, and have them inform you of any changes. If there have been significant increases in fees or new restrictions that you can't live with, cross it off your list and move on. If the facility is still a contender, request a tour.

Once you have determined that the physical elements of the place suit you, it's time to discuss details. Ask about services and amenities or fees that may not be listed in the book and make a note of them. Outline your plans to the representative and make sure that the facility can accommodate your particular needs. If you don't want to handle all the details yourself, find out what the facility is willing and able to do, and if there will be additional fees for their assistance. Facilities often provide planning services for little or no extra charge. If other in-house services are offered, such as flowers or music, you need to inquire about the quality of each service provider and whether or not substitutions can be made. If outside vendors are called in to supply these services, you might want to ascertain whether the facility receives a commission. If you prefer to use your own vendors, will the facility charge you an extra fee?

The Importance of Rapport

Another factor to consider is your rapport with the person(s) you are working with. Are you comfortable? Do they listen well and respond to your questions directly? Do they inspire trust and confidence? Are they warm and enthusiastic or cold, businesslike and aloof? If you have doubts, you need to resolve them before embarking on a working relationship with these folks—no matter how wonderful the facility itself is. Discuss your feelings with them, and if you're still not completely satisfied, get references and call them. If at the end of this process you still have lingering concerns, you may want to eliminate the facility from your list even though it seems perfect in every other way.

Working with a Caterer

Get References and Look for Professionalism

If you are selecting your own caterer, don't just pick one at random out of the yellow pages. Get references from friends and acquaintances or, better yet, call the caterers listed in the *Perfect Places* service directory. We've thoroughly screened these companies and can unequivocally assure you that they are in the top 5% of the industry in terms of quality and service. We keep all of their references on file, just in case you'd like to get more details about them. Feel free to call us and ask questions.

Every caterer is different. Some offer only preset menus while others will help you create your own. Prices and menus vary enormously, so know what you want and what you are willing to spend. After you have talked to several caterers and have decided which ones you want to seriously consider, get references for each one and call them. Ask not only about the quality of the food, but about the ease of working with a given caterer. You'll want to know if the caterer is professional: fully prepared and equipped, punctual and organized. You may also want to know if the caterer is licensed and whether he/she has a kitchen approved by the Department of Health. Ask the caterer where the food is being prepared. Does he/she carry workmen's compensation and liability insurance? Although this level of inquiry may seem unnecessary or complicated, these questions are intended to increase your critical thinking about your catering choices.

Facility Requirements

Often the facility which allows outside caterers will have specific requirements. Whether they have to be licensed and bonded, out by 11pm or fastidiously clean—make sure that before you hire a caterer, he or she is compatible with your site. In fact, even if the facility does not require it, it's a good idea to have your caterer visit the place in advance to become familiar with any special circumstances or problems that might come up. You'll notice throughout *Perfect Places* the words "provided" or "preferred" after the word Catering. Sites that have an exclusive caterer or only permit you to select from a preferred list do so because each wants to eliminate most of the risks involved in having a caterer on the premises who is not accustomed to working in that environment. Exclusive or preferred caterers have achieved this exalted status because they provide consistently good services. If your facility has confidence in them, generally you can, too. Whether you are working with one of your facility's choices or your own, make sure that your contract includes everything you have agreed on before you sign it.

Working with an Event or Meeting Planner

Consultants Handle Details

Hiring a professional may be a wise choice. If you can afford it, engaging someone to "manage" your event can be a godsend. A good consultant will ask all the right questions, determine exactly what you want, and put together your entire affair. Although your role will largely be to select from the options presented and write checks, you should not give up being a decision-maker. It's your event—no one else should decide what's right for you.

A consultant is also valuable if you have difficulty coping with the often overwhelming number of details and decisions involved. He or she can provide whatever guidance, support and decision making you need to implement your party. Event planners can sometimes be hired on a meeting-by-meeting basis, too. If you don't need much more than some advice and structure, this arrangement can be extremely beneficial.

So if the planning process is just too much for you to handle, and you don't mind the expense, definitely consider hiring a professional. Most of the principles used in selecting a caterer apply to hiring an event coordinator. Try to get suggestions from friends or facilities, follow up on references the consultants give you, compare and contrast service fees and make sure you and the consultant are compatible. The range of professionalism and experience varies greatly, so it really is to your advantage to investigate consultants' track records. We've actually done that for you in our Service Directory—the event planners we feature are all first-rate. Again, once you have found someone who can accommodate you, get everything in writing so that there won't be any misunderstandings down the road.

Insurance Considerations

You may want to get extra insurance coverage for your event. Since this is now a major consideration for many facilities (and service providers), you may not have an option. More and more facilities are requiring either proof of insurance or a certificate guaranteeing additional coverage.

Deep Pockets

These days, if someone gets injured at a party or something is damaged at or near the event site, it's likely that somebody will be sued. Unfortunately, that's the way it is. Event sites and service providers are very aware of their potential liability and all have coverage of one kind or another.

In the past, only the facility was sued. Nowadays, everybody gets sued, and that may mean you. Whoever has the most insurance is said to have the "deepest pockets" and will be pursued to pay the bulk of the claim. To protect themselves, facilities have begun to require additional insurance from service providers and their clients. The goal is to spread the risk among all parties involved. Don't panic. Although event insurance, per se, is impossible to obtain, extra insurance for a specified period of time is easy to get and relatively inexpensive.

Obtaining Extra Insurance

Facilities often require between $500,000 and $1,000,000 worth of extra coverage. If you are a home owner, just ask your insurance agent to tack on a rider to your home owner's policy to cover the event date and time period. The company will issue you a certificate of insurance specifically for your function in the amount selected. To finalize your rental agreement, you will have to present this certificate to the facility owner or representative as proof of insurance.

If you're not a home owner, many facilities are able to offer additional insurance through their own policies. You will pay an extra charge, but it's usually nominal.

It Can't Happen To Me

Don't be lulled into the notion that it can't happen to you. Naturally, there is more likelihood of risk with a late night New Year's eve party or a high school prom night than at the annual company Christmas party. But we could tell you stories of upscale parties where something did happen and a lawsuit resulted. Many event sites have plenty of coverage and are willing to assume the "deep pocket" risk. Others don't and won't. Take into account the type of event and the factors that may affect liability. Even if extra insurance is not required, you may want to consider additional coverage anyway, especially if alcohol is being served. You are the best judge of your guests' temperaments. If you plan on having a wild party, a little additional insurance could be a good thing.

Do Your Part: Reduce, Reuse and Recycle

If you're wondering why we're including information about environmental issues in a book like *Perfect Places*, it's because most of the time, special events generate excessive waste, recyclable materials and surplus food.

Meetings, Seminars and Conferences Can Become "Green" Events

Meetings and seminars create piles of extra materials—much of which can be reused or recycled. Consider a five-day seminar for 500 people, with multiple breaks per day. If each meeting-goer drinks from a foam insulated, paper or plastic cup at each break, that can add up to 7,500 cups! Here are a few general suggestions to help make your next function a "green" event. For specific programs and operational procedures, you can call Eco-Logical Solutions™ in Boston (617/457-2411), a company that specializes in environmental programs for the hospitality and event planning industries. Ask for Tedd Saunders or Liz Kay. Their address: 64 Arlington St., Suite 314, Boston, Massachusetts, 02116.

Begin early in the planning process. Make environmental concerns a priority. Review all the printed materials you're going to produce and have recycled products included in the budget: invitations, posters, give-aways, signs, manuals, brochures, exhibit floor directories, follow-up mailers, etc. Try to get one printer to produce everything and don't make more promotional materials than you really need. Contrary to popular belief, recycled xerox paper, computer paper and office paper supplies can be less expensive than non-recycled products.

Integrate your "green" initiatives into your program. Create environmental awareness and participation on the part of attendees. Let your guests know what environmental steps you've taken by creating an eco-information page in the participants' handbook. Clearly indicate on all of your printed communications that your event is a "green" event and use the recyling logo (three circular arrows) so that your reader knows you've used recyled paper. Make it easy for attendees to participate in your program by letting them know what they can do to help. Ask participants for their suggestions and create incentives for involvement.

There are lots of things you can do. Make sure all paper products are made from recycled materials. Recycle plastic badges and aluminum cans. You can leave your distinct message on give-away items: give attendees their own reusable plastic cup with a logo or name on it so they can use it over and over again. Put a recycling message on plastic badges or better yet, use stick-on paper badges with a recycling message. Let everyone know that well-marked bins will be made available on the last day to collect plastic badges, unwanted meeting manuals, cardboard or any other recyclable products. Instead of cheap, throw-away plastic bags for meeting materials, hand out reusable canvas bags made from recycled fiber. Durable totes, with your company's name or message, can provide a lasting memento from an event. *Simply printing information on both sides of paper will cut usage in half.* Ask for a soda dispensing system and glassware to reduce the need for aluminum cans. Eliminate the use of helium balloons. They can't be recyled or reused, and will cause harm to marine life and create havoc with electrical wires if released outdoors.

Create smoke-free environments. Have friendly signs telling participants that conference and breakout areas will be smoke-free, and that outdoor areas will be made available for smokers. Always provide receptacles for cigarette butts in designated indoor or outdoor smoking areas.

Select a location that has strong environmental initiatives. Let facility contenders know that site selection criteria will include environmental factors. Does the facility have in-house recycling containers for paper, glass, metal and plastic? Are recycled products provided? Are light fixtures energy efficient? Ask to see documentation or a demonstration of each site's environmental program. Vendors will respond to consumer demand if they know it's of concern to you.

Recycling Food

Many caterers often have leftover food that no one wants to take home. Nowadays, you and the caterer can feel good about doing your part by donating the excess. Added benefits are that food donations are tax deductible for either you or the caterer, and, if you recycle, the cost for extra garbage bins can be eliminated or reduced.

Food donations are distributed to teenage drop-in centers, youth shelters, alcoholic treatment centers, AIDS hospices, senior centers and refugee centers throughout the region. You should also know that a 1989 state law was passed that protects the donor from liability resulting from the use of donated food.

Your packaged food can be picked up the day of the event or brought back to the caterer's kitchen to be picked up later on. You can also transport food via taxi. Sometimes only a $10 taxi fare is needed to take food to an appropriate center. To ensure that food is dropped off in a timely fashion, ask the taxi driver to leave a receipt at the center with the date and time of delivery.

Place food in clean plastic bags, plastic containers or boxes. Other recyclable materials must be separated. Food must be edible. For example, if dressing has been poured over a salad, most likely it won't be worth eating the next day.

Call your local recycling center to arrange a pickup or look through your phone book to find a local Food Bank. How do you make a donation? Call the following organizations to make advance arrangements.

San Francisco:	Food Runners	415/929-1866
	Food Bank	415/957-1076

	The Episcopal Sanctuary	415/863-3893
Berkeley:	Daily Bread Project	510/540-1250
Oakland:	Oakland Pot Luck	510/272-0414

San Mateo & Santa Clara Counties:

	Second Harvest	408/266-8866
Marin County:	Food Bank	415/883-1302
Sacramento:	Food Bank	916/452-3663
	Loaves & Fishes	916/446-0874

Taking Little Steps

Although it may seem that implementing environmental concerns is an overwhelming task, it can be done. The reality is that we live in a market driven society. If companies experience consumer demand, they will respond to meet the need and if we start taking little steps now, over the long term, our combined efforts will make an enormous difference.

Services/Amenities & Restrictions Key

SERVICES/AMENITIES

Restaurant Services
yes: the facility has a restaurant available on site for catering your event or is accessible to your guests

Catering
provided: the facility provides catering • *provided, no BYO:* the facility arranges catering; you cannot arrange your own • *preferred list:* you must select your caterer from the facility's approved list • *provided, can BYO; provided, BYO ok:* the facility will arrange catering or you can select an outside caterer of your own • *BYO, must be licensed:* arrange for your own licensed caterer • *provided, if BYO buy-out required:* a fee will be charged to "buy out" the facility's preferred caterer if you wish to make your own arrangements

Kitchen Facilities
ample: large and well-equipped • *moderate:* medium-sized and utilitarian • *minimal:* small with limited equipment, may not have all basic appliances • *n/a:* not applicable when facility provides catering • *fully equipped:* major appliances and space

Tables & Chairs
some provided or provided: facility provides some or all of the tables and chairs • *BYO:* make arrangements to bring your own

Linens, Silver, etc.
same as above

Restrooms
wca: wheelchair accessible • *no wca:* not wheelchair accessible

Dance Floor
yes: an area for dancing (hardwood floor, cement terrace, patio) is available • *CBA, extra charge, or extra fee:* you can arrange for a dance floor to be brought in by paying an extra fee

Parking
descriptions are self explanatory; • *CBA:* can be arranged

Overnight Accommodations
if overnight accommodations are available on site, the number of guestrooms is listed

Telephone

restricted: calls made on the house phone must be local, collect or charged to a credit card • *guest phones:* private phones in guestrooms • *house phone:* central phone used by all guests • *emergency only:* self explanatory

Outdoor Night Lighting

yes: indicates that there is adequate light to conduct your event outdoors after dark • *access only or limited:* lighting is sufficient for access only

Outdoor Cooking Facilities

BBQ: the facility has a barbecue on the premises • *BBQ, CBA:* a barbecue can be arranged through the facility • *BYO BBQ:* make arrangements for your own barbecue

Cleanup

provided: facility takes care of cleanup • *caterer:* your caterer is responsible • *caterer, renter:* both you and your caterer are responsible for cleanup

Other, Special

description of any service or amenity not included in above list

RESTRICTIONS

Alcohol

provided, no BYO: the facility provides alcoholic beverages (for a fee) and does not permit you to bring your own • *BYO:* you can arrange for your own alcohol • *corkage, $/bottle:* if you bring your own alcohol, the facility charges a fee per bottle to remove the cork and pour • *WCB only (or any combination of these three letters):* only wine, champagne and/or beer are permitted

Smoking

allowed: smoking is permitted throughout the facility • *outside only:* smoking is not permitted inside the facility • *not allowed:* smoking is not permitted anywhere on the premises • *designated areas:* specific areas for smoking have been designated

Music

Almost every facility allows acoustical music unless stated otherwise. Essentially, restrictions refer to amplified music • *amplified ok:* amplified music is acceptable without restriction • *amplified outside only:* no amplified music allowed inside • *inside only:* no amplified music permitted outside • *amplified with limits or restrictions:* amplified music allowed but there are limits on volume, hours of play, number of instruments, etc.

Wheelchair Access
Accessibility is based on whether a facility is wheelchair accessible or not • *yes:* the facility is accessible • *limited:* the facility is accessible but with difficulty • *no:* the facility is not accessible

Insurance
Many facilities require that you purchase and show proof of some insurance coverage. The type and amount of insurance varies with the facility, and some facilities offer insurance for a minimal charge. • *required, certificate required or proof of insurance required*: additional insurance is required • *not required:* no additional insurance is required

Other
decorations restricted: the facility limits the use of tape, nails, tacks, confetti or other decorations

Find-It-Fast

We know your time is valuable.

If you've got to find a place to get married fast and you don't have enough time to leisurely read through all the location descriptions, use this convenient chart. It lists each facility by region and city in alphabetical order and highlights essential information for each one. This makes it easy to quickly identify the event locations that are most appropriate for you.

Once you've identified a handful of places that seem to meet your needs, read each *Perfect Places* entry for more complete information.

Target your area of geographical preference first.

Pick the cities that are best for you, your family and guests, keeping in mind the location selection advice in the *How To Use This Guidebook* section.

Identify the facilities that fit your needs.

Read through the columns, from left to right noting which features are essential to your function. If a site seems to offer what you need, put a light check mark next to it or better yet, *xerox the pages and use color highlighters*. Page numbers for all locations are listed in the first column of the matrix, making it easy to flip to the sites you've checked to read the full descriptions. If you still need more information, call the facility.

Remember, the find-it-fast section is not perfect.

The purpose of this matrix is to reduce your searching time. However, because the information presented is abbreviated, it won't be perfect. A bullet (•) in the *Amplified Music Restricted* column, for example, may mean that amplified music is not allowed, or it may only mean that you can't have it outside. To find out how the restriction will affect your party, *you have to read the full description.* The following is a brief explanation of the matrix headings.

Matrix Headings

Maximum Capacity

The capacity numbers shown are for total seated or standing capacities. The numbers marked with asterisks (*) indicate that the figure may be very inexact. For instance, we may have been given the maximum capacity for only the largest room in a multi-room facility. Consequently, the maximum capacity if all the rooms are combined is unknown. A facility with a large total capacity may also be able to comfortably accommodate a small event in one of its rooms. If a location seems perfect but the numbers are not quite right, we suggest you read the entry and then call to make sure.

Indoor and Outdoor Facilities
These columns are self explanatory.

In-house Catering and BYO Catering
In-house means that the facility can cater your event or arrange to have it catered. *BYO* indicates that you can make arrangements for your own caterer.

Alcohol Provided or Alcohol BYO
If you see a bullet (•) in the *Alcohol Provided* column and a bullet in the *Alcohol BYO*, that means the facility can provide alcohol and they will also let you bring your own. Note that many facilities charge a corkage fee if you BYO. If there's a bullet in the *Alcohol Provided* column, but not in the *Alcohol BYO* column, you cannot bring your own alcohol. If there isn't a bullet in either column it means that alcohol is not allowed.

Restaurant On Site and Guestrooms Available
These columns are self explanatory.

Event Coordination
Many facilities provide event planning and coordination, everything from catering to

flowers and custom party favors. This service may be free or there may be an additional charge. Be sure to ask.

Wheelchair Access Restricted
Indicates access problems ranging from a single step into a building to total inaccessibility. It doesn't mean you can't get into a site—it just denotes that there may be some degree of difficulty.

Smoking Restricted
Means no smoking or smoking in designated areas only.

Insurance Required
Proof of insurance or a certificate of insurance may be required.

Amplified Music Restricted
Means amplified music is not allowed or is permitted with inside/outside constraints and/or volume limits.

FIND-IT-FAST MATRIX

Private Dining Room Guide

FACILITY	PAGE	MAX. SEATED CAPACITY	MAX. STANDING CAPACITY	Indoor Facilities	Outdoor Facilities	In-house Catering	BYO Catering	Alcohol Provided	Alcohol BYO	Restaurant On Site	Guestrooms Available	Event Coordination	Handicap Restricted	Smoking Restricted	Insurance Required	Amplified Music Restricted
SAN FRANCISCO																
Asta	46	110	200	•		•		•	•	•		•				•
Atrium	47	175	300	•	•	•		•	•	•		•				•
Blue Fox, The	48	80	150	•		•		•	•	•		•	•	•		•
Cafe Majestic	49	120	n/a	•		•		•	•	•	•	•		•		•
Carnelian Room	50	800*	2000*	•		•		•	•	•		•				•
Cliff House, The	51	135	160	•	•	•		•	•	•		•	•			
Cypress Club	52	110	300	•		•		•	•	•		•				•
Delancey Street Restaurant	53	45	75	•		•		•	•	•		•	•	•		•
Elka	54	105	125	•		•		•	•	•	•	•				•
Greens	55	150	250	•		•		•	•	•		•				
Julius' Castle	56	100	n/a	•		•		•	•	•		•	•			•
Kuleto's Machiavelli Room	57	50	100	•		•		•	•	•		•				
La Fiammetta	58	50	60	•		•		•	•	•			•	•		
Lascaux	59	140	n/a	•		•		•	•	•		•		•		
MacArthur Park	60	280	500	•		•		•	•	•		•	•	•		•
Miss Pearl's Jam House	61	400*	800*	•	•	•		•	•	•	•	•				•
Palio d'Asti	62	250	300	•		•		•	•	•		•		•		•
Portico	63	100	150	•		•		•	•	•	•	•	•			•
Postrio	64	36	50	•		•		•	•	•	•	•		•		•
Rotunda at Neiman Marcus, The	65	200	350			•		•	•	•		•				
Sailing Ship Dolph Rempp	66	150	800*	•	•	•		•	•	•		•				
Splendido	67	150*	200*	•	•	•		•	•	•		•		•		•
Square One	68	45	n/a	•		•		•	•	•		•				•
Stars	69	44	70	•		•		•	•	•		•				•
Stinking Rose, The	70	125	95	•		•		•	•	•			•	•		•
Vinoteca	71	140	300	•		•		•	•	•		•		•		•
NORTH BAY																
Fairfax																
Deerpark Villa	72	225	300*	•	•	•			•	•	•		•				•
Larkspur																
Lark Creek Inn, The	73	200	250	•	•	•		•	•	•		•		•		•

FACILITY	PAGE	MAX. SEATED CAPACITY	MAX. STANDING CAPACITY	Indoor Facilities	Outdoor Facilities	In-house Catering	BYO Catering	Alcohol Provided	Alcohol BYO	Restaurant On Site	Guestrooms Available	Event Coordination	Handicap Restricted	Smoking Restricted	Insurance Required	Amplified Music Restricted
Ross																
Ross Garden Restaurant	74	150	150*	•	•	•		•		•		•		•		•
Tiburon																
Guaymas	75	100	150	•	•	•		•		•		•	•			•
PENINSULA																
Menlo Park																
Allied Arts Guild Restaurant	76	155	200	•	•	•				•		•	•			
Palo Alto																
California Cafe	77	90	100	•	•		•	•	•	•		•		•		•
MacArthur Park	78	272	120	•	•	•		•	•	•		•		•		•
EAST BAY																
Berkeley																
Bette's Oceanview Diner	79	44	70	•		•		•	•	•		•				
Oakland																
Oliveto	80	26	n/a	•		•		•	•	•			•			•
Piemonte Ovest	81	110	200	•	•	•		•	•	•		•	•			•
Scott's Restaurant	82	250	450	•	•	•		•	•	•		•	•			
Silver Dragon, The	83	350	400	•		•		•	•	•		•				•
San Ramon																
Mudd's Restaurant	84	150	70	•	•	•		•	•	•		•		•		•
Walnut Creek																
Spiedini	85	143	200	•	•	•		•	•	•		•		•		
SOUTH BAY																
Campbell																
Campbell House Restaurant	86	16	n/a	•		•		•	•	•		•	•	•		•
Martha's Restaurant and Cafe	87	180	200	•		•		•	•	•		•				
Los Gatos																
Village House & Garden Restaurant	88	130	130	•	•	•		•	•	•		•		•		
San Jose																
La Pastaia	89	175	n/a	•		•		•		•	•	•		•		

FACILITY	PAGE	MAX. SEATED CAPACITY	MAX. STANDING CAPACITY	Indoor Facilities	Outdoor Facilities	In-house Catering	BYO Catering	Alcohol Provided	Alcohol BYO	Restaurant On Site	Guestrooms Available	Event Coordination	Handicap Restricted	Smoking Restricted	Insurance Required	Amplified Music Restricted
WINE COUNTRY																
Santa Rosa																
Mark West Lodge	91	200	500	•	•	•		•	•	•		•		•		•
Sonoma																
Depot 1870 Restaurant	92	140	140	•	•	•		•	•	•		•				•
Yountville																
Cafe Kinyon! Restaurant	93	400*	250	•	•	•		•	•	•		•				
SANTA CRUZ AREA																
Aptos																
Veranda, The	94	70	175*	•	•	•		•	•	•	•	•		•		
MONTEREY PENINSULA																
Carmel Valley																
Ridge Restaurant, The	95	200*	300*	•	•	•		•	•	•	•	•				
SACRAMENTO VALLEY																
Sacramento																
Casa de los Niños	96	93	200*	•	•	•		•	•	•				•		•
TAHOE REGION																
Carnelian Bay																
Gar Woods Grill & Pier	98	220	300	•	•	•		•	•	•		•				
Tahoe Vista																
La Playa	99	175	200	•	•	•		•	•	•		•				
Truckee																
Cottonwood Restaurant	100	230*	250	•	•	•		•	•	•		•		•		
Zina's	101	75	90	•		•		•	•			•		•		•

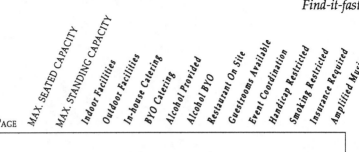

Special Event Locations

SAN FRANCISCO

FACILITY	PAGE	MAX. SEATED CAPACITY	MAX. STANDING CAPACITY	Indoor Facilities	Outdoor Facilities	In-house Catering	BYO Catering	Alcohol Provided	Alcohol BYO	Restaurant On Site	Guestrooms Available	Event Coordination	Handicap Restricted	Smoking Restricted	Insurance Required	Amplified Music Restricted
Alamo Square Inn	104	125	200	•	•	•		•	•		•	•	•	•	•	•
Ansel Adams Center/Opts. Art	105	400*	500*	•		•	•	•	•			•		•	•	•
Aquatic Park Bayview Room	106	150	190	•			•		•					•		
Archbishop's Mansion	107	50	100	•		•	•	•	•		•	•	•			•
Asta & The Rincon Center Atrium	108	200*	500*	•		•		•	•	•		•				
Balclutha	109	125	300	•	•		•		•					•	•	
Blue and Gold Fleet	110	200	300	•	•	•		•	•			•	•			
Cable Car Barn and Museum	111	400	800	•			•		•						•	
Caffe Esprit	112	125	300	•	•	•		•	•	•		•				
California Academy of Sciences	113	550	3000	•		•	•		•			•		•		•
California Culinary Academy	115	200	500*	•		•		•	•	•		•				•
California Spirit, The	116	80	149	•	•	•		•	•			•				
Campton Place	117	26	80	•		•		•	•	•	•	•		•		•
Cartoon Art Museum	118	40	250	•			•		•				•	•		
Casa de la Vista	119	180	300	•	•	•		•	•			•				
Circle Gallery	120	n/a	350	•			•		•			•		•	•	•
City Club, The	121	200	700	•		•		•		•		•				
Coit Tower	122	12	60	•			•		•				•	•	•	•
Conservatory of Flowers, The	123	70	200	•			•		•				•	•		
Contract Design Center	124	250	500	•	•	•		•	•			•		•		
Delancey Street	126	300	500	•	•	•	•	•	•	•		•		•		•
De Young Memorial Museum	127	340	800	•			•		•			•		•	•	•
Eureka, The	128	250	600	•	•		•		•				•	•	•	
Ferryboat Santa Rosa	129	500	500	•	•	•	•	•	•			•	•	•		
Flood Mansion, The	130	300	450	•	•		•		•			•		•	•	
Forest Hill Club House	132	100	200	•	•		•		•			•				•
Fort Mason Conference Center	133	230	350	•			•		•			•		•		
Fort Mason Firehouse	134	100	150	•			•		•			•		•	•	
Galleria Design Center	135	1200	2500	•		•	•	•				•		•		
GiftCenter Pavilion	136	300	450	•		•	•	•	•			•		•		
Ginsberg Collection, The	137	100	350	•			•		•			•		•	•	
Golden Gate Park	138	call	25000		•		•		•							•
Golden Sunset	139	40	100	•	•	•		•	•		•	•	•	•		
Grand Hyatt, San Francisco	140	640	1000	•		•		•	•	•	•	•		•		
Green Room, The	141	300	500	•			•		•			•	•	•	•	•

FACILITY	PAGE	MAX. SEATED CAPACITY	MAX. STANDING CAPACITY	Indoor Facilities	Outdoor Facilities	In-house Catering	BYO Catering	Alcohol Provided	Alcohol BYO	Restaurant On Site	Guestrooms Available	Event Coordination	Handicap Restricted	Smoking Restricted	Insurance Required	Amplified Music Restricted
Haas-Lilienthal House	143	80	200	•		•		•				•	•	•		•
Hamlin Mansion	144	200	350	•		•		•				•	•			•
Herbst & Festival Pavilions	145	3500	5000	•		•		•				•			•	
Hornblower Dining Yachts	146	800*	1000*	•	•	•		•	•		call	•	call			
Houston, The	148	12	12	•		•		•			•	•	•	•		
Mansions Hotel, The	149	90	150	•	•	•		•	•	•	•	•	•			
Marines' Memorial	150	250	250	•		•		•	•	•	•	•		•		
Mark Monroe Productions	151	200	600	•		•		•				•		•	•	
Miyako Hotel	152	500	600	•		•		•	•	•	•	•				
Nimitz Conference Center	153	389	500*	•	•	•		•				•				
Old Federal Reserve Bank Bldg.	155	400	800	•		•	•	•	•		•	•		•		
Pacific Heights Mansion	156	60	120	•	•	•		•				•		•		
Pacific Spirit, The	157	35	90	•	•	•		•				•	•	•		
Palace of Fine Arts, The	158	300	500		•		•	•				•			•	•
Pan Pacific Hotel	159	360	500	•	•	•		•	•	•	•	•				
Park Hyatt San Francisco	161	150	300	•	•	•		•	•	•	•	•				
Pier 35	162	625*	1000*	•	•		•	•		•		•		•	•	
Prescott Hotel, The	163	n/a	125	•		•	•	•	•	•		•				•
Queen Anne, The	164	85	150	•	•	•		•	•			•	•			
Rincon Center Atrium	108	200	500	•		•		•	•	•		•				
Rock & Bowl	165	n/a	300	•			•	•								
Rococo Showplace	166	140	350	•		•		•				•		•	•	•
San Francisco Maritime Museum	167	120	400	•		•		•				•		•	•	
San Francisco Mart	168	500	800	•		•	•	•				•			•	
San Francisco Spirit, The	169	300	700	•	•	•		•	•			•		•		
San Francisco Zoo	170	call	500	•	•	•	•	•				•		•	•	•
Sharon Arts Center & Carrousel	171	80	100	•	•	•		•				•		•	•	•
Sheraton Palace Hotel	172	600	1000	•		•		•	•	•	•	•				
Sherman House, The	174	60	100	•	•	•		•	•	•	•	•		•		•
Showplace Design Center	175	250	500	•		•	•					•	•		•	
South Beach Billiards	176	125	500	•		•	•					•	•			•
Spectrum Gallery	178	400	650	•		•	•					•			•	
SS Jeremiah O'Brien	179	210	300	•	•	•		•				•	•	•		
Stanford Court, The	180	550	800*	•		•		•	•	•	•	•				•
St. Francis Hotel, The	181	1000	1500*	•		•		•	•	•	•	•				
St. Paulus Church	182	250	450	•		•	•	•					•	•		
Trocadero, The	184	125	150*	•	•	•		•				•				
Wattis Room, The	185	100	200	•		•	•	•				•				
1409 Sutter	186	150	275	•		•		•	•			•		•	•	

Facility	Page	Max. Seated Capacity	Max. Standing Capacity	Indoor Facilities	Outdoor Facilities	In-house Catering	BYO Catering	Alcohol Provided	Alcohol BYO	Restaurant On Site	Guestrooms Available	Event Coordination	Handicap Restricted	Smoking Restricted	Insurance Required	Amplified Music Restricted
HALF MOON BAY																
Half Moon Bay																
Douglas Beach House	188	95	150	•		•		•				•				
Mill Rose Inn	189	125	125	•	•	•		•			•	•	•	•		
Strawberry Ranch	190	50	50	•	•	•		•				•	•	•	•	
Montara																
Point Montara Lighthouse	191	60	60	•	•			•			•			•	•	
NORTH BAY																
Belvedere																
China Cabin	193	48	65	•	•			•						•	•	•
Mill Valley																
Mill Valley Outdoor Art Club, The	194	120	200	•	•			•								•
Mountain Home Inn	195	80	110	•	•	•		•	•	•	•	•				
Nicasio																
Shadows, The	196	30	120	•	•			•		•				•	•	
Ross																
Caroline Livermore Room	197	130	500	•	•			•						•		•
San Rafael																
Dominican College	198	340	500	•	•			•							•	•
Falkirk Mansion	200	60	125	•	•			•						•	•	•
Forty Twenty Civic Center Drive	201	300	500	•	•			•						•	•	
Foster Hall	202	250	500	•	•	•		•	•			•		•		
San Rafael Improvement Club	203	125	160	•	•			•						•	•	
Villa Altura	204	75	200	•	•			•					•	•	•	•
Sausalito																
Alta Mira, The	205	150	200*	•	•	•		•	•	•	•	•		•		•
Casa Madrona Hotel & Restaurant	206	100	140*	•	•	•		•	•	•	•	•	•			
Sausalito Woman's Club	207	175	200*	•	•			•					•	•	•	•
Stinson Beach																
Stinson Beach Creekside Center	208	200	400	•	•			•				•		•	•	
Tiburon																
Corinthian Yacht Club	210	250	400	•	•	•		•	•	•		•	•			•

Facility	Page	Max. Seated Capacity	Max. Standing Capacity	Indoor Facilities	Outdoor Facilities	In-house Catering	BYO Catering	Alcohol Provided	Alcohol BYO	Restaurant On Site	Guestrooms Available	Event Coordination	Handicap Restricted	Smoking Restricted	Insurance Required	Amplified Music Restricted
NORTH COAST																
Bodega Bay																
Terra Nova Institute	212	50	n/a	•	•	•	•				•			•		•
Cazadero																
Timberhill Ranch	213	40	40*	•	•	•		•	•	•	•		•	•		•
Fort Bragg																
Mendocino Coast Botanical Gardens	214	30	30		•		•	•	•					•		•
Shoreline Properties	215	call	50*	•	•		•	•						•	•	•
Jenner																
Murphy's Jenner Inn	216	call	90*	•		•		•	•	•	•	•		•		•
Little River																
Glendeven	217	40	50	•		•		•		•		•	•			•
Inn at School House Creek	218	70	100*	•	•	•	•	•		•	•	•	•	•		•
Little River Inn	219	80	call	•	•	•	•	•		•	•	•	•	•		•
Rachel's Inn	220	30	125	•	•	•		•	•	•	•	•	•			•
Stevenswood Lodge	221	call	250*	•	•	•		•	•	•	•	•		•		
Marshall																
Marconi Conference Center	222	60	100	•		•		•		•		•	•			
Mendocino																
Ames Lodge	223	30	30	•	•	•		•		•			•		•	•
Mendocino Hotel	224	110	150	•	•	•		•		•	•	•		•		•
Monte Rio																
Huckleberry Springs	225	65	65		•	•	•	•			•		•	•	•	
Occidental																
Inn at Occidental	226	60*	200*	•	•	•		•	•	•	•	•		•		•
PENINSULA																
Atherton																
Holbrook Palmer Park	228	250	250	•	•	•	•	•				•	•		•	•
Belmont																
Ralston Hall	229	200	250	•	•		•		•				•	•	•	

Facility	Page	Max. Seated Capacity	Max. Standing Capacity	Indoor Facilities	Outdoor Facilities	In-house Catering	BYO Catering	Alcohol Provided	Alcohol BYO	Restaurant On Site	Guestrooms Available	Event Coordination	Handicap Restricted	Smoking Restricted	Insurance Required	Amplified Music Restricted
Burlingame																
Hyatt Regency S. F. Airport	231	2025	1930	•		•		•		•	•	•		•		
Kohl Mansion	232	250	450	•	•		•	•						•	•	•
Hillsborough																
Crocker Mansion, The	233	100	300	•	•		•	•					•	•	•	•
Menlo Park																
Latham Hopkins Gatehouse	235	45	100	•	•		•	•				•	•			•
Stanford Park Hotel	236	250	250	•	•	•		•	•	•	•	•		•		•
Mountain View																
Rengstorff House	237	24	85	•	•		•	•						•	•	•
Palo Alto																
Garden Court Hotel	238	250	300	•	•	•		•	•	•	•	•		•		
Stanford Barn	240	290	350	•	•	•	•	•	•			•		•		
Portola Valley																
Ladera Oaks	241	350	350	•	•		•	•								•
Thomas Fogarty Winery	242	200	225*	•	•		•	•				•	•	•	•	•
Woodside Priory	244	3000*	3000*	•	•	•	•					•	•	•	•	
Redwood City																
Hotel Sofitel	245	200	400	•	•	•		•	•	•	•	•		•		
Pacific Athletic Club	246	600	1000	•	•	•		•	•			•		•		
Woodside																
Green Gables	248	call	1200		•	•		•				•			•	
EAST BAY																
Benicia																
Camel Barn Museum	250	154	330	•			•	•					•			
Captain Walsh House	251	175	175	•	•		•	•	•		•	•		•	•	•
Fischer-Hanlon House	252	50	100	•	•		•	•					•	•		•
Berkeley																
Bancroft Club, The	253	250	350	•		•		•	•	•	•	•		•	•	•
Berkeley City Club	254	300	325*	•	•	•		•			•	•		•	•	
Berkeley Conference Center	256	220	350*	•		•		•	•		•	•		•		
Brazilian Room	257	150	225	•	•	•	•		•					•	•	•
Hillside Club	259	150	200	•			•		•				•	•		

FACILITY	PAGE	MAX. SEATED CAPACITY	MAX. STANDING CAPACITY	Indoor Facilities	Outdoor Facilities	In-house Catering	BYO Catering	Alcohol Provided	Alcohol BYO	Restaurant On Site	Guestrooms Available	Event Coordination	Handicap Restricted	Smoking Restricted	Insurance Required	Amplified Music Restricted
Concord																
Centre Concord	260	400	400	•			•		•					•	•	
Danville																
Behring & U.C. Museums	261	500	600*	•	•		•		•					•	•	•
Crow Canyon Country Club	263	**320**	400	•		•		•	•	•		•		•		
El Rio	264	150	300	•	•	•	•	•	•		•	•	•	•	•	
Victorian & Executive Estate, The	265	200	500*	•	•	•	•	•	•		•	•	•	•	•	•
Emeryville																
Chalkers Billiard Club	266	n/a	300	•		•		•	•			•		•		•
Fremont																
Ardenwood Historic Preserve	268	**call**	500		•	•		•				•				•
Palmdale Estate, The	269	150	1000	•	•		•		•			•		•		•
Lafayette																
Lafayette Park Hotel	270	280	500	•	•	•		•	•	•	•	•				•
Livermore																
Concannon Winery	271	500	750	•	•		•	•				•		•		
Ravenswood	272	150	150	•	•		•		•					•	•	•
Tri Valley Event Center	273	540	1000	•		•			•			•		•	•	
Wente Bros. Estate Winery	274	250	500	•	•	•		•				•				
Wente Bros. Sparkling Wine Cellars	275	700	200	•	•	•		•		•		•				
Moraga																
Hacienda de las Flores	276	128	200*	•	•		•		•					•	•	•
Oakland																
Athenian Nile Club	278	250	350	•		•		•	•			•	•			
Cafe Fontebella	279	275	1000	•	•	•		•	•	•		•		•		
California Ballroom	280	350	600	•			•		•			•		•		
Camron-Stanford House	282	call	250	•	•		•		•				•	•	•	•
Claremont Resort, The	283	350	400*	•	•	•		•		•	•	•				
Commodore Dining Cruises	284	350	450	•	•	•	•	•		•	•	•	•	•		
Dunsmuir House	286	3000	3000	•	•		•		•			•		•	•	
Lake Merritt Hotel, The	287	225	275	•		•		•	•	•	•	•	•			•
Oakland Hills Tennis Club	288	110	200	•	•	•	•		•	•		•		•	•	•
Oakland Museum	290	150	240*	•	•	•	•	•	•			•		•	•	•
Preservation Park	291	185	400	•	•	•		•	•			•		•	•	
Sailboat House	292	155	225	•			•		•				•	•		

FACILITY	PAGE	MAX. SEATED CAPACITY	MAX. STANDING CAPACITY	Indoor Facilities	Outdoor Facilities	In-house Catering	BYO Catering	Alcohol Provided	Alcohol BYO	Restaurant On Site	Guestrooms Available	Event Coordination	Handicap Restricted	Smoking Restricted	Insurance Required	Amplified Music Restricted
Scottish Rite Center	293	1500	1300*	•		•	•	•						•	•	
Sequoia Lodge	294	100	150	•	•		•	•						•		
Piedmont																
Piedmont Community Center	295	200	300*	•	•		•	•						•	•	
Pleasanton																
Pleasanton Hotel, The	296	300	400	•	•	•		•	•	•		•				
Point Richmond																
East Brother Light Station	297	250	250	•	•	•	•	•	•		•	•	•	•		
San Leandro																
Best House	299	150	150	•	•		•	•			•		•	•		
San Pablo																
Rockefeller Lodge	300	250	500	•	•	•		•	•			•				•
San Ramon																
San Ramon Community Center	301	250	450	•	•		•	•				•		•	•	•
San Ramon Senior Center	302	115	250	•	•		•	•				•		•	•	•
Sunol																
Elliston Vineyards	304	240	300	•	•	•		•	•			•		•		•
Vallejo																
Foley Cultural Center	305	500	600	•	•		•	•				•				
Marine World Africa, USA	306	call	7500		•	•		•				•				•
Walnut Creek																
Scott's Gardens	307	200	300	•	•	•		•		•		•		•		•
Shadelands Ranch	309	50	250	•	•		•	•				•		•	•	
Turtle Rock Ranch	310	1200	1200	•	•	•		•				•		•	•	
SOUTH BAY																
Cupertino																
Marianist Center	311	24	n/a	•	•	•		•			•	•		•		•
Gilroy																
Fortino Winery & Deli	312	call	250	•	•		•	•								
Hecker Pass	313	300	400		•	•		•					•			
Gilroy Historical Museum	314	n/a	75	•			•		•				•	•		•

FACILITY	PAGE	MAX. SEATED CAPACITY	MAX. STANDING CAPACITY	Indoor Facilities	Outdoor Facilities	In-house Catering	BYO Catering	Alcohol Provided	Alcohol BYO	Restaurant On Site	Guestrooms Available	Event Coordination	Handicap Restricted	Smoking Restricted	Insurance Required	Amplified Music Restricted
Los Gatos																
Byington Winery	315	150	250	•	•		•	•				•	•	•	•	•
Mirassou Champagne Cellars	316	120	200	•	•		•	•				•	•	•		
Opera House	317	500	750	•			•	•				•				
San Jose																
Briar Rose, The	319	150	150	•	•	•	•	•	•		•	•	•	•	•	•
Children's Discovery Museum	320	200	1200*	•	•	•		•				•		•	•	
Event Center	321	6500	6500	•		•	•	•	•					•	•	
Fairmont Hotel	322	1000	1000	•		•		•		•	•	•		•		
Hotel De Anza	323	150	170	•	•	•		•		•	•	•		•		
Mirassou	325	125	call	•	•	•		•				•				•
San Jose Athletic Club	326	300	400	•		•		•				•				
San Jose Historical Museum	327	1000	1000*	•	•		•		•			•		•	•	•
Tech Museum of Innovation, The	329	call	400	•		•		•				•		•	•	
Valentino's	330	650	800	•			•	•				•			•	
Winchester Mystery House	331	450	1000	•	•	•	•	•	•			•	•	•		•
Santa Clara																
Adobe Lodge Faculty Club	332	100	300	•	•	•		•	•			•		•	•	
Decathlon Club	333	400	600*	•	•	•		•		•		•		•		
Madison Street Inn	334	75	75	•	•	•	•		•		•	•	•	•		•
Saratoga																
Chateau La Cresta	335	1500	1500	•	•	•		•		•		•	•	•	•	•
Saratoga Foothill Club	337	126	185	•	•		•		•			•	•	•	•	•
Villa Montalvo	338	175	200	•	•		•		•				•	•	•	
WINE COUNTRY																
Alexander Valley																
Chateau Souverain	339	150	250	•	•	•		•		•				•	•	
Calistoga																
Clos Pegase	340	500	call	•	•		•	•						•		•
Mount View Hotel	341	100	125	•	•	•		•	•	•	•			•		•
Geyserville																
Isis Oasis Retreat Center	343	150	150	•	•	•	•	•	•		•		•	•	•	•
Guerneville																
Surrey Inn, The	344	500	1500	•	•	•	•		•			•	•	•	•	•

FACILITY	PAGE	MAX. SEATED CAPACITY	MAX. STANDING CAPACITY	Indoor Facilities	Outdoor Facilities	In-house Catering	BYO Catering	Alcohol Provided	Alcohol BYO	Restaurant On Site	Guestrooms Available	Event Coordination	Handicap Restricted	Smoking Restricted	Insurance Required	Amplified Music Restricted
Healdsburg																
Madrona Manor	345	135	135	•	•	•		•		•	•	•		•		•
Villa Chanticleer	346	600	600	•	•		•	•							•	
Kenwood																
Kenwood Inn	348	125	125	•	•	•	•	•				•	•	•		
Landmark Vineyards	349	500	700	•	•		•	•					•	•		•
Napa																
Chimney Rock Winery	350	250	250	•	•		•	•	•			•				
Hess Collection, The	351	80	n/a	•	•	•		•				•				
Inn at Napa Valley	352	250	250	•		•		•	•	•	•					
Napa River Boat	354	90	100	•	•	•		•				•	•			•
Napa Valley Wine Train	355	240	n/a	•		•		•				•	•			•
Willow Retreat	356	100	100	•	•		•	•			•			•		
Petaluma																
Garden Valley Ranch	357	250	250		•		•	•								
Rutherford																
Auberge du Soleil	358	110	180*	•	•	•		•		•	•	•				•
Rancho Caymus Inn	359	115	150	•	•	•		•	•	•	•	•				
Santa Rosa																
Chateau DeBaun Winery	360	800	800	•	•		•	•				•		•		
Sonoma																
Buena Vista Winery	361	200	400	•	•		•	•				•	•	•		
Las Castañas	362	300	500*	•	•	•	•	•	•		•	•	•	•	•	•
Sears Point Raceway	363	100	100*	•	•	•		•				•	•	•	•	
Sonoma Mission Inn and Spa	364	150	275	•		•		•	•	•	•	•				
Viansa Winery	365	112	275	•	•		•	•				•		•		•
Westerbeke Ranch Conf. Center	367	100	100	•	•	•		•	•		•	•	•	•		
St. Helena																
Charles Krug Winery	368	1500	1500	•	•		•	•	•			•		•	•	
Meadowood Resort	369	250	300*	•	•	•		•	•	•	•	•				•
Merryvale Vineyards	371	160	160	•	•	•	•					•		•		
V. Sattui Winery	372	250	350	•	•		•	•	•			•		•	•	

FACILITY

Facility	Page	Max. Seated Capacity	Max. Standing Capacity	Indoor Facilities	Outdoor Facilities	In-house Catering	BYO Catering	Alcohol Provided	Alcohol BYO	Restaurant On Site	Guestrooms Available	Event Coordination	Handicap Restricted	Smoking Restricted	Insurance Required	Amplified Music Restricted
LAKES BASIN																
Clearlake																
Windflower Island	373	60	60	•	•	•		•	•		•	•	•		•	
SANTA CRUZ AREA																
Ben Lomond																
Highlands House & Park	374	200	200	•	•		•	•						•		•
Capitola																
Inn at Depot Hill	375	call	75	•	•	•	•	•	•		•	•		•		•
Felton																
Roaring Camp	376	2000*	2000*	•	•	•			•			•	•			•
Santa Cruz																
Chaminade	377	180	225	•	•	•		•		•	•	•				•
Hollins House	378	45	250	•	•	•		•	•	•		•				
MONTEREY PENINSULA																
Carmel																
Highlands Inn	380	100	180*	•	•	•		•		•	•	•	•			•
La Playa Hotel	381	100	150*	•	•	•		•	•	•	•	•				
Mission Ranch	382	180	300*	•	•	•		•		•	•	•		•		•
Monterey																
La Mirada	384	150*	200*	•	•	•	•	•				•		•		•
Monterey Bay Aquarium	385	250	2000	•		•		•	•	•		•		•	•	
Old Monterey Inn	387	20	20	•	•	call		•	•		•	•	•	•		•
Old Whaling Station	388	150	150	•	•		•	•					•	•		•
Pacific Grove																
Asilomar Conference Center	389	1300	1500	•	•	•		•	•		•	•		•	•	•
Martine Inn	390	125	125*	•	•	•		•			•	•		•		•
Pebble Beach																
Beach & Tennis Club	391	250	250*	•	•	•		•	•		•					
Inn at Spanish Bay, The	392	300	300*	•	•	•		•		•	•	•				
Lodge at Pebble Beach, The	393	250	330*	•	•	•		•	•	•	•	•				

Facility	Page	Max. Seated Capacity	Max. Standing Capacity	Indoor Facilities	Outdoor Facilities	In-house Catering	BYO Catering	Alcohol Provided	Alcohol BYO	Restaurant On Site	Guestrooms Available	Event Coordination	Handicap Restricted	Smoking Restricted	Insurance Required	Amplified Music Restricted
GOLD COUNTRY																
Amador City																
Imperial Hotel	395	60	75	•	•	•		•		•	•	•				•
Auburn																
Auburn Valley Country Club	396	150	400	•	•	•		•	•	•						
Power's Mansion Inn	397	75	75	•	•	•		•	•		•	•	•			•
Columbia																
Angelo's Hall	398	150	200	•		•	•				•	•				•
Avery Ranch	399	250	250	•	•	•	•	•	•		•	•	•	•		
City Hotel	400	60	100	•		•		•	•	•	•	•				•
Fallon House Theatre	401	250	100*	•	•	•	•	•				•	•	•		
Jamestown																
Historic National Hotel	402	60	100	•	•	•		•	•	•	•	•	•			
Jamestown Hotel	403	84	140	•	•	•		•	•	•	•	•	•			
Railtown 1897	405	325	450	•	•	•		•				•	•			•
Sutter Creek																
Gold Quartz Inn	406	48	call	•	•	•		•	•		•	•			•	•
YOSEMITE AREA																
Groveland																
Iron Door Saloon, The	408	75	150	•		•		•		•		•	•			
Oakhurst																
Estate by the Elderberries	409	125	150	•	•	•		•		•	•	•	•			
Yosemite																
Yosemite Facilities	410	168	300*	•	•	•		•		•	•	•	•			•
SACRAMENTO VALLEY																
Oroville																
Jean Pratt's Riverside B&B	412	34	n/a	•	•		•	•		•		•	•	•		•
Rancho Murieta																
Rancho Murieta Country Club	413	200	350	•	•	•		•	•	•		•	•		•	•

FACILITY	PAGE	MAX. SEATED CAPACITY	MAX. STANDING CAPACITY	Indoor Facilities	Outdoor Facilities	In-house Catering	BYO Catering	Alcohol Provided	Alcohol BYO	Restaurant On Site	Guestrooms Available	Event Coordination	Handicap Restricted	Smoking Restricted	Insurance Required	Amplified Music Restricted
Rocklin																
Finnish Temperance Hall	415	144	309	•			•		•							•
Sunset Whitney Country Club	416	300	300	•	•	•		•		•					•	
Roseville																
Maidu Community Center	417	280	450	•	•		•		•					•	•	
R.J.'s Victorian Palms	418	100	100	•	•	•		•	•			•		•	•	
Roseville Opera House	419	250	320	•			•		•			•	•	•	•	
Sacramento																
Amber House	420	65	65	•			•		•	•	•	•		•		•
Aunt Abigail's Bed & Breakfast	421	35	35	•	•		•		•	•		•	•	•		•
California State Railroad Museum	422	400	600	•			•		•					•	•	
Capitol Plaza Halls	423	300	500	•		•	•	•	•			•		•		
Driver Mansion Inn	424	100	100	•	•	•		•			•	•	•	•		•
Fairytale Town	425	500	3500		•	•		•					•	•	•	•
Hyatt Regency Sacramento	426	1075	1650*	•	•	•		•		•	•	•				•
Matthew McKinley, The	435	150	150	•	•	•		•	•			•	•	•		•
Penthouse, The	427	240	300	•		•		•	•	•		•	•			
Radisson Hotel	428	1000	1800	•	•	•		•	•	•	•	•				
Rancho Arroyo	429	2400	6000*	•	•	•		•	•	•		•		•	•	
Sacramento Grand Ballroom	431	500	700	•		•	•	•				•		•	•	
Sacramento History Museum	432	call	700	•			•		•					•	•	
Sacrmento Horsemen's Ass'n	433	200	200	•	•		•		•					•	•	
Shot of Class, A	434	250	400	•		•		•				•				
Spirit of Sacramento, The	435	350	350	•	•	•		•	•			•		•		•
Sterling Hotel	437	110	200	•		•		•	•	•	•			•		•
Towe Ford Museum	438	300	500	•			•		•					•	•	
Yuba City																
Harkey House	439	60	125	•	•		•		•		•		•	•		
THE DELTA																
Ryde																
Grand Island Inn	440	250	700	•	•	•		•	•	•	•	•				
Walnut Grove																
Grand Island Mansion	441	200	1000	•	•	•		•	•				•	•	•	

FACILITY	PAGE	MAX. SEATED CAPACITY	MAX. STANDING CAPACITY	Indoor Facilities	Outdoor Facilities	In-house Catering	BYO Catering	Alcohol Provided	Alcohol BYO	Restaurant On Site	Guestrooms Available	Event Coordination	Handicap Restricted	Smoking Restricted	Insurance Required	Amplified Music Restricted
SAN JOAQUIN VALLEY																
Lodi																
Japanese Pavilion & Gardens	443	175	175	•	•	•	•		•					•		
Wine & Roses Country Inn	444	400	400	•	•	•		•	•	•	•	•		•	•	
Stockton																
Boat House	445	32	50	•	•	•	•		•					•		
TAHOE REGION																
Big Bend																
Rainbow Lodge	447	120	150	•	•	•		•	•	•	•	•	•			
Norden																
Sugar Bowl Resort	448	400	400	•	•		•		•		•	•	•	•		
South Lake Tahoe																
Tallac Vista	449	75	75	•	•		•		•					•		•
Squaw Valley																
Resort at Squaw Creek	450	500	700*	•	•	•		•		•						
Tahoe City																
Sunnyside Restaurant & Lodge	451	100	100*	•	•	•		•	•	•	•	•	•			
Tahoma																
Ehrman Mansion	453	150	150		•		•		•					•	•	•
Truckee																
Northstar	454	200	300*	•	•	•		•	•		•	•				

Northern California

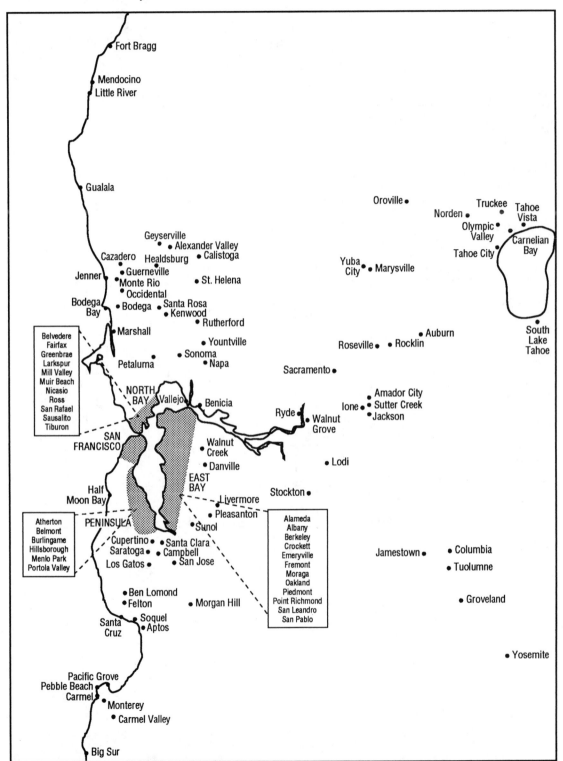

Fort Bragg

Mendocino
Little River

Gualala

Oroville

Norden

Truckee
Tahoe Vista

Olympic Valley

Carnelian Bay

Tahoe City

South Lake Tahoe

Geyserville
Alexander Valley
Calistoga

Cazadero
Healdsburg

Jenner
Guerneville
Monte Rio
Occidental

St. Helena

Yuba City
Marysville

Bodega Bay
Bodega
Santa Rosa
Kenwood

Rutherford

Marshall

Yountville

Auburn

Roseville
Rocklin

Belvedere
Fairfax
Greenbrae
Larkspur
Mill Valley
Muir Beach
Nicasio
Ross
San Rafael
Sausalito
Tiburon

Petaluma

Sonoma
Napa

Sacramento

NORTH BAY

Vallejo

Benicia

Ryde

Amador City
Sutter Creek

Ione
Jackson

Walnut Grove

SAN FRANCISCO

Walnut Creek

Danville

Lodi

EAST BAY

Stockton

Half Moon Bay

Livermore

Pleasanton

Atherton
Belmont
Burlingame
Hillsborough
Menlo Park
Portola Valley

PENINSULA

Sunol

Alameda
Albany
Berkeley
Crockett
Emeryville
Fremont
Moraga
Oakland
Piedmont
Point Richmond
San Leandro
San Pablo

Cupertino
Saratoga
Los Gatos

Santa Clara
Campbell
San Jose

Jamestown

Columbia

Tuolumne

Groveland

Ben Lomond
Felton

Morgan Hill

Santa Cruz

Soquel
Aptos

Yosemite

Pacific Grove
Pebble Beach
Carmel

Monterey

Carmel Valley

Big Sur

Restaurant Private Dining Room Guide

San Francisco

ASTA

One Rincon Center
101 Spear Street
San Francisco, CA 94105
(415) 495-2782
Reserve for Events: 3–6 months in advance

If you like the sultriness of *The Thin Man* movies, you're gonna like Asta. Taking its name from the feisty terrier who often upstaged detectives Nick and Nora Charles, played by William Powell and Myrna Loy, this sleek and sophisticated restaurant pays homage to the supper clubs of the thirties and forties. In fact, old movies (with the sound off) run continuously on small screens over the bar. Like most of the decor, they're in classy black and white. Everything here is custom designed—the period furniture, metal and glass light fixtures, and unusual 3-d wall sculptures. The main dining room curves around the lower level of the restaurant, while the bar occupies the upper level. The area in front of the bar can be used as a dance floor, and there is a place for a small band. A private room tucked away in the back is perfect for more intimate private parties. So whether you're planning a gathering of friends and family or a business luncheon or dinner, Asta can handle either with style. And if you're contemplating a really large party, Asta can cater your function in the Rincon Center Atrium. For more details, see its entry in the Special Event Facilities section.

CUISINE: Modern regional American

CAPACITY:

	Seated	*Standing*
Asta Restaurant	110	200
Private Dining Room	30	45

FEES & DEPOSITS: A deposit in the amount of 25% the estimated total is required 4 weeks prior to the event. Half of the estimated total is due the day of the event, and the remaining charges are due within 2 days of the event's conclusion. There is a 10% facility fee for all parties of less than 18 guests in Asta's private room, and for events held in the Rincon Center Atrium or the entire Asta Restaurant where the number of guests is less than 120 people. Per person food service rates are: $15–25 for luncheons or $30–40 for dinners. Tax and an 18% service charge are additional.

CANCELLATION POLICY: The deposit is refunded only if the date can be rebooked with a party of equal or greater value.

AVAILABILITY: The entire restaurant can be reserved Monday night, all day Sunday, and Saturday during the day. Other times can be arranged. The Private Dining Room is available Tuesday–Friday night, and weekday times can be arranged.

OTHER INFORMATION:

Credit Cards: all major
Parking: Rincon Center Garage, valet CBA
Full Bar: yes
Corkage: $9/bottle

Smoking: allowed
Dance Floor: yes
Wheelchair Access: yes

ATRIUM

101 California Street
San Francisco, CA 94111
(415) 788-4101
Reserve for Events: 1 day–3 months in advance

Located in the award-winning 101 California building, Atrium is one of the most elegant restaurants we've seen. As you enter the foyer, an oriental runner leads you past a marble-topped bar into the main dining room. The soothing atmosphere created by gray carpet, deep mauve upholstered chairs and light peach walls is punctuated dramatically by the exotic colors of azaleas, orchids and palms. Polished marble dividers define the dining areas in this split-level room, creating separate, homey spaces. One mirrored wall reflects the light and greenery of the atrium on the opposite side. The glass-enclosed atrium is ideal for small private parties, cocktails and hors d'oeuvres or after-dinner dancing. Hanging pots of kangaroo ivy provide a lush canopy, and bud vases with festive seasonal flowers complete the greenhouse effect. The adjacent granite plaza, lined with hundreds of planters overflowing with impatiens, is a lovely spot for a champagne reception. And during the Christmas season, a fifty-foot redwood Christmas tree with 35,000 lights, surrounded by a sea of red poinsettias creates a dazzling display. For small meetings or dinners, the executive dining room offers intimacy and seclusion. Behind plantation shutter doors, an oriental carpet, cherrywood buffet, antique mirror and striking contemporary pastel produce a rich, tasteful decor. With its special touches, imaginative cuisine, and convenient downtown location, Atrium can satisfy even the most demanding clientele.

CUISINE: California (French based)

CAPACITY:

	Seated	Standing		Seated	Standing
Main Dining Rm	40–130	100–300	Executive Dining Rm	14	—
Atrium	34	80	Entire Restaurant	175	300

FEES & DEPOSITS: A $500–1,000 non-refundable deposit (depending upon the number of guests) is required at the time of booking and is applied to the total bill. Payment schedules are individually arranged with the final bill due at the conclusion of the event. Buffets, lunches and dinners range from $15–40 per person. Beverage, tax and gratuity are additional. There is no minimum number of guests, and the final guest count is due 48 hours before the event.

CANCELLATION POLICY: The deposit is not refundable.

AVAILABILITY: Year-round, every day, 7am–2am.

OTHER INFORMATION:

Credit Cards: all major
Parking: validated lot (extra charge)
Full Bar: yes
Corkage: $10/bottle

Smoking: allowed
Dance Floor: yes
Wheelchair Access: yes

THE BLUE FOX

659 Merchant St.
San Francisco, CA 94111
(415) 981-1177
Reserve for Events: 2 weeks–12 months in advance

A long-time San Francisco institution, The Blue Fox is a restaurant with a history. Located on the first block of San Francisco, it began as a popular bohemian cafe and became a well-known speakeasy during prohibition. In 1933, an Italian from Viareggio opened the original Blue Fox, naming it after the restaurant he'd left behind in Italy. Today, it's still a family business. Nationally recognized for its elegant Italian and Continental cuisine, the restaurant also offers several dining areas that are perfect for corporate dinners or family celebrations. The Palatina and Alfieri rooms are classic, with crystal chandeliers, ambered mirrors and softly draped wall panels. The decor is soothing, in peach, mauve and cream tones. In complete contrast, the private dining rooms downstairs are two of the most unique spaces we've seen. Both serve as wine cellars, and guests are surrounded by thousands of wine bottles. The Large Wine Cellar has brick and stone walls and a dark wood-beamed ceiling. Guests dine by lantern light, kept low to protect the wine. As you survey the elaborately carved, high-backed chairs with their scarlet upholstery, and the deep red carpet, you feel like you're in the depths of a castle. The Original Wine Cellar is smaller, but similar in style. It's a bit more whimsical, however, with chianti bottles, salamis, grapes—and even a fox—suspended from the ceiling. Whether you want an ambiance that's formal and sophisticated, or one that's unconventional and fun, The Blue Fox delivers the best of both worlds.

CUISINE: Italian and Continental

CAPACITY:

Area	Seated	Standing	Area	Seated	Standing
Palatina Room	80	—	Original Wine Cellar	30	—
Alfieri Room	65	100	Large Wine Cellar	80	150

FEES & DEPOSITS: A non-refundable deposit is required when reservations are confirmed. The deposit is $250 for groups under 25, $500 for 25–50 guests and a minimum of $1,000 for over 50. There is a room charge of $100 for groups of 12 or less in the Wine Cellars. A guaranteed guest count is required 48 hours prior to the event. The balance is due 15 days after receipt of invoice. Luncheons start at $30/person, dinners at $50/person. Tax and a 20% gratuity are additional.

CANCELLATION POLICY: The deposit is not refundable.

AVAILABILITY: Monday-Saturday, flexible hours. Special events may be arranged on Sundays.

OTHER INFORMATION:

Credit Cards: all major
Parking: valet ($5/car), inexpensive garages
Full Bar: yes
Corkage: $15/bottle

Smoking: designated areas
Dance Floor: CBA
Wheelchair Access: main floor only

CAFE MAJESTIC

1500 Sutter Street at Gough
San Francisco, CA 94109
(415) 776-6400
Reserve for Events: 4 weeks in advance

Cafe Majestic, built in 1902 and authentically restored, is an appetizing restaurant in both cuisine and decor. We were surprised to learn that many of the menu selections are derived from old San Francisco cookbooks. The owner, Tom Marshall, has a penchant for 'vintage' recipes, and is enthusiastic about offering a dining environment reminiscent of the City's genteel past. For dinner parties or luncheon meetings, this is a splendid spot. The refreshing bright and airy interior has peach walls, a high ceiling and tall windows along the street side of the room. The warm wall color contrasts nicely with light teal wainscotting, shutters and trim. Small Kentia palms provide the perfect green accent next to the crisp white table settings. In addition to a charming ambiance and superb food, overnight accommodations are available in the adjacent Hotel Majestic.

CUISINE: Continental

CAPACITY: The Main Dining Room can hold 20–120 seated guests.

MEETING ROOMS: The Board Room, 10–20 guests.

FEES & DEPOSITS: A refundable deposit of $300 is required when the date is confirmed. To rent the entire restaurant (75 guests minimum to waive rental fee), a non-refundable $500 deposit is required. With food, there's usually no rental fee. Meal service per person rates: luncheon entrees $10–14, dinner entrees $15–23, first courses $4–8, hors d'oeuvres start at $6. The balance is due the day of the event. Tax and service charges are additional.

CANCELLATION POLICY: With 2 months' notice, your deposit will be refunded.

AVAILABILITY: Year-round, every day from 7am–midnight. Closed Memorial Day, July 4th, Labor Day, December 26th and January 2nd. Groups of 40 or more guests can reserve the entire restaurant any night except Saturday from 6pm–midnight. Groups of 40 or fewer guests can reserve it Sun–Fri, 6pm–midnight, and Saturday, 8pm–midnight.

OTHER INFORMATION:

Credit Cards: all major
Parking: valet

Smoking: in bar only
Dance Floor: yes

Full Bar: yes
Corkage: $12/bottle

Wheelchair Access: yes

CARNELIAN ROOM

555 California Street, 52nd Floor
San Francisco, CA 94104
(415) 433-7500
Reserve for Events: 2–26 weeks in advance

The Carnelian Room is truly a "room with a view." Occupying an enviable location on the top floor of the Bank of America building, it overlooks the Bay, both bridges, the Embarcadero and the East Bay hills. Inside, the atmosphere is reminiscent of an English manor, warm and elegant with rich walnut paneling and masterworks of 18th and 19th-century art and cabinetry. Complementing the view from the main dining room is an equally imposing backdrop: the West's finest wine cellar, some 40,000 bottles in all. Imaginative menus are available featuring American cuisine—or consult with the catering director and create your own. Experienced staff are also on hand to coordinate any details of your special event.

CUISINE: Continental

CAPACITY: The Main Dining Room and 11 private suites, each with a glittering vista of the Bay Area, can be scaled for groups as small as 2 or as large as 500 guests.

MEETING ROOMS: The Giannini Auditorium is a 200-seat theatre–style room with a small stage and full audio/visual support.

FEES & DEPOSITS: A refundable deposit of $150 is required when reservations are confirmed. Small suites rent for $50/event and the large suites, $150/event. Pre-selected menus are developed in advance of any event. Dinners start at $34/person and substantial hors d'oeuvres start at $16/person. 80% of the estimated event total is payable 10 days prior to the function. The balance is due the day of the event. Tax and a 15% service charge will be applied to the final bill.

For meetings, the Giannini Auditorium rents for $300/half day and $600 full day/evenings/weekends. Use of audio visual equipment is extra.

CANCELLATION POLICY: With 14 days' notice, the deposit will be refunded.

AVAILABILITY: Year-round, Monday–Friday from 3pm, Saturday and Sunday all day. Closed most major holidays.

OTHER INFORMATION:

Credit Cards: all major
Parking: garage, $7 after 5pm or on weekends
Full Bar: yes
Corkage: $10/bottle

Smoking: allowed
Dance Floor: CBA
Wheelchair Access: yes
Meeting Equipment: CBA

THE CLIFF HOUSE

1090 Point Lobos
San Francisco, CA 94121
(415) 386-3330 Betty or David
Reserve for Events: 1 month in advance

From here you can smell the salt air, feel the ocean breezes and watch the sea lions cavort on the rocks below. This historic spot has actually been the home of several Cliff Houses. The first, a modest 1863 structure, the second a grand and elaborate Victorian resort built in 1896, and the current restaurant, built in 1909, which is now part of the Golden Gate National Recreation Area. The upstairs restaurants are favorite destinations for both tourists and locals to eat (and have a few martinis) while experiencing a California sunset. Downstairs, however, is the Terrace Room, a private, contemporary dining room which can be reserved for special events, receptions or business functions. Painted in cool grays, with window treatments in burgundies, pinks and grays, the Terrace Room has some terrific benefits. Let's start with the views—three sides of this space have multiple windows which overlook the Pacific. It also has a small, outdoor terrace for al fresco dining or mingling with cocktails. Next, it's large enough to handle a crowd. And there's more. This room is separated from the rest of the Cliff House's public spaces, so it's completely private and quiet. If you've been searching for an event spot next to the ocean, the Terrace Room is worth a look. Also note that other spaces in the Cliff House can be reserved for private parties but availability will depend on the season and number of guests.

CUISINE: Seafood

CAPACITY: The Terrace Room can hold 135 seated guests; 160 standing guests.

MEETING ROOMS: For meetings, the Terrace Room can accommodate 100, theater-style.

FEES & DEPOSITS: To reserve, a $250 non-refundable deposit (which is applied towards the final bill) is required when reservations are confirmed. Half the estimated event total is due 4 weeks prior to the event, the balance payable at the end of the function. A guest count confirmation is due 48 hours in advance. Food service is provided. Per person costs are approximately $30, minimum, for buffets, $24–31 for seated dinners, $16–20 for luncheons and $9 for continental breakfasts. Tax and 15% service charge are additional. The room charge for meetings without food service is $250 for half day; $400 for all day.

AVAILABILITY: Year-round, every day 6am–1am except Sunday days, Mother's Day, Christmas, New Year's Day, Thanksgiving and Easter.

OTHER INFORMATION:

Credit Cards: all major
Parking: on street, 2 free lots, valet CBA
Full Bar: yes
Corkage: $10/750 ml bottle

Smoking: allowed
Dance Floor: CBA, extra charge
Wheelchair Access: limited

CYPRESS CLUB

500 Jackson
San Francisco, CA 94133
(415) 296-8555
Reserve for Events: 1–2 weeks in advance

Step into the Cypress Club and get knocked off your feet. Hard to believe, but its design was inspired by old San Francisco restaurants like Taddich, Sam's, and Jack's and yet it may be the wildest and most voluptuous interior we've ever seen. Your eyes are drawn immediately to the titillating lights suspended from the ceiling. Fashioned out of airplane propeller fittings and colorful spotted blown glass, they resemble...well you'll just have to come to your own conclusion. Half a dozen enormous, urn-shaped pillars draw your eye around the Main Dining Room and give it a grand scale. Plump copper dividers separate the sunken center of the room from the raised banquettes on either side. Every detail down to the door handles is custom designed, and the architect, himself, painted the mural of Northern California which wraps around the room. A towering, balloon-like copper arch draws you into The Club Room, a great spot for an intimate dinner, party or business meeting. Copper wall sconces wash the room with subtle light, accenting another vibrantly colored mural. Dark velour drapes and a deep purple carpet add to the soft, round, richness of the decor. Downstairs, the Wine Cellar Dining Room provides a unique space for functions. Adjacent to the Club's 14,000+ bottle wine collection, it's also a gallery, displaying contemporary art. For a visually stunning experience you'll never forget, the Cypress Club is in a class by itself.

CUISINE: North American (featuring a wood burning clay oven)

CAPACITY:

Area	*Seated*	*Standing*
Main Dining Room	110	300
The Club Room	40	50
The Wine Cellar Room	16	30

FEES & DEPOSITS: A signed reservation agreement and a 50% deposit is required 10 days after booking. Minimum per person food costs are $25 for lunch and $48 for dinner for a 3 course meal. These rates do not include beverage, 20% gratuity or tax. The entire restaurant can be reserved for $25,000 minimum. Club Room food and beverage minimums are as follows: 5:30pm–close, $3,200; 5:30–8:30pm, 22 people or $1,600; 9:00pm to close, 22 people or $1,600. The Wine Cellar Dining Room has a 10-guest lunch minimum, an 8-guest dinner minimum, and a room charge of $200 for parties under 12.

CANCELLATION POLICY: 72-hour advance notice is required for cancellation and full return of deposit. Half the deposit is returned if cancellation is received with less than 72-hour notice.

AVAILABILITY: Daily except Thanksgiving, Christmas, New Year's Day, and July 4th. You can rent The Club Room for either dinner seating, or for the entire evening. Evening hours for The Wine Cellar Dining Room are 5:30pm–close. Luncheon hours for both private rooms are 11:30am–4pm. The entire restaurant cannot be rented on Friday or Saturday nights.

OTHER INFORMATION:

Credit Cards: all major
Parking: Valet after 5:30 (CBA for lunch), on street
Full Bar: yes
Corkage: $15/bottle

Smoking: allowed
Dance Floor: only if entire restaurant reserved
Wheelchair Access: yes

DELANCEY STREET RESTAURANT

600 Embarcadero
San Francisco, CA 94107
(415) 957-9800
Reserve for Events: 2 weeks–3 months in advance

Named after the part of New York City's Lower East Side where immigrants congregated at the turn of the century, Delancey Street has evolved over the last twenty years into "the world's greatest halfway house." Once crowded into a small San Francisco apartment, this extraordinary rehab program now occupies most of a city block. One of its most successful endeavors is the Delancey Street Restaurant. Built and operated by residents (with the help of staff from some of San Francisco's finest restaurants), this American bistro has a lot to offer. The Main Dining Room features hand-crafted wood, brass and copper details. Guests sitting at the highly polished copper bar can watch the chef prepare delicacies on the open Italian rotisserie. Right outside, a brick patio with white umbrellas provides a breath-taking view of the waterfront and Bay Bridge. Two private dining rooms offer unique surroundings for meetings or parties. The Boardroom has a more formal ambiance, with Oriental-style table and chairs, wainscotting and original wildlife portraits. It overlooks both the bay and a small garden. In the Southwestern Room, guests are seated around large carved pine tables on rough-hewn chairs—all crafted by Delancey Street residents. Native American sculptures, weavings, pottery and art make this room a colorful and interesting space. Since it opened in 1991, the Delancey Street Restaurant has received great press: according to critics and diners alike, the food is very good, the service is excellent and the atmosphere is one that will lift your spirits.

CUISINE: Ethnic American

CAPACITY:

Area	Seated	Standing
Boardroom	45	75
Southwestern Room	20	—

FEES & DEPOSITS: Half the estimated total is due 2 weeks prior to the event, and the balance is payable at the conclusion of the event. The final guest count is due 48 hours before the event. There is no minimum fee for lunch. The dinner minimum is $400 for the Southwest Room, and $600 for the Boardroom. Per person food costs range from $12.50–30 for lunch and $20–46 for dinner. Beverage, tax and a 15–18% gratuity are additional.

AVAILABILITY: Tuesday–Friday, 11am–11pm; Saturday–Sunday, 10am–11pm. Closed Monday, Thanksgiving, Christmas and New Year's.

OTHER INFORMATION:

Credit Cards: all major, no checks
Parking: on street and valet
Full Bar: wine & beer only
Corkage: $8/bottle

Smoking: designated area
Dance Floor: no
Wheelchair Access: yes
Other: 5 course spa menus (under 600 cal.) avail.

ELKA

1611 Post Street
San Francisco, CA 94115
(415) 922-3200
Reserve for Events: 1 week–6 months in advance

Located in Japantown's Miyako Hotel, Elka displays an innovative and eclectic mix of Asian and contemporary influences. When you enter from Post Street, a rich black, white and burgundy marble foyer offers a dramatic welcome. A glance down and to the right provides a unique overhead view of the restaurant below, and just beyond the foyer, an elegant Japanese garden beckons through a glass wall. The lounge in front of the garden is perfect for intimate dining, and the adjacent bar area works well for cocktails and dancing. As you descend to the main dining room, you pass a school of vibrantly colored blown glass tropical fish, suspended in the stairwell. The dining room, itself, is a work of art. One wall features a mural adapted from an Edo period painting in the Tokyo Museum. The rest of the room has been painted rouge, ochre, deep blue-gray and turquoise, echoing the colors in the mural. Graceful lighting fixtures, many with Japanese-style paper shades, have been hand-crafted by local artisans. A string of delicate tubular lanterns bathes diners in a soft glow, while Shoji panels screen them from the street. Black lacquer chairs and decorative orchids add a final oriental touch to a truly original dining experience.

CUISINE: Innovative Seafood

CAPACITY: The Dining Room can seat up to 105 guests or 125 for a standing reception. The Lounge can seat 35 guests or 125 standing.

FEES & DEPOSITS: The deposit varies depending on the size of the group. Per person food costs are $15–20 for lunch or $28–45 for dinner not including beverage. A 16% gratuity and tax are additional.

CANCELLATION POLICY: The deposit will be refunded in full with 2 months' notice.

AVAILABILITY: For small groups, the restaurant is available Sunday-Thursday from 6:30am to 10:30pm, and Friday–Saturday 6:30–11pm. The entire restaurant is available every day 2–5pm. Other times can be arranged.

OTHER INFORMATION:

Credit Cards: all major
Parking: valet, on street, lot
Full Bar: yes
Corkage: $6.50+/bottle

Smoking: allowed
Dance Floor: CBA
Wheelchair Access: yes

GREENS

Fort Mason, Building A
San Francisco, CA 94123
(415) 771-7955 Rick Jones
Reserve for Events: 1–6 months in advance

Greens is a special restaurant, not just because it's located at Fort Mason, or because it's owned by a Zen Buddhist organization, or because it only serves gourmet vegetarian fare with flair. This place is special because the space makes you feel so good. Greens has enormous multi-paned windows extending the entire length of the restaurant. These windows have superb views of the Golden Gate Bridge and of the boat harbor which lies directly beyond the building. At sunset, the waning light reflected off the bridge and boats is a stunning sight to see. The interior of Greens is also exceptional, with really good original art work, unusual carved wood seating and tables, plus a high vaulted ceiling. The overall impression is light, airy and comfortable.

CUISINE: Innovative Vegetarian

CAPACITY: Greens can accommodate 150 for a seated meal or 250 for a standing hors d'oeuvres reception. There's also a 30-person private dining room, ideal for business functions and smaller special events.

FEES & DEPOSITS: A $250 non-refundable damage deposit is required to secure your event date. It's due when the event date is booked, and is credited to the final billing. Full meal service is provided. Rates vary according to group size: $50–60/person for a 50–person dinner; $30–40/person for 100 guests. These figures include space rental for 4 hours, labor, linens, flowers and candles. Gratuity and tax will be added to the final bill. Beyond 4 hours, there is a $200/hour fee.

AVAILABILITY: The private dining room is available every day. Larger private parties restricted to Sundays from 5pm onwards and Mondays from 3pm onwards.

OTHER INFORMATION:

Credit Cards: MC or Visa
Parking: large lot
Full Bar: B&W only
Corkage: $10/bottle

Smoking: allowed
Dance Floor: CBA, extra fee
Wheelchair Access: ramp

JULIUS' CASTLE

1541 Montgomery Street
San Francisco, CA 94133
(415) 362-3042
Reserve for Events: 2 months in advance

Julius' Castle, located in the heart of Northbeach, is situated high atop Telegraph Hill. Built in 1922 by Julius Roz, who used materials and craftsmen from the 1915 Panama-Pacific Exposition to design a restaurant to look like a "medieval castle," it's an unusual place to hold a private party. The restaurant's main attractions, besides the cuisine, are its unparalleled panoramic views of the Bay from interior windows and outdoor deck on the upper floor. This deck opens off of the second floor Penthouse Dining Room and is an exceptional spot for cocktails before dinner. You may rent the second floor or the entire restaurant with enough advance notice.

CUISINE: French

CAPACITY: The Penthouse Dining Room has seating capacity for 60 people; the Main Dining Room up to 100.

FEES & DEPOSITS: The deposit is approximately $1,000, depending on the size of your party. No rental fee is required. Food service costs range from hors d'oeuvres at $4–21/person to full meals at $35–75/person. Gratuity and taxes are not included in the above prices.

AVAILABILITY: From noon to 1am, every day.

OTHER INFORMATION:

Credit Cards: all major
Parking: valet only
Full Bar: yes
Corkage: $10/bottle domestic wine, $15/bottle, imports & champagne

Smoking: allowed
Dance Floor: limited
Wheelchair Access: no

KULETO'S MACHIAVELLI ROOM

221 Powell Street
San Francisco, CA 94102
(415) 397-7720
Reserve for Events: 4 days in advance

If you've ever had a tough time finding an intimate spot for a business breakfast or luncheon, board meeting or pre-theater dinner party, the Machiavelli Room may compel you to shout "Eureka!" What's so nice about this room is that it's completely private. You can make as much noise as you want or have a hush, hush conversation without worrying. And you'll enjoy Kuleto's Northern Italian fare, prepared by executive chef Robert Helstrom. Another plus is that it's ideally located in the heart of Union Square. To find the Machiavelli Room, go through Kuleto's or through the adjacent Villa Florence Hotel lobby. Wind your way to the stairway leading to the Machiavelli entry and descend into a small foyer with a black and white marble floor. This is a wonderful area for a bar setup. Guests can sip cocktails and mingle here before dining or getting down to business. The Machiavelli Room decor is rich yet subtle: mahogany wainscotting, onyx sconces, a wall of mirrors and art depicting scenic views of Italy impart a simple, old-world elegance. Given the combination of great food and attractive ambiance, this spot will appeal to the most discerning of guests.

CUISINE: Northern Italian

CAPACITY: 50 for a seated breakfast, lunch or dinner; 50 for an all-day meeting with lunch or 100 guests for cocktail receptions. Minimum, 20 guests.

FEES & DEPOSITS: When you finalize your menu, half the estimated total is requested. The balance is payable at the end of your function. Food service is provided by Kuleto's. You can select from Kuleto's preset menu or customize a special menu. The setup/cleanup charge is $100 additional. If you're just having cocktails or hors d'oeuvres, $100 is charged for the bar with bartender. For meetings with no meals, the Villa Florence Hotel will provide service. Tax and an 18% service charge are additional.

CANCELLATION POLICY: With less than 30 days' notice, any deposit is forfeited.

AVAILABILITY: Year-round, every day from 7:30am–midnight except Christmas and Thanksgiving.

OTHER INFORMATION:

Credit Cards: yes
Parking: on street, nearby garages
Full Bar: yes
Corkage: $15/bottle
Meeting Equipment: yes

Smoking: allowed
Dance Floor: CBA
Wheelchair Access: limited
Overnight Accommodations: Villa Florence, upstairs
Other: event coordinator

LA FIAMMETTA

1701 Octavia
San Francisco, CA 94109
(415) 981-1177
Reserve for Events: 2 weeks–12 months in advance

Sometimes less is more, and that's the case with La Fiammetta. Straight-forward and unpretentious, this not-so-well-known Italian restaurant is a real charmer. (It's also a favorite of SF Examiner restaurant critic, Jim Wood.) Housed on the ground floor of a pink Victorian, it's a cozy, intimate dining room that lends itself splendidly to small private or corporate parties. The interior is fresh and warm, with cream-colored walls, white linens and sunlight pouring in through storefront windows. Dozens of "pill" drawers—remnants of a past life as a pharmacy—line the walls. Above and below the drawers, rows of colorful wine bottles are displayed and stored. Juan Loeza, La Fiammetta's chef, is also its manager and host. He not only creates delectable dishes, but mingles with guests, erasing the separation between kitchen and dining room. His friendliness and accessibility are rare qualities in a chef, and he makes everyone feel welcome and comfortable.

CUISINE: Central and Southern Italian

CAPACITY: The dining room accommodates 50 seated, or 60 for a standing reception.

FEES & DEPOSITS: A deposit in the amount of 25–30% of the anticipated cost is required when reservations are confirmed. The balance is due at the conclusion of the event. There is no room rental charge. Luncheons run $25–30/person, and dinners start at $30. Prices include beverage; tax and gratuity are additional.

CANCELLATION POLICY: The deposit is refunded with 1 week's notice.

AVAILABILITY: Every day, 11am–midnight; closed Thanksgiving, Christmas, New Year's Day and July 4th.

OTHER INFORMATION:

Credit Cards: all major
Parking: on street
Full Bar: B&W only
Corkage: $10/750ml bottle

Smoking: no pipes or cigars
Dance Floor: CBA
Wheelchair Access: no

LASCAUX

248 Sutter Street
San Francisco, CA 94108
(415) 391-1555   Manager
Reserve for Events: 30 days in advance

A descent into this subterranean restaurant evokes the beauty and mystery of the Lascaux caves in France. Subdued lighting casts a soft, warm blush throughout. Wall surfaces suggest a cave's interior—uneven, tactile, earthy. A large stone fireplace provides a glowing focal point. Another contributor to the restaurant's unique ambiance is a rotisserie for meat specialties. Adjacent to the dining area, it is completely visible to all partons, actively including them in the cooking experience. It's not surprising that Lascaux won San Francisco Focus Magazine's "Best Restaurant Design Award" two years in a row. For small business dinners and parties, Lascaux is a real gem.

CUISINE: Mediterranean

CAPACITY: Partially rented, groups of 25–40 guests. The entire facility (which can seat 140) can be reserved for a private party by prior arrangement; food and beverage minimums apply.

FEES & DEPOSITS: A refundable deposit of 20% of the estimated food and beverage total is required when reservations are confirmed. The balance is payable upon completion of the event. Luncheons range from $22–25/person, dinners $35–40/person. Tax and 15% service charge are additional.

CANCELLATION POLICY: A 14-day advance notice is required for a refund.

AVAILABILITY: Year-round, every day from 11:30am–11pm except for major holidays.

OTHER INFORMATION:

Credit Cards: all major
Parking: adjacent garages
Full Bar: yes
Corkage: $10/bottle
Meeting Equipment: no

Smoking: designated areas
Dance Floor: no
Wheelchair Access: yes, elevator
Overnight Accommodations: no

Need a caterer, cake maker, florist? The Service Directory starting on page 614 features the best in the business.

MacARTHUR PARK

607 Front Street
San Francisco, CA 94111
(415) 398-5700
Reserve for Events: 2–4 weeks in advance

Housed in a pre-1906 brick warehouse—built when the area was the infamous Barbary Coast—MacArthur Park is located just blocks from the Financial District. The Main Dining Room is light and airy with eighteen-foot ceilings, skylights and a couple of towering indoor trees. The lower part of the room, called The Arcade, is frequently used for cocktail parties. It features brick arches and an expanse of tall windows that overlook the park across the street. The Aviary, once a roosting place for peacocks and other tropical birds, offers a private and soothing atmosphere for meetings and other events. A skylight ceiling, terra cotta floor and brick walls hung with modern prints create warmth and intimacy. The adjacent Patio provides a unique sheltered setting for open-air events, particularly luncheons and cocktail receptions. Guests can enjoy the fresh air, protected from the elements by a canvas roof and banks of heaters. The West Room accommodates larger groups with wood-paneled walls featuring limited edition American watercolors, windows that open out onto an ivy-covered courtyard and a large brick fireplace. Connected by French doors, these three rooms can be used individually or in combination. Blending rustic and sophisticated elements, MacArthur Park is a warm and inviting location for almost any event.

CUISINE: Creative American

CAPACITY:

Area	Seated	Standing	Area	Seated	Standing
Arcade	50	90	West Room	75	125
Aviary	38	50	Main Dining Room	120	200
Bar Area	50	250	Entire Restaurant	280	500
Patio	25	50			

FEES & DEPOSITS: A $100 deposit is required at the time of booking. The balance is due the day of the event. Per person food costs range $15–27 for luncheons, and $19–33 for dinners. Tax and an 18% gratuity are additional.

CANCELLATION POLICY: The deposit is fully refundable with 48 hours' notice.

AVAILABILITY: Private dining rooms are available every day except Thanksgiving and Christmas. The entire restaurant can be reserved Saturday and Sunday during the day. The restaurant is closed on all Monday holidays for lunch, and open July 4th for dinner only.

OTHER INFORMATION:

Credit Cards: all major
Parking: complimentary valet (dinners only), on street
Full Bar: yes, extensive Calif. wine list
Corkage: $10/bottle

Smoking: in private dining rooms only
Dance Floor: yes
Wheelchair Access: yes, except Aviary
Other: extensive wine list

MISS PEARL'S JAM HOUSE

601 Eddy St
San Francisco, CA 94109
(415) 775-5267
Reserve for Events: 2 weeks in advance

Paradise in the Tenderloin? It exists in the form of Miss Pearl's Jam House. This place vibrates with color: brilliant paintings hang everywhere, and the coral hues of a Caribbean sunset cover an entire wall. Chairs in the Main Dining Room are purple and straw; in the Sun Room they're covered with zebra stripes. The drama intensifies in the Bar, with its yellow floor, black ceiling and giant fish tank. Ceiling fans waft delectable smells throughout, and the half hull of a sailboat suspended over the Main Dining Room bar clinches the tropical feel. Right outside the restaurant is a spacious patio, pool and courtyard. Terra cotta planters with palms and flowers add splashes of color. People often have cocktails outdoors, followed by a seated dinner inside. By special arrangement you can even go swimming! Thursday through Sunday nights there's live music, so your guests can dance if the spirit moves them. And if you need to stay over, Miss Pearl's just happens to be located in the Phoenix Hotel, favorite hangout for touring rock stars and other celebs. Upbeat, funky, and just plain fun, Miss Pearl's is something completely different.

CUISINE: California-inspired Caribbean

CAPACITY:

Area	Seated	Standing	Area	Seated	Standing
Restaurant & poolside	400	800	Bar	50	120
Restaurant	150	250	Poolside tented	40	75
Sun Room	40	—	Poolside open	250	550

FEES & DEPOSITS: A deposit in the amount of half of the estimated total charges is required 1 month in advance, and the balance is due 3 days prior to the event. There is no security or cleaning deposit. Food and beverage costs run $7–15 for hors d'oeuvres, $12–20 for lunch or $15–35 for a seated or buffet dinner. Meals include house wine and beer. Tax and a 15% gratuity are additional.

CANCELLATION POLICY: All deposits are non-refundable.

AVAILABILITY: Year-round, every day except New Year's Day, 4th of July, Thanksgiving and Christmas.

OTHER INFORMATION:

Credit Cards: all major except American Express
Parking: on street, valet CBA Thurs–Sat
Full Bar: yes, specializing in wild, tropical drinks
Corkage: $7/bottle

Smoking: allowed
Dance Floor: yes
Wheelchair Access: yes
Overnight Accommodations: yes

PALIO D'ASTI

640 Sacramento Street
San Francisco, CA 94111
(415) 395-9800
Reserve for Events: 2 weeks–12 months in advance

Named after a medieval bare-back horse race that's held annually in the Northern Italian city of Asti, Palio d'Asti is a contemporary restaurant with old-world roots. Built in 1990, it was chosen "best dressed" by Restaurant Design Magazine the following year. Their choice was well justified—this sleek Milano styled trattoria is a visual delight. Steam rises from the open kitchen where chefs prepare dozens of delicacies. You can witness the speed-production of fresh pasta, savor a pizza cooked to perfection in their wood-burning oven, or sample antipasti from a specially designed cart brought to your table. Everything here is made on the premises, using the best imported products as well as fresh items from local farms and ranches. Weathered concrete columns, unique lighting fixtures and festive banners create a colorful interior. Have a luncheon meeting or party in the completely private San Pietro Room or a company dinner the in semi-private San Secondo Room, and give your eyes, nose and tastebuds a treat.

CUISINE: Italian

CAPACITY:

Area	*Seated*	*Standing*
San Pietro Room	50	75
San Secondo Room	50	75
Entire Restaurant	250	300

FEES & DEPOSITS: A non-refundable $200 deposit is required when booking a private dining room. If you reserve the entire restaurant, there's a $6,000 minimum, with 50% of the anticipated total required when reservations are confirmed. A guaranteed guest count is required 48 hours prior to the event. The balance is due 15 days after receipt of invoice. Luncheons start at $22.50/person, dinners at $35. Tax and a 20% gratuity are additional.

CANCELLATION POLICY: The deposit is not refundable.

AVAILABILITY: Monday–Saturday, flexible hours. Special events may be arranged on Sundays.

OTHER INFORMATION:

Credit Cards: all major
Parking: valet ($4/car), inexpensive garage
Full Bar: yes
Corkage: $10/bottle

Smoking: designated areas
Dance Floor: CBA if you reserve entire rest.
Wheelchair Access: yes

PORTICO

246 McAllister Street
San Francisco, CA 94102
(415) 861-2939
Reserve for Events: 2 weeks in advance

It's hard to believe that this hideaway restaurant was a carriage house complete with horse and buggy until 1990. A subterranean café in its current incarnation, Portico provides a cozy, Mediterranean ambiance for parties. When you step down into the restaurant, your eye is immediately drawn to the lush garden window at the end of the room. Artfully lit at night, it's a dramatic focal point. Fields of tall grasses are painted on the walls, giving the impression of surrounding countryside. Dried manzanita branches poised over tables enhance the sensation of being outdoors. And the tables themselves are works of art: each one is a hand-painted abstract fresco in rich earth tones. Upstairs, the foyer and bar serve as a great staging area for cocktails and hors d'oeuvres. Tall arched windows, sunkissed walls and the hint of a balcony take you to...southern Italy, perhaps? Copper-topped tables and unique upholstered adirondacks make for some unusual seating. And those wonderful painted tables in the bar appear to glow at night, thanks to special track lighting. This blending of antique and contemporary elements works well, making the Portico Restaurant a charming and relaxed urban refuge.

CUISINE: Mediterranean

CAPACITY: The Restaurant seats 100 or 150 standing guests; the Bar 30 seated, 50 standing.

FEES & DEPOSITS: A deposit in the amount of half of the estimated total charges is required 1 month in advance, and the balance is due 3 days prior to the event. There is no security or cleaning deposit. Food and beverage costs run $7–15 for hors d'oeuvres, $12–20 for lunch and $15–35 for a seated or buffet dinner. Meals include house wine and beer. Tax and a 15% gratuity are additional.

CANCELLATION POLICY: All deposits are non-refundable.

AVAILABILITY: Year-round, every day except New Year's Day, 4th of July, Thanksgiving and Christmas.

OTHER INFORMATION:

Credit Cards: all major except American Express
Parking: on street, valet CBA
Full Bar: no, WBC only
Corkage: $5/bottle

Smoking: allowed
Dance Floor: yes
Wheelchair Access: bar only
Overnight Accommodations: yes

POSTRIO
Garden Patio Room

454 Post Street at Mason
San Francisco, CA 94102
(415) 776-7825
Reserve for Events: 1–6 months in advance

Designed by Pat Kuleto and run by executive chefs Wolfgang Puck and Anne and David Gingrass, Postrio is one of the most sought-after dining spots in the City. Its dramatic design encompasses three levels and displays a variety of styles. Tucked away in a corner of the main dining room is the Garden Patio Room, a gem of a space that many Postrio regulars probably don't even know about. Here you can have a meeting or private dinner, shielded from the hubub of the main dining area. The Patio has its own special ambiance—it looks and feels just like a garden terrace. One of its most delightful features is its "ceiling," actually a very high, white canvas canopy that filters the sun's rays. When it rains, you can hear the delicate pitter-patter of raindrops overhead; when it's sunny, the room glows. A clever combination of brick walls, windows and greenery create the impression that you really *are* in a garden courtyard. Glimpses of wine bottles in storage, homemade salami, and distant diners are visible through tall, multi-paned windows. Contemporary art, pastel colors and crisp white linens add zest. Light, airy and totally private, the Garden Patio Room is a little oasis in Postrio's culinary paradise.

CUISINE: California Cuisine with Asian and Mediterranean influences

CAPACITY: Garden Patio seats 36 guests; 50 for a standing reception.

FEES & DEPOSITS: A deposit in the amount of 50% of the anticipated total is required at the time of booking. The balance is due upon completion of the event. Per person food costs average $30 for lunch and $50 for dinner, with minimums of $1,500 for lunch and $3,500 for dinner. Beverage, tax and a 17% gratuity are additional.

CANCELLATION POLICY: With 72 hours' notice, the deposit is refunded in full. With less notice, only 50% of the deposit is returned.

AVAILABILITY: Call for availability.

OTHER INFORMATION:

Credit Cards: all major
Parking: curbside valet, on street eves.
Full Bar: yes
Corkage: $15/bottle
Meeting Equipment: CBA

Smoking: designated area
Dance Floor: no
Wheelchair Access: yes
Overnight Accommodations: Prescott Hotel

THE ROTUNDA
At Neiman Marcus

150 Stockton Street
San Francisco, CA 94108
(415) 362-4777
Reserve for Events: 2–48 weeks in advance

The Rotunda at Neiman Marcus is famous for good reason. Located on the top floor, it has seating in the round beneath an extraordinary stained glass dome. The skylight is really a painting in glass—a sea theme with Neptune presiding. Constructed of 2,600 pieces of clear, rust and variegated green glass, the "ceiling" bathes diners in a warm glow. Every table here has a view of Union Square through a curved wall of glass descending four stories down to street level. Decorated in muted colors, much of the seating is arranged in tiered, private banquettes. Also well known for its San Francisco "taste tour," the restaurant creates numerous buffet tables decorated in themes of famous San Francisco spots such as Chinatown, Fisherman's Wharf, the Mission, North Beach and Japantown. Each table, of course, serves a theme-related food. Equally popular are NM's formal seated dinners which set the tone for a more upscale, elegant function. Note that The Rotunda is also available for breakfast group meetings.

CUISINE: California American

CAPACITY: The entire Rotunda can hold 350 for a reception or 200 seated guests.

FEES & DEPOSITS: A refundable deposit of half the total estimated food and beverage cost is due when the contract is submitted. There is no rental fee with food service. The balance is due the day of the event. Per person rates: hors d'oeuvres $2–5, dinners start at $40, buffets at $18. Tax and 18% gratuity are additional. For you Neiman Marcus cardholders, note that you can make payment using your NM card to gain *Incircle* points.

CANCELLATION POLICY: With 2 weeks' notice, the deposit is refunded.

AVAILABILITY: Year-round, every day from 6pm–midnight. Breakfast meetings from 8:30am–10:30am.

OTHER INFORMATION:
Credit Cards: Amer. Exp., Neiman Marcus, checks & cash
Parking: Union Square garage
Full Bar: yes
Corkage: $5/bottle
Meeting Equipment: PA sound system
Music: amplified ok
Smoking: allowed
Dance Floor: yes
Wheelchair Access: yes
Overnight Accommodations: no
Music: amplified ok

SAILING SHIP DOLPH REMPP

Pier 42–44 on the Embarcadero,
South of Market St.
San Francisco, CA 94107
(415) 777-5771 or **(415) 543-4024**
Reserve for Events: 1–8 weeks in advance

This impressive, hundred-year-old three-masted schooner combines all the advantages of being "out to sea" without any of the disadvantages. Because the vessel rests in an earthquake-proof concrete cradle at the southwest end of San Francisco's waterfront, guests will not miss the boat if late, can leave at will, and can enjoy the salt air, the sights and sounds of being on the water while remaining motionless. The Sailing Ship Dolph Rempp was built in 1884 as a trading vessel in the Baltic Sea, and has had an illustrious career. Jules Verne was aboard for exploratory journeys and used the schooner as inspiration for his novels. It was also a rum-runner, pleasure craft and a World War I supply carrier (used for espionage!). You and your guests will feel like stars in your own movie production when you board the Sailing Ship since it was, in fact, featured in more than a hundred Hollywood films. It now combines its rich history with indoor dining and fabulous views of the City, Bay Bridge and the colorful South Beach Harbor Marina.

CUISINE: California/French

CAPACITY: 800 people can be accommodated for a standing reception, up to 150 for a seated meal and 400 for a buffet dinner or luncheon. Outdoor tents on the front deck and canopies on the back deck can be erected for an additional 200 or more guests.

FEES & DEPOSITS: A negotiable fee is due 1 month before your event to secure the date and cover the security deposit. A rental fee/person is required, based on the guest count. Food service is provided. Cocktail hors d'oeuvres run $5–14.50/person, luncheons or dinners are $20–50/person. Sales tax and 18% gratuity are applied to the final bill.

CANCELLATION POLICY: Normally, 3 months' notice is allowed unless you have booked during the holiday season, in which case, 4 months' notice is required.

AVAILABILITY: 7 days a week, including major holidays.

OTHER INFORMATION:

Credit Cards: all major
Parking: on street, valet optional
Full Bar: yes
Corkage: $10/bottle wine, $13/bottle champagne
Meeting Equipment: yes, extra fee

Smoking: allowed
Dance Floor: no
Wheelchair Access: yes

SPLENDIDO

Four Embarcadero Center
Promenade Level
San Francisco, CA 94111
(415) 986-3222
Reserve for Events: 1–6 months in advance

Walk through the two hundred-year-old Spanish olivewood doors and you're in for a big surprise. This restaurant draws you into a fantastic world where no matter where you look, an uncanny mix of Mediterranean architectures surrounds you. Over the foyer is a circular, hand-chiseled stone dome. Nearby, Moorish arches blend into rustic French stone walls; Italian hand-painted tiles complement a Spanish wrought iron bannister. The handcrafted, one-ton pewter bar was flown from Portugal in ten sections, along with its builder, to ensure problem-free reassembly. Stone archways and columns, constructed of rubble collected from ancient ruins, form intimate dining areas. Hand-painted wormwood cabinetry, massive hand-hewn beams and warm hues of teal, gray, rose and muted peach create an earthy quality throughout. Unusual and fanciful light fixtures suggest octopi and Greek jugs. In the center of the restaurant, a massive European bread oven made of stone and brick stands on display. Overhead, the ceiling areas vary, from grapevine stakes and willow branches to vaulted brick and fabric canopies. For guests who like to watch food being artfully prepared, Splendido offers an exhibition kitchen, with open grill and wood-burning pizza oven. Outdoors, the restaurant has a large, permanent, cream-colored canopy and granite-topped bar for al fresco functions. Warmed by heaters and captivated by the view, you may forget you're in San Francisco and think you're relaxing on the tranquil Mediterranean.

CUISINE: Mediterranean Contemporary—emphasis on French and Italian food.

CAPACITY: Indoors, 24 seated guests in a separated area; outdoor patio 75 seated guests or 150-200 for a standing reception. On Sunday or Monday night, the entire restaurant for 150-200 seated guests.

FEES & DEPOSITS: For groups of 20 or more guests, a $200 deposit is required within a few days of booking. A guaranteed guest count is required 72 hours in advance. For parties of 10 or more, a special large party menu is available with prices ranging from $20–45/person for cocktail parties and seated luncheons. Dinners run $30–50/person. Approximately 50–75% of the anticipated food and beverage total is due 1 week prior to the event. Alcoholic beverages, tax and 15% service charge are additional. Customized cakes can be prepared with 3 days' notice from the Splendido bakery.

CANCELLATION POLICY: With less than 5 days' notice, the deposit is forfeited.

AVAILABILITY: Year round. Splendido is available every day based on guestcount and availability. Closed July 4th, Christmas, New Year's, Thanksgiving and Labor days.

OTHER INFORMATION:

Credit Cards: yes
Parking: Embarcadero garages, after 5pm free w/validation
Full Bar: yes
Corkage: $10/bottle

Smoking: designated areas
Dance Floor: no
Wheelchair Access: yes
Overnight Accommodations: no
Meeting Equipment: no

SQUARE ONE

190 Pacific at Front Street
San Francisco, CA 94111
(415) 788-1110
Reserve for Events: 2–4 weeks in advance

Often rated as one of the top ten restaurants in the US, Square One consistently delivers a sublime culinary experience. In keeping with its name, this San Francisco eatery makes almost everything from scratch (even ice cream and pickles!), using seasonal foods and fresh local produce. Bread and dessert aficionados will feel they've gone to heaven. The menu, an eclectic mix of robust and sensual international dishes, changes daily. Not only is the food splendid, but the far-ranging wine list has won five prestigious awards. The main dining room is contemporary and appealing, but for those who want to savor the essence of Square One, the Private Dining Room is where to go. Artist Carlo Marchiori has transformed two dimensional walls into an intimate Italian garden, replete with topiary, song birds and misty Tuscan landscape. You don't have to worry about a thing—restaurant staff will cheerfully handle all the arrangements and with enough notice, they'll customize any menu. And, master sommelier Peter Granoff will help you choose the perfect wine to accompany your meal. At Square One, wine and dine business associates, have delectable breakfast meetings or intimate workshops while enjoying views of Walton Park. If you've ever wondered how to make a birthday or anniversary party really special, wonder no more. This place is run by people who love to cook for people who love to eat, and they do it with a warmth and friendliness that will make you want to come back for more.

CUISINE: Eclectic international, with a strong emphasis on Mediterranean dishes.

CAPACITY: The Private Dining Room seats up to 45 guests.

FEES & DEPOSITS: To reserve the Private Dining Room, a $600 deposit is required for dinners, $300 for luncheons. Any menu can be customized. Alcohol, tax and service charge are additional. The balance is payable on completion of the event. The average luncheon is $400, dinners $600 Sunday–Thursday, Friday and Saturday $1,000 depending on number of guests. Flowers, cakes and other services can be arranged with advance notice.

CANCELLATION POLICY: With 1 week's notice, the deposit is refunded.

AVAILABILITY: Year-round from 11:30am to midnight. Luncheons Monday–Friday only, dinners daily.

OTHER INFORMATION:

Credit Cards: all major	*Smoking:* allowed
Parking: valet at night & adjacent garages	*Dance Floor:* no
Full Bar: yes	*Wheelchair Access:* yes
Corkage: $10/bottle	*Overnight Accommodations:* no
Meeting Equipment: CBA, extra fee	*Other:* award-winning wine cellar

STARS
The Grill Room

565 Golden Gate Ave.
San Francisco, CA 94102
(415) 431-2716
Reserve for Events: 6 weeks in advance

You don't have to be a star to use the Grill Room for a working lunch, cocktail party or private celebration. This renowned eatery, owned by Jeremiah Towers, has a very appealing private dining room that comes (amazingly) with its own private kitchen, chef and special events director. Private dining room guests don't have to walk through the restaurant—the shining, copper-clad door is situated nearer the Restaurant's entry. Inside you'll find a private retreat. The Grill Room's curved ceiling is its most striking element with artfully rendered and realistic sunset-colored clouds in hues of pinks and oranges painted against a gray-blue sky. A few scattered gold stars, rosy cheeked cherub and man fly effortlessly overhead, in the center of the room. The dining room's floor is in cherry hardwood, all cut on the diagonal and its walls are in soft terra cotta, with warm wood wainscotting on the lower portion. Contemporary art work graces the walls, an eye-level wood burning fireplace is tucked in one corner and a floor-to-ceiling cabinet of glassware, all backlit, separates the dining room from its own kitchen. Treat your guests to a luxurious repast—almost all the food prepared for the Grill Room comes directly from the private dining room's own kitchen and chef. If you haven't discovered the Grill Room yet, it's time to pay Stars another visit.

CUISINE: American Contemporary

CAPACITY: The Grill Room can seat 44 guests; 70 standing. Star Mart, next to Stars, is available for cocktail parties of up to 150 standing guests.

FEES & DEPOSITS: For private parties, menus are customized. A $500 deposit or more may be required, depending on guest count and menu desired. The balance is due the day of the event. Occasionally, a room rental fee for groups under 15 guests may be required.

CANCELLATION POLICY: The deposit is non-refundable.

AVAILABILITY: Year-round, anytime.

OTHER INFORMATION:

Credit Cards: all major	*Smoking:* allowed
Parking: on street, nearby garages	*Dance Floor:* no
Full Bar: yes	*Wheelchair Access:* yes
Corkage: $10/bottle	*Overnight Accommodations:* no
Meeting Equipment: limited in-house	*Other:* event coordinator, private chef

THE STINKING ROSE

325 Columbus Ave.
San Francisco, CA 94133
(415) 781-ROSE
Reserve for Events: 1 month in advance

No rose ever smelled as delectable as this North Beach eatery. Garlic—to the tune of one and a half tons a month—is the restaurant's reason for being. Bulbs of garlic fly across the fields of Gilroy in a mural painted on the front of the restaurant; a necklace of garlic is strung throughout the main dining room; and a whole wall of gorgeously bottled products claim the ancient herb as a main ingredient. A black and white tile floor, green booths and marble-topped tables give the restaurant a casual Italian flavor. The two private dining rooms upstairs will knock you out: local artist, Chuck Kennedy, has covered the walls and ceilings with irreverent cartoon murals. 2,635 cloves of garlic run wild—garlic mermaids ride the bus, garlic fish smooch beneath Fisherman's Wharf, and garlic survivors roast hot dogs over 1906 earthquake flames. The Chuck Kennedy Room also has two large skylights and a cozy outdoor terrace that's bound to convince you you're in Italy. Terra cotta walls, a bubbling fountain, and planter sconces overflowing with geraniums create a refreshing getaway in the heart of North Beach. The Stinking Rose has to be inhaled as well as seen to be fully appreciated. If you're looking to ward off vampires, lower you blood pressure or simply have fun—this is the place.

CUISINE: California-Northern Italian

CAPACITY:

Area	Seated	Standing
Main Dining Room	125	—
Washington Room	20	30
Chuck Kennedy Room	80	95

FEES & DEPOSITS: 30% of the estimated food and beverage total is required when reservations are confirmed. The balance is payable upon completion of the event. The per person food cost is $20–35 not including beverage, and customized banquet menus are available. Tax and a 15% gratuity are additional.

CANCELLATION POLICY: 72 hour advance notice is required for a full refund. With less notice, the deposit will be forfeited.

AVAILABILITY: Open daily, 11am–11pm. Closed Christmas.

OTHER INFORMATION:

Credit Cards: most major
Parking: garages, on street
Full Bar: yes
Corkage: $7/bottle

Smoking: designated areas
Dance Floor: no
Wheelchair Access: downstairs only

VINOTECA

586 Bush
San Francisco, CA 94108
(415) 983-6200
Reserve for Events: 1 weeks-6 months in advance

Conveniently located across the street from the Stockton-Sutter Street garage, Vinoteca has some of the friendliest staff we've encountered. And the hospitality extends to the restaurant's interior. In the main dining room, red and white checkered tablecloths set an informal tone. Beautiful watercolors of the Italian coastline and a mural of the Italian Riviera make you want to take off for Italy as soon as possible. The deeply coffered ceiling is painted a rich blue and walls and beams are a warm off-white. Flowers, a Campari poster and a wooden bin full of garlic are inviting accents. The middle and semi-private dining rooms feature high wooden wainscotting, warm sconce lighting and more art on the walls. A huge antique sideboard is laden with a colorful display of seasonal vegetables or fruits and five-foot long baguettes. The relaxed atmosphere and attentive service make Vinoteca a great place for a casual breakfast meeting or private dinner party.

CUISINE: Southern Italian

CAPACITY: Semi-private dining room can hold 55 seated, 70 standing; the entire restaurant can hold 140 seated, 300 standing.

FEES & DEPOSITS: A deposit in the amount of 20% of the anticipated cost is required when reservations are confirmed. The balance is due at the conclusion of the event. There is no room rental charge. Breakfast is $10/person, luncheons average $14–16/person, and dinners start at $22. Tax and a 20% service charge are additional.

CANCELLATION POLICY: The deposit is refunded with 1 week's notice.

AVAILABILITY: Every day, 7:30am–10pm; closed Thanksgiving, Christmas, New Year's Day and July 4th.

OTHER INFORMATION:

Credit Cards: all major
Parking: on street, inexpensive garage
Full Bar: yes
Corkage: $10/750ml bottle

Smoking: no pipes or cigars
Dance Floor: CBA
Wheelchair Access: yes

Prices and policies <u>do</u> change. Call each facility and confirm everything you read in Perfect Places.

Fairfax

DEER PARK VILLA

367 Bolinas Road
Fairfax, CA 94930
(415) 456-8084
Reserve for Events: 1–6 months in advance

The Villa is nestled among four acres of redwoods, oaks and lush hydrangeas. This homey Italian restaurant is supported by a very professional catering and restaurant staff with plenty of experience hosting parties and business functions. The facility includes a front garden with outdoor dance area, bar, covered and heated patio, towering redwood trees and a small Japanese pagoda and foot bridge. The main dining area is decorated in muted pinks and dark mint green with windows on three sides; adjacent to the dining area is a full bar. The split level, back deck is intimate and surrounded by dense greenery. Operated by the Ghiringhelli family since 1937, the Deer Park Villa is a Marin County dining and banquet tradition.

CUISINE: Italian Continental

CAPACITY: The Redwood Grove holds up to 300 guests; the Redwood Deck and adjoining indoor room, 125. The Villa can accommodate up to 225, but can be partitioned so that smaller groups have privacy.

FEES & DEPOSITS: No banquet room rental fee is charged if you choose a group brunch, lunch or dinner plan, however, a $2/person non-refundable deposit is required to confirm your date. Meal prices are quoted with tax and gratuity and cover a 4-hour function. Brunch at $14.75/person or lunch $14.75–16.75/person are available for 25 guests or more. Seated dinners or buffets start at $18/person. Packages, including the "Celebration Day Special" are available for group functions and include a variety of Deer Park Villa spaces and services. Menus and prices are mailed on request.

AVAILABILITY: For groups of 100 or more, any day, anytime. Less than 100 guests, Wednesday–Sunday, anytime.

OTHER INFORMATION:

Credit Cards: checks and cash	*Smoking:* allowed
Parking: large lot	*Dance Floor:* CBA $75 fee
Full Bar: yes	*Wheelchair Access:* yes
Corkage: $5.50/bottle	*Meeting Equipment:* VCR, TV, PA systems

Larkspur

THE LARK CREEK INN

234 Magnolia Avenue
Larkspur, CA 94939
(415) 924-1602 or **924-7766** Banquet Manager
Reserve for Events: 1–2 months in advance

The Lark Creek Inn, one of the most popular restaurants in the Bay Area, is a delightful place for a private party or business function. Built in 1888, this former Victorian country home is nestled in a grove of redwoods, next to a flowing creek. Muted colors, rich wood paneling and rotating original art create a tasteful interior. The private dining room upstairs and the sun porch downstairs accommodate small parties, rehearsal dinners, or business luncheons or dinners. Outdoors, the garden patio provides a tranquil spot under the trees for warm weather gatherings. The Lark Creek Inn has received national acclaim as well as local restaurant awards, and we have found the food here to be some of the best we've ever tasted. Note that the banquet manager is available to coordinate all aspects of your party planning. Add that to the outstanding ambiance and you'll understand why any event here will receive rave reviews. The Lark Creek Inn rates high on our list.

CUISINE: Farm Fresh Regional American

CAPACITY, FEES & DEPOSITS:

Area	*Standing*	*Seated*	*Rental/Event*
Private Dining Room	—	32	$50
Garden	100	60	100
Sun Porch	65	44	100
Sun Porch & Garden	150	100	100
Entire Restaurant	250	200	500

The entire restaurant can be reserved on Saturdays 11am–4pm. Other time frames are available by special arrangement. The minimum food and beverage cost is $6,000. The minimum food and beverage requirement for the private dining room is $600 at lunch or brunch, and $1,000 at dinner. Minimums for the private dining room in the month of December are $750 for lunch and $1,500 for dinner. The minimum food and beverage requirements for the patio and sun porch vary depending on the day of the week. A deposit of half the food and beverage minimum is due when reservations are confirmed. The balance is due the day of the function. Tax and an 18% gratuity are additional.

CANCELLATION POLICY: Half the deposit is refundable with 30 days' written notice.

AVAILABILITY: Year-round, every day, anytime. Closed Christmas eve and day and New Year's day.

OTHER INFORMATION:
Credit Cards: yes   *Smoking:* bar and patio only

Parking: large lot
Full Bar: yes
Corkage: $10/bottle

Dance Floor: yes
Wheelchair Access: yes
Meeting Equipment: BYO

Ross

MARIN ART AND GARDEN CENTER
Ross Garden Restaurant

30 Sir Francis Drake Blvd.
Ross, CA 94957
(415) 457-2151
Reserve for Events: 4–6 months in advance

Within the Marin Art and Garden Center located in lovely residential Ross, is the Ross Garden Restaurant. Parties can take place indoors or on the spacious patio which has umbrella-shaded tables for balmy al fresco dining. Converted from a 1930s home and set off from the rest of the garden complex, the restaurant derives its secluded, woodsy ambiance from the surrounding canopy of trees and the adjacent ten acres of beautiful gardens. Consequently, it's a wonderful place for a relaxed, comfortable outdoor function, especially during spring and summer months. In wintertime, enjoy the fireplace indoors.

CUISINE: California

CAPACITY: The restaurant and garden patio can accommodate 150 guests spring through fall. The private dining room can hold 75 guests year-round.

FEES & DEPOSITS: The $500 rental fee is the deposit required to secure your date for a 4-hour function. For 1 additional hour, the fee is $175. Other fees include a security guard fee of $75 for outdoor functions. Hors d'oeuvres run $18/person; the Elegant Buffet is $20/person; the Grand Buffet, $21/person. Tax and 15% gratuity are additional. The event balance is payable by the end of the function.

CANCELLATION POLICY: The deposit is non-refundable unless the space can be rebooked.

AVAILABILITY: For outdoor functions, weekdays, 4pm–dusk; Saturdays and Sundays, anytime–dusk. Indoor events 4pm–11pm Friday–Sunday. The restaurant is closed 2 weeks over the Christmas holiday.

OTHER INFORMATION:
Credit Cards: checks & cash
Parking: large lot
Full Bar: no, W&C only
Corkage: $7/bottle

Smoking: outdoors only
Dance Floor: patio
Wheelchair Access: yes
Other: special events director

Tiburon

GUAYMAS

5 Main Street
Tiburon, CA 94920
(415) 435-6300
Reserve for Events: 2–4 weeks in advance

Guaymas features authentic regional Mexican cuisine in a truly spectacular location. Set at the edge of the Tiburon Harbor, the restaurant has a sweeping view of the Marin hills and San Francisco, as well as the local boats docked a stone's throw from the dining room. The restaurant has a festive ambiance: vibrantly colored hand-cut paper flags hang from wooden beams and flutter in the breeze; displays of tropical fruit and whimsical Mexican artwork decorate walls and counters. Rough hewn chairs and tables covered with sun gold tablecloths and pink napkins add zest. And in winter, a huge adobe fireplace warms the semi-private area in the Main Dining Room. The real attraction, however, is the Arriba (upstairs) Deck. Bordered by sky and water, this patio is open to sun, stars and sea breezes. Geranium-filled planters provide color and greenery, and a wind shield and heaters keep guests comfortable. The Private Dining Room is also upstairs and features a large decorative fireplace, glass doors which open onto the deck, and the same wonderful vistas shared by the rest of the restaurant. For a change of pace, have a business luncheon meeting or an informal party up here. Whatever the occasion, you'll understand why people come from all over to dine and celebrate at Guaymas.

CUISINE: Authentic Regional Mexican

CAPACITY:

Area	Seated	Standing
Main Dining Room	55	—
Private Dining Room	28	40
Arriba Deck	100	150

FEES & DEPOSITS: Rental fees are $100 for the Private Dining Room and $500 for the Arriba Deck. A deposit may be required to hold your date. The rental fee and deposit are due at the time of booking. Per person food service costs are: $15–24 for luncheons, $15–24 for dinners and $15–24 for buffets. Beverages, tax and a 16% gratuity are additional.

CANCELLATION POLICY: Rental fees are refundable with 2 weeks notice.

AVAILABILITY: Every day except Christmas and Thanksgiving.

OTHER INFORMATION:
Credit Cards: all major
Parking: validated M–F, 11:30am–4pm
Full Bar: yes, $8 corkage/wine and champagne

Smoking: allowed
Dance Floor: no
Wheelchair Access: main dining level only

Menlo Park

ALLIED ARTS GUILD RESTAURANT

95 Arbor Road at Cambridge
Menlo Park, CA 94025
(415) 324-2588
Reserve for Events: 3–9 months in advance
Reserve for Meetings: 1–6 months in advance

Enclosed by a low adobe wall, the Allied Arts Guild complex of arts and crafts shops and historic structures is hidden away in a quiet, residential neighborhood not far from the Stanford campus. In 1929, Mr. and Mrs. Garfield Merner bought three and a half acres of what was once the vast Rancho de las Pulgas, a Spanish land grant dating back to the 1700s, and developed it into a crafts guild similar to those in Europe. The site retains the original Hispanic ambiance of white adobe walls, red tile roofs and patio courtyards. The grounds are nicely landscaped and meticulously maintained. Private parties are held in the restaurant, which is also of Spanish colonial design. Guests will enjoy strolling in the relaxed setting of the Guild's beautiful gardens, fountains and Spanish objects d'art. The restaurant is operated by the Palo Alto Auxiliary solely for the benefit of the Lucile Salter Packard Children's Hospital at Stanford.

CUISINE: Continental

CAPACITY: A 100-guest minimum is required for buffets and luncheons. Between May 1st and September 30th, the guest maximum is 155; in October the maximum is 100. For hors d'oeuvres receptions, the maximum is 200 guests.

FEES & DEPOSITS: The rental fee is required as a deposit and is payable when reservations are confirmed. For receptions, the fee is $500. There will be additional charges for special rental requests. Food service for buffets, hors d'oeuvres or seated receptions starts at $18/person. Non-alcoholic beverages only. Sparkling cider service runs $1.25/person.

CANCELLATION POLICY: With 6 weeks' notice, the rental fees are refundable.

AVAILABILITY: January 2–October 31st from 11am–4:30pm. No holiday weekend parties. Closed Sundays, Christmas Eve and Christmas Day, New Year's Day and the week between Christmas and New Year's.

OTHER INFORMATION:

Credit Cards: checks and cash only
Parking: large lots, on street
Full Bar: no alcohol allowed
Corkage: n/a
Meeting Equipment: no

Smoking: outside only
Dance Floor: yes
Wheelchair Access: yes
Overnight Accommodations: no
Other: event coordination

Palo Alto

CALIFORNIA CAFE

700 Welch Road
Palo Alto, CA 94304
(415) 325-2233
Reserve for Events: 1–52 weeks in advance

An upbeat and friendly eatery, the California Cafe is well known among locals as a destination for lunches and dinners. However, it's also a great spot if you've got an office party, out-of-town guests or a special occasion to celebrate. The Cafe offers three separate private dining rooms. The Banquet Room is to your left as you enter the restaurant. Swing shut the wall of metal and glass folding doors and voilà, total privacy. The other two, the Candy Room and Cafe Room, are towards the back of the main dining room. Long and linear, both are well suited for office parties, rehearsal dinners or luncheon meetings. In each dining area, walls, ceilings and furnishings in various tones of peach, dusky pink and teal create a lively environment; colorful framed prints, featuring works by Wayne Thiebaud, grace the walls. White linens, fresh flowers on tables and spot lighting add zest. No matter whether you're working or socializing, the California Cafe will provide the ambiance to do either in style.

CUISINE: California/Mediterranean

CAPACITY: Banquet Room can hold 45 seated guests, the Candy Room 50 and the Cafe Room 40.

FEES & DEPOSITS: For private parties, a refundable deposit is required when you book your event. The deposit is $5/person for luncheons or $10/person for dinners. The balance is payable by the end of the function. If your group is not dining, a room rental fee applies. Food costs range from $9–13 for luncheons to $15–24 for dinners or buffets. Tax and a 15% gratuity are additional.

CANCELLATION POLICY: With 72 hours' notice, you get your deposit back.

AVAILABILITY: Year-round 11:30am–2am, except for Christmas and Thanksgiving.

OTHER INFORMATION:

Credit Cards: all major
Parking: large lot
Full Bar: yes
Corkage: $7.50/bottle
Meeting Equipment: CBA

Smoking: not allowed
Dance Floor: no
Wheelchair Access: yes
Overnight Accommodations: no

Need a caterer, cake maker, florist? The Service Directory starting on page 614 features the best in the business.

MacARTHUR PARK

27 University Avenue
Palo Alto, CA 94301
(415) 321-9990
Reserve for Events: 1–3 weeks in advance

Although a popular restaurant, MacArthur Park's biggest secret is that it's also a great venue for luncheon meetings, prenuptial dinners and cocktail receptions. The landmark building which houses MacArthur Park was designed in 1918 by renowned architect Julia Morgan, and originally served as a recreation facility for World War I troops. The structure's simple yet handsome design was dictated by a rock-bottom $1,800 YWCA budget, and is a fine example of Morgan's ability to combine craftsman style with utilitarian needs. The main dining room has a vaulted ceiling with exposed wood trusses and beams. Details include several balconies and two large brick fireplaces situated at either end of the room. The decor is subdued. Black chairs contrast against white linens; attractive framed artwork graces board and batten walls. Rooms are painted in rich, soothing café au lait colors. The small, but very attractive private dining rooms feature the same warm tones and wall treatments as the main dining room. They are bright and airy with windows on two sides and French doors opening onto porches. Both are well suited for board meetings, working luncheons or private parties. For outdoor functions, take a peek at the enclosed courtyard. An aggregate patio supports white chairs and matching linen-covered tables. Striped fabric shades guests from the sun and ample heat lamps take the chill off during cooler months or during evening affairs.

CUISINE: American Regional

CAPACITY: The main dining room holds up to 222 seated guests, with balconies, an additional 50 guests. The Camp Fremont Room can seat up to 32 guests, the Julia Morgan Room up to 50. The patio courtyard accommodates 90 seated guests or 120 for a standing cocktail party.

FEES & DEPOSITS: A refundable $100 deposit is required to secure your date and is applied to the final bill. Food service is provided. Complete dinners, including tax and gratuity, run from $28–35/person.

CANCELLATION POLICY: With 10 days' notice, your deposit is returned.

AVAILABILITY: Year-round. Special events are held Sun–Fri from 11:30am–2am, Saturday from 9am–4pm.

OTHER INFORMATION:

Credit Cards: all major
Parking: valet available, large lot
Full Bar: yes
Corkage: $7–10/bottle
Meeting Equipment: CBA

Smoking: outside or private rooms
Dance Floor: CBA
Wheelchair Access: yes
Overnight Accommodations: no

Berkeley

BETTE'S OCEANVIEW DINER

1807 Fourth Street
Berkeley, CA 94710
(510) 601-6939
Reserve for Events: 2 weeks–6 months in advance

Bette's Diner is a legend in its own time. There's usually a line out the door—a sure sign of a successful restaurant. Why do folks flock to Bette's? Primarily for the food, which is just plain good. But Bette's also has an irresistible ambiance that makes people feel comfortable and...well, happy. It's a thirties-style diner with black and white checked linoleum floor, red leather booths, art deco lighting and snazzy metal detailing. Like all true diners, it has a long counter where patrons relax on tall stools and watch their orders being whipped up. When you have a private dinner party here, you can play the juke box all night, dance in the aisles and wax nostalgic. Cozy, friendly and unabashedly fun, Bette's Diner has captured the spirit of what a neighborhood eatery should be, and garnered a following that keeps coming back year after year.

CUISINE: American

CAPACITY: The diner accommodates 44 seated or 70 standing.

FEES & DEPOSITS: A $200 deposit is required at the time of booking. The balance is due at the conclusion of the event. A final guest count is due 48 hours prior the the event. Per person food costs run $35–40 including beverage and gratuity. Special menus are available as quoted. Tax is additional.

CANCELLATION POLICY: The deposit is refunded with 30 days' notice.

AVAILABILITY: Every day after 7pm. Closed Christmas.

OTHER INFORMATION:

Credit Cards: check or cash only
Parking: on street
Full Bar: B &W only
Corkage: $5/ bottle

Smoking: allowed
Dance Floor: dance in aisles
Wheelchair Access: yes

Oakland

OLIVETO

5655 College Avenue
Oakland, CA 94618
(510) 547-5356
Reserve for Events: 1 week–12 months in advance

A passion for Mediterranean cooking was the inspiration for this Northern Italian restaurant, situated on the second floor of the Rockridge Market Hall. Oliveto's main dining room is a fragrant, high-ceilinged space with tall windows that open out onto the street below. Sunset-colored stucco walls are reminiscent of Tuscany, and old Italian flower pots have been cleverly transformed into wall sconces. On the day we paid a visit, a vibrant display of fall leaves and flowers, framed by two enormous pumpkins, gave the room a colorful and festive ambiance. The open kitchen adds a bit of drama, and almost everything here is prepared from scratch, using plenty of fresh ingredients grown by local farmers, and organically raised beef, pork and duck. Have a luncheon meeting or dinner party in the Siena Room, a private space at the far end of the dining room. A wall of interior windows gives you a great view of the activities in the rest of the restaurant, while maintaining total privacy. Natural light, warm colors and its own floral arrangement makes this an inviting spot for a family get-together. Once considered a "mad project" by the owners' friends, Oliveto has become an East Bay favorite, creating imaginative and consistently delicious food.

CUISINE: Northern Italian

CAPACITY: The Siena Room can accommodate 26 seated guests.

FEES & DEPOSITS: A $100 deposit for dinner or $50 for lunch is required to confirm your reservation. The balance is due at the conclusion of the event. Lunches are $18.50/person, dinners range from $28.50–36.50/person depending on the number of courses. Tax and gratuity are included.

CANCELLATION POLICY: With 1 week's notice, the deposit is fully refunded.

AVAILABILITY: Monday–Friday for lunch, and every evening for dinner

OTHER INFORMATION:

Credit Cards: most major, checks ok
Parking: lot in back, on street
Full Bar: wine & beer only
Corkage: $8/bottle

Smoking: not allowed
Dance Floor: no
Wheelchair Access: yes

PIEMONTE OVEST

3909 Grand Avenue
Oakland, CA 94610
(510) 601-0500
Reserve for Events: 1 week–12 months in advance

Piemonte Ovest serves up innovative Italian specialties in one of the most appealing restaurants in the East Bay. As you walk through the gentle arches in the entry, your eye is drawn to vivid flower arrangements, reflected in an enormous mirror behind the bar. The Main Dining Room has a wall of floor-to-ceiling windows and a softly draped skylight, both designed to follow the peaked contours of the roofline and admit lots of natural light. Warmth emanates from the beautifully painted walls, roughly brushed with ochre, pink, cream and pale yellow hues. These sunkissed tones also give the Back Room and upstairs Private Dining Room a special glow. Both spaces have plenty of windows and the Back Room overlooks Piemonte's garden courtyard. This two-level patio is a lovely spot for a party on a balmy evening. It's enclosed by latticed fencing and an overhead trellis, and Magnolia, lemon and Japanese Maple trees grow through and around the wooden deck and brick areas. Impatiens and ferns create colorful clusters at the patio's edge. And on cooler evenings, a fire in the large brick oven takes the chill off. The restaurant is also an art gallery, with eye-catching, rotating exhibits in every room. Given its inviting ambiance and creative cuisine, it's no surprise that Piemonte has become a popular choice with Bay Area diners.

CAPACITY:	Area	Seated	Standing	Area	Seated	Standing
	Main Dining Room	28	—	Patio	55	70
	Private Dining Room	55	70	Entire Restaurant	110	200
	Back Room (semi-private)	18	—			

FEES & DEPOSITS: A non-refundable $100 is required when you reserve a private dining area. The entire restaurant can be reserved for a minimum of $5,000, with half the anticipated total due at the time of booking. The balance in either case is payable at the conclusion of the event. Luncheons start at $13/person, dinners at $25. Beverage, tax and gratuity are additional.

CANCELLATION POLICY: The deposit is not refundable.

AVAILABILITY: The private dining areas are available Sunday–Thursday, 11am–midnight. Special events can be arranged Friday and Saturday.

OTHER INFORMATION:

Credit Cards: Visa, MC or checks
Parking: on street
Full Bar: wine and beer only
Corkage: $8/bottle

Smoking: designated area
Dance Floor: CBA
Wheelchair Access: no

SCOTT'S RESTAURANT

#2 Broadway at Jack London Square
Oakland, CA 94607
(510) 444-5969 Catering
Reserve for Events: 1 week in advance
Reserve for Meetings: 1 day in advance

Surprise! Scott's has great private facilities that are not part of their main dining room. Located on the Oakland Estuary, the Harbor View Rooms and Bay View Terrace have views of Alameda, San Francisco and passing ships. Recently developed, the Harbor View Rooms are sophisticated in color and decor, plus they have the advantage of multiple folding doors, which can be opened or closed to create a combination of spaces. Scott's can arrange these rooms to meet the needs of your special event. If you're looking for a waterfront location for a special business party or social function—this is an unexpected find.

CUISINE: Seafood

CAPACITY:

Room	Seated	Standing	Room	Seated	Standing
Harbor View A	80	120	Combined ABC	250	450
Harbor View B	60	80	Bay View/Terrace	45	75
Harbor View C	70	80			

FEES & DEPOSITS: A $500/room deposit is required to secure your date. A $100 room charge may apply for groups under 20 guests. Per person prices: seated meals and buffets $20–30 and hors d'oeuvres $15–25. Tax and an 18% service charge are additional.

CANCELLATION POLICY: Deposits will be refunded only if the space(s) rented can be rebooked.

AVAILABILITY: Year-round, closed Christmas day. Every day from 7am–2am.

OTHER INFORMATION:

Credit Cards: all major
Parking: valet or parking lot
Full Bar: yes
Corkage: $10/bottle

Smoking: designated area
Dance Floor: yes, extra fee
Wheelchair Access: yes
Meeting Equipment: podium, microphone

THE SILVER DRAGON

835 Webster Street
Oakland, CA 94607
(510) 893-3748
Reserve for Events: 1 week–9 months in advance

There are dozens of Chinese restaurants in Oakland, but the Silver Dragon seems to be the overwhelming choice for people planning an event in Chinatown. The staff take great pride in ensuring that every detail is properly handled from customizing menus to arranging the best setup for a multi-activity event. The banquet rooms are spacious and adaptable. In the Second Floor Room, a rich red carpet with an oriental-inspired design and golden tablecloths create a colorful setting. Warm, off-white walls are hung with a variety of Asian art. Lighting is adjustable and a portable podium and bar are available. The Third Floor Room is slightly smaller and cooler in tone. A floor-to-ceiling beveled glass mirror reflects light from a graceful arched window that spans the entire wall on the opposite side of the room. A small stage and bar give this space added versatility. Whether you're planning a reception, business luncheon or private party, the Silver Dragon offers the facilities and service to make it a success.

CUISINE: Chinese

CAPACITY: The 2nd floor room accommodates 350 seated, 400 standing; the 3rd floor room holds 250 seated, 300 standing.

FEES & DEPOSITS: A $300–500 deposit, the amount depending on guest count, menu selection and time of event, is required when reservations are confirmed. The balance is due at the conclusion of the event. Food costs are $200–300 per table (8–10 guests) for a traditional 8-course banquet. Per person service can also be requested and runs $12–15 for lunch and $18–25 for dinner. Special menus are available as quoted. Beverage, tax and gratuity are additional.

CANCELLATION POLICY: The deposit is non-refundable.

AVAILABILITY: Every day, noon–3pm for lunch; 5pm–11pm for dinner. Closed Thanksgiving and Christmas.

OTHER INFORMATION:

Credit Cards: Am. Express, MC, VISA
Parking: on street, inexpensive lot
Full Bar: yes
Corkage: $10/table

Smoking: allowed
Dance Floor: CBA
Wheelchair Access: yes

San Ramon

MUDD'S RESTAURANT

10 Boardwalk
San Ramon, CA 94583
(510) 837-9387   Patty McCurdy
Reserve for Events: 3–6 months in advance
Reserve for Meetings: 1 week in advance

Surrounded by ten acres of open space and situated next to a two-acre garden, this restaurant is in a world of its own. Virginia Mudd, the restaurant's founder and namesake, had a vision—she wanted to combine the features of a peaceful, quiet rural setting with an urban-chic eating establishment. Luckily for us, she succeeded. Stroll among the acres of organic flowers, herbs and fruit trees. Bite an apple. Smell the lavender. There are vegetables galore, many of which find their way into Mudd's dishes. Under the shade of large oaks, elms and bay trees, the Fireside Deck and adjacent lawns form a nice spot for an outdoor party. If it's a small group, you can repair to the Fireside Room for cocktails and hors d'oeuvres. Or you can try the Board Room, which is terrific for intimate business dinners and luncheons. The Board Room has its own private deck, surrounded by oaks. Larger groups can reserve the entire Mudd's dining room, an appealing combination of spaces with distinctive curved ceilings. It's a contemporary design with enough wood detailing and warmth to suggest a feeling of country. Windows are everywhere, in all sorts of shapes and sizes. Most provide guests with views of the garden tapestry—vivid colors and soft, subtle shades of green. For outdoor dining, several French doors open to patios, screened by overhead trellises. All in all, Mudd's is a rare find. If you are looking for the optimum garden setting, yet would like the benefits of a full service restaurant, we suggest that you start your search here.

CUISINE: California Cuisine with an emphasis on fresh ingredients from Mudd's garden.

CAPACITY: Board Room 20 seated; Fireside Room 45 seated; Fireside Room & Deck 60–70 for a standing reception, Main Dining Room 150 seated.

FEES & DEPOSITS: There's a $750 fee to reserve the entire restaurant; there's no rental fee for the Fireside Room or Board Room. Breakfasts start at $6.50/person, luncheons $8–15/person, dinners $10–21/person, buffets $15–25/person. Tax and a 15% service charge are additional. Payment in full is due by the end of the function.

AVAILABILITY: Main Dining Room and grounds are available Saturday from 11am–5pm. Board Room and Fireside Room, year-round, anytime.

OTHER INFORMATION:

Credit Cards: all major
Parking: large lot
Full Bar: yes
Corkage: $5/bottle

Smoking: outside only
Dance Floor: in bar area
Wheelchair Access: yes
Overnight Accommodations: no

Walnut Creek

SPIEDINI

101 Ygnacio Valley Road
Walnut Creek, CA 94596
(510) 939-2100
Reserve for Events: 2 weeks–12 months in advance

Winner of Focus Magazine's award for the "Best Restaurant in Contra Costa County" for the last four years, Spiedini is as satisfying to the eye as it is to the palate. A glass and granite skylit foyer creates an airy and inviting entrance. Sea-green granite tabletops and counters contrast beautifully with the blond wood of the bar, and contemporary art adds interest. Light peach walls deepening to a terra cotta ceiling, extend the warmth generated by the open kitchen, visible from every corner of the restaurant. The Main Dining Room is softened by comfortable upholstered chairs and banquettes, and subtle sconce lighting. A semi-private dining area bordered by tall windows is a delightful spot for small parties. And outdoors, two angular patios create an herb-scented oasis where guests can savor a sun-drenched luncheon, or enjoy the evening breeze during dinner or cocktails.

CUISINE: Northern Italian

CAPACITY:

Area	Seated	Standing
Entire restaurant	143	200
Semi-private dining area	58	58
Terraces	40	40

FEES & DEPOSITS: A deposit of half the estimated total is due at the time of booking. The balance is payable 30 days prior to the event. Per person catering costs run $20–35 and do not include wine. A 15% gratuity and tax are additional.

CANCELLATION POLICY: If you cancel up to 90 days in advance, the deposit minus $200 will be refunded. With less than 90 days' notice, the deposit is forfeited.

AVAILABILITY: The semi-private dining area and terraces are available year-round, every day except Thanksgiving, Christmas and Easter. The entire restaurant can be reserved Saturday or Sunday 9am–4pm (special arrangement can be made for other times).

OTHER INFORMATION:

Credit Cards: all major
Parking: complimentary valet, on street
Full Bar: yes
Corkage: $7.50/bottle wine, $10/bottle champagne

Smoking: designated area in bar and outside only
Dance Floor: CBA
Wheelchair Access: yes

Campbell

CAMPBELL HOUSE RESTAURANT

106 E. Campbell Ave.
Campbell, CA 95008
(408) 374-57571
Reserve for Events: 1–4 weeks in advance

A quaint old stucco house that you could easily drive right by, Campbell House is one of those unexpected little gems. Aesthetically it has its charms: beautiful multi-paned windows, wood trim around everything, tables set elegantly with white cloths over dark green and illustrations of different grape varieties on the walls. It's a small, very homey restaurant which serves good food. The chef here, however, improves on a good thing by adding his special touch. For a party of no more than sixteen, he will set up a long table in the middle of the main room and grace it with candelabras. The effect is romantic and intimate, the service highly personalized. If your guest list is short, the Campbell House merits consideration.

CUISINE: New American

CAPACITY: 16 seated guests for a private party.

FEES & DEPOSITS: No deposit or rental fees are required for group functions. Luncheons range from $15–20/person; dinners from $35–40/person. Menus for groups are pre-arranged at least 1 week prior to the event.

AVAILABILITY: Year-round, closed Monday. Luncheons are served Tuesday–Friday, dinners Tuesday–Sunday.

SERVICES/AMENITIES:

Credit Cards: all major
Full Bar: WBC only
Corkage: $13/bottle
Dance Floor: no

Parking: small lot
Overnight Accommodations: no
Smoking: not allowed
Wheelchair Access: limited

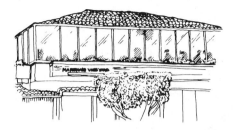

MARTHA'S RESTAURANT & CAFE

1875 S. Bascom Avenue #2400
Campbell, CA 95008
(408) 377-1193
Reserve for Events: 3 months in advance

Martha's Restaurant & Cafe is located on the second floor of the PruneYard where it overlooks the landscaped courtyard below. This newly designed restaurant, with a color scheme in alabaster, teal and magenta has a bright, cheerful ambiance. Fine contemporary art is tastefully displayed on interior walls. The greenhouse terrace, glassed in on three sides and affording a view of surrounding hills and the courtyard's century-old palm, is one of the facility's best features. Dining here is enhanced by colorful murals, rattan furniture and glass tables on a terra cotta floor. Another popular space for small hors d'oeuvres celebrations is the Wine Room, with arched white ceiling and glass encased wine racks. The Fireplace Lounge also accommodates smaller groups.

CUISINE: California with Asian influence

CAPACITY: The entire facility can accommodate 180 seated guests. The Wine Room can hold up to 40 standing guests; the Fireplace Room and Cafe up to 75 standing guests.

FEES & DEPOSITS: A $300 refundable deposit is due when reservations are confirmed. There is a rental charge of $50 if the group is under 15 guests. Per person rates are: luncheons $9–16, dinners $14–25 and hors d'oeuvres starting at $7.50. Tax and a 15% gratuity are additional.

CANCELLATION POLICY: With 3 month's notice, your deposit will be refunded.

AVAILABILITY: Year-round, every day from 8am–1am except Sundays (unless the group is over 100 guests). Closed major holidays.

OTHER INFORMATION:

Credit Cards: all major
Parking: large lot
Full Bar: yes
Corkage: $8/bottle
Meeting Equipment: no

Smoking: allowed
Overnight Accommodations: no
Dance Floor: yes
Wheelchair Access: yes, elevator

Los Gatos

VILLAGE HOUSE AND GARDEN RESTAURANT

320 Village Lane
Los Gatos, CA 95030
(408) 354-1040
Reserve for Events: 2 weeks in advance
Reserve for Meetings: 2 weeks in advance

The first thing you notice about the Village House and Garden Restaurant is the large outdoor patio, a wonderful area for al fresco dining during warm weather. Trees and flowers border the patio, while a trellis provides shade and the added beauty of hanging plants and wind chimes. The restaurant's interior also conveys a feeling of spring. Decorated in white and green, the ambiance is fresh and relaxed. The main dining room and patio combined make a popular setting for business luncheons or dinners. The Copper Corner, a smaller room with brick fireplace and copper "hood," is suitable for groups of up to thirty-six people and is often used for meeting luncheons.

CUISINE: Gourmet American

CAPACITY:

Area	Season	Seated	Minimum Required
Main Dining Room	all	90	50 (days), 60 (eves)
Copper Corner	all	36	16
Inside/Outside	Oct 1–May 14	130	100
Inside/Outside	May 15–Sept 30	130	100

FEES & DEPOSITS: For weekday functions, no deposit is required. A confirmed guest count is due 4 days prior to the event. For evening or Saturday functions, a non-refundable $250 deposit is required when reservations are confirmed. No rental fees are required for evening functions if food is served; Saturday reception rental is $350 for 3 hours, $500 for 4 hours. The balance is due at the end of the event. Per person rates: luncheons $14 (Saturday luncheons start at $17.50), dinners at $25, hors d'oeuvres by arrangement. Sales tax and 15% gratuity are additional.

AVAILABILITY: Year-round, Mon–Fri 9am–3pm; Saturday 11am–6pm. Closed Sundays, major holidays and the week between Christmas and New Year's day.

OTHER INFORMATION:

Credit Cards: Visa/MasterCard
Parking: street, public parking lot nearby
Full Bar: CBW only
Corkage: $5/bottle
Meeting Equipment: no

Smoking: patio only
Overnight Accommodations: no
Dance Floor: yes
Wheelchair Access: yes

San Jose

LA PASTAIA

233 West Santa Clara Street
San Jose, CA 95113
(408) 286-8686
Reserve for Events: 1–3 months in advance

For those of you who want to have an upscale business or social gathering in the South Bay, take heart! The relatively new La Pastaia, located in the recently refurbished Hotel De Anza, is a sophisticated, contemporary setting for both luncheons, dinners or receptions. La Pastaia (which means pastamaker in Italian) is a feast for the eyes. Designed in a Northern Italian mode, La Pastaia is serious about food, yet slightly irreverent. (The woman on the classic-looking logo proudly flourishes what appears to be a flag. Upon closer inspection, we notice it's a fork topped with wind blown pasta). Slate tile in a subtle gray with green overtones covers many of the outer surfaces, including banquettes, booths and the softly curving arches that help divide the restaurant's spaces. Lemony yellow walls are hand painted in a faux marble pattern and the stone floor is broken up into subdued greens, browns and ochres. Black lacquered chairs contrast nicely with white linens, and enlivening the perimeters are large framed Italian posters from the 1920s and 30s. The exhibition kitchen area is compelling. Laden with delectable desserts and fresh baked bread, the long marble counter draws guests in for a closer look. Linger here a while and watch the chefs work with a wood burning oven that glows continuously at one end of the counter. Small alcoves and a mixture of banquettes and tables create cozy, intimate spaces. Treat your guests to genuine Italian cuisine—fresh pastas, lively appetizers and Italian country-style entrees—or design your own menu. La Pastaia's staff is extremely flexible. No matter what you select, your guests will appreciate the great food, professionally served in a Tuscan-chic atmosphere.

CUISINE: Northern Italian

CAPACITY: 150 seated guests with dance floor; 175 without. For private parties, a guaranteed 70-guest minimum is required. Private rooms and patio are available for smaller groups.

FEES & DEPOSITS: A $250 refundable deposit is required to secure your date, due when reservations are confirmed. With food service, no rental fee is required. La Pastaia can customize any menu, with prices ranging from $25–50/person. Half of the estimated food and beverage total is payable when the contract is signed; the balance is due one week prior to the event. Tax and 17% service charge are additional.

CANCELLATION POLICY: With 2 weeks' notice, your deposit will be refunded.

AVAILABILITY: Year-round, except Christmas Day.

OTHER INFORMATION:

Credit Cards: all major
Parking: nearby lots
Full Bar: yes
Corkage: no
Meeting Equipment: no

Smoking: not allowed
Dance Floor: yes
Overnight Accommodations: Hotel De Anza
Wheelchair Access: yes
Other: cakes, coordination

Santa Rosa

MARK WEST LODGE

2520 Mark Springs Road
Santa Rosa, CA 95404
(707) 546-2592
Reserve for Events: 2 weeks–3 months in advance

It's impossible to miss Mark West Lodge—an enormous grape arbor which spans the entire highway lets you know you've arrived. Planted over a hundred and fifty years ago, these gnarled vines grow up through the lodge's deck and, according to Ripley's "Believe It or Not," are the largest in the world. Once an important stage stop between San Francisco and the Northwest, the Lodge is now a traditional French restaurant. The main dining room is French Provincial, with ornate chandeliers, gold framed mirrors and gold-toned drapes. Large 18th-century portraits add an old-world, European flavor. At the end of the room, light filters through stained glass panels with a grapevine and flower motif, illuminating a bubbling fountain. Two other rooms are available for smaller parties, cocktail receptions or meetings. The real treat here, though, is the back patio. Sheltered on three sides by the restaurant, it's an idyllic spot for an afternoon or evening get-together. Guests can enjoy the surrounding tree-covered hills, shielded from the bright sun by a colorful parachute suspended overhead. Have a seated affair inside and dance under the stars, or dine al fresco on the terrace. Cocktails and dancing can also take place in the bar area, where guests often wander out onto the deck and relax under the grapevine canopy. Owned and operated by French chef, Robert Ayme, Mark West Lodge offers affordable French cuisine and hospitality just a few minutes from Santa Rosa.

CUISINE: French

CAPACITY:

Area	Seated	Standing
Banquet Room	20–60	100
Dining Room	70–200	500
Patio	130	200
Patio w/lawn	200	300

FEES & DEPOSITS: A $200 non-refundable deposit is required when reservations are confirmed. 80% of the total anticipated cost is due 2 weeks prior to the event, and the final guest count is due 1 week before the event. Any remaining balance is due at the conclusion of the event. Per person food costs are $9–13 for seated luncheons, $18 for buffets and $15–25 for seated dinners. Alcoholic beverages, tax and gratuity are additional. If the entire restaurant needs to be closed for the event, a $200–500 facility use fee may apply.

CANCELLATION POLICY: The initial $200 deposit is not refundable. If you cancel 2 weeks prior to the event, a refund will depend on the amount of preparations already completed.

AVAILABILITY: Year-round, Tuesday–Sunday, 9am–midnight.

OTHER INFORMATION:

Credit Cards: Visa/MC

Parking: ample

Full Bar: yes

Corkage: $5.50/bottle

Smoking: outside & lounge only

Dance Floor: yes

Wheelchair Access: yes

Sonoma

DEPOT 1870 RESTAURANT

241 First Street, West
Sonoma, CA 95476
(707) 938-2980 Gia Ghilarducci
Reserve: 6–9 months in advance

Originally a private home, Depot 1870 has played an active role in Sonoma's past as a bar, restaurant and hotel. It is currently housed in an historic stone building near the Plaza in downtown Sonoma. Enter through the fireplace parlor, comfortably furnished with overstuffed chairs and couches. The crisp white walls, luxurious burgundy upholstery and simple bar make the room cheerful and homey. Glass doors lead out onto a covered terrace encircling the formal garden. The garden is serene and secluded, landscaped with flowers, hedges and a large reflecting pool. An elegant and comfortable dining area adjacent to the bar is enlarged by a glass-enclosed garden room. Here you have the benefits of indoor dining while feeling that you're outdoors. The Depot offers the services of Chef Ghilarducci, who received the prestigious national award, Grand Master Chef of America.

CUSINE: Northern Italian

CAPACITY: The Depot can accommodate up to 140 guests.

FEES & DEPOSITS: A $200 deposit is required when you make your reservation and is applied towards the food and beverage cost. There is no rental fee. Food service is provided, and prices range from an hors d'oeuvres reception at $13–19/person to seated meals at $10–30/person. All event costs are payable by the day of your party.

CANCELLATION POLICY: The deposit will only be refunded if your date can be rebooked.

AVAILABILITY: Smaller functions, anytime; larger parties (over 30 guests) on weekends from noon to 4pm, or anytime on Monday or Tuesday.

OTHER INFORMATION:

Credit Cards: Visa/MasterCard, Amer. Exp & Discover   *Smoking:* allowed

Parking: large lots
Full Bar: B&W only
Corkage: $8/bottle

Dance Floor: outside
Wheelchair Access: yes

Yountville

CAFE KINYON! RESTAURANT

6525 Washington Street
Yountville, CA 94599
(707) 944-2788
Reserve for Events: 1–6 months in advance

Cafe Kinyon! is located in the Vintage 1870 complex and is an attractive event space as well as a restaurant. For private or corporate parties, Cafe Kinyon! is an excellent location. The main dining room has French doors and multiple windows overlooking a garden area, making it light and airy. Soft pink and rose colors predominate. By opening several doors, a large 'L' can be formed with an adjacent dining area. It has a large skylight and more doors leading into a garden. The smaller dining room is appealing, with a terra cotta-colored brick wall and softwood floors. Overall, the decor is clean and fresh—sophisticated with a touch of elegance.

CUISINE: California

CAPACITY: Cafe Kinyon! can accommodate 175 seated, 250 standing inside; with outdoor spaces, 400 seated total.

FEES & DEPOSITS: With food service, there's no rental charge. Per person rates: luncheons from $11.50–15, dinners $16.50–27.50, buffets $18–23 and hors d'oeuvres $2.50–5. A refundable $500 deposit is required when reservations are confirmed; half of the estimated food and beverage is required with the returned contract. The balance is payable at the end of the event. Tax and a 17% service charge are additional.

CANCELLATION POLICY: If the event space can be rebooked, the deposit will be refunded.

AVAILABILITY: Year-round, closed Christmas and New Year's. Every day 8am–1am.

OTHER INFORMATION:
Credit Cards: American Express, checks
Parking: multiple lots
Full Bar: B&W only
Corkage: $8/bottle

Smoking: allowed
Dance Floor: yes
Wheelchair Access: yes

Aptos

THE VERANDA

8041 Soquel Drive
Aptos, CA 95003
(408) 685-1881
Reserve for Events: 1 week–3 months in advance

The Veranda is a restaurant occupying the main floor of the vintage 1878 Victorian Bayview Hotel in historic Aptos Village. All has been restored with attention to detail. The interior boasts two glass-walled verandas as well as a main dining room and outstanding bar. Muted colors in roses, off-whites and pinks blend to create a visually appealing space. The bar is in a separate room, accessible by double doors. There's a newly designed and constructed patio for outdoor events with brick pavers, roses and white lattice. Note, the food here is distinctive and very good. For group functions, The Veranda creates an environment of casual elegance.

CUISINE: New American/California

CAPACITY: Capacities are as follows: the Veranda indoors accommodates 70 seated guests, main dining room 36, side veranda 28, front veranda 20, anteroom 10. The garden patio holds up to 50 seated guests or 125 standing. The entire facility holds up to 150–175 guests.

FEES & DEPOSITS: A refundable $300 deposit is required when reservations are confirmed. For groups, luncheons start at $12/person, dinners at $22/person and hors d'oeuvres start at $10/person. The rental fee for use of the garden and interior dining room is $150/event; either space rents for $75/event. A confirmed guest count is required 48 hours prior to your function and your event balance is payable by the end of the event.

CANCELLATION POLICY: Your deposit will be refunded with 30 days' notice or if the space can be rebooked.

AVAILABILITY: Year-round, everyday by arrangement.

OTHER INFORMATION:

Credit Cards: all major
Parking: large lot
Full Bar: yes
Corkage: $10/bottle
Meeting Equipment: CBA, extra fee

Smoking: designated areas and times
Dance Floor: CBA
Wheelchair Access: yes
Overnight Accommodations: 8 guestrooms

Carmel Valley

THE RIDGE RESTAURANT
at Robles Del Rio Lodge

200 Punta Del Monte
Carmel Valley, CA 93924
(408) 659-0170
Reserve for Events: 2–12 weeks in advance

Getting to the Ridge Restaurant is half the fun. It's located up a beautiful, winding road leading to a hilltop where the restaurant overlooks Carmel Valley. Charming and rustic in appearance, The Ridge is actually part of the old Robles Del Rio Lodge which has the best ambiance and views at twilight when the sun sets and the lights come up in the Valley. Seated meals are generally the rule inside. The interior of the restaurant has two main dining areas, one with a glassed-in terrace with terrific panoramas of the Valley. The Fireside Room, which has a grand piano, adjoins the dining room and there's a full service cantina. Outdoor functions are a delight. Sizable groups can have cocktails and hors d'oeuvres, barbeques or more formal receptions on the lawns or the Lodge's garden patios.

CUISINE: French and California

CAPACITY: The main dining room can hold up to 60 seated guests; the deck, 50 and the Fireside Room, 40. For large groups outdoors, the garden can hold up to 200 seated or 300 standing guests.

MEETING ROOMS: Fireside Room, 40 guests; Oak Meadow Cottage, 25 guests.

FEES & DEPOSITS: A non-refundable deposit secures your date. For small groups staying overnight, the deposit is sometimes waived. Half of the estimated food and beverage cost is due 30 days prior to the function and the balance is due on the day of the event. Per person rates: luncheons start at $7.50, dinners start at $16, buffets range from $10–40 and Sunday brunch from $16. Tax and an 18% gratuity are added to the final bill.

CANCELLATION POLICY: Confirm the cancellation policy when you book your function to be clear about obtaining a refund.

AVAILABILITY: Year-round, daily.

SERVICES/AMENITIES:

Credit Cards: all major
Parking: large lots
Full Bar: yes
Corkage: $10–12/bottle for W&C
Overnight Accommodations: 33 guestrooms

Smoking: allowed
Dance Floor: several areas
Wheelchair Access: yes
Meeting Equipment: CBA

Sacramento

CASA DE LOS NIÑOS

2760 Sutterville Road
Sacramento, CA 95820
(916) 452-2809
Reserve: 1–3 months in advance

You might not expect much from a restaurant run by volunteers, but in the case of Casa de los Niños you'd be mistaken. Operated for the benefit of the Sacramento Children's Home, the restaurant is a delightful place to have a party or business function. From the moment you walk through the vine-laden entryway, you're impressed by the meticulously maintained grounds. Branches form a delicate canopy over the walkway, bordered by ferns, bushes and clusters of impatiens. An outdoor terrace is surrounded by magnolias, oaks, sycamores and redwoods, and a variety of flowers weave color throughout the garden. The terrace is a versatile space that can be set up for al fresco dining or dancing. The Garden Room overlooks the terrace, and tall windows on three sides provide each guest with a garden view. A vaulted ceiling, light peach walls and chintz valences give the room an airy, pleasant ambiance, while black lacquer chairs, white linens and pink carnations add a touch of formality. For small parties, meetings or corporate dinners, the Patio Room offers a more intimate space, overlooking yet another lush landscape. A little deck with flower pots and white wrought iron table and chairs brings the freshness of the garden into the dining room. In addition to hosting a wide range of events, Casa de los Niños also serves as an art gallery, featuring a different artist's work every two months.

CUISINE: California

CAPACITY:

Area	Seated	Standing
Garden Room	93	150
Patio Room	36	—
Terrace	30	50

FEES & DEPOSITS:

Weekends: On weekends, you must rent the entire restaurant for special events. A $300 deposit, which is applied to the final bill, is due when you make reservations. There is no rental fee for a 3-hour event, but a $200 fee is charged for each additional hour. There is an 80-person minimum, and per person food costs are $12.50 for hors d'oeuvres or a seated luncheon, and $17.50 for a buffet. Tax and gratuity are additional (any gratuity is tax deductible). The food balance is due 10 working days before the event. Beverages, damages and fees are billed after the event.

Weekdays: Rental of the Patio Room requires a 20-person minimum and a $25 deposit which is applied to the final bill. The Garden Room has a 60-person minimum and requires a $50 deposit. Per person food costs are $8 for a full breakfast, $5 for a continental breakfast and $8.75 for a full luncheon (including dessert). A full dinner (including hors d'oeuvres, dessert and non-alcoholic beverage) can also be served in the Garden Room for $15/person, with a minimum of 40 people and a $100 deposit. Alcoholic beverages, tax and gratuity are additional (any gratuity is tax deductible).

CANCELLATION POLICY: For weekend events, deposits are refundable up to 3 months before the event. Weekday breakfast and luncheon deposits are refundable until 3 days before the event. Weekday dinner deposits are refundable until 10 days before the event.

AVAILABILITY: Year-round, everyday 7am–9pm except major holidays.

OTHER INFORMATION:

Credit Cards: MC/Visa

Parking: large lot

Full Bar: B&W only

Smoking: terrace only

Dance Floor: terrace or indoor CBA

Wheelchair Access: yes

Need a caterer, cake maker, florist? The Service Directory starting on page 614 features the best in the business.

Carnelian Bay

GAR WOODS GRILL AND PIER

5000 N. Lake Blvd.
Carnelian Bay, CA 96140
(916) 546-3366
Reserve for Events: 1–6 months in advance

Gar Woods is a restaurant located right on the rim of Lake Tahoe. For outdoor wedding receptions, there's a substantial deck complete with blue, yellow and red umbrellas, wind screens and heat lamps for chilly days. The deck has fabulous views—of Gar Woods' private pier, the lake and the mountains beyond. If the weather is unfriendly, guests just relocate to the adjacent indoor dining room. Don't worry. The vistas through floor-to-ceiling windows make you feel like the water is only an arm's length away. The interior is easy on the eyes—everything is in soft and muted taupe and creams and the walls feature framed photos of boats on the lake. The restaurant has two floors, each with a dining room. Dressed up for a special party, Gar Woods presents a very pretty picture, inside and out.

CUISINE: California Grill

CAPACITY: Indoors, 220 seated guests; 300 for a standing reception. The deck seats 150 or 200 guests for a standing reception.

FEES & DEPOSITS: A refundable deposit equaling 25% of the estimated food and beverage total is required to secure your date. If you want to change the table and chair arrangement, the setup fee is $100/room. Buffets start at $15/person, seated luncheons $12/person and dinners $16/person. The balance is due the day of the event. Tax and a 15%–20% service charge are additional.

CANCELLATION POLICY: With 60 days' notice, the deposit will be refunded.

AVAILABILITY: Year-round, everyday 11am–1am.

OTHER INFORMATION:

Credit Cards: MC & Visa
Parking: large lot
Full Bar: yes
Corkage: $5/bottle

Smoking: allowed
Dance Floor: CBA
Wheelchair Access: yes

Tahoe Vista

LA PLAYA

7046 North Lake Blvd.
Tahoe Vista, CA 96148
(916) 546-5903
Reserve for Events: 1 week–3 months in advance

The lake becomes a part of the experience at La Playa—a brilliant and ever-changing body of blue that makes a stunning backdrop for a special event. Have cocktails in front of the fireplace or outdoors, on the lawn or sandy beach. The restaurant's dining rooms and outdoor patios have panoramic views of Lake Tahoe and the encircling mountains. Wind screens are provided for offshore breezes, and if it gets a bit chilly, move the party indoors. La Playa's light interior is really attractive. It's an eclectic blend of styles and artifacts—sea-faring paraphernalia is part of the decor as is nice looking contemporary art on the walls. A huge fireplace (with pot-belly stove inside) dominates one end of the room, wall-to-wall glass the other. Tables, with white linens and flowers, can be arranged as you like—set up for formal, seated dinners or casual buffets. Here, guests can enjoy a few hours in the sun and relax to the sound of waves lapping at the shore.

CUISINE: Fresh Seafood and Continental

CAPACITY: Indoors, 100 seated guests—combined with outdoors, 175 seated guests.

FEES & DEPOSITS: A refundable deposit of 30% of the estimated food total secures your date and is due when reservations are confirmed. With food service, no rental fee is required. La Playa can customize any menu, with prices ranging from $18–42/person. The balance is payable by the end of the event. La Playa will close for a guaranteed minimum guest count.

CANCELLATION POLICY: With 1 month's notice, your deposit will be refunded.

AVAILABILITY: Year-round, everyday 9am–9pm.

OTHER INFORMATION:

Credit Cards: all major
Parking: several lots
Full Bar: yes
Corkage: $$7/bottle

Smoking: allowed
Dance Floor: deck or indoors
Wheelchair Access: yes
Meeting Equipment: BYO

Truckee

COTTONWOOD RESTAURANT

10142 Rue Hilltop
Truckee, CA 96160
(916) 587-5711
Reserve for Events: 1 week–12 months in advance
Reserve for Meetings: 1 week–12 months in advance

Cottonwood is wonderful. Located on a high bluff overlooking Truckee, this one-time railway stop, lumbermill and lodge was the site of the first ski area in California. Pictures of Charlie Chaplin and other notables grace one of the walls since *Gold Rush* and other films were shot here in the 1920s. Cottonwood preserves a bit of the Old West—nothing about this place is ordinary. Parts of the building are constructed of railroad ties and remnants of the tracks that once ran in front of the structure are still visible. The road that takes you here is unpaved and the railing in front of Cottonwood is suggestive of old-time hitching posts. Inside, the entry rooms feature an old brick fireplace, a heavily beamed ceiling and stone and plank flooring on the diagonal. The main room, by contrast, has a more contemporary feeling of an art gallery. Large and airy, with an open truss ceiling, it offers a bird's-eye view of the city below through a wall of windows. Crisp white linens and flowers on every table add a touch of elegance. At twilight, the mood becomes romantic as candles glow on each table and the lights from Truckee begin to twinkle.

CUISINE: Eclectic American

CAPACITY: Indoors, 150 seated guests; with the deck, add an additional 80 guests.

FEES & DEPOSITS: The $200 rental fee is the deposit required to secure your date. Group buffets and seated meals run about $20/person. Tax and a 15% service charge are additional.

CANCELLATION POLICY: With 7 days' notice, your deposit will be refunded.

AVAILABILITY: Year-round, everyday, anytime except Monday. Closed Christmas and Thanksgiving.

OTHER INFORMATION:

Credit Cards: Visa/MasterCard
Parking: large lot
Full Bar: yes
Corkage: $5/bottle

Smoking: bar or outside only
Dance Floor: yes
Wheelchair Access: yes
Meeting Equipment: no, BYO

ZINA'S!

10292 Donner Pass Road
Truckee, CA 96160
(916) 587-1771
Reserve for Events: 1–3 months in advance

This Queen Anne Eastlake mansion, the C.B. White house, says welcome the moment you step across the threshold. Built in 1873, it's a Victorian reminder of Truckee's golden years at the turn of the century and has the distinction of being the only building in the Truckee area chosen for the National Register of Historic Places. Originally the home of Henry Kruger, the owner of a successful lumber mill, it was purchased by Bank of America executive Charles Bernard White in 1904. Restored with a great deal of care and filled with antique furnishings and fixtures collected by Zina, this stately house embraces you with a sense of place. Lace curtains filter incoming light through numerous windows. High ceilings give small rooms a spacious feeling. Subdued, patterned wallpapers, historic photographs, hanging plants and soft colors create a warm environment for a special occasion. A long, enclosed front porch, glassed in on three sides, offers a view of the mountains beyond. Glorious aromas waft in from the kitchen. Here Zina works her magic, preparing creative foodstuffs for parties. And, if you'd like to have an impressive cake, Zina can concoct something truly special. Her intricate designs and ability to decorate with flowers sets her cakes apart from the ordinary. (They also taste divine.) Not for large celebrations, Zina's! is just right for business or rehearsal dinners, and small, cozy gatherings of friends and family.

CUISINE: Gourmet Continental

CAPACITY: 50–75 seated guests, up to 90 standing.

FEES & DEPOSITS: As a refundable deposit, half of the estimated event total is due when reservations are confirmed. A $250 refundable security/cleaning deposit is due 1 week before the event. There is no room rental fee with food service. Food costs per person: luncheons start at $12, buffets and/or seated dinners, $22–50. Tax and 15% gratuity are additional. The balance is payable the day of the event.

CANCELLATION POLICY: With 30 days' notice, the deposit is refundable, less any expenses incurred.

AVAILABILITY: Year-round, everyday except Thanksgiving and Christmas days.

OTHER INFORMATION:

Credit Cards: Visa, MC, Am Exp.
Parking: several lots
Full Bar: B&W only
Corkage: $5/bottle

Smoking: outside only
Dance Floor: on porch & patio
Wheelchair Access: yes
Special: cakes and custom desserts

Event Locations

San Francisco

ALAMO SQUARE INN

719 Scott Street at Fulton
San Francisco, CA 94117
(415) 922-2055 Wayne Corn
Reserve for Events: 1–6 months in advance
Reserve for Meetings: 1–6 months in advance

Located along the perimeter of the much photographed Alamo Square, made famous by the row of colorful, restored Victorians, the Alamo Square Inn is a special place for business conferences, retreats, special events and holiday parties. Built in 1895, the mansion combines both Queen Anne and Neoclassical Revival styles with rich woodwork and oak floors, high ceilings, chandeliers and a stately staircase illuminated by a stained glass skylight. The Inn is actually a bed and breakfast complex of two houses adjoined in back by a garden and solarium/atrium. All of the downstairs rooms in both houses are available for functions. Of special note are the triple bay windows in the drawing room and the formal parlor which has a vista overlooking Alamo Square, the adjacent hilltop park.

CAPACITY: The Inn can accommodate 200 people for a standing reception or 125 for a seated affair.

FEES & DEPOSITS: For special events, $1,000 is required to secure your event date; $500 of this is a refundable security deposit. For business conferences, the fee is $50/person per day and includes breakfast, coffee service, lunch and mid-afternoon treats. For events, the facility costs $250/hour with a 3-hour minimum rental required. Event staff run $15/hour/person (5 hour min.). Catering is provided. Mid-afternoon buffets start at $25/person and seated functions start at $35/person. Tax and a 15% gratuity are additional. The remaining balance, based on an agreed on minimum head count, is due, in full, at the beginning of the event week.

AVAILABILITY: Year-round, anytime. Events must end by 10:30pm, with guests out by 11pm.

SERVICES/AMENITIES:

Restaurant Services: no
Catering: provided, no BYO
Kitchen Facilities: n/a
Tables & Chairs: provided
Linens, Silver, etc.: some provided, linens at cost
Restrooms: no wca
Dance Floor: yes

Parking: off street lot, valet CBA
Overnight Accommodations: 15 guestrooms
Telephone: guest phone
Outdoor Night Lighting: yes
Outdoor Cooking Facilities: no
Cleanup: provided
Meeting Equipment: audio-visual equipment

RESTRICTIONS:

Alcohol: BYO, corkage $5/bottle,
red wine at seated meals only
Smoking: smoking porch only

Music: amplified within reason
Wheelchair Access: no
Insurance: events binder required

THE ANSEL ADAMS CENTER
For Photography and Opts. Art

250 Fourth Street
San Francisco, CA 94103
(415) 546-7844
Reserve for Events: 1 month–2 years in advance
Reserve for Meetings: 2 weeks in advance

Two exciting new contemporary galleries, located right across from the Moscone Center, are now available for special events, meetings and conferences. If you are an admirer of Ansel Adams' work or you have a special interest in photography, then you're in luck! Once a semi-industrial warehouse, both have been transformed into very appealing spaces. The downstairs Ansel Adams Center is composed of multiple, contemporary rooms, all in subdued creams and grays. Interesting and colorful photographic exhibits are changed frequently. The largest room downstairs has a splendid, cork tile floor in rich brown-golds. Not for seated functions, the Ansel Adams Center is great for champagne and hors d'oeuvres receptions. Upstairs is Opts. Art, a spacious 7,000 sq. ft. room broken up by round concrete columns which flare out at the ceiling some fourteen feet above. During the day, a long row of windows provide substantial light. At night, the ceiling becomes an architectural element, equipped with a track and theatrical lighting system which is a major feature in itself. Paintings, photography and sculpture, exclusively from local artists, capture your attention in an otherwise unadorned space. Styled with neutral colors, it can be dressed up or down depending on your needs. This newcomer is a real find considering its proximity to Moscone Center, Union Square and downtown hotels. We also like the fact that highly experienced Opts. Catering and Events is the lease holder. They can orchestrate the most complex of events with ease.

CAPACITY: The Ansel Adams Center can accommodate 300 for a standing reception; Opts. Art 400 for a seated function or 500 for a standing reception.

FEES & DEPOSITS: A refundable deposit equaling 50% of the rental fee plus a refundable $500 cleaning/security deposit are required to secure your date.

Space	Rental Fee	Hours
Both Spaces	$4,000	Unlimited evening hours.
Ansel Adams Center	1,500	6pm–1am
Opts. Art	2,500	6 hour period, anytime

If you use Opts. to cater your event, per person rates are as follows: hors d'oeuvres receptions start at $20, seated meals at $40 and buffets start at $25. The service charge is included in these fees. If you select another caterer, a 10% surcharge for use of the building and a buy-out fee must be arranged in advance.

CANCELLATION POLICY: With 9 months' notice, deposits will be refunded.

AVAILABILITY: Year-round. Ansel Adams Center rentals are contingent on the gallery's event schedule. Opts. Art, any day, anytime until 2am.

SERVICES/AMENITIES:
Restaurant Services: no   *Parking:* nearby garage, street parking at night

Catering: provided, BYO requires buy-out
Kitchen Facilities: minimal
Tables & Chairs: provided or BYO
Linens, Silver, etc.: provided or BYO
Restrooms: wca
Meeting Equipment: CBA
Other: event coordination & design

RESTRICTIONS:
Alcohol: provided, corkage fee if BYO
Music: amplified needs approval
Smoking: not allowed

Overnight Accommodations: no
Telephone: pay phone
Outdoor Night Lighting: access only
Outdoor Cooking Facilities: no
Cleanup: caterer or renter
Dance Floor: yes

Wheelchair Access: yes
Insurance: extra liability required

AQUATIC PARK BAYVIEW ROOM

890 Beach Street at Aquatic Park
San Francisco, CA 94109
(415) 775-1866
Reserve for Events: 3–6 months in advance
Reserve for Meetings: 2–4 weeks in advance

Imagine your party a stone's throw from the water's edge! Make your vision a reality by renting the Bayview Room which occupies the east end of the Maritime Museum building, across from Ghirardelli Square. The entire structure was cleverly designed to resemble a cruise ship, even down to the nautical looking decks (loggias) with railings. Constructed in the round, the Bayview Room has a high ceiling, inlaid terrazzo floor and large glass windows on almost all sides providing sensational views overlooking the Aquatic Park pier, Alcatraz, Sausalito and historic ships berthed nearby. An additional benefit is the adjacent open-air loggia (balcony), resembling a long, narrow deck except with a tile floor. Bay breezes will enliven any celebration and the loggia's nautical paraphernalia will capture your guests' attention. They'll be able to touch parts from old ships, look at the dry-docked nineteen-foot sloop *The Mermaid*, Benny Buffano sculptures and unblemished examples of 1930s Art Deco tile murals along the wall facing the Bay. You can extend your party by bringing tables onto the loggia—or just have the bar set up here so everyone can enjoy the views.

CAPACITY: The Bayview Room seats 150 guests or 190 for a standing reception. Use of the loggia will increase the number of guests. For larger parties, the Maritime Museum may also be rented in conjunction with the Bayview Room.

MEETING ROOMS: Some meeting rooms are available.

FEES & DEPOSITS: For special events, a refundable $200 cleaning and security deposit is required when reservations are confirmed. The rental fee is $700 for the Bayview Room plus $10/hour for an event staff person. The rental fee for the loggia is an additional $100. All rental fees are due 2 weeks prior to the event. For meetings, the rental fee is negotiable. Call for rates.

CANCELLATION POLICY: With 60 days' notice, the deposit is refunded.

AVAILABILITY: Year-round. Weekdays after 5pm. Saturdays 9am–12:30am, Sundays 4pm–12:30am.

SERVICES/AMENITIES:

Restaurant Services: no
Catering: BYO
Kitchen Facilities: setup only
Tables & Chairs: provided
Linens, Silver, etc.: BYO
Restrooms: wca
Dance Floor: yes

Parking: on street, adjacent public lot
Overnight Accommodations: no
Telephone: pay phone
Outdoor Night Lighting: yes
Outdoor Cooking Facilities: no
Cleanup: caterer or provided, extra fee
Meeting Equipment: limited

RESTRICTIONS:

Alcohol: BYO
Wheelchair Access: yes
Smoking: outside only

Music: amplified within reason
Insurance: may be required

ARCHBISHOP'S MANSION

1000 Fulton Street at Steiner
San Francisco, CA 94117
(415) 563-7872 Kathleen Austin
Reserve for Events: 2 months in advance
Reserve for Meetings: 2 months in advance

Built in 1904 as the residence for the archbishop of San Francisco, this elegant historic landmark with hand-painted ceilings, fine woodwork and distinguished period furnishings, has been restored to its original splendor. The first floor dining room, main hallway and parlor are available for ceremonies and receptions. The great hall stairway landing is a terrific spot to take your vows, allowing the bride to make a grand entry. Facing Alamo Park, the Mansion is a regal bed and breakfast inn.

CAPACITY: For a standing reception, 100 people, or for a sit-down meal, approximately 50.

FEES & DEPOSITS: A non-refundable deposit of 50% of the estimated fee is needed in order to secure your event date. A $375 refundable security deposit is also required. This facility is rented at $150–200/hour, measured from the arrival of the caterers to their departure. A 4-hour minimum rental is required. The balance and security deposit are due 1 week prior to the event.

AVAILABILITY: Sun–Thurs, all day up to 11pm; Fri & Sat up to 5pm only.

SERVICES/AMENITIES:

Restaurant Services: no
Catering: CBA or BYO, must be licensed
Kitchen Facilities: ample
Tables & Chairs: some provided
Linens, Silver, etc.: caterer

Parking: on street, valet CBA
Overnight Accommodations: 15 guestrooms
Telephone: house phone
Outdoor Night Lighting: access only
Outdoor Cooking Facilities: no

Restrooms: no wca
Dance Floor: no dancing
Meeting Equipment: CBA

RESTRICTIONS:
Alcohol: provided, corkage fee if BYO
Smoking: outside only
Music: no amplified

Cleanup: caterer
Other: baby grand piano

Wheelchair Access: no
Insurance: not required
Other: decorations restricted

ASTA and the
RINCON CENTER ATRIUM

One Rincon Center
101 Spear Street
San Francisco, CA 94105
(415) 495-2782
Reserve for Events: 3–6 months in advance
Reserve for Meetings: 3–6 months in advance

Located in the heart of the recently renovated Rincon Center, the Atrium is a phenomenal setting for a large function. This circular space glows under a skylight roof, soaring eighty feet or more overhead. In the middle of the skylight, a fountain of water descends like soft rain, filling a shallow pool below. Palms and other plants add to the sensation of actually being outdoors. Terraced seating is arranged around the perimeter of the Atrium, and the spacious main floor has plenty of room for additional dining and dancing. For an interesting contrast, serve cocktails and hors d'oeuvres from Asta, the sophisticated 1930s-style restaurant on the premises that caters Atrium events (see Asta Restaurant's entry in the Private Dining Room section). This is definitely a unique spot—where else can you watch *Thin Man* movies, and enjoy an indoor waterfall and a view of the sky all year-round?

CAPACITY: The Atrium can hold 200 seated or 500 standing guests. Asta Restaurant can seat 110 or up to 200 standing guests.

MEETING ROOMS: Private room holds up to 30 people.

FEES & DEPOSITS: A deposit in the amount of 25% of the estimated total is required 4 weeks prior to the event. Half the estimated total is due on the day of the event, and the remaining charges are due within 2 days of the event's conclusion. There is a 10% facility fee for all parties of less than 18 guests in Asta's private room, and for events held in the Rincon Center Atrium or the entire Asta Restaurant where the number of guests is less than 120 people. Per person food service rates are: $15–25 for luncheons or $30–40 for dinners. Tax and an 18% service charge are additional.

CANCELLATION POLICY: The deposit is refunded only if the date can be rebooked with a party of equal or greater value.

AVAILABILITY: Asta is available Monday night, all day Sunday and Saturday during the day. Other times can be arranged. The Atrium is available Monday–Friday after 4:30pm, and all day Saturday and Sunday year-round.

SERVICES/AMENITIES:

Restaurant Services: yes

Catering: provided, no BYO

Kitchen Facilities: n/a

Tables & Chairs: most provided

Linens, Silver, etc.: provided

Restrooms: wca

Dance Floor: yes

Parking: Rincon Center Garage, valet CBA

Overnight Accommodations: no

Telephone: pay phone

Outdoor Night Lighting: access only

Outdoor Cooking Facilities: n/a

Cleanup: provided

Meeting Equipment: CBA

RESTRICTIONS:

Alcohol: provided, corkage $9/bottle

Smoking: allowed

Music: amplified ok

Wheelchair Access: yes

Insurance: not required

BALCLUTHA

San Francisco Maritime National Historic Park
Hyde Street Pier
San Francisco, CA 94109
(415) 929-0202 Daria Booth
Reserve for Events: 1–2 months in advance
Reserve for Meetings: 1 month in advance

The Balclutha, a three-masted, square-rigged sailing ship, made her maiden voyage from Wales to San Francisco in 1887. After her long and varied career, the ship was purchased and restored by the San Francisco Maritime Museum in 1954, as a memorial to the by-gone days of sailing. This impressive and historic floating national landmark is available as a public exhibit *and* for private functions. Hors d'oeuvres and cocktails can be served on the top (poop) deck or in the 'tween deck, which is covered. Surprise your friends! This is a very unusual site for a special event.

CAPACITY: For a standing reception, 200–300 guests; for a seated function, 125 guests.

FEES & DEPOSITS: A $1,500 refundable security deposit is required and is usually returned within 2 weeks after the event. The rental fee is $900, minimum. The total fee will depend on the length of your event and the number of guests. Work out the details with the National Maritime Museum Association. Fees include a National Park Ranger on duty during events.

CANCELLATION POLICY: All deposits are refundable 21 days prior to your event.

AVAILABILITY: Nov–May, 5pm–midnight; June–Oct, 6pm–midnight.

SERVICES/AMENITIES:

Restaurant Services: no

Catering: BYO

Kitchen Facilities: no

Tables & Chairs: BYO

Parking: on street, garage nearby

Overnight Accommodations: no

Telephone: pay phone nearby

Outdoor Night Lighting: deck lighting

Linens, Silver, etc.: BYO
Restrooms: none, restrooms on pier
Dance Floor: deck

RESTRICTIONS:
Alcohol: BYO
Smoking: only on pier
Music: amplified until 11pm

Outdoor Cooking Facilities: no
Cleanup: caterer
Meeting Equipment: none

Wheelchair Access: limited
Insurance: required

BLUE AND GOLD FLEET

Pier 39
San Francisco, CA 94133
(415) 705-5555
Reserve for Events: 2–3 months in advance
Reserve for Meetings: 2–3 months in advance

Ready to accommodate big and small parties alike, the Blue and Gold Fleet proudly offers three vessels for private charter. The Golden Bear, Old Blue and Oski make it possible to have a scenic and entertaining meeting or social event while cruising San Francisco Bay. Note that there are alternate docking sites available for your party for a minimal extra charge. The B&G staff are extremely helpful with DJ selection, live entertainment, flowers and decoration, plus theme party planning.

CAPACITY: These boats usually carry over 100 people. Each vessel can accommodate 200 for a buffet dinner dance or 300 for standing receptions.

FEES & DEPOSITS: A $500 deposit is required 10 working days after arranging a tentative date. The fees vary depending on season and day of the week:

	Friday	*Saturday*	*Sunday*	*Mon–Thurs*
April-October	$2,700	$3,000	$2,500	$2,300
November-March	2,400	2,700	2,300	2,100

The above rental fees are for a 4-hour minimum cruise. Fees are increased for major holidays. Catering is provided. Blue and Gold catering costs range from $7/person to over $20/person, depending on menu arrangements. Sales tax and a 15% service charge are additional.

CANCELLATION POLICY: Your deposit is returned if you cancel 60 days prior to the event.

AVAILABILITY: From June–Sept 5, no charters are available before 6pm. Sept 5–May 30, 1 boat is available during the day, with a 4-hour minimum rental required. Evenings are generally available for private functions.

SERVICES/AMENITIES:
Restaurant Services: no
Catering: provided, no BYO

Parking: Pier 39 garage
Overnight Accommodations: no

Kitchen Facilities: no
Tables & Chairs: provided
Linens, Silver, etc.: provided
Restrooms: no wca
Dance Floor: yes

RESTRICTIONS:
Alcohol: provided, corkage $3/bottle
Smoking: allowed
Music: amplified ok

Telephone: emergency only
Outdoor Night Lighting: yes
Outdoor Cooking Facilities: BBQ
Cleanup: provided
Meeting Equipment: not provided, CBA

Wheelchair Access: on main deck only
Insurance: not required

CABLE CAR BARN AND MUSEUM

1201 Mason St. at Washington
San Francisco, CA 94108
(415) 923-6202   Jim Tomes
Reserve for Events: 3 months–2 years in advance

Looking for something a bit different? The Barn and Museum are two really unusual sites to host a party. For a very dramatic entry, you and your group can even arrive riding a cable car! The cavernous Barn is a working "corporation yard" for the cable cars. The Museum houses historical displays and has an interesting view down into the drive wheels that run the cable car system. During special events, cable cars are lined up in the Barn to section off actual working areas from the party spaces. Note that neighborhood parking is impossible; guests may arrive by cable car or other forms of public transit. A Muni-approved parking plan must be in place before they'll allow the rental to occur.

CAPACITY: Barn and Museum, combined, can hold 800 for a standing reception or 400 seated guests.

FEES & DEPOSITS: $1,000 plus a $500 refundable cleaning deposit are required to secure a date. The deposit is payable 2 weeks from making a tentative booking. The refundable portion is usually returned within a week after the event. The fee for the Barn and Museum combined is $1,850. Any remaining unpaid balance plus use permit and insurance paperwork are due 2 weeks prior to the event.

CANCELLATION POLICY: During the holiday season or peak use periods, you must cancel at least 2 months in advance to receive a full refund.

AVAILABILITY: Year-round, daily. The Barn is available 5pm–10:30pm. The Museum, during the summer 6pm–11pm, during the winter 5pm–11pm. Guests must be out by 11pm. No events are scheduled on major holidays.

SERVICES/AMENITIES:
Restaurant Services: no
Catering: BYO
Kitchen Facilities: no

Parking: no
Overnight Accommodations: no
Telephone: office phone

Tables & Chairs: BYO
Linens, Silver, etc.: BYO
Restrooms: wca
Dance Floor: no
Meeting Equipment: no

RESTRICTIONS:
Alcohol: BYO
Smoking: allowed
Music: amplified until 10pm

Outdoor Night Lighting: access only
Outdoor Cooking Facilities: no
Cleanup: caterer
Other: cable car arrivals CBA

Wheelchair Access: yes
Insurance: event liability required

CAFFE ESPRIT

235 16th St.
San Francisco, CA 94107
(415) 777-5558
Reserve for Events: 1 week–12 months in advance
Reserve for Meetings: 1 week–12 months in advance

Caffe Esprit is far more than just a delightful place for lunch, cappucino or a snack. It's a great space for practically any type of event. The front of the café is actually two enormous glass roll-up doors which connect the attractively landscaped patio with the open two-level interior, flooding it with light. The high-tech style of burnished metal fixtures is softened by the serpentine bar and tables finished in natural ash. An oversized wire basket of lemons and large jars of pickled olives and peppers add spots of color behind the bar. Caffe Esprit's spacious patio with large round tables, umbrellas and curved benches is ideal for day or evening functions. When the weather obliges, the roll-up doors can be raised, allowing both party-goers and breezes to mingle. The semi-private area upstairs overlooks the café's main floor below, and has a bank of windows with a view of the bay, occasional sailboats and sea lions, and the East Bay hills. An artful combination of functionality and elegance, Caffe Esprit can host a casual or dressed up affair with equal ease.

CAPACITY: The Main Floor can hold 65 seated or over 300 standing guests; the Mezzanine 65 seated; the Patio up to 64 seated.

FEES & DEPOSITS: A $250 deposit is due when reservations are confirmed. "Bar only" parties require an additional $500 security deposit. Half of the total is payable 2 weeks before the function; the balance is due the evening of the event. Per person food costs are $10-25 for lunch and $18.25-75 for dinner. Tax and a 15% service charge are extra.

CANCELLATION POLICY: The deposit is not refundable with less than 1 week's notice.

AVAILABILITY: The entire restaurant can be reserved Monday–Saturday, 5pm–2am, and all day Sunday. The mezzanine is available for small groups Monday–Saturday, 11:30am–3pm. Closed Thanksgiving, Christmas and New Year's Day.

SERVICES/AMENITIES:

Restaurant Services: yes

Catering: provided, no BYO

Kitchen Facilities: n/a

Tables & Chairs: provided

Linens, Silver, etc.: provided, fee for extras

Restrooms: wca

Dance Floor: yes

Parking: large lot (no fees)

Overnight Accommodations: no

Telephone: pay phone

Outdoor Night Lighting: yes

Outdoor Cooking Facilities: no

Cleanup: provided

Meeting Equipment: BYO

RESTRICTIONS:

Alcohol: provided, corkage, $9/bottle

Smoking: allowed

Insurance: not required

Wheelchair Access: yes

Music: amplified ok

Other: no mylar balloons or tape

CALIFORNIA ACADEMY OF SCIENCES

Golden Gate Park
San Francisco, CA 94118
(415) 750-7221 Deidre Kernan
Reserve for Events: 3 months in advance
Reserve for Meetings: 3 months in advance

Although first and foremost a public museum, the California Academy of Sciences offers an incredibly wide range of sensational spaces for private parties. Located in Golden Gate Park, the museum is one of the largest natural history museums in the world and the oldest in the Western U.S. Use the dynamic and dramatically lit exhibits as backdrops for events, and reserve well in advance for parties scheduled between September and Christmas.

African Hall: Authentic sights and sounds of a busy savannah watering hole, featuring majestic dioramas filled with exotic birds and animals.

Earth and Space Hall: Features celestial bodies, a neon solar system and earthquake simulation. Note that laser shows at night have public access.

Hall of Human Cultures: Otherwise known as Wattis Hall, this large room holds dioramas depicting man's adaptation to his natural environment.

Temporary Exhibit Space: Special exhibits, like the most recent Caribbean Festival Arts show, are changed often. Call to find out what's current.

Life Through Time: Dinosaur fossils and moving models demonstrate the evidence for evolution. Available for cocktail receptions only.

Wild California: Wild California is remarkable for its lifelike exhibits. The battling sea lions and coastal dioramas are terrific.

Aquarium: Sensational exhibits of reptiles and amphibians, exotic fish, penguins, dolphins and seals.

The fish roundabout is a spiral ascending ramp with tanks along the outer wall. The top platform, a circular space surrounded by blue-green lit tanks, with large fish swimming in one direction, is one of the most extraordinary party spaces we've seen. Also, check out the swamp with crocodiles—it's a favorite spot for unique celebrations.

Museum Store: Can be opened on request. Guests must be notified in advance so they can remember to bring funds and credit cards for purchases.

CAPACITY, FEES & DEPOSITS: A non-refundable deposit of 30% of the estimated fee is due within 21 days of contract receipt. The remaining 70% and a $500 refundable security deposit are due 3 weeks prior to the event. For holiday rentals (December 1–24) the remaining fees are due 90 days prior to the event. The security deposit is returned after your function, pending assessment of the facility's condition. If cleanup assistance is necessary, $150/hour will be billed.

	Fees	*Standing Capacity*	*Seated Capacity*	*Standing & Seated*
African Hall	$3,500	400	300	150
Hohfeld I & II	1,500	capacity varies	—	—
Lovell White	1,500	capacity varies	—	—
Space Hall	1,500	150	100	60
Wattis Hall	3,500	400	150	100
Aquarium, Swamp, Roundabout Combo	3,500	400	200	—
Roundabout Only	1,500	125	60	60
Wild California	3,500	300	150	150
Life Thru Time/Oceans	3,500	capacity varies	—	—
Auditorium	1,000	—	400	—
Planetarium	1,200	—	300	—
Entire Academy	8,000–12,000	to 3,000		

Combinations of different halls can be arranged for any sized gathering. The above fees include an Academy representative and security guards. For meetings, you can rent the auditorium for $1,000 or the Goethe Room for $200.

AVAILABILITY: The Academy is available September 1–July 3 from 6pm–12:30am; July 4–September 1 from 8pm–12:30am; and the first Wednesday of every month from 10pm–12:30am. With prior notice, you can extend your party for an extra $150/hour.

SERVICES/AMENITIES:

Restaurant Services: no

Catering: provided, or BYO from approved list

Kitchen Facilities: no

Tables & Chairs: BYO

Linens, Silver, etc.: BYO

Restrooms: wca

Dance Floor: CBA

Parking: museum lot

Overnight Accommodations: no

Telephone: pay phones

Outdoor Night Lighting: access only

Outdoor Cooking Facilities: no

Cleanup: caterer and museum janitorial

Meeting Equipment: limited

RESTRICTIONS:

Alcohol: BYO, license required
Smoking: not allowed
Music: amplified ok except for aquarium

Wheelchair Access: yes
Insurance: indemnification clause required
Other: decorations need approval, catering restrictions

CALIFORNIA CULINARY ACADEMY

625 Polk Street
San Francisco, CA 94102
(415) 771-3500
Reserve for Events: 1–12 months in advance

Located in a lovely and architecturally significant landmark building, the California Culinary Academy makes available a number of interesting and varied spaces for private parties. The main dining room, The Carême Room, was once a formal theater. It's ornate, large and formal with an awesome ceiling extending up three floors. When dining here, you can observe hundreds of young, aspiring chefs cooking for you. Circling above the main floor is Cyril's, a balcony restaurant with fabulous views of the lower dining room and ceiling. The main bar is lovely, warm and intimate with dark wood, mirrors and an old bar. The Private Dining Room is a comfortable place for small gatherings. The Academy Grill is a more informal space. Wine tasting, cooking demonstrations and a Grand Buffet are available. Note that the food service here is exceptional; the Academy is one of the world's foremost culinary schools.

CAPACITY, FEES & DEPOSITS: To secure your date, a refundable $1,000 deposit is required when you book reservations.

Room	Standing	Seated	Room	Standing	Seated
Main Dining Room	500	280	Cyril's	150	80
Main Bar	150	60	Academy Grill	200	200
Private Dining Room	40	30			

Fees are based on guest count, menu selection and time of function. The Academy requires 50% of the estimated total prior to the event. Also note that for private parties, a combination of rooms with special rates can be arranged. Food service is provided. Hors d'oeuvres start at $5.50/person, luncheons at $19/person and dinners at $26/person. Sales tax and an 18% service charge will be applied to the final bill.

CANCELLATION POLICY: Your deposit will be refunded up to 30 days prior to your event.

AVAILABILITY: Because the Academy operates a school, weekday seatings for lunch are at 12, 12:30 or 1pm. Luncheons must conclude by 3pm. Dinner seatings are at 6, 6:45 or 7:30pm with a 5-hour maximum. Weekend reservations can be made anytime. You need a minimum of 100 people to open the Culinary Academy on a weekend, for which there may be an additional opening fee. There's no minimum rental block, but there's a 5-hour maximum.

SERVICES/AMENITIES:

Restaurant Services: yes

Catering: provided, no BYO

Kitchen Facilities: ample

Tables & Chairs: provided

Linens, Silver, etc.: provided

Restrooms: wca

Dance Floor: $350 setup charge

Meeting Equipment: no

Parking: garage nearby

Overnight Accommodations: no

Telephone: pay phone

Outdoor Night Lighting: access only

Outdoor Cooking Facilities: no

Cleanup: provided

Other: ice sculpture and cakes

RESTRICTIONS:

Alcohol: provided, corkage $7.50/bottle

Smoking: allowed

Music: amplified after 7:30pm

Wheelchair Access: yes

Insurance: not required

THE CALIFORNIA SPIRIT
Pacific Marine Yacht Charters

Berthed at Pier 39, East Basin
San Francisco, CA 94133
(415) 788-9100
Reserve for Events: 1–9 months in advance
Reserve for Meetings: 1 week in advance

The hundred-foot custom-designed California Spirit is one of four luxury yachts in Pacific Marine's elegant fleet. This vessel features a grand salon with dance area, a plush observation salon with leather couches and an upper salon in rich woods complemented by soft colors. A spacious outdoor deck provides guests with breathtaking views of the Bay Area's premier sights. First-class service and award-winning cuisine ensure that you and your guests will have an experience you won't soon forget.

CAPACITY: The California Spirit can accommodate up to 149 guests for cocktails and hors d'oeuvres. Formal seating is available for 80.

FEES & DEPOSITS: A $2,000 deposit is required to reserve your date and half the food and beverage cost is due 30 days prior to your event.

	Weekdays (before 6pm)	*Weekdays (after 6pm)*	*Weekends/Holidays*
Yacht rental rates	$625/hr	$750/hr	$900/hr

A 3-hour minimum rental is required, 4 hours on Saturday evenings and holidays. A guaranteed guest count is required 7 days prior to departure and the remaining balance is due 5 days prior to your event.

CANCELLATION POLICY: With 60 days' notice, 85% of the reservation deposit will be refunded; with less notice, the deposit will be forfeited.

AVAILABILITY: Anytime, no limits.

SERVICES/AMENITIES:

Restaurant Services: no
Catering: provided, no BYO
Kitchen Facilities: on board
Tables & Chairs: provided
Linens, Silver, etc.: provided
Restrooms: 4, wca
Dance Floor: yes
Meeting Equipment: podium, microphone

Parking: Pier 39 garage, validations available
Overnight Accommodations: no
Telephone: cellular phone & radio
Outdoor Night Lighting: yes
Outdoor Cooking Facilities: no
Cleanup: provided
Other: event coordination

RESTRICTIONS:

Alcohol: provided, corkage $7/bottle
Smoking: outside only
Music: amplified ok

Wheelchair Access: yes, CBA
Insurance: not required

CAMPTON PLACE

340 Stockton Street
San Francisco, CA 94108
(415) 781-5555
Reserve for Events: 2 weeks in advance
Reserve for Meetings: 1 week in advance

Campton Place is a small hotel with an understated elegance that becomes apparent the moment you enter the lobby. The beige marble floor, stunning floral centerpiece and warm background colors invite you to linger a while. Upstairs, the Conference Room and Boardroom accommodate small business functions in comfort and style. Both have beautiful custom-made mahogany tables and upholstered chairs. For a more informal atmosphere, two suites include a bedroom, sitting room and many of the comforts of home. Done in off-white, pastels and beige, the suites are perfect spots for small intimate gatherings. Campton Places pays attention to small details. Colors throughout are soothing, there are flowers in every room and dining here can be a sublime experience.

CAPACITY: The Conference Room seats 10; the Board Room 16; the Penthouse Suites can accommodate up to 26 for a reception.

FEES & DEPOSITS: No deposits are required. Prior to the event, credit and payment are established. The Conference and Board Rooms rent for $225 (8 hours) and $125 (4 hours) and the Penthouse Suites $350 (3 hours). For functions with banquet service, the room rental fees for the Conference and Board Room may be waived. Food service per person: continental breakfasts $13, luncheons $20–40, dinners $45–55 and hors d'oeuvres start at $24. Tax and 15% service charge are additional. The balance is due the day of the event.

CANCELLATION POLICY: 24 hours' notice is requested for cancellation. A small fee will be charged.

AVAILABILITY: Year-round, any day, anytime.

SERVICES/AMENITIES:

Restaurant Services: yes
Catering: provided, no BYO
Kitchen Facilities: n/a
Tables & Chairs: provided
Linens, Silver, etc.: provided
Restrooms: wca
Dance Floor: no
Other: event coordination provided

Parking: valet $19/day
Overnight Accommodations: 126 guestrooms
Telephone: pay phones
Outdoor Night Lighting: access only
Outdoor Cooking Facilities: no
Cleanup: provided
Meeting Equipment: CBA, extra charge

RESTRICTIONS:

Alcohol: provided, corkage $15/bottle
Smoking: designated areas
Music: no amplified

Wheelchair Access: yes
Insurance: not required

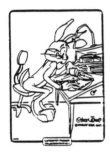

CARTOON ART MUSEUM

665 3rd Street at Townsend, Fifth Floor
San Francisco, CA 94107
(415) 546-3922
Reserve for Events: 1 month in advance
Reserve for Meetings: 2 weeks in advance

Housed on the fifth floor of what was once the Hills Bros. Coffee corporate offices, the Museum consists of three galleries with over 2,000 square feet of space. The floor plan has an open feel, with high ceilings, exposed fixtures, white walls and gray carpet. An original brick wall adds to the ambiance. Changing exhibits of matted, framed original cartoon art are displayed on the walls and in free-standing display cases. Cartoon Art Museum shows are both fun and thought-provoking, and range from Batman and Spiderman to Japanese animation and political cartoons. Since three exhibits are shown at any given time, and the exhibits change three times a year, there's always something new for your guests to see. Conveniently located just blocks from Moscone Convention Center, major highways and the Financial District, the Cartoon Art Museum is a popular place for corporate functions.

CAPACITY: The Museum can accommodate up to 250 guests for a standing reception.

MEETING ROOMS: A large conference room/classroom that can be partitioned and accommodates up to 40 people.

FEES & DEPOSITS: A $400 deposit (including a cleaning deposit) is required to secure your date. The fee for your first 2 hours' usage is $550; additional hours are $165/hr. Since the Museum houses valuable artwork, security guard charges are included in the fees. Full payment is due 3 business days prior to the event.

CANCELLATION POLICY: To obtain a refund, cancellation must be made 15 days prior to your function. All deposits are refundable less $100.

AVAILABILITY: Year-round. Mon and Tues, noon–midnight; Wed–Sun, 5pm–midnight.

SERVICES/AMENITIES:

Restaurant Services: no
Catering: BYO
Kitchen Facilities: minimal
Tables & Chairs: BYO
Linens, Silver, etc.: BYO
Restrooms: wca
Dance Floor: no
Special: caricaturist CBA, extra fee

Parking: on street, 2 inexpensive lots nearby
Overnight Accommodations: no
Telephone: emergency only
Outdoor Night Lighting: access only
Outdoor Cooking Facilities: no
Cleanup: caterer
Meeting Equipment: BYO

RESTRICTIONS:

Alcohol: BYO, no red wine
Smoking: not allowed
Music: ok until midnight

Wheelchair Access: yes
Insurance: indemnification clause required
Other: no gas-producing devices allowed in galleries

CASA DE LA VISTA

Building 271, Avenue of the Palms
Treasure Island
San Francisco, CA 94130
(415) 395-5151
Reserve for Events: 1–18 months in advance
Reserve for Meetings: 1–18 months in advance

If Treasure Island actually possesses any treasures, Casa de la Vista could very well be one of them. This is a terrific spot for those who have a sponsor (Military person on active duty, retired or reservist). Situated on the edge of the island, it has unobstructed views of the entire San Francisco skyline, both bridges, Alcatraz, and Marin. The facility itself is quite pleasant. It's light and airy with a long wall of floor-to-ceiling glass that overlooks the Bay. Painted in a soft mauve, the vaulted ceiling is accented by light blue beams and pink pillars which provide colorful support. A modern fireplace with brass chimney and a convenient bar are located near one end, leaving the majority of the room open for flexible arrangements. In back, olive trees shade a large brick patio which can also be arranged for your event. Casa de la Vista is a great place for parties and company functions because it's very private *and* has knockout views. Additionally, there's the benefit of having a central location, great for guests coming from either San Francisco or the East Bay.

CAPACITY: This facility can hold 300 for a reception or 180 guests for a seated affair.

FEES & DEPOSITS: A non-refundable deposit is required at the time of booking (25% of the estimated total cost of the event). The estimated balance and a final guest count are due one week prior to the event. There is a $200 setup fee which may be waived with meal service. After 11pm, overtime hours are available for an additional charge. Per person rates: dinners/buffets $10–30, hors d'oeuvres trays $35–200. Any menu can be customized, no tax is required and the service charge is 15%.

AVAILABILITY: Year-round, every day from 11am–4pm and 6pm–11pm.

SERVICES/AMENITIES:

Restaurant Services: no

Catering: provided

Kitchen Facilities: n/a

Tables & Chairs: provided

Linens, Silver, etc.: provided

Restrooms: wca

Dance Floor: yes

Meeting Equipment: yes

Parking: large lot

Overnight Accommodations: no

Telephone: pay phone

Outdoor Night Lighting: yes

Outdoor Cooking Facilities: CBA

Cleanup: provided

Other: event coordination, piano

RESTRICTIONS:

Alcohol: provided, corkage $6.50/bottle

Smoking: allowed

Music: amplified ok

Wheelchair Access: yes

Insurance: not required

Other: votive candles only

CIRCLE GALLERY

140 Maiden Lane
San Francisco, CA 94108
(415) 989-2100
Reserve for Events: 1–2 months in advance

Located in the only Frank Lloyd Wright designed building in San Francisco, the Circle Gallery is found on a small, trendy street off Union Square. It's a superb address for corporate or nonprofit organization cocktail parties. Developed as a prototype for the Guggenheim Museum in New York City, the Circle Gallery offers a distinguished environment, with rotating exhibits that profile different artists, for people who appreciate contemporary art. Wright's design creates perfect spaces with excellent acoustics for both large and small functions, with two levels connected by a spiral ramp. Since this is a popular place for holiday parties, reserve the gallery well in advance. No non-business parties are permitted.

CAPACITY: The Gallery can hold up to 350 guests for a reception. No seated functions.

FEES & DEPOSITS: A letter of intent is required to reserve your date. A non-refundable deposit of 50% of the rental fee is required 2 weeks prior to your function and the balance is due at the beginning of the event. The rental fee is usually $1,600 for a 4-hour block which includes staff and security along with the gallery space. The fee may vary depending on the guest count and the time of day. For hours beyond 9pm, extra charges may apply.

AVAILABILITY: Year-round, every day for group events (depending on group size) from 5pm–midnight. Closed Christmas, Thanksgiving and New Year's days.

SERVICES/AMENITIES:

Restaurant Services: no

Catering: preferred list or BYO with approval

Kitchen Facilities: no

Linens, Silver, etc.: BYO

Restrooms: no wca

Dance Floor: no dancing

Tables & Chairs: BYO
Overnight Accommodations: no
Telephone: office phone
Outdoor Night Lighting: access only
Meeting Equipment: no

Parking: major garages nearby
Outdoor Cooking Facilities: no
Cleanup: caterer

RESTRICTIONS:
Alcohol: BYO, no red wine
Smoking: outside only
Music: amplified within limits

Wheelchair Access: yes
Insurance: sometimes required

THE CITY CLUB

155 Sansome Street
San Francisco, CA 94104
(415) 362-2480
Reserve for Events: 1–12 months in advance
Reserve for Meetings: 1–6 weeks in advance

Just walking into the lobby of the Stock Exchange Tower, situated in the heart of the financial district, gives you an inkling of what's to follow. The entry has highly polished black and green marble floors and black and white marble walls, gold ceiling and finely detailed metal elevators that whisk you up to the tenth floor. Here you enter the former watering hole for the Pacific Stock Exchange which has been painstakingly restored to its original integrity. The Club is located on the tenth and eleventh floors and features one of the most striking and exquisite Art Deco interiors we've seen. The Club's tenth floor entry is through bronze-framed elevator doors decorated in silver, bronze and brass appliqué. A remarkable interior staircase complete with an original thirty-foot high Diego Rivera fresco leads to the eleventh floor. Furnishings are original Art Deco pieces and appointments are generously clad in black marble, silver and brass. The ceiling is stunning, covered with burnished gold leaf squares. The white baby grand piano is an elegant touch, and reflects the facility's attention to detail. This is a truly exceptional place to hold a sophisticated party.

CAPACITY: For events, the entire club (10th and 11th floors) must be reserved. The total capacity is 700 for a standing reception or 200 for a seated function.

FEES & DEPOSITS: A deposit is required, the amount dependent on several variables, so make sure you get specific information over the phone. For Saturday parties, the minimum rental fee is $1,250 for a 4-hour block. For Sunday, the rental fee is $500/4-hour block. Should you desire more time, additional fees may apply. On week nights, Monday through Friday, the fee for the Main Dining Room is $300 and for both floors, $500.

CANCELLATION POLICY: Deposit refund varies contingent on date of notification to the Club.

AVAILABILITY: The Club's dining rooms are available every day after 4pm. On Saturdays and Sundays, it's available earlier.

SERVICES/AMENITIES:

Restaurant Services: yes

Catering: provided, no BYO

Kitchen Facilities: n/a

Tables & Chairs: provided

Overnight Accommodations: no

Telephone: pay phone

Outdoor Night Lighting: access only

Meeting Equipment: CBA

Linens, Silver, etc.: provided

Restrooms: wca

Dance Floor: yes

Parking: CBA

Outdoor Cooking Facilities: no

Cleanup: provided

Other: white baby grand piano

RESTRICTIONS:

Alcohol: provided

Smoking: allowed

Music: amplified ok

Wheelchair Access: yes

Insurance: not required

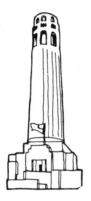

COIT TOWER

Telegraph Hill
San Francisco, CA
(415) 666-7080
Reserve for Events: 2–12 months in advance

Before the Transamerica Pyramid, this was *the* symbol of San Francisco. Rising 210 feet above Telegraph Hill, Coit Tower is famous for its view of the City and the Bay. Upon her death, Lilly Coit left a sizable donation with which the Tower was built in 1933. At the age of 15, she was the official mascot of Knickerbocker Engine Co. #5 Volunteer Fire Department, and was best known for her life-long passion for firefighting. A real trooper, Lilly rarely missed a blaze. The historic murals inside were the first WPA-commissioned art project. Because of the fragility of these recently renovated frescoes, the caterer must set up outdoors. Bar setups are permitted in the upper level of the Tower.

CAPACITY: The Tower can accommodate up to 60 guests for cocktail receptions, 12 for seated affairs.

FEES & DEPOSITS: A non-refundable deposit of 10% of the total rental cost is due when the reservation is made. The rental fee ranges from $600–1,200 depending on setup arrangements. The fee balance plus any security and/or cleaning deposits are required 10 business days prior to the event.

CANCELLATION POLICY: For cancellations made more than 10 working days prior to the event, a full refund will be given minus a $25 administration fee and/or the deposit.

AVAILABILITY: Year-round, after 5pm.

SERVICES/AMENITIES:

Restaurant Services: no

Catering: BYO

Kitchen Facilities: no

Tables & Chairs: BYO

Linens, Silver, etc.: BYO

Restrooms: wca

Dance Floor: no

Parking: shuttle buses or valet recommended

Overnight Accommodations: no

Telephone: pay phone

Outdoor Night Lighting: access only

Outdoor Cooking Facilities: no

Cleanup: whoever caters event

Meeting Equipment: no

RESTRICTIONS:

Alcohol: BYO

Music: no amplified

Wheelchair Access: no

Smoking: outside only

Insurance: certificate required

Other: security guard required, decorations restricted

THE CONSERVATORY OF FLOWERS

Golden Gate Park
San Francisco, CA 94117
(415) 641-7978
Reserve for Events: 6–9 months in advance
Reserve for Meetings: 1 week in advance

This large, graceful, ornate and mostly glass structure is the oldest existing building in Golden Gate Park and probably the best example of Victorian Greenhouse Architecture in the United States. Built in 1879, it's a California historic landmark, visited by thousands of people every year. (Be careful that you don't confuse this structure with the Hall of Flowers building.) The entire Conservatory is available for parties and special events. The West Wing is particularly well-suited for dinners, featuring an interior patio with trellis and displays of seven seasonal flower types. The East Wing has two ponds, waterfalls, rare aquatic plants and flowers. Palms and orchids abound in exotic profusion. The Conservatory is such a sensational and historically unique facility, your guests will never forget your event!

CAPACITY: The Conservatory accommodates 200 standing guests or 70 seated.

FEES & DEPOSITS: A non-refundable $150 deposit is due when the contract is signed. The rental fee is $1,200 for the evening and a refundable $300 damage deposit is also required. These fees are payable 2 weeks prior to your party and include the services of 2 security guards and 1 staff person. The damage deposit will be returned within 6 weeks following your party.

CANCELLATION POLICY: If you cancel, your $150 deposit is forfeited.

AVAILABILITY: From April 1st to October 30th, 6:30pm–midnight, daily and holidays. From October 30th to April 1st, 5:30pm–midnight. Everyone, including the caterer, must vacate the premises by midnight. There are no day-time rentals.

SERVICES/AMENITIES:

Restaurant Services: no
Catering: BYO, licensed
Kitchen Facilities: minimal
Tables & Chairs: BYO
Linens, Silver, etc.: BYO
Restrooms: wca
Dance Floor: CBA

Parking: large lot
Overnight Accommodations: no
Telephone: office phone
Outdoor Night Lighting: access only
Outdoor Cooking Facilities: BYO BBQ
Cleanup: caterer
Meeting Equipment: CBA by renter

RESTRICTIONS:

Alcohol: BYO
Music: amplified ok
Wheelchair Access: yes

Smoking: outside only
Insurance: liability required

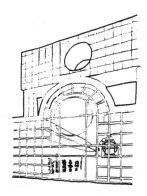

CONTRACT DESIGN CENTER

600 Townsend Street
San Francisco, CA 94103
(415) 864-1500
Reserve for Events: 3–6 months in advance
Reserve for Meetings: 1 week–12 months in advance

The Contract Design Center Atrium has a crisp, cool, clean style. White terrazzo flooring leads to a wall of uniquely constructed glass, and a white vaulted ceiling gives the center height and interest. Behind the atrium, visible through the glass wall, is a very versatile courtyard. Tented or left open to the sun, the spacious white aggregate patio lends itself to a variety of outdoor events, including office parties and receptions.

CAPACITY, FEES & DEPOSITS:

Area	*Seated*	*Reception*	*Rental Fees*
Atrium	225	500	$3,000*
The Courtyard	250	500	—
Atrium & Courtyard	—	—	$3,500*
Conference Center	—	—	$500/day

*The basic rental fee may vary depending on the specific details of your event.

A non-refundable deposit of 50% of the rental fee is required when the contract is submitted. The balance is due 30 days prior to the event. Fees include a house technician.

MEETING ROOMS: Conference Center up to 200 seated; the room can be divided into smaller sections.

CANCELLATION POLICY: Fees and deposits can be applied to another event within a 90-day period.

AVAILABILITY: Year-round, Monday–Friday after 3pm, Saturday and Sunday from 8am. The Conference Center, daily from 8am.

SERVICES/AMENITIES:

Restaurant Services: no
Catering: preferred list or BYO w/approval
Kitchen Facilities: minimal
Tables & Chairs: provided
Linens, Silver, etc.: BYO
Restrooms: wca
Dance Floor: terrazzo floor
Meeting Equipment: sound system, proj. screens, gallery lighting

Parking: street, garage
Overnight Accommodations: no
Telephone: pay phones
Outdoor Night Lighting: yes
Outdoor Cooking Facilities: yes
Cleanup: provided
Other: event coordination, technician provided

RESTRICTIONS:

Alcohol: provided, no BYO
Smoking: allowed
Music: amplified ok

Wheelchair Access: yes
Insurance: certificate required

Need a caterer, cake maker, florist? The Service Directory starting on page 614 features the best in the business.

DELANCEY STREET

600 Embarcadero
San Francisco, CA 94107
(415) 957-9800
Reserve for Events: 2–12 months in advance
Reserve for Meetings: 3 weeks–6 months in advance

Named after the part of New York City's Lower East Side where immigrants congregated at the turn of the century, Delancey Street has evolved over the last twenty years into "the world's greatest halfway house." Once crowded into a small San Francisco apartment, the successful rehab program now occupies most of a city block. Constructed almost entirely by the residents, it includes a variety of spaces that are available for parties and meetings. The Town Hall is not your standard auditorium. Its triangular shape, vaulted pine tongue-and-groove ceiling and hardwood floor make it an interesting place for large functions. Glass doors on two sides admit plenty of light, and a huge sliding barn door opens onto a spacious patio. The Theatre is a real gem featuring plush seating, a stage, and state-of-the-art lighting, screen and projector. Host an anniversary cocktail party in the Theatre foyer, and then treat your guests to a "this is your life" film or video. The Club Room is popular for cocktail parties and awards ceremonies. Pool tables are transformed into buffet tables, balcony doors can be opened to the sea breeze and there's a bird's-eye view of the Bay Bridge you don't see every day. The Dining Room is the clean, fresh and functional heart of Delancey Street. Memorabilia and awards are displayed on the walls, and there's a stunning Tiffany-style stained glass window designed and executed by the residents. Right outside, the Gallery is a wonderful open-air spot for either cocktails and hors d'oeuvres or al fresco dining. A vaulted skylight provides protection while keeping the space open to the sun and stars. And for an upscale dining experience, have your business luncheon or small party in one of Delancey Street Restaurant's private dining rooms. For more details on the Restaurant, see its entry in our Private Dining Room section.

CAPACITY:

Area	Seated	Standing	Area	Seated	Standing
Town Hall	50-300	500	Dining Room	250	—
Theatre	150	—	Gallery	60	100
Club Room	80	80-200	Discussion Room	10-50	50

MEETING ROOMS: All the above areas (except the Gallery and Dining Room) as well as the private dining rooms in the restaurant can be used for meetings.

FEES & DEPOSITS: Facility rental fees range from $600 to $1,500 depending on the room used. The Theatre rents for $125/hour, including projectionist. A non-refundable deposit in the amount of half the rental fee is required when the final booking is made. This deposit will be applied to the total. 80% of the anticipated cost of the event is due 2 weeks prior to the event, and the balance is payable at the conclusion. Per person food costs are $14-50. Beverage, tax and a 15% gratuity are additional.

CANCELLATION POLICY: The booking deposit is non-refundable. Refunds for cancellations within the 2 weeks prior to the event are handled individually.

AVAILABILITY: Year-round, every day from 8:30am-2am. Closed Thanksgiving, Christmas and New Year's days.

SERVICES/AMENITIES:

Restaurant Services: yes

Catering: provided or BYO

Kitchen Facilities: no

Tables & Chairs: some provided

Linens, Silver, etc.: BYO

Restrooms: wca

Dance Floor: Town Hall only

Meeting Equipment: podium and PA system

Parking: on street

Overnight Accommodations: no

Telephone: pay phone

Outdoor Night Lighting: Gallery and Town Hall patio

Outdoor Cooking Facilities: no

Cleanup: renter & Delancey Street

RESTRICTIONS:

Alcohol: provided or BYO for fee

Smoking: outside only

Insurance: not required

Wheelchair Access: yes

Music: amplified ok in Town Hall only

Other: decorations limited, children must be supervised

M. H. DE YOUNG MEMORIAL MUSEUM

Golden Gate Park
San Francisco, CA 94118
(415) 750-3683
Reserve for Events: 1–12 months in advance

We think this is a very special site. Others agree—President Reagan hosted a State dinner for Queen Elizabeth II in the de Young's grand Hearst Court, a large, airy and regal space, with Spanish tile, arched ceiling and skylights. You can have your event here, too, if you're a corporation or a business association. The Museum sits in the heart of Golden Gate Park, next to the Japanese Tea Gardens. It's not every day you can get treated to private tours of one of our country's finest collections of American art, featuring the works of Copley, Paul Revere, Remington, Winslow Homer, Grant Wood and Mary Cassatt. For corporate breakfasts, luncheons, cocktail receptions or formal dinners, the de Young offers impressive spaces for private entertaining. And, if your guests are interested in expanding their libraries, the museum book shop can be opened for any function.

CAPACITY: The Museum can hold up to 340 seated guests, 800 for a reception.

FEES & DEPOSITS: A refundable deposit of 30% of the rental fee is required to confirm reservations and the balance is due 2 weeks prior to the function. An event plan must be submitted at least 1 month prior to the event. The rental fee for 4 hours is $9,500, for 2 hours, $7,000. Fees include security, technician, custodial service, docents, coat check and event staff.

AVAILABILITY: Year-round, Monday and Tuesday from 8am, Wednesday–Sunday from 6:30pm.

SERVICES/AMENITIES:

Restaurant: no

Catering: BYO w/approval

Kitchen Facilities: no

Tables & Chairs: BYO

Linens, Silver, etc.: BYO

Restrooms: wca

Dance Floor: Hearst Court

Parking: large lot in front of building

Overnight Accommodations: no

Telephone: pay phone

Outdoor Night Lighting: access only

Outdoor Cooking Facilities: BYO

Cleanup: caterer and custodian

Other: docent tours, coat check, security, engineer, event staff

RESTRICTIONS:

Alcohol: BYO

Smoking: outside only

Music: amplified restricted

Wheelchair Access: yes

Insurance: certificate required

Other: no open flames

THE EUREKA

San Francisco Maritime National Historic Park
Hyde Street Pier
San Francisco, CA 94109
(415) 929-0202 Daria Booth
Reserve for Events: 1 month in advance

Once the world's largest passenger ferry, the 277-foot side-wheel paddle steamboat, the Eureka, is now permanently docked at the end of the Hyde Street Pier along with other historic vessels of note. Built in 1890 as a railroad ferry and later converted for passenger service, the Eureka is one of the few remaining relics of San Francisco's grand era of ferry transport. Unbelievably, she was still in service as recently as 1957. Now the old girl is a national landmark, available as a public exhibit and as a very unique space for special events. (Due to repairs, the Eureka will not be available until Fall, 1993.)

CAPACITY: The Eureka can accommodate up to 600 guests.

FEES & DEPOSITS: A $1,500 refundable security deposit is required and is usually returned 2 weeks after your function. The rental fee is $900 minimum. The total fee will depend on the length of your event and the number of guests. Work out the details with the National Maritime Museum Association. Fees include a National Park Ranger on duty during events. A non-profit rate is available.

AVAILABILITY: (Note that the Eureka will not be available until Fall, 1993.) Available November–May from 5pm to midnight and June–October from 6pm–midnight.

CANCELLATION POLICY: Deposits are refundable 21 days prior to your event.

SERVICES/AMENITIES:

Restaurant Services: no

Catering: BYO

Kitchen Facilities: no

Tables & Chairs: some provided

Linens, Silver, etc.: BYO

Restrooms: wca limited

Dance Floor: wood deck

Parking: on street, adjacent garage

Overnight Accommodations: no

Telephone: pay phone

Outdoor Night Lighting: yes

Outdoor Cooking Facilities: no

Cleanup: caterer or renter

Meeting Equipment: no

RESTRICTIONS:

Alcohol: BYO

Smoking: only on pier

Music: amplified until 11pm

Wheelchair Access: limited, lower deck only

Insurance: required

Other: decorations restricted

FERRYBOAT SANTA ROSA

Permanently moored at Pier 3
The Embarcadero
San Francisco, CA 94111
(415) 394-8900
Reserve for Events: 2 weeks–12 months in advance
Reserve for Meetings: 2 weeks–12 months in advance

Permanently moored at Pier 3, this historic 1927 ferryboat has been meticulously restored to her former grandeur and now commands a stately presence at the foot of San Francisco's financial district. 240 feet long, the Ferryboat Santa Rosa's main deck has ten-foot ceilings, two open-air fantail decks and floor-to-ceiling windows that wrap around the entire facility. You can have a meeting on the West Deck, and then dine on the East Deck, where the view of the bay is spectacular. Go up to the Sun Deck for a breath of sea air and a 360-degree panorama of downtown, Telegraph Hill, Treasure Island and the Bay Bridge. At night, your guests can sip cocktails and dance beneath a glittering city skyline and the Bridge's necklace of lights. And the Santa Rosa's convenient dockside location allows everyone to come and go as they please, while enjoying the unique ambiance of the waterfront.

CAPACITY:

Space	Seated	Standing	Space	Seated	Standing
Entire Ferryboat	500	500	West Deck	300	500
East Deck	200	300			

MEETING ROOMS: Both the East and West Decks serve as meeting rooms.

FEES & DEPOSITS: A $2,000 deposit is required within 7 days after booking, and the balance is due 5 days before the event. On board charges must be paid the evening of the function. Rental fees are as follows:

Day	*Hours*	*Fee*	*Min. Rental*
Mon-Fri	Before 5pm	$150-250/hr	3 hours
Sun-Thurs	After 5pm	$300-500/hr	3 hours
Weekends	5pm Fri–5pm Sun	$300-500	4 hours Sat Eve
			3 hours Sun

CANCELLATION POLICY: The deposit is fully refundable with 120 days notice, or if the date can be rebooked.

AVAILABILITY: Year-round, anytime.

SERVICES/AMENITIES:

Restaurant Services: no

Catering: select from list or BYO

Kitchen Facilities: setup only

Tables & Chairs: provided, extra charge

Linens, Silver, etc.: caterer

Restrooms: wca

Dance Floor: CBA, extra charge

Other: event coordination

Parking: on street

Overnight Accommodations: no

Telephone: boat phone

Outdoor Night Lighting: CBA for extra charge

Outdoor Cooking Facilities: allowed

Cleanup: provided

Meeting Equipment: CBA

RESTRICTIONS:

Alcohol: provided, corkage $7/bottle

Smoking: designated areas only

Insurance: required with own caterer

Wheelchair Access: main deck only

Music: amplified ok

THE FLOOD MANSION

2222 Broadway

San Francisco, CA 94115

(415) 563-2900 Mrs. Hackman

Reserve for Events: 3–12 months in advance

Reserve for Meetings: 3–12 months in advance

The Flood Mansion is a symphony of classical styles—Italian Renaissance, Rococo, Tudor and Georgian. This elegant marble building, constructed in 1915, has remained well preserved since Mrs. Flood donated her home to the Religious of the Sacred Heart in 1939. Although the building is now used as a private school, it is available for special events after school hours. The Mansion is impressive. Its Grand Hall is 140 feet long with marble floors and great views of the Bay. The Adam Room, near the entry, is quite lovely with high, ornate ceilings, specially designed wood tables and chairs plus a marble fireplace. The beautiful Reception Room, at the end of the Grand Hall, boasts magnificent coffered ceiling, painted murals in golds, blues and greens, and hardwood parquet floors. This room is architecturally complex and detailed. A pretty, enclosed courtyard off of the Grand Hall is available for outdoor gatherings, weather permitting. The Mansion is definitely the place for a stately and elegant party.

CAPACITY: The entire main floor has a standing capacity of 450 people or a seated capacity of approximately 300. Individual seated capacities: the Grand Hall, 200; the Adam Room, 60; and the Reception Room, 80–100 people. In addition, there's a theater area downstairs.

FEES & DEPOSITS: Half of the rental fee is the deposit required to secure your event date. Also required is a $1,000 custodial and security fee, some of which may be reimbursable. The rental fee is $5,000 for the facility. The final balance is due 2 weeks prior to the event.

CANCELLATION POLICY: Should you cancel, the rental deposit is not refundable. The $1,000 custodial and security deposit is refundable.

AVAILABILITY: Fridays after 3pm, Saturday and Sunday all day. All events must end by midnight. No hourly minimum rental block is required.

SERVICES/AMENITIES:

Restaurant Services: no
Catering: select from list
Kitchen Facilities: ample
Tables & Chairs: BYO
Linens, Silver, etc.: BYO
Restrooms: wca
Dance Floor: yes
Meeting Equipment: no

Parking: valet parking required
Overnight Accommodations: no
Telephone: pay phone
Outdoor Night Lighting: access only
Outdoor Cooking Facilities: no
Cleanup: caterer
Other: 2 baby grand pianos

RESTRICTIONS:

Alcohol: BYO
Smoking: outside only
Music: amplified until 11:30pm

Wheelchair Access: yes
Insurance: extra liability required

Prices and policies do change. Call each facility and confirm everything you read in Perfect Places.

FOREST HILL CLUB HOUSE

381 Magellan Ave.
San Francisco, CA 94116
(415) 664-0542 Will Connolly
Reserve for Events: 4–6 months in advance
Reserve for Meetings: 2–3 weeks in advance

The Club House, an architectural gem designed by Bernard Maybeck, is tucked away in a very nice neighborhood of private residences. Completed in 1919, the building's exterior and interior are decorative yet rustic, representing the final phase of the turn-of-the-century American Arts and Crafts movement. The interior features a large, long room with hardwood floors and a sizeable fireplace. The furniture in several rooms may have been designed by Bernard Maybeck. The adjacent brick patio and garden, completed in 1966, is a great spot for outdoor garden parties if the weather cooperates. For weekday meetings, the Club House is available with little advance notice; weekends are more problematic. This is a small but charming facility.

CAPACITY: The Club House can accommodate 200 standing guests or approximately 100 seated guests. The dance floor is large enough for 50 dancers.

FEES & DEPOSITS: Half the rental fee is required when you reserve your date. A $350 refundable security/cleaning deposit is due 6 weeks prior to the event and is usually returned within 30 days after the event. On Friday, Saturday and Sunday, the fee is $1,100. Weekdays, it's $500. Overtime is permissible at $75/hour. The remaining 50% balance is due when the contract is signed, about 6 weeks before the event.

CANCELLATION POLICY: Half the rental fee is retained if the date can not be rebooked. If rebooked, the entire rental deposit will be refunded.

AVAILABILITY: Anytime, up to midnight. An 8-hour block is the required minimum.

SERVICES/AMENITIES:

Restaurant Services: no
Catering: BYO
Kitchen Facilities: moderate
Tables & Chairs: some provided
Linens, Silver, etc.: BYO
Restrooms: wca limited
Cleanup: caterer or renter

Dance Floor: yes
Parking: on street
Overnight Accommodations: no
Telephone: pay phone
Outdoor Night Lighting: yes
Outdoor Cooking Facilities: BYO BBQ
Meeting Equipment: movie screen

RESTRICTIONS:

Alcohol: BYO
Smoking: allowed
Music: amplified inside only

Wheelchair Access: limited
Insurance: not required

FORT MASON
CONFERENCE CENTER

Fort Mason Center
San Francisco, CA 94123
(415) 441-5706 Conference Center Director
Reserve for Events: 6 months in advance
Reserve for Meetings: 2–6 months in advance

Located at the south end of Landmark Building A at Fort Mason, the Conference Center is well situated to provide an extraordinary environment for special events. Three different sized rooms, with track lighting, carpets, high ceilings and hanging banners offer varied party opportunities. The view of the Golden Gate Bridge is outstanding, as is the view of the nearby yacht harbor, especially when lit up at night. A real plus for this facility is the abundant parking nearby.

CAPACITY: The Conference Center can accommodate 350 guests for a reception; 230 for seated functions.

FEES & DEPOSITS: A $300–350 security deposit is required, depending on the size and type of event, and is returned after the function. The deposit is payable when you book your date. Rental rates vary depending on the type of event, day and number of rooms rented. For the largest room, the rental fee is $685. For that room plus two additional adjacent rooms, the fee is $785. The rental fee is due 30 days prior to the event date.

CANCELLATION POLICY: Call for cancellation policy.

AVAILABILITY: Any day from 8am. Guests and caterer must vacate the premises by midnight; 1am by request.

SERVICES/AMENITIES:

Restaurant Services: no
Catering: BYO
Kitchen Facilities: no
Tables & Chairs: provided
Linens, Silver, etc.: BYO
Restrooms: wca
Dance Floor: CBA

Parking: large lot
Overnight Accommodations: no
Telephone: pay phone
Outdoor Night Lighting: access only
Outdoor Cooking Facilities: CBA
Cleanup: caterer & Fort Mason
Meeting Equipment: limited

RESTRICTIONS:

Alcohol: BYO
Smoking: outside only
Music: amplified ok

Wheelchair Access: yes
Insurance: not required

FORT MASON FIREHOUSE

Fort Mason Center
San Francisco, CA 94123
(415) 441-5706   Conference Center Director
Reserve for Events: 2–12 weeks in advance
Reserve for Meetings: 2–6 months in advance

The Firehouse is a separate warehouse-type building within Fort Mason Center, located right on the water's edge next to the docked Liberty Ship, SS Jeremiah O'Brien. This *is* an old firehouse which has been renovated to accommodate events. The 27' x 47' central room is airy and pleasant, with Casablanca fans and colorful pastel banners flying from the tall ceiling. Views of Alcatraz and the Bay are visible from the main room and adjoining side room.

CAPACITY: The Firehouse can accommodate 150 standing or 100 seated guests.

FEES & DEPOSITS: A $300 security deposit is required to book the facility and is returned after the function. Payment of the deposit secures your event date. The $510 rental fee is payable 30 days prior to the event.

CANCELLATION POLICY: Call for cancellation policy.

AVAILABILITY: Any day, from 8am. Guests and caterer must vacate premises by 1am.

SERVICES/AMENITIES:

Restaurant Services: no
Catering: BYO
Kitchen Facilities: no
Tables & Chairs: provided
Linens, Silver, etc.: BYO
Restrooms: wca
Dance Floor: CBA

Parking: large lot
Overnight Accommodations: no
Telephone: pay phone
Outdoor Night Lighting: access only
Outdoor Cooking Facilities: BYO BBQ
Cleanup: caterer & Fort Mason
Meeting Equipment: limited

RESTRICTIONS:

Alcohol: BYO
Smoking: outside only
Music: amplified ok

Wheelchair Access: yes
Insurance: not required

GALLERIA DESIGN CENTER

101 Henry Adams Street
San Francisco, CA 94103
(415) 864-1500
Reserve for Events: 3–6 months in advance
Reserve for Meetings: 4–6 weeks in advance

The Galleria Design Center is renowned throughout the Bay Area as *the* place to celebrate. This spectacular four-story atrium soars sixty feet to a retractable skylight. Daylight floods the building, and at night you really can see the stars. Hundreds of glittering lights, giant palm trees and lush indoor gardens create a unique environment, and a large, theatrical stage is ready-made for superb parties. Tiered levels provide dining or standing reception space with excellent views of the stage. Vast and inviting, the Galleria is a grand showcase for all occasions.

CAPACITY, FEES & DEPOSITS: The Atrium seats 1,200 (4 floors), and accommodates 2,500 for a standing reception. The basic rental fee of $6,000 may vary, depending on the specific details of your event. A non-refundable deposit of half the rental fee is required when the contract is submitted. The balance is due 30 days prior to the event. Fees include a house technician.

CANCELLATION POLICY: The fees and deposits can be applied toward another event within a 90-day period.

AVAILABILITY: Year-round, Monday–Friday after 3pm, Saturday and Sunday from 8am except for seasonal market periods.

SERVICES/AMENITIES:

Restaurant Services: no
Catering: in-house caterer or BYO w/approval, extra fee
Kitchen Facilities: minimal
Tables & Chairs: some provided
Linens, Silver, etc.: BYO
Restrooms: wca
Dance Floor: terrazzo floor
Meeting Equipment: full ausio visual

Parking: street, garage
Overnight Accommodations: no
Telephone: pay phones
Outdoor Night Lighting: access only
Outdoor Cooking Facilities: yes
Cleanup: provided
Other: event coordination, stage, equipment & technician provided

RESTRICTIONS:

Alcohol: provided, no BYO
Smoking: allowed
Music: amplified ok

Wheelchair Access: yes
Insurance: certificate required

GIFTCENTER PAVILION

888 Brannan Street
San Francisco, CA 94103
(415) 861-7733　Evelyn Marks
Reserve for Events: 1–12 months in advance
Reserve for Meetings: 4–6 weeks in advance

The GiftCenter Pavilion is one of San Francisco's most appealing event spaces. Four stories high, it's capped by a skylight that covers the ceiling and opens to the stars. The center of the room makes a great area for dancing. Seating is often arranged on the surrounding elevated tiers, giving guests a great view of the activities below. The Gift Center also has a large stage and a quarter of a million dollars in state-of-the-art sound and lighting equipment. We like this space! It's impressive and spacious, yet designed well enough to make a smaller party here feel comfortable. And what's also nice is that everything can be arranged for you—from flowers and food to elaborate event planning.

CAPACITY: The Pavilion can hold 150–2,500 for a cocktail reception, 1,100 seated guests or 1,800 for a reception with food service.

FEES & DEPOSITS: A non-refundable deposit of half the total rental package is due when the contract is submitted. The total balance is due 10 days prior to the event. Rental fees range from $3,500–6,000 depending on the day of the week, level(s) rented and guest count. The fee includes setup, janitorial services, 2 security guards plus lighting and sound services. For technical personnel, there will be additional charges.

AVAILABILITY: Year-round, every day from 6am–2am, except during gift shows.

SERVICES/AMENITIES:

Restaurant Services: no
Catering: inside caterer, BYO w/approval
Kitchen Facilities: fully equipped
Tables & Chairs: provided
Linens, Silver, etc.: provided or BYO
Restrooms: wca
Dance Floor: yes

Parking: large lots, street
Overnight Accommodations: no
Telephone: pay phone
Outdoor Night Lighting: access only
Outdoor Cooking Facilities: no
Cleanup: provided
Meeting Equipment: state-of-the-art AV, podium, etc.

RESTRICTIONS:

Alcohol: caterer, corkage $5–7/bottle
Smoking: allowed
Music: amplified ok

Wheelchair Access: yes
Insurance: certificate required

THE GINSBERG COLLECTION

190 San Bruno Avenue
San Francisco, CA 94103
(415) 621-6060 Norman List
Reserve for Events: 1–12 months in advance
Reserve for Meetings: 1 week–1 year in advance

And now for something completely different... The Ginsberg Collection showroom is the handiwork of world-renowned designer, Ron Mann, who brings together an enticing mix of Mediterranean, North African and Southwest influences. The two primary event rooms look as though they might have been hewn from an upscale cave. Their uneven, textured adobe walls reveal dozens of niches—all filled with artifacts, antiques and decorative objects from around the world. And even though every nook, raised surface and corner overflows with exotic items, the showroom appears spacious thanks to thirty-foot ceilings and a fluid floor plan. A built-in concrete, serpentine table is perfect for seated dinners or buffets, and multi-leveled platforms create unique spaces for sampling hors d'oeuvres, dancing, or just plain mingling. The kitchen is another fascinating element—it blends in so thoroughly with the overall interior design that it's practically invisible. Want to have a private conversation? Two spiral staircases take you upstairs, where several slightly mysterious and angular rooms offer a quiet retreat. There's always something to discover at the showroom, and if you happen to be smitten with an oversized urn or Thai rain drum, take it home with you—everything is for sale!

CAPACITY: The showroom can accommodate 100 for a seated meal or 350 for a standing buffet.

MEETING ROOMS: The entire facility can be used in a variety of ways, and the Back Meeting Room itself can accommodate 25–30 guests.

FEES & DEPOSITS: The facility rents for $3,000. A $500 deposit is required to reserve your date, and the balance is due 10 days prior to the event.

CANCELLATION POLICY: The deposit is not refundable.

AVAILABILITY: Weekdays, 3pm–12am; weekends anytime.

SERVICES/AMENITIES:

Restaurant Services: no
Catering: preferred list or BYO
Kitchen Facilities: ample
Tables & Chairs: BYO, some gallery pieces avail.
Linens, Silver, etc.: BYO
Restrooms: wca
Dance Floor: yes
Other: event coordination

Parking: lot, on street
Overnight Accommodations: no
Telephone: emergency phone
Outdoor Night Lighting: access only
Outdoor Cooking Facilities: no
Cleanup: caterer
Meeting Equipment: no

RESTRICTIONS:

Alcohol: BYO
Smoking: outside only
Insurance: required

Wheelchair Access: yes
Music: amplified ok

GOLDEN GATE PARK

Golden Gate Park
San Francisco, CA 94117
(415) 666-7035
Reserve for Events: 1–12 months in advance

In Golden Gate Park, the variety of locations for parties and corporate outdoor functions is almost unlimited. The City's Recreation and Parks Department even offers deluxe "Play Packages" which can include activities such as paddleboating, mountain biking, tennis, flycasting and golf, to name a few. Whether it's exclusive use of the Carrousel, the Conservatory of Flowers or tours through the Strybing Arboretum and Japanese Tea Garden, it can be arranged. There's even an equestrian arena to accommodate a private rodeo. Specific locations include but are not limited to the following:

The Shakespeare Garden	Japanese Tea Garden	Carrousel
Queen Wilhelmina Tulip Garden	Equestrian Arena	Strybing Arboretum
The Rose Garden	Conservatory of Flowers	Pioneer Log Cabin Area
Marx Meadow	Lindley Meadow	Children's Playground
Sharon Arts Building	County Fair Building	

CAPACITY: Varies greatly, from 100–25,000 people. Call for specifics.

FEES & DEPOSITS: Fees and deposits vary depending on the space(s) desired and the number of people attending. Corporate picnics average $600/day; private parties $125/day.

CANCELLATION POLICY: If you cancel 30 days prior to the event, 90% of the deposit is refunded; if less than 5 working days prior to your event, no refund.

AVAILABILITY: Park areas are usually available from 9am to dusk every day. Special arrangements must be made for evening use.

SERVICES/AMENITIES:

Restaurant Services: no
Catering: BYO
Kitchen Facilities: no
Tables & Chairs: BYO
Linens, Silver, etc.: BYO
Restrooms: location and wca varies
Dance Floor: no

Parking: on street
Overnight Accommodations: no
Telephone: pay phones in park
Outdoor Night Lighting: access only
Outdoor Cooking Facilities: designated areas
Cleanup: caterer or renter
Meeting Equipment: no

RESTRICTIONS:

Alcohol: BYO
Smoking: allowed
Music: no amplified

Wheelchair Access: yes
Insurance: not required
Other: you must provide your own security

GOLDEN SUNSET
Pacific Marine Yacht Charters

Berthed at Pier 39, West Basin
San Francisco, CA 94133
(415) 788-9100
Reserve for Events: 1–9 months in advance
Reserve for Meetings: 1 week in advance

The sleek, seventy-five-foot Golden Sunset is one of four luxury yachts in Pacific Marine's elegant fleet. This yacht features three decks, an open air wing bridge with wet bar and an intimate private stateroom with queen bed, VCR and marble bath with jacuzzi. A state-of-the-art sound system complete with compact disc and cassette capabilities is also available.

CAPACITY: The Golden Sunset can accommodate up to 100 guests, weather permitting. Formal seating is available for up to 40 guests.

FEES & DEPOSITS: A $1,500 deposit is required to reserve your date, and half the food and beverage cost is due 30 days prior to your event.

	Weekdays (before 6pm)	*Weekdays (after 6pm)*	*Weekends/Holidays*
Yacht rental rates:	$500/hr	$550/hr	$625/hr
Groups of 20 or less:	425/hr	475/hr	550/hr

A 3-hour minimum rental is required, 4 hours on Saturday evenings and holidays. A guaranteed guest count is required 7 days prior to departure and the remaining balance is due 5 days prior to your event.

CANCELLATION POLICY: With 60 days' notice, 85% of the reservation deposit will be refunded; with less notice, the deposit will be forfeited.

AVAILABILITY: Anytime. No limits.

SERVICES/AMENITIES:

Restaurant Services: no
Catering: provided, no BYO
Kitchen Facilities: on board
Tables & Chairs: provided
Linens, Silver, etc.: provided
Restrooms: 3, no wca
Dance Floor: yes
Meeting Equipment: podium, microphone

Parking: Pier 39 garage, validations available
Overnight Accommodations: yes, limited
Telephone: emergency cellular phone and radio
Outdoor Night Lighting: yes
Outdoor Cooking Facilities: no
Cleanup: provided
Other: event coordination

RESTRICTIONS:

Alcohol: provided, corkage $7/bottle
Smoking: outside only
Music: amplified ok

Wheelchair Access: no
Insurance: not required

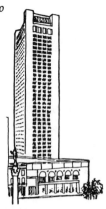

GRAND HYATT
SAN FRANCISCO
At Union Square

345 Stockton Street
San Francisco, CA 94108
(415) 398-1234
Reserve for Events: 1 week–12 months in advance
Reserve for Meetings: 1 week–12 months in advance

Located in the heart of The City, just minutes from the financial district and convention center, the Grand Hyatt offers exceptional facilities for business events. Featuring 22,000 square feet of meeting space and a 7,000 square foot ballroom, the hotel is the perfect choice for meetings and conferences. The Hyatt's Conference Theater is a fabulous room for presentations. In addition to the functional elements of stage, screen and audio-visual equipment, it was carefully designed with plush leather upholstered seating and individual curved table areas with lighting in front of each seat. The Executive Business Center is another feature businesses will appreciate: word processing, secretarial, notary public, language translation, fax and airline ticketing services are all available. The Grand Hyatt is not just a business person's paradise, however. Many areas easily accommodate all types of events. The Bayview and Union Square rooms on the 36th floor are perfect for parties or receptions. Designed with an abundance of glass and subtle decor, they offer a spacious and inviting environment with extraordinary views of the city and bay below. Winner of the American Automobile Association's Four Diamond Award, and the only hotel in San Francisco staffing four members of Les Clefs d'Or, the prestigious concierge organization, the cosmopolitan Grand Hyatt has the staff, facilities and services to satisfy the needs of every guest.

CAPACITY:	*Area*	*Classroom-style*	*Banquet*	*Theater-style*	*Reception*
	Plaza Ballroom	640	720	1,000	1,000
	Conference Theater	70	—	—	—
	Union Square/Bayview Rooms	150	250	—	300

MEETING ROOMS: 19 rooms accommodate 5–1,000 guests.

FEES & DEPOSITS: A deposit is required to secure your date and is due when the contract is submitted. The amount is negotiable depending on the guest count, date and room(s) reserved. Room rental charges vary from $150–10,000 and normally apply only when there is no food or other service required; these may be waived depending on the total amount of services provided. Usually, the estimated food and beverage total plus the final guest count are required 72 hours prior to the event. The final balance is due 7 working days prior to the event unless credit has been established. Average rates, per person: hors d'oeuvres $15, continental breakfast $10, seated breakfast $16, brunch $30, luncheon $24 and dinner $33. Tax and a 17% gratuity are additional.

CANCELLATION POLICY: If the space(s) can be rebooked, the deposit is refunded.

AVAILABILITY: Year-round, every day, anytime.

SERVICES/AMENITIES:

Restaurant Services: yes

Catering: provided, no BYO

Kitchen Facilities: n/a

Dance Floor: yes

Parking: valet

Overnight Accommodations: no

Telephone: pay phones

Other: event coord., conf. & convention planning

Tables & Chairs: provided

Linens, Silver, etc.: provided

Restrooms: wca

Outdoor Night Lighting: yes

Outdoor Cooking Facilities: CBA

Cleanup: provided

Meeting Equipment: full range of audio-visual

RESTRICTIONS:

Alcohol: provided, corkage $15/bottle

Smoking: designated areas

Music: amplified ok

Wheelchair Access: yes

Insurance: not required

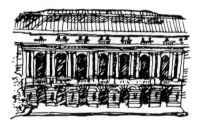

THE GREEN ROOM

Veterans Building, Second Floor
San Francisco, CA 94102
(415) 621-6600 Elizabeth or Alberta
Reserve for Events: 9–12 months in advance
Reserve for Meetings: 2–12 months in advance

The Green Room is actually green. But don't let that stop you from taking a healthy interest in this fabulous party facility. It's an outstanding and elegant place for a meeting, reception or performance and it's priced well below most comparable spaces. The Room has an incredibly high ivory and gold leaf ceiling, hardwood parquet floor, large pillars, mirrors and five stunning chandeliers adorning its interior. The Green Room opens onto a terra cotta-tiled loggia (balcony) which overlooks the enormous rotunda of City Hall. At night, from the loggia's vantage point, the view of the lighted City Hall is truly breathtaking.

CAPACITY: The room can accommodate 500 standing and 300 seated guests if there's no dancing. Dancing will reduce guest capacity.

FEES & DEPOSITS: To secure your date, a non-refundable $100 deposit is required plus a $200 refundable cleaning deposit. The rental fee is $525 plus the event manager's cost at $23.30/hour. Holidays are an additional $100. Fees include pre-custodial service. Any other assistance, such as setup/breakdown attendant, security or custodial services, is additional.

AVAILABILITY: Anytime. If you rent this facility before 8am or after midnight, you will be charged for staff at time and a half.

SERVICES/AMENITIES:

Restaurant Services: no

Catering: BYO

Tables & Chairs: provided, extra charge

Linens, Silver, etc.: BYO

Restaurant Services: no
Catering: BYO
Kitchen Facilities: minimal
Dance Floor: yes
Parking: nearby garage
Overnight Accommodations: no
Telephone: pay phone, lines CBA at extra cost

Tables & Chairs: provided, extra charge
Linens, Silver, etc.: BYO
Restrooms: wca
Outdoor Night Lighting: on loggia
Outdoor Cooking Facilities: no
Cleanup: caterer
Meeting Equipment: sound system, lecturn, staging extra charge

RESTRICTIONS:

Alcohol: BYO
Smoking: outside only
Music: amplified ok with restrictions

Wheelchair Access: no
Insurance: extra liability & damage required
Other: decorating restrictions

Need a caterer, cake maker, florist? The Service Directory starting on page 614 features the best in the business.

HAAS-LILIENTHAL HOUSE

2007 Franklin Street at Washington
San Francisco, CA 94109
(415) 441-3011 Events Coordinator
Reserve for Events: 4 months in advance
Reserve for Meetings: 2–4 weeks in advance

The Haas-Lilienthal House is a stately gray Victorian located in Pacific Heights and is one of the few houses that remains largely as it was when occupied by the Haas and Lilienthal families from 1886–1972. The house provides a unique and intimate environment for a private party or business event (the ballroom is great for business presentations). The main floor has thirteen-foot ceilings, two large parlors and formal dining room, foyer and hall. The interior is very attractive, with subtle colors, oriental carpets, rich woodwork and turn-of-the-century furnishings. This architectural treasure is very comfortable and warm inside.

CAPACITY: The house can accommodate 200 guests for a standing reception; 80 seated in the ballroom or 50 seated on the main floor.

MEETING ROOMS: The ballroom can seat 100 auditorium-style.

FEES & DEPOSITS: A $500 refundable deposit is required and is returned 30 days after the event. Fees range from $650–2,000, depending on the number of guests.

CANCELLATION POLICY: You must cancel 90 days prior to your party to receive a refund.

AVAILABILITY: Monday, Tuesday and Thursday until 10pm; Friday and Saturday until 11pm; Wednesday and Sunday 5pm–10pm.

SERVICES/AMENITIES:
Restaurant Services: no
Catering: BYO, select from list
Kitchen Facilities: moderate
Tables & Chairs: most provided
Linens, Silver, etc.: BYO
Restrooms: no wca
Dance Floor: yes

Parking: on street, valet CBA
Overnight Accommodations: no
Telephone: emergency only
Outdoor Night Lighting: access only
Outdoor Cooking Facilities: BYO BBQ
Cleanup: caterer
Meeting Equipment: no

RESTRICTIONS:
Alcohol: BYO, no red wine at standing events
Smoking: outside only
Music: amplified with restrictions

Wheelchair Access: no
Insurance: not required

HAMLIN MANSION

2120 Broadway
San Francisco, CA 94115
(415) 331-0544
Reserve for Events: 6–12 months in advance
Reserve for Meetings: 6 weeks in advance

The Hamlin Mansion is an impressive structure inside and out. The interior features the elegant and spacious Foyer and the two-story Great Hall, complete with ornate oak columns, herringbone hardwood floors and crowned by a richly detailed leaded glass skylight. The magnificent staircase, backed on the landing by a huge leaded glass window, is perfect for dramatic entries. The Main Dining Room has a striking black marble and gold fireplace and great views of the Bay. With Italian hand-laid mosaic tile on its floor and walls plus lovely leaded Tiffany-style skylights, the Solarium is a jewel of old-fashioned craftsmanship. Upstairs are several rooms with sensational ornate plaster ceilings, painted detailing and fireplaces. Use the downstairs rooms or setup bar and tables on the upstairs balcony. With classic lines and plenty of rich detailing, the Mansion makes a wonderful place for an upscale celebration or business function.

CAPACITY: The Mansion can hold up to 200 seated guests or 350 for a standing reception.

FEES & DEPOSITS: A non-refundable $500 security deposit is required when the contract is signed. The rental fees vary according to day of week and guest count. Fees are payable 2 months prior to the event. Valet service runs $400–1,000 and a security guard is about $150/event.

AVAILABILITY: Sunday–Thursday to 10pm, Friday–Saturday to 11:30pm.

SERVICES/AMENITIES:

Restaurant Services: no
Catering: provided, no BYO
Kitchen Facilities: n/a
Tables & Chairs: provided
Linens, Silver, etc.: caterer
Restrooms: wca
Dance Floor: yes
Meeting Equipment: in-house PA system, podium

Parking: valet
Overnight Accommodations: no
Telephone: pay phone
Outdoor Night Lighting: access only
Outdoor Cooking Facilities: no
Cleanup: caterer
Other: baby grand piano

RESTRICTIONS:

Alcohol: BYO
Smoking: allowed
Music: amplified with volume limit

Wheelchair Access: limited, elevator
Insurance: recommended
Other: decorations restricted

HERBST AND FESTIVAL PAVILIONS

Fort Mason Center
San Francisco, CA 94123
(415) 441-5706 Director of Sales
Reserve for Events: 3 months–2 years in advance
Reserve for Meetings: 2–3 months in advance

Theme parties, festivals, trade shows, exhibits and conventions all come alive in these waterfront spaces located on historic covered piers. The Festival Pavilion has an extraordinary 50,000 sq. ft. of clear-span space, which includes a mezzanine cafe/bar with great views of the Bay and Golden Gate Bridge. The Herbst Pavilion has 30,000 sq. ft. of open space and offers the same flexible and highly unique surroundings. Both facilities have undergone extensive renovations and have white interiors, stunning glass entries, stainless steel food preparation areas and tiled restrooms. If you've got a large crowd, the Pavilions can handle it.

CAPACITY: Festival Pavilion up to 5,000; Herbst Pavilion up to 3,000 people.

FEES & DEPOSITS: A $2,000–3,000 portion of the rental fee reserves your date. A $2,000–3,000 refundable security deposit is also required. The rental fee is $3,500–5,000/day, depending on the type of event and Pavilion selected. The balance of the rental fee and security deposit are due 30 days prior to the event. If food and/or drink is served on site, there is a $1.00/person catering fee. Inquire about rental rates for non-profit organizations.

CANCELLATION POLICY: Call for cancellation policy.

AVAILABILITY: Year-round, every day 8am–midnight.

SERVICES/AMENITIES:

Restaurant Services: no
Catering: BYO
Kitchen Facilities: large food prep
Tables & Chairs: limited numbers
Linens, Silver, etc.: BYO
Restrooms: wca
Dance Floor: BYO

Parking: Fort Mason Center & Marina Green lots
Overnight Accommodations: no
Telephone: pay phone, private lines for clients
Outdoor Night Lighting: access only
Outdoor Cooking Facilities: BYO BBQ (permit req'd)
Cleanup: client provides
Meeting Equipment: no

RESTRICTIONS:

Alcohol: BYO
Smoking: allowed
Music: amplified ok

Wheelchair Access: yes
Insurance: required

HORNBLOWER DINING YACHTS

Berkeley and San Francisco
(415) 394-8900 ext 6
Reserve for Events: see each vessel below
Reserve for Meetings: see each vessel below

Hornblower Dining Yachts offers a wide range of vessels for hire, from sleek yachts to a replica of a turn-of-the-century coastal steamer. You'll travel in style with standard amenities that include white linens, flowers, china and silver service. All vessels are fully enclosed and carpeted. Hornblower staff can help you order everything from invitations and favors to balloons, flowers and entertainment. Also note that remote pickups and dropoffs can be arranged at many locations for a modest additional charge. For winter and early spring parties, Hornblower offers a "good weather" guarantee that applies to rentals made between November 1st and March 31st.

FEES AND DEPOSITS: The deposit amount varies depending on which vessel you select. Event packages range from $29 per guest for a 2-hour mid-week luncheon cruise to $92 per person for a 4-hour Saturday night dinner cruise. A 15–20% gratuity and tax are additional. Hornblower's Charter Coordinators are available to customize your special event or business function, offering a multitude of special services. For all vessels, the final balance is due 5 working days prior to your cruise.

AVAILABILITY: Year-round, anytime.

CAPTAIN HORNBLOWER & ADMIRAL HORNBLOWER

These two vessels are similar in design, including full galley, two decks, parquet dance floor, bar and sound systems. **Reserve:** 1 week–1 year in advance.

CAPACITY: Each yacht can accommodate 60 for a seated function and 75 standing.

DEPOSITS: A $1,000 deposit is due 7–10 days after setting a tentative date.

CANCELLATION POLICY: You must cancel 60 days prior to the event or forfeit the deposit. If the date can be rebooked, it will be refunded.

COMMODORE HORNBLOWER

A gracious, custom built motor yacht which offers two decks, all wood interiors, two parquet dance floors, two bars, full galley and sound system. **Reserve:** 2 weeks–1 year in advance.

CAPACITY: This vessel can carry up to 130 for a seated affair or 150 for a standing reception.

DEPOSITS: A $2,000 deposit is due after setting a tentative date.

CANCELLATION POLICY: You must cancel 90 days prior to your event or forfeit the deposit. If the date can be rebooked, it will be refunded.

EMPRESS HORNBLOWER

This hundred-foot vessel offers two large indoor decks, one large outdoor deck, two parquet dance floors, three bars, full galley and sound system. **Reserve:** 2 weeks–1 year in advance.

CAPACITY: 500 for a standing reception or 270 for a seated meal. You may also charter a single deck for a smaller group.

DEPOSITS: A $2,000–3,000 deposit is due 7–10 days after setting a tentative date.

CANCELLATION POLICY: You must cancel 120 days prior to the event or forfeit the deposit. If the date can be rebooked, your deposit will be refunded.

CALIFORNIA HORNBLOWER

Patterned after a classic steamer of the early 1900s, this large vessel has three decks, three dining salons, three parquet dance floors, three bars, full galley, sound system and expansive sun deck. **Reserve:** 1–12 months in advance.

CAPACITY: This vessel can accommodate 1,000 for cocktails or standing buffet, 800 for a seated meal. You can also charter a single deck for smaller groups. The capacity would then range from 100–900.

DEPOSITS: A $1,000–5,000 deposit is due 7–10 days after setting a tentative date.

CANCELLATION POLICY: You must cancel 120 days prior to the event or forfeit the deposit. If the date can be rebooked, your deposit will be refunded.

PAPAGALLO II

This sleek yacht features two decks, two salons, bar, full galley and a master suite with spa. She has an intimate living room feel with two state rooms on the lower deck. This yacht is available for overnight and extended cruises. **Reserve:** 2 weeks–1 year in advance.

CAPACITY: 24 guests for a seated meal and 50 for a standing reception, 6 for an overnight cruise.

DEPOSITS: A $1,000 deposit is due 7–10 days after setting a tentative date.

CANCELLATION POLICY: You must cancel 60 days prior to your event or forfeit the deposit. If the date is rebooked, your deposit will be refunded.

SERVICES/AMENITIES FOR ALL VESSELS:

Restaurant Services: no
Catering: provided
Kitchen Facilities: n/a
Tables & Chairs: provided
Linens, Silver, etc.: provided
Restrooms: varies each vessel
Meeting Equipment: CBA

Parking: various locations
Dance Floor: provided, except Papagallo II
Overnight Accommodations: Papagallo only
Telephone: credit card phone on board
Outdoor Night Lighting: varies
Outdoor Cooking Facilities: no
Cleanup: provided

RESTRICTIONS:

Alcohol: provided, corkage $7/bottle
Smoking: allowed
Music: amplified ok

Wheelchair Access: varies/vessel
Insurance: not required

THE HOUSTON
Uncommon Journeys

703 Market Street, Ste 711
San Francisco, CA 94103
(415) 543-1072
Reserve for Events: 1–6 months in advance
Reserve for Meetings: 2–3 months in advance

Built in 1926, The Houston is a time capsule of plush 1920's train travel. Once reserved for the very rich or very famous, this elegantly understated private railcar epitomized first class business travel before the advent of commercial airlines. It has the traditional open-air observation platform and a wood-paneled observation lounge which is the center of daytime activity, from mid-morning coffee to pre-dinner cocktails. For overnight trips, there is a bedroom with upper and lower berths and an 8 ft x 17 ft master suite with large closets and built-in dressers. Morning coffee, bathrobes, nightcap and chocolate mint on your pillow are all part of your non-stop impeccable service. Also on board is a formal dining room with antique chairs, wood paneling and table seating for eight. Aft is a fully equipped kitchen complete with charcoal broiler. The Houston is one of the few cars to feature 'track lights' which illuminate the passing scene at night. This railcar can be attached to any AMTRAK train or can be 'parked' in a number of cities for stationary special events. For a nostalgic and exciting environment, The Houston is ideal for special celebrations, corporate meetings or promotional events. Pamper your friends or associates by inviting them aboard! It'll be the highlight of their lives.

CAPACITY: For day trips, up to 12 passengers; overnight stays, up to 5 passengers.

FEES & DEPOSITS: For trips, a deposit of 20% of the total estimated cost is required. For stationary functions, a $500 deposit is required. Both are non-refundable and due when the contract is submitted. For an event with extended travel, costs will run $3,400/day, which includes chef, butler, all meals, snacks, wine, cocktails, transportation costs, rental fees, operational charges, personalized stationary and flowers. To "park" nearby (primarily Oakland and San Francisco locations) the cost is $500–$1,000 for 4–5 hours depending on whether it's for afternoon tea, cocktails or a formal, seated dinner. The balance is payable 7 days prior to any event or departure.

CANCELLATION POLICY: Determined on an individual basis.

AVAILABILITY: Year-round, every day with no hourly restrictions.

SERVICES/AMENITIES:

Restaurant Services: no
Catering: provided, no BYO
Kitchen Facilities: n/a
Tables & Chairs: provided
Linens, Silver, etc.: provided
Restrooms: no wca
Meeting Equipment: no

Dance Floor: no
Parking: available
Overnight Accommodations: for 5 guests
Telephone: cellular
Outdoor Night Lighting: no
Outdoor Cooking Facilities: no
Cleanup: provided

RESTRICTIONS:
Alcohol: provided, no BYO
Smoking: rear platform only
Music: amplified okay

Wheelchair Access: no
Insurance: not required

THE MANSIONS HOTEL

2220 Sacramento Street
San Francisco, CA 94115
(415) 929-9444
Reserve for Events: 2–6 months in advance
Reserve for Meetings: 2–4 weeks in advance

Two large adjoining historic homes combine to form The Mansions Hotel. Each features a different ambiance but both have fine art, fanciful sculpture and eclectic furniture. There is a billiard room, cabaret with stage and theatrical lighting, courtyard sculpture gardens with gazebo and several dining rooms. Featuring treasured antiques, fine art, stained glass walls and panoramic murals, the Mansions Hotel is a unique spot for a great celebration, office party or unusual business meeting.

CAPACITY: The Mansions can hold up to 150 for a standing reception or 90 for seated meals.

MEETING ROOMS: 4 meeting rooms that can hold between 8–35 guests.

FEES & DEPOSITS: A refundable $350 deposit is required when a tentative date is set. 50% of estimated total food and beverage cost is due 10 working days prior to the event. The fee is $350 for a 8-hour rental depending on day of the week. Catering is provided and food service rates start at $15/person for luncheons up to $40/person for seated meals. Saturday night a minimum of $4,500 in food, alcohol and room rental is required. Gratuity 18% and tax are not included in the above fees.

AVAILABILITY: Parties are usually held 11am–4pm on Saturdays, noon–10pm on Sundays. Saturday night bookings are negotiable. Weekday events or business functions any day 8am–10pm.

SERVICES/AMENITIES:
Restaurant Services: yes
Catering: provided, no BYO
Kitchen Facilities: ample
Tables & Chairs: provided
Linens, Silver, etc.: provided
Restrooms: no wca
Dance Floor: yes
Meeting Equipment: TV, VCR screen, flip charts

Parking: Webster/Clay garage
Overnight Accommodations: 21 guestrooms
Telephone: pay phone
Outdoor Night Lighting: yes
Outdoor Cooking Facilities: no
Cleanup: provided
Other: 2 pianos, billiard room

RESTRICTIONS:
Alcohol: provided, corkage $10/bottle
Smoking: allowed
Music: amplified until 10pm

Wheelchair Access: no
Insurance: not required

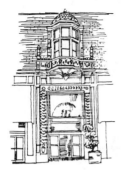

MARINES' MEMORIAL

609 Sutter Street
San Francisco, CA 94102
(415) 921-2689
Reserve for Events: 4–6 months in advance
Reserve for Meetings: 2–4 months in advance

Marines' Memorial Club is a hidden jewel in the heart of downtown San Francisco. Although you need to find a sponsor to host an event here, almost anyone can find someone who has served in any branch of the U.S. military to act as a sponsor. Built in 1910 as a formal woman's club, it was transformed in 1946 as a memorial to marines who lost their lives in the Pacific during World War II. The non-profit Club has suites, restaurant, health club, indoor pool, library, museum and wonderful banquet rooms. Most people don't know that the Club has an exquisite, take-your-breath-away Crystal Ballroom that is available for grand receptions. Ornate chandeliers, detailed ceiling and wall paintings, raised stage plus a gleaming hardwood parquet floor all combine to form an exceptional venue for private parties. The Regimental Room, with vaulted, painted ceilings, marble fireplace and lots of wood detailing, is great for hors d'oeuvres receptions. The Heritage and Commandants Rooms are also available. If you're going to have a party, conference or seminar in the City, make sure you don't overlook this facility.

CAPACITY: 600 seated guests, maximum.

MEETING ROOMS:	*Seated*	*Standing*	*Classroom*	*Conference*	*Theater*
Crystal Ballroom	200	—	125	100	300
Crystal Lounge	40	200	30	40	—
Commandants Room	250	300	150	—	300
Heritage Room	50	—	30	40	60
Regimental Room	50	—	30	40	70

FEES & DEPOSITS: A $100–500 refundable deposit is required within 14 days of reserving a banquet room. There's no rental fee if you achieve a minimum guest count, however house catering is required. A guest count along with 90% of the estimated event total are required 7 days prior to the event; a final guest count 72 hours before. Any remaining balance is due and payable the day of the event. Seated luncheons and dinners run $13–24/person; hors d'oeuvres $4–10/person; buffets (min. 75 people) $17–25/person. All rates are subject to tax and a 15% gratuity. As an added bonus, they offer special rates for events held during June, July, January or February.

CANCELLATION POLICY: Your deposit is returned if you cancel at least 60 days prior to the event.

AVAILABILITY: Any day, from 7am–11pm. There are overtime charges for holidays.

SERVICES/AMENITIES:

Restaurant Services: yes
Catering: provided, no BYO
Kitchen Facilities: n/a
Tables & Chairs: provided

Parking: nearby garages
Overnight Accommodations: 128 guestrooms
Telephone: pay and guest phones
Outdoor Night Lighting: access only

Linens, Silver, etc.: provided
Restrooms: wca
Dance Floor: yes
Other: full event coordination

RESTRICTIONS:
Alcohol: provided, corkage $5/bottle
Smoking: designated areas
Music: amplified ok

Outdoor Cooking Facilities: no
Meeting Equipment: yes
Cleanup: provided

Wheelchair Access: yes, elevator
Insurance: not required
Other: sponsor required

MARK MONROE PRODUCTIONS

449 Powell Street
San Francisco, CA 94102
(415) 928-7359
Reserve for Events: 1–12 months in advance
Reserve for Meetings: 1 week or more in advance

Don't let the nondescript entryway on Powell Street deter you. Take the elevator to the third floor, where you'll find yourself in a completely captivating Italian villa. Rose-entwined lattices make their way up the walls; windows, balconies and lush countryside surround you. And the amazing thing is, all these wonderful details are illusions, painted by a very clever artist. Not everything is trompe l'oeil, however. The Concession Room has real trees, a softly weathered black and white tile floor and tall windows overlooking the central courtyard. Circling the courtyard are three other spaces which can be used independently or in combination. The Main Ballroom, with its exceptionally high ceiling, hardwood floor and large stage is well suited for theater productions or dining and dancing. The Salon Room has a smaller stage, a twenty-foot coffered ceiling and original turn-of-the-century chandeliers. Brushed terra cotta-colored walls, ochre wainscoting and tall windows that open out onto Powell Street give this room an earthy elegance, perfect for small lectures or concerts. The Sutter Street Room derives its romantic ambiance from coral hued walls and flowing drapes. It's a lovely setting for an intimate dinner. And last but not least, the courtyard itself is a great little place to relax. When the weather's fine, guests can bask in the afternoon sun or stargaze at night. Looking for a unique spot? Mark Monroe Productions veers well off the beaten path and is still conveniently located just off Union Square.

CAPACITY: The facility can accommodate 30-300 guests, depending on the spaces reserved.

FEES & DEPOSITS: Rental rates start at $500. A deposit in the amount of the rental rate and a security deposit based on the space rented is required at the time of booking. The balance of the anticipated total cost is due 2 weeks prior to the event. Call for current catering rates.

CANCELLATION POLICY: The circumstances of the cancellation dictate the amount of refund.

AVAILABILITY: Year-round, every day.

SERVICES/AMENITIES:

Restaurant Services: no
Catering: provided
Kitchen Facilities: n/a
Tables & Chairs: some provided
Linens, Silver, etc.: provided
Restrooms: wca
Dance Floor: yes
Other: event coordination

Parking: nearby inexpensive garages, on street
Overnight Accommodations: CBA
Telephone: pay phone, house phone
Outdoor Night Lighting: courtyard only
Outdoor Cooking Facilities: no
Cleanup: provided
Meeting Equipment: BYO

RESTRICTIONS:

Alcohol: provided
Smoking: designated areas
Insurance: required

Wheelchair Access: yes
Music: amplified ok

MIYAKO HOTEL

1625 Post Street
San Francisco, CA 94115
(415) 922-3200
Reserve for Events: 2 weeks–6 months in advance
Reserve for Meetings: 1 week–6 months in advance

Japantown's Miyako Hotel reflects an interesting blend of Japanese and California cultures. Traditional Japanese gardens are visible from many of the meeting and event spaces, bringing a touch of greenery and serenity indoors. The Imperial Ballroom, with its Oriental art and soft beige tones, is an elegant, formal space for large meetings or parties. A custom-designed carpet adds vibrance, taking its rich blue and coral tones from antique obi sashes. Smaller in scale and more relaxed in style, the Sakura Ballroom can also host a variety of events. Its Japanese ambiance is enhanced by a shoji panel coffered ceiling and a floor-to-ceiling view of the Summer Garden. Small formal meetings and intimate dinners are often held in the Boardroom. Silk wallpaper, a large oval cherry wood table and soft overhead lighting create a comfortable atmosphere, and built-in audiovisual equipment is available. For a visual treat, have your party in Elka, the Hotel's unique restaurant. Painted in striking colors, it features art, sculptures and lighting fixtures created by local artisans. (For more information about Elka, see its entry in the Private Dining Room section.) Whether you're planning a business function or private party, The Miyako Hotel's multilingual staff and emphasis on service will make it a success.

CAPACITY:	Seated	Standing	Classroom	Theatre
Imperial Ballroom*	250–500	300–600	150–340	350–750
Sakura Ballroom*	60–300	75–400	45–240	75–400
Kosakura	12	—	—	—

* These rooms can be sectioned

MEETING ROOMS: There are 14 meeting rooms including those listed above, accommodating from 12 to 750 people.

FEES & DEPOSITS: A $500 deposit is due at the time of booking. It is applied to the final payment due 72 hours prior to the event. Per person food costs not including wine are $15-23 for lunch and $25-36 for dinner. Tax and a 16% gratuity are additional.

CANCELLATION POLICY: The deposit will be refunded in full with 2 months' notice.

AVAILABILITY: Year-round, anytime.

SERVICES/AMENITIES:

Restaurant Services: yes
Catering: provided, no BYO
Kitchen Facilities: n/a
Tables & Chairs: provided
Linens, Silver, etc.: provided
Restrooms: wca
Dance Floor: yes
Other: event coordination, piano, stage

Parking: Valet, on street, lot
Overnight Accommodations: 218 guestrooms
Telephone: pay phones, guest phones
Outdoor Night Lighting: n/a
Outdoor Cooking Facilities: no
Cleanup: provided
Meeting Equipment: provided

RESTRICTIONS:

Alcohol: provided, $6.50+ corkage/bottle
Smoking: allowed
Music: amplified ok

Wheelchair Access: yes
Insurance: not required

NIMITZ
CONFERENCE CENTER

410 Palm Ave., Bldg. 140
Treasure Island-90
San Francisco, CA 94130
(415) 395-5151
Reserve for Events: 1–18 months in advance
Reserve for Meetings: 2 weeks–18 months in advance

The Conference Center offers a variety of meeting and event spaces to those who have a sponsor (Military person on active duty, retired or a reservist). The largest is the Grand Ballroom, featuring a vaulted beamed ceiling, chandeliers, a hardwood dance floor and a thirty-two-foot stage. A forest green carpet and light peach walls create a fresh ambiance. At the entrance to the Grand Ballroom, the thirty-foot L-Bar runs the entire length of the Foyer, ending at a glass wall that overlooks the tennis courts. Comfortable chairs and contemporary art make this a more casual space. The Garden Ballroom has a view of surrounding lawns, and a huge skylight and floor-to-ceiling windows flood the room with light. This space is ideal for conferences or parties. The adjacent Garden Foyer is a wonderful pre-function area, often used for cocktails and hors d'oeuvres. Three skylights and a glass wall keep this room bright and airy, too. For business luncheons or dinners, the Treasure Room is a rustic, homey dining room. Part of the old Nimitz house, it has a vaulted ceiling, a large working fireplace and subdued evening lighting. The Captain's Lounge was designed for meetings. It can be easily darkened for audio-visual presentations, and when it's time to break for lunch, participants simply walk through the door into the Patio Room. A tile floor, café tables and an outdoor terrace overlooking a landscaped lawn, make this a delightful spot. Whatever area you choose, the Conference Center will set it up any way you like, and insure that your event goes smoothly.

CAPACITY:

Area	Seated	Standing	Area	Seated	Standing
Grand Ballroom	389	500	Treasure Room	60	100
Garden Room	200	350	Captain's Lounge	20	40
L-Bar	60	100	Patio Room	50	100

MEETING ROOMS: All of the above rooms may be used for meetings.

FEES & DEPOSITS: A non-refundable deposit is required at the time of booking (25% of the total estimated cost for the Grand Ballroom and Garden Ballroom, $75 for smaller rooms). The estimated balance and a final guest count are due 1 week prior to the event. There is a $200 setup fee for conferences and receptions, which may be waived with meal service. Overtime hours are available after 11pm for an additional charge. Per person rates: dinners/buffets $10-30, hors d'oeuvres trays $35-200. Any menu can be customized, no tax is required, and the service charge is 15%.

CANCELLATION POLICY: Deposits and pre-payment are non-refundable.

AVAILABILITY: Year-round, every day from 11am-4pm and 6pm-11pm.

SERVICES/AMENITIES:

Restaurant Services: no
Catering: provided
Kitchen Facilities: n/a
Tables & Chairs: provided
Linens, Silver, etc.: provided
Restrooms: wca
Dance Floor: yes

Parking: large lot
Overnight Accommodations: no
Telephone: pay phone
Outdoor Night Lighting: yes
Outdoor Cooking Facilities: CBA
Cleanup: provided
Meeting Equipment: yes

RESTRICTIONS:

Alcohol: provided
Smoking: allowed
Music: amplified ok

Wheelchair Access: yes
Insurance: not required

OLD FEDERAL RESERVE BANK BUILDING

400 Sansome Street
San Francisco, CA 94111
(415) 392-1234 Catering
Reserve for Events: 3-6 months in advance
Reserve for Meetings: 3-6 months in advance

We always get asked about mansions in San Francisco, and to tell you the truth, there are not many which can accommodate large functions indoors. Although the Old Federal Reserve Bank Building is not a mansion, it comes close to the kind of stately, elegant and understated grandeur you'd expect from a palatial estate. And, it can handle quite a crowd. Originally part of the lobby of the 1924 Federal Reserve Bank, the building has been fully restored and is included in the National Register of Historic Places. The Old Federal Reserve serves as a fine example of San Francisco's banking "temple" tradition and the government's penchant for monumental classical architecture of that era. Inside, you'll find one of the most dramatic staircases we've ever seen. If you'd like to make a theatrical entrance, try descending the bronze and marble double stair which starts from two separate places and curves seamlessly onto the gleaming marble floor below. Everywhere you look, you'll see French and Italian marble (or a close facsimile). Expertly painted faux marbling has transformed the two rows of twenty-five foot tall Ionic columns that flank the room into "rock-solid" architectural elements. Entry doors are solid bronze. Drawing your eyes to the awe-inspiring thirty-four foot ceiling overhead are two bronze chandeliers, originals (designed by the architect) from the 1920s. All in all, if you have an extended guest list and are searching for a grand location in the City, you couldn't ask for a better spot.

CAPACITY: The Old Federal Reserve can hold 150–400 seated or 600 for a standing cocktail reception. For seminars or conferences, 500 theater-style, 350 classroom-style.

FEES & DEPOSITS: The rental fee is $1,800 weekdays or $2,800 weekends. The fee may be waived depending upon the size of the event and the selection of caterer. A deposit, also based on event size, is due when the space is booked. The balance of all fees is payable 14 days prior to the event.

CANCELLATION POLICY: With less than 60 days' notice, 50% of deposit is refunded; with 60-90 days' notice, 75% of deposit is returned; with more than 90 days' notice, the deposit is returned in full.

AVAILABILITY: Year-round, daily from 5pm-2am. For day use, it's by special arrangement.

SERVICES/AMENITIES:

Restaurant Services: no
Dance Floor: CBA
Catering: select from preferred list
Restrooms: wca
Kitchen Facilities: no
Tables & Chairs: caterer
Linens, Silver, etc.: caterer
Meeting Equipment: CBA

Parking: adjacent garage, discounted weekdays, complimentary on weekends
Overnight Accommodations: 360 guestrooms at Park Hyatt San Francisco, including 37 suites
Telephone: pay phones
Outdoor Night Lighting: no
Outdoor Cooking Facilities: no
Cleanup: provided

RESTRICTIONS:

Alcohol: provided, corkage W $10/bottle

Smoking: outside only

Music: amplified ok

Wheelchair Access: yes

Insurance: not required

PACIFIC HEIGHTS MANSION

Address withheld to maintain privacy.
San Francisco, CA
(415) 864-0803
Reserve for Events: based on availability

What a treat to discover this Italian Palladian mansion, with neoclassic entrance, glorious views and designer interior. Built in 1919, this showcase home is a very special place for intimate, elegant functions. The large foyer sets the tone. Here you'll find a floor of bleached oak, beveled mirrors, oversized stone planters and a dramatic split staircase leading upstairs. To your left is the living room, a refreshing vision in an off-white color scheme, with accents in pale soft peaches, melons, greens and ivories. In this room, comfortable contemporary furnishings blend with French antiques. And, of course, the best feature is the bank of windows that provide a stunning view of San Francisco Bay, the Golden Gate Bridge and the Palace of Fine Arts. If you can tear yourself away from this panorama, head in the other direction, towards the dining room, where a 17th-century Waterford chandelier is suspended from an unusual recessed oval ceiling. There's a grand-size travertine table in the room's center, behind which are French doors overlooking the garden. Adjacent is the breakfast nook. This is the most fanciful room downstairs—an artistic delight. All the moldings and walls are hand painted with ornate, very Italian garden motifs. Like a renaissance fresco, the fruit, flowers and leaves are entwined in soft terra cottas and greens. Saunter outside where you can smell salt water breezes and savor unobstructed views of the Bay.

CAPACITY: The Mansion can hold 60 seated guests for dinner; 120 for a standing reception. Only the ground floor is available for functions.

FEES & DEPOSITS: A $500 refundable security deposit plus 50% of the rental fee is payable upon reservation, the balance 1 week prior to the event. The rental fee is $3,500. Food costs for luncheons or dinners is at the client's discretion.

CANCELLATION POLICY: The deposit is refundable if cancellation occurs 1 month prior to the event date. For December events, the deposit is not refundable.

AVAILABILITY: Year-round, daily.

SERVICES/AMENITIES:

Restaurant Services: no

Catering: provided, no BYO

Kitchen Facilities: n/a

Parking: valet or street

Overnight Accommodations: no

Telephone: house phone

Tables & Chairs: some provided
Linens, Silver, etc.: caterer
Restrooms: no wca
Dance Floor: no
Other: grand piano

RESTRICTIONS:
Alcohol: provided
Smoking: outside only
Insurance: certificate required

Outdoor Night Lighting: access only
Outdoor Cooking Facilities: no
Cleanup: provided
Meeting Equipment: no

Wheelchair Access: ramp available
Music: no amplified

THE PACIFIC SPIRIT
Pacific Marine Yacht Charters

Berthed at Pier 39, East Basin
San Francisco, CA 94133
(415) 788-9100
Reserve for Events: 1–9 months in advance
Reserve for Meetings: 1 week in advance

The Pacific Spirit is an eighty-three-foot classic Broward Yacht with two enclosed decks and a full open flybridge. It features a comfortably appointed main salon with wet bar and an adjoining aft salon with a teak wood dance floor. Below deck are three intimate lounge salons. Professional service and award-winning cuisine will make your special occasion an exceptional experience.

CAPACITY: The Pacific Spirit can accommodate up to 90 guests, weather permitting. Formal seating is available for up to 35 guests.

FEES & DEPOSITS: A $1,000 deposit is required to reserve your date, and half the food and beverage cost is due 30 days prior to your event.

	Weekdays (before 6pm)	*Weekdays (after 6pm)*	*Weekends/Holidays*
Yacht rental rates:	$350/hr	$375/hr	$450/hr
Groups of 20 or less:	325/hr	350/hr	375/hr

A 3-hour minimum rental is required, 4 hours on Saturday evenings and holidays. A guaranteed guest count is required 7 days prior to departure and the remaining balance is due 5 days prior to your event.

CANCELLATION POLICY: With 60 days' notice, 85% of the reservation deposit will be refunded; with less notice, the deposit will be forfeited.

AVAILABILITY: Anytime, no limits.

SERVICES/AMENITIES:
Restaurant Services: no
Catering: provided, no BYO
Kitchen Facilities: on board

Parking: Pier 39 garage, validations available
Overnight Accommodations: no
Telephone: emergency cellular and radio

Tables & Chairs: provided
Linens, Silver, etc.: provided
Restrooms: 3, no wca
Dance Floor: yes
Meeting Equipment: podium and microphone

RESTRICTIONS:

Alcohol: provided, corkage $7/bottle
Smoking: aft enclosed salon
Music: amplified ok

Outdoor Night Lighting: yes
Outdoor Cooking Facilities: no
Cleanup: provided
Other: event coordination

Wheelchair Access: no
Insurance: not required

THE PALACE OF FINE ARTS

Lyon at Marina Boulevard
San Francisco, CA
(415) 666-7035 Recreation & Parks
Reserve for Events: 1–12 months in advance

Designed by architect Bernard Maybeck for the Panama-Pacific Exposition of 1915, the Palace of Fine Arts is a magnificent San Francisco landmark and one of the most glorious spots you can imagine for an outdoor party. Located in the Marina District, the picturesque shaded lagoon, ducks and swans, landscaped island and spraying fountain offer an exceptional setting for a celebration. Seated functions are possible under the grand and impressive classic Roman rotunda. Your guests can roam anywhere around the lagoon's perimeter; the entire setting is idyllic and highly romantic. Although this is a public park space, you are allowed to rope off an area for your event or hire security personnel. Given the low fees for use of this spectacular park, we'd say this is a real find.

CAPACITY: The rotunda and park can accommodate 300–500 guests.

FEES & DEPOSITS: A 10% non-refundable deposit of the total fee is due 5 working days from the time you make your reservation. The rental fee for 2 hours is $225, and for each hour over that, the fee is $35/hour. Any remaining fees are required 30 days prior to your event.

AVAILABILITY: Daily, from 9am to dusk.

SERVICES/AMENITIES:

Restaurant Services: no
Catering: BYO
Kitchen Facilities: no
Tables & Chairs: BYO
Overnight Accommodations: no
Telephone: pay phone
Outdoor Night Lighting: access only

Linens, Silver, etc.: BYO
Restrooms: by Exploratorium
Dance Floor: no
Parking: on street
Outdoor Cooking Facilities: no
Cleanup: caterer
Meeting Equipment: no

RESTRICTIONS:
Alcohol: BYO
Smoking: allowed
Music: no amplified

Wheelchair Access: yes
Insurance: sometimes required

PAN PACIFIC HOTEL

500 Post St.
San Francisco, CA 94102
(415) 771-8600
Reserve for Events: 3–9 months in advance
Reserve for Meetings: 2–4 weeks in advance

Elegant. Sophisticated. Tasteful. The Pan Pacific is all of these and then some. World-renowned architect, John Portman, has successfully blended Asian and American elements, warm colors and graceful design themes in this twenty-one-story architectural gem. Eye-pleasing arches abound, from the exterior windows to interior entranceways. A Portuguese rose marble is used for flooring and columns throughout, and Oriental antiques and art lend a timelessness to an otherwise contemporary structure. Most of the event spaces work well for either parties or meetings. The Executive Conference Center, with its four meeting rooms and private dining area offers a secluded location for any business function. The second floor is the Olympic Ballroom level, with a spacious foyer and four auxiliary rooms. You can use these spaces in any combination, as the rooms flow conveniently into one another. The foyer is lovely with its marble floor and brilliant cut glass columns. The Ballroom features four enormous brass and crystal chandeliers, and a rear wall of beveled glass panels that let in natural light and add sparkle to the room. All of the rooms have the Hotel's custom teal, rose and mauve heather carpet, rose banquet chairs and blush colored walls. State-of-the-art audio-visual equipment is available at the touch of a few buttons. Upstairs on the third floor is the main lobby, including a lounge and conversation areas anchored by two imposing rectangular fireplaces. The focal point of the room is a bronze sculpture entitled "Joie de Danse," four fluid, larger-than-life dancers circling round a marble fountain. This area can be used for cocktails and hors d'oeuvres. Take the elevator to the 21st floor Terrace Room where wrap-around windows offer incredible views—especially at sunset, when the light glowing off thousands of highrise windows can take your breath away. A coffered ceiling, rosewood bar, and arched fireplaces create an intimate ambiance. From the Terrace Room, guests can stroll into the Solarium, an open-air brick patio that also shares a wonderful panorama of the City and bay. And if you want to stay overnight, the Penthouse is only a few steps away. More like a gracious home than a hotel suite, it features two bedrooms, custom designed furniture, a baby grand piano and a terrific view. The Boardroom on the same floor is also available for smaller functions. Original Imogene Cunningham photos on the walls are as striking as the view. And with a staff to guest ratio of 1 to 1, the Pan Pacific makes service its top priority. What more could you ask for?

CAPACITY:

Area	Seated	Standing	Area	Seated	Stanting
Conference Center	30–90	35–150	Boardroom	14	35
Olympic Ballroom	25–360	100–500	Patio Room	50	100
(can be sectioned)			The Terrace	52–120	175
Prefunction Area	180	300	Terrace Solarium	30–50	50
Bar	100	50–300	Penthouse	10	80

MEETING ROOMS: All of the areas listed above are available for meetings except the Bar.

FEES & DEPOSITS: A non-refundable $250–1,000 deposit is required 30 days after booking to secure your date, and the balance is due on the day of the event. Rental fees vary, based on the event. Per person food costs range from $25–80 for lunch and $40–120 for dinner. Beverage, tax and an 18% gratuity are extra.

CANCELLATION POLICY: With less than 90 days notice, a cancellation fee in the amount of 50% of the anticipated revenue will be charged.

AVAILABILITY: Year-round except Christmas and New Year's Day.

SERVICES/AMENITIES:

Restaurant Services: yes
Catering: provided, no BYO
Kitchen Facilities: n/a
Tables & Chairs: provided
Linens, Silver, etc.: provided
Restrooms: wca
Dance Floor: yes
Other: event coordination

Parking: valet and nearby lots
Overnight Accommodations: 330 guestrooms
Telephone: pay phones, guest phones, house phones
Outdoor Night Lighting: Terrace Solarium only
Outdoor Cooking Facilities: n/a
Cleanup: provided
Meeting Equipment: yes

RESTRICTIONS:

Alcohol: provided, corkage $7–10
Smoking: allowed
Insurance: not required

Wheelchair Access: yes
Music: amplified ok
Other: live music in the Terrace Room ends at 11pm

PARK HYATT
SAN FRANCISCO

333 Battery Street
San Francisco, CA 94111
(415) 392-1234 Catering
Reserve for Events: 3–6 months in advance
Reserve for Meetings: 1–14 days in advance

The Park Hyatt is a different kind of hotel. Understated and upscale, the Hotel provides an environment conducive to elegant affairs in the heart of the financial district. It not only has a tasteful interior, but the Park Hyatt's professional staff is one of the best we've encountered. From the doorman to the catering manager, each hotel employee offers the kind of friendly, impeccable service that is rare in today's world. No matter what type of function you have here, you'll be able to relax and enjoy it knowing that this hostelry bends over backwards to provide a worry-free experience. Events take place in an exclusive, club-like atmosphere that is warm and elegant throughout: rich polished wood, translucent onyx fixtures, detailed ceilings, spiral staircase and a black baby grand piano are additional accoutrements. Solid granite tables, leather swivel chairs and handsome Australian lacewood paneling create a business environment that is subdued yet sumptuous. If you need additional support, Park Hyatt offers a twenty-four-hour concierge, reference library and full secretarial assistance, too. The Park Grill, a popular restaurant with a strong culinary as well as visual appeal, can host receptions or luncheon meetings. This is a top notch eatery, with lounge alcoves and a beautiful bar. For outdoor entertaining, the adjacent patio can be dressed up with black tables, white linens and large umbrellas. A sophisticated place with flawless style and service, Park Hyatt San Francisco actually delivers what most other places just talk about.

CAPACITY: Level 2 can accommodate 8–200 guests; B Level 150 guests. The Park Grill holds up to 150 guests.

MEETING ROOMS: 14 rooms, ranging from 8–100 people.

FEES & DEPOSITS: A deposit of 10% of the total estimated food and beverage bill is due at the time of booking. The balance is due 2 weeks prior to the event.

CANCELLATION POLICY: With 30 days' notice, your deposit will be refunded.

AVAILABILITY: Year-round, daily from 6am–2am.

SERVICES/AMENITIES:

Restaurant Services: yes
Catering: provided, no BYO
Overnight Accommodations: 360 guestrooms including 37 suites
Telephone: pay phone
Tables & Chairs: provided
Linens, Silver, etc.: provided
Meeting Equipment: CBA, extra fee

Parking: adjacent garage, discounted weekdays, complimentary on weekends
Restrooms: wca
Kitchen Facilities: n/a
Dance Floor: yes
Outdoor Night Lighting: n/a
Outdoor Cooking Facilities: no
Cleanup: provided

RESTRICTIONS:
Alcohol: provided, $10/corkage
Smoking: allowed
Insurance: not required

Wheelchair Access: yes
Music: amplified ok

PIER 35
Cruise Ship Passenger Terminal

Pier 35
San Francisco, CA 94109
(415) 243-8161
Reserve for Events: 1 week-6 months in advance
Reserve for Meetings: 1 week-6 months in advance

Who would have thought that a cruise ship passenger terminal could be such an outstanding event space? Located at Pier 35, the terminal sits right on the water and has unobstructed views of the bay, Treasure Island and the Bay Bridge. Two spacious rooms on the upper level are the pièce de résistance of the complex. Both are light and airy thanks to a wall of floor-to-ceiling windows which faces the bay. Scarlet, yellow, purple and blue banners suspended from an open, beamed ceiling create a festive atmosphere. Each room opens out onto a wide deck which runs the length of the building. Dine in the banquet room, and dance on the parquet floor of the reception area, or treat your guests to an al fresco lunch or dinner on the deck. It's easy to imagine a balmy afernoon party with the sun sparkling on the water and the waves gently lapping below. Or picture an evening affair—the deck aglow with lights, a sprinkle of stars overhead and the illuminated outline of the Bay Bridge off in the distance. There's also easy access to another area downstairs that can handle a crowd by itself, or provide additional space for a bash that's too big for the upper floor alone. Roll-up doors and a deck give guests here the same vistas and sea breezes they'd enjoy up above. All three rooms can be reserved individually or in combination, and there's plenty of sheltered parking available downstairs on the main floor of the terminal. And if you just happen to be looking for a place to hold a trade show, festival or other large function, Pier 35 has an additional 218,000 square feet available.

CAPACITY:

	Area	*Seated*	*Standing*	*Area*	*Seated*	*Standing*
Upper Level	Banquet Room	250	400	Deck	175	300
	Reception Area	200	400	Entire Upper Level	625	1,000
Lower Level		600	1,000			

MEETING ROOMS: All of the above areas are available for meetings.

FEES & DEPOSITS: Rental rates range from $500–5,000 depending on the room(s) booked and time of year. A deposit of 25% of the rental fee is due when the contract is signed. The balance is due 30 days prior to the event. Call for information regarding rental of the entire pier.

CANCELLATION POLICY: With 30 days' notice, 50% of the deposit will be refunded.

AVAILABILITY: Year round, 6am–2am, subject to cruise ship schedule.

SERVICES/AMENITIES:

Restaurant Services: no
Catering: select from list or BYO
Kitchen Facilities: prep only
Tables & Chairs: caterer or CBA, extra fee
Linens, Silver, etc.: caterer or CBA, extra fee
Restrooms: wca
Dance Floor: yes
Other: event coordination

Parking: inside terminal for nominal fee
Overnight Accommodations: CBA
Telephone: pay phone
Outdoor Night Lighting: access only
Outdoor Cooking Facilities: no
Cleanup: caterer or provided, extra fee
Meeting Equipment: CBA, extra fee

RESTRICTIONS:

Alcohol: provided, if BYO license required
Smoking: in terminal only
Insurance: required

Wheelchair Access: yes
Music: amplified ok

THE PRESCOTT HOTEL
Penthouse Suites

545 Post Street
San Francisco, CA 94102
(415) 563-0303
Reserve for Events: 1–3 months in advance
Reserve for Meetings: 2 weeks in advance

If you've got to host a small but prestigious meeting, cocktail party or reception in the City, we'd suggest you preview the Penthouse Suites on the seventh floor of the Prescott Hotel. Adjacent to and sharing a lobby with Wolfgang Puck's famous Postrio Restaurant, the Prescott is an especially warm and appealing hostelry that's conveniently located near Union Square. Your guests will enter through the elegant lobby, highlighted by oriental carpets, alabaster chandeliers and richly upholstered custom furnishings. They'll be directed across the polished marble floor to the elevators where they are whisked up to the Penthouse. For private business functions or small, upscale receptions, the four suites on this floor are one of the City's best kept secrets. The decor is à la Ralph Lauren, with rich floral patterns and appointments in hunter green, burgundy, taupe and gold. The Mendocino Suite, largest of the four, features custom-made cherry furniture, oil paintings and green faux-marble accessories. Everything's been designed to resemble a distinguished residence—there's little here to suggest you're in a hotel. Oak floors with orientals, a baby grand piano, dining room with chandelier and wood-burning fireplace are all part of the residential atmosphere. There's even a rooftop deck with hot tub for guests who'd like to relax a bit more. For those who have no time to plan an event, the Prescott Hotel has a staff coordinator to handle all the details for you. And, the ultimate extra benefit is that Postrio can cater any function held in the Penthouse.

CAPACITY: The entire 7th floor can accommodate up to 125 for a standing reception. The Mendocino Suite holds up to 40. The other 2 suites can hold up to 10 guests, each.

FEES & DEPOSITS: You can rent the entire 7th floor for $1,000–1,500. The room rental is due 30 days in advance. Room tax is additional. For just the Mendocino Suite, the room rental is $200–475; the remaining suites run $200–225 per suite.

CANCELLATION POLICY: You need to cancel 72 hours in advance if you've rented the entire floor; 24 hours if you've rented one suite.

SERVICES/AMENITIES:

Restaurant Services: yes

Catering: provided or preferred list

Kitchen Facilities: n/a

Tables & Chairs: provided

Linens, Silver, etc.: provided

Restrooms: wca

Dance Floor: no

Other: baby grand piano

Parking: valet, garages nearby

Overnight Accommodations: 167 guestrooms

Telephone: house and pay phones

Outdoor Night Lighting: no

Outdoor Cooking Facilities: no

Cleanup: provided

Meeting Equipment: CBA

RESTRICTIONS:

Alcohol: provided or BYO

Smoking: allowed

Music: no amplified

Wheelchair Access: yes

Insurance: not required

THE QUEEN ANNE

1590 Sutter Street
San Francisco, CA
(415) 441-2828
Reserve for Events: 4–6 months in advance
Reserve for Meetings: 2 weeks–6 months in advance

Built in 1890 by a Comstock silver king, this former girl's school and one-time gentlemen's club is now a popular forty-nine-room bed and breakfast hotel which has maintained its old world charm. It is handsomely furnished with English antiques that set off the oak paneling and inlaid floors. The small patio located off the garden can also accommodate seated guests.

CAPACITY: The Hotel can serve 65 guests for a seated meal in the Parlor and 85 in the Salon; both can hold up to 150 standing guests.

FEES & DEPOSITS: A $375 non-refundable security deposit is payable when you reserve your date. It will be applied towards the total charge. The rental fee for a reception is $750. If you or your party stay overnight, special rates apply. There is also a group rate available if multiple overnight accommodations are requested, minimum 10 rooms. Food service is provided.

SERVICES/AMENITIES:

Restaurant Services: no

Catering: provided

Parking: valet recommended

Overnight Accommodations: 49 guestrooms

Kitchen Facilities: n/a
Tables & Chairs: provided
Linens, Silver, etc.: provided
Restrooms: wca
Dance Floor: yes

RESTRICTIONS:
Alcohol: BYO, corkage $3–4/bottle
Smoking: allowed
Music: amplified until 10:30pm

Telephone: pay phone
Outdoor Night Lighting: yes
Outdoor Cooking Facilities: no
Meeting Equipment: CBA
Cleanup: provided

Wheelchair Access: yes
Insurance: not required

ROCK & BOWL

1855 Haight Street
San Francisco, CA 94117
(415) 826-BOWL
Reserve for Events: 3–12 months in advance

This is one of those places you just have to experience. By day, it's a mild-mannered bowling alley. By night (Friday and Saturday, that is) it becomes the infamous, raucous and outrageous Rock & Bowl. TV monitors over each lane run nonstop rock videos long into the night. Music blasts from overhead speakers, making every cell in your body vibrate with heretofore unknown energy. And—people actually bowl! Celebrations here are nothing if not unique. Reserve a bunch of lanes, bring in some swell food and knock down those pins! Dancing is ok, talking loud is ok (and often required), and looking cool is de rigueur.

CAPACITY: This facility can hold 300 guests (4 is the minimum for a group reservation). With over 60 guests, you can reserve the entire facility.

FEES & DEPOSITS: The deposit for 3 or more lanes is $2/person. To reserve the entire facility, the deposit is 33% of the $1,000–2,500 rental fee, which varies with the day, time and league bowling schedules. Deposits are refundable and due when the reservation is confirmed. Fees include bowling lanes, shoes, balls and use of pool tables.

CANCELLATION POLICY: If lanes can be rebooked, the deposit is refunded.

AVAILABILITY: Year-round, every day from 10am–2am except Christmas day.

SERVICES/AMENITIES:
Restaurant Services: snack bar
Catering: BYO
Kitchen Facilities: CBA
Tables & Chairs: some provided
Linens, Silver, etc.: BYO
Restrooms: no wca

Parking: street, Kezar Stadium lot
Overnight Accommodations: no
Telephone: pay phones
Outdoor Night Lighting: access only
Outdoor Cooking Facilities: BYO
Cleanup: renter or provided, extra charge

Dance Floor: bowling areas

RESTRICTIONS:

Alcohol: provided, no BYO
Smoking: allowed
Music: amplified ok

Wheelchair Access: yes
Insurance: not required

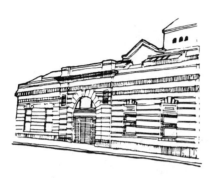

ROCOCO SHOWPLACE

165 Tenth Street
San Francisco, CA 94103
(415) 552-5600 Kate
Reserve for Events: 1–6 months in advance
Reserve for Meetings: 3–6 weeks in advance

Rococo's ranks high on our list. Its ample space, uptempo decor and tremendous flexibility make it a perfect place for celebrating. Rococo is housed in an historic, south-of-Market building which was rebuilt after the 1906 earthquake. The entry is an attractive mix of old brick wall and modern glass and the interior looks much like an art gallery, with lofty ceilings and skylights. Original brick archways blend with modern plasterwork to form two comfortable rooms where small groups can gather for intimate chats. The main event room, Rococo Showplace, is a fantastic party space. The interior walls are brick. Natural, ambient light filters in through a large skylight running the entire length of the unfinished wood ceiling. Paved in white marble with black detail along the border, the floor is a visual treat. In Rococo Showplace, you'll find faux colonnades, a massive white marble bar and an enormous old iron door above which hangs a terrific modern frieze of Trojan soldiers on horseback. Behind one balcony is a room with a pool table where guests can sharpen their cues or watch the activities below. The decor changes frequently—depending on which paintings are featured, the kind of events held and the whims of the owners. We think Rococo is a superb, one-of-a-kind event space. If you've got a sizable party, don't worry. It can accommodate large groups with lots of panache.

CAPACITY: 350 for a standing reception; 140 seated guests.

FEES & DEPOSITS: Rococo's entire space rents for $1,500 for day use, and $2,600 for evening use. For evening use, a $700 non-refundable deposit is due when reservations are booked (this is the maximum deposit required).

AVAILABILITY: Year-round, seven days a week, including holidays.

SERVICES/AMENITIES:

Restaurant Services: no
Catering: preferred list, flexible
Kitchen Facilities: limited
Tables & Chairs: provided
Linens, Silver, etc.: BYO
Restrooms: wca

Parking: street, nearby lot
Overnight Accommodations: no
Telephone: pay phone
Outdoor Night Lighting: access only
Outdoor Cooking Facilities: no
Cleanup: provided

Meeting Equipment: no
Dance Floor: yes

RESTRICTIONS:

Alcohol: BYO
Smoking: designated areas
Music: amplified within reason

Other: event planning

Wheelchair Access: yes
Insurance: extra liability required

SAN FRANCISCO MARITIME MUSEUM

SF Maritime National Historic Park
900 Beach Street at the foot of Polk
(415) 929-0202 Daria Booth
Reserve for Events: 1–2 months in advance
Reserve for Meetings: 1 month in advance

Across from Ghirardelli Square, in the heart of Aquatic Park, stands the Maritime Museum. It houses hundreds of artifacts, photographs and documents of West Coast seafaring history. The building was cleverly designed to resemble a cruise ship, even down to the nautical looking air vents. The Museum is superb for an event because it is a marvel of Art Deco style, terrazzo floors, murals and chrome detailing. Loaded with marine artifacts and historic memorabilia, the main exhibit room is terrific. Adjacent to it is the Museum's open-air veranda featuring artifacts from old ships, a nineteen-foot sloop *The Mermaid*, Benny Buffano sculptures and 1930s Art Deco tile murals along the wall facing the Bay. From here the views towards the harbor and Alcatraz are unobstructed, and the water so close you can hear the waves lapping against the sand. Do yourself a favor and ask for a tour. This is a real find.

CAPACITY: For a standing reception, the building can accommodate 400 guests. For a seated function, approximately 120 guests.

FEES & DEPOSITS: A $1,500 security deposit is required. The deposit is usually returned 2 weeks after the event. A minimum of $900 is needed to rent the Museum. The total fee is based on the length of your event and the number of guests. Work out the fee details with the National Maritime Museum Association. The fee includes a National Park Ranger on duty during your event. Non-profit rates are available.

CANCELLATION POLICY: All deposits are refundable 21 days prior to your event.

AVAILABILITY: Year-round, 5pm–midnight.

SERVICES/AMENITIES:

Restaurant Services: no
Catering: BYO
Kitchen Facilities: minimal
Tables & Chairs: BYO
Linens, Silver, etc.: BYO

Parking: on street, nearby garage
Overnight Accommodations: no
Telephone: pay phone
Outdoor Night Lighting: access only
Outdoor Cooking Facilities: no

Restrooms: wca

Dance Floor: no

RESTRICTIONS:

Alcohol: BYO

Smoking: outside only

Music: amplified until 11pm

Cleanup: caterer or renter

Meeting Equipment: none

Wheelchair Access: yes

Insurance: required

SAN FRANCISCO MART
Grand Lobby and Mart Exchange

1355 Market Street
San Francisco, CA 94103
(415) 381-2311 Bartenders Unlimited
Reserve for Events: 1–12 months in advance
Reserve for Meetings: 1 week–12 months in advance

A walk into the restored San Francisco Mart Grand Lobby is a walk into an Art Deco wonderland. Dramatic and glamorous, the central rotunda sparkles with unexpected colors, textures and lighting. Nine structural columns clad in polished stainless steel overlaid with an intricate brass pattern support a ceiling ringed by concentric circles of incandescent and neon lights. A trip up the escalator to the mezzanine gives you an overview of the space below and a fuller appreciation of the terrazzo floors, laid out in a complex star pattern. Two large rectangular areas on either side of the rotunda accommodate dining, presentations, and other event activities. One of these areas serves as an exhibition space which may be incorporated into your event. Up on the ninth floor, the Mart Exchange is a more intimate ballroom setting for meetings or parties. Soft pastel hues create a warm ambiance while Art Deco chandeliers and wall sconces add distinction. Controlled lighting allows you to define the mood. A sleek, fully-appointed bar, professional kitchen and a baby grand piano are just a few of the amenities the Mart offers. No matter what your event, The San Francisco Mart will leave an indelible impression.

CAPACITY: The Grand Lobby can hold 500 seated or 800 standing. The Mart Exchange can hold 275 seated or 500 standing.

MEETING ROOMS: The Mart Exchange is available for meetings.

FEES & DEPOSITS: The Mart Exchange rents for $1,200. The Grand Lobby rental fee is based on the number of guests: $2,000 for up to 500, and $500 more for each additional 100 guests. The maximum fee is $3,500 for 800 guests. A refundable deposit of 50% of the rental fee is due when reservations are confirmed. A refundable $1,000 security and cleaning deposit, certificate of insurance plus the balance of the rental fees are payable 10 days prior to the function. Extra security is occasionally required.

CANCELLATION POLICY: With 90 days' notice, a full refund; with 60 days', a 50% refund. For December dates, no deposits are refunded. The security and cleaning deposit is usually refunded.

AVAILABILITY: Year-round, daily. Weekday, daytime restrictions may apply to the Grand Lobby.

SERVICES/AMENITIES:

Restaurant Services: no
Catering: preferred list or BYO
Kitchen Facilities: prep only
Tables & Chairs: caterer
Linens, Silver, etc.: caterer
Restrooms: wca
Dance Floor: terrazzo floor

Parking: on-site, secured garage extra charge, behind building, free
Overnight Accommodations: no
Telephone: pay phones
Outdoor Night Lighting: no
Outdoor Cooking Facilities: no
Cleanup: caterer and Mart
Meeting Equipment: podium, screen, limited PA

RESTRICTIONS:

Alcohol: provided or BYO
Smoking: allowed
Music: amplified ok

Wheelchair Access: yes
Insurance: certificate required
Other: no open flames

THE SAN FRANCISCO SPIRIT
Pacific Marine Yacht Charters

Berthed at Pier 39, East Basin
San Francisco, CA 94133
(415) 788-9100
Reserve for Events: 1–9 months in advance
Reserve for Meetings: 1 week–9 months in advance

In June 1991, Pacific Marine Yacht Charters christened their luxurious, 150-foot custom-built flagship, the San Francisco Spirit, making it the fourth member of its elegant fleet. Warm neutral tones, plush furnishings and tasteful appointments in glass, brass, marble and stone provide a sophisticated backdrop for a special event. Two spacious dance floors, three bars, a central sound system, grand staircase and attractive interior are just some of the amenities this yacht has to offer. Add Pacific Marine's impeccable service and award-winning cuisine, and you have an exceptional choice for entertaining on the bay.

CAPACITY: The San Francisco Spirit can accommodate up to 700 guests for receptions. Formal seated service is available for 300 in the Main Salon, 180 in the Upper Salon and 30 in the VIP Lounge.

FEES & DEPOSITS: For the entire vessel, a $4,000 deposit is required when you reserve your date; for half the vessel, $3,000. Half of the food and beverage cost is due 30 days prior to your event.

	Weekdays (before 6pm)	*Weekdays (after 6pm)*	*Weekends/Holidays*
Full boat rental fees are:	$1,800/hr	$2,200/hr	$2,700/hr
Half boat rental fees are:	1,000/hr	1,200/hr	1,500/hr

A 3-hour minimum rental is required, 4 hours on Saturday evenings and holidays. A guaranteed guest count is required 7 days prior to departure and the remaining balance is due 5 days prior to your event.

CANCELLATION POLICY: With 90 days' notice, 85% of the reservation deposit will be refunded; with less notice, the deposit will be forfeited.

AVAILABILITY: Anytime, no limits.

SERVICES/AMENITIES:

Restaurant Services: no

Catering: provided, no BYO

Kitchen Facilities: on board

Tables & Chairs: provided

Linens, Silver, etc.: provided

Restrooms: 16, 1 wca

Dance Floor: yes

Meeting Equipment: podium, microphone

Parking: Pier 39 garage, validations available

Overnight Accommodations: no

Telephone: emergency cellular phone & radio

Outdoor Night Lighting: yes

Outdoor Cooking Facilities: no

Cleanup: provided

Other: event coordination

RESTRICTIONS:

Alcohol: provided, corkage fee $7/bottle

Smoking: outside only

Music: amplified ok

Wheelchair Access: yes

Insurance: not required

SAN FRANCISCO ZOO

One Zoo Road

(415) 753-7171

Reserve for Events: 1–2 months in advance

Reserve for Meetings: 2–26 weeks in advance

The San Francisco Zoo? Oh yes, you can rent this place, too! The Aviary, Children's Zoo, Insect Zoo, Lion's House, Terrace Cafe, Wildlife Theater and Carrousel plus areas that can be tented are all available for private functions. With Zebra Train Tours, theme parties and 'Behind the Scene' tours, your business associates, friends and family will have a wonderful time.

In addition, the Zoo hosts children's birthday parties, providing all eating utensils, cups, juice, ice cream and cake. They also throw in party hats, favors and tickets for a Carrousel ride for each child. The price includes admission to the Zoo and Children's Zoo. By prearrangement, box lunches can be provided. What a deal!

CAPACITY: Varies from 10–500 people. Call for specific area capacities.

FEES & DEPOSITS: For special events the rental fees vary. Picnic areas are $50 and up. Call for specific rates. A deposit of 25% of the rental fee is required. Children's birthday parties cost $7.50/child and $12.50/adult.

CANCELLATION POLICY: The deposit is refunded in full if you cancel 30 days prior to your function.

AVAILABILITY: Year-round; special events can be arranged for day or evening hours.

SERVICES/AMENITIES:

Restaurant Services: no
Catering: provided or BYO
Kitchen Facilities: minimal
Tables & Chairs: BYO, some provided
Linens, Silver, etc.: BYO, some provided
Restrooms: wca
Dance Floor: yes

Parking: on street
Overnight Accommodations: no
Telephone: pay phones
Outdoor Night Lighting: in certain areas
Outdoor Cooking Facilities: CBA, approval needed
Cleanup: whoever caters event
Meeting Equipment: no

RESTRICTIONS:

Alcohol: BYO
Smoking: restricted
Music: restricted

Wheelchair Access: yes
Insurance: liability required

SHARON ARTS CENTER AND CARROUSEL

Golden Gate Park
San Francisco, CA 94117
(415) 666-7035
Reserve for Events: 3–12 months in advance
Reserve for Meetings: 2 weeks–12 months in advance

The Sharon Arts Center is a stately, historic stone building that's located not too far from the bocci ball lanes. It was originally used as a "mother's" building for families visiting Golden Gate Park. Adjacent to the Carrousel, it has recently been renovated and features a large room with cathedral ceiling, chandeliers, wood paneling and French doors that open onto a balcony overlooking the park and children's play area.

The Herschel Spillman Carrousel, circa 1912–1914, was painstakingly restored from 1977–1984. Originally carved in upstate New York, it was housed in several parks on the West Coast before coming here where it continues to be one of Golden Gate Park's extraordinary highlights. It was also the main carrousel of the 1939 Exposition World's Fair on Treasure Island. A Gebruder band organ made in Germany in the 1920s provides lively musical accompaniment. Do something really different! Rent it as wonderful entertainment for your guests—young and old, alike. Tents can be set up in front of the Carrousel for large outdoor receptions. The Carrousel is available only in the evenings after 5pm, when it's not open to the public.

CAPACITY: The Sharon Center can hold 80 seated or 100 standing. The Carrousel can accommodate 70 seated on the fanciful animals!

FEES & DEPOSITS: 10% of all fees are required as a deposit to secure your date. 30 days prior to your event, the balance of the refundable security/cleaning deposit is required: Sharon Center $150; Carrousel $750. The deposit is normally returned after the event if the premises are clean and undamaged. The base rental fee for the Sharon Arts Center is 5 hours for $250. Each additional hour is $50. The Carrousel is $200–500 for 4 hours, with rates depending on staff availability. A private security guard is required for Carrousel use, usually $20/hour.

CANCELLATION POLICY: If you cancel 30 days prior to your event, you will receive 90% of your deposit; if you cancel less than 10 working days in advance, no refund.

AVAILABILITY: The Sharon Center: Saturdays 6pm–11pm; Sundays 10am–4pm and 5pm–11pm. The Carrousel: any day after 5pm.

SERVICES/AMENITIES:

Restaurant Services: no

Catering: BYO

Kitchen Facilities: ample

Tables & Chairs: provided

Linens, Silver, etc.: BYO

Restrooms: wca in Sharon Center

Dance Floor: yes

Parking: park lots

Overnight Accommodations: no

Telephone: pay phone

Outdoor Night Lighting: access only

Outdoor Cooking Facilities: no

Cleanup: caterer or renter

Meeting Equipment: no

RESTRICTIONS:

Alcohol: BYO

Smoking: no

Insurance: sometimes required

Wheelchair Access: yes

Music: amplified inside only, requires permit outside

SHERATON PALACE HOTEL

2 New Montgomery Street
San Francisco, CA 94105
(415) 392-8600
Reserve for Events: 6–9 months in advance
Reserve for Meetings: 3–6 months in advance

There is nothing quite like the Sheraton Palace. Following a stunning multi-million dollar renovation, it has reclaimed its role as San Francisco's premier historic hotel. If you've dreamed of an elegant function in a royal setting, the Palace is the perfect location. You can host a tea in the world renowned Garden Court, one of the most exquisite rooms we've ever seen. The magnificent domed ceiling of pale yellow leaded glass floods the restaurant with warm natural light, and the original crystal chandeliers add old-world sparkle. The Ralston Room, which served as The Men's Grille at the turn of the century is reminiscent of a Gothic cathedral. This room soothes with its cream, gold and jewel tones. For large events, the Grand Ballroom lives up to its name. English classical in style, its charm comes from unique lace plasterwork, and shimmering chandeliers decorated with carved crystal pears and apples. The Gold Ballroom is the most popular reception site. Once the Hotel's music room, it has the feel of a ballroom in a manor house. Tall draped windows highlight the intricate lattice plasterwork and gold leaf detailing throughout. An antique orchestra balcony, grand fireplace, and rich blue and gold carpet complete the lovely decor. For smaller receptions, the French Parlor features stained glass skylights, crystal chandeliers, marble fireplaces and a birds-eye view of the Garden Court ceiling that is guaranteed to take your breath away. And for a more contemporary space, the Sunset Court accommodates intimate gatherings beneath an arched glass dome. Business clients will appreciate the three wood-paneled boardrooms and numerous modern meeting rooms, some with built-in, state-of-the-art audio-visual equipment. A full service Business Center is also available to provide for all AV and basic office needs. Grand and gorgeous, the Sheraton Palace Hotel is a place worth visiting even if you're not planning an event. Come and see for yourself why it's been a San Francisco landmark for over 100 years.

CAPACITY:

	Seated	*Standing*		*Seated*	*Standing*
Grand Ballroom	600	1,000	French Parlor	100	150
Gold Ballroom	275	600	Sunset Court	300	600
Ralston Room	275	600	Boardrooms	12–20	—

MEETING ROOMS: All of the areas listed above, as well as 14 additional rooms that can accommodate 10–250 people, are available for meetings.

FEES & DEPOSITS: For events, a deposit in the amount of 10% of the estimated cost is required with the signed contract. The balance is due 48 hours prior to the event. Per person food service rates are: $25–35 for luncheons, $38–50 for dinners and $50–70 for buffets. Tax and a 17% service charge are additional. Call for meeting rate information.

CANCELLATION POLICY: To be discussed with the Hotel.

AVAILABILITY: Year-round, every day.

SERVICES/AMENITIES:

Restaurant Services: yes
Catering: provided
Kitchen Facilities: n/a
Tables & Chairs: provided
Linens, Silver, etc.: provided (specialty linens avail.)
Restrooms: wca
Dance Floor: yes

Parking: valet CBA at a charge, or lot
Overnight Accommodations: 550 guestrooms
Telephone: pay phones
Outdoor Night Lighting: access only
Outdoor Cooking Facilities: no
Cleanup: provided
Meeting Equipment: full range

RESTRICTIONS:

Alcohol: provided, corkage $10/bottle
Smoking: allowed
Music: amplified ok

Wheelchair Access: yes
Insurance: provided by Hotel

THE SHERMAN HOUSE

2160 Green Street between Webster & Fillmore
San Francisco, CA 94123
(415) 563-3600
Reserve for Events: 3 months in advance
Reserve for Meetings: 1 month in advance

This tastefully and artfully decorated house, originally built in 1876 by the founder of the Sherman/ Clay Music Company, opened as a hotel seven years ago and is rated one of the top ten hotels in the Zagat U.S. Hotel Survey. It's well known for its fine dining, providing an intimate atmosphere with impeccable service—just the right combination for a sophisticated business function or special party. The Sherman House butlers escort guests into the house through a separate entry for private functions. Guests then move on to the music room featuring wood paneling, fireplace, leaded glass skylight, mirrors and a double staircase that descends into the room from an upper level gallery. The musicians' balcony, overlooking the music room, is a perfect spot for a harpist, guitarist or trio. The lush gardens in the back of the house are quite lovely, with a cobbled courtyard, gazebo and fountain. If you want a place that is really private and quiet, ask to see the Garden Suite. These quarters can be rented separately and come with private salon, bedroom, bath and two private gardens. The Sherman House staff offers personal, attentive service and will help you with all the party planning details.

CAPACITY: 100 for an hors d'oeuvres reception, carried by silver tray butler service; 60 seated.

FEES & DEPOSITS: A refundable deposit is required to secure your event date. The rental fee for use of the music room and gallery is $500–2,000 depending on the number of guests, season and time of day. Use of the Garden Suite is $750. Food service costs range from hors d'oeuvres receptions $25-55/person to seated functions ranging from $55–80/person. Service charge of 20% and tax are added to the final bill. The balance is due at least 30 days prior to your function.

CANCELLATION POLICY: Cancellation is required 30 days prior to your event to receive a refund and 45 days prior to your party during peak periods.

AVAILABILITY: Not restricted. Guests must vacate the premises by 10pm during the week, 10:30pm on weekends.

SERVICES/AMENITIES:

Restaurant Services: yes
Catering: provided, no BYO
Kitchen Facilities: n/a
Tables & Chairs: provided
Linens, Silver, etc.: provided
Restrooms: wca
Meeting Equipment: CBA

Parking: valet CBA
Overnight Accommodations: 14 guestrooms
Telephone: house phone
Outdoor Night Lighting: access only
Outdoor Cooking Facilities: no
Cleanup: provided
Dance Floor: no

RESTRICTIONS:
Alcohol: provided, WBC only
Smoking: outside only
Music: no amplified

Wheelchair Access: yes
Insurance: not required

SHOWPLACE DESIGN CENTER

2 Henry Adams Street
San Francisco, CA 94103
(415) 864-1500
Reserve for Events: 3–6 months in advance
Reserve for Meetings: 1 week–12 months in advance

Built in the early 1900s, this historic, versatile Cabaret encompasses an Italian piazza setting accented by natural teak wood furnishings. Floor-to-ceiling, multi-paned windows flood the reception area with natural light. State-of-the-art club sound and stage lighting create the mood. Guests can enjoy the festivities from the main dining area as well as the balcony level.

The Showplace Penthouse features spectacular views of the San Francisco skyline and the Bay Bridge from a glass-enclosed space and a rooftop terrace. In the evening, it's perfect for receptions, dining and dancing. During the day, it's a popular choice for meetings and luncheons.

CAPACITY, FEES & DEPOSITS:

Area	*Seated*	*Reception*	*Rental Fees*
Cabaret	250	500	$2,500*
Penthouse	up to 120	125	$850*

*The basic rental fee may vary depending on the specific details of your event.

A non-refundable deposit of 50% of the rental fee is required when the contract is submitted. The balance is due 30 days prior to the event. Fees include a house technician.

CANCELLATION POLICY: The fees and deposits can be applied toward another event within a 90-day period.

AVAILABILITY: Year-round. The Cabaret Monday–Thursday after 3pm, Sunday from 8am; no Friday or Saturday nights. The Penthouse every day from 8am.

SERVICES/AMENITIES:
Restaurant Services: no
Catering: in-house caterer or BYO w/approval, extra fee
Kitchen Facilities: minimal
Tables & Chairs: provided
Linens, Silver, etc.: BYO
Restrooms: wca

Parking: street, adjacent lot
Overnight Accommodations: no
Telephone: pay phones
Outdoor Night Lighting: access only
Outdoor Cooking Facilities: no
Cleanup: provided

Dance Floor: yes
Meeting Equipment: full AV

RESTRICTIONS:
Alcohol: provided, no BYO
Smoking: allowed
Music: amplified ok

Other: event coordination, technician

Wheelchair Access: limited
Insurance: certificate required

SOUTH BEACH BILLIARDS

270 Brannan Street
San Francisco, CA 94107
(415) 495-5939
Reserve for Events: 1 week-12 months in advance
Reserve for Meetings: 1 week in advance

Tired of parties where everyone just stands around with drink in hand making small talk? Why not try something fun, engaging and conducive to social interaction like...pool! You don't need to be an Olympic athlete to play pool, and whether you're on intimate terms with bank shots or have never wrapped your fingers around a pool cue, South Beach Billiards is a terrific place to play the game. Not only are their 37 tables in impeccable condition, they can provide an in-house pro to demonstrate trick shots, run tournaments or give basic lessons. While the standard pool hall may be cramped, smoky and a tad sleazy, South Beach is anything but. It's a spacious room with a 20-foot ceiling, cool gray-blue walls and a knock-out art exhibit that changes every six weeks. And because it was originally a licorice factory, it still has a high-powered ventilation system that keeps the air practically smoke-free. A red and white checkerboard ramp runs down the middle of the room, and if you like, it can be set up with tables for dining. The cafe adjacent to the pool tables offers additional space for seating. If your party is small, host it in the VIP Room. You'll have your own pool table, leather couch and, of course, privacy. And if you want a swell place to dance, the Special Event Room upstairs has the perfect set-up: DJ booth with dazzling sound system, convenient bar and plenty of space for trippin' the light fantastic. So next time you're wracking your brain to come up with a party idea that your guests won't expect and definitely won't forget, give South Beach Billiards a call.

CAPACITY:

Room	Seated	Standing	Room	Seated	Standing
Entire Room	—	500	Cafe	50	—
Ramp	80	—	Special Event Room	125	250
VIP Room	20	30			

MEETING ROOMS: The Cafe, VIP Room and Special Event Room are available for meetings.

FEES & DEPOSITS: A deposit of 25% of the anticipated total is required at the time of booking. The balance is due at the conclusion of the event. Reservations are accepted for 4 or more tables with a minimum play time of 3 hours. A guest count is required 72 working hours prior to the event. The whole downstairs rents for $600/hr, half for $200/hr. The VIP Room rents for $20/hr during the week and $25/hr Fri and Sat night. To rent part of the downstairs, tables are $10/hr weekdays, and $12/hr Fri and Sat after 7pm. The Special Event Room rents for $200/hr with a $600 maximum. A bar guarantee based on guest count is required. There is a $10,000 minimum for reserving the entire downstairs on a Fri or Sat night. Per person food service runs $7 for breakfast or desserts, $4.50 for snacks, $10 for deli selection, $12.50 for oyster bar and $20 for buffet. Tax and an 18% gratuity are additional.

CANCELLATION POLICY: A full refund will be given with 15 days' notice; a 50% refund with 7–14 days notice. With less notice the deposit is forfeit.

AVAILABILITY: Every day, noon–2am weekdays, 2pm–2am Sat and Sun. The Private and Special Event Rooms are available anytime, and other areas can be reserved during off hours by special arrangement. Note that guests must be 21 or over.

SERVICES/AMENITIES:

Restaurant Services: yes
Catering: select from list or BYO, extra fee
Kitchen Facilities: prep only
Tables & Chairs: CBA
Linens, Silver, etc.: caterer
Restrooms: wca downstairs only
Dance Floor: upstairs
Other: event coordination

Parking: large free lot
Overnight Accommodations: no
Telephone: pay phone
Outdoor Night Lighting: access only
Outdoor Cooking Facilities: no
Cleanup: caterer
Meeting Equipment: BYO or CBA, extra fee

RESTRICTIONS:

Alcohol: provided, no BYO
Smoking: allowed
Insurance: not required
Other: no food or drink on pool tables

Wheelchair Access: downstairs only
Music: amplified ok upstairs, downstairs if you rent entire floor

Prices and policies <u>do</u> change. Call each facility and confirm everything you read in Perfect Places.

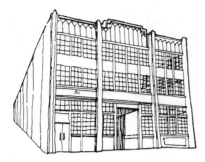

SPECTRUM GALLERY

511 Harrison Street (at First St.)
San Francisco, CA 94105
(415) 495-1111 Thomas Roedoc
Reserve for Events: 2 weeks in advance
Reserve for Meetings: 2 weeks in advance

Designed and built by an event professional, this spacious fine art gallery has a twenty-foot high wall of windows facing the entire downtown skyline. At night, the view sparkles with thousands of lights twinkling just four blocks away. Spectrum also offers almost every amenity you could want: a state-of-the-art lighting and dimming system; a whisper-clear sound system; huge restrooms, a 1,200-sq foot caterer's area and abundant free parking nearby. This gallery allows you to create your own environment: place the portable stage and dance floor where you wish, hang draperies for room separation or to black out the room for daytime projection. You can also move or remove the paintings and sculpture. As few as seventy-five or as many as four hundred can be seated comfortably, all in the same room. Located at the peak of Rincon Hill, Spectrum is just a few blocks from Moscone Convention Center, the financial District, and the bay. In addition to its many social uses, Spectrum can handle all types of business events, and product intros are their speciality.

CAPACITY: This facility can hold 75–400 seated guests (with stage and dance floor), 150–650 for a standing reception, up to 275 theater-style and 165 classroom-style.

FEES & DEPOSITS: A non-refundable deposit of 50% of the rental fee is due when reservations are confirmed. The balance is due 90 days prior to your event. Rental rates are $2,750 for evenings, $1,375 for daytime events and $1,750 for Sundays. A refundable $1,000 cleaning/damage deposit is due 10 days prior to your function. Rates during December are higher.

CANCELLATION POLICY: The deposits, other than the cleaning/damage deposit, are non-refundable. If the date can be rebooked, most of the deposit will be returned.

AVAILABILITY: Year-round, every day from 8am–2am.

SERVICES/AMENITIES:
Restaurant Services: no
Catering: any insured caterer
Kitchen Facilities: moderate
Tables & Chairs: provided
Linens, Silver, etc.: BYO
Restrooms: wca
Dance Floor: yes
Parking: abundant on-street

Overnight Accommodations: no
Telephone: pay phones
Outdoor Night Lighting: access only
Outdoor Cooking Facilities: no
Cleanup: caterer and Spectrum
Other: stage, riser, projection screen
Special: theatrical lighting and sound
Meeting Equipment: full range

RESTRICTIONS:
Alcohol: provided
Smoking: allowed
Music: amplified ok

Wheelchair Access: yes
Insurance: required, available

SS JEREMIAH O'BRIEN

Fort Mason
San Francisco, CA 94123
(415) 441-3101 Marci Hooper
Reserve for Events: 1–6 months in advance
Reserve for Meetings: 1–6 weeks in advance

This is America's last unaltered Liberty Ship. Out of more than 2,700 nearly identical ships, the Jeremiah O'Brien is the only known Liberty Ship that is in original and full operating condition! Preserved as a National Historic Landmark, the 441-foot long ship is now docked at Fort Mason and is available for Bay charter cruises, tours and special events. The forward gun tub and deck are great places to have toasts and serve hors d'oeuvres because the views of Alcatraz, Angel Island and Aquatic Park are sensational. This is a wonderful spot (especially if you're a World War II buff) and there is an additional bonus—during events, the ship's staff is available to give highly interesting tours of the multiple decks and machine rooms.

CAPACITY: 300 standing guests or 210 for seated functions.

FEES & DEPOSITS: A $125 cleaning deposit is required. There's a flat rental fee of $65–250 (depending on which space is reserved) plus an additional $3/person.

CANCELLATION POLICY: A 10-day advance notice is required for a full refund.

AVAILABILITY: 9:30am to midnight. No events on New Year's, Christmas, Easter or Thanksgiving holidays.

SERVICES/AMENITIES:
Restaurant Services: no
Catering: BYO
Kitchen Facilities: no
Tables & Chairs: provided
Linens, Silver, etc.: BYO
Restrooms: no wca
Dance Floor: yes

Parking: large lot
Overnight Accommodations: no
Telephone: office phone
Outdoor Night Lighting: yes
Outdoor Cooking Facilities: no
Cleanup: caterer
Meeting Equipment: no

RESTRICTIONS:
Alcohol: BYO
Smoking: outside preferred
Music: amplified until 11:30pm

Wheelchair Access: no
Insurance: sometimes required
Other: gangway entry steep & narrow

THE STANFORD COURT

905 California Street
San Francisco, CA 94108
(415) 989-3500
Reserve for Events: 1 week–1 year in advance
Reserve for Meetings: 1 week–1 year in advance

Conveniently located atop prestigious Nob Hill, this historic five-star hotel will transport you to an earlier era of gracious service and refined luxury. Enter through the elegant carriage courtyard, covered by a dramatic, Tiffany-style stained glass dome. The lobby evokes the 19th-century splendor of Nob Hill with Baccarat chandeliers, fine French antiques and wood paneling. Carrara marble floors, Oriental carpets, original artwork and collectibles such as an 1806 grandfather clock once owned by Napoleon add to the richness of the decor. For parties, the International Terrace just off the lobby offers a unique setting overlooking San Francisco's only cable car crossing and the downtown skyline. The award-winning Fournou's Ovens restaurant features four private dining rooms ideal for special luncheons and dinners. For large events, the hotel offers the Stanford Ballroom, sparkling with Baccarat chandeliers originally from Paris' Grand Hotel, and the India Suite, decorated with hand-painted murals depicting romantic scenes from India circa 1810. Three recently added executive dining rooms, featuring burlwood paneling, crystal chandeliers and state-of-the-art lighting, are available for smaller gatherings and business meetings.

CAPACITY:	*Room*	*Reception*	*Seated*
	Stanford Ballroom	800	550
	India Suite	275	200
	Telegraph Hill Room	40	30
	Russian Hill	50	40
	Nob Hill	90	70
	Fournou's Ovens Private Rooms (4)	—	10–24
	International Terrace	150	80

FEES & DEPOSITS: An advance deposit is payable when reservations are confirmed. The estimated food and beverage total and final guest count are due 3 days prior to the event. Per person rates: luncheons at $22, dinners at $32, buffets start at $32–46, and hors d'oeuvres at $10. Tax and a 15% gratuity are additional.

CANCELLATION POLICY: If the space(s) can be rebooked, the deposit will be refunded.

AVAILABILITY: Year-round, every day, anytime.

SERVICES/AMENITIES:

Restaurant Services: yes
Catering: provided, no BYO
Kitchen Facilities: n/a
Tables & Chairs: provided

Linens, Silver, etc.: provided
Restrooms: wca
Dance Floor: yes
Parking: valet

Overnight Accommodations: 400 guestrooms
Telephone: pay phones
Outdoor Night Lighting: access only
Meeting Equipment: CBA

RESTRICTIONS:
Alcohol: provided, no BYO
Smoking: designated areas
Music: amplified w/approval

Outdoor Cooking Facilities: no
Cleanup: provided
Other: event coordination, piano

Wheelchair Access: yes
Insurance: sometimes required
Other: no open flames

THE ST. FRANCIS HOTEL

335 Powell Street, Union Square
San Francisco, CA 94102
(415) 774-0126   Catering Manager
Reserve for Events: up to 9 months in advance
Reserve for Meetings: 3 months in advance

Named The Westin St. Francis in 1982, this famous San Francisco landmark has been the hotel of choice for internationally prominent guests since 1904. From royalty to presidents and society notables to Hollywood stars, The St. Francis has offered first class dining and lodging for almost a hundred years. This stately, twelve-story building facing Union Square was one of the few structures to survive the 1906 earthquake. Considerably damaged by fire, it was quickly refurbished using California's most skilled artists and craftsmen to recreate the ornate and opulent interior and many innovations were added to make it the most sophisticated hotel of its time. Marble Corinthian columns, paneled ceilings with gold leaf trim and crystal chandeliers are highlights of the newly restored Powell Street Lobby. A grand and impressive place, The St. Francis is more than qualified to host your special event or business function.

CAPACITY: The St. Francis has 26 rooms that can accommodate events. Here are a few:

Room	Seated	Reception
Grand Ballroom	1,000	1,500
Colonial Room	340	400
California Ballroom	450	600
4 Elizabethan Rooms (ea)	100–110	120–130
St. Francis Suite (3 sections)	100	100–200
Oz, Victor's, St. Francis Grill	*By Special Arrangement*	

MEETING ROOMS: 35,000 square feet of meeting rooms are conveniently located on the mezzanine and second floors of the hotel. The variety of rooms can easily handle a board meeting of 10 or an elegant seated banquet for 1,500.

FEES & DEPOSITS: A refundable $500–1,000 deposit is payable when you confirm your reservation and 100% of the estimated event total is due 1 week prior to the function. Deposits and fees vary with guest count, type of function and room(s) rented. The balance is invoiced, payable 30 days following the function. If food service is provided, rental fees are reduced. Per person rates: luncheons $23–50, dinners $34–70, hors d'oeuvres start at $10 and buffets range from $27–65. Tax and an 18% service charge are added to the final bill. If your party is staying here, be sure to ask for special room rates which are based on availability.

AVAILABILITY: Year-round, every day, anytime up to 2am.

SERVICES/AMENITIES:

Restaurant Services: yes
Catering: provided, no BYO
Kitchen Facilities: n/a
Tables & Chairs: provided
Linens, Silver, etc.: provided
Restrooms: wca
Dance Floor: yes
Parking: hotel garage or adjacent lots

Overnight Accommodations: 1,200 guestrooms
Telephone: pay phone
Outdoor Night Lighting: access only
Outdoor Cooking Facilities: no
Cleanup: provided
Other: event coordination, grand piano
Meeting Equipment: yes
Special: theme party coordination

RESTRICTIONS:

Alcohol: provided, WB corkage $12/bottle
Smoking: allowed
Music: amplified ok

Wheelchair Access: yes
Insurance: not required

ST. PAULUS CHURCH

950 Gough Street
San Francisco, CA 94102
(415) 673-8088
Reserve for Events: 1 month in advance
Reserve for Meetings: 1 month in advance

Often referred to as the "Wedding Cake Church" because of its ornate exterior detailing, St. Paulus Church has been a part of San Francisco's history for a century. With its soaring spires, triple arched portal and elegant rose window, St. Paulus is reminiscent of the Gothic cathedrals of Europe. The church's Hall is an unpretentious space for a wide variety of events: meetings, speaker forums, classes, parties and even square dancing! A high ceiling, creamy white walls and arched windows create a light, airy ambiance. Ficus trees in planters add a dash of greenery, and a stage is available for lectures, speeches and plays. During the 1906 quake, St. Paulus was within seconds of being dynamited to create a fire break. A frantic pastor begged firemen to try a hydrant on the corner, despite the fact that almost all water mains were broken. Much to the astonishment of everyone, the hydrant worked and the church was saved. Divine intervention? Maybe. Have your function here and who knows—the church's good luck might rub off on you.

CAPACITY: The Hall accommodates 250 seated and 450 standing.

FEES & DEPOSITS: A $500 fee covering a four-hour period is required at the time of booking. Additional time costs $50/hour, and must be arranged in advance. All fees must be paid two weeks prior to the event. The renter is responsible for removing any items they bring in; St. Paulus will clean the facility after the event.

CANCELLATION POLICY: With 90 days notice, all but $50 will be refunded. With 89-30 days notice, 50% of payments will be refunded. No refunds will be made if cancellation occurs less than 30 days from the event.

AVAILABILITY: The Hall can be reserved anytime.

SERVICES/AMENITIES:

Restaurant Services: no

Catering: provided or BYO with approval

Kitchen Facilities: CBA for fee

Tables & Chairs: provided

Linens, Silver, etc.: caterer or BYO

Restrooms: wca

Dance Floor: yes

Parking: on street, Opera Plaza

Overnight Accommodations: no

Telephone: pay phone

Outdoor Night Lighting: no

Outdoor Cooking Facilities: no

Cleanup: renter responsible for own items

Meeting equipment: no

RESTRICTIONS:

Alcohol: wine and beer ok, liquor license may be required for mixed drinks

Smoking: not allowed

Music: amplified ok

Wheelchair Access: CBA

Insurance: not required

Other: decorations restricted

THE TROCADERO
Sigmund Stern Grove Clubhouse

19th Ave. and Sloat Blvd.
San Francisco, CA 94116
(415) 666-7035   Recreation & Parks
Reserve for Events: 1–12 months in advance
Reserve for Meetings: 2 weeks–12 months in advance

In the middle of Stern Grove, approached from a lovely entry drive flanked by eucalyptus and stone walls, sits The Trocadero Clubhouse. This turn-of-the-century, two-story Victorian is available for special events and features a spacious veranda, river rock fireplace, hardwood floors, old fashioned bar and fully equipped industrial kitchen. Adjacent park amenities include a pond, redwood grove, bridge, meadow, outdoor stone fireplaces and picnic tables. In Stern Grove, you can ignore the fact that you're in urban San Francisco; this is an oasis in the heart of the City.

CAPACITY: The Trocadero can hold up to 150 guests for a standing reception and 125 for seated meals. The outdoor picnic area can accommodate 1,000 with seating for 100–150 guests.

FEES & DEPOSITS: The fees and a refundable cleaning/security deposit of $150 are due 30 days prior to your event. The rental fee is $300 for a 6-hour function on weekdays. From 5pm Friday to 11pm Sunday and holidays, the fee is $400.

CANCELLATION POLICY: If you cancel 30 days prior to your event, you will receive 90% of your deposit; if less than 10 working days in advance, no refund.

AVAILABILITY: Rental times are 10am–4pm and 5–11pm in 6-hour blocks any day of the week. Extended hours 9–10am and 11am–1pm can be arranged with advance notice.

SERVICES/AMENITIES:

Restaurant Services: no
Catering: BYO
Kitchen Facilities: moderate
Tables & Chairs: provided
Linens, Silver, etc.: BYO
Restrooms: wca
Dance Floor: yes
Meeting Equipment: no

Parking: 50–75 cars
Overnight Accommodations: no
Telephone: distant pay phone
Outdoor Night Lighting: yes
Outdoor Cooking Facilities: stone fireplaces
Cleanup: caterer
Other: wooded area and gardens nearby

RESTRICTIONS:

Alcohol: BYO
Smoking: allowed
Music: amplified until 11pm

Wheelchair Access: yes
Insurance: not required

THE WATTIS ROOM
At Davies Symphony Hall

201 Van Ness Avenue
San Francisco, CA 94102
(415) 552-4089
Reserve for Events: 1–6 months in advance

Most folks don't know that The Wattis Room, a private Club for major donors in Davies Symphony Hall, is available for social events. Well, luckily for us, it is. This is a space tucked away on the first floor, approached through the main doors on Grove Street. As you enter the room, you'll notice the large art pieces on the walls, rotating exhibits from the San Francisco Museum of Art. The lighting is subdued and the room's decor is sophisticated and understated. From private dinners to formal seated receptions, this location is versatile enough to handle any type of crowd.

CAPACITY: The Wattis Room can hold 100 seated guests or 200 guests for a reception.

FEES & DEPOSITS: No deposit is required. The $450 rental fee covers a 4-hour block. Rental includes a symphony staff member, flowers, piano and custodial services. Any time over 4 hours costs $100/hour. Food service is provided. Buffets range $15–25/person, luncheons start at $15/person, dinners at $20/person and hors d'oeuvres start at $6/person. Staff, table service equipment, tax and a 20% production charge are additional.

AVAILABILITY: Year-round, any day, anytime. Dates in June, July, August and Christmas holidays are more available because the Symphony is in recess. Overtime will be charged for functions past midnight.

SERVICES/AMENITIES:
Restaurant Services: no
Catering: in-house caterer, Creative Catering, has first right of refusal
Kitchen Facilities: fully equipped
Tables & Chairs: some provided
Linens, Silver, etc.: provided, extra fee
Dance Floor: CBA

Parking: Grove & Franklin garage
Overnight Accommodations: no
Telephone: pay phone
Outdoor Night Lighting: access only
Outdoor Cooking Facilities: no
Cleanup: provided
Meeting Equipment: easels, podium, platform

RESTRICTIONS:
Alcohol: provided, corkage $3.50–5/bottle corkage negotiable
Smoking: allowed
Music: amplified ok

Wheelchair Access: yes
Insurance: not required
Other: red wine at seated events only, votive candles only

1409 SUTTER

1409 Sutter St.
San Francisco, CA 94109
(415) 561-0855 or **(415) 561-0856**
Reserve for Events: 2 months in advance
Reserve for Meetings: 2–4 weeks in advance

You may think that 1409 Sutter is an odd name for an event site, but this is one address with a very long history. Built in 1881 by Theodore Payne, a forty-niner who made his fortune in business, his house is one of San Francisco's Victorian treasures, surviving both the 1906 earthquake and subsequent fire. If you're coming for a site visit, slow down and look carefully for the address which is partially screened by large trees. From the ornate, wrought iron fence encircling the front yard to the colorful mosaic landing at the foot of impressive front doors, 1409 Sutter is a great example of 1880 architecture. As you enter the formal, deep burgundy foyer with high oak wainscotting, you'll immediately notice the fifteen foot ceilings, windows with stained glass panels at the top and inlaid hardwood floors. The foyer leads directly into the Great Hall and the Parlor. Both are large spaces which can separately or together accommodate receptions, fundraisers, corporate or social events. The Great Hall is a very large room with chandeliers, fireplace and a massive oak staircase. The Parlor is slightly smaller with a window alcove perfect for a band setup. Also on the event floor are the Main Bar, a room with a long, dark mahogany bar and lovely, intricate patterned wallpaper and the Red Room Bar, which has striking cranberry wallpaper and a small bar. Around the corner is the Atrium, which has floor-to-ceiling glass at one end, which makes it the lightest room in the house. Downstairs, there's another room for meetings and seminars. The third floor contains a professional kitchen which supports an in-house chef, available for all functions. Other caterers can be selected from a preferred list. If you're looking for a spacious mansion in San Francisco to host your next event, this is a new addition we recommend you preview.

CAPACITY: The entire main floor 150 seated guests; for a reception, 275 guests. Downstairs meeting room, 50 max. theater style; less if seated at tables.

FEES & DEPOSITS: Rental rates range from $100–2,000 based on guest count, hours and season. 10% of anticipated costs are required as a deposit to hold your date. The rental fee balance is payable 60 days prior to the event plus a $100–500 refundable security deposit.

CANCELLATION POLICY: With 45 days' notice, you will receive a refund less a $50 cancellation fee. Food cancellations within 72 hours of the function will incur a 50% charge of quoted food cost.

SERVICES/AMENITIES:

Restaurant Services: no
Catering: provided or select from list
Kitchen Facilities: professional
Tables & Chairs: provided, extra fee

Parking: on street, nearby garages, valet CBA
Overnight Accommodations: no
Telephone: pay phones
Outdoor Night Lighting: access only

Linens, Silver, etc.: provided, extra fee
Restrooms: wheelchair access
Dance Floor: yes
Other: bar service available

RESTRICTIONS:
Alcohol: wine & hard alcohol provided,
corkage fee $7/bottle
Music: amplified ok until 11pm

Outdoor Cooking Facilities: no
Cleanup: caterer
Meeting Equipment: some provided

Wheelchair Access: yes
Insurance: proof of liability may be required
Smoking: outside only

Half Moon Bay

DOUGLAS BEACH HOUSE

Miramar Beach
Half Moon Bay, CA 94018
(415) 726-4143
Reserve for Events: 1 week–1 year in advance
Reserve for Meetings: 1 week–1 year in advance

You can't get much closer to the ocean than this. On a secluded stretch of coast just north of Half Moon Bay lies the Douglas Beach House, otherwise known as The Bach Dancing and Dynamite Society which is famous for its concerts. It's actually a rambling complex of a house with recital/music hall, decks and dining rooms. The proprietor, Pete Douglas, is well known for his jazz and classical programs presented regularly on Sundays. Saturdays and weekdays are set aside for private parties or business meetings. The decor has been described as "comfy-funky in that rustic Northern California style of hanging ferns, dark wood and stained glass." The multiple decks and ocean vistas make this a great place to have a social gathering, special event or an out-of-the-ordinary business function.

CAPACITY: The dining area can hold 95 guests for seated meals. The entire facility can accommodate up to 150 for a standing reception.

MEETING ROOMS: The meeting room can accommodate 80 guests.

FEES & DEPOSITS: For social events, a non-refundable deposit of half the total estimated rental fee is due on confirmation. The rental fee is $800–1,200, depending on the date, time and number of guests. For weekday meetings, the rental fee is $300.

CANCELLATION POLICY: Fees will be refunded only if the space can be rebooked on the event date.

AVAILABILITY: Year-round. Parties are scheduled for Saturdays 2pm–7pm, or 3pm–8pm; and occasional Friday nights may be scheduled, if available. Meetings can be held weekdays.

SERVICES/AMENITIES:

Restaurant Services: no
Catering: BYO
Kitchen Facilities: ample
Tables & Chairs: provided
Linens, Silver, etc.: BYO
Restrooms: no wca
Dance Floor: yes

Parking: parking lot
Overnight Accommodations: no
Telephone: pay phone
Outdoor Night Lighting: yes
Outdoor Cooking Facilities: BYO
Cleanup: provided
Meeting Equipment: yes

RESTRICTIONS:

Alcohol: BYO, no kegs
Smoking: allowed
Music: amplified ok

Wheelchair Access: limited
Insurance: not required

MILL ROSE INN

615 Mill Street
Half Moon Bay, CA 94019
(415) 726-9794
Reserve for Events: 8–12 months in advance
Reserve for Meetings: 1–3 weeks in advance

The Mill Rose Inn is an outstanding location for business retreats or seminars. With its English country garden setting, dormers and bay window alcoves overlooking the garden, this venue offers a first-rate experience. Framed by a sensational floral palette with hundreds of roses in bloom, the gardens and courtyards offer intimate spaces for meetings. For outdoor, informal get-togethers, the flagstone courtyard behind the Inn, sheltered by a handsome maple and embraced by multi-color flowers, is especially nice. Inside, every room is appealing. The Conference Room, which has 10 sets of French doors overlooking the garden, is light and fresh, with rose carpets, fireplace and decorative wallpaper. The library and parlor make excellent break-out spaces. The parlor is warm and inviting with lots of color and appointments that reflect attention to detail. The library is a small jewel-of-a-room that features a beautifully painted fireplace and window alcove with views the blooms outside. For overnight guests, the 6 guestrooms have private phones, baths and separate entrances. Most feature bay windows, tv's and fireplaces. There's even a 7-person jacuzzi for groups which want to relax after a long day. For a business get-away, you couldn't pick a lovelier spot. And you won't have to worry about anything—the Inn will take care of all the details.

CAPACITY: The Conference Room accommodates up to 35 guests.

FEES & DEPOSITS: Groups have exclusive use of the facility. The rental rate, $60–80/person, varies depending on the selection of A/V equipment, continental or full breakfast, deli or full lunch, unlimited beverage service, wine and cheese or high tea service.

CANCELLATION POLICY: No refunds. If you cancel, credit can be applied towards another function.

AVAILABILITY: Year-round, any day in an 8-hour block, starting at 8am.

SERVICES/AMENITIES:

Restaurant Services: no
Catering: BYO or select from preferred list
Kitchen Facilities: ample
Tables & Chairs: provided
Linens, Silver, etc.: some provided
Restrooms: no wca
Meeting Equipment: yes
Special: event coordination, floral arrangements, piano

Dance Floor: garden patio
Parking: on and off street
Overnight Accommodations: 6 guestrooms
Telephone: house & guest phones
Outdoor Night Lighting: yes
Cleanup: provided
Outdoor Cooking Facilities: BBQs

RESTRICTIONS:

Alcohol: BYO
Smoking: outside only
Music: amplified ok

Wheelchair Access: limited
Insurance: recommended

STRAWBERRY RANCH

Redondo Beach Rd. at Highway 1
Half Moon Bay, CA 94019
(415) 726-5840
Reserve for Meetings: 3 days–3 months in advance

Strawberry Ranch is a bit off the beaten path, but well worth the effort if you're looking for a unique retreat or mini-conference environment. Follow the bumpy and largely unpaved Redondo Beach Road to the end and turn left. Sitting by itself, within a hundred yards of the ocean, is an attractive, two-story gray and blue wood structure with decks and garden. The original building was constructed in the early 1900s and has seen a colorful past, from rum runners during prohibition to military operations through World War II. Remodeled and restored, it provides unobstructed panoramic views of the ocean through wall-to-wall windows while getting down to business in a comfortable and casual workshop setting. Strawberry Ranch offers its guests an outstanding oceanfront location with quiet and privacy, away from phones and the bustle of the office.

CAPACITY: Strawberry Ranch can accommodate up to 50 guests.

FEES & DEPOSITS: Half the estimated cost of the conference is due when reservations are confirmed. The rental fee is $55/person which includes meeting space, continental breakfast, buffet lunch, all beverages throughout the day, all conference-related equipment, tax and gratuity. For the upstairs room, the minimum rental cost is $1,100 for up to 20 guests. The fee for each additional guest is $55. Dinners and hors d'oeuvres, wine, beer and BBQ events can be arranged.

CANCELLATION POLICY: With 30 days' notice, the deposit is fully refundable.

AVAILABILITY: Year-round, 8am–9pm. Closed the last 2 weeks of December.

SERVICES/AMENITIES:

Restaurant Services: no
Catering: provided, no BYO
Kitchen Facilities: n/a
Tables & Chairs: provided
Linens, Silver, etc.: provided
Restrooms: no wca
Meeting Equipment: full range

Dance Floor: no
Parking: large lot
Overnight Accommodations: no
Telephone: house phones
Outdoor Night Lighting: CBA
Cleanup: provided
Outdoor Cooking Facilities: no

RESTRICTIONS:

Alcohol: provided, corkage $6/bottle
Smoking: outside only
Music: amplified ok

Wheelchair Access: limited
Insurance: required

Montara

POINT MONTARA LIGHTHOUSE

16th Street at Highway 1
Montara, CA 94037
(415) 728-7177 (7:30–9:30am, 4:30–9:30pm)
Reserve for Events: 3–6 months in advance
Reserve for Meetings: 2–3 months in advance

Time may actually have stopped here. Twenty-five miles from San Francisco off Highway 1, the picturesque Point Montara Lighthouse occupies a phenomenal location right above the ocean. Built here because several ships ran aground at Point Montara in the 1860s, the light house started as a fog station in 1875. In 1900 a red oil lantern was added and a fresnel lens followed. In 1928 the lighthouse took its present form. Now a youth hostel operated by a non-profit group, the lighthouse and an appealing mix of modern and restored turn-of-the-century buildings provide an unusual environment for business retreats, community events and workshops. Much of it is similar to a village right out of the 1880s. In between the old lighthouse and the largest Victorian structure, is a lush rectangular lawn dotted by venerable cypress trees and surrounded by a white picket fence. Pollyanna would be right at home here. This is a place where old fashioned picnics or family reunions are appropriate. Get-togethers can take place on the lawn or at the ocean's edge. Views of the rugged coastline are magnetic, and November through April, migrating whales can be spotted from shore. If you'd like a glimpse of the past century, this garden setting will take you back.

CAPACITY: Maximum 50 guests.

FEES & DEPOSITS: A $100–300 refundable rental fee (based on the number of guests and the length of stay) is due at the time of booking. A $100 refundable damage deposit is also required 30 days prior to the event.

CANCELLATION POLICY: With 30 days' notice, the deposit is refunded.

AVAILABILITY: Year-round, daily 10am–4pm.

SERVICES/AMENITIES:

Restaurant Services: no
Catering: BYO
Kitchen Facilities: fully equipped
Tables & Chairs: provided
Linens, Silver, etc.: BYO
Restrooms: wca
Dance Floor: inside CBA
Meeting Equipment: no

Parking: large lot
Overnight Accommodations: 13 guestrooms, space for 30 guests
Telephone: pay phone
Outdoor Night Lighting: access only
Outdoor Cooking Facilities: BYO or BBQ CBA
Cleanup: caterer or renter

RESTRICTIONS:

Alcohol: use limited
Smoking: outside only
Music: amplified until 3pm

Wheelchair Access: yes
Insurance: sometimes required
Other: no pets

Need a caterer, cake maker, florist? The Service Directory starting on page 614 features the best in the business.

Belvedere

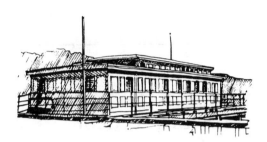

CHINA CABIN

54 Beach Road
Belvedere, CA 94920
(415) 435-2251 Beverly Bastian
(415) 435-1853 Landmarks Society
Reserve for Events: 10 days in advance
Reserve for Meetings: 10 days in advance

In 1866, the Pacific Steamship Company commissioned W.M.Webb to construct a sidewheel steamer. Unfortunately, with a wood hull, the ship was destined for a short career and was burned for scrap metal in 1886. The China Cabin, the First Class social salon, was removed intact from the ship and set on pilings in the Belvedere Cove. The Cabin consists of a large room and two small state rooms. Its plain exterior belies the ornate and regal appointments inside. This place is impressive. The walls and domed ceiling are panels of elaborately carved wood that have been painted a crisp white and highlighted with gold leaf. Along the sides of the Cabin are a series of small, delicately etched glass windows; handsome crystal chandeliers hang at each end of the room. The Cabin also has decks on three sides that have wonderful views of the San Francisco skyline and boats of the nearby yacht harbor. The China Cabin offers a glimpse of old world elegance and attention to detail; the result is a rich, sophisticated appearance that makes this a very unique setting for a special event or corporate function.

CAPACITY: The Cabin can hold up to 55 standing or 48 seated guests. The outdoor deck allows for 65 guests during summer months.

FEES & DEPOSITS: A $100 deposit and a $250 refundable damage deposit are required when you make your reservation. The rental fee is $520 for a 5-hour minimum rental block and $100 for each additional hour. The total fee is due 30 days prior to your party.

CANCELLATION POLICY: Should you cancel 30 days before the event, your deposit will be refunded less a $50 administrative fee.

AVAILABILITY: Any day, anytime until midnight, except Wednesday and Sunday afternoons from April–October.

SERVICES/AMENITIES:

Restaurant Services: no
Catering: BYO, must be approved
Kitchen Facilities: no
Tables & Chairs: 2 tables, chairs available
Linens, Silver, etc.: available
Restrooms: wca
Dance Floor: yes

Parking: CBA
Overnight Accommodations: no
Telephone: house phone
Outdoor Night Lighting: deck only
Outdoor Cooking Facilities: no
Cleanup: caterer
Meeting Equipment: no

RESTRICTIONS:

Alcohol: BYO
Smoking: not allowed indoors or on deck
Music: no amplified

Wheelchair Access: yes
Insurance: proof of personal coverage required
Other: no rice, seeds, confetti or petals; decorations restricted

Mill Valley

THE MILL VALLEY OUTDOOR ART CLUB

1 West Blithedale
Mill Valley, CA
(415) 383-2582
Reserve for Events: 12 months in advance
Reserve for Meetings: 3–6 months in advance

The Outdoor Art Club, located in downtown Mill Valley, is one of Marin's favorite event spots. You enter through a wooden arch into a restful garden patio that immediately removes you from the bustle of every day life. Centered in the large patio is a sprawling grand oak that provides a canopy, allowing dappled light to filter through. The flowers and other landscaping add to the serenity of this outdoor space. The clubhouse, designed in 1904 by Bernard Maybeck, displays his trademark peaked roof line. Inside, the main hall is spacious and majestic with a very high ceiling of dark exposed beams. Windows across the south side lighten the room and can be opened to admit breezes. There's a large stage at one end of the clubhouse for a dance band and a smaller room, running the full length of the clubhouse, which is perfect for a lavish buffet. There's no question why the Outdoor Art Club is so popular—this is a great location.

CAPACITY: The facility can hold up to 200 standing or 120 seated guests. The Sun Room holds an additional 40 seated guests. Various rooms can be used for meetings and can accommodate 40–200 people.

FEES & DEPOSITS: For events, a refundable deposit of half the rental fee is required to reserve a date. The remaining half is due 10 days before your function. The Club's rental fee is $1,200. A security deposit of $500 is also required and is refunded after the keys are returned. Call for rate information regarding meetings.

CANCELLATION POLICY: The deposit is refunded only if the date can be rebooked.

AVAILABILITY: Weekends 8am–1am. Weekdays are negotiable.

SERVICES/AMENITIES:

Restaurant Services: no
Catering: BYO

Parking: street only
Overnight Accommodations: no

Kitchen Facilities: ample
Tables & Chairs: most provided
Linens, Silver, etc.: some provided
Restrooms: wca
Dance Floor: yes
Meeting Equipment: BYO

RESTRICTIONS:
Alcohol: BYO
Smoking: allowed
Music: amplified until midnight, indoors only

Telephone: pay phone
Outdoor Night Lighting: yes
Outdoor Cooking Facilities: no
Cleanup: caterer
Other: caretaker provided

Wheelchair Access: yes
Insurance: not required

MOUNTAIN HOME INN

810 Panoramic Highway
Mill Valley, CA 94941
(415) 381-9000
Reserve for Events: 1–6 months in advance
Reserve for Meetings: 2–6 weeks in advance

Perched on the eastern slope of Mt. Tamalpais is a modern wooden structure with spectacular views of Marin, San Francisco Bay and Mt. Diablo. The decor in Mountain Home Inn's main dining room is simple, but elegant. Furnishings and rugs are in muted pastels and a large stone fireplace enhances a feeling of cozy intimacy. There's a bar area which is light and airy with high ceilings adorned with natural redwood tree trunks and nearby is a large deck that takes full advantage of the panoramic views below. An additional dining room downstairs uses mirrors to draw the light through double glass doors off the neighboring deck. For business luncheons, dinners or private parties, the Mountain Home Inn offers a sensational setting on Mount Tamalpais.

CAPACITY:	*Area*	*Season*	*Standing*	*Seated*
	Upper & Lower Floor and Deck	March–Oct	110	40–110
	Upper & Lower Floor	Oct–March	80	80
	Lower Floor	—	40	35

FEES & DEPOSITS: A non-refundable deposit in the amount of your rental fee is required to secure your date. The Upper and Lower Floor rental rate is $1,500. The Lower Floor rental fee is $250. The rate for each of the 10 guest rooms ranges from $112–178/night. Food service is provided. Food costs run $15–20/person for hors d'oeuvres, lunch or light meals, $25–35/person for buffets and seated meals. Bar service, sales tax and 15% gratuity are added to the final bill.

AVAILABILITY: Every day, from 11:30am–4pm and 5:30–11pm.

SERVICES/AMENITIES:

Restaurant Services: yes
Catering: provided, no BYO
Kitchen Facilities: n/a
Tables & Chairs: provided
Linens, Silver, etc.: provided
Restrooms: wca
Dance Floor: yes

Parking: easy eves, difficult weekend days
Overnight Accommodations: 10 guestrooms
Telephone: pay phone
Outdoor Night Lighting: yes
Outdoor Cooking Facilities: no
Cleanup: provided
Meeting Equipment: projection screen, flip chart

RESTRICTIONS:

Alcohol: provided, WBC only, corkage $8/bottle
Wheelchair Access: yes
Smoking: allowed

Music: amplified until 11pm
Insurance: not required

Nicasio

THE SHADOWS

1901 Nicasio Valley Road
Nicasio, CA 94946
(415) 662-2012
Reserve for Events: 2–4 months in advance
Reserve for Meetings: 4 weeks in advance

Ensconced in a circle of towering redwoods, The Shadows is a woodsy and private spot for small social and business groups looking for something a bit different. A cultural and educational retreat, perfectly suited for overnight stays, it's located in a secluded redwood forest in West Marin County. It is a quiet getaway for an undisturbed meeting, workshop, seminar or gathering of any sort. The buildings here are relatively new, tastefully designed in an elegant yet rustic style with stone fireplaces and beamed ceilings. There's also a pool house and pool which can be used for meetings or parties. Close by are wooded hiking and biking trails leading to adjoining State and Federal parks or to a nearby golf course. Although just nineteen miles from the Golden Gate Bridge, The Shadows has that intangible quality of making you feel like you're in another world.

CAPACITY: Indoor meeting and guest rooms can accommodate 15–30 people. Outdoor facilities can hold up to 120 guests.

FEES & DEPOSITS: A $500 refundable deposit is required to reserve a date. Rental fees: $1,400/day for the exclusive use of the entire facility, including room accommodations, pool, pool house and picnic area.

CANCELLATION POLICY: With 90 days' notice, the deposit is refunded.

AVAILABILITY: Year-round, every day 10am–10pm unless you are an overnight guest.

SERVICES/AMENITIES:

Restaurant Services: no
Catering: BYO or CBA
Kitchen Facilities: ample
Tables & Chairs: BYO or CBA
Linens, Silver, etc.: BYO or CBA
Restrooms: wca
Dance Floor: outdoor
Meeting Equipment: audio-visual

Parking: large area
Overnight Accommodations: 12 bedrooms
Telephone: guest phone
Outdoor Night Lighting: yes
Outdoor Cooking Facilities: BBQ
Cleanup: caterer
Other: kids' play area

RESTRICTIONS:

Alcohol: BYO
Smoking: outside only
Music: amplified & DJ ok

Wheelchair Access: yes
Insurance: certificate required
Other: no pets

Ross

MARIN ART AND GARDEN CENTER
Caroline Livermore Room

30 Sir Francis Drake Blvd.
Ross, CA 94957
(415) 454-1301
Reserve for Events: 9–12 months in advance
Reserve for Meetings: 2–6 weeks in advance

The Caroline Livermore Room is located in a rustic building set way back into the lovely ten acres of the Marin Art and Garden Center. Just off Sir Francis Drake Boulevard in Ross, this special indoor-outdoor space is perfectly suited for meetings, seminars and workshops as well as special events. Inside, there's a large party room with multiple glass doors opening out onto the deck and stone patio. The adjacent outdoor gravel and paved areas are surrounded by large trees and flowers which provide spots of color. This facility, a favorite among Marin residents because of its park-like setting, attracts groups from all over the Bay Area.

CAPACITY: This facility can accommodate 225 standing or 130 seated guests. In combination with the outdoor areas, it can hold up to 500 guests.

FEES & DEPOSITS: For special events, a $300 non-refundable deposit is required to secure your date; for business functions, the deposit is a non-refundable $20. For special events, the fees vary depending on season and guest count:

Number of Guests	Winter Fee	Spring/Summer Fee
50–75	$550	$650
75–300	—	850
301–400	—	1,000
401–500	—	1,200

Fees must be received 10 days prior to your event. For business meetings of less than 50, the rental fee is $50/day; over 50 people, $75/day. For all-day business functions, non-profits are charged $200/day and others are charged $300/day.

AVAILABILITY: Year-round. Wintertime indoor functions: Friday eves, Saturday and Sunday until 11pm. Spring/Summer outdoor events: weekends until dusk. Weekday functions until 11pm.

SERVICES/AMENITIES:

Restaurant Services: no

Catering: BYO, must be licensed

Kitchen Facilities: ample

Tables & Chairs: provided

Linens, Silver, etc.: caterer

Restrooms: wca

Dance Floor: yes

Meeting Equipment: large screen

Parking: large lot

Overnight Accommodations: no

Telephone: pay phone

Outdoor Night Lighting: yes

Outdoor Cooking Facilities: no

Cleanup: caterer

Other: security guard

RESTRICTIONS:

Alcohol: BYO, caterer must serve

Smoking: allowed

Music: inside only

Wheelchair Access: yes

Insurance: liability required

San Rafael

DOMINICAN COLLEGE

50 Acacia Avenue
San Rafael, CA 94901
(415) 485-3228
Reserve for Events: 6–12 months in advance
Reserve for Meetings: 3–4 months in advance

This facility is situated in a quiet residential area of San Rafael, on an eighty-acre wooded campus developed at the turn of the century. For an outdoor affair, the Anne Hathaway Garden provides a lovely lawn, ringed with roses and other annuals, which can be equipped with a dance floor or decorated with night lighting. Housed in a modern building nearby, the Shield and Creekside Rooms offer spaces for smaller parties and meetings. Also located on campus is Meadowlands, a grand, three-story Victorian structure that has been meticulously maintained. Broad steps lead up to a sunny veranda, and the massive front door seems a threshold into another era. Spacious and inviting, the interior entry hall and dining room feature polished wood paneling and patterned ceilings. Downstairs you'll see the dance hall and stage alcove lit by brilliant sunlight coming through stained glass windows. The Meadowlands can accommodate a very large group by offering variety—the veranda and grounds for sun, the main floor for quiet dining and conversation and the downstairs for lively dancing. The campus is also a popular spot for conferences, seminars, workshops and retreats. During the summer, the college offers overnight accommodations for business guests.

CAPACITY, FEES & DEPOSITS: The full rental fee is the deposit required to secure your date.

Area	*Standing*	*Seated*	*Rental Fee*
Meadowlands	250	150	$800
Anne Hathaway Garden	200+	100	220
Shield Room	500	300	650–750
Creekside Room	100	50–75	220–380

CANCELLATION POLICY: With 90 days' notice, you'll receive a full refund.

AVAILABILITY: Meadowlands: Mid-May to mid-June. Anne Hathaway Garden: weekends only. The Creekside Room is available any time; however, the Shield Room has restricted hours.

SERVICES/AMENITIES:

Restaurant Services: no

Catering: select from preferred list Rooms, preferred caterer

Kitchen Facilities: varies

Tables & Chairs: some provided

Linens, Silver, etc.: through caterer

Restrooms: wca

Dance Floor: yes or CBA

Parking: large lot, on street

Overnight Accommodations: summer only

Telephone: pay phone

Outdoor Night Lighting: CBA

Outdoor Cooking Facilities: BBQ CBA

Cleanup: caterer

Other: baby grand piano

Meeting Equipment: CBA

RESTRICTIONS:

Alcohol: BYO, permit required

Smoking: allowed

Music: Shield Room only

Wheelchair Access: mostly yes

Insurance: certificate required

FALKIRK MANSION

1408 Mission Street
San Rafael, CA 94901
(415) 485-3328
Reserve for Events: 3–5 months in advance
Reserve for Meetings: 1–2 months in advance

Magnificent oaks and colorful magnolias frame the historic Falkirk Mansion, a lovely Queen Anne Victorian built in 1888, nestled on eleven acres in the heart of San Rafael. Spacious foyer, parlor and dining room lend themselves beautifully to elegant parties or receptions. Workshops, change-of-pace business meetings or small seminars can also be held here. The interior's redwood paneling, ornate mantelpieces, shiny hardwood floors and elegant wall coverings are noteworthy. The dining area has a huge fireplace and floor-to-ceiling stained glass windows overlooking the deck. Curving around two sides of the Mansion is a wide veranda, great for dancing and casual dining, bordered by colorfully planted flower boxes. Located on the hill above City Hall, this century-old Victorian mansion has a charm and intimacy along with a central location to be found nowhere else in Marin.

CAPACITY: October–April, standing capacity is 85; seated capacity 50–60 guests. April–October, the house and veranda up to 125 guests.

FEES & DEPOSITS: A non-refundable deposit of half the rental fee is required to reserve your date. Weekends, from October 15–April 15, there is a $90/hour rental fee for a 6-hour minimum block; $135/hour overtime. From April 16–October 14, the fee is $115/hour for a 6-hour minimum (weekends only); $165/hour overtime. A refundable $500 security deposit and any remaining balance are payable 45 days in advance of your event. Weekday rates vary; call for more information.

AVAILABILITY: Year-round. Saturdays from 1pm–11pm, Sundays all day. Weekdays 9am–11pm by arrangement.

SERVICES/AMENITIES:

Restaurant Services: no

Catering: select from approved list

Kitchen Facilities: minimal

Tables & Chairs: CBA, extra charge for chairs

Linens, Silver, etc.: BYO

Restrooms: wca

Dance Floor: yes

Parking: large lot

Overnight Accommodations: no

Telephone: pay phone

Outdoor Night Lighting: CBA

Outdoor Cooking Facilities: no

Cleanup: caterer

Meeting Equipment: no

RESTRICTIONS:

Alcohol: BYO

Smoking: outside only

Music: amplified to 90 decibels

Wheelchair Access: yes

Insurance: extra liability required

Other: no candles, decorations restricted

FORTY TWENTY CIVIC CENTER DRIVE
The Event Center

4020 Civic Center Dr.
San Rafael, CA 94903
(415) 507-1000
Reserve for Events: 1–3 months in advance
Reserve for Meetings: 1–3 months in advance

The Marin Association of Realtors offers a relatively new site for Marin special events. Four rooms in their new facilities have been completely remodeled: these spaces are clean, light and, a novelty in this county, air conditioned. The decor is sparse and modern. The larger space, designed in shades of gray, has a movable stage, a large dance floor, recessed lighting and wall-to-wall carpeting. This attractive room is flexible, breaking down into three different-sized spaces, depending on your guest count. Windows lining the west-facing wall look out onto a small landscaped side yard. In the corner of the building is the Garden Room. This space, with its high tongue-in-groove ceiling, wood rafters and pleasantly patterned gray ceramic tile floors, has a more open feel. Afternoon light streams in through large windows and glass doors that lead to a well-landscaped patio area surrounded by high stucco walls. Overall, this is a clean, well-lighted place for cocktail parties, seminars or workshops, with ample space, great kitchen facilities and a friendly, accommodating staff.

CAPACITY: Indoors, 300 seated guests; 500 for a standing reception. The Garden Room and adjoining patio can each accommodate 75 seated.

FEES & DEPOSITS: A refundable $200 deposit, which is applied towards the rental fee, is required to secure your date. The fee is $700 for the entire facility for 4 hours; $100/hour for each additional hour. A refundable $200 damage/cleaning deposit is payable, along with the rental fee, at least 30 days prior to the function.

CANCELLATION POLICY: With 30 days' notice, the deposit is returned.

AVAILABILITY: Year-round, any day, anytime.

SERVICES/AMENITIES:

Restaurant Services: no
Catering: BYO
Kitchen Facilities: ample
Tables & Chairs: provided
Linens, Silver, etc.: BYO
Restrooms: wca
Meeting Equipment: full spectrum of audio-visual

Parking: large lot
Overnight Accommodations: no
Telephone: pay phone
Outdoor Night Lighting: no
Outdoor Cooking Facilities: no
Cleanup: renter or caterer
Dance Floor: yes

RESTRICTIONS:

Alcohol: BYO, licensed server
Smoking: outside only
Insurance: proof of liability

Wheelchair Access: yes
Music: amplified ok
Other: decorations restricted

FOSTER HALL
At Marin Academy

1600 Mission Ave.
San Rafael, CA 94901
(415) 258-9211   Debra
Reserve for Events: 3–6 months in advance
Reserve for Meetings: 2–4 weeks in advance

Rejoice. If you've despaired of finding an event site for over 200 guests in Marin, here is a new spot that can handle both business functions and sizable parties. Set back from Mission Avenue by a large circular lawn and drive, stately neo-classic Foster Hall is now available for private events. This historic building on the Marin Academy campus has a combination of spaces that can easily handle a party, seminar, conference or board meeting. The two-story structure's long veranda is perfect for tables with umbrellas. Several sets of French doors connect the veranda to interior rooms, some of which can be combined by opening interior sliding doors. The long entry hall has a unique, geometric parquet floor and features a grand staircase with a handsome bannister railing. The color scheme indoors is in eye-pleasing tan and cream, and each event space has multi-paned windows overlooking landscaped grounds. Although unadorned, Foster Hall has some fine architectural details that make it a great spot for special events. When this building is "dressed up," it can look positively sensational.

CAPACITY: Foster Hall can hold up to 250 seated guests, 500 for a standing reception. The front lawn can seat 200 for an outdoor function.

MEETING ROOMS: 3 rooms, each can seat up to 250.

FEES & DEPOSITS: A $250 deposit, which is applied towards the rental fee, is required when you book this facility. The rental fee is $250 for the largest event space or $450 for the entire building. A $500 refundable security/cleaning deposit plus 90% of the anticipated food and beverage total is due 1 week prior to the event. The balance is due the day of the event. Tax and a 15% service charge are additional. Food service is provided by All Seasons Party Productions who will customize any menu depending on your needs and budget. For weekday meetings or conferences, the rental fee is $250. Coffee and food service can be arranged for any business function.

CANCELLATION POLICY: With 90 days' notice, your deposit will be refunded.

AVAILABILITY: Year-round. Evenings from 5pm–2am, Saturday and Sunday anytime until 2am. June 10 through September 3, anytime.

SERVICES/AMENITIES:

Restaurant Services: no
Catering: provided, no BYO
Kitchen Facilities: n/a
Tables & Chairs: provided
Linens, Silver, etc.: provided
Restrooms: wca
Dance Floor: yes

Parking: ample
Overnight Accommodations: no
Telephone: pay phone
Outdoor Night Lighting: yes
Outdoor Cooking Facilities: CBA
Cleanup: provided
Meeting Equipment: CBA

RESTRICTIONS:

Alcohol: provided, corkage $5/bottle
Smoking: outside only
Music: amplified ok indoors

Wheelchair Access: yes
Insurance: not required

SAN RAFAEL
IMPROVEMENT CLUB

Corner of 5th and H Streets
San Rafael, CA 94901
(415) 459-9955
Reserve for Events: 2 weeks–6 months in advance
Reserve for Meetings: 1–12 weeks in advance

The San Rafael Improvement Club is one of the few structures remaining from the 1914 San Francisco Pan Pacific Exhibition. The building, designed by William B. Faville, was brought over to San Rafael in 1915 and purchased by the Improvement Club. It's now an historic landmark, ensconced in a small garden setting with an adjacent brick patio. Its interior is sophisticated and attractive, accented with scalloped pillars, large windows and a sculpted ceiling. Light and airy, this facility is great for parties and business functions of any kind.

CAPACITY: The Club can hold up to 160 for a buffet or 125 seated guests.

FEES & DEPOSITS: A $200 refundable security deposit is required to reserve a date. On weekends, the rental fee is $350. The rental fee for luncheons during the week is $225, evening events $275. The final rental balance is due 10 days prior to the event along with an insurance certificate.

CANCELLATION POLICY: The deposit for weekend events is fully refundable with 60 days' notice October–April, 90 days' notice May–September.

AVAILABILITY: Weekends, 10am–midnight. During the week, 8am–midnight. Thursdays and Fridays from 10am–5pm are not available for bookings.

SERVICES/AMENITIES:

Restaurant Services: no
Catering: BYO
Kitchen Facilities: minimal
Tables & Chairs: provided
Linens, Silver, etc.: BYO
Restrooms: wca
Dance Floor: yes

Parking: lot and street
Overnight Accommodations: no
Telephone: pay phone
Outdoor Night Lighting: yes
Outdoor Cooking Facilities: no
Cleanup: caterer
Meeting Equipment: no

RESTRICTIONS:

Alcohol: BYO
Smoking: not allowed
Music: amplified until 10pm

Wheelchair Access: yes
Insurance: liability required
Other: decorations restricted, no candles

VILLA ALTURA

Address withheld to maintain privacy.
San Rafael, CA 94901
(415) 456-7440
Reserve for Events: subject to availability
Reserve for Meetings: subject to availability

Villa Altura is a rare, one-of-a-kind location for an elegant affair. This striking Beaux Arts mansion sits atop a two-acre knoll with filtered views of the Bay and the surrounding hills. Guests travel up a gently curving private road through a large gate that automatically swings open, revealing the white mansion at the end of the drive. It was built for U.S. Senator Truxton Beale in 1909 by Arthur Brown, the notable architect responsible for Coit Tower, and San Francisco's City Hall and War Memorial Opera House. Formal architectural elements predominate—Doric columns, balustrades, verandas and an oval loggia. Meticulously restored with exquisite detailing throughout, the mansion's interior is impressive. The generous foyer, dining and living rooms have beautiful herringbone hardwood floors with oriental carpets, and each room has decorative moldings and marble mantels. The decor is softened by pastel shades and sophisticated floor-to-ceiling draperies. Twelve-foot ceilings and French doors and windows that open to the garden create light and inviting interior spaces. The stately home presides over formal grounds with fountains and classical statuary, so if you've ever wondered where you could host the ultimate garden party, look no further.

CAPACITY: Indoors, 75 seated; outdoors 200, maximum.

FEES & DEPOSITS: A $500–1,000 refundable security deposit is required to reserve a date. Half of the rental fee is payable when your contract is submitted, the remaining half 2 weeks prior to the event along with a certificate of insurance. The rental fee ranges from $2,000–4,000 depending on the number of guests.

CANCELLATION POLICY: The deposit is fully refundable with 90 days' notice. With 60 days' notice, the deposit is returned less $200; with less than 30 days' notice, less $500.

AVAILABILITY: Year-round.

SERVICES/AMENITIES:

Restaurant Services: no
Catering: select from preferred list
Kitchen Facilities: prep only
Tables & Chairs: BYO or thru caterer
Linens, Silver, etc.: BYO or thru caterer
Restrooms: no wca
Dance Floor: CBA or thru caterer

Parking: valet
Overnight Accommodations: no
Telephone: emergency only
Outdoor Night Lighting: yes
Outdoor Cooking Facilities: thru caterer
Cleanup: caterer
Meeting Equipment: BYO

RESTRICTIONS:

Alcohol: BYO or CBA
Smoking: designated area
Music: amplified restricted

Wheelchair Access: limited
Insurance: liability required
Other: decorations by approval only

Sausalito

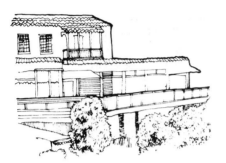

THE ALTA MIRA

125 Bulkley Avenue
Sausalito, CA 94965
(415) 332-1350
Reserve for Events: 2 weeks–6 months in advance
Reserve for Meetings: 1 week–1 year in advance

The Alta Mira is one of Marin's oldest and most renowned hotels. The property was originally the residence of Thomas Jackson, who later converted his villa into a hotel. After the original structure was lost in a fire, Jackson's son rebuilt the Alta Mira as a Spanish-style villa. The main dining room has a huge deck, reminiscent of the Riviera with its round tables and bright umbrellas. The deck also has one of the most spectacular panoramic views of the San Francisco skyline, Sausalito Harbor and Angel Island. It's understandably a very popular spot for private gatherings. The main dining area is relaxed but elegant, highlighted with leaded glass mirrors and floral designs. A private dining room called the Fiesta Room has high ceilings, chandeliers and a gorgeous fireplace with hand-painted tiles displaying a country garden. Large mirrors extend the open, sunny feeling of this beautiful room and the adjoining deck has a lovely view of the San Francisco skyline. Outdoors, the Garden Terrace, with its surrounding flowers and bay view provides a delightful setting for cocktails and hors d'oeuvres. Rooms at the hotel are available, including a suite in an adjacent Victorian house that includes sitting room, kitchen and deck.

CAPACITY: The Annex Dining Room and Deck can hold 200 standing guests and 150 seated. There is a 130-guest minimum requirement for this space. The Fiesta Room can accommodate 110 for a buffet and 100 seated guests, with a 35-guest minimum. The Outdoor Patio seats 150, and the Garden Terrace accommodates 150 seated and 200 standing.

MEETING ROOMS: The Fiesta room seats 10–80 guests, and the Cottage Meeting Suite accommodates up to 15.

FEES & DEPOSITS: For special events, a $500 refundable deposit is required to reserve a date and is applied towards the food and beverage bill. For a luncheon or dinner, there's no rental fee. Half the anticipated total is due 30 days prior to your function and the balance is due the day of the event. Food service is provided. Receptions average $35–45/person and seated meals $30–45/person, including bar service. Tax and 15% gratuity will be added to the final bill.

CANCELLATION POLICY: If you give notice 6 months in advance, your deposit will be returned.

AVAILABILITY: The Annex and Deck are available Saturdays, 2:30pm–6:30pm, and Sundays, 5pm–10pm. The Fiesta Room is available any time during the week, noon–5pm and 6:30pm–11pm Saturday and 4pm–10pm Sunday. The Garden Terrace is available daily for a $300 fee.

SERVICES/AMENITIES:

Restaurant Services: yes
Catering: provided, no BYO
Kitchen Facilities: n/a
Tables & Chairs: provided
Linens, Silver, etc.: provided
Restrooms: limited wca
Dance Floor: yes
Meeting Equipment: CBA, extra fee

Parking: valet CBA, on street
Overnight Accommodations: 29 guestrooms
Telephone: pay phone
Outdoor Night Lighting: patio only
Outdoor Cooking Facilities: no
Cleanup: provided
Special: event planning services

RESTRICTIONS:

Alcohol: provided, corkage $10/bottle
Smoking: allowed
Music: no amplified

Wheelchair Access: limited, entry CBA
Insurance: sometimes required

CASA MADRONA HOTEL AND RESTAURANT

801 Bridgeway
Sausalito, CA 94965
(415) 322-0502
Reserve for Events: 1–12 months in advance
Reserve for Meetings: 1 day–12 months in advance

Located in the hills of Sausalito, Casa Madrona Hotel and Restaurant are a haven of comfort and retreat. Built in 1885, the original Victorian mansion has been expanded to include three cottages and the New Casa—sixteen uniquely decorated rooms set into the hillside. The result is a grand establishment that offers a variety of services and settings. Casa Madrona Restaurant has a dramatic, glass-enclosed terrace, with retractable sliding glass roof and walls that create an open, outdoor feeling. It is situated high on a hill and has spectacular views. Below the Restaurant is a 1,300 square foot outdoor tiled terrace. Again, views of Angel and Belvedere Islands, Sausalito Harbor, the Bay Bridge and San Francisco skyline are unsurpassed. Villa Madrona Suite is a unique location for smaller gatherings. Imagine a conference room with two private terraces, a fireplace and an extraordinary view of the bay! This room, like all others, shows meticulous attention to detail, and best of all, you feel a million miles away from the every day office setting.

CAPACITY:

	Seated	Standing	Facility Fee	5-Hour Availability
Restaurant	100	140	$850	12–5pm or 5–10pm*
Villa Madrona Suite	26	60	300	3–10pm
Lower Terrace	40	120	100	open

* call for more information on evening events

MEETING ROOMS: The Villa Madrona Suite accommodates 22 and the Lower Casitas holds 6.

FEES & DEPOSITS: A $750 deposit is required at the time of booking. 80% of the anticipated event total (including the deposit) is due 1 month prior to the event, and the balance is payable on the day of the event. The average per person food cost including beverage is $40 (the beverage charge is based on consumption). Reduced rates are offered November through February.

CANCELLATION POLICY: Your deposit will be refunded in full with at least 120 days' written notice.

AVAILABILITY: Year-round, every day.

SERVICES/AMENITIES:

Restaurant Services: yes

Catering: provided, no BYO

Kitchen Facilities: n/a

Tables & Chairs: provided

Linens, Silver, etc.: provided

Restrooms: no wca

Dance Floor: yes

Parking: lot, valet for overnight hotel guests only

Overnight Accommodations: 34 rooms

Telephone: pay phone, house phone, guest phones

Outdoor Night Lighting: access only

Outdoor Cooking Facilities: no

Cleanup: provided

Meeting Equipment: CBA, extra fee

RESTRICTIONS:

Alcohol: provided, corkage $10/bottle

Smoking: in designated areas

Music: amplified ok

Wheelchair Access: no

Insurance: not required

SAUSALITO WOMAN'S CLUB

120 Central Ave.
Sausalito, CA 94965
(415) 332-0354
Reserve for Events: 2–6 months in advance
Reserve for Meetings: 6 weeks in advance

This Sausalito landmark is a classic, craftsman-style Julia Morgan building nestled in the hills overlooking the Bay. Since its dedication as a woman's club in 1918, it has been a preferred place for meetings and social functions through the years. The structure is clad in brown shingles and is designed with simple and understated detailing. The large auditorium room has a stage, original fixtures, hardwood floor and large paned windows, perfect for receptions or business presentations. Multiple doors open onto a small brick patio sheltered by mature oaks. The landscaping is well maintained and the canopy of trees surrounding the Woman's Club filters glimpses of the Bay beyond. Unpretentious yet stately, this structure fits into the hillside landscape perfectly. It's a bit hard to find, but worth the exploratory trip into the always interesting and visually stimulating Sausalito hills.

CAPACITY: The Club can hold 125–150 seated guests, 150–175 for buffets and 200 theater-style.

FEES & DEPOSITS: For weekend events, a refundable $500 deposit is due when the rental contract is submitted. The rental fee is $825 for 48 hours for Friday, Saturday and Sunday. For weekday events the deposit is $275 and the rental fee is $300 for 12 hours. The rental balance is due 10 days prior to the function.

CANCELLATION POLICY: The deposit is refunded with 6 months' notice.

AVAILABILITY: Year-round, every day until midnight except Thursdays.

SERVICES/AMENITIES:

Restaurant Services: no

Catering: BYO

Kitchen Facilities: setup only

Tables & Chairs: provided

Linens, Silver, etc.: BYO

Restrooms: wca

Dance Floor: yes

Parking: street, shuttle encouraged

Overnight Accommodations: no

Telephone: house phone

Outdoor Night Lighting: access only

Outdoor Cooking Facilities: no

Cleanup: caterer or renter

Meeting Equipment: screen on stage

RESTRICTIONS:

Alcohol: BYO

Smoking: outside only

Music: acoustical only, until 10pm

Wheelchair Access: limited

Insurance: certificate required

Other: decorations restricted

Stinson Beach

STINSON BEACH "CREEKSIDE" COMMUNITY CENTER

32 Belvedere Ave.
Stinson Beach, CA 94970
(415) 868-1444
Reserve for Events: 2–6 months in advance
Reserve for Meetings: 2 weeks–6 months in advance

Looking for a special spot near the ocean? Here's one you'd never know about unless you went looking for it. Situated alongside a meandering creek and in front of coastal foothills is the Stinson Beach Community Center. Sitting on a quiet, residential side street away from the bustle of town activities, the Center is a modest one-story, with a sloping shake roof and a wide porch. In spring, the oaks in front of the building are covered with long, delicate white flowers which hang in such profusion, you can hardly see the entry. Inside, the Main Hall is a large, open space with a vaulted wood beam ceiling, hardwood floor, working stone fireplace and large windows overlooking a creekside patio. Adjacent to the Hall, the Community Church, with its tall windows and quiet interior makes an interesting spot for a meeting. Another popular room for meetings is the "Little Room," the Community Center's historical room, with picture of old Stinson Beach on the walls. The outdoor area is lovely: the patio borders the creek (actually the confluence of two bubbling creeks) and makes a delightful space for al fresco dining. An added feature is a huge maple tree which creates a shaded, leafy canopy overhead. The Center offer a casual, warm and friendly environment for parties and meetings.

CAPACITY:

Area	Seated	Standing
Main Hall	150	300
Center with Patio Space	200	400
Community Church	110	—
Little Room	30	—

MEETING ROOMS: All the above areas except the patio are available for meetings.

FEES & DEPOSITS: For special events, a $225 deposit applied to the total is required when you book the facility. A partially refundable $175 security/cleaning deposit is required 60 days prior to the function. The rental fee is $450 plus $100 for full use of the kitchen, payable 1 week in advance of the event. The fee covers a block from 7am–1am. The Church rents for $100/day. Call for information regarding meeting rates.

CANCELLATION POLICY: With 21 days' notice, all deposits are refundable. With less notice, only the security/cleaning deposit will be refunded.

AVAILABILITY: Year-round, every day from 7am–1am except 1 week in mid July.

SERVICES/AMENITIES:

Restaurant Services: no
Catering: BYO
Kitchen Facilities: new, fully equipped
Tables & Chairs: some provided
Linens, Silver, etc.: some provided
Restrooms: wca
Dance Floor: yes
Other: some event coordination, grand piano

Parking: Center's pkg area & on street
Overnight Accommodations: no
Telephone: emergency only
Outdoor Night Lighting: access only
Outdoor Cooking Facilities: BBQ
Cleanup: caterer or renter
Meeting Equipment: no

RESTRICTIONS:

Alcohol: BYO
Smoking: outside only
Insurance: certificate required

Wheelchair Access: yes
Music: amplified ok

Tiburon

CORINTHIAN YACHT CLUB

End of Main Street
Tiburon, CA 94920
(415) 435-4771
Reserve for Events: 2–12 months in advance
Reserve for Meetings: 1 week–12 months in advance

Reminiscent of a ship captain's parlor, the Corinthian Yacht Club Ballroom is a spacious room that is popular for receptions, business luncheons and banquets. It features wood paneling with hardwood floors plus high ceilings which are draped with nautical flags and lit by two chandeliers made from wooden ship wheels. There is an enormous stone fireplace above which soars a majestic bronze eagle. Adjacent is a glass-enclosed solarium with a fantastic view of the Tiburon Harbor and San Francisco Bay. When there's a full moon, this panoramic view is absolutely breathtaking (not to mention romantic). Downstairs, the newly remodeled main dining room is also available for parties. The neighboring deck overlooks the picturesque marina and has a similar sensational view of the harbor and Bay.

CAPACITY: The Ballroom can hold up to 400 guests; the Main Dining Room up to 135.

MEETING ROOMS: The above areas are available for meetings of 12 to 250 people.

FEES & DEPOSITS: A refundable deposit (ranging from $800–1,800 depending on the space and date booked) is applied towards the total cost and is required at the time of booking. The rental fee for the Ballroom starts at $800 and can exceed $2,000, depending on the day of rental. The Dining Room fee varies between $4.50 and 6.50/person. These fees are for a 5-hour maximum rental. 80% of the anticipated total is due 2 weeks prior to the event, and the balance is due at the conclusion.

Food service is provided, and ranges from $20–45/person. A $400 minimum for bar service is required; an open bar usually costs $14–20/person. Tax and 17% gratuity are added to the final bill. Note that rental discounts of up to 50% are available Monday–Friday for events.

CANCELLATION POLICY: With 3 months' advance notice in writing, you will receive a full refund. With less than 3 months, the deposit is forfeited.

AVAILABILITY: The Ballroom is available every day from 9am–midnight. The Dining Room, Monday–Thursday, from 9am–midnight.

SERVICES/AMENITIES:

Restaurant Services: yes
Catering: provided, no BYO
Kitchen Facilities: n/a
Tables & Chairs: provided
Linens, Silver, etc.: provided

Parking: public lot nearby
Overnight Accommodations: no
Telephone: pay phone
Outdoor Night Lighting: yes
Outdoor Cooking Facilities: no

Restrooms: limited wca downstairs
Dance Floor: yes

RESTRICTIONS:

Alcohol: provided, BYO possible
Smoking: on decks only
Music: amplified restricted

Cleanup: provided
Meeting Equipment: limited

Wheelchair Access: downstairs only
Insurance: not required
Other: security required

Bodega Bay

TERRA NOVA INSTITUTE

Address withheld for privacy.
Bodega Bay, CA 94923
(707) 865-2377
Reserve: 1–2 months in advance

The Institute is a unique facility. Situated at the convergence of natural springs, white sandy beaches, acres of dunes, Salmon Creek and the ocean, it is a place for people to meditate, rest, commune with nature and generally disengage. The main house was built in the mid 1800s, but the current focal point of the Institute is the floral solarium added nearly forty years ago. A 2,000 square foot greenhouse, it houses dozens of varieties of coastal and semi-tropical plants. It is here, in the midst of greenery and sunlight, that people participate in workshops and seminars. The Institute is only available for use by non-profit organizations involved in educational, spiritual or holistic pursuits.

CAPACITY: The facility can accommodate 50 guests.

MEETING ROOMS: The Solarium has a capacity of 50 guests.

FEES & DEPOSITS: The Solarium and grounds rent for $250/day, $500/weekend. If the entire house is rented, including overnight accommodations, the fee is $750. A $200 deposit is due when reservations are made, the balance payable on arrival. Catering fees need to be arranged.

CANCELLATION POLICY: A full refund will be given with 30 days' notice. With less notice, a refund will apply only if the spaces can be rebooked.

AVAILABILITY: Year-round, daily.

SERVICES/AMENITIES:

Restaurant Services: no
Catering: provided, select from preferred list
Kitchen Facilities: n/a
Tables & Chairs: caterer
Linens, Silver, etc.: caterer
Restrooms: no wca
Dance Floor: no
Meeting Equipment: CBA

Parking: on and off street
Overnight Accommodations: 4 guestrooms, 5 nearby homes
Telephone: house phone
Outdoor Night Lighting: no
Outdoor Cooking Facilities: BBQ
Cleanup: caterer or renter

RESTRICTIONS:

Alcohol: not permitted
Smoking: outside only
Music: no amplified

Wheelchair Access: yes
Insurance: not required
Other: no shoes worn in house

Cazadero

TIMBERHILL RANCH

35755 Hauser Bridge Road
Cazadero, CA 95421
(707) 847-3258
Reserve for Events: 4–6 months in advance
Reserve for Meetings: 4–6 months in advance

Timberhill Ranch is a little like Shangri-la—a place steeped in beauty and harmony, far removed from the rest of the world. Set on a sunlit ridge, surrounded by high meadows and towering redwoods, Timberhill is an oasis of tranquility, perfect for small conferences, seminars and group retreats. The Main Lodge provides an intimate yet open space for private celebrations. Floor-to-ceiling windows and skylights bring the outdoors in and the warmth of a parquet floor, wood and stone fireplace, exposed beams and comfortable seating invite wedding guests to relax and stay a while. Fifteen private cottages work a similar magic: each has its own fireplace, private deck and tiled bath and is fragrant with scents of cedar and fresh flowers. Add tennis courts, a swimming pool, a jacuzzi and exceptional cuisine and you have a resort that is, perhaps, the ultimate escape.

CAPACITY: The Dining Room and Main Room in the Lodge can accommodate 40 people. This number is negotiable, depending on the function.

MEETING ROOMS: The Conference Center can hold up to 30 guests.

FEES & DEPOSITS: Use of the facility is only available to overnight guests. Rates for accommodations are $350 per couple/double occupancy on weekends, and $296 per couple/double occupancy on weekdays. Fees include breakfast and dinner. There are special policies for holidays. A 1 night deposit is required at the time of booking and the balance is due on departure.

CANCELLATION POLICY: With 7 days' notice, a full refund less a 5% processing fee is given. With less notice, a full refund less a 10% processing fee is given only if the accommodations are rebooked.

AVAILABILITY: Every day except 2 weeks in January.

SERVICES/AMENITIES:

Restaurant Services: yes
Catering: provided, no BYO
Kitchen Facilities: n/a
Tables & Chairs: provided
Linens, Silver, etc.: provided
Restrooms: wca
Dance Floor: CBA

Parking: off street
Overnight Accommodations: 15 cottages
Telephone: house phone
Outdoor Night Lighting: minimal
Outdoor Cooking Facilities: no
Cleanup: provided
Meeting Equipment: CBA

RESTRICTIONS:

Alcohol: BW provided, BYO in cottages only

Wheelchair Access: limited

Smoking: designated areas only
Insurance: not required

Music: with approval

Fort Bragg

MENDOCINO COAST BOTANICAL GARDENS

18220 N. Highway 1
Fort Bragg, CA 95437
(707) 964-4352
Reserve: 2–3 months in advance

It's hard to believe that a garden as spectacular as this exists a mere five hundred feet from the highway. When you walk through the entrance, a seemingly endless landscape of colorful and varied plants unfolds before you. Meandering paths take you past plant species from all over the world—the Mediterranean, South Africa, Australia and more! Nestled between the pine forest and the main garden is the Meadow Lawn, a lovely, semi-private clearing surrounded by trees, bushes and flowers. On a sunny day the setting is just right for a company picnic or family retreat. There's also the Cliff House, Dahlia Garden and Headlands to consider. With 47 acres of garden and pine forest to explore, this is a one-of-a-kind event location.

CAPACITY: The Meadow Lawn accommodates 30.

FEES & DEPOSITS: A fee of $5/person is required when you make reservations.

CANCELLATION POLICY: A full refund will be given with 30 days' notice.

AVAILABILITY: Every day except Thanksgiving, Christmas, and second Saturday in September. Hours are 9am–5pm, March–October; 9am–4pm, November–February. The rainy season is mid-October through mid-March.

SERVICES/AMENITIES:

Restaurant Services: yes
Catering: BYO
Kitchen Facilities: no
Tables & Chairs: BYO
Linens, Silver, etc.: BYO
Restrooms: wca
Dance Floor: no

Parking: lot
Overnight Accommodations: no
Telephone: pay phone
Outdoor Night Lighting: no
Outdoor Cooking Facilities: no
Cleanup: renter or caterer
Meeting Equipment: no

RESTRICTIONS:

Alcohol: BYO
Smoking: designated areas only
Music: no power available

Wheelchair Access: yes
Insurance: required
Other: no vehicle access to site; 500-foot walk from lot

SHORELINE PROPERTIES

18300 Old Coast Highway
Fort Bragg, CA 95437
(707) 964-1444 or (800) 942-8288
Reserve for Events: 2–3 months in advance
Reserve for Meetings: 2–3 months in advance

If you want to experience the ocean as part of your event, Shoreline Properties has what you have been looking for. Most of their homes are less than a hundred feet from the water's edge! Each home is unique and the majority have decks, barbecues, hot tubs, fireplaces and panoramic views of the coast. Families, businesses and organizations can rent one or more homes (usually just a short walk from one another) depending on the size of the group. The Mendocino coast offers unlimited quiet, privacy and salt air along with a wide variety of activities: hiking, horseback riding, fishing, canoeing and of course, whale watching. Whether you're planning an extended meeting, retreat or casual get-together, Shoreline Properties can arrange facilities to meet all your special event needs.

CAPACITY: There are approximately 25 properties which range in capacity from 2–15 guests.

MEETING ROOMS: Many of the properties can be used for meetings.

FEES & DEPOSITS: Houses rent for $110–275/night with significant discounts for week-long stays. A deposit is due within 10 days of contract receipt. The balance along with bed tax, cleaning fee and refundable security deposit are due at least 3 weeks prior to arrival. Call for exact fees.

CANCELLATION POLICY: A full refund is given within 7 days of making the reservation. With 2 weeks' notice prior to the event date, the charge is 50% of all deposits. With less than 2 weeks' notice, no refund.

AVAILABILITY: Year-round, every day.

SERVICES/AMENITIES:

Restaurant Services: no
Catering: BYO
Kitchen Facilities: adequate
Tables & Chairs: provided
Linens, Silver, etc.: provided
Restrooms: some wca
Dance Floor: no
Cleanup: caterer

Parking: off street
Overnight Accommodations: yes, varies
Telephone: house phone
Outdoor Night Lighting: varies
Outdoor Cooking Facilities: yes
Cleanup: provided
Meeting Equipment: CBA
Special: full event coordination

RESTRICTIONS:

Alcohol: BYO
Smoking: designated areas only
Wheelchair Access: yes
Music: with approval

Insurance: required
Other: children under 12, smoking & pets allowed in some homes

Jenner

MURPHY'S JENNER INN

10400 Coast Highway 1
Jenner, CA 95450
(707) 865-2377
Reserve for Events: 3–6 months in advance
Reserve for Meetings: 2–6 months in advance

Jenner by the Sea is surrounded by fifteen miles of sandy beaches, the ocean and hundreds of acres of state park. And, if you're planning a small getaway, meeting or seminar, the Inn can address all your needs. It's conveniently located right off of the coastal highway, has its own restaurant and offers a variety of overnight accommodations. The Salon, with fireplace, antiques and cut flowers, has a Victorian coastal charm, suitable for private parties. The Solarium, an attractive, fully landscaped 2,000 square foot greenhouse with spectacular views of the coast, is also available. Note that the Inn is an ideal location for a retreat, featuring numerous guestrooms and cottages that have hot tubs, fireplaces and ocean views.

CAPACITY: The Salon holds up to 45 guests; the Solarium, up to 90 guests.

MEETING ROOMS: The Salon up to 50, Captain's Cabin 10–15 and the Pelican 10–15 guests.

FEES & DEPOSITS: Meeting room fees are $75/hour (2-hour minimum) up to $350/day. If 5 or more overnight accommodations are booked with the meeting, the room rental fee is $100/day. For special events, the Inn rents for $100/hour, maximum $500 per day. This includes 1 staff person and beverage service. Catering fees run $10–15/person for lunch and $15–25 for dinner. Half the rental fee is due as a deposit when reservations are confirmed; the balance is payable the day of the event. For overnight stays, rooms are available. Call for specific rates.

CANCELLATION POLICY: A full refund is given with 45 days' notice. With less notice, the refund depends on whether the spaces can be rebooked.

AVAILABILITY: Year-round, daily.

SERVICES/AMENITIES:

Restaurant Services: yes
Catering: provided or BYO if entire inn rented
Kitchen Facilities: ample
Tables & Chairs: provided
Linens, Silver, etc.: provided
Restrooms: no wca
Dance Floor: yes
Meeting Equipment: CBA, extra fee

Parking: on and off street
Overnight Accommodations: 11 rooms, several rental homes
Telephone: pay phone
Outdoor Night Lighting: no
Outdoor Cooking Facilities: no
Cleanup: caterer

RESTRICTIONS:

Alcohol: provided, corkage $5/bottle
Smoking: outside only
Music: no restrictions if entire inn rented

Wheelchair Access: limited
Insurance: not required

Little River

GLENDEVEN

8221 N. Highway 1
Little River, CA 95456
(800) 822-4536 or (707) 937-0083
Reserve for Events: 1–12 months in advance
Reserve for Meetings: 2 weeks–12 months in advance

Glendeven is a delightful small country inn located in a restored 1867 farmhouse. Set back on a headland meadow with the bay of Little River in the distance, the inn's two acres of tended grounds invite you to have a picnic, take a walk, or enjoy the gardens from the brick terrace. The innkeepers have blended antiques with contemporary ceramics, paintings and prints, creating an appealing and interesting decor. Gallery Glendeven, an art gallery on the ground floor of the renovated hay barn, is available for limited special events. The Barnhouse Suite above the gallery is an excellent place for small meetings and team-building retreats.

CAPACITY: The gallery accommodates up to 40, and the maximum for the entire facility is 50.

MEETING ROOMS: Two meeting rooms have a capacity of 12–15 guests.

FEES & DEPOSITS: A refundable deposit of 50% of the total anticipated rental is due when reservations are confirmed, and the balance is due prior to the arrival date. For Friday, Saturday or Sunday, the entire facility rents for $1,500/night and midweek $1,325/night. Breakfast is included in these fees. Room, breakfast tax and 15% gratuity are additional. Individual areas of Glendeven are available for functions. Call for rates.

CANCELLATION POLICY: With 30 days' notice the deposit is returned, less a service charge.

AVAILABILITY: Year-round, every day.

SERVICES/AMENITIES:

Restaurant Services: no
Catering: preferred list or BYO
Kitchen Facilities: moderate
Tables & Chairs: some provided
Linens, Silver, etc.: some provided
Dance Floor: no
Meeting Equipment: BYO or CBA, extra fee

Parking: off street
Overnight Accommodations: 10 guestrooms, 1 suite
Restrooms: no wca
Telephone: designated guest and conference line
Outdoor Night Lighting: minimal
Outdoor Cooking Facilities: no
Cleanup: provided extra fee

RESTRICTIONS:

Alcohol: BYO
Smoking: outside only
Music: with approval

Wheelchair Access: limited
Insurance: not required
Other: no pets

INN AT SCHOOLHOUSE CREEK

7051 N. Highway 1
Little River, CA 95456
(707) 937-5525 Linda Wilson
Reserve for Events: 2–6 months in advance
Reserve for Meetings: 2–3 weeks in advance

Once part of a large coastal ranch, the Inn has offered lodging to visitors since the 1930s. Quaint cottages built at the turn of the century are surrounded by tall cypress trees and gardens. White picket fences add old-fashioned charm. Most of the rooms and cottages have ocean views, small decks and fireplaces. The main inn building, known as the old Ledford home, was built in 1862 and offers a relaxed space for meetings, receptions and dining. Redwood walls and ceilings, wide-plank fir floors, a brick fireplace and baby grand piano create a warm, homey ambiance. The dining room has views of the sea and the adjacent forest. Businesses will appreciate the fact that the Inn can provide all meals, enabling guests to focus on work without interruption. This writer also had an opportunity to sample the Inn's hospitality and clam chowder, and found them both to be exceptional.

CAPACITY: The Inn's main building accommodates 50 standing or 20 seated guests; outdoors, an additional 50 guests. Maximum overnight capacity is 36 guests.

MEETING ROOMS: 5 rooms with a capacity of 6–30 guests.

DEPOSITS & FEES: A deposit of one night's stay is due at the time of booking and the balance is due on arrival. Use of the main building may require rental of the entire Inn. Fees vary depending on the use of the facilities and whether food is included with the event. Per person catering costs run about $7–20 for lunch and $15–25 for dinner.

CANCELLATION POLICY: A full refund less a $10 cancellation fee is given with 1 month's notice or if the rooms are rebooked.

AVAILABILITY: Year-round, every day.

SERVICES/AMENITIES:

Restaurant Services: yes
Catering: provided or BYO licensed
Kitchen Facilities: ample
Tables & Chairs: provided
Linens, Silver, etc.: provided

Parking: off street
Overnight Accommodations: 6 cottages, 7 rooms
Telephone: house phone
Outdoor Night Lighting: no
Outdoor Cooking Facilities: no

Restrooms: no wca
Dance Floor: no
RESTRICTIONS:
Alcohol: provided, BWC only
Smoking: designated areas only
Music: amplified ok if entire inn rented

Cleanup: provided
Meeting Equipment: no

Wheelchair Access: no
Insurance: not required

LITTLE RIVER INN

Highway 1
Little River, CA 95456
(707) 937-5942
Reserve for Events: 2–12 months in advance
Reserve for Meetings: 2–12 months in advance

Built in 1853 by settler Silas Coombs, Little River Inn offers small-town hospitality in the only resort facilities on the Mendocino Coast. The Highway One landmark is owned and operated by the Coombs' great-grandchildren who bring family pride and graciousness to the 225-acre enclave. The inn's rooms are located in and around the original building with some in a lodge-type facility and others in comfortable cottages. Many have fireplaces and commanding views of the magnificent bay. The ocean-view country bar is filled with Little River and family photographs and memorabilia. The Garden Dining Room features chef Judy Griswold's country cuisine, noted for its use of fresh, local products. Adding to the charm of the inn are beautifully landscaped gardens, a challenging golf course, lighted tennis courts and the redwood trails in the adjacent Van Damme State Park.

CAPACITY:	Mallory House (incl. outside area)	30
	Bay Suite Meeting Room	15
	Dining Room	80

MEETING ROOMS: The above rooms are available for meetings, but there are restrictions on the use of the dining room.

FEES & DEPOSITS: A deposit in the amount of the first night's lodging and any special events fee is due by personal or business check shortly after booking. The balance is due at checkout.

CANCELLATION POLICY: A full refund is given with 2 weeks' notice or if all rooms are rebooked.

AVAILABILITY: Year-round, every day. Note that the Dining Room has restricted hours when used as a meeting space, and is closed for several weeks in January.

SERVICES/AMENITIES:
Restaurant Services: yes (breakfast & dinner)
Catering: provided or BYO
Kitchen Facilities: ample

Parking: off street
Overnight Accommodations: 55 rooms
Telephone: guest phones

Tables & Chairs: provided and CBA, extra fee
Linens, Silver, etc.: provided
Restrooms: mostly wca
Dance Floor: yes
Other: event coordination, golf & tennis facilities

Outdoor Night Lighting: yes
Outdoor Cooking Facilities: yes
Cleanup: provided or CBA
Meeting Equipment: yes

RESTRICTIONS:
Alcohol: provided
Smoking: designated rooms or outside
Insurance: not required

Wheelchair Access: limited
Music: amplified ok with approval
Other: no pets

RACHEL'S INN

8200 N. Highway 1
Little River, CA 95456
(707) 937-0088 Rachel Binah
Reserve for Events: 3 months in advance
Reserve for Meetings: 4–6 weeks in advance

The first thing you notice when you drive up to the Inn is the old-fashioned garden. Rachel has a way with flowers—they blossom wildly, creating a tapestry of color all around the grounds. Inside, the Inn is fresh and tasteful. The fireplace in the dining room, piano in the parlor and newly-cut flowers everywhere are the kinds of touches that make guests feel right at home. The space in the Inn is also very flexible and can be arranged to accommodate any of your business or special event needs.

CAPACITY: 30 seated or 125 standing guests. The Inn can hold up to 24 overnight guests.

MEETING ROOMS:

Room	*Capacity*
Dining Room & Parlor	30 at tables, 60 assembly
Sitting Rooms (3)	10

FEES & DEPOSITS: When you hold an event here, your reservation also includes all overnight accommodations. A deposit for 1 night's lodging ($1,171) is due when reservations are made. Catering starts at $25/person and a 20% deposit for catering is required. The balance of all fees is due on departure.

CANCELLATION POLICY: A full refund is given with 1 month's notice or more, otherwise a refund is only given if the rooms are rebooked.

AVAILABILITY: Year-round, every day.

SERVICES/AMENITIES:
Restaurant Services: no
Catering: provided, no BYO
Kitchen Facilities: n/a
Tables & Chairs: provided

Parking: off street
Overnight Accommodations: 9 guestrooms
Telephone: house phone
Outdoor Night Lighting: yes

Linens, Silver, etc.: provided
Restrooms: wca
Dance Floor: no
Other: event coordination

RESTRICTIONS:
Alcohol: provided, corkage $5/bottle
Smoking: allowed
Music: no amplified

Outdoor Cooking Facilities: no
Cleanup: provided, extra fee
Meeting Equipment: CBA

Wheelchair Access: 1st floor only
Insurance: not required

STEVENSWOOD LODGE

8211 Highway 1
Little River, CA 95460
(800) 421-2810
Reserve for Events: 1 month in advance
Reserve for Meetings: 1 month in advance

Stevenswood is located two miles south of Mendocino. Named for Isaiah Stevens, pioneer settler and postmaster of historic Little River, Stevenswood blends the natural beauty of its setting by forest and sea with an elegant and spacious contemporary lodge design. The result of meticulous planning, the inn offers a custom Executive Conference Room, an inviting lounge with a warm wood floor and fireplace, and all the amenities you could want for an overnight stay. The inn also serves as a first-rate gallery, exhibiting paintings and sculpture throughout.

CAPACITY:

Room	Capacity
Executive Conference Room	10 (with conference table)
Lounge	30–40
Suites (2)	3 each

The Inn can accommodate 250 people maximum in the Lounge, Foyer, and outdoors combined.

FEES & DEPOSITS: These vary according to how many guestrooms are booked with your event. 25% of the cost is due at the time of booking, an additional 50% is due 1 month before the event and the rest is due the day of the event. Catering runs about $20–50 per person.

CANCELLATION POLICY: The amount of notice required to receive a refund depends on the number of rooms reserved. Generally it is 4 days for 2 rooms, 1 week for 3 rooms, and 2 weeks for over 4 rooms. Some events require a non-refundable deposit.

AVAILABILITY: Year-round, every day.

SERVICES/AMENITIES:
Restaurant Services: no
Catering: provided, no BYO
Kitchen Facilities: n/a

Parking: off street
Overnight Accommodations: 9 suites, 1 guestroom
Telephone: guest phones

Tables & Chairs: provided
Linens, Silver, etc.: provided
Restrooms: wca
Dance Floor: yes
Other: concierge service, gallery, complimentary wine bar, airport pickup

Outdoor Night Lighting: yes
Outdoor Cooking Facilities: yes
Cleanup: provided, extra fee
Meeting Equipment: VCR

RESTRICTIONS:

Alcohol: provided or BYO
Smoking: outside only
Music: amplified ok

Wheelchair Access: yes
Insurance: not required
Other: limited kinds of functions allowed

Marshall

MARCONI CONFERENCE CENTER

18500 Highway 1
Marshall, CA 94940
(415) 663-9020
Reserve for Events: 1 month–2 years in advance
Reserve for Meetings: 1 month–2 years in advance

Situated on sixty-two acres of wooded hillside overlooking Tomales Bay, the Center is the perfect setting for productive conferences. Meeting areas are designed with break-out rooms and in-house AV equipment. Overnight accommodations support the purpose of the center by providing a smoke-free environment, study desks and a simple, uncluttered decor. The Center prepares all meals and has games, books, films and snacks for evening relaxation. Tranquil and free from urban distractions, the Marconi Conference Center is a great place in which to think.

CAPACITY:

Room	Informal Seating	Classroom	Room	Informal Seating	Classroom
Pine Lodge	30	60	Cypress Lodge	30	60
Break-Out A	6	12	Break-Out A	6	14
Break-Out B	6	10	Pelican Shores	12	24
Buck Hall	60	100			

FEES & DEPOSITS: Rates include lodging, use of meeting spaces, 3 meals and all conference center amenities. The range per person/day is $50–100 depending on the type of accommodation and the room occupancy. A booking deposit is required to hold your space.

CANCELLATION POLICY: The deposit is refundable, less a $100 processing fee, with written notice 180 days prior to the conference date.

AVAILABILITY: Year-round, every day.

SERVICES/AMENITIES:

Restaurant Services: snack/beverage only
Catering: n/a
Kitchen Facilities: n/a
Tables & Chairs: provided
Linens, Silver, etc.: provided
Restrooms: wca
Dance Floor: n/a

Parking: off street
Overnight Accommodations: 40 guestrooms, 96 beds
Telephone: pay phones
Outdoor Night Lighting: access only
Outdoor Cooking Facilities: no
Cleanup: provided
Meeting Equipment: provided, extra fee

RESTRICTIONS:

Alcohol: BYO
Smoking: outside only
Music: amplified ok

Wheelchair Access: yes, hilly terrain
Insurance: not required

Mendocino

AMES LODGE

42287 Little Lake Road
Mendocino, CA 95460
(707) 937-0811
Reserve for Events: 1–2 months in advance
Reserve for Meetings: 1–2 months in advance

Located in a secluded forest near Mendocino, this casual, comfortable family-run lodge is a unique facility for small, private functions. Guests can relax in the main room with its fireplace, stereo, library and piano or gather on the sundeck beneath surrounding redwoods. Nearby trails meander through redwood and pygmy forests or to the river. Only minutes from town and the coast, Ames Lodge provides privacy and intimacy in a truly rustic setting.

CAPACITY: This facility can accommodate day groups of up to 30 guests, overnight up to 18 guests.

FEES & DEPOSITS: You must rent the entire facility. A 2-night deposit for all 7 rooms ($660) is due when reservations are confirmed. The balance is due on arrival. Partial day use rates are $100/day, available in conjunction with overnight use only.

CANCELLATION POLICY: A full refund will be given with 1 month's notice. A sliding fee is imposed on short notice cancellations.

AVAILABILITY: Every day, except for occasional closures.

SERVICES/AMENITIES:

Restaurant Services: no
Catering: BYO, vegetarian only
Kitchen Facilities: ample
Tables & Chairs: provided
Linens, Silver, etc.: provided
Restrooms: wca
Dance Floor: no

Parking: off street
Overnight Accommodations: 7 guestrooms
Telephone: house phone
Outdoor Night Lighting: limited
Outdoor Cooking Facilities: no
Cleanup: provided except for kitchen
Meeting Equipment: BYO

RESTRICTIONS:

Alcohol: BYO BW, hard alcohol discouraged
Smoking: outside only
Music: no amplified

Wheelchair Access: no
Insurance: not required
Other: no pets, no meat

MENDOCINO HOTEL

45080 Main St.
Mendocino, CA 95460
(800) 548-0513 or (707) 937-0511
Reserve for Events: 6–12 months in advance
Reserve for Meetings: 4 months–2 years in advance

The Mendocino Hotel occupies a select spot on the village's Main Street—directly overlooking the rugged Mendocino coast. Built in 1878, the hotel has been carefully remodeled. While the original Victorian style is maintained with antiques, rich wood detailing and stained glass, guests will appreciate the Hotel's many modern amenities. In the main Hotel, the Garden Room is an unusual place to hold a private affair. Once an outdoor patio, it is now enclosed by a translucent ceiling which lets in plenty of light. Plants abound, increasing the sensation of being outside. For meetings, guests gather in two comfortable and quaint board rooms. This is an exceptional place for corporate planning sessions: surrounded by beautiful and quiet surroundings, people relax and are more creative and productive. And the Mendocino Hotel's location couldn't be better—visitors not only have the ocean right across the street, but the entire town with its shops, galleries and distinctive architecture! Whether you come here for a personal or business getaway, the Mendocino Hotel will make your stay a memorable one.

CAPACITY: About 50–80 guests is ideal for private parties, although the Hotel can accommodate more. The Garden Room seats 110, maximum.

MEETING ROOMS: 1 board room can accommodate 16 seated guests; the other holds 32.

FEES & DEPOSITS: The Garden Room's fee varies, call for current rates. Catered luncheons run $8–15/person, dinners $15–30/person, hors d'oeuvres start at $5/person and buffets can be arranged. Half the estimated cost is due 30 days prior to the event and the balance is due upon departure. If you'd like to use the board rooms, the rate is $75/half day, $125/full day; fees may be waived if your group books a minimum of 10 guestrooms.

CANCELLATION POLICY: The cancellation policy depends on the number of rooms reserved.

AVAILABILITY: Year-round, every day, anytime.

SERVICES/AMENITIES:

Restaurant Services: yes
Catering: provided, no BYO
Kitchen Facilities: n/a
Tables & Chairs: provided
Linens, Silver, etc.: provided
Restrooms: wca
Dance Floor: yes

Parking: on and off street
Overnight Accommodations: 51 guestrooms
Telephone: guest phones
Outdoor Night Lighting: limited
Outdoor Cooking Facilities: no
Cleanup: provided
Meeting Equipment: standard audio-visual

RESTRICTIONS:

Alcohol: provided, no BYO
Smoking: not in Garden Room
Music: with approval

Wheelchair Access: yes
Insurance: not required
Other: event coordination

Monte Rio

HUCKLEBERRY SPRINGS

8105 Old Beedle Rd.
Monte Rio, CA 95462
(800) 822-2683 or **(707) 865-2683**
Reserve for Events: 1–12 months in advance
Reserve for Meetings: 2–8 weeks in advance

Above the Russian River is Huckleberry Springs, an unusual country inn with accommodations for a larger party or for just a few guests. With its fresh, regional cuisine and natural hot springs, this retreat facility with five cabins gives guests the advantages of the French auberge and the Japanese ryokan. Located on fifty-six heavily wooded acres, the inn enjoys spectacular views of the surrounding hills. The main lodge is comfortable and airy with lots of light from windows and skylights. A new Solarium dining addition is also available for events. Parties often take place outdoors, in the redwood groves nearby or on the water garden deck, which also has wonderful vistas. Guests can sunbathe on the deck and at the swimming pool or totally relax in the spa. Each cabin is unique in design, but all offer privacy, wood stoves and the soothing, restful feeling that comes from communing in the forest. Huckleberry Springs can arrange private dinners, formal seated meals and/or buffets, all in-house.

CAPACITY: The facility accommodates 65 guests for events, and 17 for an overnight stay.

MEETING ROOMS: The Main Lodge accommodates 40–50, the Dining Solarium 20 and the Conference House, 15–20.

FEES & DEPOSITS: Most events require that you reserve all overnight accommodations. If you book the entire inn, the fee is approximately $600 per night (double occupancy for 4 cabins). For Mon–Fri day use only, the fee is $450 for 4-1/2-hours. A 2-night minimum is required for events on weekends. Half the rental fee is due when reservations are confirmed; the balance is payable on departure. Catering costs range from $11–19/person, depending on guest count and menu selections.

CANCELLATION POLICY: Special events require 30 days' notice for a full refund.

AVAILABILITY: Open Wednesday–Sunday; closed Monday & Tuesday. Closed January and February.

SERVICES/AMENITIES:

Restaurant Services: no
Catering: provided or BYO, must be licensed
Kitchen Facilities: ample
Tables & Chairs: provided
Linens, Silver, etc.: provided or BYO
Restrooms: wca, main building only
Dance Floor: pool area or deck

Parking: off street
Overnight Accommodations: 5 cabins
Telephone: house phone
Outdoor Night Lighting: limited
Outdoor Cooking Facilities: BBQ
Cleanup: caterer
Meeting Equipment: CBA, no extra fee

RESTRICTIONS:

Alcohol: BW provided, no BYO
Smoking: outside only
Music: amplified ok

Wheelchair Access: limited
Insurance: required for day use
Other: no pets

Occidental

INN AT OCCIDENTAL

3657 Church Street
Occidental, CA 95465
(707) 874-1311
Reserve for Events: 1–6 months in advance
Reserve for Meetings: 1 week–3 months in advance

Nestled against a hillside of berries and fruit trees, the Inn at Occidental combines the warmth and charm of a country inn with the services of a big-city hotel. It was built in 1988 as a replica of the original Victorian that once occupied the site, and fits in perfectly with the restored village of Occidental. When you walk through the front door, a pine harvest table with a beautiful floral arrangement sets the tone, and all of the rooms are furnished with antiques and original art. The inn is especially well-suited for corporate seminars or retreats, with comfortable meeting areas on two levels. The Gallery Lobby downstairs serves as both a conference room and an art gallery. Oil paintings and watercolors primarily by local artists adorn the walls, and a crackling fire in the massive stone fireplace takes the chill off during winter months. The dining room upstairs is light and airy thanks to a wall of French windows overlooking the garden. A set of French doors opens onto a Victorian porch that wraps around the entire inn. When the weather's warm, the porch is a delightful spot for a private dinner party or reception. To fully appreciate the country air, host a party in the lushly landscaped courtyard. A moss-covered fountain flows softly in the center, and azaleas, rhododendrons, hydrangeas and many other varieties of flowers form a colorful border. The Inn's restaurant uses only local, organically grown produce, meats and breads, and features wines exclusively from Russian River wineries. Inn staff are extremely service-oriented, and are available to take care of business needs, help guests plan activities in the surrounding countryside and even provide room service. If you're looking for an intimate setting for a family get-together, conference or party, the Inn at Occidental offers everything you need.

CAPACITY:

	Seated	*Standing*		*Seated*	*Standing*
Gallery Lobby	30	50	Victorian Porch	20	40
Dining Room	26	50	Courtyard	60	100

Maximum capacity of the inn is 200

MEETING ROOMS: All of the above areas can be used for meetings (porch and courtyard subject to weather).

FEES & DEPOSITS: For events, you are usually required to rent the entire inn for 2 nights on weekends or 1 night mid-week. The weekend rate is $1,515/night; the mid-week rate is $1,280/night. An 8% tax is additional. A deposit of 1 night's room rental fees is due when reservations are confirmed. An additional deposit for food, beverages and any other services is negotiated and required the following week along with a $500 facility fee. The facility fee may be waived depending on food and beverage consumption. The balance of the room rental fees is due at checkout; the balance of the food/services fees is due 48 hours prior to the event. Per person food costs run $25–75 for events. Beverage, tax and a 15% gratuity are additional. For meetings, a deli service is available and other food arrangements can be made.

CANCELLATION POLICY: A full refund is given with 30 days' notice. With less notice, the food/services deposit will be forfeit, and the room rental deposit will only be returned if the rooms can be rebooked.

AVAILABILITY: Year-round, 7am–2am.

SERVICES/AMENITIES:

Restaurant Services: yes
Catering: provided, no BYO
Kitchen Facilities: n/a
Tables & Chairs: provided
Linens, Silver, etc.: provided
Restrooms: wca
Dance Floor: portable CBA, extra fee
Other: concierge service

Parking: on and off street
Overnight Accommodations: 9 guestrooms, additional CBA
Telephone: guest phones
Outdoor Night Lighting: yes
Outdoor Cooking Facilities: no
Cleanup: provided
Meeting Equipment: CBA

RESTRICTIONS:

Alcohol: provided, corkage $10/bottle
Smoking: outside only
Insurance: not required

Wheelchair Access: yes
Music: amplified ok if entire inn rented
Other: no children or pets

Atherton

HOLBROOK PALMER PARK

150 Watkins Avenue
Atherton, CA 94027
(415) 688-6534
Reserve for Events: 2 years in advance
Reserve for Meetings: 1 week in advance

Holbrook Palmer Park is what's left of an old estate, complete with historic buildings, mature oak trees and an 1870 water tower. Located on Watkins Avenue between El Camino and Middlefield Road, the park consists of twenty-two acres of open space in exclusive residential Atherton. The main house rests in the center of the property and has wide, gracious steps that lead from the main event room down to a spacious patio framed by large trees. The patio and steps are perfect for an outdoor celebration. Nearby is the Jennings Pavilion, a modern structure which can accommodate large events and bands. Outside the Pavilion is another patio which is appropriate for seated functions. Additionally, the 1896 Carriage House is available for special parties and business functions. The Carriage House is particularly good for meetings, seminars and workshops. Although you might think that a facility in Atherton would require formality, just the opposite is true. The main house, Carriage House and Pavilion can accommodate a wide variety of functions, and on warm days, the feeling here is one of relaxed informality.

CAPACITY: The Main House indoors, 75 seated guests; with outdoor seating, 100 guests. The Jennings Pavilion holds 250 guests including outside seating; the Carriage House seats 85 guests.

FEES & DEPOSITS: A $250 refundable security/damage deposit is required when reservations are made. Resident refers to a resident of Atherton.

Special Events:

Guests	Resident Fee	Non-Resident Fee
1–100	$700	$1,000
101–200	1,200	1,500
201–250	1,600	1,900

The use fee is payable 1 month before the event. Fees are based on a 7-hour use period; 1–2 hours for setup, 4–5 hours for the event, 1 hour for cleanup. For events exceeding 7 hours, a charge $50/hour charge will apply. Additional hours must be arranged in advance.

Meetings:

Area	Guests	Fee Half Day (4 hrs)	Fee Full Day (over 4 hrs or evenings)
Main House	1–75	$100	$125
Carriage House	1–100	125	150
Jennings Pavilion	1–100	125	175
	101–200	150	250

Evening meetings are charged the full day rate plus a $25/hour supervisory fee which applies after 6pm.

CANCELLATION POLICY: With 6 months' notice, the deposit is refunded; with 4–6 months' notice, $200; and 2–3 months' notice, $175 is refunded.

AVAILABILITY: Saturdays 10am–5pm or 5pm–midnight, including setup and cleanup. Sundays, only one event which must end by 9pm. Cleanup must be completed by 10pm. Weekday business functions are held Mon–Fri 7:45am–11pm.

SERVICES/AMENITIES:

Restaurant Services: no
Catering: BYO or provided
Kitchen Facilities: yes
Tables & Chairs: some provided
Linens, Silver, etc.: BYO
Restrooms: wca in Pavilion only
Dance Floor: CBA

Parking: several lots
Overnight Accommodations: no
Telephone: pay phones
Outdoor Night Lighting: yes
Outdoor Cooking Facilities: BYO
Cleanup: caterer
Meeting Equipment: no

RESTRICTIONS:

Alcohol: BYO
Smoking: outside only
Music: amplified inside only

Wheelchair Access: yes
Insurance: included in fees, not required if no alcohol is served

Belmont

RALSTON HALL

1500 Ralston Avenue
Belmont, CA 94002
(415) 508-3501 ext. 501
Reserve for Events: 12 months in advance
Reserve for Meetings: 6 weeks in advance

Ralston Hall is a stunning Victorian mansion, completed in 1867 by William Chapman Ralston, founder of the Bank of California. Ralston purchased the land in 1864 and modified the original Italian villa with touches of Steamboat Gothic and Victorian details to create a lavish and opulent estate. The exterior of this three-story mansion is meticulously maintained. The front doors have delicately etched glass panes. Inside, Ralston Hall is an outstanding example of a by-gone era. The first floor consists of a large ballroom, several parlors, dining rooms and a sun porch. Each room is decorated with beautiful antiques, stunning crystal chandeliers and elegant oriental rugs. The ballroom is particularly sensational. The patterned hardwood floors are encircled by mirrored walls. Three delicate chandeliers hang gracefully from the huge skylight. At the far end of the ballroom is a large bay window with a curving green moiré bench seat and regal matching draperies. Musicians can set up in a ballroom alcove without interfering with the grandeur and flow of the ballroom floor. The spacious dining rooms were decorated with an attention to detail that is mind-boggling by today's standards. Because of its size and layout, you can choose from a variety of setups that include the entire first floor or the West or East wings. This facility is a special and outstanding location for an elegant, sophisticated and memorable event.

CAPACITY: The entire facility can accommodate 250 guests. The East Wing, 150 seated guests and the West Wing, 100 guests with partial seating.

FEES & DEPOSITS: A $500 refundable deposit is required when you make reservations. For an 8-hour social or business function, the fee for the first floor, Sunday–Thursday, is $3,800, Friday or Saturday $4,000. For business functions only, Monday–Thursday (up to 5 hours 9am–4pm, not to exceed 100 guests) the rental fee for the West Wing is $100/hour, East Wing $125/hour or the entire first floor $150/hour.

CANCELLATION POLICY: If you cancel 120 days prior to your event, your deposit minus a $50 administration fee is refunded.

AVAILABILITY: Ralston Hall is open for events every day 9am-1am, except Thanksgiving Day, December 24–25th, December 31st and January 1st.

SERVICES/AMENITIES:

Restaurant Services: no
Catering: BYO from approved list
Kitchen Facilities: moderate
Tables & Chairs: CBA, extra charge
Linens, Silver, etc.: BYO
Restrooms: wca
Dance Floor: yes except for West Wing
Meeting Equipment: podium, microphone

Parking: ample
Overnight Accommodations: no
Telephone: local calls only
Outdoor Night Lighting: no
Outdoor Cooking Facilities: BBQ
Cleanup: caterer
Other: hostess available

RESTRICTIONS:

Alcohol: BYO
Smoking: not permitted
Music: amplified ok

Wheelchair Access: limited
Insurance: extra liability required
Other: candles not permitted

Need a caterer, cake maker, florist? The Service Directory starting on page 614 features the best in the business.

Burlingame

HYATT REGENCY
San Francisco Airport

1333 Bayshore Highway
Burlingame, CA 94010
(415) 347-1234
Reserve for Events: 5–7 months in advance
Reserve for Meetings: 3 months in advance

How often have you walked into a hotel and thought, "This place is so spacious, light, and incredibly pleasant, I could stay in here all day"? If you've never had the experience, pay a visit to the San Francisco Airport Hyatt. The heart of the hotel is its soaring atrium lobby. Warmed by sunlight and soft earth tones, it gives the spirit an immediate lift. An open cafe/lounge in the center is an irresistible place for a bite after a meeting. Gently burbling water flows down several waterfalls and through a series of tableside aqueducts and pools, creating a soothing undercurrent. And as you sit beneath a redwood gazebo, surrounded by lush ficus trees, enormous ferns, birds of paradise and golden bamboo, it's hard to believe you're indoors. Both ballrooms are also designed in appealing, neutral colors, and the Regency Ballroom is unique in its triangular shape and use of art deco lighting. Corporate clients will appreciate not only the variety of meeting spaces, but the full-service business center and health club as well. A fun place for a private party is the Knuckles Sports Bar. Reminiscent of "Cheers," it features a massive wood bar and an abundance of wood paneling. A colorful mural of a 1920s baseball game overlooks the pool tables at one end of the room, and photos of famous local athletes adorn the walls. Glassware hangs over the bar, illuminated by the wall of windows behind it. Barrels of peanuts and plenty of vintage sports paraphernalia add old-fashioned touches. Conveniently located near the San Francisco Airport, the Hyatt offers a versatile environment for any type of event.

CAPACITY:	*Area*	*Banquet*	*Reception*	*Classroom*	*Theatre*
	Grand Peninsula Ballroom	120–1,500	160–1,930	110–1,258	170–2,025
	Regency Ballroom	130–420	189–608	120–350	150–644
	Harbour Room	60–120	90–195	30–100	80–180
	Sandpebble Room	48–240	61–311	24–120	60–300

All of the above rooms can be sectioned.

MEETING ROOMS: The hotel has over 45,000 square feet of meeting space, including 3 boardrooms and 8 conference rooms.

FEES & DEPOSITS: A non-refundable $200–500 deposit is required when reservations are confirmed. The balance is due prior to the event. Per person food costs start at $18 for lunch, $23 for dinner and $25 for buffets. Beverage, tax and an 18% service charge are additional.

CANCELLATION POLICY: The deposit is non-refundable.

AVAILABILITY: Year-round, every day, 8am–1:30am.

SERVICES/AMENITIES:

Restaurant Services: yes

Catering: provided, no BYO

Kitchen Facilities: n/a

Tables & Chairs: provided

Linens, Silver, etc.: provided

Restrooms: wca

Dance Floor: yes

Other: event coordination, pianos, stage

Parking: large complimentary lot or valet

Overnight Accommodations: 793 guestrooms

Telephone: pay phones, guest phones

Outdoor Night Lighting: n/a

Outdoor Cooking Facilities: no

Cleanup: provided

Meeting Equipment: provided, extra fee

RESTRICTIONS:

Alcohol: provided, no BYO

Smoking: designated areas

Music: amplified ok

Wheelchair Access: yes

Insurance: not required

KOHL MANSION

2750 Adeline Drive
Burlingame, CA 94010
(415) 591-7422
Reserve for Events: 12 months in advance
Reserve for Meetings: 6 months in advance

Commissioned by C. Frederick Kohl and his wife in 1912, the Kohl Mansion was built on forty acres of oak woodlands in Burlingame. Kohl, heir to a shipping fortune, loved to entertain and created this grand estate to include manor house, tennis court, pool, green houses, rose garden and large carriage house. The elegant rosebrick Tudor mansion is again available for parties and has many spectacular rooms for events and business functions. The wood-paneled Library, with large granite fireplace, book cases and graceful French doors opening to a center courtyard, ends in a Gothic bay window which catches the light filtered through the oaks on the lawns outside. The sizable Great Hall, a copy of the Arlington Tudor Hall in Essex, England, was built for music and entertaining. It has very high ceilings, plus its oak paneling and walnut floors create a fine acoustical setting for music. A lighter twin of the Library, the spacious and airy Dining Room has delicate, pristine white plaster relief on the walls and ceiling. This marvelous dining environment is complete with views of oaks and lawns from bay windows. Guests can roam outdoors, surrounded by a courtyard combination of green lawns, red brick bordered by aggregate and a large terrace. The Kohl Mansion is a perfect facility for those who want a grand and elegant environment.

CAPACITY: Indoors, the Mansion can hold 450 standing or 250 seated guests. The indoor facilities plus outdoor tents can hold up to 600 for a reception or 400 seated guests.

FEES & DEPOSITS:

	Guests	Saturday and Sunday		Guests	Friday	
		Oct–Mar	Apr–Sept		Oct–Mar	Apr–Sept
Use of the entire mansion:	80–100	$2,700	$3,000	80–100	$2,400	$2,600
	100–150	2,900	3,200	—	—	—
	151–250	3,400	3,600	150–250	3,000	3,200
	251–350	4,000	4,200	251–350	3,600	3,800

A $500 security deposit is due when you reserve your date; the final balance is due 30 days in advance of the party. There is also a $12/table setup charge and $100 fee for use of the baby grand piano. The rental fee for tents is about $1,200, depending on size.

CANCELLATION POLICY: The deposit, minus $50, will be refunded only if the date can be rebooked.

AVAILABILITY: From Sept–June, parties can be held after 4pm on Fridays and anytime on Saturday and Sunday. June through mid-August, every day, anytime.

SERVICES/AMENITIES:

Restaurant Services: no

Catering: BYO, select from list

Kitchen Facilities: ample

Tables & Chairs: provided

Linens, Silver, etc.: BYO

Restrooms: wca

Dance Floor: yes

Meeting Equipment: podium, black boards

Parking: lot or on street

Overnight Accommodations: no

Telephone: pay phone

Outdoor Night Lighting: limited

Outdoor Cooking Facilities: BBQ

Cleanup: caterer

Other: baby grand piano

RESTRICTIONS:

Alcohol: BYO, bartender required

Smoking: outside only

Music: amplified inside until 10pm

Wheelchair Access: yes

Insurance: certificate required

Hillsborough

THE CROCKER MANSION

6565 Skyline Boulevard
Hillsborough, CA 94010
(415) 348-2272
Reserve for Events: 6–12 months in advance

The Crocker Mansion, a palatial estate designed by the architect of San Francisco's Opera House and City Hall, was built for W.W. Crocker in the 1930s. The large white facade and arches create an atmosphere of permanence and stability. Guests are ushered into the Mansion through impressive wood double doors into a round foyer and second set of double doors leading into the Ballroom. The Ballroom, complete with lofty arched glass doors and fireplace with mantel, is light and airy. The room has a wide stone balcony with sensational views of the adjacent property that is landscaped with orange and olive trees. The building is bordered by impeccably kept gardens and a serene woodland running thirty-five acres along Hillsborough's Skyline Ridge. Several areas are especially well suited for outdoor celebrations: the wide lawns joined by a winding fieldstone stairway and a cloistered courtyard are graced by manicured hedges and bright flowers. The Italian Renaissance-style mansion, now a private school for children, is a beautiful and versatile event setting for large or small private parties.

CAPACITY: In summer, the Mansion can accommodate 300 guests using both indoor and outdoor spaces. In winter, 100–150 guests, depending on use.

DONATION: The minimum donation is $2,500 and includes use of the Mansion for one 8-hour event.

AVAILABILITY: Saturday and Sunday only.

SERVICES/AMENITIES:

Restaurant Services: no

Catering: BYO, select from preferred list

Kitchen Facilities: moderate

Tables & Chairs: provided for 150 guests

Linens, Silver, etc.: caterer

Restrooms: no wca

Dance Floor: yes

Meeting Equipment: no

Parking: large lot

Overnight Accommodations: no

Telephone: pay phone

Outdoor Night Lighting: limited

Outdoor Cooking Facilities: CBA

Cleanup: caterer

Other: baby grand piano

RESTRICTIONS:

Alcohol: BYO, service by caterer only

Smoking: outside only

Music: amplified inside, acoustical outside

Wheelchair Access: limited

Insurance: required

Menlo Park

LATHAM HOPKINS GATEHOUSE

555 Ravenswood
Menlo Park, CA 94025
(415) 858-3470
Reserve for Events: 3–6 months in advance
Reserve for Meetings: 2–4 weeks in advance

The Gatehouse is a Victorian structure that has been tastefully restored to its former splendor. This facility is rather small, and lends itself to more intimate gatherings. With mansard roof and decorative Victorian shingling, the Gatehouse is an attractive reminder of days gone by. The main entrance for functions is at the back of the house, where a circular lawn is ringed by large oaks. Beyond the small lawn is a much larger lawn backdrop, separating the Gatehouse from City Offices. At the lawn's edge is an old-fashioned fountain supported by two Mermen (as opposed to Mermaids), with water spouting out of the mouths of fanciful turtles and lion-like animals. The Gatehouse has a medium-sized wood deck with stairs gracefully cascading down to the lawn. (This is a splendid place for a ceremony). Its interior is decorated with understated floral wallpaper and attractive appointments. The dining room, living room and kitchen are available for functions. Even though the Latham Hopkins Gatehouse can accommodate only very small parties, it has considerable charm and appeal.

CAPACITY: In the winter, the Gatehouse can accommodate 44 guests including 15 seated. In the summer, the facility can hold up to 100 total for a standing buffet with 45 seated guests using the patio area.

FEES & DEPOSITS: The total rental fee is required as a refundable deposit: $400 cleaning/security deposit plus the $60–72/hour rental fee multiplied by the number of hours anticipated. The cleaning/security deposit is usually returned 2–3 weeks after your event. The rental fee is $60/hour for Menlo Park residents and $72/hour for non-residents. This fee includes a staff person for your function and applies to a 3-hour block minimum.

CANCELLATION POLICY: If you give more than 2 weeks' notice, the total deposit is refunded less $25.

AVAILABILITY: Monday–Friday 1pm–10pm; Saturday and Sunday, all day to 8pm.

SERVICES/AMENITIES:
Restaurant Services: no
Catering: BYO
Kitchen Facilities: minimal
Tables & Chairs: BYO
Linens, Silver, etc.: BYO

Parking: on street, lot
Overnight Accommodations: no
Telephone: no
Outside Night Lighting: limited
Outdoor Cooking Facilities: BBQ

Restrooms: no wca
Dance Floor: no

RESTRICTIONS:
Alcohol: BYO, WBC only
Smoking: outside only
Music: no amplified

Cleanup: caterer
Meeting Equipment: no

Wheelchair Access: no
Insurance: not required

STANFORD PARK HOTEL

100 El Camino Real
Menlo Park, CA 94025
(415) 322-1234   Rita Hubner
Reserve for Events: 3–9 months in advance
Reserve for Meetings: 1–2 months in advance

Opened just seven years ago, the Stanford Park Hotel offers several choice spaces for your celebration. Inside the brass entry doors is a softly lit lobby with an immense brick fireplace and oak staircase. Just past the lobby is a beautiful inner courtyard with old world ambiance that we enthusiastically recommend for outdoor functions. Although the Stanford Park is located on busy El Camino Real, its tranquil courtyard is completely insulated from the noise of traffic and urban bustle. It is beautifully landscaped, with lots of multi-colored flowers, good-sized trees and handsome, stone benches. The upper courtyard is separated from the larger, lower courtyard by a vine-covered brick wall. Permanently seated on a bench in the upper area is a full bronze statue of Benjamin Franklin, a guest at every event here. The lovely walkway is bordered by blooming flowers. Free-standing beige canvas umbrellas are available to shade guests in the lower courtyard. Inside the Hotel, the Atherton, Menlo and Woodside Rooms are popular spaces for small indoor functions or dinner parties. These pleasant spaces are all designed in a classic style with a contemporary touch. They have high vaulted ceilings, soft muted colors and are furnished with pieces designed specifically for the Stanford Park. And for guests who'd like to stay overnight, we like the fact that special room rates are offered groups.

CAPACITY, FEES & DEPOSITS:

Area	*Seated*	*Standing*	*Rental Fee* (4 1/2 hours)
Menlo Room	64	—	$100
Atherton Room	64	—	100
Woodside Room	130	180 (incl. foyer)	250
The Courtyard	250	250	450

A non-refundable deposit of $500 is required to secure your date and is payable when reservations are confirmed. 80% of the estimated event total is due 2 weeks prior to the event with the balance payable by the end of the function. For anytime over 4-1/2 hours there will be $100/hour charge. Food service is provided. Per person rates: luncheons start at $16, dinners at $22 and buffets range from $24–41. Tax and a 17% gratuity are additional.

AVAILABILITY: Year round, every day from 9am–midnight. The Courtyard is available May–September, 9am–10pm.

SERVICES/AMENITIES:

Restaurant Services: yes

Catering: provided, no BYO

Kitchen Facilities: n/a

Tables & Chairs: provided

Linens, Silver, etc.: provided

Restrooms: wca

Meeting Equipment: CBA, extra fee

Other: event coordination

Parking: large lot

Overnight Accommodations: 163 guestrooms

Telephone: pay phones

Outdoor Night Lighting: yes

Outdoor Cooking Facilities: no

Cleanup: provided

Dance Floor: yes, Woodside room $50 extra fee

RESTRICTIONS:

Alcohol: provided, WC corkage $10/bottle

Smoking: designated areas

Insurance: not required

Wheelchair Access: yes

Music: amplified within reason

Mountain View

RENGSTORFF HOUSE

Shoreline at Mountain View
Mountain View, CA 94039
(415) 903-6088 Events coordinator
Reserve for Events: 3–12 months in advance
Reserve for Meetings: 2 weeks in advance

Some old homes have such character, historic interest and charm, that concerned citizens rescue them from the wrecking ball at the last minute. Such is the case with Rengstorff House, an Italianate-style Victorian that has received a new lease on life from the City of Mountain View. Purchased by the City, the house was relocated to its current site and completely renovated. A circular walkway leads to the cream-colored home with its widow's walk and green-trimmed windows. The surrounding yard has been well-landscaped. To one side is a pretty brick patio surrounded by hedges and perennials and handsome park benches. An expansive green lawn extending beyond the patio is bordered by a white picket fence; beyond is a fifty-acre saltwater lake. Inside the Rengstorff House are three front parlors and a dining area downstairs available for your celebration. Each has wainscotted walls, polished oak floors, carved marble fireplaces and stunning Bradbury & Bradbury period reproduction wallpapers. The home has Eastlake furnishings, mixed with some beautiful antique pieces donated by local residents. Original paintings by John Rengstorff decorate the walls. The dining room, running the width of the house, has a brick fireplace with marble hearth, wood wainscotting, walls in burgundy and gold, lovely large Persian rugs on the hardwood floor and two large antique dining tables with matching burgundy upholstered chairs. Although it is situated in an urban environment, the Rengstorff House affords its guests the privacy of the country. It is a nice location for an afternoon meeting with a garden luncheon.

CAPACITY: Indoors 24 seated; 60 standing. Indoors and outdoors combined, 85 guests maximum.

FEES & DEPOSITS: A refundable deposit of 50% of rental fee is payable when reservations are confirmed. The balance plus a $500 refundable security deposit are due 30 days prior to the event. The rental fee Monday–Friday is $300 for a 3-hour minimum, with $100 for each additional hour. Weekend rates: $375 for a 3-hour minimum, with $125 for each additional hour. For a full 8-hour day, the rate is $850.

CANCELLATION POLICY: With 60 days' notice, deposits refunded, less a $50 fee.

AVAILABILITY: Daily, except for Sun, Tues or Wed 11am–5pm, when the House has public tours.

SERVICES/AMENITIES:

Restaurant Services: no
Catering: BYO
Kitchen Facilities: fully equipped
Tables & Chairs: BYO
Linens, Silver, etc.: BYO
Restrooms: wca
Meeting Equipment: no
Other: service referrals

Parking: large lot and special lot
Overnight Accommodations: no
Telephone: pay phone
Outdoor Night Lighting: yes
Outdoor Cooking Facilities: no
Cleanup: renter or caterer
Dance Floor: terraces

RESTRICTIONS:

Alcohol: BYO, BWC only
Smoking: outside only
Insurance: liability required

Wheelchair Access: yes
Music: acoustic only
Other: no red wine

Palo Alto

GARDEN COURT HOTEL

520 Cowper Street
Palo Alto, CA 94301
(800) 824-9028 or **(415) 322-9000**
Reserve for Events: 4–12 months in advance
Reserve for Meetings: 2–3 months in advance

Designed as a re-creation of a European village square, this four-story hotel looks more like something you'd see in a Tuscan town than in bustling downtown Palo Alto. Yet it offers one of the few spots on the Peninsula where you can host your special event and house all your guests at the same location. The Garden Court Hotel provides a warm Mediterranean ambiance combined with modern facilities and top-notch service. All is visually appealing: dark green and white trim contrast against terra cotta-colored walls, potted planters are filled to the brim with colorful annuals and perennials. Built in the shape of a square, the structure encloses an inviting interior courtyard. Guests can relax in the warm sun, sip champagne or sample hors d'oeuvres before returning to the expansive Courtyard Ballroom for a seated meal. Just like in an Italian village, a multitude of balconies allow guests to watch and enjoy the activities from above. Additional rooms, which can accommodate seminars, meetings and conferences on the Garden Court's second floor, come with terraces and feature large, arched windows. Another benefit of having your function here is that the in-house caterer is Il Fornaio, a restaurant renowned for its Northern Italian cuisine.

CAPACITY:

	Theater	*Reception*	*Banquet*	*Classroom*	*Conference*	*U-Shape*
Grove I &II, each	35	50	30	20	14	14
Grove III	100	100	60	50	35	35
Grove I, II & III	200	200	175	100	65	60
Courtyard I	30	30	20	20	10	10
Courtyard II & III, each	50	70–75	50–60	40–45	20–22	20–22
Courtyard IV	120	150	100	70	48	40
Courtyard I–IV	—	300	250	—	—	—
Terrace Room	70	80	50	30	25	25
Board Room	20	25	20	10	15	—

FEES & DEPOSITS: A $500 non-refundable deposit is due within 2 weeks of booking, which is applied to the event balance. The estimated total is due 2 weeks prior to the event, and any remaining balance is due 30 days after of the event. The rental fee for the Grove Room is $250 Sunday–Friday and Saturday during the day, and $500 Saturday evening. The rental fee for the courtyard is $500. There is no rental fee for the Terrace Room, however there is a guaranteed 30-guest minimum. Meals run $25–35 per person; beverages, tax and 17% service charge are additional. For daytime meetings, the rental rates are $200–1,000, depending on the number of rooms and days of week rented.

AVAILABILITY:

	Weekday	*Saturday*	*Sunday*
	any 5 hours	*any 5 hours*	*any 5 hours*
Terrace Room or Grove Ballroom	8am–5pm	11:30am–4:30pm	10am–midnight
	6pm–midnight	6pm–midnight	
Courtyard Ballroom	8am–5pm	10am–8pm	10am–8pm

SERVICES/AMENITIES:

Restaurant Services: yes
Catering: provided, no BYO
Kitchen Facilities: n/a
Tables & Chairs: provided
Linens, Silver, etc.: provided
Restrooms: wca
Dance Floor: yes

Parking: complimentary valet, large lot
Overnight Accommodations: 61 guestrooms
Telephone: pay phones
Outdoor Night Lighting: access only
Outdoor Cooking Facilities: no
Cleanup: provided
Meeting Equipment: full AV, extra cost

RESTRICTIONS:

Alcohol: provided, corkage $10 /bottle, WC only
Smoking: designated areas
Music: amplified ok

Wheelchair Access: yes
Insurance: not required

STANFORD BARN

Corner of Welch and Quarry Roads
Palo Alto, CA 94304
(415) 322-4341
Reserve for Events: 1–12 months in advance
Reserve for Meetings: 2 weeks–12 months in advance

This landmark building has just become the newest spot for special events on the Peninsula. Built by Leland Stanford in 1888, it's had a long and illustrious past as a working winery, dairy barn and cattlemen's association headquarters. A handsome, three-story brick structure shaded by mature palms and softened by ivy clinging to its walls, it now houses offices, the California Cafe and attractive retail shops. One of the last reminders of a time when Stanford was really a farm, the Barn is a survivor of a bygone era. It stayed intact through the 1906 quake and luckily avoided the wrecking ball during the urban encroachments of the 40s, 50s and 60s. And even though the Stanford Shopping Center, Hospital and University have mushroomed around it, the Barn still stands, its exterior virtually unchanged since it was built. The southwest portion of the ground floor and adjacent wind-protected courtyard are available for events and business functions. The main interior room is brightened by French windows, several of which overlook the patio. Dark green shutters and window trim complement the terra cotta color of old brick walls, and a fifteen-foot ceiling is supported by three wood posts which punctuate an otherwise open and uncluttered space. One set of doors opens onto a landscaped courtyard, perfect for seated luncheons, outdoor receptions or cocktails and hors d'oeuvres. A nearby lawn can also be used for prefunction activities. This combination of spaces is the answer for those who beg us for the perfect Peninsula event location: a garden spot with an interior space that can handle a large group when the weather proves uncooperative.

CAPACITY: Inside, up to 200 seated guests, 275 standing. In combination with the courtyard, up to 290 seated, 350 standing guests.

MEETING ROOMS: 1 breakout room with a seated capacity of 30 guests.

FEES & DEPOSITS: A deposit in the amount of half the rental fee is the refundable deposit required to secure your date. The rental fee balance plus a $500 cleaning/security deposit are due 7 days prior to the event. Please call for current rental rates.

CANCELLATION POLICY: With 30 days' notice the deposit will be returned.

AVAILABILITY: Year-round, daily from 8am–2am.

SERVICES/AMENITIES:

Restaurant Services: CBA
Catering: CBA or BYO
Kitchen Facilities: set up only
Tables & Chairs: CBA or BYO
Linens, Silver, etc.: BYO
Restrooms: wca
Dance Floor: CBA or courtyard

Parking: large lot
Overnight Accommodations: no
Telephone: pay phones
Outdoor Night Lighting: yes
Outdoor Cooking Facilities CBA
Cleanup: caterer or CBA
Meeting Equipment: CBA

RESTRICTIONS:
Alcohol: CBA or BYO
Smoking: outside only
Music: amplified ok

Wheelchair Access: yes
Insurance: not required

Portola Valley

LADERA OAKS

3249 Alpine Road
Portola Valley, CA 94028
(415) 854-3101 Annie
Reserve for Events: 1–6 months in advance
Reserve for Meetings: 1 week–12 months in advance

Located off Alpine Road in Portola Valley, the Ladera Oaks' shingled clubhouse and beautifully landscaped grounds provide a really pleasant indoor and outdoor event facility. The building's exterior is covered with vines and the courtyard garden between clubhouse and pools has an extremely attractive interior garden, with two-tiered lawn areas surrounded by oak trees, flowering annuals and perennials. There's also a raised brick patio, well suited for presentations and non-amplified bands. The clubhouse offers a sizable space for indoor dining, with hardwood floors and large picture windows overlooking the garden. An adjoining lounge can be used in conjunction with the large event space or separately for smaller gatherings. Private and quiet, this is a great location for business functions, parties and special events.

CAPACITY: The Ballroom can seat 100–150 guests in the daytime, 180 in the evening and, in combination with the garden, 350 seated guests. Alone, the Courtyard Garden can accommodate 200 seated guests. The Lounge can hold up to 35 seated.

FEES & DEPOSITS: To make a reservation, a partially refundable $500 deposit is required.

	Month	*Hours Available*	*Fee*
Mon–Thurs	year-round	7am–6pm	$6/guest ($300 min)
		6pm–10pm	$6/guest ($500 min)
Friday	year-round	7am–6pm	$6/guest ($300 min)
	Jan, Feb, Nov	6pm–1am	$9/guest ($900 min)
	Mar–October	6pm–1am	$9/guest ($1,000 min)
	December	6pm–1am	$9/guest ($1,200 min)
Saturday	Jan, Feb, Nov	7am–1am	$9/guest ($900 min)
	Mar–October	7am–5pm	$9/guest ($1,350 min)
Saturday	Mar–October	5pm–7pm	$9/guest ($2,000 min)
		7pm–1am	$9/guest ($1,200 min)

	December	7am–4pm	$9/guest ($900 min)
	December	4pm–1am	$9/guest ($1,200 min)
Sunday	Jan, Feb, Nov, Dec	7am–10pm	$9/guest ($900 min)
	Mar & Oct	7am–10pm	$9/guest ($1,350 min)
	April–Oct	—	not available

CANCELLATION POLICY: If you cancel within 5 days of making the reservation, half your deposit will be refunded. Thereafter, only 50% of the deposit will be refunded only if your date can be rebooked.

AVAILABILITY: Monday–Thursday, 6pm–10pm. Fridays 6pm–1am and Saturdays 7am–1am. Occasional Sundays are available. Call for specific dates and times.

SERVICES/AMENITIES:

Restaurant Services: no

Catering: BYO

Kitchen Facilities: ample

Tables & Chairs: provided

Linens, Silver, etc.: BYO

Restrooms: wca

Dance Floor: yes

Parking: large lots, limited weekdays

Overnight Accommodations: no

Telephone: pay phone

Outdoor Night Lighting: yes

Outdoor Cooking Facilities: BBQ

Cleanup: caterer and club staff

Meeting Equipment: no

RESTRICTIONS:

Alcohol: BYO

Smoking: allowed

Music: amplified inside only

Wheelchair Access: yes

Insurance: not required

THOMAS FOGARTY WINERY AND VINEYARDS

19501 Skyline Blvd.
Portola Valley, CA 94028
(415) 851-1946
Reserve for Events: 2–12 months in advance
Reserve for Meetings: 4–6 weeks in advance

If we were to rate facilities on a scale from one to ten, the Fogarty Winery would be deemed a ten! Located off Skyline Boulevard, this has got to be one of the best places we've seen for corporate meetings, seminars, private parties and special events. Commanding an extraordinary view of the Bay and Peninsula, the Winery sits high on a ridge in a quiet, vineyard setting. A small, lovely pond with circling swans and vineyards all around greet you as you drive in. At the top of the ridge is a large lawn, beautifully landscaped around the perimeter—a perfect spot for an outdoor reception. The building steps down the hill, and is designed with incredible attention to detail, with stone fireplaces, fine woodwork, skylights and lots of decks. The Tasting Room is light and airy, arranged with custom-built "barrel" tables, handcrafted leather chairs, wood burning stove and full kitchen. In the restroom, there's even a blue-green slate and stone bath tub! The Hill House is at the lower level. It has a semi-enclosed deck, stone fireplace, wine bar and professional kitchen. This is an exceptionally pleasant environment for a meeting or company retreat. It has wood parquet floors, comfortable seating and windows overlooking the adjacent vineyard and distant Bay. The Board Room is outstanding, featuring floor-to-ceiling windows and a sunken area for informal group sessions. The Tasting Room and Hill House both reflect the ambiance of the surrounding environment with taste and sophistication. We can't recommend this facility more highly.

CAPACITY: Hill House can hold 200 seated guests, maximum. The Tasting Room and lawn can accommodate 125 guests. The Board Room holds 4–24 people.

FEES & DEPOSITS: A non-refundable deposit of 25% of the rental fee is due when reservations are confirmed. The balance is payable 30 days prior to your function.

Area	*Monday–Thursday*		*Friday–Sunday*	
	Half Day	*Full Day*	*Half Day*	*Full Day*
Tasting Room	$350	$500	$500	$750
Hill House	750	1,200	900	1,500
Conference Room	200	350	200	350

For functions running past 5pm Monday–Thursday or on Sunday, the full day rate will apply. Rental fees do not include food, beverages or audio/visual rentals.

AVAILABILITY: Year-round, weekends until 11pm. Closed Thanksgiving, Christmas Day and January 1st.

SERVICES/AMENITIES:

Restaurant Services: no

Catering: must select from preferred list

Kitchen Facilities: fully equipped

Tables & Chairs: some provided

Linens, Silver, etc.: BYO

Restrooms: no wca

Dance Floor: deck or lawn

Parking: large lots or valet

Overnight Accommodations: no

Telephone: pay phone

Outdoor Night Lighting: yes

Outdoor Cooking Facilities: CBA

Cleanup: caterer

Meeting Equipment: audio-visual

Special: wine tasting

Other: event coordination

RESTRICTIONS:

Alcohol: WC provided, no BYO

Smoking: outside only

Music: must select band from preferred list

Wheelchair Access: no

Insurance: certificate required

WOODSIDE PRIORY

302 Portola Road
Portola Valley, CA 94025
(415) 822-7218 Opts Catering
Reserve for Events: 3–6 months in advance
Reserve for Meetings: 2 weeks in advance

By day, Woodside Priory is a private Benedictine school. But, on weekends, a number of indoor and outdoor spaces for parties and special events are available. The largest and most popular of these are the playing fields at the front of the property. Two wide open spaces, ringed by redwoods, can be set up for huge events such as corporate picnics. This works especially well when one of the fields is tented and the adjacent field is left open. Another playing field, that can be approached through a walnut orchard, is also available for use. Our favorite space for indoor functions is the Founders Hall inside the school's administration building. This room features a baby grand piano, large stone fireplace, parquet floors and a high, wood-beamed ceiling. A bank of doors along one wall opens onto a brick, split-level patio bathed in dappled light and planted with an assortment of flowers. The Assembly Hall, situated on a hillside, is a good-sized space with a permanent stage at one end, a parquet dance floor and tall windows along both side walls. The adjacent Seminar Hall is a very pleasant reception spot with white walls, beamed ceilings and recessed spot lighting. It has a baby grand piano, nicely finished wood floors covered with a Persian rug and two walls of windows overlooking a patio that has a Spanish-style fountain and rose garden. The school's modern gymnasium, with stage and dance floor, is yet another option for indoor celebrations. The main advantages of this site are the diversity, flexibility and openness it affords. In an area where event sites are hard to come by, we feel the Woodside Priory is an option well worth exploring.

CAPACITY:

Area	Seated	Standing		Area	Seated	Standing
Assembly Hall	250	400		Outdoor Areas	3,000	3,000+
Dining Hall	250	400		Gymnasium	500	750
Founders Hall	75	125				

FEES & DEPOSITS: A refundable deposit in the amount of 25–50% of the estimated food and beverage total, plus rental fee, is required to secure your date. The rental fee is $600–2,500 depending on location selected and guest count. The balance is due the day of the event. Food service is provided by Opts Catering and runs approximately $35/person for a wedding buffet; seated meals start at $60/person. The service charge is built into these figures. Tax is additional.

CANCELLATION POLICY: With 60 days' notice, deposit will be refunded.

AVAILABILITY: Year-round, Saturday and Sunday anytime until 10pm.

SERVICES/AMENITIES:

Restaurant Services: no
Catering: provided, BYO requires buyout
Kitchen Facilities: fully equipped

Parking: large lot
Overnight Accommodations: no
Telephone: pay phones

Tables & Chairs: provided, extra charge
Linens, Silver, etc.: provided, extra charge
Restrooms: wca varies per building
Meeting Equipment: some available
Other: event coordination

RESTRICTIONS:
Alcohol: provided, no BYO
Smoking: outside only
Insurance: sometimes required

Outdoor Night Lighting: yes
Outdoor Cooking Facilities: BBQ
Cleanup: provided
Dance Floor: yes

Wheelchair Access: varies
Music: amplified ok

Redwood City

HOTEL SOFITEL
at Redwood Shores

223 Twin Dolphin Drive
Redwood City, CA 94065
(415) 598-9000
Reserve for Events: 6–12 months in advance
Reserve for Meetings: 1–8 weeks in advance

The Hotel Sofitel is special because, unlike most large hotels, this one conveys a sense of warmth and intimacy. It has friendly and experienced staff that make you feel right at home. The Hotel offers lots of choices for meetings, seminars, receptions or parties. The author's favorite space is Baccarat, a sophisticated restaurant on the premises which overlooks the water. With floor to ceiling bay windows, Baccarat is light and warm. This is a small, intimate space where you can eat at square tables instead of typical six-foot rounds. Colors are soft and muted, in creams, pale teals and greens. At one end of the restaurant is the Crystal Room, named for the brilliant Baccarat chandelier suspended from the ceiling. When the etched glass doors are closed, this is a private dining room. Open them and voila, another room for a buffet setup, bar or head table. Adjacent to Baccarat is La Terrasse, an appealing two-tiered area with great views of the water and the Hotel pool and patio. La Terrasse's floor is sensational—a geometrical woven pattern of black, tan and rose colored rectangles of polished marble. Cocktails, champagne and hors d'oeuvres can be served here before moving elsewhere for a seated meal. For the adventurous, the outdoor pool and patio can be tented for al fresco receptions. If your guest list is large, don't worry. Hotel Sofitel's 6,200 square foot Grand Ballroom can accommodate a sizable crowd. Guests will enter through the impressive marble-floored Hotel Lobby, and head to the Ballroom foyer for prefunction champagne and hors d'oeuvres. Inside, the Grand Ballroom can be left whole or divided into sections, depending on the size of your party. All is designed in pastels—soft peach with silver and teal accents. For smaller functions such as meetings, anniversary or retirement parties, use the adjacent Grand Salon. No matter what space you eventually select for your event, the Hotel Sofitel will handle it with attentive service and a sense of style.

CAPACITY:

Room	Seated	Standing	Room	Seated	Standing
Half Grand Ballroom	180	325	Pool & Patio Tented	200	400
Grand Ballroom	450	700	La Terrasse	—	15
Baccarat Dining Room	85	—	Grand Salon	70	125

FEES & DEPOSITS: A refundable $1,000 deposit is due when you book your special event. For meetings, the equivalent of the room rental charge is required as a deposit. Full payment of the estimated balance is due 5 working days before the function. Any remaining balance is due at the conclusion of your event. Room rental charges, food and beverage costs will vary depending on the room and number of guests. A service charge of 17% and tax will apply to the total food and beverage bill.

CANCELLATION POLICY: With over 90 days' notice, your deposit is refunded. With less, the deposit is applied toward another event.

AVAILABILITY: The Grand Ballroom and other spaces are available any day, anytime. The Baccarat Dining Room is available Saturdays 11–4:30pm and Sunday evenings from 4pm–midnight.

SERVICES/AMENITIES:

Restaurant Services: yes
Catering: provided
Kitchen Facilities: n/a
Tables & Chairs: provided
Linens, Silver, etc.: provided
Restrooms: wca
Dance Floor: provided
Other: event planning services

Parking: large lot, valet
Overnight Accommodations: 326 guestrooms
Telephone: pay phones
Outdoor Night Lighting: no
Outdoor Cooking Facilities: no
Cleanup: provided
Meeting Equipment: full spectrum available

RESTRICTIONS:

Alcohol: provided, corkage $12/bottle
Smoking: designated areas
Music: amplified ok

Wheelchair Access: yes
Insurance: not required

PACIFIC ATHLETIC CLUB at Redwood Shores

200 Redwood Shores Parkway
Redwood City, CA 94065
(415) 593-9100
Reserve for Events: 4–12 months in advance
Reserve for Meetings: 2–6 weeks in advance

You know you're almost there once you see the distinctive, green copper pyramid-shaped roofs of a new seven-acre complex of event spaces, restaurant, pools and athletic courts. Enter the foyer and step onto the tan mosaic flagstone floor. The space soars to thirty-five feet, with huge Douglas fir poles supporting an enormous skylight. Guests are led to the lounge and reception areas, the latter, an octagon-shaped room with an unusual two-tone floor of Brazilian walnut and cherry hardwoods. There are several mirrored arches, one of which cleverly pushes back to provide a place for a band. Hors d'oeuvres and cocktails are served here before an event, and after a seated meal elsewhere, guests often return to dance. The adjacent Main Dining Room is a large, light-filled room with a sizable skylight and two walls of floor-to-ceiling glass. The other two walls feature pastel-colored landscapes. Four large Douglas fir poles that match those in the foyer, support a very high, vaulted ceiling. Attached to these poles are multi-tiered pinpoint fixtures, making evening functions sparkle. Tables are dressed with crisp white linens overlapping chintz fabric prints. Beyond the glass walls and doors is the garden courtyard, lushly planted and landscaped to accommodate outdoor parties. Nearby is a large pergola, tennis court and croquet lawn. If you'd like to have just an outdoor function on the patio, it can be screened off from the pool; lawn functions can be tented. And, if you've got a whopping guest list, the interior tennis court complex is perfect. Three courts combined can hold an indoor convention, trade show or cocktail party for up to 5,000 guests! This is a must-see location. Be prepared to be impressed—we think that the Pacific Athletic Club is one of the best new event sites on the Peninsula.

CAPACITY:

Room	Seated	Standing	Room	Seated	Standing
Dining Room	250	600	Outdoor Patio	200	500
Lounge & Reception	—	250	Lawn Area	600	750
Dining Room Courtyard	80	150	Indoor Tennis Courts	—	2,000–5,000
2 Conference Rooms, ea.	12–45	—			

FEES & DEPOSITS: A $1,000 non-refundable deposit is required to secure your date. The room rental fee is $800-1,500 depending on the day of week reserved, and covers a 5-hour block of time. Half the anticipated food and beverage cost is payable 30 days in advance and the balance, along with a confirmed guest count, are due 72 hours prior to the function. Seated meals start at $23.50/person, not including hors d'oeuvres or beverages. Tax and an 18% service charge are additional. Coat check service is $100 extra. For meetings, the rental fee for conference rooms is $150 each. The cost for use of the indoor tennis courts varies, depending on guest count and day(s) reserved.

AVAILABILITY: Year-round, daily. The only time the Dining Room is not available for private functions is Monday–Friday 11:30am–2pm.

SERVICES/AMENITIES:

Restaurant Services: yes
Catering: provided
Kitchen Facilities: n/a
Tables & Chairs: provided
Linens, Silver, etc.: provided
Restrooms: wca
Dance Floor: yes
Other: full event coordination

Parking: valet available, large lot
Overnight Accommodations: no
Telephone: pay phones
Outdoor Night Lighting: yes
Outdoor Cooking Facilities: yes
Cleanup: provided
Meeting Equipment: full audio visual & other

RESTRICTIONS:

Alcohol: provided, corkage $/bottle
Smoking: designated areas
Music: amplified ok

Wheelchair Access: yes
Insurance: not required
Other: no helium balloons

Woodside

GREEN GABLES

Address withheld.
Woodside, CA
(415) 952-1110
Reserve for Events: 1–12 months in advance
Reserve for Meetings: 1–12 months in advance

For special events, Green Gables is one of the most exclusive and one of the loveliest private estates we've seen. This 1912 country estate was built by Green and Green, famous architects from the turn of the century who had a talent for fitting man-made elements into the natural environment without destroying it. The property is sizable, with ancient oaks, native grasses and an undisturbed California landscape surrounding an enclave of formal terraced lawns, gardens and pools. All has been designed to take advantage of the panorama of the Woodside hills and spectacular views of the coastal range beyond. When you arrive, you'll come up a series of steps to the mansion's lovely brick terrace, which can be set up with umbrella-shaded tables for champagne and hors d'oeuvres. Very large seated receptions, with or without tents, can be held on the sloping lawns. Guests can wander through the garden, enjoying the colorful profusion of annuals and perennials which contrast nicely against the darker greens of background trees. Standing at one edge of the lawn, you'll be in for a surprise. Look down to an unbelievably beautiful green rectangular reflecting pool which is surrounded by walls and archways of multi-colored stone. Narrow lawns and clay pots filled with white flowers are laid out on either side of the reflecting pool, creating a feeling of order and symmetry while just beyond these man-made features, is an untouched natural landscape of flowering trees, oaks and bays. For corporate afternoon outings, elegant picnics or company retreats, Green Gables is an exceptional location guaranteed to impress any guest.

CAPACITY: 1,200 guests, maximum.

FEES & DEPOSITS: A security deposit of $1,000 is payable when reservations are made. The rental fee is $5,000. Half of the rental fee is due 60 days in advance and the balance is payable 1 week prior to the event. Event planning and design can be provided. Any menu and any service can be customized for your party. Estimates for catering and other services are developed on a per function basis depending on your budget. The security deposit is usually refunded if the site is left in good condition.

AVAILABILITY: Green Gables is normally available September–May or June. Only 1 event per day is scheduled.

SERVICES/AMENITIES:
Restaurant Services: no
Catering: provided, no BYO
Kitchen Facilities: n/a

Parking: valet CBA, private lot
Overnight Accommodations: no
Telephone: emergency only

Tables & Chairs: provided by caterer
Linens, Silver, etc.: provided by caterer
Restrooms: wca
Dance Floor: CBA

RESTRICTIONS:
Alcohol: provided, no BYO
Smoking: outside only

Outdoor Night Lighting: CBA
Outdoor Cooking Facilities: CBA
Cleanup: provided by caterer
Meeting Equipment: CBA

Wheelchair Access: yes
Insurance: required

Benicia

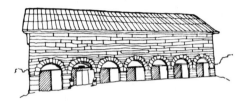

CAMEL BARN MUSEUM

2024 Camel Road
Benicia, CA 94510
(707) 745-5435
Reserve for Events: 1–12 months in advance
Reserve for Meetings: 1 month in advance

Once a military storehouse, the building acquired some distinction in 1864 when thirty-five camels were housed there pending auction. They stayed for approximately six weeks, during which time folks started referring to the place as the Camel Barn. Needless to say, the name stuck. Today, the museum is housed upstairs and celebrations take place on the first floor. The building's interior is cool, with twenty-two-inch-thick sandstone walls. Down the center of the first floor are a series of graceful arches which support the upper level, and arched windows along the length of one side let in some natural light. White and unadorned, the room lends itself to decoration. Way off the beaten path, the Camel Barn Museum is an interesting and little known part of Benicia's history.

CAPACITY: The Camel Barn can accommodate 154 for banquets, 330 for standing reception.

FEES & DEPOSITS: The rental fee is $400. A $100 refundable deposit is due when reservations are confirmed, and is applied towards the fee. A $200 damage/cleaning deposit plus the rental balance is due 3 weeks before the function. For local non-profits, meetings are $25/hour with a 2-hour minimum.

CANCELLATION POLICY: With 14 days' notice, the deposit will be returned.

AVAILABILITY: Year-round, every day 8am–1am.

SERVICES/AMENITIES:
Restaurant Services: no
Catering: BYO
Kitchen Facilities: moderate
Tables & Chairs: provided
Linens, Silver, etc.: BYO
Restrooms: wca
Dance Floor: wood floor
Meeting Equipment: lecturn

Parking: large lot
Overnight Accommodations: no
Telephone: restricted, emergencies only
Outdoor Night Lighting: access only
Outdoor Cooking Facilities: yes, needs prior approval
Cleanup: caterer or renter
Other: raised platforms

RESTRICTIONS:
Alcohol: BYO, license required
Smoking: outside only
Music: amplified ok

Wheelchair Access: yes
Insurance: not required

CAPTAIN WALSH HOUSE

235 East L Street
Benicia, CA 94510
(707) 747-5653
Reserve for Events: 3–6 months in advance
Reserve for Meetings: 2–4 weeks in advance

This is a rare find—a classic Carpenter's Gothic Cottage. Purchased as a derelict relic in 1989, the house has undergone a complete renovation. Selected out of a catalog by General Vallejo in the mid-1800s, it was built in Boston, dismantled, packed in crates and sent around Cape Horn to be finally erected across from Benicia City Hall in 1849. The first occupant was General Vallejo's daughter Epifinia. The second, and most notable occupants were Captain John and Eleanor Walsh. They and their descendants occupied the house through the 1960s. Now restored, the house sports a warm, pale taupe color; its white trim highlights the classic Gothic detailing around the roof edge. Landscaping has been selected so that green and white predominate, except for the multi-colored rose garden in the rear. Under the shade of a large pine, the front drive turns into a quartzite patio, perfect for outdoor receptions and ceremonies. Get ready for a surprise. Although the house exterior is subdued, the architect-designed interior is a fanciful, eclectic blend of old and new. Softwood floors have been painted a glossy white with black faux marble diamonds. The entry foyer features mauve, bird's-eye maple veneer which complements cool gray walls. Mirrors with gold gilt molding, antiques and a stately stair with curved bannister and shining wood treads invite guests in for a closer look. The Grand Parlor has numerous details that capture the eye. Drapes are artistically hung over windows with tie backs, tassels and braids in gold, raspberry and green. Ceiling medallions and rosettes, marble fireplace and gold harp all add to the high level of detail. The adjacent Small Parlor has received similar attention, with Regency-style furniture and panels featuring Gothic Carpenter's wallpaper. No matter where you look, you'll notice custom-designed and hand painted elements: yellow walls with gray stripes, hand faux finished surfaces, gold accents and trim. Epifinia's Room upstairs is the honeymoon suite, complete with claw foot tub and gold plated faucets. The owners deserve a pat on the back for taking on two years of intense, back-breaking work. Their home, the Captain Walsh House, reflects a labor of love.

CAPACITY: Inside, 40 seated guests; 100 for a standing reception. With outdoor spaces, 175 guests, maximum.

FEES & DEPOSITS: A non-refundable deposit of $250 is due when reservations are confirmed and a $200 refundable security/cleaning deposiit is payable with your finished contract. The event balance is due 3 weeks prior to the function. The rental fee for 4 hours is $750–1,500 based on guest count and day of week. Extra hours are $100/hour. For weekday meetings, the rental fee is $375 for up to 25 people.

AVAILABILITY: Year-round, every day from 10am–10pm.

SERVICES/AMENITIES:

Restaurant Services: no
Catering: preferred list only
Kitchen Facilities: ample

Dance Floor: outside only
Parking: street
Overnight Accommodations: 4 guestrooms

Tables & Chairs: caterer or CBA, extra fee
Linens, Silver, etc.: caterer or CBA, extra fee
Restrooms: wca
Meeting Equipment: CBA
Other: event coordination & referrals

RESTRICTIONS:
Alcohol: BYO
Smoking: outside only
Music: amplified restricted, none after 10pm

Outdoor Night Lighting: yes
Outdoor Cooking Facilities: BBQ CBA
Telephone: house phone
Cleanup: caterer

Wheelchair Access: yes
Insurance: certificate required
Other: no open flames, red wine or confetti indoors

FISCHER-HANLON HOUSE

135 West G. Street
Benicia, CA 94510
(707) 745-3385
Reserve for Events: 2 months in advance
Reserve for Meetings: 2 weeks in advance

This lovely old Federal style house is located in the center of historic Benicia, next door to the Capital. Filled with period artifacts and antiques, the house is a relic of yesteryears. Outside, the rear brick patio and gardens serve as a setting for festivities. Surrounded by a wide variety of trees, bushes and a garden, the patio has a secluded, intimate quality. Even on warm days, the nearby water cools the local breezes and guests can wander leisurely along the brick paths through the gardens.

CAPACITY: The parlor is limited to a maximum of 20 people; the grounds 100 standing guests or 50 seated.

FEES & DEPOSITS: There is a $25 refundable cleaning deposit due at the time of booking. The parlor and upstairs changing room rent for $50 each. There is a minimum $50 fee for the use of the garden, with an additonal charge of $2 per person over 25 people.

AVAILABILITY: Weekdays 9am–9pm. Weekends, the parlor is unavailable noon–4pm during public tours. However, the gardens are still available.

SERVICES/AMENITIES:
Restaurant Services: no
Catering: BYO
Kitchen Facilities: no
Tables & Chairs: some chairs provided
Linens, Silver, etc.: BYO
Restrooms: no wca
Dance Floor: BYO
Meeting Equipment: no

Parking: on street, limited
Overnight Accommodations: no
Telephone: no
Outdoor Night Lighting: no
Outdoor Cooking Facilities: no
Cleanup: caterer
Other: vintage carriage CBA

RESTRICTIONS:

Alcohol: BYO
Smoking: outside only
Music: amplified ok, low volume

Wheelchair Access: no
Insurance: not required

Berkeley

THE BANCROFT CLUB

2680 Bancroft Way
Berkeley, CA 94704
(510) 549-1000
Reserve for Events: 2–6 months in advance
Reserve for Meetings: 2 weeks in advance

Here's a relatively new discovery! The Bancroft Club, located across the street from the University of California and next door to the University Art Museum, is now open to the public for the first time since it was built in 1928. Originally the home of the College Women's Club, it was designed by Walter Steilberg (an associate of Julia Morgan) and is currently a National Register landmark building. An absolute must see is the Club's one-of-a-kind event space. Immediately to the right of the foyer is a large room with three parts featuring floor-to-ceiling woodwork, Mediterranean detailing, leaded stained glass windows and hardwood floors. The raised stage is suitable for musicians while the recessed middle could be transformed into an intimate dance floor. The other end could be set up for wining and dining. The room is large and the space extremely flexible—you could probably arrange your party in a multitude of ways and still have it work beautifully. Upstairs is a light-filled conference room with fireplace that has Bay views. The Bancroft Club has recently undergone restoration and it's now perfect for a warm, comfortable gathering. This is a small boutique hotel, ideal for housing out-of-town relatives and friends—a real find. If you are looking for an indoor party or meeting site that is distinctive, has warmth and imparts a sense of history, the Bancroft Club is a wonderful choice.

CAPACITY: The Bancroft Club can hold up to 250 seated guests; 350 for a standing reception.

MEETING ROOMS: Conference Room accommodates 15–40 depending on the seating configuration.

FEES & DEPOSITS: To secure your date, a deposit in the amount of the rental fee is payable when the contract is submitted. The deposit is applied towards the event total. A refundable $500 security/cleaning deposit is also required. The rental fee averages $400 and varies depending on season and day of week. Please call for specifics. Half the fee is payable 60 days prior; the balance due 2 weeks before the event. For business functions in the Conference Room, the rental fee averages $80/half day, $120/full day.

CANCELLATION POLICY: With 90 days' notice, your deposit will be refunded.

AVAILABILITY: Year-round, every day beginning Summer 1993.

SERVICES/AMENITIES:

Restaurant Services: yes

Catering: provided, no BYO

Kitchen Facilities: n/a

Tables & Chairs: provided

Linens, Silver, etc.: provided

Restrooms: wca

Dance Floor: yes

Meeting Equipment: provided or CBA

Overnight Accommodations: 22 guestrooms

Telephone: pay phones

Outdoor Night Lighting: CBA

Outdoor Cooking Facilities: no

Cleanup: provided

Other: event coordinator

Parking: adjacent lot or valet CBA

RESTRICTIONS:

Alcohol: provided, corkage fee if BYO

Smoking: not allowed

Music: amplified restricted

Wheelchair Access: yes

Insurance: sometimes required

Other: decorations restricted

BERKELEY CITY CLUB

2315 Durant Avenue
Berkeley, CA 94704
(510) 848-7800
Reserve for Events: 3–6 months in advance
Reserve for Meetings: 4–8 weeks in advance

The Berkeley City Club is a sensational landmark building, located just one block from the U.C. Berkeley campus. It's a private social club, designed in 1927 by Julia Morgan in a Venetian-Mediterranean style with inner landscaped courtyards and fountains. The Club includes a seventy-five-foot swimming pool, dining room, bar lounges, conference and reception rooms, many of which are available for celebrations. Throughout, the detailing and craftsmanship are impressive. The Drawing and Patio Rooms are large, gracious rooms with beamed ceilings, fireplaces, wall tapestries, tile floors, oriental carpets and sizeable leaded glass windows. The Ballroom is a large, spacious theater-like space with stage, parquet floor and leaded glass windows. A wonderful outdoor spot on a warm day for a party, the Terrace is an appealing reception area that has a terra cotta-colored canopy overhead. Berkeley campus and downtown life bustles all around the City Club, yet it remains a quiet, old world haven of comfort.

CAPACITY, FEES & DEPOSITS: A $500 non-refundable deposit is required when the reservations are confirmed and is applied toward the rental fee.

Room	Reception	Seated	Fees
Drawing Room	80	60	$200
Drawing Rm, Patio & Courtyard	125 total	—	500

Room	Reception	Seated	Fees
Courtyard	30	25	100
Loggia Court	—	12	50–75
Ballroom	275	250	300
Venetian Room	50	—	100
Ballroom & Venetian Rooms	325 total	300	400
The Terrace	120	100	200
Julia Morgan Room	—	40	100

All fees cover a 4-hour rental period. An additional flat fee of $500 is applied to Sunday and holiday weekend events. The balance and a final guest count are due 10 days prior to the function. For a separate bar setup, there's a $100 bartender fee. Food service is provided. Per person rates are: hors d'oeuvres buffet $18, seated luncheons $9.50–15.50, dinner buffets $23–27, luncheon buffets $14–18 and seated dinners by arrangement. If your guests would like to stay overnight, bed and breakfast rates will apply. Call for more information.

AVAILABILITY: Year-round, every day from 6am–10pm; extra hours can be arranged. Closed Christmas and Thanksgiving.

SERVICES/AMENITIES:

Restaurant Services: yes

Catering: provided, no BYO

Kitchen Facilities: n/a

Tables & Chairs: provided

Linens, Silver, etc.: provided

Restrooms: wca

Dance Floor: yes

Parking: $4/car if reserved City Club spaces, lots nearby, street

Overnight Accommodations: 18 guestrooms

Telephone: pay and guest phones

Outdoor Night Lighting: yes

Outdoor Cooking Facilities: no

Cleanup: provided

Other: reception coordinator

Special: candelabras

Meeting Equipment: CBA

RESTRICTIONS:

Alcohol: provided, no BYO

Smoking: designated areas

Music: amplified ok

Wheelchair Access: yes

Insurance: sometimes required

Other: security sometimes required

Need a caterer, cake maker, florist? The Service Directory starting on page 614 features the best in the business.

BERKELEY CONFERENCE CENTER

2105 Bancroft Way
Berkeley, CA 94704
(510) 848-3957
Reserve for Events: 1–2 months in advance
Reserve for Meetings: 3–4 weeks in advance

Don't let the modest, understated entry on Bancroft fool you. The Berkeley Conference Center has remarkable facilities for conferences and meetings. Housed in an historic, four-story landmark building, the Center has over 11,000 sq. ft. of meeting and banquet space. Built in 1905 as a Masonic Temple, this building has an amazing assortment of highly detailed, classically beautiful spaces great for small gatherings or large functions. The Ballroom is magnificent. This is an enormous and elegant room with high ceilings, diffused lighting and a color palette that is superb. The Carleton and Haste Rooms are also large, with lots of wood moulding and high ceilings. The Board Room is at the top, featuring bay views out of a long wall of windows. This is a medium-sized room, equipped with a small bar, which can handle small groups for intimate company retreats. Throughout, the facility maintains a high standard of excellence, not only in the decor, but in the high level of staff support. The Berkeley Conference Center is an unexpected and delightful surprise.

CAPACITY:

Room	Seated	Standing	Room	Seated	Standing
Grand Ballroom	220	350	Haste	160	275
Carleton	150	250	Board Room	60	125
Bancroft	60	75	Ashby	40	40
Evans	40	30	Channing	40	30

FEES & DEPOSITS:

Room	4-hour fee	8-hour fee	Room	4-hour fee	8-hour fee
Grand Ballroom	$400	$800	Haste	$200	$400
Carleton	200	400	Board Room	150	250
Bancroft	125	200	Ashby	100	150
Evans	80	120	Channing	80	120

A deposit equal to the room rental is required to secure the date. Half of the estimated food and beverage balance is due 2 months prior to the event, the remaining balance due 2 weeks before the event. For extended hours, there are additional fees.

CANCELLATION POLICY: For events, 60 days' notice is required for a refund.

AVAILABILITY: Year-round, every day from 6am to midnight.

SERVICES/AMENITIES:

Restaurant Services: no
Catering: provided, no BYO
Kitchen Facilities: n/a

Parking: lot nearby
Overnight Accommodations: Shattuck Hotel
Telephone: pay phone

Tables & Chairs: provided
Linens, Silver, etc.: provided
Restrooms: mostly wca
Dance Floor: yes
Meeting Equipment: CBA, extra fee

RESTRICTIONS:
Alcohol: provided, corkage $6/bottle
Smoking: restricted
Music: amplified ok

Outdoor Night Lighting: no
Outdoor Cooking Facilities: no
Cleanup: provided
Other: full event planning and coordination

Wheelchair Access: mostly yes
Insurance: not required
Other: security guards sometimes required

BRAZILIAN ROOM

Tilden Park
Berkeley, CA 94708
(510) 540-0220 Jeri Honderd
Reserve for Events: 2–12 months in advance
Reserve for Meetings: 2 months in advance

Once a part of the 1939 Golden Gate Exposition on Treasure Island, the Brazilian Room was presented as a gift to the East Bay Regional Park District by the country of Brazil. The original interior hardwood paneling and parquet flooring were kept intact, while a new exterior of local rock and timber was constructed to permanently house the room. Natural light flows through the floor-to-ceiling leaded glass windows that run the length of the room on both sides and a huge stone fireplace gives the space an added charm and warmth. Outside, the large flagstone patio overlooks a sloping lawn and the adjacent botanical garden. Located in Tilden Park, nestled high in the Berkeley Hills above UC Berkeley, the serene, pastoral surroundings offer an environment free from noise and distraction. It's no surprise that the Brazilian Room has become one of the most popular special event sites in the East Bay.

CAPACITY: The Main Room holds 225 standing guests, 150 seated.

FEES, DEPOSITS & AVAILABILITY: A $250 non-refundable reservation deposit wil be required at the time of booking. This deposit will become the refundable cleaning/damage deposit after your event takes place, as long as all the terms of the contract are met.

Weekend Rates (min. 5 hours)	Fee	Timeframes
Saturday, Sunday, holidays	$575	9am–4pm or 5pm–12am
Friday evening	575	6–12am
Additional hours	100/hr	

Weekday Rates (min. 3 hours)

Monday, Wednesday, Thursday	150	8am–midnight
Friday day (any 3-hour block)	150	8am–4pm
Each additional hour costs $50		
Special all day rate	200	8am–4pm

Seasonal Sunday Rates (min. 6 hours)

November through April, any 6-hour block	675	9am–midnight
Each additional hour	75	

The fee balance is due 90 days prior to the event. Optional services are available for a fee. If using a non-preferred caterer, add $75. For non-residents of Alameda and Contra Costa counties, add $100 on weekends and holidays only. Caterers must be licensed and have insurance.

CANCELLATION POLICY: The reservation deposit will be forfeited if you cancel. Any money paid for room rental will also be non-refundable.

SERVICES/AMENITIES:

Restaurant Services: no

Catering: provided or BYO

Kitchen Facilities: ample

Tables & Chairs: some provided

Linens, Silver, etc.: BYO

Restrooms: wca

Dance Floor: yes

Parking: lot

Overnight Accommodations: no

Telephone: pay phone

Outdoor Night Lighting: yes

Outdoor Cooking Facilities: yes

Cleanup: caterer

Meeting Equipment: some available

RESTRICTIONS:

Alcohol: WCB only, kegs of beer restricted to patio and kitchen

Smoking: outside only

Music: amplified inside only

Wheelchair Access: yes

Insurance: extra liability required

Other: decorations restricted

HILLSIDE CLUB

2286 Cedar Street
Berkeley, CA 94709
(510) 848-3227
Reserve for Events: 1 month in advance
Reserve for Meetings: 1 week in advance

The Hillside Club was founded by a group of Berkeley citizens who wished to protect the hills of their town from "unsightly grading and the building of unsuitable and disfiguring houses." The original 1906 Club building was designed by renowned architect Bernard Maybeck. Destroyed in the great fire of 1923, it was redesigned by Maybeck's partner, John White, and rebuilt that year. Its style is that of an English Tudor hall, featuring a high wood-beamed ceiling and massive fireplace. Afternoon light traverses the tall, multi-paned windows, warming the dark wood interior. Recitals often make use of the stage, piano and newly improved lighting system. The hardwood floor is perfect for dancing. An integral part of Berkeley's history, the Hillside Club is a warm, friendly place to host your event.

CAPACITY: The Club accommodates 200 standing or 150 seated.

FEES & DEPOSITS: $150 or half the rental fee, whichever is larger, is due at the time of booking. Weekdays and evenings (except Friday evening) the facility rents for $200. Friday evening, Saturday or Sunday it rents for $300. The balance of the fee is due a week before the event. The basic rental is for a 4-hour block of time. For each hour over 4 hours, there is a $40 charge. There are additional fees for use of certain items.

CANCELLATION POLICY: Cancellations are handled on an individual basis.

AVAILABILITY: Until 11pm every day.

SERVICES/AMENITIES:

Restaurant Services: no
Catering: BYO
Kitchen Facilities: yes
Tables & Chairs: provided
Linens, Silver, etc.: BYO
Restrooms: no wca
Dance Floor: yes
Meeting Equipment: yes

Parking: on street
Overnight Accommodations: no
Telephone: no
Outdoor Night Lighting: access only
Outdoor Cooking Facilities: no
Cleanup: caterer or renter
Other: sound system, movie screen, piano

RESTRICTIONS:

Alcohol: BYO, BWC only
Smoking: not allowed
Music: amplified ok

Wheelchair Access: no
Insurance: not required
Other: no confetti

Concord

CENTRE CONCORD

5298 Clayton Road
Concord, CA 94521
(510) 671-3466
Reserve for Events: 9–12 months in advance
Reserve for Meetings: 1–6 months in advance

The best kept secret in this neck-of-woods is Centre Concord. Hidden in the back of the Clayton Faire Shopping Center, it's a bit hard to find, but you'll be well rewarded. The building has been totally remodeled, with subtle and attractive decor. Its most outstanding feature is the Ballroom. Easy on the eyes, the room's colors are neutral grays, with a rose carpet and teal-green accents. The walls are covered with fabric, and even the ceiling has a soft, textured appearance. But the minute you hit the light switch, it's showtime—multiple sets of chandeliers glitter and sparkle, setting an upscale tone. The room is bright when fully lit, and quite glamorous when the lights are dimmed. Each section of lights can be individually controlled. This is a large room, but because it can be divided into three sections, small groups won't be overwhelmed. Conferences, meeting luncheons or dinners and parties can all be accommodated in style. And for weekday or multiple day use, the entire building can be rented, including other meeting and break-out rooms.

CAPACITY: The Ballroom can accommodate a maximum of 400 guests.

MEETING ROOMS: 1 classroom, 50 people, maximum. Overflow rooms are also available, each 35 people, theatre-style.

FEES & DEPOSITS: The rental fee for the Ballroom, Friday night-Sunday, is $100/hour (non-residents $120/hour) for 4-hours, minimum. Half the anticipated rental fee, plus a non-refundable setup/cleanup fee, is required to secure your date. The setup/cleanup fee is $300 for the entire Ballroom, 2/3 the space $225, 1/3 the space $180. The balance of the rental fee and any additional fees are due 2 weeks prior to the event. Dance floor and portable risers are extra. A $500 refundable security deposit is required 2 weeks in advance along with another $500 security deposit if you use the Centre's kitchen.

For meetings, the classrooms are $25/hour, with a 2-hour minimum. The non-profit rate for Ballroom use Monday–Tuesday is $50/hour. On other days, the rates are: full Ballroom, $100/hour, 2/3 Ballroom, $75/hour, 1/3 Ballroom $60/hour. To rent the entire building or for multiple day use, rates are negotiable. Non-residents using the building Monday–Friday pay an additional $20 per hour.

CANCELLATION POLICY: With more than 60 days' notice, you will receive a full refund of the rental deposit, minus a $5 service charge. The security deposit is only refunded if the room(s) are left in good condition.

AVAILABILITY: Year-round, daily. The Centre is open weekends until 2am, weekdays until 11pm.

SERVICES/AMENITIES:

Restaurant Services: no

Catering: BYO

Kitchen Facilities: fully equipped industrial

Tables & Chairs: provided

Linens, Silver, etc.: BYO, table skirts available

Restrooms: wca

Dance Floor: yes, extra fee

Parking: community lot

Overnight Accommodations: no

Telephone: pay phone

Outdoor Night Lighting: no

Outdoor Cooking Facilities: no

Cleanup: caterer or renter

Meeting Equipment: CBA

RESTRICTIONS:

Alcohol: BYO

Smoking: outside only

Music: amplified ok

Wheelchair Access: yes

Insurance: sometimes required

Danville

BEHRING AUTO MUSEUM & U.C. Berkeley Museum of Art, Science and Culture

Blackhawk Plaza Circle
Danville, CA 94506
(510) 736-2280
Reserve for Events: 3–6 months in advance
Reserve for Meetings: 6 weeks in advance

The U.C. Berkeley Museum and Behring Auto Museum are exciting places for private parties. The Behring Museum is a study in glass, granite and stainless steel. Overlooking Blackhawk Plaza, this multi-million dollar museum showcases rare classic automobiles in elegant, sumptuous surroundings. The lobby is impressive with its soaring skylights and dusty rose Italian marble floors and walls. The juxtaposition of metal and stone with soft rich colors creates a vivid impression. As the sun sets through the tinted glass facade, the entire space is bathed in a warm hazy glow. The dining room presents a striking contrast: black from its granite floor to unadorned ceiling. Vintage car galleries border the dining area and can be illuminated or rendered invisible by a network of computerized lights. Here guests are dazzled by colorful fender curves, gleaming metal and sparkling chrome. The new U.C. Museum of Art, Science and Culture is a handsome and stately structure located adjacent to the Behring Museum. Designed along classical lines and presented in terra cotta colors, this is the crowning touch to an already impressive mercantile center, Blackhawk Plaza. Although functions are not set up in this museum, guests can roam through the exhibits during dining and dancing festivities at the Behring Museum. Whether you come here to savor Ken Behring's ultra-modern vision or you simply like the idea of a private celebration or upscale business function amidst classic cars and a showcase of living history, prehistory and scientific discovery, the Museums at Blackhawk will make your event unforgettable.

CAPACITY: The Dining Room in the Behring Museum accommodates up to 500 seated guests. For more than 300 guests, additional fees may be required for a special dining room setup. The Lobby holds 600 standing.

FEES & DEPOSITS: The Museums rent space only. All services are provided by others.

Security/Maintenance Fees				*Rental Fees*		
Reception Only	2hrs	$280		Reception Only	2hrs	$500
(Over 100 Guests, $40 per each 50 guests)				Each Additional Hour	—	150
Reception & Seated Dinner	2hrs	520		Reception & Dinner	2hrs	1,000
Reception, Seated Dinner				Reception, Dinner & Dancing	2hrs	1,500
& Dancing	2hrs	650				

A non-refundable deposit of half the total maintenance and rental fees is due when reservations are confirmed; the balance is due the day of the event. A $1,000 refundable security deposit is due 30 days prior to the event. Caterers must be selected from a preferred list.

CANCELLATION POLICY: The security deposit will be refunded if you cancel 30 days in advance of your function.

AVAILABILITY: Tuesdays–Sundays 6:30pm–12:30am. Private parties can only be arranged when museums are closed to the public and there are no conflicting activities.

SERVICES/AMENITIES:

Restaurant Services: no

Catering: preferred list only

Kitchen Facilities: no

Tables & Chairs: caterer

Linens, Silver, etc.: caterer

Restrooms: wca

Dance Floor: granite foyer

Parking: large lots

Overnight Accommodations: no

Telephone: pay phone

Outdoor Night Lighting: yes

Outdoor Cooking Facilities: no

Cleanup: caterer

Meeting Equipment: microphone, podium

RESTRICTIONS:

Alcohol: through licensed caterer

Wheelchair Access: yes

Smoking: outside only

Music: amplified limited

Insurance: certificate required

CROW CANYON
COUNTRY CLUB

711 Silver Lake Drive
Danville, CA 94526
(510) 735-8200
Reserve: 6–8 months in advance
Reserve for Meetings: 1 week in advance

Crow Canyon Country Club is a private club which has banquet facilities for parties, special events and business functions. All activities take place in the Clubhouse, a versatile group of rooms surrounded by a championship eighteen-hole golf course, swimming pool and tennis courts. Large functions can be accommodated in the Mark Twain Room, Crow Canyon's main dining area. The windowed east side of this room overlooks the golf course and offers a spectacular view of Mt. Diablo. For added flexibility, a stage and hardwood dance floor are located in the center of the room. Smaller groups are comfortably accommodated in the Jack London Lounge, a section of the Mark Twain Room. And for more intimate functions, the Eugene O'Neill Room, which also has a dramatic view of the Diablo Valley, provides a private and sophisticated retreat. With its nine meeting and banquet rooms, Crow Canyon is one of the few places in this area that can meet all your business and private party needs.

CAPACITY, FEES & DEPOSITS:

Room	Seated	Standing	Rental Fee	Food & Bev Min
Jack London Lounge	120	150	$150–300	$750
Mark Twain Room	320	400	300	1,500
Eugene O'Neill Room	80	100	125	750
Grill Room	80	100	35	1,000
John Steinbeck Room	20	30	30–50	75
Bret Hart Room	40	50	50–80	200

For functions of 50 or more guests, a $1,000 deposit is required. To open the clubhouse for banquet functions during non-member hours, a 75-person minimum is required. Saturdays, for large events, a $4,000 minimum food and beverage total is required. Ninety percent of the estimated event cost is due 30 days prior to the function, with the final 10% payable at the end of the event. Food service is provided. Catered functions require 72-hour advance confirmation of guest count. Approximate per person rates for in-house service: breakfasts from $6–12, luncheons $11–17, dinners $18–26, buffet menus $19–24. Menus for catered functions can be created for specific events. Tax and 17% service charge are additional.

MEETING ROOMS: 9 rooms, capacity 8–320 seated guests.

AVAILABILITY: Year-round, every day from 6am–11pm.

SERVICES/AMENITIES:
Restaurant Services: yes
Catering: provided

Parking: parking lot, valet available
Overnight Accommodations: no

Kitchen Facilities: n/a
Tables & Chairs: provided
Linens, Silver, etc.: provided
Restrooms: wca
Dance Floor: yes
Other: baby grand piano, upright piano

RESTRICTIONS:
Alcohol: provided, corkage $8.50/bottle
Smoking: designated areas
Music: amplified ok

Telephone: pay phones
Outdoor Night Lighting: yes
Outdoor Cooking Facilities: BBQ CBA
Cleanup: provided
Meeting Equipment: yes

Wheelchair Access: yes
Insurance: not required

EL RIO

Danville, CA
Address withheld to maintain privacy.
(510) 837–0777
Reserve for Events: 1–6 months in advance
Reserve for Meetings: 1 day in advance

This is a very large, private residence available for parties and business functions. With over 8,000 square feet of living space and a sizeable garden, it offers flexibility and a variety of event spaces. El Rio has seven bedrooms, eight baths, a wet bar, French doors, new hardwood floors, fireplaces and a large, well–equipped kitchen. Outdoors are a pool with poolhouse, a sunken heated/conversation pit and expansive courtyard. Even the poolhouse has two bathrooms and a bar. If you would like to have your event in a very private location in the East Bay, and need accommodations for up to fourteen guests, this is the place. In addition, any service you can dream of, from maid service and entertainment to flowers and catering, can be provided by the house management.

CAPACITY: Indoors 150 seated or 200 standing guests; outdoors 150 seated or 600 standing guests.

FEES & DEPOSITS: A non-refundable deposit of 100% of the rental fee is due when the contract is signed. A refundable cleaning and security deposit will be required, and will be returned within 2 weeks following the event. The rental fee for a 4-hour minimum period is $100/hour. Call for corporate meeting rates.

CANCELLATION POLICY: The cleaning and security deposit will be returned as per the rental contract.

AVAILABILITY: Year-round, every day from 9am.

SERVICES/AMENITIES:
Restaurant Services: no
Catering: provided or BYO
Kitchen Facilities: ample
Tables & Chairs: BYO or CBA

Dance Floor: yes
Parking: valet required, extra charge
Overnight Accommodations: 7 guestrooms
Telephone: house phone, extra charge

Linens, Silver, etc.: BYO or CBA
Restrooms: no wca
Meeting Equipment: no
Special: event coordination

RESTRICTIONS:
Alcohol: BYO or CBA
Smoking: outside only
Music: amplified with approval

Outdoor Night Lighting: yes
Outdoor Cooking Facilities: BBQs
Cleanup: caterer or provided, extra charge

Wheelchair Access: yes
Insurance: extra liability required
Other: decorations restricted

THE VICTORIAN and the EXECUTIVE ESTATE

Addresses withheld to maintain privacy.
Danville, CA
(510) 837–0777
Reserve for Events: 1–6 months in advance
Reserve for Meetings: 1 day in advance

These two sizeable homes occupy the same parcel, yet are separated by considerable open space, including a tennis court. The first house you encounter is a remodeled white Victorian with cream walls and carpets, hardwood floors, fireplaces, sunken tubs and seven bedrooms. In the backyard garden, you'll find a spa and heated pool. Parties can take place either outdoors around the pool or inside. The interior rooms are large, making it a very flexible event site. The second residence, The Executive Estate, is a recently built 6,600 square foot home with state-of-the-art kitchen and baths. The kitchen in this house is very sophisticated, with gray granite and white cabinets. The bathrooms all feature raised marble tubs and other elegant amenities. The interior is light and airy, with a multitude of windows overlooking the hillsides beyond. There are many rooms in this enormous house, some of which connect to form large event spaces. Both houses provide guest accommodations for those who'd like to spend the night. And for those who need assistance planning an event, the staff is able to coordinate catering, limousines, entertainment and maid/valet services.

CAPACITY: The Victorian's indoor capacity is 75 seated or 125 for a standing reception. Outdoor capacity is 200 standing guests; add 500 to that figure if you use the tennis court. Indoors, The Executive Estate can hold up to 80 seated guests or 150 for a standing reception. Using its terraces, you can plan for an additional 50 seated people.

FEES & DEPOSITS: A non-refundable deposit of 100% of the rental fee is due when the contract is signed. A refundable cleaning/security deposit is also required and will be returned within 2 weeks following the event. The Victorian's rental fee for a 4-hour minimum is $200/hour. The Executive Estate's rental fee is $300/hour. Overnight stays can be arranged for both places; call for rates.

CANCELLATION POLICY: The cleaning and security deposit is refundable as per the rental contract.

AVAILABILITY: Year-round, every day from 9am.

SERVICES/AMENITIES:

Restaurant Services: no

Catering: provided or BYO

Kitchen Facilities: ample

Tables & Chairs: BYO or CBA

Linens, Silver, etc.: BYO or CBA

Restrooms: no wca, both residences

Dance Floor: CBA

Special: event coordination, heated pool, spa, tennis court

Parking: valet required, extra charge

Overnight Accommodations: 7 guestrooms w/ private baths each residence

Telephone: house phone, extra charge

Outdoor Night Lighting: yes

Outdoor Cooking Facilities: BBQs

Cleanup: caterer or provided, extra fee

Meeting Equipment: no

RESTRICTIONS:

Alcohol: BYO or CBA

Smoking: outside only

Music: amplified inside only with approval

Wheelchair Access: no

Insurance: extra liability required

Other: decorations restricted

Emeryville

CHALKERS BILLIARD CLUB

5900 'S' Hollis Street
Emeryville, CA 94608
(510) 658-5821   Sue or Hal
Reserve for Events: 1 week–6 months in advance
Reserve for Meetings: 1 week–6 months in advance

Chalkers is an upscale "pool hall." The decor is reminiscent of an art gallery: clean lines, sophisticated colors and good artwork on the walls. Chalkers not only provides its customers with billiard and snooker lessons, it offers a full bar, hors d'oeuvres and light meals, too. Located in the back of a renovated industrial complex on 59th Street at Hollis, Chalkers offers an interesting and fun event venue for those who want to play pool or snooker. There are two floors of pool tables. The upper floor, private rooms or the entire facility can be made available for your private party. Bring your own custom-made cue and impress your friends or workmates. A house pro can be booked for demonstrations and "mini-lessons" for the novice players in your group.

FEES, DEPOSITS & CAPACITY: A deposit in the amount of the first hour's rental is required to secure your date. If you rent the entire facility, the deposit will increase.

Area	Hours	Fee/hr	Capacity
Entire Facility	until 7pm	$ 250	300
(34 tables)	after 7pm (Sun–Thurs)	350	
	after 7pm (Fri & Sat)	550	
Upper Floor	until 7pm	130	100

	after 7pm (Sun–Thurs)	185	
	after 7pm (Fri & Sat)	275	
Party Annex	until 7pm	75	50
(7 tables, includes	after 7pm (Sun–Thurs)	100	
Club Room)	after 7pm (Fri & Sat)	120	
VIP Room	anytime	17–26	12
Club Room	anytime	24–42	16

Capacities are for standing affairs only. There is a 3-hour minimum for group rentals of 15 or more after 7pm. Per person food costs for a standing buffet are $7–20. Beverage and a 15% gratuity are additional. A bar guarantee will be applied to groups of 50 or more.

MEETING ROOMS: The VIP Room and the Annex are available for meetings.

CANCELLATION POLICY: The deposit will be refunded with 1 week's notice for events with food or if the entire facility is rented. Small parties with no food service require a 24-hour notice.

AVAILABILITY: For events with groups of 15–300. Note that guests must be 21 years and older.

Mon: noon–7pm (15–50 guests, 7pm–2am)
Tues, Wed, Thurs, & Sun: noon–2am

Fri & Sat: noon–9pm
VIP Room: Mon–Fri, noon–2am; Sat & Sun, 2pm–2am. Closed Christmas.

SERVICES/AMENITIES:

Restaurant Services: cafe only
Catering: provided, no BYO
Kitchen Facilities: no
Tables & Chairs: provided for meetings only
Linens, Silver, etc.: provided
Restrooms: wca
Dance Floor: CBA, extra fee

Parking: large lot
Overnight Accommodations: no
Telephone: pay phone
Outdoor Night Lighting: access only
Outdoor Cooking Facilities: no
Cleanup: provided
Meeting Equipment: CBA, extra fee

RESTRICTIONS:

Alcohol: provided, corkage $6/bottle
Smoking: designated areas
Other: decorations limited, no confetti or glitter

Music: amplified ok when entire facility is rented
Wheelchair Access: yes
Insurance: not required

Prices and policies do change. Call each facility and confirm everything you read in Perfect Places.

Fremont

ARDENWOOD
HISTORIC PRESERVE

34600 Ardenwood Blvd.
Fremont, CA 94555
(510) 462-1400 Reservations Office
Reserve for Events: 3–12 months in advance
Reserve for Meetings: 2 weeks–12 months in advance

Ardenwood is a 205-acre working farm, established during the last half of the 19th-century. Here, you can travel back in time—draft horses still pull wagons, ladies wear Victorian dresses and the land still grows the kinds of crops it did a hundred years ago. Guests can stroll through the beautiful gardens, tour the impressive Patterson Mansion and enjoy historic farm demonstrations and other remnants of a past way of life. Ardenwood offers a unique atmosphere for group picnics and special events. A short ride on the horse-drawn railroad brings you to the Deer Park Picnic Areas, where your group can relax and enjoy the simple pleasures of a time gone by.

CAPACITY: The Deer Park Picnic Area can hold groups between 75–1,200 people.

FEES & DEPOSITS: A non-refundable deposit, ranging from $100–1,200 (depending on group size) is required to secure your date. It's due when the date is booked and is credited to the final billing. Picnic site rental includes sports and recreation activities, tours, demonstrations and wagon rides. Site rental rates from $395–2,900 depending on the size of the site(s) rented. Purchase of beverages is required (beer, wine, soft drinks, coffee & tea) at $3.25/person. Catered all-you-can-eat meals, BBQ-style, range from $3.75–$14/person. Moonlighting Parties start at $18/person with rental, food and beverages included.

AVAILABILITY: May–October, Saturday and Sunday from 10am–5pm. Moonlighting Party hours are 6:30pm to midnight.

SERVICES/AMENITIES:

Restaurant Services: no
Catering: provided or cater yourself, no outside caterers
Kitchen Facilities: n/a
Tables & Chairs: provided
Linens, Silver, etc.: provided
Restrooms: wca
Dance Floor: yes
Meeting Equipment: CBA

Parking: ample lots
Overnight Accommodations: no
Telephone: pay phone
Outdoor Night Lighting: yes
Outdoor Cooking Facilities: BBQs
Cleanup: caterer
Other: horse-drawn carriage CBA, complete event services

RESTRICTIONS:

Alcohol: WBC provided
Smoking: allowed
Music: amplified after 4:30pm only

Wheelchair Access: yes
Insurance: not required
Other: park open to public from 10am to 4:30pm

THE PALMDALE ESTATE

159 Washington Blvd.
Fremont, CA 94539
(510) 651-8908
Reserve for Events: 2–12 months in advance
Reserve for Meetings: 1 week–12 months in advance

The Palmdale Estate is an unexpected jewel in Fremont. Towering palm trees, lakes, rose gardens and expansive lawns grace this twenty-three-acre estate. Best House (built by Mrs. Best) is a white, brown-trimmed Tudor-style home. Built in 1915, it features a large ballroom with burgundy drapes, hardwood floors and murals on the walls and ceilings. The Music room is decorated in gold leaf and has artwork everywhere you look. French doors, chandeliers, hardwood and marble floors make this an attractive and special spot to celebrate.

CAPACITY: The gardens can hold 1,000 guests for a reception and Best House can hold 150 seated indoors and, combined with outdoor spaces, up to 500 guests.

FEES & DEPOSITS: To rent the house and garden, a $250 refundable security deposit is due when the rental agreement is submitted. Rental fees are as follows:

	Fees	*Timeframe*
Weekend	$1,500/8 hours	8am–1am*
Weekday	$500/8 hours or $100/hour	9am–5pm
Weekday Evenings	$150/hour	5pm–midnight

CANCELLATION POLICY: The security deposit is forfeited if you cancel.

AVAILABILITY: Year-round, every day except Easter and Christmas. *On Saturdays between April and October, there are 2 time periods for parties: 9am–5pm and 5:30pm–1am.

SERVICES/AMENITIES:
Restaurant Services: no
Catering: BYO
Kitchen Facilities: minimal
Tables & Chairs: provided to 150 guests
Linens, Silver, etc.: CBA
Restrooms: wca
Dance Floor: ballroom
Meeting Equipment: some provided

Parking: large lot
Overnight Accommodations: no
Telephone: lounge phone
Outdoor Night Lighting: CBA
Outdoor Cooking Facilities: BBQ
Cleanup: CBA
Other: event coordination

RESTRICTIONS:
Alcohol: BYO WCB only, hard alcohol restricted
Smoking: outside only
Music: amplified within limits

Wheelchair Access: yes
Insurance: not required

Lafayette

LAFAYETTE PARK HOTEL

3287 Mt. Diablo Blvd.
Lafayette, CA 94549
(510) 283-3700 or **(800) 368-2468**
Reserve for Events: 3–12 months in advance
Reserve for Meetings: 30 days in advance

The Lafayette Park is truly a different kind of hotel because comfort, ambiance and attentive service are the hallmarks here. The staff treats you like royalty, offering a level of service rarely found in hotel environments nowadays. You'll have no difficulty locating it—the distinctive Norman French architecture, with dormers, French windows, green shutters and peaked roofline, makes the Hotel a landmark in Lafayette. Designed around three European-style courtyards, it has spacious rooms for meetings, conferences and receptions. If you're interested in an outdoor party, the interior Fountain Courtyard is especially lovely. Here you'll find ivy-trellised urns which support flowering trees and multi-colored flowers. Umbrella-shaded tables encircle a hand-carved Italian limestone fountain. The pool courtyard is another great spot for outdoor luncheons or barbecues near the swimming pool. Smaller, more intimate dinner parties can be held in the Diderot Library. With an 18th century imported marble mantel, wood burning fireplace, oak floors and cherrywood furnishings, the Library makes a perfect venue for an elegant business or rehearsal dinner. All meals in the Library, created by the hotel's award-winning chef, are served on china and crystal.

CAPACITY:

Room	Reception	Banquet	Room	Reception	Banquet
Independence Hall	220	175	Fountain Courtyard	300	150
George Washington Room	130	100	Independence Hall		
Benjamin Franklin Room	50	42	with Courtyard	500	280
Diderot Library	24	20	Wishing Well Courtyard	100	50-60
Board Room	—	14			

FEES & DEPOSITS: A $125 deposit or more is required depending on guest count and number of rooms reserved. Per person food costs: Breakfasts $8.50–14, luncheons $14–23, dinners $20–38. Hors d'oeuvres and specialty break options are available, such as ice cream breaks or afternoon teas. Tax and service charge are additional. A meeting room charge may also apply.

SERVICES & AMENITIES:

Restaurant Services: yes
Catering: provided
Kitchen Facilities: n/a
Tables & Chairs: provided
Linens, Silver, etc.: provided

Parking: lot, garage and valet
Overnight Accommodations: 139 guestrooms
Telephone: pay phones
Outdoor Night Lighting: yes
Outdoor Cooking Facilities: CBA

Restrooms: wca
Dance Floor: yes
Other: event coordination, piano available

RESTRICTIONS:
Alcohol: provided, corkage $10/bottle
Smoking: outdoors only
Music: amplified within limits

Cleanup: provided
Meeting Equipment: audio-visual company in-house

Wheelchair Access: yes
Insurance: not required

Livermore

CONCANNON VINEYARD

4590 Tesla Road
Livermore, CA 94550
(510) 447-3760
Reserve for Events: 3–6 months in advance

An arch with the Concannon name on it welcomes you to this historic family winery. Surrounded by acres of vineyards, Concannon offers quite a few options for business and social functions. When you arrive, you'll see the lawn area in front of the winery, shaded by large trees and bordered by roses and vineyards. Nearby is a vine-covered arbor with carriage lamps hung on every other post and another lawn area, which can accommodate seated groups. Stand underneath the arbor and look up. Overhead is a ceiling of intertwined grape vines with grapes dangling delicately through the greenery. Sunlight filters through to the herringbone brick arbor floor. In cooler months the arbor can be covered by a custom-made tent, creating an indoor/outdoor reception spot. Through the archway is a lovely green lawn, next to which sits a new arch with climbing roses. Not too far away is the Concannon home, an old-fashioned white Victorian farmhouse, with a wisteria-covered veranda. For company picnics, try La Pergola, a two-acre open space across Tesla Road, which has a grassy field lined with willows and eucalyptus and shaded by pepper and oak trees. For indoor functions, the Tasting Room has a warm feel, with both brick and redwood walls. In winter, the old fashioned wood-burning fireplace is aglow and for color, local art is displayed on the walls, with shows rotating every month. For evening dining or dancing, the Tasting Room Courtyard is wind-protected and intimate. Here guests can sit at candlelit tables or dance without worrying about an evening chill.

CAPACITY:

Area	Seated	Standing	Area	Seated	Standing
Arbor	150	200	Heart-shaped Lawn	75	100
Arbor Lawn	150	300	Trellis Archway Garden	50	100
Gazebo Lawn	300	450	La Pergola	500	750
Tasting Rm & Ctyd	80	160			

FEES & DEPOSITS: A refundable security deposit of $350 is required to reserve your event date. The security deposit is refundable 1 week after the event. The rental fee for functions is $12/person and is due 2 weeks in advance. The fee includes setup, tables, chairs, glassware and wine service staff. Wine may be purchased at a case discount. Horse and carriage rental can be arranged for $150; dance floor for $250. For catered parties, meetings and seminars, the rental fee is included in the food and beverage total.

CANCELLATION POLICY: With 90 days' notice, the deposit will be refunded less 20%.

AVAILABILITY: Every day, year-round. Outdoors from 8am–midnight; Tasting Room 5pm–midnight. Closed Thanksgiving, Easter and Christmas.

SERVICES/AMENITIES:

Restaurant Services: no
Catering: preferred list
Kitchen Facilities: minimal
Tables & Chairs: provided
Linens, Silver, etc.: by caterer
Restrooms: wca
Dance Floor: tasting room or courtyard
Other: event coordination

Parking: large lot
Overnight Accommodations: no
Telephone: house phone
Outdoor Night Lighting: yes
Outdoor Cooking Facilities: BBQ
Cleanup: by caterer
Meeting Equipment: no

RESTRICTIONS:

Alcohol: provided, no BYO
Smoking: outside only
Music: amplified ok

Wheelchair Access: yes
Insurance: not required

RAVENSWOOD

2647 Arroyo Road
Livermore, CA 94550
(510) 373-5700 Park District Office
Reserve for Events: 3–12 months in advance
Reserve for Meetings: 3–12 months in advance

Ravenswood is one of those places you want to explore the minute you see it. A pepper tree-lined driveway draws your eye straight up to the two houses set far back from the main road. The Cottage House, built in 1885, looks out over a lovely little garden. As you walk toward the main house, the fragrance of roses accompanies you. A Queen Anne Victorian, the larger house on the estate has real old-fashioned charm. A comfortable wrap-around veranda encourages lazy afternoon socializing, and the palm-ringed front lawn is a perfect spot for an al fresco repast. Inside, high ceilings, a fireplace, hardwood floors and simple decor make you feel right at home. Behind both houses is grassy area with a gazebo. Surrounded by a dozen trees, it rests in dappled shade, completing a picture of country serenity.

CAPACITY: The Main House holds 150 standing or 71 seated, the grounds 150 maximum and the Billiard Room, 75 standing or 50 seated.The facility accommodates a maximum of 150 guests.

FEES & DEPOSITS: A $50 rental deposit is required to secure a date. The balance of the rental fee and a $150 cleaning deposit are due 30 days prior to the event. The rental fee is $480 for Livermore residents, and $720 for non-residents. There is also an additional liquor permit charge.

CANCELLATION POLICY: If the event is cancelled 3 months or more prior to the event, 50% of the rental deposit is returned. If you cancel within 3 months of the event, the deposit will be forfeited. For either period, any prepaid rental charges in excess of the facility rental deposit are refunded. With less than 1 month's notice, only the cleaning deposit is returned.

AVAILABILITY: Every day 8am–9pm, except Tuesdays.

SERVICES/AMENITIES:

Restaurant Services: no
Catering: BYO
Kitchen Facilities: moderate
Tables & Chairs: some provided
Linens, Silver, etc.: BYO
Restrooms: wca
Dance Floor: yes
Meeting Equipment: no

Parking: lot
Overnight Accommodations: no
Telephone: restricted use
Outdoor Night Lighting: no
Outdoor Cooking Facilities: no
Cleanup: caterer and renter
Other: horse-drawn carriage allowed

RESTRICTIONS:

Alcohol: WCB only with license
Smoking: outside only
Music: no amplified music

Wheelchair Access: yes
Insurance: damage and liability required
Other: decorations restricted

TRI VALLEY EVENT CENTER
Aahmes Hall

170 Lindbergh Ave.
Livermore, CA 94550
(510) 582-5147
Reserve for Events: 1–6 months in advance
Reserve for Meetings: 1–3 weeks in advance

This brand new facility has two things going for it. The first is that it can hold a really large crowd (up to 650 seated guests!) for parties, and the second is that Beets Catering is the exclusive caterer/coordinator. We know of no other site in the tri valley area that offers this square footage indoors. Although the space is an unpretentious auditorium with stage and vaulted ceiling over an expansive linoleum floor, Beets can transform it into something special. Whatever you want, whether it's budget-minded or skies-the-limit, Beets can probably do it. We'd also like to point out that Beets does a fine job in the catering department, too. From gourmet, fancy finger foods to modest but tasty morsels for a gathering of six hundred, this caterer does a professional job. So if you've got a sizable guest list, and Livermore is geographically well suited to your needs, call and ask for a tour.

CAPACITY: The facility accommodates 650 seated guests; 1,000 for a standing cocktail party.

FEES & DEPOSITS: A $200 non-refundable deposit is required when the contract is submitted. The rental fee for Friday, Saturday or Sunday is $450. Rental includes a 5-hour period plus 2 hours for setup. The full rental fee and half the estimated food total are due 60 days prior to the event. The balance is due 1 week prior to the function, with any remainder due the day of the event. Additional event staff are available. Call for hourly rates.

AVAILABILITY: Fridays and weekends 8am–midnight.

SERVICES/AMENITIES:

Restaurant Services: no
Catering: provided, no BYO
Kitchen Facilities: n/a
Tables & Chairs: provided
Linens, Silver, etc.: CBA
Restrooms: wca
Dance Floor: yes
Meeting Equipment: no

Parking: large lot
Overnight Accommodations: no
Telephone: pay phone
Outdoor Night Lighting: CBA
Outdoor Cooking Facilities: CBA
Cleanup: provided
Other: event coordination

RESTRICTIONS:

Alcohol: BYO
Smoking: outside & foyer only
Music: amplified ok

Wheelchair Access: yes
Insurance: certificate required

WENTE BROS. ESTATE WINERY

5565 Tesla Road
Livermore, CA 94550
(510) 447-3603
Reserve for Events: 6–12 months in advance

The Estate Winery is located in the scenic Livermore Valley wine country in a lovely vineyard setting. This hundred-year-old winery has charm and a rustic ambiance perfect for special meetings, corporate parties, leisurely brunches or evening dinners in the Estate Tasting Room or on the adjacent patio. During the summer, the patio is shaded by a canopy of fruitless mulberry trees offering protection from the sun.

CAPACITY: The banquet room holds up to 100 standing or 70 seated guests; the patio up to 500 standing or 250 seated guests.

FEES & DEPOSITS: A deposit of half the estimated total is due when reservations are made. The remainder is due 30 days prior to the event. For events of up to 250 people, there is a $250 fee for the use of any part of the facility. For over 250 people, add $2 per person. Per person catering costs run between $15–40 and do not include wine. Sales tax and a 15% gratuity are additional.

CANCELLATION POLICY: With 90 days' notice, the deposit minus $200 will be refunded. With less than 90 days' notice, the deposit is forfeited.

AVAILABILITY: The facility is available every day 10am–midnight.

SERVICES/AMENITIES:

Restaurant Services: no
Catering: provided, no BYO
Kitchen Facilities: n/a
Tables & Chairs: provided
Linens, Silver, etc.: provided
Outdoor Night Lighting: yes
Outdoor Cooking Facilities: no

Restrooms: wca
Dance Floor: CBA
Parking: lot
Overnight Accommodations: no
Telephone: pay phone
Cleanup: provided
Meeting Equipment: no

RESTRICTIONS:

Alcohol: provided, WC only
Smoking: outside only
Music: amplified ok

Wheelchair Access: yes
Insurance: not required

WENTE BROS. SPARKLING WINE CELLARS

5050 Arroyo Road
Livermore, CA 94550
(510) 447-3023
Reserve for Events: 6–12 months in advance
Reserve for Meetings: 1–12 months in advance

Situated in a picturesque canyon at the southern end of the Livermore Valley, Wente Bros. Sparkling Wine Cellars is surrounded by vineyards, sycamore groves and rolling hills. The site offers guests unparalleled vistas and an appealing, natural environment for meetings and parties. The grounds also include a Visitor's Center, Conference Center and an award-winning, casually elegant restaurant serving top-notch cuisine. The white, Spanish-style stucco buildings are accented with tile roofs and floors, terra cotta pots full of flowering plants and acres of vineyards which convey a strong Mediterranean feeling. Shimmering white and green in the soothing afternoon sun, this winery is an oasis in the midst of our dry California hills.

CAPACITY:	Area	Standing	Seated	Area	Standing	Seated
	Restaurant	200	185	Garden Area	—	700
	Visitor's Center	200	170	Veranda Area Restaurant	—	75

MEETING ROOMS:

Room	Capacity	Room	Capacity
VIP Room	10	Conference Room A	120
Vineyard Room	20	Conference Room B	20

FEES & DEPOSITS: A deposit is due when the contract is submitted. The remainder is due 30 days prior to the event. The facility fee is based on the size of the group, the time of day and the type of event. Hors d'oeuvres, buffets, seated luncheons and dinners can be arranged. Call for specific rates.

CANCELLATION POLICY: For events, if you cancel 6 months in advance, the deposit minus $600 will be refunded. With less than 6 months' notice, the deposit will be forfeited unless Wente is able to rebook the event date. For meetings, cancellation refunds are handled individually.

AVAILABILITY: The facility is available year-round, every day from 10am–11pm for events and 8am–6pm for meetings. Closed Thanksgiving, Christmas and New Year's Day.

SERVICES/AMENITIES:

Restaurant Services: yes

Catering: provided

Kitchen Facilities: n/a

Tables & Chairs: provided

Linens, Silver, etc.: provided

Outdoor Night Lighting: yes

Outdoor Cooking Facilities: no

Restrooms: wca

Dance Floor: yes

Parking: lot

Overnight Accommodations: no

Telephone: pay phones

Cleanup: provided

Meeting Equipment: AV equipment

RESTRICTIONS:

Alcohol: provided, WC only

Smoking: outside only

Music: amplified ok

Wheelchair Access: yes

Insurance: not required

Moraga

HACIENDA DE LAS FLORES

2100 Donald Drive
Moraga, CA 94556
(510) 376-2520
Reserve for Events: 2–12 months in advance
Reserve for Meetings: 2–3 weeks in advance

An authentic Spanish-style mansion, the Hacienda de las Flores sits on land that was once the hunting ground for Miwok Indians. The historic structure is painted white with blue trim, and is surrounded by park grounds. A large lawn spreads out behind the building, enhanced by blue spruce trees, weeping willows, palms and flowers. A circular flower bed and fountain in the middle of the patio serve as the focal point for private parties. Inside the building, hardwood floors, beamed ceilings, a fireplace and red leather furniture create a warm and inviting setting. La Sala and the Pavilion, which features an enclosed courtyard, are available for meetings. Conveniently located, the Hacienda and grounds offer a tranquil and secluded spot for your next event or business function.

CAPACITY: The Hacienda accommodates 200 guests outdoors or 128 for a seated meal indoors. The Pavilion seats 40 inside and has an outdoor capacity of 100.

MEETING ROOMS: La Sala accommodates up to 80 and the Pavilion seats 40.

FEES & DEPOSITS: The following rates and times apply to events only. Please call for meeting information. A security deposit is due at the time of booking and will be refunded within 30 days after the event, provided all conditions have been met.

	Residents*		Non Residents	
Friday (8 hr)	*Deposit*	*Fee*	*Deposit*	*Fee*
Hacienda	$475	$510	$475	$790
Pavilion	475	370	475	645
Hacienda & Pavilion	475	735	475	1,205
Sat/Sun (8 hr)	*Deposit*	*Fee*	*Deposit*	*Fee*
Hacienda	$475	$765	$475	$1,125
Pavilion	475	580	475	955
Hacienda & Pavilion	475	1,175	475	1,860

Completed rental packet and final fees are due 60 days before the event. May–Oct there is a $125 surcharge, and there is a mandatory $75 insurance premium for special events.

CANCELLATION POLICY: Cancellations must be made in writing. Refunds will be made as follows: over 120 days' notice, 100% of deposit less a $50 bookkeeping fee; 90–120 days' notice, 50% returned.

AVAILABILITY: Fridays from 3–11pm, Saturdays and Sundays, 8 consecutive hours 10am–11pm.

SERVICES/AMENITIES:

Restaurant Services: no

Catering: BYO, must be licensed

Kitchen Facilities: ample

Tables & Chairs: provided

Linens, Silver, etc.: BYO

Restrooms: wca

Dance Floor: yes (small)

Parking: on street and lot

Overnight Accommodations: no

Telephone: pay phone

Outdoor Night Lighting: no

Outdoor Cooking Facilities: no

Cleanup: provided

Meeting Equipment: varies according to bldg.

RESTRICTIONS:

Alcohol: BYO, WCB only

Smoking: outside only

Wheelchair Access: yes

Insurance: extra insurance required

Oakland

ATHENIAN NILE CLUB

410 14th Street
Oakland, CA 94612
(510) 451-0693
Reserve for Events: 2–6 months in advance
Reserve for Meetings: 2–6 months in advance

This location may be one of the best kept secrets in the East Bay. Operating for a hundred and ten years as a private club, the Athenian Nile Club is now available to the public for private functions. Don't let the nondescript front door on 14th Street deter you. Once inside, you'll be ushered upstairs to the facility's light and airy Dining Room, with stage, hardwood dance floor and plenty of room for a sizable party. The room is the size of a small ballroom, with a thirty-foot ceiling. The decor is in grays, whites and burgundies. Comfortable, upholstered chairs contrast against crisp, white linens. Silver flatware, crystal and china are provided for all events. A working fireplace with decorative white mantle adds a homey touch and soft lighting is provided by wall sconces around the room. If you've got a large crowd, and you'd like to be close to downtown, come by for a site review.

CAPACITY: The Dining Room can accommodate 250 seated, 350 guests for a standing reception. For smaller functions, the room can be split into 2 sections. For Saturday and Sunday events, a minimum of 100 guests is required.

MEETING ROOMS: 5 meeting rooms can accommodate 10–300 guests.

FEES & DEPOSITS: A $250 non-refundable deposit applied toward the event total is required when reservations are confirmed. A final guest count is required 72 hours in advance. The food & beverage total is payable on the day of the event. Functions after 6pm require a security guard at $15/hour. Seated luncheons start at $15/person, dinners at $22/person and buffets at $20/person. Tax and a 15% service charge are additional. Bartenders cost $75 per 5-hour function.

CANCELLATION POLICY: The deposit is forfeited if you cancel at anytime.

AVAILABILITY: Year-round, every day from 7am–2am.

SERVICES/AMENITIES:

Restaurant Services: no
Catering: provided
Kitchen Facilities: n/a
Tables & Chairs: provided
Linens, Silver, etc.: provided
Restrooms: no wca
Dance Floor: yes

Parking: valet
Overnight Accommodations: no
Telephone: house phone
Outdoor Night Lighting: no
Outdoor Cooking Facilities: no
Cleanup: provided
Meeting Equipment: podium, PA system

RESTRICTIONS:

Alcohol: provided, corkage $5-6/bottle
Smoking: allowed
Music: amplified ok

Wheelchair Access: yes
Insurance: not required

CAFE FONTEBELLA

1111 Broadway
Oakland, CA 94607
(510) 452-2500
Reserve for Events: 3–12 months in advance
Reserve for Meetings: 1 week–6 months in advance

Talk about a sophisticated environment. Clad in a stunning combination of granite and glass, Cafe Fontebella has heretofore been a secret favorite of this author. Hidden inside an understated, glass-walled highrise in downtown Oakland, this facility is on the ground floor of the American President's Companies Building. The Cafe, which bustles during the work week, is quiet and peaceful on weekends. It occupies a small portion of the total floor space and its decor reflects an Art Deco and craftsman influence with contemporary black tables and chairs and large, colorful paintings. The rest of the open space is divided between the conservatory and the impressive lobby. Thirty-foot floor-to-ceiling glass panels on three sides allow abundant light to flood into the atrium during the day. The soaring ceiling caps a space that is simultaneously open yet intimate. A contemporary sculpture exhibit, which is changed every four months, acts as a centerpiece. Adjacent is the grand foyer which has one of the most exquisite floors we've ever seen. High-polished granite, in geometric patterns of rose, black, tan and gray, is a design element that visually holds all the spaces together. Adding warmth are tasteful leather furniture and wood paneled walls. Several glass display cases hold large ship replicas, which can be moved if the need arises. Outside the glass and chrome doors is a lovely landscaped courtyard with a raised lawn area, ringed by a granite benchseat. Large sculptures and granite stepping stones provide visual interest and slabs of gray granite with polished surfaces form a patio. Tall trees surround the perimeter, enclosing the space. Off to one side is a fabulous waterfall, constructed of stone. The rush of water creates an inviting sound that eliminates the feeling you are in the heart of the city.

CAPACITY: Cafe Fontebella can seat 75 guests. Including the conservatory and lobby, the entire ground floor can seat up to 275 or 1,000 standing guests. A minimum party of 25 is required.

FEES & DEPOSITS: A $500 refundable cleaning/damage deposit is payable when reservations are confirmed. There's no fee for renting the Cafe, alone. The rental fee for the entire ground floor, including the Cafe space, is $750–2,000 depending on day of week, guest count and services required. Food service is provided by Cafe Fontebella. Any menu can be customized and prices will vary accordingly. Tax and a 15% service charge are additional. Half the total estimated event cost is payable 6 weeks prior to your function and the final half, plus a confirmed guest count, are due 1 week in advance. Any remaining balance is payable at the event's conclusion.

CANCELLATION POLICY: With 120 days' notice, your deposit will be refunded minus $100 administration fee. The deposit is non-refundable on major holidays or during the holiday season. If your date can be rebooked with comparable size party, your deposit will be refunded less a $100 fee.

AVAILABILITY: Year-round, every day. Evenings from 6pm–midnight. Saturday and Sunday from 9am–1am.

SERVICES/AMENITIES:

Restaurant Services: yes
Catering: provided, no BYO
Kitchen Facilities: n/a
Tables & Chairs: provided for 75 guests or CBA
Linens, Silver, etc.: provided for 75 guests or CBA
Restrooms: wca
Dance Floor: yes
Other: event coordination, fresh flowers

Parking: adjacent garage for free
Overnight Accommodations: no
Telephone: pay phone
Outdoor Night Lighting: yes
Outdoor Cooking Facilities: no
Cleanup: provided
Meeting Equipment: CBA

RESTRICTIONS:

Alcohol: provided, corkage $8/bottle
Smoking: bar only
Music: amplified ok

Wheelchair Access: yes
Insurance: not required
Other: decorations restricted

CALIFORNIA BALLROOM

1736 Franklin Street
Oakland, CA 94612
(510) 834-7761
Reserve for Events: 1–12 months in advance
Reserve for Meetings: 1–7 days in advance

The California Ballroom and Rose Room are just a few blocks from Lake Merritt in Oakland. The former was built in 1926 as the grand ballroom of the elegant old Leamington Hotel, and showcases a majestic 45-foot gold-leafed ceiling, a 500-square foot stage with curtain and spotlights, and a 700-square foot dance floor—possibly the largest in the Bay Area. Although the Leamington no longer exists, its impressive Art Deco Ballroom is still going strong. Renovated in 1986, this landmark space is one of few locations in the East Bay that can seat over 300 for receptions or seminars. Large, original Art Deco lights are suspended from the soaring ceiling. Burgundy draperies and carpet contrast nicely with the cream-colored walls and gold detailing above the doors and mirrors. The stage is impressive, and can be used for the head table or to feature a band or DJ. Tables can be arranged around the hardwood dance floor which occupies the center of the room. The Rose Room is a distinctive space for smaller events, featuring a beautiful marble entry, black stone bar and a baby grand piano. On-site staff is happy to coordinate the details of your corporate or social event, and butler sevice is available to handle errands, faxes and secretarial services.

CAPACITY:

	Banquet	Standing	Classroom	Seminar
California Ballroom	350	600	300	400
Rose Room	100	150	80	100

FEES & DEPOSITS: Half the rental fee is required when you book this facility. The balance is payable 90 days prior to the event. Any function beginning after dusk will require a security guard. Non-refundable rental fees are as follows:

	Saturday & Holidays		Sunday–Friday	
	Ballroom	Rose Room	Ballroom	Rose Room
8am–5pm	$600	$300	$500	$300
7pm–2am	800	500	500	500
Each additional hour after 2am	150	—	125	—
All day up to 12 hours	1,000	650	500	450
Corporate 9am–5pm	—	—	250	200
Non-Profit Groups	—	—	400	250
Optional cleanup & setup	—	—	50	50

AVAILABILITY: Year-round, every day until 2am. Saturday receptions can be held from 8am–5pm or 7pm–2am or you can rent the Ballroom all day, up to 12 hours.

SERVICES/AMENITIES:

Restaurant Services: no
Catering: BYO with approval
Kitchen Facilities: minimal
Tables & Chairs: provided
Linens, Silver, etc.: caterer or BYO
Restrooms: wca
Dance Floor: yes
Other: wet bar

Parking: adjacent garages, private lot
Overnight Accommodations: no
Telephone: pay phone
Outdoor Night Lighting: access only
Outdoor Cooking Facilities: no
Cleanup: caterer or renter
Meeting Equipment: podium, overhead projector, screen, microphone

RESTRICTIONS:

Alcohol: BYO
Smoking: outside only
Music: amplified allowed

Wheelchair Access: yes
Insurance: not required
Other: decorations restricted, no tacks, staples or tape

Need a caterer, cake maker, florist? The Service Directory starting on page 614 features the best in the business.

CAMRON-STANFORD HOUSE

1418 Lakeside Drive
Oakland, CA 94612
(510) 836-1976   Elizabeth Way
Reserve for Events: 1–6 months in advance
Reserve for Meetings: 6 weeks in advance

Gracing the shore of Lake Merritt, the Camron-Stanford House is the last of the grand Victorian homes that once ringed the lake. Constructed in 1876, it derives its name from the Camrons who built it and the Stanfords who occupied it for the longest period. When the building was scheduled for demolition in the late 1960s, concerned citizens formed the Camron-Stanford House Preservation Association and spent the intervening years raising funds to return the home to its former splendor. Elaborate molding, authentic wallpaper and fabrics have all been recreated to match the originals as closely as possible. Rooms filled with period artifacts, antiques and photos take you back to the late 1800s. The only operational gas chandelier in Northern California is located here. Outside, an enormous rear veranda overlooks Lake Merritt. Events can take place in the house, the veranda or on the expansive lawn that extends to the lake. The veranda is an especially popular spot for business functions. An iron fence enclosing the site ensures privacy while allowing guests to appreciate the colorful tapestry of boats, birds and joggers that surrounds them.

CAPACITY: The facility accommodates 125 guests inside; 250 outside.

MEETING ROOMS: The Dining Room can hold 45–80 guests; one other room up to 20.

FEES & DEPOSITS: Half the rental fee and a refundable $50 cleaning deposit are due at the time of booking.

Area	*Fee*
Veranda, Hall, Dining Room, Kitchen (2 hours)	$325
Veranda, Hall, Dining Room, Kitchen (4 hours)	525
Additional Time	100/hr.
Period Room (maximum 2 hours)	50/hr.

CANCELLATION POLICY: If less than 30 days' notice is given, half the rental fee will be forfeited. The remainder of the fee and the cleaning deposit are usually returned.

AVAILABILITY: Until 10pm weekdays, and 11pm Saturdays.

SERVICES/AMENITIES:

Restaurant Services: no

Catering: BYO licensed

Parking: on street, lot

Overnight Accommodations: no

Meeting Equipment: projector, screen, rostrom

RESTRICTIONS:

Alcohol: BYO
Smoking: outside only
Music: amplified outside only
Wheelchair Access: limited

Insurance: proof required
Other: decorations restricted, no candles, flame-heated chafing dishes, confetti

THE CLAREMONT RESORT, SPA & TENNIS CLUB

Ashby and Domingo Avenues
Oakland, CA 94623
(510) 843-3000　Jan Hager
Reserve for Events: 1–12 months in advance
Reserve for Meetings: 2 days in advance

The Claremont rises up from the Oakland/Berkeley Hills where it has been a Bay Area landmark for decades. The resort and spa offer an extensive range of services and amenities and numerous rooms for business conferences and special events. This is a full-service facility with over 32,000 sq. ft. of event space. You can choose from among private rooms, balconies, trellised patios or lawns and gardens. The Claremont can cater a small cocktail party, a formal sit-down feast for hundreds, or anything in between. If you need help with any aspect of your event, the Claremont has the staff to assist you—there's even a conference service department as well as an on-site audio-visual company. So whether you want an affair on a grand scale or a small informal gathering of business associates, the Claremont can accommodate your needs.

CAPACITY: 2 of the ballrooms can accommodate 400 standing or 350 seated guests. Capacities for the 20 other available rooms vary.

MEETING ROOMS: There are 22 meeting rooms.

FEES & DEPOSITS: For special events, a $500 non-refundable deposit, which is applied toward the fee, is due at the time of booking. 95% of the total estimated bill is due 5 days prior to the event, and the balance is due at the conclusion. For business functions, deposits and fees vary. The fee schedule is based on the room(s) selected and the number of guests attending.

AVAILABILITY: Any day, 6am–1am.

SERVICES/AMENITIES:

Restaurant Services: yes
Catering: provided, no BYO
Kitchen Facilities: n/a
Tables & Chairs: provided
Linens, Silver, etc.: provided
Restrooms: wca
Dance Floor: yes

Overnight Accommodations: 239 guestrooms
Telephone: pay phone
Outdoor Night Lighting: no
Outdoor Cooking Facilities: yes
Cleanup: provided
Special: spa, tennis courts, swimming pool
Other: event coordination

Parking: lot, valet

RESTRICTIONS:

Alcohol: provided
Smoking: allowed
Music: no music at poolside

Meeting Equipment: microphone, movie screen

Wheelchair Access: yes
Insurance: not required
Other: receptions held inside only

COMMODORE DINING CRUISES

Docked at Embarcadero Cove
Port of Oakland, CA
(510) 256-4000
Reserve for Events: 1–12 months in advance
Reserve for Meetings: 2–4 weeks in advance

You'll have no problem locating Commodore Dining Cruises—its fleet of four white yachts is lined up in a row at the dock next to Quinn's Lighthouse in Port of Oakland's historic Embarcadero Cove. Each vessel is well equipped and especially designed for entertaining on San Francisco Bay. Parquet dance floors, full galley, bars and even sleeping quarters are on board. During the cruise, weather permitting, canvas coverings can be rolled up for unobstructed views of San Francisco, Alameda and the bridges. Take a deep breath. Relax. Nothing beats a party on the water. Guests can stroll about the decks or join the captain in the pilot house for a chat. Enjoy the sea lions while gliding by Pier 39. Sail beneath the Bay Bridge or circle Treasure Island. Whether you come aboard for a business function or social occasion, Commodore Dining Cruises will host your event in a personalized and gracious style without straining your pocketbook (offering a tremendous service at very competitive prices). Transform any outing into an adventure. Your guests will rave about the great time they had, taking home memories of salt water breezes and the excitement of yachting on the Bay.

CAPACITY:

Vessel	Seated	Standing	Vessel	Seated	Standing
Commodore Stockton	72	86	Showtime Commodore	150	150
Argo Commodore	50–60	10	Jack London Commodore	350	450

FEES & DEPOSITS: A $500–2,000 refundable deposit, which is applied toward the event total, is required to secure your date. The food and beverage balance is payable 2 weeks prior to the function. Fees run from $25–60/person, including yacht rental and food. Tax and gratuity are additional.

CANCELLATION POLICY: With 90 days' notice, the deposit will be refunded. With less notice, refunds will be given only if the yacht can be rebooked, minus a $200 rebooking fee.

AVAILABILITY: Year-round, anytime.

SERVICES/AMENITIES:
Restaurant Services: no

Overnight Accommodations: Argo sleeps 32 guests

Catering: provided, BYO by arrangement
Kitchen Facilities: fully equipped
Tables & Chairs: provided
Linens, Silver, etc.: provided
Restrooms: no wca
Dance Floor: yes
Other: event coordination, decorations

Telephone: ship to shore
Outdoor Night Lighting: access only
Outdoor Cooking Facilities: no
Cleanup: provided
Parking: free parking, large lot
Meeting Equipment: CBA

RESTRICTIONS:

Alcohol: provided, BYO by arrangement
Smoking: some restrictions
Music: amplified ok

Wheelchair Access: yes
Insurance: not required

DUNSMUIR HOUSE

2960 Peralta Oaks Court
Oakland, CA 94605
(510) 562-0328
Reserve for Events: 12 months in advance
Reserve for Meetings: 2 weeks–6 months in advance

Nestled in the East Bay foothills, the historic Dunsmuir House and Gardens offer a lovely and secluded setting featuring a turn-of-the-century white mansion and a forty-acre expanse of lawn and trees, evoking the serenity of a bygone era. The House was a romantic wedding gift from Alexander Dunsmuir to his bride on the occasion of their marriage in 1899. The Pond Area, with its weeping elms and delicate white gazebo, is a popular site for outdoor events. Parties are often held on its beautiful lawn with vistas of the Mansion and gardens. The Carriage House is a unique, rustic setting for indoor receptions. Its quaint seating nooks and mahogany paneling add an old-fashioned feel. Lit up with hundreds of twinkling lights and draped with evergreen garlands throughout, the Pavilion, with its large dance floor, is an especially lovely room for evening parties. Built in the 1930s as a summer guest house, Dinkelspiel House has an English cottage ambiance. Six sets of glass French doors open out onto a patio, surrounded by huge pine trees and flowers. Inside, the knotty pine trim and fireplace make this a cozy place for small functions. The grounds here are private, peaceful and beautiful throughout the year. This is one of the most exceptional sites in the Bay Area for any kind of celebration.

CAPACITY:

Area	Standing	Seated
Carriage House	200	100 or more
Pavilion	400	200
Pond area	400	300
Meadow (partial use)	200–500	200–500
Meadow (full use)	3,000	2,000
Dinkelspiel House	80	60

MEETING ROOMS: The Carriage House, Pavilion and Dinkelspiel House are available for meetings.

FEES & DEPOSITS: For events, a minimum refundable $500 deposit reserves your date. The balance of fees is due 30 days prior to the event. If you select a caterer not from the preferred list, there is a $300 charge. Use fees below are for a 6-hour time block and include use of some tables and chairs as well as setup and breakdown. Call for information about meeting rental rates.

Locations	Use Fees			
	75 Guests	*100 Guests*	*150 Guests*	*200 Guests*
Carriage House	$1,575	$1,650	$1,910	$2,175
Pavilion or	1,725	1,800	2,060	2,325
Meadow (partial use)		*by special arrangement*		
Meadow (full use)		*by special arrangement*		
Pond Area	1,725	1,800	2,060	2,325
Dinkelspiel House	950	—	—	—

Any additional equipment must be rented through Dunsmuir House.

CANCELLATION POLICY: No refund will be given 72 hours after reservations are made.

AVAILABILITY: Any day, February–November.

SERVICES/AMENITIES:

Restaurant Services: no
Catering: select from preferred list
Kitchen Facilities: no
Tables & Chairs: limited
Linens, Silver, etc.: BYO
Restrooms: wca
Parking: on street, or $100/parking lot
Meeting Equipment: CBA, extra fee

Dance Floor: Greenhouse only; lawn area CBA, extra fee
Overnight Accommodations: no
Telephone: pay phone
Outdoor Night Lighting: access only
Outdoor Cooking Facilities: CBA
Cleanup: provided

RESTRICTIONS:

Alcohol: provided or BYO, BWC only
Smoking: outside only
Music: amplified ok

Wheelchair Access: yes
Insurance: may be required
Other: decorations limited

THE LAKE MERRITT HOTEL

1800 Madison Street at Lakeside
Oakland, CA 94612
(510) 832-2300
Reserve for Events: 3–12 months in advance
Reserve for Meetings: 2 weeks in advance

Totally enclosed in twenty-foot floor-to-ceiling windows, the Lake Merritt Hotel's Terrace Room presents a spectacular panorama of Lake Merritt, Lakeside Park and the Oakland hills. At night, the lake glitters below, reflecting the Necklace of Lights gracing its perimeter. Recently, over $1.5 million was spent to turn the Hotel and restaurant into one of Oakland's premier entertainment sites. This classic, 1927 Art Deco landmark has been renovated with new furnishings, carpeting and soft colors throughout. During the day, the multi-level Terrace Room is bathed in light. In the evening, it has an intimate, almost cabaret feeling. Here you'll find a semi-circle hardwood dance floor, very good original watercolor paintings and a sizeable mural along one wall (circa 1927) depicting Lake Merritt before the Depression. Fresh flowers, a black baby grand piano and Art Deco fixtures are nice finishing touches. In addition to having a great location along the perimeter of Lake Merritt and a good restaurant in-house, the staff aims to please by offering highly personalized services, many of which can be specifically tailored to your special event.

CAPACITY: The Terrace Room accommodates 275 standing or 225 guests for a seated affair.

MEETING ROOMS: The Paramount Room holds 75; the Terrace Room 300.

FEES & DEPOSITS: A $500 non-refundable security deposit is required to reserve your date. 50% payment is required 1 month prior and the balance is due 2 weeks prior to your event. For events, the Terrace Room rental fee varies from complimentary to $1,000 based on your event. Food and beverage service is provided in-house. For full seated service including food and beverage, rates run approximately $25/person. Buffets start at $20/person; hors d'oeuvres start at $10/person. Sales tax and a 17% service charge are additional.

AVAILABILITY: The Terrace Room is available every day from noon to midnight.

SERVICES/AMENITIES:

Restaurant Services: yes
Catering: provided
Kitchen Facilities: n/a
Tables & Chairs: provided
Linens, Silver, etc.: provided
Restrooms: no wca
Dance Floor: yes
Meeting Equipment: CBA

Parking: valet CBA
Overnight Accommodations: suites & packages available
Telephone: pay phone
Outdoor Night Lighting: no
Outdoor Cooking Facilities: no
Cleanup: provided
Special: full event coordination in-house

RESTRICTIONS:

Alcohol: provided, champagne corkage $4/bottle
Smoking: designated areas
Music: amplified restricted

Wheelchair Access: limited
Insurance: not required

OAKLAND HILLS TENNIS CLUB

5475 Redwood Rd.
Oakland, CA 94619
(510) 531-3300
Reserve for Events: 12 months in advance
Reserve for Meetings: 1 week in advance

Here's a new introduction with a killer view of the Bay. Set on ten acres atop the Oakland Hills, this facility is now hosting private parties. Don't be deterred by the front door which says 'members only'. For those who have reserved the Club for functions after regular hours, this place is definitely open. The entry walk to the front door is shaded by old oaks and new landscaping. The swimming pool is on your right and the multiple tennis courts are below, on your left. Inside, you'll find the usual paraphernalia of a tennis club: sports clothing, equipment, lockers and the like. However, on the west part of the building is the aerobics room, a large, uncluttered space with a shiny, oak hardwood floor, a vaulted wood-beamed ceiling, a wall of mirrors and wall-to-wall windows with a remarkable, unobstructed view of the Bay Area. For outdoor entertaining, the long deck running the length of the room can be arranged with tables, chairs and umbrellas. The Club's Cafe is next door, which is connected to the aerobics room by way of double doors. Both can be used simultaneously for larger functions. The Club is a good choice if you're looking for light and contemporary spaces for informal receptions, meetings, anniversary or birthday parties.

CAPACITY: 110 seated guests; 200 for a standing reception. Additional seating for 40 available on adjacent deck.

MEETING ROOMS: One room; classroom style 120 seated, with tables, 80 seated. For business functions with food, a 25 person minimum is required.

FEES & DEPOSITS: A $250 non-refundable security deposit reserves your date. The rental fee is $500 per event, due 30 days prior to the function. An extra $75/hour will be charged for any use of the facility after 10pm. For business functions, the rental fee with food service runs about $10–20/person.

CANCELLATION POLICY: If you cancel, the security deposit can be allocated to hold another event date.

AVAILABILITY: Year-round, Friday, Saturday and Sunday after 4pm. Rentals prior to 4pm will only be considered during the Club's non-peak times.

SERVICES/AMENITIES:

Restaurant Services: yes
Catering: provided or BYO
Kitchen Facilities: fully equipped
Tables & Chairs: provided, extra charge
Linens, Silver, etc.: BYO or provided, extra charge
Restrooms: wca
Dance Floor: yes
Meeting Equipment: BYO

Parking: large parking lot
Overnight Accommodations: no
Telephone: pay phone
Outdoor Night Lighting: yes
Outdoor Cooking Facilities: CBA
Cleanup: provided and/or caterer
Other: some event coordination provided

RESTRICTIONS:

Alcohol: BYO, some restrictions
Smoking: outside only
Music: amplified volume restricted

Wheelchair Access: yes
Insurance: required

Need a caterer, cake maker, florist? The Service Directory starting on page 614 features the best in the business.

OAKLAND MUSEUM

1000 Oak Street
Oakland, CA 94607
(510) 238-2264
Reserve for Events: 6 months in advance
Reserve for Meetings: 3 weeks in advance

Located in the heart of downtown Oakland near Lake Merritt, the Museum provides a surprisingly quiet and aesthetic setting. Meetings, events and receptions can be held in the restaurant or on the adjacent tree-lined terraces and patios. The restaurant, with its carpeting, upholstered chairs and floor-to-ceiling windows, has a casual, relaxed ambiance. There's even a baby grand piano in here for your use. The sculptured gardens outdoors, however, are what make the Museum a special site. Guests can enjoy the openness of a grassy courtyard, find a little solitude among the many levels of terraces or enjoy the Koi pond.

CAPACITY: The Museum Restaurant accommodates 240 standing guests and 150 seated. The Gardens and Terraces have space for a sizable party.

FEES & DEPOSITS: 50% of the total estimated fee plus a refundable cleaning/damage deposit are required when the contract is signed. The balance of payment is required prior to the event. The Restaurant rents for $850–1,020 for up to 4 hours and $1,050–1,260 for more than 4 hours, depending on whether you're a nonprofit organization. Call for Garden and Terrace fee information.

CANCELLATION POLICY: If notice is received within 5 working days of the event, the 50% deposit will be refunded. Any direct costs incurred in preparing for the event will be charged.

AVAILABILITY: Mon–Tues 10am–9pm; Wed–Sun 6pm–midnight. You may be able to arrange other times during the hours the Museum is open to the public.

SERVICES/AMENITIES:

Restaurant Services: open during hours of public access
Catering: provided or BYO
Kitchen Facilities: ample, $175 use fee
Tables & Chairs: some provided
Linens, Silver, etc.: BYO
Restrooms: no wca
Dance Floor: outside terrace or CBA, extra charge
Other: baby grand piano

Parking: garage and on street
Overnight Accommodations: no
Telephone: pay phone
Outdoor Cooking Facilities: no
Outdoor Night Lighting: CBA
Cleanup: caterer or renter
Meeting Equipment: projectors, video equip., podium, microphone

RESTRICTIONS:

Alcohol: provided or corkage fee required
Smoking: outside only
Music: amplified with restrictions

Wheelchair Access: yes
Insurance: liability required

PRESERVATION PARK

660 & 668 13th St at Martin Luther King Jr. Way
Oakland, CA 94612
(510) 874-7580
Reserve for Events: 1–6 months in advance
Reserve for Meetings: 60 days in advance

Occupying two blocks a heartbeat away from Oakland's City Center, Preservation Park is a recreation of a Victorian neighborhood where historic residences have been transformed back to their original splendor. Sixteen beautifully restored and colorfully painted Victorian homes have been relocated here, replicating a turn-of-the-century small town setting, with period park benches, ornate wrought-iron fences and 19th-century street lamps. A large, two-tiered fountain with the moon goddess Diana resting atop, acts as the Park's centerpiece. It is located in the center of a cul-de-sac, framed by manicured lawns and well-maintained landscaping. Two houses, in particular, are well-suited for special events. The Ginn House, circa 1890, features two delightful light and airy parlors which are reminiscent of an English country home. The Nile Club, circa 1911, is a craftsman-style building connected to the Ginn house via a spacious hallway. Walk through and enter Nile Hall, which is a sensational space for a grand and elegant party. It has a soaring 30-foot high ceiling, skylights, multiple windows, stage plus theatrical lighting and sound system. This room is well designed, with soft colors, nice detailing and attractive appointments—and, enough room to please any group with an extensive guest list. We think Preservation Park is an outstanding addition to the East Bay. This is a "must see" facility.

CAPACITY:

Area	*Standing*	*Seated*	*Area*	*Standing*	*Seated*
Ginn House	125	—	Nile Hall	250	140
Large Parlor	105	50	Ginn & Nile	400	185
Small Parlor	20	15			

FEES & DEPOSITS: A non-refundable $250 rental deposit, applied to the rental fee, is required to secure your date. The balance of the rental fee, together with a refundable cleaning/damage deposit, are payable 60 days prior to the event. The fee for Nile Hall is $800; for Nile Hall plus the Ginn House, $1175. For functions during the Christmas season, the non-refundable rental deposit is $500. Fees for meetings (3-hour minimum) range from $25/hour to $500 per day.

CANCELLATION POLICY: The rental deposit is non-refundable. With less than 30 days' notice, the rental fee is forfeited.

AVAILABILITY: Year-round, every day from 8am–1am.

SERVICES/AMENITIES:

Restaurant Services: no
Catering: provided, no BYO
Kitchen Facilities: setup only
Tables & Chairs: provided, no BYO
Linens, Silver, etc.: provided by caterer

Parking: on street or City lot nearby
Overnight Accommodations: no
Telephone: pay phone
Outdoor Night Lighting: yes
Outdoor Cooking Facilities: no

Restrooms: wca
Dance Floor: CBA
RESTRICTIONS:
Alcohol: provided, no BYO
Smoking: outside only
Music: amplified ok

Cleanup: caterer
Meeting Equipment: yes

Wheelchair Access: yes
Insurance: may be required

SAILBOAT HOUSE

568 Bellevue in Lakeside Park
Oakland, CA 94612
(510) 238-3187 Parks and Recreation Office
Reserve for Events: 11 months in advance
Reserve for Meetings: 2 weeks in advance

Resting on the edge of Lake Merritt within Lakeside Park, the Sailboat House offers a wonderful view of the water. The large upstairs room that is available for parties and receptions is totally enclosed in glass and has an outdoor deck which runs the length of the lake side of the building. The atmosphere is especially light and airy during sunny afternoons, and at night the lakeside necklace of lights lends an added sparkle to events.

CAPACITY: The room accommodates 225 standing, 155 seated or 125 seated banquet style.

FEES & DEPOSITS: A refundable security deposit of $200 and the minimum rental fee are due when reservations are made. The facility rents for $50/hr between 9am–midnight; $60/hr between midnight–1am (Fri & Sat only) and $60/hr before 9am. There is a 4-hour minimum rental. Setup and teardown are available for $50 and $75, respectively. If champagne, beer or wine are served, there's an extra fee of $50; hard alcohol $75. Entry into Lakeside Park is $2/car.

CANCELLATION POLICY: With more than 31 days' notice, you forfeit $25. With less notice, $200 is forfeited.

AVAILABILITY: The facility is available from 8am–midnight Monday–Friday and until 1am on Friday and Saturday nights.

SERVICES/AMENITIES:
Restaurant Services: no
Catering: BYO
Kitchen Facilities: moderate
Tables & Chairs: provided
Linens, Silver, etc.: BYO
Restrooms: no wca
Dance Floor: yes
Meeting Equipment: no

Parking: lot ($2/car)
Overnight Accommodations: no
Telephone: pay phone
Outdoor Night Lighting: access only
Outdoor Cooking Facilities: no
Cleanup: whoever caters event, CBA extra fee
Other: piano

RESTRICTIONS:

Alcohol: BYO (permit fee)

Smoking: outside only

Music: amplified ok

Wheelchair Access: yes, elevator

Insurance: usually not required

SCOTTISH RITE CENTER

1547 Lakeside Drive
Oakland, CA 94612
(510) 832-0819
Reserve for Events: 3–6 months in advance
Reserve for Meetings: 1 week in advance

Although you might not pay too much attention to the rather nondescript facade of the Scottish Rite Center, once you're inside, it's an entirely different story. This historic building houses some of the most remarkable and impressive interior spaces we've ever seen. Constructed for the Masonic Order in 1927, it's just a stone's throw from Lake Merritt in Oakland. Here, you'll find a wide selection of differently designed small and large rooms. We were impressed by inlaid terrazzo and mosaic floors, walls of ornate design, soaring, hand-carved ceilings, grand staircases and period fixtures that create an old world ambiance. We were 'wowed' by two rooms in particular. The Grand Ballroom, on the first floor, is magnificent. Five chandeliers, suspended from an exquisite ceiling, light a 10,000 square foot hardwood floor. The twenty-eight foot vaulted ceiling is hand-painted mostly in golds, with highlights of greens, pinks and taupe. The decorative plaster friezes are delicate, almost lace-like as they curve down to meet the walls. The Ballroom has a refined elegance. On one side, a large, formally draped stage is perfect for a band—along the opposite wall, a balcony stretches the length of the room. Take the walnut-clad elevators to the top floor and step out into the auditorium foyer. This splendid space is the prefunction or waiting area for the Center's theater. It has its own loggia (balcony), overlooking Lake Merritt and has a remarkable ceiling. In fact the foyer, in its own right is so beautiful, it's hard to believe that what comes next could top it. Talk about a space that takes your breath away—this is a room you *must* see. The expansive theater is capped by a dome which rises eighty feet from the floor, partially supported by multiple Corinthian columns. Brass lamps, artfully suspended from the perimeter, provide a subtle glow. Curved theater seating in tiers is oriented towards the very large, professional stage. Heavy, burgundy velvet with gold and burgundy tie-backs, tassels and braids plus a hand-sewn canopy create a one and a half-ton theater curtain that was, in 1927, the largest curtain outside of Metropolitan Opera house in New York. Used for formal showings of film or videos, seminars, comedy competitions, fashion shows, talent competitions and theater productions, this auditorium is extraordinary. If you are looking for an East Bay location that can offer variety, distinction and a sense of grandness, we urge you to take a full tour of this facility. We think you'll be pleasantly surprised.

CAPACITY, FEES & DEPOSITS: For special events, a $200 non-refundable deposit is required when your date is confirmed. The rental fee plus a $250 refundable security/cleaning deposit are payable 30 days prior to your function. A stage electrician is an additional charge. For meetings, the rental rate

Monday–Friday ranges from $300–1,200/day. The charge for shorter meetings will be pro-rated on an hourly basis.

Area	Seated	Standing	Fee
Grand Ballroom	1,000	1,300	$1,000–1,300
Banquet Room	250-300	350	500–700
Auditorium/Theater	1,500	—	1,200–1,800

MEETING ROOMS: 7 rooms, from 8–1,000 guests.

AVAILABILITY: Year-round, any day 10am–midnight.

SERVICES/AMENITIES:

Restaurant Services: no
Catering: BYO or CBA
Kitchen Facilities: fully equipped
Tables & Chairs: provided
Linens, Silver, etc.: BYO
Restrooms: wca
Meeting Equipment: yes

Parking: private lot
Overnight Accommodations: no
Telephone: pay phone
Outdoor Night Lighting: access only
Outdoor Cooking Facilities: no
Cleanup: renter or caterer
Dance Floor: yes

RESTRICTIONS:

Alcohol: BYO
Smoking: designated areas
Music: amplified ok

Wheelchair Access: yes
Insurance: proof of liability required

SEQUOIA LODGE

2666 Mountain Blvd.
Oakland, CA
(510) 238-3187 Parks and Recreation Office
Reserve for Events: 11 months in advance
Reserve for Meetings: 2 weeks in advance

Located among the trees at the base of the Oakland Hills, Sequoia Lodge has the feel of a mountain retreat. The interior features rustic wood paneling, a stone fireplace and a high pitched roof with skylight. A sunken seating area in front of the fireplace gives guests an intimate spot for conversation and an outside deck area adds to the serene setting in the trees.

CAPACITY: The Lodge accommodates 150 standing, 100 seated or 80 seated guests at banquet tables.

FEES & DEPOSITS: A refundable security deposit of $200 and the minimum rental fee are due at the time of booking. The facility rents for $50/hr between 9am–midnight; $60/hr between midnight–1am and before 9am. On Fri & Sat, the minimum rental is 4 hours. If champagne, beer or wine are served, there's an extra $50 fee; hard alcohol $75. If needed, setup fee is $50 and teardown is $75.

CANCELLATION POLICY: With more than 31 days' notice, you forfeit $25; with less than 31 days' notice, $200 is forfeited.

AVAILABILITY: Monday–Thursday 3:30pm–midnight (9am–midnight during summer), Friday–Saturday 9am–1am, Sunday 9am–midnight.

SERVICES/AMENITIES:

Restaurant Services: no

Catering: BYO

Kitchen Facilities: ample

Tables & Chairs: provided

Linens, Silver, etc.: BYO

Restrooms: wca

Dance Floor: yes

Parking: on and off street, lot

Overnight Accommodations: no

Telephone: pay phone

Outdoor Night Lighting: yes

Outdoor Cooking Facilities: no

Cleanup: caterer

Meeting Equipment: no

RESTRICTIONS:

Alcohol: BYO for $50 fee

Smoking: outside only

Music: amplified ok

Wheelchair Access: yes

Insurance: usually not required

Piedmont

PIEDMONT COMMUNITY CENTER

711 Highland Ave.
Piedmont, CA 94611
(510) 420-3081 Penny Robb
Reserve for Events: 9–12 months in advance
Reserve for Meetings: 2 weeks in advance

Brick steps lead down to the Center, situated in a park setting. Mediterranean in style, the light taupe building with its tile roof and landscaped plaza is surrounded by redwoods and flowering cherry trees. Azaleas and camellias provide splashes of color near the round patio, and behind the building, a stream and more trees complete the circle of greenery. The Center's interior has recently undergone renovation and looks better than ever. This is a great party room, with high beamed ceiling, shining herringbone hardwood floors and chandeliers. Floor-to-ceiling windows allow lots of natural light and ensure that the feeling of the park carries over to your gathering. This is a refined, nicely designed space suitable for an elegant dinner party, fundraiser, corporate seminar or retreat.

CAPACITY: The Center accommodates 223 standing or 104 seated guests. The patio area holds 300 standing or 200 seated guests.

FEES & DEPOSITS: A security deposit of $300 is due 2 weeks after booking and is refundable 4 weeks after the event. For residents, the facility is rented in 6-hour blocks; the fee is $700. For non-residents, a 6-hour block is available for $1,200. These rates are for Friday, Saturday and Sunday. Payment is due 30 days prior to the event. For Monday–Thursday rates for business functions, please call for specifics.

CANCELLATION POLICY: If notification of cancellation is given 2 months prior to the event, half of the security deposit will be refunded. A full refund minus $30 will be given with 6 months' notice.

AVAILABILITY: The Center is available (1 event per day) from 8am to midnight daily, with extensions possible if requested in writing 30 days in advance. The summer months are booked quickly.

SERVICES/AMENITIES:

Restaurant Services: no

Catering: BYO

Kitchen Facilities: minimal

Tables & Chairs: provided

Linens, Silver, etc.: BYO

Restrooms: wca

Dance Floor: yes

Parking: on and off street

Overnight Accommodations: no

Telephone: pay phone

Outdoor Night Lighting: yes

Outdoor Cooking Facilities: BYO

Cleanup: caterer or renter

Meeting Equipment: podium, microphone, movie screen

RESTRICTIONS:

Alcohol: BYO, must have controlled bar

Smoking: not allowed

Music: amplified ok

Wheelchair Access: yes

Insurance: included in weekend rates, you must provide for any weekday use

Pleasanton

THE PLEASANTON HOTEL

855 Main St.
Pleasanton, CA 94566
(510) 846-8112 or **(510) 846-8106**
Reserve for Events: 6–12 months in advance
Reserve for Meetings: 2–4 weeks in advance

The Pleasanton Hotel, which sits in the center of Pleasanton's historic downtown, is conveniently located near Bishop Ranch and Hacienda Business Parks. This 130-year-old building, flanked by stately Magnolia and palm trees, is a turn-of-the-century Victorian with "gingerbread" detailing. The recently redecorated interior (which features a comfortable mix of Victorian appointments and antiques) works equally well for both business functions and social events. The Hotel boasts two large rooms and several adjacent rooms, all of which can be connected via folding doors to accommodate large parties. For corporate luncheons or dinners, use the Magnolia-shaded patio outdoors, which features a built-in bar and barbecue. A bubbling fountain adds to the ambiance of this vintage setting.

CAPACITY: The Hotel can seat 180 guests indoors; the Patio 100 guests. For cocktail receptions, the maximum capacity is 300 guests.

FEES & DEPOSITS: A $250 non-refundable deposit is required to secure your date. Full meal service is provided. Luncheons range from $11–17/person and dinners from $15–22/person. Under certain conditions, a room fee will apply. Tax and 15% service charge will be added to the final estimated bill which is payable at the conclusion of the event.

CANCELLATION POLICY: The deposits are not refundable unless the space can be rebooked with a party of equal or larger size.

AVAILABILITY: Monday–Friday, any time. Saturdays 11am–4pm and 6pm–11pm; Sunday 5pm–11pm.

SERVICES/AMENITIES:

Restaurant Services: yes
Catering: no BYO
Kitchen Facilities: n/a
Tables & Chairs: provided
Linens, Silver, etc.: provided
Restrooms: wca
Parking: lot
Meeting Equipment: full spectrum available

Overnight Accommodations: no
Telephone: pay phone
Outdoor Night Lighting: yes
Outdoor Cooking Facilities: BBQ
Cleanup: provided
Dance Floor: yes
Other: event coordination

RESTRICTIONS:

Alcohol: provided, corkage $7.50/750 ml bottle
Smoking: allowed
Music: amplified ok

Wheelchair Access: yes
Insurance: not required

Point Richmond

EAST BROTHER LIGHT STATION

San Francisco Bay, off Point San Pablo
(510) 233-2385
Reserve for Events: 2–6 months in advance

A short but exhilarating boat ride takes you to the island. On this one-acre, sun-washed speck in the ocean sits the oldest operational lighthouse in or around San Francisco Bay. Constructed in 1873–74, the light station continues to preserve a little bit of maritime history. Gone are the telephone poles, cars, crowds and noise of the mainland. Here the only sound comes from seagulls, the sea and the foghorn. Have a thoroughly relaxing family or corporate picnic, reunion or anniversary party in the tangy sea air. From the island, visitors have a clear, unobstructed view of the San Francisco skyline and the coast of Marin. The main house, with its lace curtains, wooden floors and fireplaces is relaxed and homey— a delightful place for an intimate Christmas party. The innkeeper is also the chef, and a visit to her kitchen is a treat. When we were there, the afternoon sun was streaming in through the window onto two freshly baked pies. The fragrant warmth of the scene still lingers, and makes us want to pay the light station another visit.

CAPACITY: The island will accommodate a maximum of 250 people. The 4-bedroom guest house can accommodate up to 8 guests for an overnight stay, and 20 for a small party.

FEES & DEPOSITS: A deposit in the amount of 25% of the fee is required at the time of booking, and the balance is due within 30 days. Island fees vary depending on the size of the group, and the duration of the stay, so call for rates. Boat transportation, catering and all other services can be arranged by East Brother Light Station for an additional charge.

CANCELLATION POLICY: If cancellation is made 60 days prior to the event, a full refund will be made; between 30 and 60 days, a 90% refund is given. With less than 30 days notice, 90% will be refunded only if the date can be rebooked.

AVAILABILITY: 11am–4pm, Friday through Sunday.

SERVICES/AMENITIES:

Restaurant Services: no
Catering: provided or BYO
Kitchen Facilities: limited
Tables & Chairs: some provided
Linens, Silver, etc.: BYO
Restrooms: wca
Dance Floor: CBA

Parking: at yacht harbor
Overnight Accommodations: 4 guestrooms
Telephone: cellular for emergencies
Outdoor Night Lighting: yes
Outdoor Cooking Facilities: yes
Cleanup: caterer

RESTRICTIONS:

Alcohol: provided or BYO
Smoking: outside only
Music: amplified ok

Wheelchair Access: difficult
Insurance: not required

Prices and policies do change. Call each facility and confirm everything you read in Perfect Places.

San Leandro

BEST HOUSE

1315 Clarke Street
San Leandro, CA 94577
(510) 351-0911
Reserve for Events: 1–6 months in advance
Reserve for Meetings: 1 week–6 months in advance

This yellow Victorian is a bright spot in the city. The yard, where parties are often held, is shaded by a variety of trees, and the brick patio and low decks give guests plenty of room to unwind. Have a relaxed meeting or an afternoon tea in the gazebo or on the covered patio. A working water wheel and miniature street lamps add quaint touches to this quiet setting. Indoors, the dining room, provides a comfortable, cozy space for a meeting or business luncheon. Two French doors overlook the garden, and the other side of the room has tall windows with a view of St. Leander's Church, an old Catholic Mission that predates the house, itself! Personalized service and an informal atmosphere make this facility terrific for private functions. Best House is also a bed and breakfast inn and guests are welcome to stay the night.

CAPACITY: The grounds accommodate a maximum of 150 people.

MEETING ROOMS: The dining room seats 25–30, the gazebo, 8 and the patio 12.

FEES & DEPOSITS: A deposit of 50% of the rental fee is required to reserve your date. An additional $200 damage/cleaning deposit is due 30 days before your event and is refundable within 1 week of your event. The total rental fee is $850 for a 5-hour block of time and the remaining balance is due 30 days prior to the event.

CANCELLATION POLICY: With less than 30 days' notice, deposits are not refundable unless the date can be rebooked.

AVAILABILITY: Any time April–October. Reserve early for summer.

SERVICES/AMENITIES:
Restaurant Services: no
Catering: BYO, licensed only
Kitchen Facilities: moderate
Tables & Chairs: some provided
Linens, Silver, etc.: BYO
Restrooms: wca in garden
Dance Floor: brick patio

Parking: lot and on street
Overnight Accommodations: 5 guestrooms
Telephone: pay phone, emergencies only
Outdoor Night Lighting: yes
Outdoor Cooking Facilities: no
Cleanup: caterer
Meeting Equipment: no

RESTRICTIONS:
Alcohol: WCB only
Smoking: outside only
Music: no amplified

Wheelchair Access: outdoors only
Insurance: not required

San Pablo

ROCKEFELLER LODGE

2650 Market St.
San Pablo, CA 94806
(510) 235-7344
Reserve for Events: 6–12 months in advance
Reserve for Meetings: 4 weeks in advance

Have you always wanted to celebrate a bit differently? Maybe have a Victorian or Western theme party? Or maybe treat your guests to milk and cookies baked on the spot. Whatever your fantasy, the owner and staff of Rockefeller Lodge love the challenge of making it a reality. And with its variety of rooms and outdoor areas, the Lodge can accommodate a wide range of creativity. Once a Japanese Buddhist Temple, the Rockefeller Lodge still offers a fragrant, woodsy serenity with waterfall and covered seating. The brown-shingled building derives its secluded feeling from the surrounding trees and quiet neighborhood. Winding brick paths and wisteria-covered arbors invite leisurely, relaxed strolls through the grounds. The back garden court has covered seating. The outdoor patios are popular for both business and private parties. The interior rooms are spacious, featuring hardwood floors, hand-hewn ceiling beams and a noteworthy fireplace constructed from burnt bricks from the 1906 earthquake.

CAPACITY: The Lodge and grounds accommodate 250 seated guests; the Lodge alone holds 150 seated, 250 for buffets. The entire site holds 500 total for a standing reception.

MEETING ROOMS: Garden Room 75 seated; Fireplace Room 40 seated; Rockefeller Room 38 seated; Lady Irene Room 28 seated.

FEES & DEPOSITS: For special events, a $300–600 refundable deposit is required to secure your date. There is a 50-guest minimum. Food service is provided. Monday–Friday, there is no rental fee, day or evening. Saturday, the fee is $600, Sunday, $300. Food service runs $10–20/person, depending on menu selection.

CANCELLATION POLICY: With 4 months' notice, a full refund minus a 20% bookkeeping charge is given. Less than 4 months, the deposit will be forfeited.

AVAILABILITY: Any day 6am–11pm. No bookings on Christmas or Thanksgiving.

SERVICES/AMENITIES:

Restaurant Services: no
Catering: provided
Kitchen Facilities: n/a
Tables & Chairs: provided
Linens, Silver, etc.: provided
Restrooms: wca
Dance Floor: yes

Parking: 2 lots
Overnight Accommodations: no
Telephone: pay phone
Outdoor Night Lighting: yes
Outdoor Cooking Facilities: yes
Cleanup: provided
Other: full event planning

Meeting Equipment: podium

RESTRICTIONS:

Alcohol: provided or BYO
$2.50/person service fee
Smoking: allowed
Music: amplified inside only, 4-piece band limit

Wheelchair Access: yes
Insurance: not required

San Ramon

SAN RAMON COMMUNITY CENTER

12501 Alcosta Blvd.
San Ramon, CA 94583
(510) 275-2300
Reserve for Events: 1–12 months in advance
Reserve for Meetings: 2 weeks in advance

Normally, we don't include park and recreation buildings because they're pretty uninteresting. In this case, however, we'd like to introduce you to a sophisticated newcomer that offers spaces that compete with the best event sites. Built in 1989, this rose-colored granite and glass community center is outstanding. The building is surrounded by pools, fountains and lush landscaping. Inside, the Fountain Room is the most popular area for large parties and conferences. Curved, laminated beams radiate from a center point, creating a domed ceiling seventy feet high. In subtle plums and lavenders, this sizable room is equally suitable for black tie affairs or more casual parties and business functions. For smaller affairs, we like the Terrace Room and Gallery, which are rented as a duo. The cool gray Terrace Room can be used for intimate dinners or meetings while the semi-circular Gallery is for hors d'oeuvres and cocktail receptions. The Gallery features different works of art each month. Its plum and lavender interior is warmed by light filtering through a forty-foot wall of windows overlooking a fountain courtyard. If you are looking for an event site in this area, come take a look. We think that the San Ramon Community Center is a real find—the price and the ambiance are sure to please.

CAPACITY: The Fountain Room can seat 250 guests; 450 for a standing reception. The Terrace Room, which comes with the Gallery, can seat 80, 150 for a standing reception.

MEETING ROOMS: 2 conference rooms which can seat 15–40 people.

FEES & DEPOSITS: A $400 security/cleaning deposit is required for the Fountain Room/Rose Garden; $200 security/cleaning deposit for the Terrace Room/Gallery and use of East Terrace to book the facility. The cleaning deposit is due 90 days prior to the event and the full rental fee is payable 30 days before the event. Weekday rentals are $20–70/hour; non-profits $10–25/hour; businesses $30–70/

hour, with a 2-hour minimum. Weekend rentals are $30–105/hour; non-profits $30–80/hour; businesses $40–115/hour, with a 2-hour minimum. San Ramon residents are charged a discounted rate.

CANCELLATION POLICY: For special events: with more than 60 days' notice, 50% of the deposit and the full rental fee is refunded. With 30–60 days' notice, the full rental fee is returned. With less notice, 50% of the rental fee is returned. For conference rooms: with more than 60 days' notice, all of the rental fee is refunded. With 30–60 days' notice, 50% of the rental fee is returned.

AVAILABILITY: Year-round, daily. Sunday–Thursday and holidays, 7am–11pm; Friday and Saturday 7am–1am.

SERVICES/AMENITIES:

Restaurant Services: no
Catering: select from preferred list
Kitchen Facilities: fully equipped
Tables & Chairs: provided
Linens, Silver, etc.: some available, extra fee
Restrooms: wca
Dance Floor: yes
Other: baby grand piano, extra fee

Parking: large lot
Overnight Accommodations: no
Telephone: pay phone
Outdoor Night Lighting: yes
Outdoor Cooking Facilities: no
Cleanup: renter or caterer
Meeting Equipment: some available, extra fee

RESTRICTIONS:

Alcohol: BYO
Smoking: outside only
Insurance: sometimes required

Wheelchair Access: yes
Music: amplified inside only
Other: some decorating restrictions, no glitter or confetti, red wine and punch discouraged

SAN RAMON
SENIOR CENTER

San Ramon, CA 94583
(510) 275-2316
Reserve for Events: 3–6 months in advance
Reserve for Meetings: 2 weeks in advance

Even though it's a senior center, this contemporary building (completed in 1992) has something for everyone. We particularly like the large Vista Grande Room—an upscale event space, well suited for parties, conferences or seminars. It can be rented in its entirety, or it can be partitioned in half for smaller rentals. The floor is light oak, which is great for dancing, and the walls are painted in a neutral, dusky peach. A high, vaulted ceiling, recessed lighting and windows which provide views of the Las Trampas ridgeline, add to its charm. The room's terrace, accessible through multiple doors, and the adjacent fully equipped commercial kitchen are additional attractions. Other rooms are available for meetings, such as the Classroom, Games and Crafts Rooms. Outdoors, the East Terrace is a peaceful courtyard, surrounded by a terraced, landscaped hillside, abloom with pink oleander and purple Mexican sage.

You can arrange tables with umbrellas in this wind-protected area for luncheons, or just set up buffet tables for champagne and hors d'oeuvres. We think the San Ramon Senior Center is very attractive and, for those on a budget, very easy on the pocketbook.

CAPACITY:

Area	*Seated*	*Standing*	*Area*	*Seated*	*Standing*
Vista Grande Room & Terrace	115	250	Classroom	20–30	—
Half Vista Grande	60	125	Crafts Room	20–30	—
East Terrace	20	40	Games Room	30	—

FEES & DEPOSITS: A $50–100 damage deposit is due when you book the facility and a $50–100 cleaning deposit is due 90 days prior to the event. Weekday rentals range from $20–55/hour; non-profits $10–20/hour. Weekend rates run from $30–90/hour; non-profits $30–60/hour depending on spaces rented and residential or commercial status. San Ramon residents are charged a discounted rate. The Vista Grande Room can be partitioned in half, and may be rented as a half space.

CANCELLATION POLICY: With 60 days' notice, half the deposit and the full rental fee is refunded. With 30–60 days' notice, the rental fee is returned. With less notice, half the rental fee is returned.

AVAILABILITY: Year-round, daily. Sunday–Thursday and holidays, 7am–11pm; Friday and Saturday 7am–1am. Public functions are scheduled around pre-arranged Senior Center programs.

SERVICES/AMENITIES:

Restaurant Services: no

Catering: select from preferred list

Kitchen Facilities: fully equipped

Tables & Chairs: provided

Linens, Silver, etc.: some available, extra fee

Restrooms: wca

Dance Floor: yes

Other: baby grand piano, extra fee

Parking: ample lot

Overnight Accommodations: no

Telephone: pay phone

Outdoor Night Lighting: yes

Outdoor Cooking Facilities: BBQ, extra fee

Cleanup: renter or caterer

Meeting Equipment: CBA, extra fee

RESTRICTIONS:

Alcohol: BYO

Smoking: outside only

Music: amplified inside only

Wheelchair Access: yes

Insurance: sometimes required

Other: decorating restrictions; no glitter or confetti; red wine & punch discouraged

Need a caterer, cake maker, florist? The Service Directory starting on page 614 features the best in the business.

Sunol

ELLISTON VINEYARDS

463 Kilkare Road
Sunol, CA 94586
(510) 862-2377
Reserve for Events: 1–6 months in advance
Reserve for Meetings: 1 week–1 month in advance

Tucked in a sheltered valley between the Pleasanton and Sunol ridges, is the 1890 Victorian estate of Gold Rush pioneer, Henry Hiram Ellis. This is an exceptional spot for corporate parties, luncheons, day seminars or private dinners. Acres of vineyards greet guests as they enter the site. Elliston Vineyard's landmark structure, constructed of thick sandstone from nearby Niles Canyon, has graceful stone arches over windows and entrances designed in a Romanesque style. The first two floors of the Mansion may be reserved for tours and group events. Especially nice is the Mansion's dining room for intimate dinners. The adjacent Carriage House has been remodeled with a tasting room and commercial kitchen to accommodate food and wine events. The Terrace Room, with expansive glass windows and doors, opens out to a secluded deck, furnished with white umbrella-shaded tables and a Victorian gazebo. Although close to civilization, it seems like you're a million miles away. The quiet, country atmosphere makes a nice contribution to any celebration. When you want to get away, but not go very far, this is the spot.

CAPACITY: The Terrace Room and adjoining deck can seat 240. The Elliston Mansion, up to 24 guests. The rose garden lawn can accommodate 250 for a lawn party.

FEES & DEPOSITS: Fees and deposits for events are determined by day of week and type of event. Fixed-price meals, with no dancing, range from $25–75/person, with an $800 minimum per event.

CANCELLATION POLICY: With 1 month's notice, the deposit, less a 25% service charge, is refunded.

AVAILABILITY: Year-round, Monday through Saturday until 10pm. Sunday until 6pm.

SERVICES/AMENITIES:

Restaurant Services: no
Catering: provided, no BYO
Kitchen Facilities: n/a
Tables & Chairs: provided
Linens, Silver, etc.: provided
Restrooms: wca
Dance Floor: yes
Meeting Equipment: some provided

Parking: large lot, parking attendants
Overnight Accommodations: no
Telephone: office phone
Outdoor Night Lighting: yes
Outdoor Cooking Facilities: no
Cleanup: provided
Other: event planning

RESTRICTIONS:

Alcohol: WC provided, corkage $5/bottle
Smoking: outside only
Music: amplified inside only

Wheelchair Access: yes
Insurance: not required

Vallejo

FOLEY CULTURAL CENTER
Dan Foley Park

East end of N. Camino Alto
Vallejo, CA 94589
(707) 648-4630   Eileen Brown
Reserve for Events: 6–11 months in advance
Reserve for Meetings: 2 weeks in advance

This community park has a multipurpose auditorium and several smaller rooms are available for private parties. The auditorium, known as The Lake Room, overlooks the large man-made Chabot Lake. Hexagonal in shape, it has a high beamed ceiling and a wall of windows with a view. The interior is light and airy and is designed for a wide variety of uses. Outside, a wide deck runs along one side of the building, providing relaxed, breezy seating right off the lake. The whole facility is situated inside a lovely 65-acre park, making a nice setting for gatherings of friends and family.

CAPACITY:

Room	Seated	Reception
Lake Room	500	600
Vista Room	50	75

FEES & DEPOSITS: A $100 deposit, applied toward the rental fee, is due when the use permit is submitted. The balance and a $100 cleaning/damage deposit is payable 60 days prior to the event. The rental for private parties is approximately $525/10 hours.

CANCELLATION POLICY: If you cancel, 10% of the total fees and charges will be forfeited; with 30 days' notice or less, 50% will be forfeited.

AVAILABILITY: Year-round, Friday–Sunday from 10:30am–2am, Monday–Thursday, only if there is a cancellation in a regularly scheduled program. Closed most major holidays.

SERVICES/AMENITIES:

Restaurant Services: no
Catering: BYO
Kitchen Facilities: fully equipped
Tables & Chairs: provided
Linens, Silver, etc.: BYO
Restrooms: wca

Parking: large lots
Overnight Accommodations: no
Telephone: pay phone
Outdoor Night Lighting: no
Outdoor Cooking Facilities: in adjacent park
Cleanup: renter or CBA for extra fee

Dance Floor: yes

Meeting Equipment: no

Other: stage, setup service, pianos, PA system

RESTRICTIONS:

Alcohol: BYO, sales need permit, surcharge $25

Smoking: designated areas

Music: amplified ok

Wheelchair Access: yes

Insurance: not required

Other: security required

MARINE WORLD AFRICA USA

Marine World Parkway
Vallejo, CA 94589
(707) 644-4000 ext. 236 or 223
Reserve for Events: 6 months in advance

For group or corporate events, you could hardly ask for a more exciting location. Marine World Africa USA is big fun! It's a one-of-a-kind combination wildlife park and oceanarium like no other in the United States. This 160-acre showcase for exotic animals is designed to allow visitors to come as close as possible to wild creatures—everything from killer whales and tigers to elephants and more. Where else could you experience a 300,000 gallon underwater shark habitat while moving through a clear acrylic tunnel, feed a giraffe or walk among a rainbow of fluttering tropical butterflies from all over the world? Most of the private group picnic areas are on lawns hugging Lake Chabot which provide the best vantage points for spectacular water shows. A variety of packages are available including all-you-can-eat barbecues and supervised activities. Special animal visits, one-on-one talks with trainers or a balloon sculpturist are some of the features that can be arranged for your group. In addition, promotional services for companies including personalized flyers, tickets and photos for company newsletters or a greeting on the main entrance marquee make Marine World Africa an especially enticing venue for corporate events.

CAPACITY: 5 outdoor group facilities can hold up to 7,500 guests, with a 100-guest minimum: Shoreline, 2,000; Chabot, 1,600; Ski Point, 500; Grove, 350; and Cypress, 200 guests.

FEES & DEPOSITS: A $1,000 deposit is required when you submit your signed contract. The balance is payable the day of the event. Group packages start at $20/person, and include food, beverages and admission into Marine World. Prices will vary depending on group size. Night parties can be arranged, which require a $3,000 deposit. Groups have exclusive use of Marine World at night, and can design events around animal appearances or special shows.

CANCELLATION POLICY: With more than 6 months' notice, the deposit is fully refundable. With less than 2 months' notice, a minimum guarantee will be billed.

AVAILABILITY: April 1–October 31, from 9:30am–5:30pm. Night parties can be arranged 4pm–10pm for 2,000–3,500 guests.

SERVICES/AMENITIES:

Restaurant Services: no
Catering: provided, no BYO
Kitchen Facilities: n/a
Tables & Chairs: provided
Linens, Silver, etc.: picnicware provided
Restrooms: wca
Dance Floor: Dolphin Plaza, asphalt surface
Other: event coordination, supervised activities, promotional assistance, special animal appearances

Parking: large lots
Overnight Accommodations: no
Telephone: pay phones
Outdoor Night Lighting: yes
Outdoor Cooking Facilities: BBQs
Cleanup: provided
Meeting Equipment: no

RESTRICTIONS:

Alcohol: provided, no BYO
Smoking: allowed
Music: provided, no BYO

Wheelchair Access: yes
Insurance: not required
Other: no glass containers

Walnut Creek

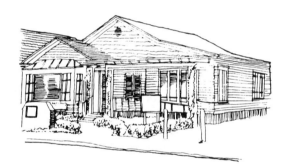

SCOTT'S GARDENS

1719 Bonanza Street
Walnut Creek, CA 94596
(510) 934-0598
Reserve for Events: 2–6 months in advance
Reserve for Meetings: 1 week–12 months in advance

Take note! If you are looking for an exceptional East Bay outdoor event spot, you must see this facility. Scott's Gardens is a site that could be aptly described as an urban oasis. Situated in the heart of Walnut Creek's retail district, Scott's has spared no cost to transform a small hillside into a brick-walled, multi-terraced courtyard garden with a conservatory cover. Under the expansive canopy of a four hundred-year-old oak tree (the site's centerpiece) you'll find handsome amenities such as designer wood benches, large heat lamps and sizable, self-standing umbrellas in addition to lush landscaping. Of special interest is a green lattice aviary, several fountains and an antique water wheel. Observe the details here. All of the terraces are paved with slate and even the outdoor bar and indoor dressing room feature marble counters. At the topmost terrace, you'll find a back stairway leading to Scott's restaurant, where there's another outdoor patio for evening dinners and small weekend parties. Inside the restaurant, additional elegantly appointed private and semi-private rooms are available for business functions.

CAPACITY: The Garden can accommodate a maximum of 200 seated guests, 300 for a standing reception; the private dining rooms hold up to 80 seated and 125 standing.

FEES & DEPOSITS: A non-refundable deposit of $1,000 and is due when the event date is booked. The rental fee is $500 Sunday–Thursday and $1,000 Friday and Saturday for blocks between 10am–4pm or 6pm–1am. Rental includes tables, chairs, linens, silverware, setup and cleanup. Hors d'oeuvres receptions start at $20/person, buffets start at $22/person, seated luncheons or dinners range from $20–30/person. Tax and an 18% service fee will be applied to the final bill. Normally, 80% of the estimated food and beverage total is due 72 hours prior to the event. The remaining portion is payable at the conclusion of the event.

CANCELLATION POLICY: The deposit is not refundable unless the date is rebooked.

AVAILABILITY: Any day, 10am–4pm and 6pm–12am. For weekday business functions, 7am–12am.

SERVICES/AMENITIES:

Restaurant Services: yes
Catering: provided, no BYO
Kitchen Facilities: n/a
Tables & Chairs: provided
Linens, Silver, etc.: provided
Restrooms: wca
Meeting Equipment: CBA for extra charge
Cleanup: provided

Dance Floor: yes
Parking: complimentary valet
Overnight Accommodations: no
Telephone: pay phone
Outdoor Night Lighting: yes
Outdoor Cooking Facilities: CBA
Special: full service event coordination, flowers,

RESTRICTIONS:

Alcohol: provided, no BYO
Smoking: outside only
Music: DJ or small combos

Wheelchair Access: yes
Insurance: not required

SHADELANDS RANCH
and Historical Museum

2660 Ygnacio Valley Road
Walnut Creek, CA 94598
(510) 935-7871
Reserve for Events: 3–6 months in advance

Shadelands is a 1903 colonial revival-style home that exists today in virtually its turn-of-the-century state, with the original owner's furnishings and memorabilia intact. Hiram Penniman, an early Walnut Creek pioneer, acquired portions of a Mexican land grant in the early 1850s. Here he planted 320 acres in fruit and nut trees. It's believed that Hiram built the homestead for his eldest, unmarried daughter who died, unfortunately, six years after the house was completed. The house and one and a half acres were passed down through family members, and in 1948, a foundation was set up to administer the estate. Donated to the City of Walnut Creek in 1970, it is now listed on the National Register of Historic Places. In the last few years, Shadelands has received some major improvements which make it an exceptional spot to have an outdoor function. Repainted in its original soft burgundy with cream trim, the house is really inviting, with broad steps that lead to a veranda that sweeps around one side of the building. The grounds have been nicely landscaped, with shade trees, roses and flowering annuals. In the back, a gazebo, designed in keeping with the house, is the centerpiece of the garden. Red roses cling to the posts, and the shady interior is perfect for sunny days. Expansive emerald lawns, beautifully maintained, surround the gazebo. For parties, you can set up tables with umbrellas on either lawns or a medium-sized patio adjacent to the house. Shadlands is pretty and pleasant, and provides and environment that has an old-world appeal. It's worth a visit.

CAPACITY: Inside, the house can accommodate 50 guests. Outside, 250 guests.

FEES & DEPOSITS: A $100 non-refundable deposit (which is applied toward the rental fee) plus a refundable $200 cleaning/security fee secures your date. Both are payable when reservations are confirmed. Indoors or outdoors rents for $85/hour. Use of both is $170/hour. Use of the kitchen is $35/event and a required custodian is $35/event.

AVAILABILITY: Daily, 8am–10pm. The house interior is not available 1pm–4pm on Sundays.

SERVICES/AMENITIES:

Restaurant Services: no

Catering: BYO

Kitchen Facilities: minimal

Tables & Chairs: BYO, some provided

Linens, Silver, etc.: BYO

Restrooms: wca

Meeting Equipment: no

Parking: large lots

Overnight Accommodations: no

Telephone: house phone

Outdoor Night Lighting: yes

Outdoor Cooking Facilities: CBA

Cleanup: renter or caterer

Dance Floor: patio

RESTRICTIONS:

Alcohol: BYO

Smoking: outside only

Music: amplified within reason

Wheelchair Access: yes

Insurance: proof of liability required

Other: no candles indoors

TURTLE ROCK RANCH

Mt. Diablo
Walnut Creek, CA 94596
(510) 837-2517
Reserve for Events: 1 week–12 months in advance
Reserve for Meetings: 1 week–12 months in advance

Located just ten miles from Walnut Creek on the slopes of Mt. Diablo, Turtle Rock Ranch is one of the most appealing recreational resorts in the Bay Area. Because it's privately owned, it offers entertainment packages not usually associated with picnic or day retreats. Why have an ordinary company picnic when you can treat your employees to a circus, complete with death-defying Fire Eater, carnival games and plenty of cotton candy. Other possibilities include Mardi Gras, Luau, Nifty 50s or Country Western themes. All packages are tailored for your group, and feature lots of fun activities. And if you're looking for a meeting place far removed from office distractions, you couldn't find a more relaxed setting. Gather around picnic tables on a huge, trellis-covered patio, or in the Ranch House living room with its large fireplace and view of the valley below. Conduct business all morning, and when it's time for lunch, ranch staff will prepare a BBQ of your choice. When you're finished with work, swim, play volleyball or baseball, or just sunbathe. Whether you reserve part or all of Turtle Rock, they will take care of all the details while your group enjoys the fresh air, natural scenery and a guaranteed good time.

CAPACITY: The facility can accommodate 60–1,200 guests.

MEETING ROOMS: The patio around the pool can hold 1,200 seated; the Ranch House 75.

FEES & DEPOSITS: A rental fee is due at the time of booking: a flat fee of $850 is for weekday events, and $380–$3,100 for weekend events (based on the area reserved). Half of the food, beverage and optional entertainment cost is required 5 days prior to the event, and the balance is payable on the day of the event. Per person food costs are $7.50–11.50 and beverages run $3.00–3.50. Entertainment packages run $200–3,500. There is no charge for children under the age of 5.

CANCELLATION POLICY: The fee is refundable if the date can be rebooked with a comparable party.

AVAILABILITY: May through October, every day 8am–9pm.

SERVICES/AMENITIES:

Restaurant Services: no
Catering: provided, no BYO
Kitchen Facilities: n/a
Tables & Chairs: provided
Linens, Silver, etc.: provided
Restrooms: wca
Dance Floor: patio and small stage
Other: special entertainment packages

Parking: large lot
Overnight Accommodations: no
Telephone: pay phone
Outdoor Night Lighting: yes
Outdoor Cooking Facilities: yes
Cleanup: provided
Meeting Equipment: PA system, microphone, easels

RESTRICTIONS:

Alcohol: provided, no BYO
Smoking: outside only
Insurance: required

Wheelchair Access: yes
Music: amplified ok
Other: no pets

Cupertino

MARIANIST CENTER

22622 Marianist Way
Cupertino, CA 95014
(408) 253-6279
Reserve for Events: 2–9 months in advance
Reserve for Meetings: 2–9 months in advance

The Marianist Center is a quiet retreat for those wanting to pursue educational and spiritual goals. Here, you'll be surrounded by lush gardens, serpentine paths and emerald green lawns. Everything is well tended. The three main structures encircle a center green, where a new fountain and landscaping has been installed. A separate building with retractable roof houses an indoor pool with jacuzzi and adjacent, is a full-size tennis court. Built in 1981, the Center was used as a novitiate, and then as a religious community. Since February 1991, it's been used as a private place for personal development, more effective communication, team building and goal setting for non-profits and executive groups. Its overnight suites have vaulted ceilings and private patios; the meeting rooms are uncluttered and simple. Each guest house has group activity spaces which feature cozy furnishings, flagstone fireplaces and extensive libraries. All is designed in warm, earth tones. Just a short way from Highway 280 (the Marianist Center is tucked away in a most unlikely spot), you'll think you've found a bit of Shangrila. This is a place guaranteed to nourish the soul.

CAPACITY: 2 meeting rooms can accommodate up to 24 guests, each. Other meeting areas can seat 14. For overnight stays, 30 guests.

FEES & DEPOSITS: A non-refundable 20% deposit is necessary to confirm reservations prior to your function. The balance is payable within 2 weeks of the function. Rental fees are as follows:

Business Use/Person		*Non-Profit or Religious Use/Person*	
Day Use	$25	Day Use/Retreats	$22
Overnight Use	65	Overnight Use	55

Day use: am/pm homemade snacks, lunch, beverages, meeting space, use of pool and tennis court included in fee. Overnight use: 3 meals, guestroom, use of pool, jacuzzi, tennis court and meeting rooms included in fee. Per person costs: breakfasts $5.75, luncheons $7 and dinners $9.25. Snacks are an extra $2.25/person. Hors d'oeuvres are $3.50/person.

AVAILABILITY: Year-round, every day. Closed Christmas.

SERVICES/AMENITIES:
Restaurant Services: no
Catering: provided
Kitchen Facilities: n/a
Telephone: guest phone

Parking: small lot, carpooling encouraged
Overnight Accommodations: 30 guests
Outdoor Night Lighting: limited
Outdoor Cooking Facilities: BBQ

Tables & Chairs: provided
Restrooms: wca
Meeting Equipment: yes, extra fees
Other: vegetarian food also offered

Linens, Silver, etc.: provided
Cleanup: provided
Dance Floor: no

RESTRICTIONS:

Alcohol: BYO, w/ meals only
Smoking: outside only
Insurance: not required

Wheelchair Access: yes
Music: no amplified

Gilroy

FORTINO WINERY & DELI

4525 Hecker Pass Highway
Gilroy, CA 95020
(408) 842-3305
Reserve for Events: 1–2 months in advance

Established in 1970, this family-owned winery is the product of three generations of winemaking. Events are held in the same rooms where the wine is stored. The largest room has barrels of wine stacked up fifteen feet high on the side. The space is left completely natural with plywood walls and tin roof. The only additions are the white and burgundy tablecloths and flower arrangements on each table. This room and two others are kept cool to protect the wine and are a refreshing retreat from the valley heat. Immediately adjacent is "the shed," an area open to the outdoors overlooking the vineyard. And right next to the rows of grapes are the BBQ facilities. Fortino is noted for great barbecues, and people can do their own cooking, dance and enjoy themselves in the company of fragrant eucalyptus trees, vineyards and sun. For a relaxed and casual party in the heart of the South Bay's wine country, try sampling the Fortino family's hospitality.

CAPACITY: This site can hold up to 250 guests.

FEES & DEPOSITS: A $300 non-refundable fee (includes cleaning, setup and rental fee) is required when reservations are confirmed.

AVAILABILITY: Spring and summer, every day, 5pm–midnight. Closed major holidays.

SERVICES/AMENITIES:

Restaurant Services: no
Catering: BYO
Kitchen Facilities: no
Tables & Chairs: provided
Linens, Silver, etc.: provided

Parking: large lot
Overnight Accommodations: no
Telephone: office phone
Outdoor Night Lighting: yes
Outdoor Cooking Facilities: BBQs

Restrooms: wca
Dance Floor: yes
Meeting Equipment: no

RESTRICTIONS:
Alcohol: BWC provided, no BYO
Smoking: allowed
Music: amplified ok

Cleanup: provided
Other: tastings & tours

Wheelchair Access: yes
Insurance: not required
Other: no hard alcohol allowed

HECKER PASS
A Family Adventure

3050 Hecker Pass Highway
Gilroy, CA 95020
(408) 842-2121
Reserve for Events: 6–12 months in advance
Reserve for Meetings: 60 days in advance

Once the private park for Nob Hill Foods employees, this facility (located one and a half miles outside Gilroy) is now open for special events. Eighty acres of the six-hundred-acre site are being transformed into a large theme park, scheduled to open in 1994. While plans for the theme park are in progress, corporate parties have become popular here because of the grounds. There's a plant nursery on site, hence Hecker Pass is beautifully landscaped, with a multitude of trees, shrubs and flowers. One of the big benefits of having an event here is that different kinds of plants can be arranged or moved to divide spaces, hence you can create different visual environments for your event. Three bridges cross a meandering creek and nearby is a party pavilion with an ivory-colored cloth canopy for protection on a warm day. This is a secluded, serene and peaceful spot at the base of the foothills. Water flowing gently down the creekbed provides the only sound.

CAPACITY: This facility has a minimum of 125 guests, but can accommodate up to 400 seated guests.

FEES & DEPOSITS: A deposit of $1 per guest is due when the contract is signed, based on an estimated guest count. Half the estimated event total is due 45 days before and final payment is due 1 week prior to the event along with a final guest count. 5 buffet menus are available, ranging $20–35/person, based on options selected. No service fee or site rental fee is required; tax is additional.

CANCELLATION POLICY: The deposit will only be refunded if an event can be rebooked for the same day.

AVAILABILITY: April–October, every day from 11am–8pm.

SERVICES/AMENITIES:
Restaurant Services: no
Catering: provided, no BYO
Kitchen Facilities: n/a

Parking: large lots
Overnight Accommodations: no
Telephone: pay phones

Tables & Chairs: provided
Linens, Silver, etc.: provided
Restrooms: wca
Dance Floor: in Pavilion
Meeting Equipment: PA system

RESTRICTIONS:
Alcohol: BWC provided, no hard alcohol
Smoking: allowed
Music: amplified within limits

Outdoor Night Lighting: access only
Outdoor Cooking Facilities: BBQ
Cleanup: provided
Other: event coordination, nursery on site

Wheelchair Access: yes
Insurance: not required

GILROY
HISTORICAL MUSEUM
Carnegie Library

195 Fifth Street
Gilroy, CA 95020
(408) 847-2685
Reserve for Events: 2–12 weeks in advance
Reserve for Meetings: 2 weeks in advance

Designed by noted architect, William H. Weeks, this Classical Revival style building has housed the Museum since 1963. The space is only available for cultural events and consists of a round foyer with skylight, flanked by rectangular rooms on either side. Glass cases in both rooms house museum artifacts, and overhead spots highlight the artwork displayed throughout. A cool, subdued pale green, the interior offers an interesting backdrop for art shows, music, historical and theater receptions.

CAPACITY: 75 guests for a reception.

FEES & DEPOSITS: A $25 refundable deposit is required when reservations are confirmed. The rental fee is $50/event for 3 hours.

CANCELLATION POLICY: With 5 working days' notice, the deposit is refunded.

AVAILABILITY: Year-round, every day from 9am–midnight.

SERVICES/AMENITIES:
Restaurant Services: no
Catering: BYO
Kitchen Facilities: no
Tables & Chairs: provided
Linens, Silver, etc.: BYO
Restrooms: no wca
Dance Floor: no
Meeting Equipment: CBA

Parking: street, parking lot
Overnight Accommodations: no
Telephone: office phone
Outdoor Night Lighting: access only
Outdoor Cooking Facilities: no
Cleanup: provided
Other: tours of historic district

RESTRICTIONS:

Alcohol: BYO, WBC only
Smoking: outside only
Music: no amplified

Wheelchair Access: no
Insurance: not required
Other: no hard alcohol allowed

Los Gatos

BYINGTON WINERY

21850 Bear Creek Road
Los Gatos, CA
(408) 354-1111 ext 206
Reserve for Events: 3–12 months in advance
Reserve for Meetings: 1 week–12 months in advance

The Byington Winery and Vineyards are located up above Los Gatos, in one of the oldest grape growing regions in the U.S. Although a relative newcomer, Byington is already reserved well in advance for events because of its great location and wonderful amenities. Step outside and look at the vista, stretching for miles around. You couldn't ask for more incredible views of the mountains and distant Monterey Bay. Most events take place in the winery. It's constructed of gray stone, with a terra cotta roof, and has several balconies dotted with blue umbrellas. Before your dinner party or business meeting, greet guests in the VIP Room which features oak hardwood floors, black baby grand piano, a long bar, stone fireplace, overstuffed sofas and wingbacked chairs. For formal, seated functions, the VIP dining area with overhead chandelier sets an elegant tone. For larger functions, both the Private Tasting Room and the Barrel Room are available. They overlook the wine cellar, which is filled with French oak barrels and large steel fermentation tanks. Byington is extremely service oriented. Only one function per day is scheduled so that staff can be flexible and provide guests with lots of personal attention.

CAPACITY: 150 seated guests; 250 for a standing reception. Summer receptions up to 400 guests.

MEETING ROOMS: The V.I.P. Room holds up to 70. The Barrel Room can accommodate 120 guests classroom-style or 200 theater-style.

FEES & DEPOSITS: A non-refundable deposit, due when the contract is signed, is one half of the rental fee. The other 50% is payable 3 months prior to the event. Rental fees for special events Monday–Friday 8am–5pm: V.I.P. Suite $200; the entire upper floor (V.I.P. Suite and Barrel Room) $450. Monday–Friday evening fees range from $300–500. The rental fee for either Saturday or Sunday is $1,550.

AVAILABILITY: Every day from 8am–11pm. Functions must conclude at 11pm, and all vendors must leave by midnight.

SERVICES/AMENITIES:

Restaurant Services: no

Dance Floor: CBA

Catering: BYO, select from preferred list
Kitchen Facilities: ample
Tables & Chairs: provided
Linens, Silver, etc.: BYO
Restrooms: limited wca
Meeting Equipment: no
Other: picnic area, BBQ, baby grand piano

RESTRICTIONS:

Alcohol: provided, no BYO
Smoking: outside only
Music: amplified indoors only

Overnight Accommodations: no
Parking: 70 spaces, carpooling recommended
Telephone: pay phone
Outdoor Night Lighting: yes
Outdoor Cooking Facilities: BBQ
Cleanup: caterer

Wheelchair Access: limited
Insurance: proof of insurance required
Other: no confetti

MIRASSOU CHAMPAGNE CELLARS

300 College Ave.
Los Gatos, CA 95032
(408) 395-3790
Reserve for Events: 1–3 months in advance
Reserve for Meetings: 1–3 weeks in advance

This is one lovely spot. Mirassou Champagne Cellars is now housed on the grounds of the Sacred Heart Novitiate, an old Jesuit seminary with stone walls, large winery, huge shade trees and lots of privacy. The road leading up to this site is through a pretty residential neighborhood, but once you go through the Novitiate's stone and wrought iron gates, you leave the world behind. It was on top of this knoll that Jesuits began missionary work in the late 1860s. The first seminary was built here in 1888, giving way to a more permanent winery building in 1893. The Jesuits stopped making Novitiate wines in 1985 and have now leased the winery to Mirassou. The original winery building still stands, forming the core of the present-day Champagne Cellars. The entry to the Tasting Room is called La Cave. It actually resembles a cave, with vaulted, stone ceiling and champagne bottles stacked on end for riddling along one wall. Antique wine and champagne-making equipment and photos depicting the history of the Novitiate Winery are on the other side of La Cave. It's dimly lit, cool and very old world. Both the Tasting and Blanc de Noir rooms can handle seated functions. Outdoors there's a sunny, quiet courtyard terrace, with an ivy-planted bank on one side and trees on the other. Recessed into the bank is a stepped, wooden platform, perfect for musicians. You couldn't ask for a more tranquil and beautiful environment for a business or social get-together.

CAPACITY:

Area	*Seated*	*Reception*
Lower Terrace	120	200
Tasting Room	75	150
Blanc de Noir Room	120	150

FEES & DEPOSITS: A refundable deposit equalling half of the estimated facility fee is payable when reservations are confirmed. Use fees for events are $10/person with a 25-person minimum. All wines and champagnes are included. A final guest count is due 48 hours prior to the event. For business functions, the cost per day for groups up to 18 guests is $180. The fee includes the conference room, continental breakfast, private tour and tasting. Gourmet box lunches can be provided for an additional $12/person.

CANCELLATION POLICY: With 6 months' notice, your deposit will be refunded.

AVAILABILITY: Year-round, meeting facilities Monday–Friday from 8am–5pm .

SERVICES/AMENITIES:

Restaurant Services: no

Catering: preferred list

Kitchen Facilities: no

Tables & Chairs: provided up to 120 guests

Linens, Silver, etc.: provided

Restrooms: wca

Meeting Equipment: flip charts

Other: event coordination

Parking: several lots

Overnight Accommodations: no

Telephone: pay phone

Outdoor Night Lighting: yes

Outdoor Cooking Facilities: no

Cleanup: caterer

Dance Floor: outdoor patio or tasting room

RESTRICTIONS:

Alcohol: WC provided by Mirassou

Smoking: outside only

Music: amplified ok

Wheelchair Access: yes

Insurance: certificate required

Other: no alcohol other than Mirassou

OPERA HOUSE

140 W. Main Street
Los Gatos, CA 95030
(408) 354-1218
Reserve for Special Events: 6–12 months in advance
Reserve for Meetings: 2–4 weeks in advance

For very large events, The Opera House is the best *and* the only game in town. Occupying a 1904 landmark building in historic Los Gatos, it offers 8,000 square feet with a seating capacity of up to five hundred guests! The restored exterior facade is an attractive brick with crisp, white trim. Enter the downstairs foyer and wind your way up the formal, sweeping staircase to the main event floor. Highly detailed Bradbury & Bradbury wallpaper adorns the stairway in blues, creams and golds. Antique light fixtures abound and walls and ceilings are covered with original pressed tin in fifteen different Victorian motifs. The grand ballroom has a twenty-four-foot ceiling, with a rectangular skylight in the center which helps bring in natural light. Up above is the Balcony which overlooks the ballroom, great for those who want to look down on dancing below. The lower portion of the room is called the Mezzanine, which has a wall of windows facing north. Soft pastels, creams and taupes predominate and a large mural on an upper wall facing the Ballroom depicts the Opera House's original theater curtain. Because of the way this facility is configured, groups of a hundred need not feel dwarfed in this space. Additional enhancements are a movable dance floor and separate cocktail bars. We think The Opera House is a splendid choice for large Christmas or New Year's parties. Note you can have exclusive all day use if your company is putting on a seminar or conference.

CAPACITY:

	Seated	*Standing*	*Reception*
Entire Facility	500	750	
Mezzanine	130	300	
Balcony	90	200	
Main Event Floor	320	500	

MEETING ROOMS: The Green Room, a separate meeting room, can seat up to 25.

FEES & DEPOSITS: A non-refundable deposit totaling one quarter of the event cost is required within 1 week of confirming reservations. A second deposit, the amount dependent on size and type of event, is due 60 days prior to the event. The balance, including a refundable damage deposit of $500, is payable 1 week in advance of the function. A $200/hour overtime charge is applied when appropriate. Food service is provided. For over 200 guests, the cost is approximately $40–60/person which includes food service, setup, cleanup, chairs, dance floor, linens, china and valet parking. Tax and 15% gratuity are additional. Beverage packages are available from no host bars to hosted bars at $5–14/person.

AVAILABILITY: Year-round. Mon–Fri 8am-midnight. Sat and Sun, 10–4pm or 6pm–midnight.

SERVICES/AMENITIES:

Restaurant Services: no

Catering: select from preferred list

Kitchen Facilities: prep only

Tables & Chairs: provided

Linens, Silver, etc.: provided

Restrooms: wca

Dance Floor: yes

Other: event coordination, theme party props

Parking: valet and attendant parking

Overnight Accommodations: no

Telephone: pay phone

Outdoor Night Lighting: access only

Outdoor Cooking Facilities: no

Cleanup: provided

Meeting Equipment: various available

RESTRICTIONS:

Alcohol: provided, no BYO

Smoking: allowed

Insurance: certificate required

Wheelchair Access: yes, elevator

Music: amplified ok

Other: decorations restricted

Prices and policies do change. Call each facility and confirm everything you read in Perfect Places.

San Jose

THE BRIAR ROSE

897 East Jackson Street
San Jose, CA 95112
(408) 279-5999
Reserve for Events: 2–4 weeks in advance
Reserve for Meetings: 1 week in advance

The Briar Rose Inn is a very attractive old Victorian home located in a quiet residential neighborhood five minutes from downtown San Jose. You enter under a vine-covered trellis and stroll up the rose-lined walkway past a small, white pitched-roof gazebo shaded by an old elm in the front yard. With a decorative wrought iron fence, lace curtains and pastel-painted exterior, the Inn presents an inviting face. Wide stairs lead you past the veranda into a warm and comfortable interior with lots of charm and Victorian detailing. The back yard has a well-tended garden and amenities for outdoor functions. Beautifully restored by its present owners, the Inn offers a variety of carefully appointed rooms for small meetings, receptions and overnight guests.

CAPACITY: The Inn can hold up to 50 guests indoors; 150 outdoors. The total capacity is 150.

Area	*Seated Only*
Parlor	15
Dining Room	35
Garden Conference Room	50
Small Conference Room	15

MEETING ROOMS: All of the above areas can be used for meetings.

FEES & DEPOSITS: For events, a non-refundable $500 deposit is required when reservations are confirmed. The rental fee is $1,250 for 5 hours; $200 for each additional hour. The total balance is payable 1 week prior to the function. Rates for meetings are $200 for a half day (including continental breakfast) and $350 for a full day. Lunch is additional and runs $10–15/person. A $100 deposit is required at the time of booking; the balance is payable at the conclusion of the event.

AVAILABILITY: Year-round, every day.

SERVICES/AMENITIES:

Restaurant Services: no
Catering: provided
Kitchen Facilities: n/a
Tables & Chairs: provided
Linens, Silver, etc.: provided
Restrooms: no wca

Parking: street
Overnight Accommodations: 5 guestrooms, 2 cottages
Telephone: guest phones
Outdoor Night Lighting: yes
Outdoor Cooking Facilities: no
Cleanup: provided

Dance Floor: brick portico
Meeting Equipment: BYO

Other: event coordination

RESTRICTIONS:
Alcohol: WCB only, provided or BYO
Smoking: outside only
Music: no amplified

Wheelchair Access: garden only
Insurance: sometimes required

CHILDREN'S DISCOVERY MUSEUM

180 Woz Way
San Jose, CA 95110
(408) 298-5437
Reserve for Events: 1–4 months in advance

Open for "hands-on" adventure during private parties, the Children's Discovery Museum is a marvel of delights for adults as well as kids. The spacious layout enables guests to enjoy a wide range of activities and interactive exhibits. The major theme of the Museum is "connection to the community and the world," with an emphasis on our relationship to the infrastructure that exists all around us. Here it is articulated by exhibits relating to typical public services on a city street. The major circulation arteries in the Museum are designed as a street scene, complete with fire hydrants, parking meters and traffic lights. You can assume the role of a fireman or ambulance driver by donning the appropriate garb and hopping onto an awaiting vehicle. The Museum highlights community elements by making each a learning experience. For example, there's a cross-section of a street showing what occurs underground, plus exhibits focusing on communications, health care and an art recycle center. It's a stimulating event environment, inviting interaction and discussion, movement and flexibility. Although the Museum is more conducive to informal gatherings, black tie events have been held here, too.

CAPACITY: The Museum can hold up to 200 seated, 800 for a standing reception indoors; with outdoor spaces, the total capacity is 1,200 guests. Note that the open space that surrounds the Museum is a public park, not private open space, and arrangements for exclusive use must be made with the City of San Jose.

FEES & DEPOSITS: A $600 non-refundable deposit is due when reservations are confirmed. The fee is $10/person or a minimum of $1,200/event. The nonprofit rate is $8/person, minimum $1,200/event. For corporate Museum members, discounts are available.

AVAILABILITY: Year-round. Mondays are for large groups only. Tuesday–Sunday, 5pm–midnight. Closed Thanksgiving, Christmas and New Year's Eve.

SERVICES/AMENITIES:
Restaurant Services: no
Catering: BYO with approval

Parking: large lots
Overnight Accommodations: no

Kitchen Facilities: setup only
Tables & Chairs: BYO
Linens, Silver, etc.: BYO
Restrooms: wca
Dance Floor: no
Meeting Equipment: no

RESTRICTIONS:
Alcohol: BYO
Smoking: outside only
Music: amplified ok

Telephone: pay phones
Outdoor Night Lighting: limited
Outdoor Cooking Facilities: BYO
Cleanup: caterer
Other: Discovery Guides included

Wheelchair Access: yes
Insurance: certificate required

EVENT CENTER
At San Jose State University

290 S. 7th Street at San Carlos
San Jose, CA 951923
(408) 924-6300
Reserve for Events: 1–6 months in advance
Reserve for Meetings: 1–6 months in advance

Although mostly recognized as a venue for sports and concerts, the Event Center is also available for corporate and special events. This is a relatively new brick and concrete structure, built near the Student Union in the heart of the San Jose State Campus. During the day, students predominate. But at night and on weekends, this facility is a great location for fashion shows, large business functions, fundraisers or awards ceremonies. The interior is a state-of-the-art mini-arena, with stadium-style tiered seating facing a center floor. The flooring can be changed to suit different functions, from a basketball hardwood court to a dance floor. You may never have thought of this place for your next party, but it's a winner for large events where theatrical lighting, good sound and great visibility are required. Check it out.

CAPACITY:

Type of Function	Guest Count
Concert-style w/seating above on center floor	6,500
Concert-style, seating in tiers only	5,400
Athletic and social events	4,600

FEES & DEPOSITS: A non-refundable deposit totaling a percentage of the rental fees and services is due when reservations are confirmed. The deposit amount is based on the type of function and its total estimated cost. The rental fee for functions where tickets are sold is $2,000 or 10% of gross ticketed sales, whichever is greater. A service fee for setup is $1,000/day. The minimal rental for banquets or events without ticket sales is $3,500. Other fees, such as security, box office, ticket takers, AV and setup/cleanup, are negotiable. The final balance or estimated direct costs are due 10 days prior to the event.

AVAILABILITY: Year-round, daily. All private functions are planned around scheduled sports events.

SERVICES/AMENITIES:

Restaurant Services: no
Catering: provided, BYO w/approval
Kitchen Facilities: fully equipped
Tables & Chairs: some provided or BYO
Linens, Silver, etc.: some provided or BYO
Restrooms: wca
Meeting Equipment: CBA, extra fee
Other: professional lighting & sound

Parking: adjacent garage, extra fee
Overnight Accommodations: no
Telephone: pay phone
Outdoor Night Lighting: yes
Outdoor Cooking Facilities: BBQ
Cleanup: caterer and janitorial
Dance Floor: yes, extra fee

RESTRICTIONS:

Alcohol: provided or BYO with restrictions
Smoking: designated areas
Insurance: certificate required

Wheelchair Access: yes
Music: amplified ok
Other: no open flames

FAIRMONT HOTEL
San Jose

170 South Market Street
San Jose, CA 95113
(408) 998-1900 ext. 3520
Reserve for Events: 8–12 months in advance
Reserve for Meetings: 1 day–12 months in advance

This luxury hotel, built in 1987, is a splendid addition to downtown San Jose. It's a facility that offers a myriad of spaces for special events: ballrooms, bistros, classy restaurants and an upscale luncheon eatery called the Fountain. The exterior and interior are designed with understated colors and quality materials: soft apricot hues, arched windows, marble floors, chandeliers, antiques, original artwork and granite columns. The entry lobby is both impressive and inviting. The lobby lounge is recessed, attractive with overstuffed, comfortable sofas and chairs and huge planters. Of special note is the Club Regent, a space designed like a nightclub. With stage lighting, dance floor, bistro seating and great acoustics, Club Regent is a sensational, sophisticated space for parties. The octagonal layout insures intimacy even though the room is very spacious. Several Ballrooms and other nicely appointed spaces are available for corporate galas, seminars and dinner parties—so ask for the full tour to examine all your options. For comfort, style and flexibility, the Fairmont is hard to beat.

CAPACITY:	*Room*	*Seated Guests*	*Room*	*Seated Guests*
	The Crystal Room	150	The Club Regent	230
	The Gold Room	150	Imperial Ballroom	500–1,000
	The Regency Ballroom	450	Other Rooms	varying capacities

FEES & DEPOSITS: A $1,000–3,000 non-refundable deposit is required to secure your date. Food service is provided. Seated meals run $40–65/person, hors d'oeuvres receptions $12–20/person and buffets $45–70/person. Tax and a 17% service charge are additional.

AVAILABILITY: Year-round, any day until 2am.

SERVICES/AMENITIES:

Restaurant Services: yes
Catering: provided, no BYO
Kitchen Facilities: n/a
Tables & Chairs: provided
Linens, Silver, etc.: provided
Restrooms: wca
Meeting Equipment: full range
Other: event coordination

Parking: large lot and valet
Overnight Accommodations: 550 guestrooms
Telephone: pay phones
Outdoor Night Lighting: no
Outdoor Cooking Facilities: no
Cleanup: provided
Dance Floor: yes

RESTRICTIONS:

Alcohol: provided, no BYO
Smoking: designated areas
Insurance: not required

Wheelchair Access: yes
Music: amplified ok

HOTEL DE ANZA

233 West Santa Clara Street
San Jose, CA 95113
(800) 843-3700 or **(408) 286-1000**
Reserve for Events: 2–6 months in advance
Reserve for Meetings: 1–3 months in advance

This place is a treasure. A recent infusion of ten million dollars has brought the Hotel De Anza back to its original Art Deco splendor—it now shines both as a restored historic hotel and as one of San Jose's most beautiful event facilities. Every detail here has been considered. Guests who are new to the De Anza will be more than impressed by the lobby, with gold accents, etched glass and distinctive fixtures. It is a refined space, with limestone floors that have green-black marble insets. Walls are nicely hand painted to match the floor. The Hotel elevator's interior is striking, with mirrors and bird's-eye maple incised with ebony. Around the corner is the Hedley Club, the De Anza's classic lounge. It is, in a word, extraordinary. The ceiling is highly detailed, painted in golds, raspberries and blues. An enormous stone fireplace glows in winter. Large paintings, eclectic furnishings and a glass-backed bar create a sensational spot for pre-party cocktails. French doors lead to the adjacent Palm Court Terrace, which offers a splendid limestone patio, complete with three fountains, terra-cotta colored walls, palm trees and white umbrellas. Multi-color impatiens dot the patio and gray-blue tiles back the wall fountains. A white lattice screen separates the patio from the street on one side, a large white canopy (which can be erected or left down depending on the weather) is at the other. For indoor functions, guests will be dazzled by the De Anza Room. This large space is richly magnificent. Walls are painted a warm gold—

hand-stenciled with gold leaf leaves, edged with a cranberry-colored shadow. The ceiling's concrete beams are intricately painted in golds, burgundies, blues and greens. A beautiful mural, created on a self-standing screen, adds color across one end of the space. Tables are dressed up with white linens; comfortable chairs come with arm rests and seats with a lovely floral pattern. In a day and age when "luxurious" and "elegant" are buzzwords, the Penthouse atop the De Anza truly is stunning. A marble bar, living room and foyer are designed in a neoclassic style, with beautiful furnishings and art. Nearby, one of the most sumptuous baths we've encountered beckons you with black marble floors, marble counters and a whirlpool bath large enough for four. A wall of mirrors and glass enclosed shower/ steam room are special features. Two small decks for sunning or breakfasting offer views of downtown San Jose and are entirely private. We can't say enough about the Hotel De Anza. If you haven't seen it yet, we urge you to take a tour, including the Hotel's on-premises restaurant, La Pastaia. Be prepared to spend some time here—the Hotel De Anza is a one-of-a-kind place that needs to be savored to be fully appreciated.

CAPACITY:

Room	Seated	Reception
Boardroom	16	n/a
De Anza	70	100
San Jose	40	60
Palm Court Terrace	120	170
La Pastaia	150	150

FEES & DEPOSITS: A room rental fee, $0–800, may apply depending on the details of your function. Catering is provided by La Pastaia, with prices ranging from $25–50/person. Menus can be customized. Half of the estimated food and beverage total is due when the contract is signed; the balance is payable 1 week prior to the event. Tax and a 17% service charge are additional. The Palm Court outdoor canopy setup charge is $250.

CANCELLATION POLICY: With more than 30 days' notice, your deposit will be returned.

AVAILABILITY: Year-round. Every day, anytime.

SERVICES/AMENITIES:

Restaurant Services: yes
Catering: provided, no BYO
Kitchen Facilities: n/a
Tables & Chairs: provided
Linens, Silver, etc.: provided
Restrooms: wca
Meeting Equipment: yes
Other: coordination & referrals

Parking: nearby lots and valet
Overnight Accommodations: 100 rooms & penthouse
Telephone: pay phone
Outdoor Night Lighting: yes
Outdoor Cooking Facilities: no
Cleanup: provided
Dance Floor: CBA, extra fee

RESTRICTIONS:

Alcohol: provided
Smoking: outside only
Music: amplified ok

Wheelchair Access: yes
Insurance: not required

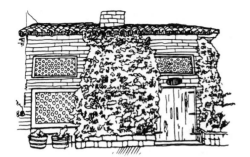

MIRASSOU

3000 Aborn Road
San Jose, CA 95135
(408) 274-4000 Melanie Bacon
Reserve for Events: 1 month in advance
Reserve for Meetings: 1 month in advance

This winery offers businesses and private parties a chance to savor Mirassou wines during events. A Conference Room provides comfortable meeting space with all the necessities. Wine bottles line the walls and there is a view of adjacent, giant wine barrels. The Tasting Room is a popular place: spacious, with an oversized suspended mirror for cooking demonstrations, windows fashioned out of bottles and a backdrop of huge wine barrels. Mirassou's two patios can accommodate either simple wine and cheese affairs or full course meals with guests seated at umbrella-shaded tables. For a slightly more formal affair, the Heritage House has several light, airy rooms with views of the back garden. Whether you're planning a meeting, secretary's luncheon or sunset dinner, Mirassou provides versatility and a beautiful, tranquil setting.

CAPACITY:

Area	Month	Max. Capacity
Outdoor Patios	June–Sept	125
Indoor Dining Room	Year-round	65–80
Conference Room	Year-round	18

FEES & DEPOSITS: Deposits are sometimes required; in December a refundable $250 deposit is required when reservations are confirmed. There are no rental fees with food service. Per person rates for meals, including wine, tax and tip: $48 for dinners and $25 for luncheons. The Conference Room Lunch Program rate is $250/day for 10 guests, which includes meeting space, business equipment, lunch, tax, tip and wine. For each guest over 10, the rate is $22/person. Seminars, minimum 25 participants, can be arranged for a $50 setup fee. Food service is $7.50–12.50/person for fruit, cheese and paté.

CANCELLATION POLICY: One month's notice is required for a refund.

AVAILABILITY: Year-round, every day except for major holidays.

SERVICES/AMENITIES:

Restaurant Services: no
Catering: provided, no BYO
Kitchen Facilities: n/a
Tables & Chairs: provided
Linens, Silver, etc.: provided
Restrooms: wca
Dance Floor: no
Other: wine tasting & tours

Parking: large lot
Overnight Accommodations: no
Telephone: pay phone
Outdoor Night Lighting: yes
Outdoor Cooking Facilities: CBA
Cleanup: provided
Meeting Equipment: yes

RESTRICTIONS:

Alcohol: CW provided, no BYO

Wheelchair Access: yes

Smoking: allowed
Music: amplified within limits

Insurance: not required
Other: no guests under 21 years

SAN JOSE ATHLETIC CLUB

196 N. Third Street
San Jose, CA 95112
(408) 292-1281
Reserve for Events: 12–18 months in advance
Reserve for Meetings: 2–4 weeks in advance

Located in the heart of historic downtown San Jose, the San Jose Athletic Club is a striking and stately Neoclassic structure. It has grand-sized columns, enormous urns and broad granite steps leading up to the impressive front doors. Inside you'll find a variety of rooms available for private parties, meetings or conferences. Most often, large seated functions are held in the Corinthian Room, which is a stunning space. Its faux marble finish and intricately detailed high ceilings are extraordinary. The decor is tasteful, with attractive appointments and huge palm trees that grace the main floor. For formal or informal events, the San Jose Athletic Club is an impressive building with interior spaces to match.

CAPACITY:	*Room*	*Standing*	*Seated*	*Room*	*Standing*	*Seated*
	Columns Lounge	250	100	Corinthian Room	400	100–300
	Olympia Room	100	80	Gold, Silver, Bronze Rm	200	150

FEES & DEPOSITS: A $300–1,000 deposit, depending on the room reserved, secures your date and is due when the reservation is made. Full payment is due prior to your event. The fee for the Corinthian Room is $250–1,000 based on the number of guests, for a 5-hour block. Other rooms range from $75–500. The Club provides full service catering. The Executive Chef and Catering Coordinator can help you customize any menu—you'll have to inquire for current prices. An 18% service charge and sales tax are applied to the final total.

CANCELLATION POLICY: The deposit is only refundable if the event date can be rebooked.

AVAILABILITY: All rooms are available, every day from 6am–1am.

SERVICES/AMENITIES:

Restaurant Services: yes
Catering: provided, no BYO
Kitchen Facilities: n/a
Tables & Chairs: provided
Linens, Silver, etc.: provided
Restrooms: wca
Dance Floor: yes
Special: poolside parties

Parking: street or nearby garage, complimentary on weekends & weekdays after 6pm
Overnight Accommodations: no
Telephone: pay phone
Outdoor Night Lighting: yes
Outdoor Cooking Facilities: BBQ
Cleanup: provided
Meeting Equipment: CBA

RESTRICTIONS:

Alcohol: provided, corkage $6/bottle
Smoking: allowed
Music: amplified ok

Insurance: not required
Wheelchair Access: yes
Other: no helium balloons/confetti in Corinthian Rm

SAN JOSE HISTORICAL MUSEUM at Kelley Park

Between Story & Tully on Senter Road
San Jose, CA 95112
(408) 287-2290   Events Dept.
Reserve for Events: 1–3 months in advance
Reserve for Meetings: 3 weeks in advance

Housed on twenty-five acres in the southernmost section of Kelley Park, the Historical Museum Complex offers a unique glimpse of the old homes and businesses that once graced the streets of early San Jose. This is a recreation of old San Jose, with historically significant buildings and exhibits depicting the history of Santa Clara Valley. Whether restored or reconstructed, each building in Kelley Park is placed as nearly as possible in its original relation to other structures. The Museum Complex features an operating, turn-of-the-century trolley with costumed conductor, a scaled-down 115-foot high replica of the San Jose 1881 Electric Light Tower, a 1927 gas station and decorative 1890-style park bandstand. In addition to various outdoor spaces for parties, there are facilities in the Firehouse and Pacific Hotel for indoor functions. This is an interesting and unusual site for a special event. Dress up and arrive in style aboard a vintage trolley or horse-drawn carriage! The Museum staff can help you be creative—period costumes, trolley rides, museum tours and ice cream parlor parties can be arranged.

CAPACITY: The Pacific Hotel's reception room can hold up to 40 seated guests, 80 standing and the Firehouse upstairs reception room can accommodate 60 seated guests, 125 standing. For outdoor functions, up to 10,000 can be accommodated.

FEES & DEPOSITS: A non-refundable deposit of 50% of the estimated use fee is required when the reservation is made. A refundable maintenance deposit of $150 (indoor events) or $250 (outdoor events) is due 30 days prior to your function and is returned 2–3 weeks afterwards.

Indoor Functions/Special Events: $50/hour 8am–5pm, $75/hour 5pm–midnight. A 3-hour minimum block is required. The security requirement of 1 off-duty police officer is required, rate varies.

Indoor Functions/Meetings & Retreats: $125 8am–5pm (only). There is no security requirement for day time business functions.

Outdoor Functions:

Guest Count	Fee	Guest Count	Fee
0–100	$360	3,001–4,000	$8,400
101–200	510	4,001–5,000	10,500
201–300	675	5,001–6,000	12,600
301–400	900	6,001–7,000	14,700

Guest Count	Fee	Guest Count	Fee
401–600	1,350	7,001–8,000	16,800
601–800	1,710	8,001–9,000	18,900
801–1,000	2,100	9,001–10,000	21,000
1,001–2,000	4,200	10,000 (capacity limit)	
2,001–3,000	6,300		

The outdoor security requirement of 1 or more off-duty police officers is required, rate varies. The total balance is due 5 days prior to the event.

AVAILABILITY: Indoor functions: 8am–5pm or 5pm–midnight. Outdoor events: 8am–6pm or 10pm, depending on type of function.

SERVICES/AMENITIES:

Restaurant Services: no

Catering: BYO

Kitchen Facilities: minimal

Tables & Chairs: some provided

Linens, Silver, etc.: BYO

Restrooms: wca varies

Dance Floor: at plaza outside, indoors CBA

Meeting Equipment: limited

Parking: large lots

Overnight Accommodations: no

Telephone: pay phone

Outdoor Night Lighting: yes

Outdoor Cooking Facilities: BBQs

Cleanup: caterer

Other: trolley, costumes & tours CBA

RESTRICTIONS:

Alcohol: BYO, BWC only, permit required

Smoking: outside only

Music: amplified restricted, permit required

Wheelchair Access: yes

Insurance: sometimes required

Need a caterer, cake maker, florist? The Service Directory starting on page 614 features the best in the business.

THE TECH MUSEUM OF INNOVATION

145 West San Carlos St.
San Jose, CA 95113
(408) 279-7156   Maureen Langan
Reserve for Events: 1–6 months in advance
Reserve for Meetings: 2–26 months in advance

Since unusual and exceptional sites are our specialty, we could hardly leave this one out. The Tech Museum's contemporary high-tech setting combines a unique atmosphere with highly imaginative and interactive exhibits. One month after opening in 1990, The Tech was named one of the top ten attractions to open in that year. Whether you're holding a corporate event or private party , The Tech is equipped with lots of hands-on activities and guests are sure to be entertained. The main Exhibit Hall has a "techy" look, with tall black ceilings and museum spotlighting, and has elaborate exhibits on microelectronics, space exploration, high-tech bikes, robotics, materials and biotechnology. If your guests are interested in or curious about science and technology and how it affects our lives, choose The Tech for your next function. Guests can have their portrait drawn by an artistic robot, conduct a simulated low-level flight over the surface of Mars or design their own bicycle at a CAD/CAM workstation. In any event, yours will be a celebration they're sure to remember.

CAPACITY: 400 guests, maximum.

MEETING ROOMS: Seating for 75 in the Info Lounge.

FEES & DEPOSITS: A $750 refundable deposit is required to secure your date. The rental fee, $10/person up to 400 guests for 3 hours, reserves the entire facility. The minimum rental fee is $1,500. An additional 30% per hour will be charged after the first 3 hours. The balance is due within 30 days after the event.

CANCELLATION POLICY: With 30 days' notice, the deposit is refundable.

AVAILABILITY: Year-round, Monday–Sunday from 6pm–midnight. Closed Thanksgiving day, Christmas eve and day, New Year's eve and day.

SERVICES/AMENITIES:

Restaurant Services: no
Catering: provided, no BYO
Kitchen Facilities: n/a
Tables & Chairs: provided
Linens, Silver, etc.: provided
Restrooms: wca
Meeting Equipment: projector, screen, microphone
Other: on-site coordinator

Parking: Convention Center garage, nearby lots
Overnight Accommodations: no
Telephone: pay phone
Outdoor Night Lighting: no
Outdoor Cooking Facilities: no
Cleanup: provided
Dance Floor: CBA

RESTRICTIONS:

Alcohol: provided
Smoking: outdoors only
Insurance: certificate required

Wheelchair Access: yes
Music: amplified ok

VALENTINO'S

8 South First Street
San Jose, CA 95113
(408) 971-7700
Reserve for Events: 2–6 months in advance

Valentino's, a new special event site on the ground floor of San Jose's original Bank of America building, is becoming one of this community's favorite sites for celebrating. The expansive ground floor, with its enormous vaulted ceilings, marble floor, balconies and floor-to-ceiling columns can accommodate a cast of hundreds and offers endless possibilities for imaginative party-givers. The style of the 12,000 square foot room is Italianate. Original 1926 pink and black marble counters and teller windows, some with frosted glass or metal bars, are still in place. These are perfect for banquet or bar arrangements, for dressing up with creative floral displays or simply for separating dining from dancing areas. The bank's ornate vault is also open for use and makes a great conversation area. Guests may wander around the upstairs balconies overlooking the event space, and separate rooms, adjacent to the balconies, can be used for buffet setups. Tall windows lining the length of the room filter in ambient light, and along the walls are brass sconces providing an after dark glow. We feel that the space is shown to best advantage in the evenings, when soft sconce lighting enhances the room's dramatic architectural lines. If you've got a large guest list and need a flexible space, request a tour.

CAPACITY: Valentino's holds 650 seated or 800 guests for a cocktail reception.

FEES & DEPOSITS: The rental fee is $6,000 for Saturday night, $5,000 for Friday night and $4,000 for Sunday–Thursday. Rental includes sound, lighting, stage and 3–5 security guards. A non-refundable $3,000 rental deposit is required to secure your date. A refundable $750 cleaning/security deposit ($400 of which is required for cleaning) plus the rental balance is payable 60 days prior to the function. Bar service for 4 hours: $10/person for beer, wine and soda; $15/person for beer, wine, soda and liquor. Bar service has a 300 person minimum charge. Tax and 17% gratuity for bar service are additional.

AVAILABILITY: Year-round, daily from 10am–1:30am.

SERVICES/AMENITIES:

Restaurant Services : no
Catering: BYO
Kitchen Facilities: very limited
Tables & Chairs: some provided
Linens, Silver, etc.: BYO
Restrooms: wca
Meeting Equipment: no

Parking: private lot & adjacent city lots
Overnight Accommodations: no
Telephone: pay phones
Outdoor Night Lighting: no
Outdoor Cooking Facilities: no
Cleanup: renter or caterer
Dance Floor: yes

RESTRICTIONS:

Alcohol: provided, no BYO
Smoking: allowed
Insurance: certificate required

Wheelchair Access: yes
Music: amplified ok

WINCHESTER
MYSTERY HOUSE

525 S. Winchester Blvd.
San Jose, CA 95128
(408) 247-2000
Reserve for Events: 3–6 months in advance
Reserve for Meetings: 2 weeks in advance

Referred to as "a pathetic $5 million dollar witness to an obviously deranged mind," the Winchester Mystery House is a 160-room Victorian mansion designed and built from 1884–1922 by Sarah Winchester, heir to the Winchester rifle fortune. Allegedly distraught by the loss of her only child and early death of her husband, she funneled all of her energy and money into the continuous construction of this extraordinary structure in order to stay her own death. Reports note that she spent the astronomical sum of five and a half million on the house from the late 1800s to the early 1920s. Today the Mansion is open to the public for tours and private functions. The house is enormous, with incredible gingerbread detailing and craftsmanship throughout. The grounds are formal, with meticulously manicured lawns, flower beds, courtyard fountains and towering palm trees. Your guests will be thrilled to attend a private party surrounded by the unique product of an eccentric who had unlimited wealth and the freedom to spend it as she pleased.

CAPACITY:

Area	Standing	Seated	Area	Standing	Seated
Front Garden	1,000	450	Central Courtyard	300	150
Central Garden	300	150	Winchester Room	65	65

For private parties of 200 guests or more, the Mansion will open for self-guided tours for up to 2 hours. For under 200, 35-minute guided tours are available. Meetings take place in the Winchester Room.

FEES & DEPOSITS: A $500 deposit is due with the rental agreement 30 days prior to your event. The Garden and Courtyard fees: $1,500 for the first 100 guests, based on 10/table seating, and $150 for each additional table of 10; $1,600 for the first 100 guests, based on 8/table seating, with $160 for each additional table of 8. The Winchester Room fee is $500 for the first 48 guests, based on 8/table seating plus $10/person for each additional guest. These fees cover a 4-hour rental period. Food and beverage service can be provided and will be catered on an individual basis. Prices will vary accordingly. Tax and gratuity are additional.

CANCELLATION POLICY: With 2 or more weeks' notice, you'll receive a full refund; with 1 week's notice, a 50% refund.

AVAILABILITY: Gardens and grounds available every day, April, May and September from 7pm–11pm; June, July and August 8pm–midnight. The Winchester Room is available year-round.

SERVICES/AMENITIES:

Restaurant Services: no
Catering: provided, can BYO but will be charged 20% of gross

Parking: large lots
Overnight Accommodations: no
Telephone: pay phone

Kitchen Facilities: minimal
Tables & Chairs: provided
Linens, Silver, etc.: BYO
Restrooms: wca
Dance Floor: CBA
Meeting Equipment: P/A system, podium

RESTRICTIONS:
Alcohol: provided, corkage $2/bottle
Smoking: garden and courtyard only
Music: amplified until 11pm

Outdoor Night Lighting: yes
Outdoor Cooking Facilities: no
Cleanup: caterer
Other: mini tours, flashlight tours
& murder mystery events

Wheelchair Access: to garden only
Insurance: not required

Santa Clara

ADOBE LODGE
FACULTY CLUB

Santa Clara University
Santa Clara, CA 95053
(408) 554-4059
Reserve for Events: 12 months in advance
Reserve for Meetings: 4 weeks in advance

In the heart of Santa Clara University sits the Adobe Lodge. Now the Santa Clara University Faculty Club, it is the only structure to have survived the 1926 fire and remains the single structural remnant of the original 1822 Mission Santa Clara. It has been remodeled extensively, but still has a Mission era flavor. To reach the Club, you stroll through the Old Mission Gardens, under an ancient, wisteria-laden pergola. This particular vine deserves mention because it's breathtaking, with 150-year-old trunks the size of small trees. In the spring, the pergola overflows with color. In fact, all of the landscaping flanking the entry path is delightful. Everything from the palms dotting the lawns to the multi-hued roses and pansies is perfectly maintained. There is no traffic noise in this interior garden, only the sound of the birds. The Spanish-tiled Faculty Club building is surrounded by a vine-covered porch and inside there's a main dining room which is formally resplendent in creams and golds. The Club's outdoor patio is inviting and intimate, with Chinese elms providing dappled shade overhead. Here you can have a business lunch, dinner or small meeting, in an historic environment.

CAPACITY: Main dining room 100 seated guests; two adjacent dining rooms, 12 seated guests each; with porch and patio, up to 300 for hors d'oeuvres during warmer months.

FEES & DEPOSITS: A $600 rental fee, which includes a refundable $50 damage deposit, is due when the rental contract is submitted. The fee covers a 4 to 4-1/2 hour time frame. A final guest count is due

1 week prior to the event. Food services are provided. Special event menus, with prices ranging from $12.50–16.50/person, are available. The bartender's fee is $15/hour for a minimum of 6 hours. Tax and 15% service charge are additional. The balance is due at the conclusion of the event.

CANCELLATION POLICY: A 90-day written notice is required for a refund. With less than 90 days, the rental fee deposit is pro-rated.

AVAILABILITY: Year-round. Mon–Friday 5pm–10pm; Saturday and Sunday, 10am–8:30pm.

SERVICES/AMENITIES:

Restaurant Services: no
Catering: provided, no BYO
Kitchen Facilities: n/a
Tables & Chairs: provided
Linens, Silver, etc.: provided
Restrooms: wca
Meeting Equipment: call for list

Dance Floor: yes
Parking: large lot
Overnight Accommodations: no
Telephone: pay phone
Outdoor Night Lighting: no
Outdoor Cooking Facilities: CBA
Cleanup: provided

RESTRICTIONS:

Alcohol: WC provided, corkage $6.50/bottle
Smoking: outside only
Music: no amplified

Wheelchair Access: yes
Insurance: certificate required

DECATHLON CLUB

3250 Central Expressway
Santa Clara, CA 95051
(408) 738-8743 or **(408) 736-3237**   Catering
Reserve for Events: 6–18 months in advance
Reserve for Meetings: 2 weeks in advance

One of Silicon Valley's finest private athletic clubs, the Decathlon Club is ingeniously designed to accommodate private parties or business meetings without disturbing its membership. As you enter, there is a shaded garden setting with a bubbling stream which flows through the building, beautifully separating the social function spaces from the Club's athletic areas. Guests for social gatherings can be ushered into the party spaces without having to mingle with Club members. The dining area is large and open, yet it gives guests a feeling of privacy. It opens onto a wide deck overlooking a lush, sloping lawn and tennis court below. Adjacent to the dining area is a raised hardwood dance floor. The deck, lawn and private tennis court combo allows a private group to design their own tournament for fund-raising, corporate fun or just a private tennis match. For unique corporate events, all the Club's sports facilities are available for rental. Corporate challenges or inter-office games can be played here, all supported by a helpful and experienced staff.

CAPACITY: Indoors, the Club can hold 600 guests for receptions with dancing; 400 seated. The outdoor stadium tennis court and outside deck areas can hold 500 guests.

MEETING ROOMS: 2 rooms, 2–22 people conference seating; 25–60 classroom seating.

FEES & DEPOSITS: A minimum guest count of 100 is required to book reservations. The $800 rental fee covers 4-1/2 hours. Overtime is available at an additional charge. A non-refundable $500 deposit, applied to final bill, is due when your reservation is confirmed. 30 days before the event, 75% of the estimated food & beverage total is due. The balance of fees and rental is due upon conclusion of your party. Food service is provided. Per person rates: luncheons and dinners from $10–30, buffets from $20–35, hors d'oeuvres from $15–30 and BBQs at $18. Tax and an 18% service charge are additional.

Meeting room fees are $200/8 hours for the large room, $150/8 hours for the small room. Invoicing for business meetings can be arranged. For meetings, continental breakfast, lunch and coffee service can be arranged starting at $6/person. For corporate sports challenges, call for rates.

AVAILABILITY: Year-round, every day in 4-1/2 hour time blocks. Closed major holidays.

SERVICES/AMENITIES:

Restaurant Services: yes
Catering: provided, no BYO
Kitchen Facilities: n/a
Tables & Chairs: provided
Linens, Silver, etc.: provided
Restrooms: wca
Dance Floor: yes
Meeting Equipment: full range

Parking: large lots
Overnight Accommodations: no
Telephone: pay phone
Outdoor Night Lighting: yes
Outdoor Cooking Facilities: BBQ
Cleanup: provided
Other: event coordination

RESTRICTIONS:

Alcohol: provided, no BYO
Smoking: outside deck only
Music: amplified ok

Wheelchair Access: yes
Insurance: not required
Other: premises must be vacated by 1am

MADISON STREET INN

1390 Madison Street
Santa Clara, CA 95050
(408) 249-5541
Reserve for Events: 2 weeks in advance
Reserve for Meetings: 2 weeks in advance

The Madison Street Inn is an inviting bed and breakfast establishment offering an unusual blend of 1890s Victorian charm with modern amenities. The house, with its white picket fence, antique furnishings, authentic wallpaper and lace curtains, maintains its period authenticity. Soothing colors, an intimate parlor with fireplace and a warm and airy dining area make anybody coming for a meeting, conference or private party feel right at home. The grounds offer a more contemporary setting with swimming pool and brick patio. In the summer, the white trellis over the patio is ablaze with colorful flowers and the adjacent lawn area is suitable for small, outdoor functions.

CAPACITY: The Inn can hold up to 30 guests indoors and 75 outdoors.

MEETING ROOMS: 1 meeting room that can hold up to 30 guests.

FEES & DEPOSITS: A non-refundable $200 deposit, applied toward the rental fee, is required when reservations are confirmed. The rental fee is $100–400 depending on the total guest count. The total estimated balance of both rental and food service is due 1 week before the event. The Inn provides catering: hors d'oeuvres run $5–20/person, luncheons $10–15/person and dinners $15–25/person. Tax and gratuity are additional. The rental fee for weekday meetings is $125.

AVAILABILITY: Year-round, every day 11am–7pm.

SERVICES/AMENITIES:

Restaurant Services: no
Catering: provided or BYO with approval
Kitchen Facilities: setup only
Tables & Chairs: some provided
Linens, Silver, etc.: some provided
Restrooms: wca
Dance Floor: yes
Meeting Equipment: CBA

Parking: on street
Overnight Accommodations: 5 guestrooms
Telephone: house phone
Outdoor Night Lighting: limited
Outdoor Cooking Facilities: BBQ
Cleanup: caterer
Other: event coordination

RESTRICTIONS:

Alcohol: BYO, BWC only
Smoking: outside only
Music: no amplified

Wheelchair Access: limited to garden
Insurance: not required

Saratoga

CHATEAU LA CRESTA
At The Mountain Winery

14831 Pierce Road
Saratoga, CA 95070
(408) 741-0763
Reserve for Events: 2 weeks–1 year in advance
Reserve for Meetings: 1 day in advance

Chateau La Cresta, located within the Mountain Winery (home of the Paul Masson Summer Series) is situated high in the Santa Cruz mountains, surrounded by vineyards. This is a lovely outdoor setting with majestic oaks and unbeatable views of the Santa Clara valley. The winery building and Chateau La Cresta, Paul Masson's home, were built in 1905 of stone masonry. These historic ivy-covered structures feature large wood beams and oak casks—the appealing aroma of aging wine lingers in the air. The Chateau, built to entertain Masson's peers, such as John Steinbeck and Charlie Chaplin, represents a fine example of French country architecture. Outdoor functions are held on lawns or on a large wood terrace overlooking the valley floor; the Chateau and Great Winery Hall are available for indoor events. At 1,400 feet up, this "vineyard in the sky" provides a tranquil and unusual setting for an unforgettable special event.

CAPACITY: Chateau La Cresta can accommodate 50–1,500 guests, depending on how the facility is used. Areas available for events: Terrace, Wishing Well, Chateau and the Great Winery Hall.

MEETING ROOMS: The Vista Room holds groups up to 40, the Board Room and the sun porch each hold up to 20, and the Bordello Room holds groups up to 12. The Great Winery Hall has 2 separate rooms, each holds up to 120 people.

FEES & DEPOSITS: The rental fee, contract and confirmed guest count are required when the facility is reserved. Half the catering total is due 1 week prior to the event, and the balance is due the day of the event.

Area	*Capacity*	*Rental Rates*
Chateau	10–80	$200–1,200
Great Winery Hall	60–280	1,000
Grounds	up to 1,500	750–3,000

Meals are $15.50–35/person, plus tax and 17% service charge. Unlimited wine, beer and champagne is $12.50/person.

AVAILABILITY: Year-round with some restrictions during the Paul Masson Summer Series which runs June–September.

SERVICES/AMENITIES:

Restaurant Services: yes

Catering: provided

Kitchen Facilities: n/a

Tables & Chairs: provided

Linens, Silver, etc.: provided

Restrooms: limited wca

Parking: large lot

Overnight Accommodations: no

Telephone: pay phone

Outdoor Night Lighting: yes

Outdoor Cooking Facilities: BBQ

Cleanup: provided

Dance Floor: CBA

Meeting Equipment: flip charts, overhead and slide projectors, screens, PA systems

RESTRICTIONS:

Alcohol: provided, WC only, no BYO

Smoking: outside only

Music: amplified with volume control

Wheelchair Access: limited

Insurance: certificate required

SARATOGA FOOTHILL CLUB

20399 Park Place
Saratoga, CA 95070
(408) 867-3428 Dianna
Reserve for Events: 9–12 months in advance
Reserve for Meetings: 9–12 months in advance

In a spot you'd never expect, on a quiet residential street near the crossroads of Big Basin and Sunnyvale/Saratoga Roads, lies the Foothill Club. This decorative 1915 Arts and Crafts-style historic landmark was designed by Julia Morgan as a women's club. The old-fashioned brown-shingled facade has a wisteria-covered trellis framing unusually shaped windows. An adjoining paved courtyard is dotted with Japanese maples. It's small but very pretty and private. The Club's formal entry is all in redwood and ushers you into a room that is perfect for a buffet arrangement. The interior's largest room has thirty-foot high ceilings, a raised platform stage, hardwood floors and an elaborate window through which glorious sunlight filters and sets the room aglow. The Foothill Club offers a formal entry space, two interior rooms and an exterior courtyard for fundraisers, business meetings or recitals. All are pleasant, intimate spaces. The final impression is one of old-world comfort and warmth.

CAPACITY: From November–May, the Club's indoor and outdoor combined maximum capacity is 150 guests. From June–October the combined capacity is 185. The indoor maximum seated capacity is 126 guests.

FEES & DEPOSITS: A $200 refundable security deposit is required when reservations are made. There is a 4-hour maximum for events and business functions.

	Business Functions & Private Parties	Nonprofits	Piano Recitals
Food served	$300	$225	$225
No food served	250	175	175

AVAILABILITY: Tuesday through Sunday, 9:30am–9pm.

SERVICES/AMENITIES:

Restaurant Services: no
Catering: BYO
Kitchen Facilities: moderate
Tables & Chairs: provided
Linens, Silver, etc.: BYO
Restrooms: wca
Dance Floor: yes
Meeting Equipment: no

Parking: adjacent church lot, $50 donation
Overnight Accommodations: no
Telephone: house phone
Outdoor Night Lighting: access only
Outdoor Cooking Facilities: no
Cleanup: caterer
Other: baby grand available

RESTRICTIONS:

Alcohol: BYO, WC only
Smoking: outside only
Music: amplified restricted

Wheelchair Access: no
Insurance: liability required

VILLA MONTALVO

15400 Montalvo Road
Saratoga, CA 95071
(408) 741-1524
Reserve for Events: 1 month in advance
Reserve for Meetings: 1 month in advance

The Villa is a stately Mediterranean-style estate nestled against a wooded slope in the private and secluded Saratoga hills. Built in 1912 as the private home of one of San Francisco's former mayors, Villa Montalvo, with its terra cotta tile roofs and light stucco exterior, is now an arboretum and a center for the arts. The Villa is approached from below by a narrow, one-way road offering a striking view of the structure as you round the last turn. An amphitheater with stage and a lovely patio with lawn are situated in back of the Villa. This open-air courtyard, called the Oval Garden, is surrounded by a wisteria-draped pergola and is a delightful place for a musical event. The acoustics are fabulous in this quiet setting. The Spanish Courtyard, another wisteria-laden courtyard, is wonderful for small, intimate parties or corporate events. The Villa's interior rooms and its verandas are also very impressive spots. The latter have sweeping views down the grand steps and main lawn corridor to the Love Temple. Reserve well in advance. Villa Montalvo is an extraordinary site for elegant and sophisticated celebrations.

CAPACITY: The maximum capacity for outdoor functions is 400; indoor capacity 200.

MEETING ROOMS: The Claire Loftus Carriage House Theatre can hold 275 for meetings.

FEES & DEPOSITS: A non-refundable 50% deposit of the total fee is required when you book your event date. A $1,000 security deposit is payable 30 days prior to the event and is usually returned 2 weeks after the event. The corporate fee for 8 hours use is $2,600. Non-corporate full day Villa rentals for 20–50 guests from 9am–5pm costs $1,500. The conference area is available for groups of 20 or less at $100/hour for the first 4 hours and $75/hour for each additional hour. The Carriage House is available for 8 hours use for $850.

AVAILABILITY: Year-round, every day.

SERVICES/AMENITIES:

Restaurant Services: no
Catering: BYO, select from list
Kitchen Facilities: ample
Tables & Chairs: provided, extra charge
Linens, Silver, etc.: caterer
Restrooms: no wca
Dance Floor: extra charge, required indoors

Parking: 125 cars, carpooling encouraged
Overnight Accommodations: no
Telephone: pay phone
Outdoor Night Lighting: yes
Outdoor Cooking Facilities: no
Cleanup: caterer
Meeting Equipment: no

RESTRICTIONS:

Alcohol: BYO, BWC only
Smoking: discouraged, not allowed inside Villa
Music: amplified with restrictions

Wheelchair Access: yes
Insurance: certificate required

Alexander Valley

CHATEAU SOUVERAIN

Independence Lane
Alexander Valley, CA 95441
(707) 433-3141
Reserve for Events: 2–6 months in advance

Located seventy miles north of the Golden Gate Bridge, Chateau Souverain is beautifully situated on a vine-covered hill, commanding a spectacular view of Sonoma's Alexander Valley. Recognized for its contemporary French and American cuisine, it's one of the few California premium wineries to offer year-round gourmet dining. When you arrive, a grand staircase leads you from a tree-lined drive below to the large upper courtyard and fountain. The winery buildings are architecturally striking, designed in the shape of hop kilns with high-peaked slate roofs and extensive window detailing. The interior of the cafe is dynamic, with vibrant wall murals painted by a local artist and a large hanging fabric sculpture. Chateau Souverain's two formal dining rooms are connected by double glass doors. The Main Dining Room, with its large fireplace and cathedral ceilings, opens onto a split-level terrace, while the Front Dining Room, a semi-private area, has a view of the fountain. The latter is great for business dinners. Both are decorated in soft colors and are well-adorned with stunning floral arrangements. A bit off the beaten path, this winery makes a lovely setting for a Wine Country party.

CAPACITY, FEES & DEPOSITS: A refundable deposit of $300 is required to secure a date. A deposit of $15/person for lunch or $25/person for dinner, plus a room rental fee, is required 2 weeks prior to your event. These deposits are credited to the final bill. A final guest count guarantee is needed 1 week prior to your function. Sales tax and an 18% service charge are additional. Payment is due in full the day of the event. Luncheons start at $25/person, dinners at $40.

Area	*Rental Fee*		*Seated*	*Standing*	*Hours*
Main Dining Room	$500		90	—	
Front Dining Room	250		40	—	vary according
Outdoor Terrace	1,500	(1 tent, heating & lighting)	150	250	to event
	2,200	(2 tents, heating & lighting)	150	250	
Cafe	varies		80	120	

CANCELLATION POLICY: With 30 days' written notice in advance of your function, your reservation deposit will be refunded.

AVAILABILITY: Private parties outdoors can take place during the time frames shown above. For indoor parties during normal business hours (approximately 11:30am–9:30pm) or with 75 guests or more, the restaurant can be opened beyond normal business hours.

SERVICES/AMENITIES:

Restaurant Services: yes
Parking: large lot
Catering: provided, no BYO
Kitchen Facilities: n/a
Tables & Chairs: provided
Linens, Silver, etc.: provided
Restrooms: wca

Dance Floor: CBA
Meeting Equipment: no
Overnight Accommodations: no
Telephone: pay phone
Outdoor Night Lighting: yes
Outdoor Cooking Facilities: no
Cleanup: provided

RESTRICTIONS:

Alcohol: provided, WC only
Smoking: outside only
Music: amplified indoors only until 9:45pm

Wheelchair Access: yes
Insurance: indemnification clause required
Other: decorations may be restricted

Calistoga

CLOS PEGASE

1060 Dunaweal Lane
Calistoga, CA 94515
(707) 942-4981
Reserve for Events: 2–6 months in advance
Reserve for Meetings: 2 weeks–2 months in advance

Both controversial and architecturally dramatic, Clos Pegase was designed as a temple to celebrate the marriage of wine and art. The terra cotta-roofed and earth-toned buildings bring to mind ancient images—a bit of Egyptian grandeur and classic Roman symmetry. This site is impressive, indeed. Although no weddings are permitted, the winery is available for corporate functions, food and beverage industry and arts groups events. The Dining Room is clean, stylish and sophisticated with detailed wood cabinets, high ceiling and subtle colors. For a very unique experience, have your group meet in Clos Pegase's underground "Cave", a tunnel into the mountainside created for cool and controlled wine storage. There's a room with a stage for formal presentations, too. Softly lit and appointed with ancient artifacts nestled into alcoves along the Cave's corridors, the Cave is extraordinary for a business lecture or cocktail party.

CAPACITY: The Dining Room can seat 70 guests, the Cave 150 and the Garden 400, theater-style 500.

FEES & DEPOSITS: A refundable $250 deposit may be required at the time of booking. For groups, there is a facility fee of $10/person, and wine is charged on consumption. Catered dinners range from $25–75/person including tour and tasting. Tax and tip are additional.

CANCELLATION POLICY: With 7 days' notice, you will receive a full refund.

AVAILABILITY: Year-round, except for Thanksgiving, New Year's and Christmas days. Anytime until midnight.

SERVICES/AMENITIES:

Restaurant Services: no
Catering: preferred list or BYO with approval
Kitchen Facilities: fully equipped
Tables & Chairs: provided
Linens, Silver, etc.: caterer or CBA
Restrooms: wca
Meeting Equipment: podium w/ microphone,
Other: wine tours & tastings, wine & art slide show

Dance Floor: in Cave
Parking: large lots
Overnight Accommodations: no
Telephone: pay phone
Outdoor Night Lighting: yes
Outdoor Cooking Facilities: BBQ
Cleanup: Clos Pegase and caterer

RESTRICTIONS:

Alcohol: W provided, no BYO
Smoking: outside only
Music: with approval

Wheelchair Access: yes
Insurance: not required

MOUNT VIEW HOTEL

1457 Lincoln Ave.
Calistoga, CA 94515
(707) 942-6877
Reserve for Events: 1–6 months in advance
Reserve for Meetings: 1–12 weeks in advance

When you need a place for a special event or business function that can provide overnight accommodations in the wine country—call the Mount View Hotel. Here, you can have parties, meetings and extended conferences. Overnight corporate retreats are Mount View Hotel's specialty. This recently renovated landmark hotel has both indoor and outdoor spaces for seated parties, a full service, upscale restaurant *plus* plenty of guestrooms for your group. For indoor dining, Valeriano's (the Hotel's in-house restaurant) is a splendid spot. The decor is upscale contemporary. Colors are in creams and tans with white trim. Gold framed pictures, textured walls and cane chairs with rush seats make Valeriano's visually appealing. For al fresco events, try the Hotel's Poolside Grill and Patio Courtyard. Tables with umbrellas are arranged around the large, heated pool. Next to the pool, terra cotta sculptures with gurgling streams of water add to the ambiance. Inside, all the Hotel's rooms have all been renovated by interior designer Michael Moore, including the small but sweet cottages that are adjacent to the Hotel. Each cottage has a private courtyard and hot tub. What more could you ask for? Well, there is more—the Hotel has a chic new European spa, all designed in marble and glass. It has every conceivable service your guests will need to look their best. From facials to massage and herbal wraps to manicures, the spa's professional staff will make them feel as terrific as they look. And if you wonder why you should have your function in Calistoga, note that the Mt. View Hotel is in the heart of town—a stone's throw from golf, tennis, hot air ballooning, bicycling, glider rides and winery touring.

CAPACITY: Valeriano's 85 seated guests; the Poolside Patio 80–100 seated guests or 125 for a standing reception; the Private Dining Room 30 seated guests; Johnny's Cafe/Bar 60 seated guests, 80 standing.

MEETING ROOMS: The private dining room can accommodate up to 30, and Valeriano's main dining room can accommodate 80–100 people depending on seating style.

FEES & DEPOSITS: Half the estimated total is due at the time of booking, and the balance is due at the conclusion of the event. A final guest count is due 72 hours in advance. The rental fees are: Valeriano's $300, the Poolside Patio $500, Private Dining Room $150, Johnny's $250. Menus can be customized for your party and must be confirmed 2 weeks in advance. Luncheons start at $15/person, dinners and buffets start at $28/person. Tax and 15% service charge are additional.

CANCELLATION POLICY: If you cancel less than 14 days before an event, the menu deposit will be forfeited.

AVAILABILITY: Year–round. Every day from 7am–10pm except Valeriano's, which is available from 7am–4:30pm.

SERVICES/AMENITIES:

Restaurant Services: yes

Catering: provided, no BYO

Kitchen Facilities: n/a

Tables & Chairs: provided

Linens, Silver, etc.: provided

Restrooms: wca

Dance Floor: yes

Other: full event coordination

Parking: on street, lot

Overnight Accommodations: 22 rooms, 8 suites, 3 cottages

Telephone: pay phones & room phones

Outdoor Night Lighting: yes

Outdoor Cooking Facilities: CBA

Cleanup: provided

Meeting Equipment: CBA, extra fee

RESTRICTIONS:

Alcohol: provided, corkage $7.50–10/bottle

Smoking: designated areas

Music: amplified ok, outside until 10pm

Wheelchair Access: yes

Insurance: not required

Prices and policies <u>do</u> change. Call each facility and confirm everything you read in Perfect Places.

Geyserville

ISIS OASIS RETREAT CENTER

20889 Geyserville Avenue
Geyserville, CA 95441
(707) 857-3524
Reserve for Events: 6 months in advance
Reserve for Meetings: 2 months in advance

This is a New Age retreat for those who wish to relax, rejuvenate or expand the mind. Isis Oasis provides a supportive environment for private celebrations or groups coming for workshops and seminars. Occupying ten acres of fertile wine country, the Center has four main buildings (some historical), yurts, a wine barrel room and an Egyptian-style meditation temple. There's also a theater, a redwood structure enhanced by stained glass with stage, balcony, and sound system. A separate dining pavilion serves as the main eating area and meeting room. The outdoor areas are a wonderful mix of the rustic and not-so-rustic. A pool, spa and sauna are available for those who want to unwind. For nature lovers, there's an expansive garden, the adjacent vineyard, a pond for waterfowl and a mini-zoo, featuring a variety of common and exotic animals. Pheasant, peacock, doves and emu are here, along with ocelots, serval cats, a llama, black sheep, pygmy goats and dwarf rabbits. Your Isis Oasis hosts are Loreon Vigne, an artist, non-denominational minister and tarot reader and her partner, Paul, a Gestalt therapist, past-life guide and counselor who presides over men's consciousness-raising groups. At Isis Oasis, you'll be able to have an out-of-the-ordinary business meeting or a personal experience connecting you with both ancient wisdoms and the evolving New Age.

CAPACITY: Groups from 9–150 people. There is a wide range of facilities, with various capacities.

MEETING ROOMS: 1 large, carpeted room that accommodates 50 seated participants; the Theater for 100 participants and the Dining Pavilion 100–150.

FEES & DEPOSITS: 15% of the total lodging cost is due when reservations are confirmed. To rent the entire facility, the fee is $1,800/night. The remaining 85% is payable on arrival. Rates for individual parts of Isis Oasis run about $20–25/person per night. Meals are served buffet style, with breakfasts at $5, luncheons at $7.50 and dinners at $12.50/person. An all-day meal rate is $24/day including tax. No gratuity is required. The payment for meals is due upon departure.

AVAILABILITY: Year-round, every day.

SERVICES/AMENITIES:

Restaurant Services: no
Catering: provided or BYO
Kitchen Facilities: ample, $75/day if BYO
Tables & Chairs: provided
Linens, Silver, etc.: provided

Dance Floor: pavilion
Parking: large lots
Overnight Accommodations: 22 guestrooms
Telephone: guest phone
Outdoor Night Lighting: yes

Restrooms: some wca
Meeting Equipment: TV, VCR, projector, easels
Other: pool available, zoo tour, massage therapist, meditation temple

RESTRICTIONS:
Alcohol: WB provided or BYO, no hard liquor
Smoking: outside only
Music: amplified within limits

Outdoor Cooking Facilities: BBQ
Cleanup: provided or renter

Wheelchair Access: limited
Insurance: sometimes required
Other: children need supervision

Guerneville

THE SURREY INN

16590 River Road
Guerneville, CA 95446
(707) 869-2002
Reserve for Events: 6–12 months in advance
Reserve for Meetings: 1–2 months in advance

Less than two blocks from the center of town, this Russian River resort has been transformed into the best combination of indoor and outdoor event spaces we've seen in this area. Totally private and enclosed by tall redwoods, the Surrey Inn is a three and a half acre enclave featuring a pool, pool house, interior banquet spaces, tennis courts and lawns. Set back from River Road, the building's ordinary creme and gray-blue facade belies an exceptional interior. The largest space, designed for special events, has a high, vaulted ceiling, enormous wood-burning fireplace and skylights throughout. With this room, you don't have to worry about your guest list—it seats 350! Equally impressive are the outdoor facilities. The Surrey Inn has one of Sonoma's largest private swimming pools, flanked by men's and women's changing areas, jacuzzi and spa. For more active guests, there are tennis courts, basketball court, horseshoes and volleyball. There's even play equipment for restless youngsters. On warm days and evenings, you can have a relaxed garden party arranged around the pool. Umbrellas provide shade and the outdoor bar is just a stone's throw away. If you've got a large guest list, you should make time to visit the Surrey Inn. No matter whether you have a company picnic or a gala dinner, this is a must see location for Russian River events.

CAPACITY: Indoors, the Inn can accommodate 500 seated guests; 800 for a standing cocktail party. Indoor and outdoor spaces can hold up to 1,500 standing guests.

FEES & DEPOSITS: A non-refundable $500 security deposit is due when reservations are made. The rental fee is $500 for up to 100 guests, $2,000 for 500 guests and $4,000 for 1,500 guests. The rental fee covers a 5-hour period and is payable 30 days prior to the event. For parties over 200 guests, professional security guard(s) are required, to be hired at the renter's expense.

AVAILABILITY: Year-round, daily from 6am–2am.

SERVICES/AMENITIES:

Restaurant Services: no
Catering: provided or BYO
Kitchen Facilities: no
Tables & Chairs: BYO or CBA
Linens, Silver, etc.: BYO or CBA
Restrooms: no wca
Dance Floor: yes

Parking: large secured lot
Overnight Accommodations: no
Telephone: phone usage with approval
Outdoor Night Lighting: yes
Outdoor Cooking Facilities: BBQ
Cleanup: caterer or renter
Meeting Equipment: no

RESTRICTIONS:

Alcohol: BYO
Smoking: outside only
Music: amplified ok indoors, limited outdoors

Wheelchair Access: yes
Insurance: liability required

Healdsburg

MADRONA MANOR

1001 Westside Road
Healdsburg, CA 95448
(707) 433-4231
Reserve for Events: 2–12 months in advance
Reserve for Meetings: 2–6 weeks in advance

Madrona Manor is an exceptionally lovely Victorian house set high over the Dry Creek Valley of Sonoma County, surrounded by eight acres of wooded and landscaped grounds. Built in 1881 by John Paxton, a wealthy San Francisco businessman, the three-story stately Manor and adjacent buildings originally served as his summer home and weekend retreat. Now a country inn, the Manor complex provides its guests with an elegant country ambiance. The Manor's interior rooms come complete with antique furniture, Persian carpets and hand-carved rosewood detailing. Outside a sizeable deck overlooks a meticulously manicured lawn and flower beds. A Carriage House providing additional guestrooms, an herb, vegetable and citrus garden, plus pool create a wonderful environment for corporate events, reunions and parties. Madrona Manor offers an extensive wine list and beautifully prepared meals containing ingredients that are always fresh. The Manor is so pleasant, pretty and tranquil, we guarantee you'll want to come back for more after the party's over.

CAPACITY: The Manor can accommodate up to 100 guests, 135 in good weather.

MEETING ROOMS: 1 meeting room for up to 35 guests.

FEES & DEPOSITS: For meetings, the rental fee is $50/day. Food service is provided and ranges from

$5/person (coffee service only) to $45/person. Half of the estimated food and beverage cost is required as a deposit. Other fees will vary according to the needs of each group. Sales tax and 15% gratuity are applied to the total bill.

CANCELLATION POLICY: If you cancel 2 weeks prior to the event, the deposit will be refunded less $50.

AVAILABILITY: Meetings, Monday–Saturday, 8am–5pm. Special events and parties, anytime.

SERVICES/AMENITIES:

Restaurant Services: yes

Catering: provided, no BYO

Kitchen Facilities: n/a

Tables & Chairs: provided

Linens, Silver, etc.: provided

Restrooms: wca

Dance Floor: CBA

Meeting Equipment: CBA

Parking: large lot

Overnight Accommodations: 21 guestrooms

Telephone: guestroom phones

Outdoor Night Lighting: yes

Outdoor Cooking Facilities: no

Cleanup: provided

Other: made-to-order special desserts

RESTRICTIONS:

Alcohol: provided, WBC only

Smoking: not in dining rooms

Music: no amplified

Wheelchair Access: yes

Insurance: not required

Other: decorating restrictions

VILLA CHANTICLEER

1248 North Fitch Mountain Road
Healdsburg, CA 95448
(707) 431-3301
Reserve for Events: 6 months–2 years in advance
Reserve for Meetings: 1–6 months in advance

Atop a gentle slope, within a seventeen-acre park at the edge of Healdsburg, you'll find Villa Chanticleer, a casual, no frills facility owned by the City of Healdsburg. The redwood tree setting is pleasant, quiet and cool. Built in 1910 as a lodge resort for San Franciscans, this one-story structure is surrounded on three sides by a wide veranda, shaded by a substantial wisteria-covered trellis. Follow the entryway which leads directly into a room containing a large U-shaped bar with a southwest-style mural painted on the back wall. On either side of the bar are two more rooms: the Ballroom and the Dining Room, 3,000 square feet each. Both have light-toned hardwood floors, redwood paneled walls and white ceilings. The Ballroom has a large (non-usable) stone fireplace at its center and a small elevated stage area built into one corner. The Dining Room has a more open, lighter ambiance and views of the adjacent hillside. Although these cavernous rooms aren't elegant, they can be dressed up for a formal affair or a relaxed, down-home party. What's nice about this facility is that it can handle large crowds and the spaces are flexible. Consequently, Villa Chanticleer is extremely popular in this area—

a great favorite among event planners.

CAPACITY: The Dining Room seats 340; the Villa's maximum capacity is 450. The Annex accommodates 150 seated guests or 250 for a standing reception. Outdoor picnic facilities up to 500 people. The bar area holds up to 100 guests.

MEETING ROOMS: All of the above rooms are available for meetings.

FEES & DEPOSITS:	*Area*	*Timeframe*	*Weekday Fee*	*Weekend Fee*
	Villa	10-hour block	$769	$962
		Additional hours	40	40
	Annex	10-hour block	285	481
		Additional hours	Call for hourly rate	
	Picnic Area	all day	150	200

If the facility is rented more than a year in advance, a $200 deposit is required at the time of booking and the balance is due 12 months prior to the event. If the facility is rented a year or less in advance, the entire fee is due when reservations are confirmed. Cleaning deposits are $400 for the Villa and $200 for the Annex. They are due 60 days prior to your event and will be refunded 30 days after the event. No deposit is required for use of the outdoor picnic area. The American Legion has a full liquor license to handle the bar. If you contract with the Legion there is no fee. If you do your own bar, there is a non-refundable $250 charge.

AVAILABILITY: Year-round, daily, including holidays.

SERVICES/AMENITIES:

Restaurant Services: no
Catering: preferred list
Kitchen Facilities: ample
Tables & Chairs: provided
Linens, Silver, etc.: BYO linens
Restrooms: wca
Meeting Equipment: BYO or CBA
Dance Floor: yes

Parking: large lot, shuttle CBA
Overnight Accommodations: no
Telephone: pay phone
Outdoor Night Lighting: yes
Outdoor Cooking Facilities: BBQ
Cleanup: caterer
Special: dishes, glassware provided

RESTRICTIONS:

Alcohol: BYO
Smoking: outdoors only
Music: amplified ok

Wheelchair Access: yes
Insurance: required
Other: no metallic balloons, streamers or confetti

Need a caterer, cake maker, florist? The Service Directory starting on page 614 features the best in the business.

Kenwood

KENWOOD INN

10400 Sonoma Highway
Kenwood, CA 95452
(707) 833-1293
Reserve for Events: 1–6 months in advance

The Kenwood Inn is an "Italian pensione" with facilities for afternoon receptions as well as intimate dinners. It's a bit hard to find, so keep your eyes open as you head into Kenwood from the South. This place has an old-world appearance and a romantic ambiance. The exterior of the building is very European, as is the interior. Walk right in. You'll find lovely slate floors, walls painted with fanciful motifs in rich shades of terra cotta and green. The style is Northern Italian Country. A medium-sized dining area is linked to the kitchen in an open, hospitable way. The kitchen has copper counters, burnt sienna-colored walls and modern amenities. All extends a subtle invitation to linger a while longer. There's even a fireplace here to warm guests in the evenings. To the left, there's a sitting room with another fireplace, also comfortably decked out with overstuffed couches, chairs and Mediterranean wrought-iron glass tables. Outside, a full-size pool and flagstone patio dominate the front garden, which is ringed by green lawn and rambling roses. This is a wonderful setting for a relaxed, poolside luncheon. At the Kenwood Inn, wedding guests can breath in fresh, country air while taking in the sights. From the Inn's windows and garden, you can marvel at the nearby hillsides covered with row upon row of grape vines. The Kenwood Inn is a fitting addition to the ever-beautiful Valley of the Moon.

CAPACITY: 125 guests, maximum. Guestrooms can accommodate 8 overnight.

FEES & DEPOSITS: A non-refundable $800 deposit is required 1 month prior to the event. For afternoon receptions, all rooms must be reserved at the Inn, approximately $765 summer, $660 winter. An additional $400 fee is required for exclusive use of the premises plus a $200 refundable cleaning deposit.

CANCELLATION POLICY: With 31 days' notice, the deposit is refundable.

AVAILABILITY: Year-round, every day.

SERVICES/AMENITIES:

Restaurant Services: no
Catering: BYO, preferred list
Kitchen Facilities: ample
Tables & Chairs: BYO or provided
Linens, Silver, etc.: provided, extra fee
Restrooms: wca limited
Meeting Equipment: no

Dance Floor: poolside or dining room
Parking: lot provided
Overnight Accommodations: 4 guestrooms
Telephone: house phone
Outdoor Night Lighting: yes
Outdoor Cooking Facilities: BBQs
Cleanup: caterer

RESTRICTIONS:
Alcohol: BW provided
Smoking: outside only
Music: amplified ok

Wheelchair Access: no
Insurance: not required

LANDMARK VINEYARDS

101 Adobe Canyon Road
Kenwood, CA 95452
(707) 833-1144
Reserve for Events: 1–6 months in advance
Reserve for Meetings: 1–6 months in advance

In the heart of the Valley of the Moon, at the junction of Adobe Canyon and Highway 12, you'll find Landmark Vineyards' new facility. Constructed in an early California style with shake roof and post-and-beam supports, the building encloses a very attractive patio courtyard with large fountain rimmed with blue tile. The courtyard is accented with terra cotta pots and pavers, and is well-situated to take advantage of the nice views of the adjacent vineyards and the hills beyond. You can set up umbrella-shaded tables or tenting during outdoor parties. There's also a private dining room for smaller, more intimate functions, that comes with its own courtyard, accessible through multiple French doors. The structure also houses a large tasting room, with high beamed ceiling, terra cotta paved floors and windows overlooking the courtyard. A colorful mural, painted on the high wall over the tasting room bar, depicts a scene of the vineyard seen through a magnified grapevine. Landmark is designed for events, which makes it easy for planning purposes. And, it provides an in-house event coordinator for those who need assistance.

CAPACITY: Landmark can accommodate 115 seated guests or 100–200 for a standing reception indoors. The Dining Room holds up to 48 seated. After hours, the Tasting Room can seat up to 67 guests. The maximum capacity outdoors is 500 guests seated or 600–700 standing.

MEETING ROOMS: The Private Dining Room can seat up to 48 guests, the Tasting Room can seat up to 67. The Dining Room can be used for seminars and all-day events.

FEES & DEPOSITS: Half of the facility use fee, which is applied toward the event, is required when reservations are confirmed. The balance of the rental fee plus a guaranteed guest count are due 7 days in advance.

Guests	Rental Fee		Guests	Rental Fee
1–40 guests	$400		101+	$4.25/guest plus
41–100 guests	$10/guest			$600 use fee

For business functions during weekdays, the rental fee is 10% off the regular use fee.

AVAILABILITY: Every day, 7am–11pm. Outdoor use is seasonal. For meetings, the Tasting Room is available from 5:30pm–11pm.

SERVICES/AMENITIES:

Restaurant Services: no
Catering: preferred list, licensed & bonded
Kitchen Facilities: ample
Tables & Chairs: provided
Linens, Silver, etc.: BYO
Restrooms: wca
Meeting Equipment: CBA

Dance Floor: CBA, extra charge
Parking: lot provided
Overnight Accommodations: no
Telephone: pay phone
Outdoor Night Lighting: yes
Outdoor Cooking Facilities: BBQs
Cleanup: provided, cleaning fee for larger groups

RESTRICTIONS:

Alcohol: WC provided
Smoking: outside only
Music: amplified, some restrictions

Wheelchair Access: yes
Insurance: not required

Napa

CHIMNEY ROCK WINERY

5350 Silverado Trail
Napa, CA 94558
(707) 257-2641 Kathy Higgins
Reserve for events: 1–2 months in advance
Reserve for meetings: 1–2 months in advance

Chimney Rock is located on the Silverado Trail near Yountville. It's a relatively new winery, set among seventy-five acres of vineyards in the famed Stags Leap District, known for its superlative wine growing conditions. Bordered by a stand of tall Lombardy poplars, the Hospitality Center was built for both wine tasting and special events. Designed in a Cape Dutch style, the building is tastefully appointed, with huge fireplace, beamed cathedral ceiling and hardwood floors. French doors lead to a large outdoor patio. The garden here is enclosed, sheltered on all sides by the walls of the buildings. On the upper portion of the winery building, facing guests as they enter the garden, is an impressive relief of Ganymede, cupbearer to the Gods. Sun plays with the relief's shadows during the day and at night when lit, the relief is stunning. The interior garden has a lush lawn, divided in half by a falling cascade. Pretty and private, Chimney Rock is well suited for entertaining.

CAPACITY: Indoors, the facility can hold up to 60 seated guests; outdoors up to 250 seated. The winery barrel room can hold up to 100 seated guests. The winery maximum is 250 guests.

FEES & DEPOSITS: A deposit of half the total estimated rental is required to secure your date. The balance is due the day of the event. The rental fee is $35/person which includes all wine (limited quantity per/person), wine service staff, glassware, flowers, tables, chairs, setup and cleanup.

CANCELLATION POLICY: If you cancel, 25% of the deposit will be forfeited.

AVAILABILITY: Year-round, except for Christmas and Thanksgiving. Outdoor events 10am–10:30pm; indoor functions 6pm–10:30pm only.

SERVICES/AMENITIES:

Restaurant Services: no
Catering: preferred list
Kitchen Facilities: fully equipped
Tables & Chairs: provided
Linens, Silver, etc.: caterer
Restrooms: wca
Dance Floor: CBA
Meeting Equipment: CBA

Parking: large lot
Overnight Accommodations: no
Telephone: business phone
Outdoor Night Lighting: yes
Outdoor Cooking Facilities: CBA
Cleanup: caterer & Chimney Rock
Other: winery tours, barrel sampling

RESTRICTIONS:

Alcohol: W provided, champagne CBA
corkage $8/bottle
Music: amplified okay
Other: no hard alcohol

Wheelchair Access: yes
Insurance: not required
Smoking: outside only

THE HESS COLLECTION

4411 Redwood Road
Napa, CA 94558
(707) 255-1144
Reserve for Events: 2–3 months in advance

For those who want a highly sophisticated and unusual location for an event, The Hess Collection winery is sure to please. Set on Mt. Veeder, on the western side of Napa Valley, the heart of the winery is a historic limestone building which underwent an extensive, two-year face lift in 1986. The result is an amazingly successful integration of historic elements with modern architecture. Owned by Swiss entrepreneur Donald Hess, the complex is part winery, part art collection. At ground level in the Visitor's Center, guests have a privileged view of French oak barrels and fermentation tanks. Inside, the winery's original stone walls are juxtaposed with new, crisp white ones. A glass elevator whisks guests upstairs to the light, airy and art-filled "museum". Here is Donald Hess' private collection, an eclectic group of 130 paintings and sculptures by contemporary European and American artists. Located off the third floor gallery, supported by an in-house chef and state-of-the-art kitchen, is the Private Dining Room. Its clean, uncluttered style, with white walls and cool gray carpet, adds a refined quality to gatherings. Tables set with damask linens, fine china and silver flatware enhance the ambiance. A wall of French multi-paned windows overlooks the terrace and the vineyards atop Mt. Veeder. An even more unusual dinner venue is the West Gallery—unusual because it's not every day that you can dine in a world-class art gallery. White walls, floors of bleached oak installed on the diagonal and wall-to-wall art create a environment that guests will remember for a long time.

CAPACITY: The Private Dining Room can hold up to 40 guests for luncheons, 80 for dinners. Seated functions only; winery or trade-related groups are preferred.

FEES & DEPOSITS: For events held in the Private Dining Room, a refundable $250 deposit (which is applied to the event total) is due when reservations are made. The balance is payable at the conclusion of the event. There is a 20-guest minimum; the final guest count is due 48 hours prior to the function. Luncheons are $45/person, dinners $85/person all inclusive. Tax is additional. Dinners may also be held in the West Gallery requiring an additional $1,000 deposit and $2,000 facility use fee.

CANCELLATION POLICY: With 30 days' notice, the deposit is refunded.

AVAILABILITY: Year-round, daily except major holidays.

SERVICES/AMENITIES:

Restaurant Services: no
Catering: provided, no BYO
Kitchen Facilities: n/a
Tables & Chairs: provided
Linens, Silver, etc.: provided
Restrooms: wca
Dance Floor: no
Other: event coordination, private gallery tour, wine service

Parking: large lot
Overnight Accommodations: no
Telephone: pay phone
Outdoor Night Lighting: access only
Outdoor Cooking Facilities: no
Cleanup: provided
Meeting Equipment: no

RESTRICTIONS:

Alcohol: provided, CW only
Smoking: outside only
Insurance: not required

Wheelchair Access: yes
Music: amplified ok

INN AT NAPA VALLEY
Crown Sterling Suites

1075 California Blvd.
Napa, CA 94559
(707) 253-9160 Catering
Reserve for Events: 1–12 months in advance
Reserve for Meetings: 1 week–12 months in advance

The Inn at Napa Valley, located near downtown Napa, offers spacious and varied accommodations for any size party. This Mediterranean-style hotel, with pastel walls, red tile roof and stone arches, greets entering guests with fountains and a circular palm-tree-lined driveway. Moving through one of the outdoor courtyards, with a working wood mill and mill pond with waterfowl, lush plantings and small waterfalls, you step into an interior restaurant atrium resplendent in Mexican tile pavers, potted trees and high ceilings. The Inn's facilities for seminars, conferences and meetings adjoin the atrium. The prefunction atrium offers high ceilings, large tropical plants, terra cotta tile floors, skylight and indoor fountain. The surrounding rooms can be combined to expand in any way to meet your guest requirements. And, if you wish to have your guests stay here, the Inn has saunas, spas and both indoor and outdoor pools in addition to distinctive suites with fireplaces and wet bars.

CAPACITY: The Inn has a variety of spaces available and can accommodate 25–200 seated or standing guests.

MEETING ROOMS: There are 11 meeting rooms which can hold up to 200 guests.

FEES & DEPOSITS: A non-refundable $500 deposit, which is applied toward the event balance, is required when you reserve your date. Per person rates: luncheons are approximately $14, seated dinners $18 and buffet service $20. Sales tax and a 17% service charge are additional. The total balance is due 72 hours prior to your event and any remaining balance is payable at the event's conclusion. If multiple rooms are reserved, the use fee is $300; if your party can be contained in 1 room, there's no charge. Bartender service is $50/function.

AVAILABILITY: Year-round, every day 6am–2am.

SERVICES/AMENITIES:

Restaurant Services: yes
Catering: provided, no BYO
Kitchen Facilities: n/a
Tables & Chairs: provided
Linens, Silver, etc.: provided
Restrooms: wca
Dance Floor: yes
Meeting Equipment: audio visual, extra charge

Parking: large lots
Overnight Accommodations: 205 suites
Telephone: pay phones
Outdoor Night Lighting: limited
Outdoor Cooking Facilities: no
Cleanup: provided
Other: grand piano

RESTRICTIONS:

Alcohol: provided, CW only, corkage $8/bottle
Smoking: allowed
Insurance: not required

Music: amplified ok
Wheelchair Access: yes

NAPA RIVER BOAT

Napa Valley Marina
1200 Milton Road
Napa, CA 94559
(707) 226-2628 Judy
Reserve for Events: 3–6 months in advance
Reserve for Meetings: 2–3 months in advance

Plan your next event aboard the authentic sternwheeler, "City of Napa" and return to a slower-paced, gentler period. Your memorable cruise can be as formal as an antebellum plantation ball or as casual as a relaxed weekend picnic. Antique lighting, oak bar and rich mahogany paneling grace the interior. Meals are served on crisp linens and beautifully presented on settings of gleaming crystal and china. You can relax here. Your business meeting or event will be uninterrupted except for the sounds of splashing water from the Napa River Boat's paddlewheel.

CAPACITY: The entire vessel holds up to 100 standing or 90 seated guests.

FEES & DEPOSITS: A deposit of 25% of the estimated total fee is required when your contract is returned. For boat rental only, the fee is $250/hour for a 2-hour minimum cruising time. Rental plus food service runs $24–46/person, depending on whether it is a brunch or a 4-course gourmet seated meal. The rental fee is for a 3-hour period. Tax and a 15% gratuity are added to the final bill which is due 3 working days prior to the event.

CANCELLATION POLICY: With 30 days' notice your deposit is fully refundable; with less than 30 days' notice, 80% is refundable if the date can be rebooked.

AVAILABILITY: Any day, anytime.

SERVICES/AMENITIES:

Restaurant Services: no
Catering: provided
Kitchen Facilities: full galley
Tables & Chairs: provided
Linens, Silver, etc.: provided or BYO if hourly rental
Restrooms: no wca
Dance Floor: yes
Meeting Equipment: no

Parking: marina lots
Overnight Accommodations: no
Telephone: radio
Outdoor Night Lighting: yes
Outdoor Cooking Facilities: no
Cleanup: caterer
Other: event coordination, remote pick-ups

RESTRICTIONS:

Alcohol: provided, corkage $5/bottle
Smoking: outside decks only
Music: amplified ok, space limited

Wheelchair Access: lower deck only
Insurance: not required

NAPA VALLEY WINE TRAIN

1275 McKinstry Street
Napa, CA 94559
(707) 253-2160 ext. 210
Reserve for Events: 1–4 months in advance

All aboard! You and your private party can return to the gracious era of elegant rail travel while gliding gently past the famous vineyards of Napa Valley. Embark at the Wine Train's station in the historic town of Napa. You are whisked away in luxury Pullman lounge and dining cars, painstakingly restored and resplendent in polished mahogany, brass and etched glass. Savor a gourmet brunch, lunch or an exquisitely prepared four-course dinner served in style: white damask linens, bone china, silver flatware and crystal. And, of course, the wine selection is superb, with over sixty Napa Valley varietals available by the glass for your own wine tasting. So hop aboard these turn-of-the-century cars. Every brunch, lunch and dinner round-trip excursion is a thirty-six-mile, three-hour nonstop adventure.

CAPACITY: The Wine Train can accommodate groups from 12 to 240 guests.

FEES & DEPOSITS: A 10–50% refundable deposit is required to hold a group reservation. For private lunch or brunch groups, the group train fare ranges from $18–26/person and food service is an additional $22–25/person. For group dinner parties, the fare ranges from $10–14.50/person and dinners are $45/person. A final guest count guarantee plus the remaining fees are due 15–30 days in advance of your scheduled train party. Sales tax and a 12% service charge will apply to food and beverages.

CANCELLATION POLICY: The deposit is refundable until 1 month prior to your event date.

AVAILABILITY: The trains operate year-round, daily.

SERVICES/AMENITIES:

Restaurant Services: yes
Catering: provided, no BYO
Kitchen Facilities: aboard train
Tables & Chairs: provided
Linens, Silver, etc.: provided
Restrooms: lounge car, no wca
Dance Floor: in station

Parking: large lot
Overnight Accommodations: no
Telephone: pay phone
Outdoor Night Lighting: yes
Outdoor Cooking Facilities: no
Cleanup: provided
Meeting Equipment: no

RESTRICTIONS:

Alcohol: provided, corkage $10/bottle
Smoking: not allowed
Music: no bands, PA system on train

Wheelchair Access: limited
Insurance: not required
Other: decorations restricted

WILLOW RETREAT

6517 Dry Creek Road
Napa, CA 94558
(707) 944-8173
Reserve for Events: 1–12 months in advance

You have to wind up the Oakville Grade a fair piece to get to Willow Retreat, but we think it's well worth it. Look sharp—the driveway into this place is very easy to miss. Once here, you'll experience a comfortable, down home environment that is absolutely private and quiet. A variety of rooms and separate guest houses offer each person something different. For those who love to hike, the entire property is surrounded by woods and vineyards. For others who just want to laze around the pool, take your pick of the many lounge chairs dotting the perimeter or grab a book and sit at one of the deck's umbrella-shaded tables. There's also an outdoor hot tub and indoor sauna. The main house has a large kitchen, dining room with pot bellied stove and living room with fireplace. The barn guest house has its own separate kitchen and an intimate deck overlooking the vineyard. (A very nice feature is that everything here is wheelchair accessible, even the hot tub). Thumbs up. Willow Retreat is a real find for any group that wants an unpretentious, private place to call their own for a while.

CAPACITY: Up to 100 guests for day use, 32 overnight guests, maximum.

FEES & DEPOSITS: A $100 non-refundable deposit is required, due when reservations are made.

Summer	*Fee*	*Winter*	*Fee*
weekends, Apr 1–Oct 31		weekends, Nov 1–March 31	
6pm Fri–4pm Sun	$2,200	4pm Fri–2pm Sun	$2,000
weekdays, 6pm–4pm the		weekdays, 4pm–2pm the	
following day	$900.	following day	$800

If you'd like multiple weekdays for workshops or seminars, fees can be negotiated. Half of the rental fee is due 60 days in advance, the balance 30 days in advance. All fees are non-refundable.

AVAILABILITY: Year-round.

SERVICES/AMENITIES:

Restaurant Services: no
Catering: BYO or CBA
Kitchen Facilities: well equipped
Tables & Chairs: some provided
Linens, Silver, etc.: some provided
Restrooms: wca
Dance Floor: CBA
Other: upright piano

Parking: parking lot
Overnight Accommodations: 11 guestrooms
Telephone: pay phone
Outdoor Night Lighting: yes
Outdoor Cooking Facilities: BBQ
Cleanup: provided and caterer
Meeting Equipment: BYO

RESTRICTIONS:

Alcohol: BYO
Music: not allowed unless you rent the entire retreat
Smoking: outside only

Wheelchair Access: yes
Insurance: not required

Petaluma

GARDEN VALLEY RANCH

498 Pepper Road
Petaluma, CA 94952
(707) 795-0919 Robert Galyean
Reserve for Events: 6–12 months in advance

If you love roses or are a gardening or horticulture buff, Garden Valley Ranch, located three miles north of Petaluma, is the perfect location for your next outdoor event. Corporate barbecues, picnics, garden tour luncheons and wine tastings can be held amidst the roses. This seven-acre ranch contains some 4,000 rose bushes cultivated for the sale of their blooms and a one-acre garden where fragrant plants are grown for potpourri blends. Several Victorian-style structures, a large lawn and adjacent gardens are available for large functions. Tents, canopies, tables with umbrellas and dance floor can be set up on lush, green lawns, creating a comfortable environment for the ultimate garden party.

CAPACITY: The facility can accommodate up to 250 guests for outdoor functions.

FEES & DEPOSITS: A non-refundable security deposit totaling 50% of the rental fee is payable when reservations are confirmed. A refundable security deposit of $400, the remaining 50% of the rental fee and equipment fees are due 2 weeks prior to the function. Rental rates: up to 50 guests $750, 51–100 guests $950, 101–150 guests $1,150, 151–200 guests $1,350, 201–250 guests $1,550. Extra time is available for an additional fee.

AVAILABILITY: May–October, Wednesday–Sunday 10am–8pm. Garden Valley Ranch only holds 1 event per day.

SERVICES/AMENITIES:

Restaurant Services: no
Catering: BYO
Kitchen Facilities: moderate
Tables & Chairs: provided extra charge
Linens, Silver, etc.: BYO
Restrooms: wca
Dance Floor: at Belvedere
Meeting Equipment: no

Parking: large lots
Overnight Accommodations: no
Telephone: emergency only
Outdoor Night Lighting: minimal
Outdoor Cooking Facilities: BBQ with approval
Cleanup: caterer or CBA, extra fee
Other: tents CBA, extra fee

RESTRICTIONS:

Alcohol: BYO
Smoking: allowed
Music: amplified ok

Insurance: suggested
Other: children must be supervised
Wheelchair Access: yes

Rutherford

AUBERGE DU SOLEIL

180 Rutherford Hill Road
Rutherford, CA 94573
(707) 963-1211
Reserve for Events: 6–12 months in advance
Reserve for Meetings: 1 week–2 months in advance

On a Napa hillside, near the Silverado Trail, rests the lovely Mediterranean-style Auberge du Soleil. This is an outstanding facility for an elegant party. The entrance is upstairs, through an exquisite garden courtyard complete with a tastefully designed fountain and shaded canopy of gray olive trees. The beautifully appointed, yet understated lobby is all in light pastels. A curved staircase leads down to the private banquet rooms. The smaller room is circular and is appropriately named The Black Room because it really is painted black. But don't worry—the black walls highlight the many French doors and windows overlooking the valley below and the upholstered chairs and couches in black, green and pink floral patterns contrast well with the dark walls. Wood ceilings and floors and a large stone fireplace make this a very comfortable room. The Black Room serves as a cocktail area, expanded dinner seating room or as a place for band and dancing. It's also ideal for small group gatherings and dinners. The adjacent banquet room, the White Room, is large and airy with white walls and furniture plus excellent views. The gravel Terrace, just outside these two rooms, has unparalleled views and, on warm days or evenings, can be arranged for outdoor dining with tables and white umbrellas. The Auberge sets the tone for a really upscale, California-style celebration.

CAPACITY: The Black Room, 50 standing or 30 seated; the White Room 76 seated; the Terrace 50.

FEES & DEPOSITS: A deposit is due 2 weeks from the booking date, with 50% of the estimated event total due 30 days prior to the event. The rental charge is $150–300. The total balance is due upon departure. Per person rates for in-house catering: buffets $25–55, luncheons $28–35 and dinners $48–55. Sales tax and a 20% gratuity are applied to the final bill.

CANCELLATION POLICY: If the space(s) can be rebooked, the initial deposit will be refunded.

AVAILABILITY: Every day, from 11am–4pm or 6pm–1am.

SERVICES/AMENITIES:

Restaurant Services: yes
Catering: provided, no BYO
Kitchen Facilities: n/a
Tables & Chairs: provided
Linens, Silver, etc.: provided
Restrooms: wca
Dance Floor: yes

Parking: valet
Overnight Accommodations: 48 guestrooms/suites
Telephone: pay phone
Outdoor Night Lighting: yes
Outdoor Cooking Facilities: no
Cleanup: provided
Meeting Equipment: CBA

RESTRICTIONS:

Alcohol: provided, corkage $15/bottle
Smoking: allowed
Music: on approval

Wheelchair Access: elevator
Insurance: not required

RANCHO CAYMUS INN

1140 Rutherford Road (Hwy 128)
Rutherford, CA 94573
(707) 963–1777 or (800) 845-1777
Reserve for Events: 3–6 months in advance

The Rancho Caymus Inn is a Spanish Mission–style inn, complete with big cacti, mosaics, red tile roof, stucco walls, arched windows, interior patios and abundant landscaping. You can hold your luncheon within the interior brick-paved courtyard, surrounded by wisteria-laden arbors or have your outdoor dinner or cocktail party here. The building encircles your guests—small tables with umbrellas, a large river rock fireplace and the sound of trickling water from a fountain add to the ambiance. For indoor parties, the Mont. St. John Room, adjacent to the patio, has a large wood bar, hardwood floors, handsome stone fireplace, piano and stained glass windows. And if you'd like your party to stay here, the Inn has a variety of lovely suites from which to choose.

CAPACITY: The garden patio can accommodate 60 guests; the Mont. St. John Room can hold up to 60 seated or 150 for a standing reception.

FEES & DEPOSITS: A refundable deposit of 50% of the rental fee is required to secure your date. The rental fee is $500. Per person rates for food service: modest hors d'oeuvres reception $9, a full buffet $20–30 and seated dinner $20–45. Sales tax and a 15% gratuity are additional.

CANCELLATION POLICY: With 4 weeks' notice, the deposit is refundable.

AVAILABILITY: Daily, from 10am to 10pm.

SERVICES/AMENITIES:

Restaurant Services: yes
Catering: provided, no BYO
Kitchen Facilities: n/a
Tables & Chairs: provided
Linens, Silver, etc.: provided
Restrooms: wca
Dance Floor: yes
Meeting Equipment: CBA

Parking: large lot
Overnight Accommodations: 26 suites
Telephone: house phone, local only
Outdoor Night Lighting: yes
Outdoor Cooking Facilities: no
Cleanup: provided
Other: event coordination services

RESTRICTIONS:

Alcohol: BWC provided, corkage $5–7.50/bottle
Smoking: allowed
Music: amplified until 10pm

Wheelchair Access: yes
Insurance: not required

Santa Rosa

CHATEAU DEBAUN WINERY

5007 Fulton Road
Santa Rosa, CA 95403
(707) 571-7500 John Burton
Reserve for Events: 3 months in advance
Reserve for Meetings: 3 months in advance

Imagine an impressive French chateau-style winery, surrounded by acres of vineyards and walnut trees. The Chateau's banquet room features brass chandeliers, French provincial furnishings, fireplace and a skylight in the vaulted, thirty-five foot ceiling. Outdoors, the spacious courtyard patio is framed by fragrant roses and native trees. This is a sizeable space, conducive to large gatherings. The vineyard and distinctive architecture make Chateau DeBaun an unusual setting in the Wine Country for business functions as well as private parties.

CAPACITY:

Area	Seated	Area	Seated
Harmony Hall (Banquet Room)	160	VIP Room	20
Concerto Courtyard	350	Symphony Hall (Tasting Room)	60
Medley Meadows	800		

MEETING ROOMS: All areas except the Tasting Room can be used during the day. The Tasting Room can be used for evening events.

FEES & DEPOSITS: A non-refundable facility fee in the amount of 25% of the estimated food, beverage and service total is required to secure your date. The remaining 75% is due 1 week prior to your function. A special midweek rate for non-profit organizations and service clubs, Monday–Thursday is $10/person. A minimum guest count of 60 is required. The facility fee is for a 5-hour function and includes all setup and cleanup, tables, chairs, linens, china, glassware, flatware and beverage service.

AVAILABILITY: Every day, except for major holidays. Individual areas (except Tasting Room) are available for events from 10am–1am. The entire facility is available for rental after 5pm.

SERVICES/AMENITIES:

Restaurant Services: no
Catering: select from preferred list
Kitchen Facilities: ample
Tables & Chairs: provided
Linens, Silver, etc.: provided
Restrooms: wca
Dance Floor: yes
Meeting Equipment: no

Parking: large lot and on private road
Overnight Accommodations: no
Telephone: pay phone
Outdoor Night Lighting: yes
Outdoor Cooking Facilities: BBQ
Cleanup: caterer and staff
Other: limo, carriage and tents CBA

RESTRICTIONS:

Alcohol: provided, WC only

Smoking: outside only

Music: amplified ok

Wheelchair Access: yes

Insurance: not required

Sonoma

BUENA VISTA WINERY

18000 Old Winery Road
Sonoma, CA 95476
(800) 926-1266
Reserve for Events: 3–12 months in advance
Reserve for Meetings: 3–12 months in advance

The Buena Vista Winery, founded in 1857 by Count Agoston Haraszthy, is generally acknowledged as the birthplace of premium wines in California. The Old Winery is a striking two-story stone building in a grotto of eucalyptus, redwoods and lush greenery. The main tasting room has exposed stone walls, very high ceilings and a second story gallery displaying local artwork. The extended bank of wine racks, the long bar and the historic displays give the room a friendly and convivial ambiance and a wood-burning stove warms chilly evenings. Outside is a large paved courtyard, dotted with huge, old wooden wine kegs. The dappled sunlight from the tall canopy of trees provides a comfortable and relaxing atmosphere for outdoor dining and events. A second vine-covered, stone building provides an impressive backdrop to the fountain courtyard.

CAPACITY: The winery requires a minimum of 50 guests. Indoor facilities can seat 100 guests. Outdoor spaces can accommodate up to 200 guests for a seated dinner or 400 for a standing reception.

FEES & DEPOSITS: A refundable security deposit is required to reserve a date. The deposit is returned within 2 weeks of the event. The rental fee is $17–30/person and is due one week prior to the event. The fee includes setup and cleanup, 2/3 bottle of wine/person, tables, chairs and staff.

CANCELLATION POLICY: With 90 days' notice, the deposit will be refunded less 20%.

AVAILABILITY: Every day, 6:30pm–10:30pm.

SERVICES/AMENITIES:

Restaurant Services: no

Catering: select from preferred list

Kitchen Facilities: n/a

Tables & Chairs: most provided

Linens, Silver, etc.: caterer

Restrooms: no wca

Parking: large lot

Overnight Accommodations: no

Telephone: pay phone

Outdoor Night Lighting: yes

Outdoor Cooking Facilities: no

Cleanup: provided

Dance Floor: yes, outdoor floor CBA

RESTRICTIONS:
Alcohol: provided, WC only
Smoking: outside only
Music: acoustic & amplified ok until 10pm

Meeting Equipment: podium

Wheelchair Access: yes
Insurance: not required

LAS CASTAÑAS

2246 Sobre Vista Road
Sonoma, CA 95476
(707) 996-5742
Reserve for Events: 2–6 months in advance
Reserve for Meetings: 1–2 months in advance

Up from the Valley of the Moon, down a private road flanked by oaks, bays and redwoods, you get the feeling that your destination will be very special. Once the Spreckels family's private estate, the forty acres of grounds and buildings are an arrestingly beautiful hybrid of casual, country charm with a touch of formal elegance. The outdoor spaces here are sensational—some of the best we've ever seen. A large concrete and flagstone patio meanders through and around the huge indigenous redwoods and is surrounded by rock-terraced lawns and lush flower beds. The grounds here are gorgeous. From the estate's greenhouses come flowers that line virtually every pathway. Stones that form the winding terrace walls that define gardens and sloping lawns have been unearthed from the surrounding vineyards. Las Castañas also has a tennis court and lovely swimming pool with brick patio—perfect for an afternoon reception. Indoor celebrations are held in the main Tudor-style house. Inside, the large dining room has a brick fireplace, a high cathedral ceiling framed with wood beams, handsome wood floors adorned with orientals and large windows overlooking the Valley's vineyards and orchards. An adjacent room, jutting out from the main building, is surrounded by windows with terrific views. This site is attractive, private, spacious and flexible. All in all, Las Castañas is a wonderful addition to Sonoma Valley.

CAPACITY:

Area	Seated	Standing	Area	Seated	Standing
Main Room	75	100	Redwood Terraces	300	500
Sun Room	40	75	Pool & Patio	75	150

FEES & DEPOSITS: The base rental fee for use is $1,500, which includes 10 guests for 1 overnight stay, use of the pool house, main house, guest cottage, tables and chairs with over 100 guests. The non-refundable guest fee, which is in addition to the base fee, is $25/guest for up to 100 guests and $15/guest for over 100 guests. Valet parking, security guards and setup/breakdown are additional. Half of the base rental and guest fee is required as a non-refundable deposit and is due when you book your date. A $1,000 refundable damage/security deposit is required 7 days before the function. The balance of the fees is due 30 days prior to the event. A purchase of estate Chardonnay, 1/2 bottle/guest, is requested.

AVAILABILITY: Year-round, daily from 9am–9pm.

SERVICES/AMENITIES:

Restaurant Services: no

Catering: BYO or CBA

Kitchen Facilities: ample

Tables & Chairs: provided

Linens, Silver, etc.: BYO or CBA

Restrooms: wca

Meeting Equipment: no

Other: event coordination CBA

Parking: large lot

Overnight Accommodations: 7 guestrooms

Telephone: use with approval

Outdoor Night Lighting: yes

Outdoor Cooking Facilities: CBA

Cleanup: renter or caterer

Dance Floor: outdoor terrace

RESTRICTIONS:

Alcohol: estate wine or corkage $5/bottle

Smoking: designated areas only

Music: amplified within reason

Wheelchair Access: limited

Insurance: certificate required

Other: no hard alcohol

SEARS POINT RACEWAY

Highways 37 & 121
Sonoma, CA 95476
(707) 938-8448
Reserve for Events: 3–6 months in advance
Reserve for Meetings: 1–2 months in advance

A business meeting that's fun? exciting? challenging? You bet! Sears Point Raceway offers, hands down, one of the most thrilling corporate meeting and special event environments we've seen. You will scream with delight behind the wheel of a high-performance race car while practicing teamwork and leadership skills. You can drive with a professional instructor through a twisting, twelve-turn, two and a half mile road course. Enjoy a full throttle hundred mile-per-hour spin around the track as part of your corporate event, and learn the dynamics of car control from professionals. The on-site racing school also provides educational and motivational driving experiences in state-of-the-art race cars or new BMW sedans. Combined with a sales meeting, conference or special event, Sears Point Raceway can become part of your company's adventurous incentive program. Hold on to your seatbelt—Sears Point's unique corporate day programs are designed to get you up to speed!

CAPACITY: The basic corporate day program can handle up to 100 guests. Special arrangements can be made for larger groups. Minimum group size is 15 guests.

MEETING ROOMS: Track-side tents can be set up for corporate meetings and seminars.

FEES & DEPOSITS: Four different corporate day programs, ranging from hot laps around the track to head-to-head driving competitions, cost $55–80/person. The Skip Barber Driving School also offers formula and BMW racing; rates will vary based on the number of guests and the amount of time spent on the track. Programs can be customized around a company's particular needs. A deposit of 25% of the anticipated food and beverage total is required to hold your date. The balance is due 15 days in advance. Food service is provided. Prices start at $10.50/person for lunch to $21/person for dinner. Add $5/person for a seated meal. Coffee and beverages can be provided for meetings. Tax and service charges are additional.

CANCELLATION POLICY: With 30 days' notice, your deposit will be refunded, less an administrative fee.

AVAILABILITY: Year-round. Corporate programs run Monday–Friday, 7am–7pm. Spectator and race-related events are available on weekends.

SERVICES/AMENITIES:

Restaurant Services: no
Catering: provided, no BYO
Kitchen Facilities: n/a
Tables & Chairs: provided
Linens, Silver, etc.: provided
Restrooms: wca
Dance Floor: CBA
Other: event coordination

Parking: large lots
Overnight Accommodations: no
Telephone: pay phone
Outdoor Night Lighting: CBA
Outdoor Cooking Facilities: BBQs
Cleanup: provided
Meeting Equipment: CBA

RESTRICTIONS:

Alcohol: provided, no BYO
Smoking: outside only
Music: amplified ok

Wheelchair Access: limited
Insurance: certificate required

SONOMA MISSION INN & SPA

Highway 12 and Boyes Boulevard
Sonoma, CA 95476
(707) 938-9000
Reserve for Events: 6 months in advance
Reserve for Meetings: 6 months in advance

Amidst eight acres of eucalyptus trees, manicured lawns and colorful gardens, the Sonoma Mission Inn & Spa is an ideal setting for business events and special celebrations. The Inn offers a variety of meeting rooms, most with high ceilings, muted colors and natural sunlight. The largest of these rooms, the Sonoma Valley Room has an inviting fireplace for cold winter evenings and French doors that open onto terraces during warm weather. Banquet menus range from simple hors d'oeuvres to elegant, seated dinners and theme buffets. To help with your event, the Inn provides a professional, efficient and courteous staff. They will oversee all aspects of the event, from initial setup to overnight accommodations for your guests. With the Spa's full range of services helping your guests to relax and feel their best, it's no wonder that this spot is so popular.

CAPACITY, FEES & DEPOSITS: The rental fee is used as a refundable deposit to reserve a date. Another non-refundable deposit of half the estimated total is payable 90 days prior to your function. Fees vary:

Room	Standing	Seated	Fees
Sonoma Valley Room	275	135–150	from $750
Harvest/Carneros Suites	50	24	from $525
(with guestroom)	25	10	—
Kenwood Room	—	32	from $250

Food service is provided. Meals start at $30/person with bar service and bartender additional. Tax and a 20% gratuity are applied to the final bill, due the day of the event.

CANCELLATION POLICY: With 180 days' notice, your deposit will be refunded in full.

AVAILABILITY: Any day, anytime.

SERVICES/AMENITIES:

Restaurant Services: yes

Catering: provided, no BYO

Kitchen Facilities: n/a

Tables & Chairs: provided

Linens, Silver, etc.: provided

Restrooms: wca

Dance Floor: yes

Meeting Equipment: full range

Parking: large lot, complimentary valet

Overnight Accommodations: 170 guestrooms

Telephone: pay phone

Outdoor Night Lighting: yes

Outdoor Cooking Facilities: yes

Cleanup: provided

Other: event coordination

RESTRICTIONS:

Alcohol: provided, corkage $8.50/bottle

Smoking: restricted

Music: amplified until 11pm

Wheelchair Access: yes

Insurance: not required

VIANSA WINERY

25200 Arnold Dr. (Highway 121)
Sonoma, CA 95476
(707) 935-4725 or (707) 935-4700
Reserve for Events: 1–6 months in advance
Reserve for Meetings: 1–2 months in advance

Viansa is one of the best and most professionally designed new facilities we've seen in a while. The owner has taken great care to develop a site that is both visually appealing and workable for events. Located on a knoll, overlooking vineyards and the northernmost part of San Francisco Bay, this Tuscan-style winery has a remarkably warm ambiance. With terra-cotta-colored walls, dark green shutters and tile roofs, it makes you feel comfortable, as though you're in Northern Italy. It's the details, such as decorative ironwork, intricate paintings on wine tanks, murals, herringbone brick floors and exceptional lighting, that make Viansa special. The interior tasting room, which includes a state-of-the-art area for food setup, is perfect for large parties. For smaller receptions, there is a wine cellar with large oak barrels and arched ceilings and a small dining room with lovely, patterned concrete floors. Outside is a circular courtyard surrounding a small, water-filled cistern. Terra cotta pots with flowers abound. The "loggia" adjacent to the courtyard has French doors, a working fireplace and dark green cafe tables and chairs which match the shutters—a fine spot to chat with guests while sampling Viansa wines. There's even a hillside garden where Viansa grows its own vegetables, ensuring that everything served here is absolutely fresh. The professional staff can handle most aspects of an event, from catering to flowers. We can't say enough about Viansa. We're very impressed by this relative newcomer and urge you to take a look for yourself.

CAPACITY: Maximum indoor seated capacity 112 guests; for indoor standing receptions, using both the tasting room and wine cellar, 275 guests.

MEETING ROOMS: The Loggia can hold 5–20 guests, the Tuscan Room 3–12 and the Barrel Aging Cellar 40–50 seated guests.

FEES & DEPOSITS: A non-refundable 10% deposit is due when the contract is submitted. 2 days prior to the event, half the remaining balance is payable along with a $500 security deposit. Final payment is due 2 days prior to the event. Food and wine service is provided; wine and hors d'oeuvres receptions can be arranged. Formal luncheons start at $45/person. Four-course dinners start at $64/person and include a before-dinner reception with hors d'oeuvres and wine, wine with each dinner course, custom-printed menus, glasses, table settings and flowers. Tax and a 7.5% gratuity are additional. For meetings, the room rental rate varies, so call for rates.

CANCELLATION POLICY: If you cancel less than 2 weeks prior to your event, only the $500 security deposit will be refunded.

AVAILABILITY: Special events, every day after 5:30pm. Business functions can be accommodated 10am–5pm, schedule permitting.

SERVICES/AMENITIES:

Restaurant Services: no
Catering: provided, no BYO
Kitchen Facilities: professional
Tables & Chairs: provided
Linens, Silver, etc.: provided
Restrooms: wca
Meeting Equipment: CBA

Parking: ample
Overnight Accommodations: no
Outdoor Night Lighting: yes
Outdoor Cooking Facilities: no
Cleanup: provided
Telephone: pay phone
Dance Floor: yes

RESTRICTIONS:

Alcohol: wine provided, no BYO
Smoking: outside only
Music: amplified requires approval

Wheelchair Access: yes
Insurance: not required

WESTERBEKE RANCH
Conference Center

2300 Grove
Sonoma, CA 95476
(707) 996-7546 Wendy Westerbeke
Reserve for Events: 3–12 months in advance
Reserve for Meetings: 3–12 months in advance

A family home for four generations, Westerbeke Ranch offers a level of hospitality, warmth and charm seldom experienced in a conference center. The grounds are beautiful—a hundred acres in the heart of Sonoma Valley, covered with ancient oaks, dried grasses, flowers and lawns. As you stroll leisurely along the earthen and brick paths that meander throughout the property, you can feel your body shift into low gear—there is no need to hurry here. Meetings are held everywhere, in quite unorthodox settings. Small groups gather informally in the dappled shade of overhanging trees or on the tile patio next to the dining room. A favorite spot is inside an enormous redwood wine vat, whose cathedral-like carpeted interior smells like wine when it rains. Even the most conventional meeting room has a fireplace and view of the pool and gardens. The soul of Westerbeke is the old adobe dining room: when the ranch bell rings, guests know they're in for something special. Delicious smells of garlic, herbs and homemade bread permeate the air. In the evening, long redwood tables are lit by candles and festooned with fresh garden flowers. A welcoming fire glows in the fieldstone hearth, and colorful Mexican serapes, pottery and Haitian metalwork decorate the walls. The food has been described as "exquisite," prepared by a gifted Cordon Bleu-trained chef, using only the freshest local ingredients. And at the end of the day, guests walk back to their rustic, cozy cabins, where they sleep the sleep of those well fed in body and spirit.

CAPACITY: The ranch can accommodate 50 guests overnight, 100 guests for day use.

MEETING ROOMS: There are 2 meeting rooms that can accommodate up to 80 guests, and many outdoor meeting areas. The Dining Room can also be used as a meeting space.

FEES & DEPOSITS: Half the anticipated total is required as a deposit within 30 days of confirming your reservation. The balance is due on arrival. Rates are $80–90/person and include 3 meals a day, overnight accommodations and use of the meeting rooms and all other ranch facilities. There is a 10% discount with an overnight mid-week stay.

CANCELLATION POLICY: The deposit is non-refundable unless the date(s) can be rebooked with another group of the same size.

AVAILABILITY: Weekends (Friday dinner–Sunday lunch), and weekdays (Sunday dinner–Friday lunch). Year-round, anytime.

SERVICES/AMENITIES:

Restaurant Services: no
Catering: provided
Kitchen Facilities: n/a
Tables & Chairs: provided

Parking: lot
Overnight Accommodations: 6 cabins (50 guests), additional guests CBA
Telephone: pay phone

Linens, Silver, etc.: provided
Restrooms: wca
Dance Floor: yes
Other: sauna, hot tub, aerobics, dance & yoga classes

Outdoor Night Lighting: yes
Outdoor Cooking Facilities: yes
Cleanup: provided
Meeting Equipment: CBA

RESTRICTIONS:
Alcohol: provided, corkage $6/bottle
Smoking: outside only
Music: amplified ok until 10:30pm

Wheelchair Access: limited (1 cabin, dining and meeting areas)
Insurance: not required

St. Helena

CHARLES KRUG WINERY

2800 Main Street
St. Helena, CA 94574
(707) 963-5057
Reserve for Events: 3–6 months in advance
Reserve for Meetings: 1–3 months in advance

Charles Krug, the oldest winery in the Napa Valley, is just two miles north of St. Helena on Highway 29. It occupies a prime location on the valley floor, surrounded by vineyards. The winery has an expansive two-acre lawn which can easily accommodate more than 1,500 guests for an outdoor corporate picnic or large party. The lawn spreads south from the Carriage House and is generously dotted by huge, hundred-year-old oaks and conifers. On the grounds are a permanent stage, with tall posts set for lighting and sound equipment and a large outdoor barbecue sheltered by a post and beam trellis structure. For more intimate gatherings indoors, the historic Carriage House, built in 1881, offers a wonderful change of pace. This California historical landmark is a remarkable structure with arched windows and doors, multiple roof lines and stone and concrete architectural elements. Inside, wine barrels and a wine library provide an interesting backdrop for a any type of special event. Candlelit Christmas or New Year's Eve celebrations in the Carriage House are particularly enchanting.

CAPACITY: Carriage House lawn, 1,500+ guests. Carriage House, 120 seated or 200 for a reception.

FEES & DEPOSITS: A deposit of 25% of the total rental fee is required to secure your date; the balance is due 2 weeks prior to the function. The rental fee includes setup, teardown, wine service, use of tables and chairs, glasses and flowers. The fee for up to 50 guests is $17/person, 51–100 guests $16/person, 101–200 guests $15/person, 201–300 guests $13.50/person. Special rates are available for larger groups. Note that wine must be purchased from Charles Krug and is available at 33% off retail cost with a minimum purchase of 2 cases for groups of 50 or less.

CANCELLATION POLICY: With 60 days' notice, the deposit is refunded in full.

AVAILABILITY: Carriage House lawn, from May–October 9am–10pm. The Carriage House is available year-round, 9am–1am.

SERVICES/AMENITIES:

Restaurant Services: no
Catering: select from preferred list
Kitchen Facilities: minimal
Tables & Chairs: some provided
Linens, Silver, etc.: BYO
Restrooms: wca
Dance Floor: no, CBA

Parking: large parking lot
Overnight Accommodations: no
Telephone: pay phone
Outdoor Night Lighting: yes
Outdoor Cooking Facilities: BBQ
Cleanup: caterer or renter
Meeting Equipment: CBA

RESTRICTIONS:

Alcohol: Charles Krug wine only; C&B permitted
Smoking: outside only
Insurance: certificate required

Wheelchair Access: yes
Music: indoors until midnight, outdoors until 9:30pm

MEADOWOOD RESORT

900 Meadowood Lane
St. Helena, CA 94574
(707) 963-3646
Reserve for Events: 12 months in advance
Reserve for Meetings: 12 months in advance

Driving into the Meadowood Resort is indeed a pleasure. You follow a narrow tree-shaded lane, flanked by immaculately tended vineyards and forested hillsides to the sophisticated resort complex, complete with wine school, executive conference center and first-rate recreational facilities. The superbly designed buildings are reminiscent of New England during the early 1900s with white balconies, gabled roofs and gray clapboard siding. All is secluded on two hundred and fifty acres of densely wooded Napa Valley landscape. The sprawling, multi-tiered Clubhouse accommodates private parties. It's set high, overlooking lush, green fairways and manicured lawns. The Vintner and Woodside Rooms are available for indoor meetings, conferences and special events. The Vintner Room is fabulous, with high ceilings and stone fireplace, decks with umbrella-shaded tables and outstanding views. The nearby lawn slopes down to steps leading to a dry creek bed planted with willows, leading to a footbridge which crosses over to golf fairways. For outdoor celebrations, Meadowood arranges tables and tents on the lawns next to the Vintner Room. There is something very special about this facility. It provides top flight cuisine prepared by French chefs, deluxe accommodations and an environment to match. Meadowood ranks high on our list for special parties and executive conferences.

CAPACITY:

Room	Standing	Seated	w/Outdoors	Classroom Style
Vintner	175	110	300	80
Madrone	35	24	40	32
Wine Library	–	20	–	20
Courthouse	–	–	–	30
Woodside	80	60	80	60

FEES & DEPOSITS: For parties, special events and 1-day meetings, the setup and use fee ranges from $200–600. To hold your date, a $500 deposit is due with a finalized contract. For conferences, including overnight stays, the deposit (due with your finalized contract) includes the first night's room rate and tax on all overnight guestrooms.

CANCELLATION POLICY: If you cancel an event or 1-day meeting within 6 months of your date, and the date can be rebooked, 50% of your deposit will be refunded. If conference space or guestrooms are cancelled with less than 90 days' notice, the deposit is forfeited. Call for additional details.

AVAILABILITY: Year-round, every day.

SERVICES/AMENITIES:

Restaurant Services: yes
Catering: provided, no BYO
Kitchen Facilities: n/a
Tables & Chairs: provided
Overnight Accommodations: 82 guestrooms plus suites
Outdoor Cooking Facilities: CBA
Cleanup: provided
Other: event planning services, spa & fitness center

Linens, Silver, etc.: provided
Restrooms: wca
Dance Floor: Vintner yes, Woodside CBA
Parking: multiple lots, no valet
Meeting Equipment: yes
Outdoor Night Lighting: CBA
Telephone: pay phones

RESTRICTIONS:

Alcohol: provided, corkage fee if BYO
Smoking: allowed
Music: amplified indoors only

Wheelchair Access: yes
Insurance: not required

Prices and policies do change. Call each facility and confirm everything you read in Perfect Places.

MERRYVALE VINEYARDS

1000 Main Street
St. Helena, CA 94574
(800) 326-6069   Director of Special Events
Reserve for events: 1–12 months in advance
Reserve for meetings: 1–12 months in advance

For an experience that's really memorable, have your company's special event in Merryvale's Cask Room. It features antique casks made in San Francisco in the late 1800s. The historic casks lining the walls hold up to 2,000 gallons, and the ones framing the steps as you enter hold an astonishing 16,000 gallons. These remarkable redwood wine barrels must be at least sixteen feet in diameter! Candle-lighted dinners and celebrations are especially lovely in here. Behind the winery is the renovated "schoolhouse," an appealing Victorian-looking building with an old world aura. It's also a great spot for cocktail receptions, with a wide wisteria-framed veranda painted in crisp white.

CAPACITY: Indoor and outdoor areas hold up to 160 guests, maximum.

FEES & DEPOSITS: A non-refundable deposit of 20% of the estimated total winery fees and signed contract are due within 1 month of making a reservation. Winery fees include: rental, wine (3/4 bottle wine/person for dinner), tables, chairs, glassware, wine service staff and candelabras. Catering can be provided, approximately $25–35/person for dinner. Tax and gratuity are additional. The balance is due the day of the event.

AVAILABILITY: Year-round, every day until midnight, except for Christmas and Thanksgiving.

SERVICES/AMENITIES:

Restaurant Services: no
Catering: CBA or BYO with approval
Kitchen Facilities: ample
Tables & Chairs: provided
Linens, Silver, etc.: some provided
Restrooms: wca
Dance Floor: yes

Parking: large lot
Overnight Accommodations: no
Telephone: business phone
Outdoor Night Lighting: yes
Outdoor Cooking Facilities: no
Cleanup: Merryvale and caterer
Meeting Equipment: some available

RESTRICTIONS:

Alcohol: provided, no BYO, no hard alcohol or beer
Smoking: outside only
Music: amplified ok

Wheelchair Access: yes
Insurance: not required

V. SATTUI WINERY

White Lane at Highway 29
St. Helena, CA 94574
(707) 963-1664
Reserve for Events: 1–12 months in advance
Reserve for Meetings: 1 week–12 months in advance

V. Sattui Winery, located in the heart of Napa Valley, is a small, family winery founded in 1885. It occupies a massive stone building reminiscent of California's early wineries and is surrounded by lush lawns, giant oak trees and 35 acres of vineyards. The surrounding scenery is really lovely, with extensive vineyards and vistas of the Napa Valley hills beyond. Guests can dine in a castle-like cellar lined with oak barrels and filled with the pungent aromas of aging wines. Through a stone archway are four caves where wines are aged behind heavy wrought iron gates. A second cellar provides a more intimate setting for smaller gatherings. Hand-hewn stone walls, heavy ceiling timbers and wine barrels create an old-world atmosphere suitable for elaborate formal buffets. Outdoor luncheons and group picnics can also be arranged on V. Sattui's two acres of tree-shaded picnic grounds.

CAPACITY: The large cellar can hold 200 seated guests, the small cellar, 50 guests; 250 total. The outside lawn and terraces can accommodate up to 350.

FEES & DEPOSITS: A $200 deposit is required to secure your date. The rental fee is based on guest count and type of event. Rental fees plus a final guest count are due 1 week prior to the event. All events are coordinated by Rebecca Kingsley Associates, for which there is a consulting fee.

CANCELLATION POLICY: The deposit is refundable only if the date is rebooked.

AVAILABILITY: Every day, 6pm–midnight.

SERVICES/AMENITIES:

Restaurant Services: no
Catering: select from preferred list
Kitchen Facilities: minimal
Tables & Chairs: provided up to 200 guests
Linens, Silver, etc.: caterer
Restrooms: wca
Dance Floor: yes

Parking: large lot
Overnight Accommodations: no
Telephone: pay phone
Outdoor Night Lighting: yes
Outdoor Cooking Facilities: BBQ
Cleanup: provided
Meeting Equipment: CBA

RESTRICTIONS:

Alcohol: V. Sattui wine only,
champagne corkage $5/bottle
Music: amplified ok
Smoking: outside only

Wheelchair Access: ramp and lift
Insurance: certificate required
Other: no hard liquor

Clearlake

WINDFLOWER ISLAND

Clearlake, CA 95422
(707) 542-1235   ESP Event Planners
Reserve for Events: 90 days in advance
Reserve for Meetings: 90 days in advance

Windflower Island is the place for those who want something extraordinary—a totally private tropical garden setting surrounded by water. Set at the base of Clearlake's twin volcanoes, this two and a half acre island paradise is often likened to Maui yet is only a two and a half hour drive from San Francisco. A leisurely boat ride transports you in minutes to this secluded island estate. What awaits you are manicured lawns with sweeping lake views of the Clearlake Basin, an open-air gazebo, flagstone patios and lush landscaping. Windflower Island sets the stage for fun-filled celebrations, company picnics or retreats. The island features a beach for sun bathing and swimming, boat docks and outdoor barbecues areas. If guests are interested in active water sports, jet skiing, windsurfing and waterskiing are available nearby. More leisurely excursions include canoeing, fishing and lake cruises. Arrangements can also be made for golf and tennis. One of the more unique and lovely locations we've encountered, Windflower Island is definitely worth the journey.

CAPACITY: The island can accommodate 60 guests.

FEES, DEPOSITS & CANCELLATION POLICY: Call for current pricing, deposit requirements and cancellation policies.

AVAILABILITY: Daily, March 1 through November 15 from 8am to sunset.

SERVICES/AMENITIES:

Restaurant Services: no
Catering: provided
Kitchen Facilities: n/a
Tables & Chairs: provided
Linens, Silver, etc.: provided
Restrooms: no wca
Dance Floor: no
Other: transportation to island provided, sound system available, event coordination

Parking: several lots
Overnight Accommodations: at Konocti Harbor Resort
Telephone: emergency only
Outdoor Night Lighting: access only
Outdoor Cooking Facilities: no
Cleanup: provided
Meeting Equipment: CBA

RESTRICTIONS:

Alcohol: BYO
Smoking: outside only
Music: amplified ok

Wheelchair Access: no
Insurance: liability required
Other: children must be supervised, limited electrical outlets, minors must wear life vests on boats

Ben Lomond

HIGHLANDS HOUSE AND PARK

8500 Highway 9
Ben Lomond, CA 95005
(408) 425-2696 Parks Department
Reserve for Events: 2–12 months in advance
Reserve for Meetings: 2–52 weeks in advance

The Highlands House is a former private residence built in the 1940s. Set in a public park, surrounded by large redwoods, the two-story white wood house is available for private parties and business functions. The house sits quite a way below Highway 9, ensuring quiet and a sense of privacy. The setting is lovely with expansive lawns, huge magnolia and pine trees, well-maintained landscaping and nearby pool. Framed by several tall palms, the Highland House is an attractive and pleasant spot for either social or business gatherings.

CAPACITY: The facility can accommodate 200.

FEES & DEPOSITS: Fees and deposits are required when reservations are made. For bookings made less than 45 days in advance, a $50 surcharge applies. The rental fee for county residents is about $550, non-county applicants, about $700. The cleaning deposit is $200 with alcohol use, $100 without. These fees are for an 8-hour block. Weekday business functions run about $70/hour for the entire house and outdoor lawn areas.

CANCELLATION POLICY: With 30 days' notice, all fees will be returned less a $100 cancellation charge. With less notice, only the cleaning deposit will be returned.

AVAILABILITY: Year-round. Monday–Thursday, 8am–10pm, Friday–Saturday, 10am–12am, Sunday, 10am–10pm.

SERVICES/AMENITIES:

Restaurant Services: no
Catering: BYO
Kitchen Facilities: ample
Tables & Chairs: some provided
Linens, Silver, etc.: BYO
Restrooms: wca
Dance Floor: yes
Meeting Equipment: no

Parking: large lot, fee on summer weekends
Overnight Accommodations: no
Telephone: pay phone
Outdoor Night Lighting: no
Outdoor Cooking Facilities: BYO BBQ
Cleanup: renter's responsibility
Other: spinet available

RESTRICTIONS:
Alcohol: BYO, WBC only
Smoking: outside only
Music: amplified to 75 decibels

Wheelchair Access: yes
Insurance: not required

Capitola

THE INN AT DEPOT HILL

250 Monterey Avenue
Capitola-by-the-Sea, California 95010
(408) 462-3376
Reserve for Events: 1–3 months in advance
Reserve for Meetings: 1–3 months in advance

Located in the beachside resort of Capitola, this new bed and breakfast has been designed with considerable attention to detail. Once a grand railroad depot in 1901, the Inn retains the large exterior columns, and inside, the original sixteen-foot ceilings and round lobby (now dining room) with the old ticket windows. The owners have had lots of fun creating an unusual interior environment for their guests. The dining room has a trompe l'oeil scene that creates the illusion of a train dining car, complete with a vista of the Big Sur coast out the window. As though you were taking a railroad journey, all of the Inn's eight suites are designed after different parts of the world such as Portofino or Paris. Light pastels and clean lines make the interior spaces very appealing. Outdoors, in the back, there's a lovely garden courtyard, with lush planting, gazebo and fishpond. The garden has been nicely put together— a great place to mingle or sit under umbrella-shaded tables and chat with guests. For receptions, small business gatherings or events, this is a surprise destination.

CAPACITY: The Depot can accommodate 16 guests indoors or up to 75 outdoors.

FEES & DEPOSITS: For business functions, the entire Inn can be reserved. The rental fee is $1,600/day including an overnight stay, breakfast, and coffee service during the day. A catered lunch can be arranged for social events noon–4pm, starting at $200 per 4–hour period. All fees are due when reservations are confirmed.

CANCELLATION POLICY: For business functions, a minimum 30 days' notice is required for a refund. If rooms can be rebooked, part or all will be returned. For social gatherings, 1 week's notice is required.

AVAILABILITY: Year-round, every day.

SERVICES/AMENITIES:
Restaurant Services: no
Catering: provided or BYO

Overnight Accommodations: 8 guestrooms
Telephone: guest phones

Kitchen Facilities: setup only
Tables & Chairs: CBA or BYO
Linens, Silver, etc.: CBA or BYO
Restrooms: wca
Dance Floor: CBA
Meeting Equipment: CBA or BYO

RESTRICTIONS:
Alcohol: CBA or BYO
Smoking: outside only
Music: no amplified

Outdoor Night Lighting: yes
Outdoor Cooking Facilities: no
Cleanup: CBA or renter
Parking: large lot across street, on street & on site

Wheelchair Access: yes
Insurance: not required

Felton

ROARING CAMP

Graham Hill Road & Roaring Camp Road
Felton, CA 95018
(408) 335-4484
Reserve for Events: 1–6 months in advance

Deep in the heart of the Santa Cruz Mountains is one of America's last steam-powered, daily-operated passenger railroads. The Roaring Camp and Big Trees Railroad still operates this narrow gauge steam train through forests of giant redwoods and over very steep grades and switchbacks to Bear Mountain. Your party group can board with other passengers or you can arrange an exclusive rental for your special event. The depot is located in the self-contained tiny crossroads "town" of Roaring Camp which is approached by foot from the main parking lot. The walk into "town" features the world's shortest covered bridge and a large, lovely pond. The train ride into the mountains is great fun for party-goers of all ages. Chuckwagon barbecues can be arranged for your party, too. Unusual celebrations could be planned to coincide with Roaring Camp's famous moonlight steam train parties which include train excursion, chuckwagon barbecue and square dancing. Moonlight parties are scheduled on certain moonlit Saturday nights between 7pm–11pm, June–October. This is a terrific getaway for company picnics and business-related entertainment.

CAPACITY: For BBQ's, the outdoor facilities can hold up to 2,000 guests; for indoor parties, the General Store Annex can hold 125 standing and 85 seated guests; the train up to 200 guests.

FEES & DEPOSITS: A deposit of 25% of the total estimated cost is due when reservations are made; the remaining 75% is due in installments of 25% each, up to 2 weeks prior to the event. For a group rate you need 25 guests minimum, and that includes a combination of BBQ and train ride. The total cost runs up to $23/person. A guaranteed headcount is due 7 days prior to your party.

CANCELLATION POLICY: The policy varies depending on the size of group and type of function—

call for details.

AVAILABILITY: Open daily, from dawn to dusk. In the summer, there are moonlight excursions, so call to get more details.

SERVICES/AMENITIES:

Restaurant Services: no
Catering: provided, no BYO
Kitchen Facilities: n/a
Tables & Chairs: provided
Linens, Silver, etc.: provided
Restrooms: wca
Dance Floor: yes
Meeting Equipment: microphone

Parking: large lots
Overnight Accommodations: no
Telephone: pay phones
Outdoor Night Lighting: yes
Outdoor Cooking Facilities: BBQ
Cleanup: provided
Other: square dancing w/caller, full event services

RESTRICTIONS:

Alcohol: BYO
Smoking: allowed
Music: amplified with restrictions

Wheelchair Access: CBA
Insurance: not required

Santa Cruz

CHAMINADE

1 Chaminade Lane
Santa Cruz, CA 95065
(408) 475-5600 or **475-5676** Catering Manager
Reserve for Events: 1–6 months in advance
Reserve for Meetings: 1 day–2 years in advance

Chaminade is primarily an exclusive conference center retreat set high on a mountain bluff overlooking Monterey Bay. Winding your way up from Highway 1, the final approach to the center is private and woodsy. The original Mission-style buildings, constructed in the 1930s as a boys' school, have been expanded and transformed into a well-designed complex that includes complete recreation facilities as well as meeting rooms and overnight guestrooms. The new structures at Chaminade have the red tile roofs, delicate arches and stucco exteriors that characterize the old school buildings. Luckily, the center is available for more than just conference retreats. For special events, there are decks, balconies, patios and expansive lawn areas for parties that take advantage of views and warm weather. Many of Chaminade's interior rooms, including a prefunction area, are also available, so ask to see them when you visit this facility. Chaminade, with its careful attention to service, culinary excellence and comfort, is a luxurious and private setting for a sophisticated celebration or business function.

CAPACITY: Chaminade can accommodate up to 200 guests; Sports Lawn up to 300.

FEES & DEPOSITS: A non-refundable deposit of half the estimated total is due when you make your reservations. Reception room fees are $1/person with no dance floor and $3/person with a dance floor. Both seated and buffet food service are provided. Luncheons run $15–25/person and dinners $23–45/person. These figures are approximate and include tax and gratuity. The remaining 50% balance is payable by the day of your event.

AVAILABILITY: Any day, morning through evening. Luncheons until 4:30pm; dinners 6:30pm–1am.

SERVICES/AMENITIES:

Restaurant Services: yes

Catering: provided, no BYO

Kitchen Facilities: n/a

Tables & Chairs: provided

Linens, Silver, etc.: provided

Restrooms: wca

Dance Floor: charge for setup

Parking: several lots

Overnight Accommodations: 152 guestrooms

Telephone: pay phone

Outdoor Night Lighting: yes

Outdoor Cooking Facilities: BBQ

Cleanup: provided

Meeting Equipment: full range

RESTRICTIONS:

Alcohol: provided, no BYO

Smoking: allowed

Music: amplified restricted in some areas

Wheelchair Access: yes

Insurance: not required

HOLLINS HOUSE

20 Clubhouse Road
Santa Cruz, California 95060
(408) 459-9177 Margy Seifert
Reserve for Events: 6–12 months in advance
Reserve for Meetings: 2 weeks in advance

The Hollins House, built in 1929 by championship golfer Marion Hollins, is located in the Pasatiempo Golf Course Complex in the Santa Cruz Mountains, not far from Highway 17. Approached through acres of green fairways, the house is situated atop a knoll and has impressive views of Monterey Bay. You can reserve either the entire facility or just the Hollins Room and patio. The main dining room is very long, with high ceilings, big mirrors and picture windows with views of the garden and ocean beyond. There's also a fireplace and hardwood parquet dance floor. The Tap Room is a more informal space, with a long wood bar, fireplace and windows overlooking garden and ocean. The adjacent garden is narrow with a lawn bordered by profusely blooming impaties. A medium-sized patio surrounded by wisteria and situated next to the Hollins Room is a picturesque place for an outdoor party. The Hollins Room is small, with a big mirror over the fireplace, chandelier, rounded bay windows with bench seat and a vista of the Pacific Ocean framed by nearby oak trees. The house staff aim to please and will assist you with all of your event arrangements, from flowers to specialized menus. And for business functions, play golf nearby and then have dinner or a barbecue after the eighteenth hole.

CAPACITY: The entire facility can accommodate up to 250 guests maximum in the summer and fall, 175 guests during cooler months. The Hollins Room and patio combined can accommodate 45 guests.

FEES & DEPOSITS: When reservations are made, a non-refundable deposit of $7 per person, based on an anticipated number of guests, is required. The rental fee for the entire Hollins House is $5 per person. For the Hollins Room and patio it's only $1.50 per person. Per person rates: hors d'oeuvres/ buffets are approximately $20 and seated meals vary from $13–21. These fees do not include sales tax or 15% service charge. You may customize your menu with help from the chef and/or event coordinator. The total balance is due in full by the end of your event.

AVAILABILITY: The entire Hollins House: Monday–Saturday 11am–4pm or Sundays 4pm–9pm. The Hollins Room and patio: 6pm–midnight Saturdays or 10am–2pm Sundays. For weekday functions, the Hollins Room and Patio are available Wednesday–Friday, 9am–3:30pm for business breakfasts or luncheons, 6pm–midnight for dinners.

SERVICES/AMENITIES:

Restaurant Services: yes
Catering: provided, no BYO
Kitchen Facilities: n/a
Tables & Chairs: provided
Linens, Silver, etc.: provided
Restrooms: wca
Dance Floor: yes

Parking: large lots
Overnight Accommodations: no
Telephone: pay phone
Outdoor Night Lighting: yes
Outdoor Cooking Facilities: BBQ CBA
Cleanup: provided
Meeting Equipment: no

RESTRICTIONS:

Alcohol: provided, corkage fee $70/case
Smoking: allowed
Music: amplified ok if entire facility rented

Wheelchair Access: ramp
Insurance: not required

Carmel

HIGHLANDS INN

Highway 1
Carmel, CA 93921
(408) 624-3801
Reserve for Events: 1 week or more in advance
Reserve for Meetings: 1 week or more in advance

Built in 1916 in the Carmel Highlands just south of Carmel, the Highlands Inn is one of the most sought-after locations in California. Noted for its breathtaking views and extraordinary cliffside setting, the Inn provides an idyllic environment for business meetings, conferences or special events. After its multi-million dollar, award-winning renovation, Highlands Inn is more stunning than ever. Commanding one of the world's most spectacular vistas, with exploding waves crashing two hundred feet below, the Inn offers a variety of first class facilities for special affairs. Several meeting rooms, offer guests a quiet place to get down to business. In the main building, they can warm themselves in front of one of two large fireplaces in the Fireside Room. The Room has a refined Arts and Crafts period feel, with hardwood floors, rough wool upholstery against butter-soft leathers and brass and polished granite appointments. A grand piano is also available for functions. After cocktails, guests are ushered into a variety of dining areas—each is elegant, with comfortable furnishings and outstanding views. The Inn's chefs are renowned for culinary excellence and the wine and champagne list is extensive. The staff can organize a traditional affair or a more creative event for the adventuresome. If you are looking for a very special place, the incomparable Highlands Inn should be high on your list.

Area	Standing	Seated	Area	Standing	Seated
Yankee Point Room	—	50	Gazebo & Deck	20	80
Monarch Room	—	14	Wine Room	—	40
Surf Room	—	110	Groves North & South	80	60
Fireside Room	180	—			

FEES & DEPOSITS: The space rental fee is the deposit and is payable when the wedding date is reserved. The rental fees are: Gazebo & Deck $350; Monarch Room $150; Yankee Point Room $400; Wine Room $150; Grove Room $250 and Surf Room $550. A dance floor is an extra $85. Approximate per person rates for food service: luncheons $19, dinners $26 and buffet brunches with champagne $24. Sales tax and 17% gratuity are additional. Half the estimated total bill is due 4 weeks before and the balance is due 7 working days prior to the event. A final confirmed guest count is required 3 working days in advance of the event.

CANCELLATION POLICY: The deposit will be fully refunded if the date can be rebooked with an equal number of guests. A partial refund may be negotiated. With less than 6 weeks' notice, the deposit is forfeited.

AVAILABILITY: Any day, anytime.

SERVICES/AMENITIES:

Restaurant Services: yes
Catering: provided, no BYO
Kitchen Facilities: n/a
Tables & Chairs: provided
Linens, Silver, etc.: provided
Restrooms: wca
Dance Floor: extra charge
Meeting Equipment: full range

Parking: complementary valet
Overnight Accommodations: 142 guestrooms
Telephone: pay phone
Outdoor Night Lighting: yes
Outdoor Cooking Facilities: BBQs
Cleanup: provided
Other: coordination services

RESTRICTIONS:

Alcohol: provided, corkage $12.50/bottle
Smoking: allowed
Music: amplified restricted

Wheelchair Access: yes
Insurance: not required

LA PLAYA HOTEL

Camino Real and 8th Street
Carmel, CA 93921
(408) 624-6476
Reserve for Events: 2–9 months in advance
Reserve for Meetings: 1–3 months in advance

Occupying several acres in the heart of residential Carmel, just two blocks from the beach, La Playa is one of the loveliest and most inviting places we've seen. Originally built in 1904 as a private residence, La Playa was converted and expanded into a hotel in 1916. Boasting an exceptionally beautiful Mediterranean style, with terra cotta tile roofs, soft pastel walls and formal gardens, this full-service resort hotel offers a contemporary freshness as well as romantic old-world appeal. Outdoor celebrations can be held amid brick patios, fountain, technicolor annuals, manicured lawns and climbing bougainvillea. The entire setting is lush and private. Inside are rooms of various size for private functions, with antiques, lithographs and memorabilia of early Carmel. Tasteful furnishings, French doors, big windows and magnificent views are standard amenities. This is a wonderful site for a social or company party and an equally great location for a relaxing getaway.

CAPACITY, FEES & DEPOSITS:

Room	Deposit	Rental Fee	Standing	Seated
Garden Room	$250	$75	36	50
Fireside Room	250	50	18	30
Poseidon Room	500	200	150	100

Deposits must be submitted within 10 days of making your reservation. All deposits are applied to the total food and beverage bill. 70% of the estimated event total is due 60 days prior to the function and the remaining balance, within 30 days after the event. Per person rates: reception buffets about $25, seated meals about $25–30. Sales tax and 16% gratuity are additional. The rental fee for meeting rooms ranges from $50–150, depending on the room selected.

MEETING ROOMS: The Patio Room holds up to 10, the Carmel Room up to 50 guests.

CANCELLATION POLICY: Refunds are given with 4 months' or more notice.

AVAILABILITY: Every day, anytime.

SERVICES/AMENITIES:

Restaurant Services: yes
Catering: provided, no BYO
Kitchen Facilities: n/a
Tables & Chairs: provided
Linens, Silver, etc.: provided
Overnight Accommodations: 75 guestrooms, 5 cottages
Meeting Equipment: audio/visual CBA

Restrooms: wca
Dance Floor: portable
Parking: on street
Telephone: pay phones, guest phones
Outdoor Night Lighting: limited
Outdoor Cooking Facilities: no
Cleanup: provided

RESTRICTIONS:

Alcohol: provided, corkage $12/bottle
Smoking: allowed
Music: booked thru La Playa, over by 10pm

Wheelchair Access: yes
Insurance: not required

MISSION RANCH

26270 Dolores
Carmel, CA 93923
(408) 624-3824
Reserve for Events: 1–15 months in advance
Reserve for Meetings: 2–4 weeks in advance

Mission Ranch has been a Carmel tradition for over fifty years. Once a working dairy, the Ranch is a delightful and rustic retreat, extensively renovated in 1992. Situated on the grounds are a turn-of-the-century farmhouse, a bunkhouse, rustic cottages, hotel rooms, and triplex cottages with spectacular views of Carmel Beach and rugged Point Lobos. These historic buildings, surrounded by hundred-year-old cypress trees and natural landscaping, offer the kind of quiet and peaceful ambiance not found in nearby bustling downtown Carmel. Parties and celebrations are often held in the two Party Barns, known for their friendly bars and great dance floors. The Patio Party Barn has a wall of full-length wood-framed glass doors opening onto a brick patio with a restful view of meadows and wetlands rolling down to Carmel River Beach. The Large Party Barn is ideal for evening parties with its lofty, three-story ceiling. Both barns feature stages for live music, upright pianos and high, open truss ceilings. The structures are appropriately painted white with barn red trim. The Ranch Catering Department prides itself in designing specialty menus for any occasion, from square dancing to theme parties. If you're looking for a place to hold a fun BBQ or upscale dinner in Carmel, this is it.

CAPACITY: The Patio Party Barn accommodates up to 150 guests seated or 200 standing. The Large Party Barn holds up to 180 seated or 300 standing guests. There is a required minimum of 50 guests in the barns.

FEES & DEPOSITS: The Party Barn rental fee ($650/Large Party Barn; $850/Patio Party Barn) is required to reserve a date. A 60% deposit of all estimated services is due 60 days prior to the event, with the remaining estimated balance due 10 days prior to the function. Party Barn rental fees cover a 5-hour period. Additional overtime charges are billed at $100/hour. Buffet and dinner prices start at $21/person and 16% gratuity plus tax are additional.

AVAILABILITY: Every day, anytime. (Note that live music is allowed Thursday–Saturday until 11pm and Sunday until 6pm.)

SERVICES/AMENITIES:
Restaurant Services: yes
Catering: provided, no BYO
Linens, Silver, etc.: provided
Restrooms: wca
Dance Floor: in Barns
Parking: large lot
Overnight Accommodations: 25 guestrooms
Meeting Equipment: CBA

Kitchen Facilities: n/a
Tables & Chairs: provided for 100 guests
Telephone: pay phones
Outdoor Night Lighting: CBA
Outdoor Cooking Facilities: CBA
Cleanup: provided
Other: special event planning

RESTRICTIONS:
Alcohol: provided, no BYO
Smoking: allowed
Music: amplified with restrictions

Wheelchair Access: yes
Insurance: not required

Need a caterer, cake maker, florist? The Service Directory starting on page 614 features the best in the business.

Monterey

LA MIRADA

The Castro Adobe, Frank Work Estate
720 Via Mirada
Monterey, CA 93940
(408) 372-3689
Reserve for Events: 2–12 months in advance
Reserve for Meetings: 2 weeks–2 months in advance

La Mirada is a historic home, situated on a three-acre knoll overlooking Lagunita Mirada and Lake El Estero. Originally built as the residence of Jose Castro, one of the most prominent men in California during the Mexican period, the old adobe portion of the house reflects the early days of Monterey. At the beginning of this century a two-story wing and drawing room were added. It has also been restored, and is filled with fine antique furnishings and decorative art. By 1993, three new galleries designed by award winning architect, Charles Moore, will be completed. Great care has been taken to insure that they will not only be state-of-the-art fine art galleries, but will maintain the character of La Mirada. Surrounding the house, galleries and colorful courtyards, are extensive rose and rhododendron gardens with old rock walls. The beauty of both buildings and landscape makes La Mirada a unique and distinctive spot for business or non-profit organizations to have gatherings. Note that private social events and weddings are not allowed.

CAPACITY: The maximum capacity indoors is 60 seated guests; the formal dining room can seat 22. The outdoor courtyards accommodate up to 150 seated and 200 standing. The new gallery wing can hold 200 for a standing reception.

MEETING ROOMS: The Conference Room seats 35.

FEES & DEPOSITS: Rental fees vary depending on the areas chosen, nature of the event and number of hours of use. Exact fees will be quoted at the time of your inquiry. A general guideline is as follows:

Group Size	*Breakfast*	*Luncheon*	*Dinner*
under 25	$100	$350	$450
25–60	150	500	750–1,250

For meetings (no meals) the rental for under 35 guests is $250 (half day); over 35 guests $350 (half day); and for a full day, the charge is $350-450, depending on the guest count.

CANCELLATION POLICY: With 4 weeks' notice you'll receive a full refund.

AVAILABILITY: Year-round, 8am–11pm

SERVICES/AMENITIES:

Restaurant Services: no
Catering: BYO or CBA
Kitchen Facilities: ample
Tables & Chairs: provided, extra charge
Linens, Silver, etc.: provided, extra charge
Restrooms: no wca
Dance Floor: CBA
Other: event coordination, gift shop

RESTRICTIONS:

Alcohol: BYO, no red wine in some rooms
Smoking: outside only
Music: no amplified

Parking: lot nearby, carpooling encouraged
Overnight Accommodations: no
Telephone: house phones
Outdoor Night Lighting: yes
Outdoor Cooking Facilities: CBA
Cleanup: whoever caters event
Meeting Equipment: no

Wheelchair Access: yes
Insurance: not required, "hold harmless" indemnification clause is required

MONTEREY BAY AQUARIUM

886 Cannery Row
Monterey, CA 93940
(408) 648-4928
Reserve for Events: 6–18 months in advance
Reserve for Meetings: 10–12 weeks in advance

If you've already been to the sensational Monterey Bay Aquarium you'll be delighted to learn that it's available for private events. If you haven't been here yet, then this is a great opportunity to see one of the most beautifully designed buildings in the United States. Constructed on the site of the old Hovden Cannery on the water's edge in the heart of Monterey's historic Cannery Row, this facility is unsurpassed in its range of Monterey Bay displays and exhibits. One extraordinary feature is a three-story tank complete with kelp forest swaying in rhythm with tidal undulations. Some of the touch-and-learn exhibits, where you can pet swimming bat rays or multi-colored sea stars, are open at night and there are countless other exotic-looking sea creatures to see. The aquarium is perfect for a variety of evening events and has facilities for meetings and other programs during the day. The nicely appointed Portola Cafe and the private Ocean View Conference Room are also available. And, as an added dimension to an already exceptional setting, aquarium guides will be available during your exclusive evening event. What a treat for your guests! No one will turn down an invitation to join in the festivities if you decide to hold your party here. Reserve early—this is a much sought-after place.

CAPACITY:

Area	Standing	Seated
Kelp Forest	100	100
Marine Mammals Gallery	300	200–250
Portola Cafe	80	80
Ocean View Conference Room	100	20–100
Entire Aquarium	2,000	—

MEETING ROOMS: The Ocean View Conference Room seats up to 30 people boardroom-style, 50 classroom-style and 85 theater-style. Audio visual equipment and lunch service is available.

FEES & DEPOSITS: An initial deposit is required 6 months in advance of the event and complete payment is required one month prior to the event. Admission fees will be quoted at the time of your inquiry. Per person food service rates: an hors d'oeuvres reception $15–30, a seated dinner or buffet $28–60. Breakfast, lunch and coffee-break menus are also available. Sales tax and 16% gratuity are applied to the final bill.

CANCELLATION POLICY: With 6 months' notice, your deposit will be fully refunded; 3–6 months, 50% will be refunded; less than 3 months, no refund.

AVAILABILITY: Every evening, 7pm–11pm. Closed Christmas. The Ocean View Conference Room is available for groups up to 100 during the day.

SERVICES/AMENITIES:

Restaurant Services: yes

Catering: provided, no BYO

Kitchen Facilities: n/a

Tables & Chairs: provided

Linens, Silver, etc.: provided

Restrooms: wca

Dance Floor: yes

Meeting Equipment: audio visual, auditorium

Parking: city lots

Overnight Accommodations: no

Telephone: pay phones

Outdoor Night Lighting: yes

Outdoor Cooking Facilities: no

Cleanup: provided

Other: full range of event services

RESTRICTIONS:

Alcohol: provided, corkage $8/bottle

Smoking: outside only

Music: amplified ok

Wheelchair Access: yes

Insurance: extra liability required plus indemnification clause

Other: decoration restrictions

OLD MONTEREY INN

500 Martin Street
Monterey, CA 93940
(408) 375-8284
Reserve for Events: 4–6 months in advance
Reserve for Meetings: 1–6 months in advance

Identified as "The Perfect Inn" by Country Inns of California, the Old Monterey Inn, a 1929 Tudor country house, is located in a quiet residential section of town. Monterey's first elected mayor built this three-story mansion, which has been thoughtfully restored and improved over the years. Surrounded by more than an acre of English-style gardens, you can breakfast or enjoy afternoon tea amongst hydrangeas, begonias, rhododendrons, fuchsias and roses. A canopy of redwoods, oaks and pines frames all the vistas from the garden. Inside, there are lovely handcrafted details such as the ceiling panels in the dining room, fireplace hood and Gothic archways. Each of the ten guestrooms is well appointed and comfortable. Although limited to the off-season, for business conferences it is a unique and desirable executive retreat.

CAPACITY: The Inn can accommodate 20 guests, only with an overnight stay.

FEES & DEPOSITS: Payment is due in full when reservations are confirmed. The Inn will book small conferences November–April. The entire house rental is $1,925/night, Sunday–Thursday, which includes a full breakfast and evening wine and cheese.

CANCELLATION POLICY: With 3 months' advance notice, you'll receive a full refund. With 2 months', a 50% refund or more, depending on what has been rebooked.

AVAILABILITY: November–April, Sunday–Thursday. Check-in is between 2:30pm–8pm, departure by noon.

SERVICES/AMENITIES:
Restaurant Services: no
Catering: provided, breakfast & lunch only
Kitchen Facilities: n/a
Tables & Chairs: provided
Linens, Silver, etc.: provided
Restrooms: no wca
Dance Floor: no

Parking: limited to 12 cars
Overnight Accommodations: 10 guestrooms
Telephone: courtesy phone, private lines
Outdoor Night Lighting: no
Outdoor Cooking Facilities: no
Cleanup: provided
Meeting Equipment: CBA, extra fee

RESTRICTIONS:
Alcohol: white wine provided, no red, BYO with approval
Smoking: in garden only

Music: no amplified
Wheelchair Access: no
Insurance: not required

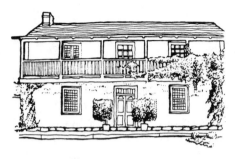

OLD WHALING STATION

391 Decatur St.
Monterey, CA 93940
(408) 375-5356
Reserve for Events: 2 weeks–3 months in advance
Reserve for Meetings: 2 weeks–3 months in advance

This historic adobe structure reflects the character and history of early Monterey. Most sources indicate that the Old Whaling Station was built in 1847 by a Scottish adventurer as a home for his wife and daughter. In 1855, The Old Monterey Whaling Company began using the building for on-shore whaling operations, hence the unusual name. Local legend has it that whalers kept their lookout from the upstairs windows which have an unimpeded view of the Bay. When the whaling business waned at the turn of the century, the building fell into disrepair. Now leased by the Junior League of Monterey County, Inc., the property has undergone an extensive restoration and the result is an appealing facility and technicolor garden available for small, private events.

CAPACITY: The Station can hold up to 50 inside; the garden up to 100 seated guests. The facility's total capacity is 150 guests.

FEES & DEPOSITS: Rental fees are $500 for the general community and $250 for non-profit organizations. A non-refundable booking deposit in the amount of half the rental fee must be submitted with a signed contract within 10 days of making a tentative reservation. The balance of the rental fee, if any, is due 21 days in advance of the rental date. A refundable $200 security deposit is due when keys are transferred to the renter. If you'd like an additional half-day rental for setup or cleanup, the fee is $150.

CANCELLATION POLICY: Rental fee payments are non-refundable. With 6 weeks notice, the booking deposit may be transferred to another date within 12 months of the original contract, subject to availability.

AVAILABILITY: Year-round, every day 9am–midnight.

SERVICES/AMENITIES:

Restaurant Services: no
Catering: BYO
Kitchen Facilities: full kitchen
Tables & Chairs: some provided
Linens, Silver, etc.: some provided
Restrooms: wca limited
Dance Floor: BYO

Parking: Heritage Harbor lots
Overnight Accommodations: no
Telephone: house phone
Outdoor Night Lighting: yes
Outdoor Cooking Facilities: BYO
Cleanup: renter
Meeting Equipment: BYO

RESTRICTIONS:

Alcohol: BYO
Smoking: outside only
Music: amplified restricted

Wheelchair Access: no
Insurance: not required
Other: no pets

Pacific Grove

ASILOMAR
Conference Center

800 Asilomar Blvd.
Pacific Grove, CA 93950
(408) 372-8016
Reserve for Events: 12–24 months in advance
Reserve for Meetings: 12–24 months in advance

Although Asilomar is not a secret, most people don't know it's available for special events. Widely recognized as one of California's most extraordinary conference facilities, Asilomar (literally "Refuge-by-the-Sea") was established as a YMCA retreat in 1913. As part of the California State Park System, it now offers the public an unparalleled environment for any kind of gathering. Architecturally, Asilomar is outstanding. Many of the buildings are historic landmarks, designed in craftsman style by Julia Morgan in the early 1900s. Even the newer structures harmonize with the surrounding beach and forest. After the meeting or festivities, guests can enjoy white sand beaches, dune boardwalks and tidepools nearby. Swimming, bicycling, oceanfront strolling and picnicking are favorite activities. Asilomar's character is unique. It combines an unbeatable 105-acre location next to the ocean with reasonably priced accommodations and distinctive meeting spaces.

CAPACITY: 1,200 guests, minimum group must be 10 guests

MEETING ROOMS: 48 rooms, ranging from a boardroom or informal living room for 10 to a large conference space for 850 participants.

FEES & DEPOSITS: To reserve a date, contact the conference office to request an application. A deposit of $10/person is required when a contract is submitted, usually 8–12 months in advance of the event. An estimated guest count is required both 90 and 60 days prior to the function with a final count due in writing 30 days in advance. Conference rates for 2 or more nights are $41–52/person. For 1 night, $43–61/person. There are reduced rates for children. Rates include accommodations, meals, tax, meeting spaces, grounds and recreation facilities. The charge for off-grounds participants is $6/person per day. The event balance is due upon departure.

CANCELLATION POLICY: With 120 days' notice, the deposit will be fully refunded minus a $25 administration fee.

AVAILABILITY: Year-round, every day. Arrival time is 3pm; departure time at noon.

SERVICES/AMENITIES:

Restaurant Services: yes
Catering: provided, no BYO
Kitchen Facilities: n/a
Tables & Chairs: provided

Parking: many large lots
Overnight Accommodations: 311 guestrooms
Telephone: guest phone, pay phone
Outdoor Night Lighting: yes

Linens, Silver, etc.: provided
Restrooms: mostly wca
Dance Floor: yes
Meeting Equipment: full spectrum of audio-visual

RESTRICTIONS:
Alcohol: BYO
Smoking: restricted
Music: amplified, DJs ok, hours & volume w/approval

Outdoor Cooking Facilities: BBQ
Cleanup: provided

Wheelchair Access: yes, except in historic bldg.
Insurance: sometimes required

MARTINE INN

255 Oceanview Blvd.
Pacific Grove, CA 93950
(408) 373-3388 Marion
Reserve for Events: 1–6 months in advance
Reserve for Meetings: 1 week–12 months in advance

For a meeting, small conference or private business function, the Martine Inn is an uplifting location. It's set high, right on the edge of Monterey Bay, overlooking the rocky coastline of Pacific Grove. Originally designed as an oceanfront Victorian mansion in 1899, it was remodeled as a Mediterranean Villa by James and Laura Park (of the Park Davis pharmaceutical company) when Victoriana went out of style in the early 1900s. Although the exterior is Mediterranean, the Inn's decor is strictly Victorian, in rose and pink hues. There are elegantly furnished rooms complete with museum-quality American antiques and from interior windows, guests have wonderful views of waves crashing against the cliffs. The Martines can help you design your business event to meet your specific requirements and will even provide a staff consultant to plan for food, music, decorations or entertainment.

CAPACITY: For events, the Inn can accommodate up to 125 guests; for meetings and conferences, 20.

FEES & DEPOSITS:

Events: For under 10 guests, there's a $100 deposit; for 10–35 guests, a $250 deposit is required. If there are more than 35 guests, you must reserve the entire Inn for which there is a $500 deposit. All deposits are non-refundable. In addition, the group must reserve the entire house, which costs approximately $3,000/night. For groups of fewer than 35 guests, there is a 2-night minimum stay for weekend events (either Fri/Sat night or Sat/Sun night). For groups of 35 or more, if the event occurs on Saturday, you must book half the guestrooms on Friday night, all the guestrooms on Saturday night and half the guestrooms on Sunday night. Arrangements for payment of the balance due are made individually. Call for current catering costs.

Meetings and Conferences: There is a $135 fee plus tax and 15 % service charge per participant, Sunday through Thursday. Spouses cost $25 extra. The fee includes breakfast, snack, wine and hors d'oeuvres and conference rooms. A deposit in the amount of half the estimated total is required at the time of booking. The balance is payable within 30 days of the event.

CANCELLATION POLICY: Cancellation refunds for events are handled individually. For meeting or conference cancellations, 50% of the deposit will be refunded with more than 30 days' notice. With less notice, the deposit is forfeited.

SERVICES/AMENITIES:

Restaurant Services: no
Catering: provided, no BYO
Kitchen Facilities: n/a
Tables & Chairs: provided
Linens, Silver, etc.: provided
Restrooms: wca
Dance Floor: yes
Meeting Equipment: easels, AV equip. CBA, extra fee

Parking: on street, medium lot
Overnight Accommodations: 19 guestrooms
Telephone: guest phone
Outdoor Night Lighting: minimal
Outdoor Cooking Facilities: BBQ
Cleanup: provided
Other: event coordination

RESTRICTIONS:

Alcohol: provided, no BYO, WBC only
Smoking: restricted
Music: amplified with volume limit

Wheelchair Access: yes
Insurance: not required

Pebble Beach

BEACH AND TENNIS CLUB

Pebble Beach, CA 93953
(408) 624-3811
Reserve for Events: 1–12 months in advance

Just two quick minutes from the Lodge at Pebble Beach is the resort's private Beach and Tennis Club which has tennis courts, pool, spa and fitness center. Although this is a private club, you don't have to be a member to reserve the banquet facilities! And that's a good thing because the Surf Room is one of the most wonderful places for a reception we've run across. The location and ambiance rivals—no, surpasses—The Lodge at Pebble Beach in providing outstanding views in an intimate setting. The main dining room juts out almost to the ocean's edge. And since three of the four dining room walls are glass, the vistas over Carmel Bay, nearby fairways and cliffs are unparalleled. With muted pastel colors, white linens and brass and mirror details, the Surf Room is sophisticated yet comfortable. The adjacent poolside patio can be tented for outdoor dancing, bar service or buffet meals. Another room that's available is the Terrace Room, which has a working black marble-faced fireplace and is decorated in whites and cream colors. This room is primarily for small, seated functions or it can be used for buffet table service when guests are seated in the Surf Room.

CAPACITY: The Surf Room holds 200–250 for a seated party (depending on use of the dance floor), the Terrace Room holds up to 50 seated guests and the Patio can hold up to 90 seated guests.

FEES & DEPOSITS: A non-refundable $1,500 deposit is due within 2 weeks after you make your reservation. A $1,000 rental fee reserves the entire club. Food service is provided. Buffets start at $48/person and dinners range from $45–50/person. Sales tax and 17% gratuity are applied to the final bill. The total is due 14 days in advance of your party.

CANCELLATION POLICY: The deposit is non-refundable.

AVAILABILITY: Every day from 6pm until midnight. This is a private club, consequently availability is limited.

SERVICES/AMENITIES:

Restaurant Services: yes
Catering: provided, no BYO
Kitchen Facilities: n/a
Tables & Chairs: provided
Linens, Silver, etc.: provided
Restrooms: wca
Dance Floor: yes

Parking: large lot
Overnight Accommodations: at Lodge
Telephone: pay phone
Outdoor Night Lighting: yes
Outdoor Cooking Facilities: CBA
Cleanup: provided
Other: tents for patio CBA, extra charge

RESTRICTIONS:

Alcohol: provided, corkage $10/bottle
Smoking: allowed
Music: amplified ok

Wheelchair Access: yes
Insurance: not required

THE INN AT SPANISH BAY

17 Mile Drive
Pebble Beach, CA 93953
(408) 647-7500
Reserve for Events: 1–3 months in advance
Reserve for Meetings: 2 weeks–3 years in advance*

Right off of the famous 17 Mile Drive, this new resort stands at the edge of the Del Monte Forest, barely 300 yards from the ocean's edge. The Inn is designed in the Old Monterey and Spanish California style, with sloping roofs, arched windows and light stucco walls. The Inn is surrounded by lush golf fairways and wind-swept dunes sloping down to the ocean. Inside, the Inn offers guests fireplaces, tasteful appointments in soft colors and various special amenities. This is a large complex featuring 270 guestrooms, restaurants, retail shops, recreation facilities as well as banquet accommodations. A wide range of rooms is available for private parties including the sizable Ballroom and the Bay Club Restaurant.

CAPACITY: The Bay Club Restaurant, available on Saturdays for lunch only, seats 60 guests. The

Ballroom seats 300 guests comfortably and the Fairway Patio can hold 250 guests for a standing reception.

FEES & DEPOSITS: A non-refundable $500–1,000 deposit, depending on the size of the room, is due when you book your reservations. For events, per person rates: luncheons $22–30, buffets start at $35, and dinners at $38. Sales tax and 17% gratuity are additional.

CANCELLATION POLICY: If you cancel less than 2 months prior to your event, your deposit will be forfeited unless the Inn can rebook the date.

AVAILABILITY: Any day, until 2am. *Day functions that do not include overnight accommodations can only be reserved up to 6 months in advance.*

SERVICES/AMENITIES:

Restaurant Services: yes
Catering: provided, no BYO
Kitchen Facilities: n/a
Tables & Chairs: provided
Linens, Silver, etc.: provided
Restrooms: wca
Dance Floor: yes

Parking: large lots
Overnight Accommodations: 270 rooms
Telephone: pay phones
Outdoor Night Lighting: CBA
Outdoor Cooking Facilities: BBQs
Cleanup: provided
Meeting Equipment: full range

RESTRICTIONS:

Alcohol: provided, no BYO
Smoking: allowed
Music: amplified ok

Wheelchair Access: yes
Insurance: not required

THE LODGE AT PEBBLE BEACH

17 Mile Drive
Pebble Beach, CA 93953
(408) 624-3811
Reserve for Events: 1 month–1 year in advance
Reserve for Meetings: 1 week–3 years in advance*

Since opening in 1919, the Lodge has served as the hub of one of the world's premier and most challenging golf courses. The emerald green, meticulously manicured fairways follow the serpentine edge of Carmel Bay and lie directly below the Lodge. With its sweeping ocean panoramas, setting and relaxed elegance, the Lodge is one of Northern California's favorite spots for conferences, parties and meetings. Inside are a variety of rooms suitable for functions that have great views and are well appointed. Plus, there's a conference center which can seat up to 330 guests. For those with limited time to coordinate an event, The Lodge's professional and courteous staff can assist you with every detail of your function.

CAPACITY, FEES & DEPOSITS:

Room	Seated	Standing	Room	Seated	Standing
Pebble Beach Room	120–150	250	Conference Center	240	330
Library Room	60	90	Card Room	30	40
Garden Room	30	40			

The exterior lawn can be rented for croquet games and lawn parties. Call for individual quotes. A non-refundable deposit of approximately $500 is due within 2 weeks after making your reservation. Per person rates for food: hors d'oeuvres start at $25, luncheons start at $22–27 and dinners at $40–50. Sales tax and 17% gratuity are additional. For parties on the lawn overlooking the ocean, the setup fee is $1,500.

MEETING ROOMS: All the above areas except the Garden Room are available for meetings.

CANCELLATION POLICY: The deposit is not refundable.

AVAILABILITY: Any day, anytime until midnight. *Day functions that do not include overnight accommodations can only be reserved up to 6 months in advance.*

SERVICES/AMENITIES:

Restaurant Services: yes

Catering: provided, no BYO

Kitchen Facilities: n/a

Tables & Chairs: provided

Linens, Silver, etc.: provided

Restrooms: wca

Dance Floor: yes

Meeting Equipment: full range

Overnight Accommodations: 161 guestrooms

Telephone: pay phone

Outdoor Night Lighting: limited

Outdoor Cooking Facilities: CBA

Cleanup: provided

Other: tents for outdoor lawn parties CBA

Parking: large lots

RESTRICTIONS:

Alcohol: provided, corkage $10/bottle

Smoking: allowed

Music: amplified until 10pm

Wheelchair Access: yes

Insurance: not required

Prices and policies __do__ change. Call each facility and confirm everything you read in Perfect Places.

Amador City

IMPERIAL HOTEL

14202 Highway 49
Amador City, CA 95601
(209) 267-9172
Reserve for Events: 2 weeks–6 months in advance
Reserve for Meetings: 2 weeks–6 months in advance

Built originally as a mercantile store, this building was developed into a hotel in 1879 because the town had insufficient lodging. In 1988, after a fifty-one-year hiatus, the Imperial Hotel was restored by its present innkeepers. It has a restaurant and bar in addition to overnight accommodations. The dining room is simple yet stylish with high ceilings, white walls and contemporary art which gives the interior an art-gallery ambiance. The bar is also appealing, with features reminiscent of an Egyptian oasis. With outstanding food and an environment to match, the Imperial is a splendid destination for a creative celebration, private party or unique business retreat.

CAPACITY: The dining room can hold up to 55 seated guests for dinner and up to 60 for lunch.

MEETING ROOMS: The dining room can be used as one meeting room for up to 60, or it can be divided into 2 areas.

FEES & DEPOSITS: For weekday meetings, the rental fee is $100. If meal service is provided, the charge is waived. Food service starts at $10/person for lunch and dinners start at $14/person. A non-refundable deposit of half the estimated event cost is due 7 days in advance of the function. The balance is due at the end of the event.

CANCELLATION POLICY: The deposit is not refundable.

AVAILABILITY: Year-round, every day except during Sunday brunch from 10am–2pm. Most Friday and Saturday group events are scheduled 5pm–7pm. Meetings can be scheduled Monday–Saturday, 8am–4pm.

SERVICES/AMENITIES:

Restaurant Services: yes
Catering: provided, no BYO
Kitchen Facilities: n/a
Tables & Chairs: provided
Linens, Silver, etc.: provided
Restrooms: wca
Dance Floor: no

Parking: on street, parking lot
Overnight Accommodations: 6 guestrooms
Telephone: house phone
Outdoor Night Lighting: no
Outdoor Cooking Facilities: no
Cleanup: provided
Meeting Equipment: CBA

RESTRICTIONS:

Alcohol: provided, no BYO
Smoking: allowed
Music: amplified restricted

Wheelchair Access: yes
Insurance: sometimes required

Auburn

AUBURN VALLEY COUNTRY CLUB

8800 Auburn Valley Road
Auburn CA 95603
(916) 269-2775
Reserve for Events: 6–12 months in advance
Reserve for Meetings: 1 week–12 months in advance

The Auburn Valley Country Club is one of those unexpected gems. You drive down a curvy scenic road for miles, wondering if the destination at the end will be worth the drive. Well, this one is. Set atop a knoll, the Club overlooks a gorgeous golf club studded with lakes, rolling hills and deep green trees. The view is breathtaking, and the surroundings so peaceful that all you hear are the birds and the breeze. The dining room faces this picture-book valley through floor-to-ceiling windows, providing a light and airy space for a private party or business dinner. A large, nicely landscaped patio is also a great place for outdoor functions.

CAPACITY:

Area	*Seated*	*Standing*
Patio	250	400
Lounge	100	—
Dining Room	175	—

FEES & DEPOSITS: A $500 deposit, which is applied to the total, is due at the time of booking. 90% of all costs and a guaranteed guest count are due 1 week prior to the event. The balance is payable on departure. Per person catering fees run about $14–23 for a seated meal and $14–20 for a buffet. There is a Club usage fee (based on guest count) for events without catering.

CANCELLATION POLICY: A refund is only given with 30 or more days' notice.

AVAILABILITY: Every day, 7am–midnight depending on group size, space(s) reserved and time of year. Closed Christmas and New Year's Day.

SERVICES/AMENITIES:

Restaurant Services: yes
Catering: provided
Kitchen Facilities: n/a

Parking: lot
Overnight Accommodations: no
Telephone: pay phone

Tables & Chairs: provided
Linens, Silver, etc.: provided
Restrooms: wca
Dance Floor: yes

RESTRICTIONS:
Alcohol: provided or BYO CW, corkage $6/bottle
Smoking: designated areas
Music: amplified ok

Outdoor Night Lighting: yes
Outdoor Cooking Facilities: BBQ
Cleanup: provided
Meeting equipment: BYO or CBA, extra fee

Wheelchair Access: yes
Insurance: not required
Other: there is a dress code

POWER'S MANSION INN

164 Cleveland Ave.
Auburn, CA 95603
(916) 885-1166
Reserve for Events: 1–2 months in advance
Reserve for Meetings: 1 day in advance

One of Auburn's landmarks, this century-old Victorian is a bed and breakfast inn with a business side. The large dining room and adjoining parlors are often used for meetings and conferences, and the concierge service is a plus that businesses will appreciate. The Inn has been completely restored with custom wallpaper, antiques, period fixtures and beautiful colors. The elegant interior, terraced garden patio, wrap-around porches and decks make this a lovely spot for private parties as well.

CAPACITY: Dining room 35 guests; 2 parlors hold up to 40; the entire facility, 75 guests total.

MEETING ROOMS: All of the above rooms can be used for meetings.

FEES & DEPOSITS: One third of the estimated charges are due at the time of booking. The balance is due the day of the event. The facility rents for $400/day if no lodging is reserved, and there is a $25 credit for each room reserved. Catering is handled by the Inn and runs $9–15/person for lunch or $16–25/person for dinner.

CANCELLATION POLICY: With partial rental, you will receive a full refund with 2 weeks' notice. If you have reserved the entire Inn, 1 month's notice is required.

AVAILABILITY: Year-round, every day.

SERVICES/AMENITIES:
Restaurant Services: breakfast only
Catering: provided, no BYO
Kitchen Facilities: n/a
Tables & Chairs: provided
Linens, Silver, etc.: provided
Restrooms: wca
Dance Floor: CBA, extra fee

Parking: on and off street
Overnight Accommodations: 11 guestrooms
Telephone: guest phones
Outdoor Night Lighting: yes
Outdoor Cooking Facilities: no
Cleanup: provided
Special Services: concierge & valet service

Meeting Equipment: CBA

RESTRICTIONS:

Alcohol: corkage $3/bottle
Smoking: outside only
Music: no restrictions if you rent entire Inn

Wheelchair Access: 1st floor only
Insurance: not required
Other: children by arrangement

Columbia

ANGELO'S HALL

State Street
Columbia, CA 95310
(209) 532-5134   Columbia House Restaurant
Reserve for Events: 1–6 months in advance
Reserve for Meetings: 1 day–1 month in advance

A Mother Lode dance hall, this has also been used as Columbia's town hall and for community gatherings over the last seventy years. Historic Angelo's Hall is a pleasant yet unassuming wood structure with one large room. Because of its hardwood floors and spacious interior, it is one of the most popular dance halls around. The Hall is a very flexible space and can support luncheons or dinners, square dancing, meetings or seminars.

CAPACITY: The Hall can hold 199 people standing, 150 seated.

FEES & DEPOSITS: A $50 maintenance fee and the estimated total rental fee is due when reservations are booked. If no food or drinks are being served, or if the Columbia House provides the catering, the rental fee is $1/person. Otherwise, the rental fee is $2/person. Per person meal costs average $5/breakfast, $8.50/lunch or $14.50/dinner, including tax and gratuity. Any balance is payable the day of the event. (Note: if Columbia House does the catering, you may not bring your own alcohol.)

CANCELLATION POLICY: Fees are fully refundable until 30 days prior to the event.

AVAILABILITY: Year-round, any day until midnight.

SERVICES/AMENITIES:

Restaurant Services: yes
Catering: provided or BYO
Kitchen Facilities: no
Tables & Chairs: provided
Linens, Silver, etc.: BYO
Restrooms: wca
Dance Floor: yes

Parking: rear lot
Overnight Accommodations: no
Telephone: no
Outdoor Night Lighting: no
Outdoor Cooking Facilities: no
Cleanup: caterer or renter
Meeting Equipment: no

RESTRICTIONS:

Alcohol: CBW provided or BYO w/some restrictions
Smoking: outside only
Music: some restrictions

Wheelchair Access: limited
Insurance: sometimes required

AVERY RANCH

Forest Service Road 3N03
Columbia, CA 95310
(209) 533-2851 or **(415) 752-6434**
Reserve for Events: 1–6 months in advance
Reserve for Events: 2 weeks–6 months in advance

Getting here is part of the fun. Avery Ranch, a full-service wilderness resort, is set in a remote and beautiful meadowland overlooking the Stanislaus River Canyon, forty minutes from historic Angel's Camp. You can elect to arrive by car, air-conditioned van, helicopter or by boat! Avery Ranch is at an elevation of 2,700 feet, encircled by thousands of acres of Stanislaus National Forest. Once an old homestead, the site still has the original Avery cabin, complete with stone fireplace. The spacious Main Lodge serves as the center for dining and entertaining plus there are private cottages and log cabins for overnight guests. Here you'll find the perfect blend of rustic comfort and really good food. Everything is homemade yet creatively prepared with attention to variety. Versatility, a commitment to good fun and good friends makes this place a rare treat. The Ranch can handle everything from spectacular theme parties, private events, stage shows, dances, group retreats to secluded "hide-outs" for famous entertainers. This is a superb and tranquil setting for business retreats. Recreation activities abound; river rafting, hiking, bicycling, horseback riding, swimming and fishing. Avery Ranch provides an extraordinary, peaceful and relaxed environment.

CAPACITY: The Avery Cabin can hold 20–30 seated guests, the Lodge dining room 75. A maximum of 250 guests can be accommodated in conjunction with the outdoor spaces.

FEES & DEPOSITS: A $100 refundable deposit secures your reservation and is due when the reservation is booked. 25% of the estimated total is due 1 week prior to the event and the final 75% is due at the end of the event. Each function is unique, so charges vary. The normal range is $25–75/person per day. Call to make specific arrangements.

CANCELLATION POLICY: With 4 weeks' notice, you'll receive a full refund.

AVAILABILITY: Year-round, every day.

SERVICES/AMENITIES:

Restaurant Services: no
Catering: provided, can BYO with extra charge
Kitchen Facilities: full industrial
Tables & Chairs: provided

Parking: lots
Overnight Accommodations: 15 guestrooms
Telephone: radio phone
Outdoor Night Lighting: CBA

Linens, Silver, etc.: provided
Restrooms: limited wca, CBA
Dance Floor: yes
Meeting Equipment: CBA

RESTRICTIONS:
Alcohol: provided, corkage $2/bottle
Smoking: outside only
Music: amplified ok

Outdoor Cooking Facilities: BBQ
Cleanup: provided
Other: outdoor stage, event coordination

Wheelchair Access: limited, CBA
Insurance: sometimes required
Other: no pets

CITY HOTEL

Main Street
Columbia, CA 95310
(209) 532-1479
Reserve for Events: 1–3 months in advance
Reserve for Meetings: 2–4 weeks in advance

Built in 1856 and located in Columbia State Historic Park, four miles north of Sonora, the City Hotel still provides hospitality on a daily basis. Small and intimate, the hotel appears to have been left intact as a remnant of California's gold mining past when Columbia had 5,000 residents, 150 saloons and shops. The parlor rooms upstairs, which can be used for meetings, are furnished with antiques and open directly onto the main sitting parlor. Dining here is a memorable event; the food is terrific and the wine list extensive. For special events, the Main Dining Room and adjacent Morgan Room are perfectly suited for business meeting luncheons or group dinners. If you want to stay overnight there are ten guest rooms upstairs and additional rooms in the nearby Fallon Hotel, operated by the same management.

CAPACITY: The Main Dining Room can seat 60 guests; 100 standing. The Morgan Room can hold a maximum of 25 seated. An additional 20 can be seated in the adjacent historic saloon.

MEETING ROOMS: Morgan Room 25 guests, maximum.

FEES & DEPOSITS:

Room	Deposit Day	Deposit Eves	Meeting Fees 3 hours max.
Morgan Room	$50	$200	$25 (no meal service)
Main Dining Room	100	200	—
Upstairs Parlor	—	—	25 (no meal service)

A refundable deposit is required, due within 2 weeks of making the reservation. The rental charge for meetings is waived if you're staying overnight or have your meals here. For the Morgan Room and Main Dining Room, the day and evening deposits are $50/200 and $100/200 respectively. For luncheon or dinner events, food service is provided. Lunch starts at $11/person, dinners at $19/person. Tax and a 15% gratuity are added to the total bill, which is payable at the end of the event.

CANCELLATION POLICY: With more than 2 weeks' notice, you will receive a full refund less $50.

AVAILABILITY: Every day; 8am–11pm, depending on the type of function arranged.

SERVICES/AMENITIES:

Restaurant Services: yes

Catering: provided, no BYO

Kitchen Facilities: n/a

Tables & Chairs: provided

Overnight Accommodations: 10 guestrooms

Telephone: pay phone

Outdoor Night Lighting: limited

Meeting Equipment: screen, blackboard

Linens, Silver, etc.: provided

Restrooms: limited wca

Dance Floor: no

Parking: lot behind Hotel

Outdoor Cooking Facilities: no

Cleanup: provided

Other: historic tours, stagecoach, gold panning

RESTRICTIONS:

Alcohol: provided, corkage $7/bottle

Smoking: restricted

Music: restricted

Wheelchair Access: limited

Insurance: not required

Other: no pets

FALLON HOUSE THEATRE

Broadway
Columbia, CA 95310
(209) 532-4644
Reserve for Events: 2–12 months in advance
Reserve for Meetings: 1 week–6 months in advance

It seems that Gold Rush audiences couldn't get enough theater. Within two years of its founding, Columbia boasted three playhouses, including one Chinese. Traveling entertainers played the Mother Lode circuit, drawing wildly enthusiastic crowds from long distances. An historic playhouse, the Fallon House Theatre has been restored to its original splendor. The interior has burgundy upholstered seating, stage, balcony and professional sound and lighting systems and is used during most of the year for local theatrical productions. Decorative wallpaper, wood wainscotting and period detailing make this a very unique setting for a business meeting, seminar, training session or private musical event. You can rent the Theatre or Ice Cream Parlor for your private party or business function in between theater productions, or the outdoor rose garden for receptions. The Fallon House Theatre serves as home to the Columbia Actors Repertory, featuring an eight-show year-round season. Group discounts and packages in conjunction with local bed & breakfasts and restaurants are available.

CAPACITY: The Theatre space can hold up to 250 seated; an additional 28 with the balcony. The adjacent Ice Cream Parlor can accommodate 75–100 standing and the outdoor rose garden another 100 standing.

MEETING ROOMS: The Theatre is available for meetings or conferences.

FEES & DEPOSITS: The Theatre rental fee is $175/event, due 2 weeks in advance of the event. Technical support may be required and the cost will vary depending on the number of technicians desired and the work involved. A refundable $100 cleaning deposit is also required, to be returned 30 days after the event if the Theatre is left in clean condition. Ice Cream Parlor and rose garden rental is $50/event, which can be credited toward ice cream purchase.

CANCELLATION POLICY: With 1 week's notice, the deposit will be refunded.

AVAILABILITY: Year-round. The Theatre and Ice Cream Parlor spaces are subject to the theater production schedule; the rose garden is available anytime.

SERVICES/AMENITIES:

Restaurant Services: no
Catering: BYO or CBA, no food in Theatre
Kitchen Facilities: no
Tables & Chairs: parlor or rose garden, BYO
Linens, Silver, etc.: BYO
Restrooms: wca
Dance Floor: no

Parking: large lot
Overnight Accommodations: Fallon Hotel
Telephone: business phone
Outdoor Night Lighting: CBA
Outdoor Cooking Facilities: nearby BBQ
Cleanup: renter
Meeting Equipment: CBA

RESTRICTIONS:

Alcohol: BYO or CBA through City Hotel
Smoking: outside only
Music: amplified until 11pm

Wheelchair Access: yes
Insurance: sometimes required

Jamestown

HISTORIC NATIONAL HOTEL

77 Main Street
Jamestown, CA 95327
(209) 984-3446
Reserve for Events: 2 weeks–6 months in advance
Reserve for Meetings: 1 week–6 months in advance

One of the ten oldest continuously operating hotels in California, The National is a good example of 1860s Mother Lode architecture. Its rooms have been authentically restored to convey a feeling of the past, and can be used for small meetings. Of special note is the saloon which has the Hotel's original bar, dating back to 1859! Here you'll find wainscotting, period furnishings, oak stools and a convivial ambiance popular with the locals. The Hotel's two dining rooms can be set up for any type of gathering, and outside is the garden courtyard, festive with white furniture and blue Campari umbrellas. Each area is readily available for business seminars or group luncheons and dinners. Overhead is an arbor with lush vines and latticework detailing. Another main attraction is the National's cuisine, touted by

Bon Appetit and Motorland magazines. The food is great and the award-winning wine list is extensive. The hotel is a delightful place to stay overnight, and if you need additional accommodations, their staff will arrange it for you. Although the National has added some new amenities, it has successfully retained its quaint, 19th-century charm.

CAPACITY: The dining room holds 60 seated or 100 standing. The courtyard accommodates 50 seated, 75 standing.

FEES & DEPOSITS: A refundable deposit in the amount of 20% of the total estimated bill is due when reservations are made. Food service is provided. Luncheons range from $9–11/person and dinners $15–18/person. Tax and service charge are included. The event balance is due the day of the function.

CANCELLATION POLICY: A full refund is given with 30 days' notice.

AVAILABILITY: Year-round, anytime.

SERVICES/AMENITIES:

Restaurant Services: yes
Catering: provided, no BYO
Kitchen Facilities: n/a
Tables & Chairs: provided
Linens, Silver, etc.: provided
Restrooms: no wca
Dance Floor: no
Meeting Equipment: some provided

Parking: on street
Overnight Accommodations: 11 guestrooms
Telephone: pay phone
Outdoor Night Lighting: yes
Outdoor Cooking Facilities: no
Cleanup: provided
Other: event coordination

RESTRICTIONS:

Alcohol: provided, corkage $3–5/bottle
Smoking: bar only
Music: amplified ok

Wheelchair Access: downstairs only
Insurance: not required

JAMESTOWN HOTEL

18153 Main Street
Jamestown, CA 95327
(209) 984-3902
Reserve for Events: 2 weeks–4 months in advance
Reserve for Meetings: 2 weeks–4 months in advance

The restored Jamestown Hotel rests in the center of this historic Gold Rush town. With brick exterior and flower boxes, it feels homey and old-fashioned. For those that want to relax before the festivities, the comfortable lounge has period furniture, an inviting fireplace and nicely detailed oak bar with large mirror. It's also a delightful room for breakfast meetings. The main dining room has light floral wallpaper and is an attractive room with both bench seating and individual tables. This is one of the most popular places in town for Christmas parties. Right outside there's a garden patio—a wood deck which is enclosed by overhead lattice and side screens. During winter, the patio is heated by a wood-burning stove and space heaters all day, making it a toasty spot for a private meeting. And, if you're from out of town, note that your group can stay overnight in cozy rooms upstairs, all nicely furnished with Gold Rush-era antiques.

CAPACITY: The dining room holds 64 seated, the lounge 36 seated and the garden patio 84 seated. The total capacity for a standing reception is 140 guests.

MEETING ROOMS: All 3 of the above areas are available for meetings, but the patio is the most private.

FEES & DEPOSITS: A $100 deposit which is applied to the final bill is required when reservations are made. No rental fees are required if food service is provided. Per person rates: luncheons range $9–11, buffet lunches start at $10, seated dinners at $20 and dinner buffets at $15. These prices generally include tax and gratuity.

CANCELLATION POLICY: With 2 weeks' notice, you'll receive a full refund.

AVAILABILITY: Year-round, every day. For meetings, the patio is available anytime, the lounge and dining room in the morning only.

SERVICES/AMENITIES:

Restaurant Services: yes
Catering: provided, no BYO
Kitchen Facilities: n/a
Tables & Chairs: provided
Linens, Silver, etc.: provided
Restrooms: wca
Dance Floor: no
Meeting Equipment: CBA

Parking: lot nearby, on street
Overnight Accommodations: 8 guestrooms
Telephone: pay phone
Outdoor Night Lighting: yes
Outdoor Cooking Facilities: BBQ
Cleanup: provided
Other: event coordination, horse-drawn carriage CBA

RESTRICTIONS:

Alcohol: provided, corkage $3–5/bottle
Smoking: dining room is non-smoking
Music: amplified ok

Wheelchair Access: yes
Insurance: not required

Need a caterer, cake maker, florist? The Service Directory starting on page 614 features the best in the business.

RAILTOWN 1897

Sierra Railway Depot
5th Ave. at Reservoir Rd.
Jamestown, CA 95327
(209) 984-3953
Reserve For Events: 2–6 months in advance
Reserve For Meetings: 6 weeks in advance

Ride a steam train and relive the past! Railtown provides an authentic glimpse of the era when America steamed innocently into the 20th Century. This is a living museum, with vintage steam locomotives which have served the Sierra Railway since its inception in 1897. Railtown, a working facility that maintains and dispatches its historic equipment for excursion rides and filming operations, has contributed to nearly 200 feature movies, television shows and commercials. Steam engine #3, Hollywood's favorite, has become the most photographed locomotive in the world. Your group can charter one car or an entire train, depending on the nature of your function. Special events have included a mystery train tour, pumpkin tours at Halloween and train dance parties. Now a twenty-six-acre State Historic Park, including a large picnic area for receptions, Railtown remains much the same as it was at the turn of the century.

CAPACITY, FEES & DEPOSITS: Railtown offers a variety of train excursion and picnic options. Train excursions can accommodate up to 450 guests, and the picnic area up to 325. Rates for adults range from $8 for a 1-hour train ride to $34.50 for a train ride with BBQ and entertainment. Call for train schedules, private charter and childrens' rates.

A 50% deposit is required when reservations are made. The balance is due the day of the event. Groups of 10 or more are required for group reservations.

CANCELLATION POLICY: With 48 hours' advance notice, you'll receive a full refund.

AVAILABILITY: Every day, year-round, depending on the type of event planned.

SERVICES/AMENITIES:

Restaurant Services: no
Catering: provided
Kitchen Facilities: no
Tables & Chairs: some provided, BYO
Linens, Silver, etc.: BYO
Restrooms: wca
Dance Floor: dance train car
Meeting Equipment: no

Parking: large lot
Overnight Accommodations: no
Telephone: pay phone
Outdoor Night Lighting: yes
Outdoor Cooking Facilities: BBQs
Cleanup: caterer or renter
Other: full event coordination

RESTRICTIONS:

Alcohol: provided, BWC only, no BYO
Smoking: outside only
Music: amplified restricted

Wheelchair Access: yes
Insurance: sometimes required

Sutter Creek

GOLD QUARTZ INN

15 Bryson Drive
Sutter Creek, CA 95685
(800) 752-8738
Reserve for Events: 2–12 months in advance
Reserve for Meetings: 2–3 months in advance

The Inn is actually a new building, but it's designed with a 19th-century ambiance and attention to historic detailing. The style is Queen Anne, with gables, peaked gray roofs and wrap-around porch. Abundant latticework and many balconies give the Inn an overall feeling of a home, rather than a hotel. The interior boasts a Victorian style with antiques, restored fixtures and floral wallpaper. For small gatherings, the cozy parlor with its overstuffed furniture and lace curtains is very comfortable. For business functions, the banquet room is designed for group meetings. Nice touches include cookie jars full of home-baked cookies and a croquet set for use on the lawn.

CAPACITY: The 2 dining rooms can hold up to 48 for a seated dinner.

MEETING ROOMS: The banquet room can hold up to 49 people.

FEES & DEPOSITS: A non-refundable deposit of 15% of the total estimated room stay is due when reservations are made. For meetings in the banquet room a $50–75/day fee is required. Weekday business luncheons start at $15/person. Friday–Sunday business retreats start at $2,500 (rooms are included); special group weekday rates are available. Food service is provided, with luncheons starting at $15/person and dinners at $25/person, 15 guests minimum. Full breakfast and afternoon tea is included in the room rate.

CANCELLATION POLICY: Business functions require a 60-day notice for a refund. Non-business events require a 30-day advance notice. There is a 15% service charge for cancellations.

AVAILABILITY: Year-round, every day.

SERVICES/AMENITIES:

Restaurant Services: no
Catering: provided, no BYO
Kitchen Facilities: no
Tables & Chairs: provided
Linens, Silver, etc.: provided
Restrooms: wca
Dance Floor: CBA for extra fee
Meeting Equipment: TV, VCR, FAX

Parking: large lot
Overnight Accommodations: 24 guestrooms
Telephone: guest phones
Outdoor Night Lighting: yes
Outdoor Cooking Facilities: BBQ CBA
Cleanup: provided
Other: event coordination

RESTRICTIONS:

Alcohol: WBC provided, corkage $2/bottle
Smoking: outside only
Music: no amplified

Wheelchair Access: yes
Insurance: required for hard liquor bar
Other: BYO hard alcohol, no pets

Groveland

THE IRON DOOR SALOON

18761 Main Street
Groveland, CA 95321
(209) 962-5947
Reserve for Events: 1 month in advance
Reserve for Meetings: 1–2 weeks in advance

On your way to Yosemite, you probably passed the oldest operating saloon in California without knowing it. Built in 1852, The Iron Door Saloon was initially called the "Granite Store" most likely because the front and back walls are made of solid granite. The sidewalls are of rock and mortar, and the roof consists of three-foot-thick sod covered with tin. Inside are reminders of the region's colorful past: bullet holes, pictures of the pre-dam Hetch Hetchy Valley and Old West paraphernalia. Although moose heads and deer antlers adorn the walls, the interior feels more like a natural history museum; the owners are ecology-minded and provide information about the status of these animals. Outside, don't miss the outstanding mural on the building's front—a collage of western scenes depicting miners, mountain men, Indians, wild horses and stampeding buffalo along with a portrait of John Muir. Peter and Bettike Barsotti refurbished The Iron Door in 1985, after falling in love with the historic lore of the building. The staff is efficient and friendly, and since both owners are producers for Bill Graham Presents, events are handled very professionally. This is a fun spot to have a party.

CAPACITY: The indoor capacity is 150 for a standing reception, 75 guests seated.

DEPOSITS & FEES: A non-refundable $500–750 deposit for Friday–Saturday night or $500 for Sunday–Thursday is due when reservations are confirmed. The rental fee is $250–500/event; however, it may be waived depending on the total amount of services requested. Both deposit and rental fee vary depending on the time of year. Per person rates: dinners start at $20, luncheons at $10, hors d'oeuvres at $10 and buffets at $15. The balance is due the day of event; tax and a 15% gratuity are additional.

AVAILABILITY: Year-round. Weekends, 10am–4pm; weekdays anytime.

SERVICES/AMENITIES:

Restaurant Services: yes
Catering: provided, no BYO
Kitchen Facilities: n/a
Tables & Chairs: provided
Linens, Silver, etc.: provided
Restrooms: no wca
Dance Floor: yes
Meeting Equipment: no

Parking: medium lot
Overnight Accommodations: no
Telephone: pay phone
Outdoor Night Lighting: no
Outdoor Cooking Facilities: no
Cleanup: provided
Other: full event coordination

RESTRICTIONS:

Alcohol: provided, no BYO
Smoking: allowed
Music: amplified ok

Wheelchair Access: yes
Insurance: sometimes required

Oakhurst

ESTATE BY THE ELDERBERRIES
Erna's Elderberry House and
Chateau du Sureau

48688 Victoria Lane
Oakhurst, CA 93644
(209) 683-6800 or (209) 683-6860
Reserve for Events: 6 months in advance
Reserve for Meetings: 3–4 weeks in advance

If you're like many Californians, half your guests hail from the north, the other half from the south. We've found a place midway that's guaranteed to make everyone happy—the Estate by the Elderberries. Nestled in the hills near Oakhurst, not far from Yosemite's south gate and forty-five minutes from Fresno, this is a place that's worth the trip—from anywhere. The seven-and-a-half-acre estate, which contains the Elderberry House Restaurant and Chateau du Sureau (the French word for elderberry), offers guests a chance to sample both an old-world European ambiance and a sublime culinary experience. The Elderberry House, renowned for its innovative prix fix menus (arguably the best cuisine in Central California) has four dining rooms. Dressed up with fine linens, crystal and fresh flowers, each provides an exceptional environment for a sophisticated reception. Guests can stay overnight in the nearby Chateau du Sureau, a castle-like inn, with turret and stone walls. Designed and furnished to resemble a nineteenth-century French country estate, this manor house has wrought-iron balconies imported from Paris, stone and red clay tile floors and hand-carved doors. The Chateau's rooms have canopied beds with goosedown comforters and are furnished with antiques, tapestries and pieces of art. Bathrooms are extraordinary—all marble and hand-painted French tiles with deep, sunken tubs. Your group can relax in front of a roaring fire and be pampered by the Chateau's caring staff. If you're looking for something special for your next event or business party, Estate by the Elderberries won't disappoint you.

CAPACITY: Indoors, the Elderberry House can seat 100 guests. With garden and terrace areas, the total capacity is 165 guests.

FEES & DEPOSITS: Both the Restaurant and Chateau require a 50% deposit of the estimated food, beverage and lodging total. The Restaurant's rental fee is $500/event. Dinners range from $35–75/person, luncheons from $18–35/person, tax and gratuity included. The remaining balance is due the day of event.

AVAILABILITY: Year-round, with the exception of the first 3 weeks in January.

SERVICES/AMENITIES:

Restaurant Services: yes
Catering: provided
Kitchen Facilities: n/a
Tables & Chairs: provided
Linens, Silver, etc.: provided
Restrooms: wca
Dance Floor: outdoor terrace
Meeting Equipment: CBA

Parking: estate lot
Overnight Accommodations: 9 guestrooms
Telephone: guest phones CBA
Outdoor Night Lighting: yes
Outdoor Cooking Facilities: no
Cleanup: provided
Other: event coordination

RESTRICTIONS:

Alcohol: provided, corkage $10/bottle
Smoking: outside or in wine cellar only
Music: amplified within reason

Wheelchair Access: yes
Insurance: not required

Yosemite

YOSEMITE FACILITIES

Yosemite Park and Curry Company
Yosemite National Park, CA 95389
(209) 372-1122
Reserve for Events: 12 months in advance
Reserve for Meetings: 4–8 months in advance

Hold your special event in the most beautiful place on earth—Yosemite. It never fails to leave its visitors with a sense of awe and wonder. The park's unparalleled beauty is an inspiring backdrop for any function, whether it's a business meeting, corporate retreat or company party. Here you'll find the classically elegant and sophisticated Ahwahnee, the versatile Yosemite Lodge, the well-equipped Curry Village and the old-world Wawona Hotel. After the festivities, enjoy a multitude of summer and winter activities. Savor Yosemite. It can transform any event into a special occasion.

CAPACITY:

The Ahwahnee		Yosemite Lodge		Wawona Hotel	
Dining Room	*Capacity*	*Dining Room*	*Capacity*	*Dining Room*	*Capacity*
Winter Club Room	10–45	Mt. Room Broiler	60	Sunroom	75
Mural Room	10–45	Redwood Room	40	Lawns	150
Solarium	40–125	Mt.Broiler & Redwd	100		
		Cliff Room	75		
		Falls Room	75		
		Cliff & Falls Rooms	150		

The Ahwahnee can accommodate any combination of the above totalling 168 seated or 300 guests for a standing function.

FEES & DEPOSITS: A $300 refundable deposit is required within 1 month after booking. There is no room rental fee for the first 3 hours of an event. A room rental fee of $125/hour is charged for every additional hour. Menu selection for groups is to be submitted at least 6 weeks in advance and a final guest count must be submitted 72 hours prior to your party. The estimated total is due 4 weeks prior to the event and the final balance is payable before departure. Overnight accommodations vary. Call for rates.

CANCELLATION POLICY: With less than 90 days' notice, the deposit is forfeited.

AVAILABILITY: Daily, 6am–11pm; October through April for business meetings.

SERVICES/AMENITIES:

Restaurant Services: various choices
Catering: provided, no BYO
Kitchen Facilities: n/a
Tables & Chairs: provided
Linens, Silver, etc.: provided
Restrooms: wca
Dance Floor: no
Meeting Equipment: slide projectors, overheads

Parking: large lots
Overnight Accommodations: wide range
Telephone: pay phones
Outdoor Night Lighting: no
Outdoor Cooking Facilities: no
Cleanup: provided
Other: event coordination

RESTRICTIONS:

Alcohol: all alcohol through Yosemite

Wheelchair Access: yes

Oroville

JEAN PRATT'S RIVERSIDE BED & BREAKFAST

45 Cabana Drive
Oroville, CA 95965
(916) 533-1413
Reserve for Events: 1 week–6 months in advance
Reserve for Meetings: 1 week–6 months in advance

This is one of those places that is off the beaten path and well worth the trip. The inn consists of three buildings located on the Feather River, surrounded by five acres of pine, cedar and toyon trees. The river meanders by at a lazy pace, providing a runway for ducks, geese, heron and jumping fish. The rear deck overlooks a lawn that slopes down to the river, while a bench swing and umbrella-shaded table invite you to enjoy the view. This is a wonderful setting for a retreat—secluded and quiet, it allows you to sever all ties with civilization. Jean Pratt, owner and Innkeeper, has created a comfortable and casual refuge that is conducive to complete relaxation and appreciation of nature. She and her inn make it easy to focus on important meetings or workshops.

CAPACITY:

Room	Capacity	Room	Capacity
Lodge*	34	Upstairs Room	12
Living Room	15–30	Cottage	10

*Use of the Lodge also includes reservation of 4 guestrooms in the same building.

FEES & DEPOSITS: Fees depend on the number of rooms and nights reserved. Rooms rent for $48.50–95 per night, single or double occupancy. Half the fees are due at the time of booking; the balance is due 1 month prior to the function. There is a 10% discount in fees if 3 or more nights are reserved.

CANCELLATION POLICY: A full refund will be given with 1 month's notice. With less notice, a refund minus a $25 handling charge is given only if the space is rebooked.

AVAILABILITY: Year-round, every day.

SERVICES/AMENITIES:

Restaurant Services: no
Catering: select from list or BYO
Kitchen Facilities: adequate
Tables & Chairs: most provided
Linens, Silver, etc.: most provided
Restrooms: wca
Dance Floor: no
Meeting Equipment: BYO

Parking: off street
Overnight Accommodations: 15 guestrooms
Telephone: separate lines in each building
Outdoor Night Lighting: yes
Outdoor Cooking Facilities: BBQ
Cleanup: provided for a fee
Special Services: custom meals CBA

RESTRICTIONS:

Alcohol: BYO
Smoking: outside only
Music: approval required

Wheelchair Access: limited
Insurance: not required

Rancho Murieta

RANCHO MURIETA COUNTRY CLUB

7000 Alameda Drive
Rancho Murieta, CA 95683
(916) 354-3400
Reserve for Events: 1–12 months in advance
Reserve for Meetings: 2 weeks–3 months in advance

Golfers from all over the country come here and think they've gone to heaven. What's surprising is that Rancho Murieta Country Club is also popular for parties and meetings. Built in a Spanish Hacienda style, the Clubhouse has unadorned cream walls, dark, wood-beamed ceilings and numerous arches. Large events are held in the Murieta Room which features a high, vaulted ceiling, mammoth beams and a striking stained glass window. Comfortable seating surrounds a central dance floor, and strings of tiny Christmas lights add sparkle overhead. A glass wall dominates the room, providing not only light, but a direct view of the 18th green. The California Room can accommodate small meetings and has some audio-visual equipment on hand. Its dark wood paneling and ceiling are lightened by an expansive view of the golf course. The Parasol Dining Room, which normally serves as the club's restaurant, is also available for special luncheons or dinners. Green walls, white ceiling and bamboo cushioned seating create a fresh, casual feeling. Shaped like a pentagon, four of the room's five sides are glass and overlook—what else?—the golf course. The main attraction at the club has to be the terrace, a curved brick patio that is wonderful for outdoor parties. From here, the rolling hills of the golf course spread out endlessly in all directions. Oaks dot the landscape, and a wild turkey is occasionally spotted amongst the trees. Meticulously landscaped rock gardens border the terrace, and in spring, they're covered with brilliantly colored blooms. And for tennis aficionados, there are six lighted tennis courts. More than a golfer's paradise, Rancho Murieta Country Club is an unexpected place for a variety of functions, just a half hour and a million miles from downtown Sacramento.

CAPACITY:	Area	Seated	Standing	Area	Seated	Standing
	Murieta Room	200	350	Terrace	200	300
	(w/o full dance floor)	250	350	19th Hole Bar	84	—
	Club Rancho Room	100	150	Parasol Dining Room	92	—
	California Room	40	60			

FEES & DEPOSITS: A deposit is required at the time of booking which is applied to the total balance. Deposits range from $100–1,500 depending upon the size and type of event. There may be a room setup fee of $50–300, depending on the food and beverage arrangements. The total estimated balance is due 10 days prior to the event. A minimum of 25 people is required for catering services, and a final guest count is due 72 hours prior to the event. Seated luncheons start at $10/person, seated dinners at $18/person. Buffet luncheons start at $12/person, buffet dinners at $17/person. Beverages, tax and a 20% service charge are additional.

CANCELLATION POLICY: With more than 90 days' notice, your deposit is fully refunded. With less notice, refunds are only given if the space can be rebooked.

AVAILABILITY: Year-round, every day except some major holidays, 6am–1am. The Parasol Dining Room and the 19th Hole Bar have limited availability.

SERVICES/AMENITIES:

Restaurant Services: yes
Catering: provided, no BYO
Kitchen Facilities: n/a
Tables & Chairs: provided
Linens, Silver, etc.: provided
Restrooms: no wca
Dance Floor: yes
Other: event coordination, piano, golf/tennis events may be arranged

Parking: 2 large lots, valet CBA
Overnight Accommodations: CBA
Telephone: pay phone
Outdoor Night Lighting: yes
Outdoor Cooking Facilities: BBQ
Cleanup: provided
Meeting Equipment: overhead projector, TV/VCR, blackboard & easels

RESTRICTIONS:

Alcohol: provided, corkage $6/bottle
Smoking: designated areas only
Music: limited amplified ok

Wheelchair Access: yes
Insurance: sometimes required
Other: decorations must be approved

Need a caterer, cake maker, florist? The Service Directory starting on page 614 features the best in the business.

Rocklin

FINNISH TEMPERANCE HALL

4090 Rocklin Road
Rocklin, CA 95677
(916) 632-4100 Diana
Reserve for Events: 3–12 months in advance
Reserve for Meetings: 8 weeks in advance

This recently remodeled 1905 hall is a surprisingly fresh and inviting space. Light pouring through tall windows with stained glass panels makes the room bright and cheerful. Painted off-white and light olive green with clean, straight lines, the Finnish Temperance Hall succeeds in creating a warm, eye-pleasing environment. A raised stage, beautiful maple flooring, and overhead spot lighting add to the room's ambiance.

CAPACITY: The Hall can accommodate 144 seated guests or 309 for a standing reception.

FEES & DEPOSITS: A $250 refundable deposit is due when the contract is submitted and the rental fee is due 15 days prior to the function. A $15 service fee is included in the rental totals below. Any hours over 12 will be billed at the hourly rate. Non-residents will be charged 20% more than the fees below.

Hourly Rate	*3 Hour min.*	*6 Hours*	*7 Hours*	*8–9 Hours*
$30	$150	$255	$295	$330

CANCELLATION POLICY: With up to 31 days' notice, 25% of the rental fee will be forfeited. With less than 30 days, 50% will be retained; less than 10 days, 100%.

AVAILABILITY: Year-round, every day, anytime.

SERVICES/AMENITIES:

Restaurant Services: no
Catering: BYO
Kitchen Facilities: fully equipped
Tables & Chairs: provided
Linens, Silver, etc.: BYO
Restrooms: wca
Dance Floor: yes
Meeting Equipment: no

Parking: adjacent lot
Overnight Accommodations: no
Telephone: pay phone
Outdoor Night Lighting: access only
Outdoor Cooking Facilities: no
Cleanup: renter or caterer
Special Services: stage

RESTRICTIONS:

Alcohol: BYO, some restrictions apply
Smoking: allowed
Music: amplified with approval

Wheelchair Access: yes
Insurance: may be required
Other: decorations restricted

SUNSET WHITNEY COUNTRY CLUB

4201 Midas Ave.
Rocklin, CA 95677
(916) 624-2402 Social Coordinator
Reserve for Events: 6–12 months in advance
Reserve for Meetings: 2–3 weeks in advance

While its main claim to fame may be its golf course, the Sunset Whitney Country Club is also a popular place for parties and business functions. Both the Sunset and Whitney Rooms have vaulted wood-beamed ceilings made of stone, wood and glass construction. They are spacious, airy, and a nice refuge from the heat during the summer. The Whitney Room has a unique four-sided fireplace that creates a warmth and intimacy in all corners of the room during cooler weather. It also opens out onto a large tree-shaded patio with pool—a delightful area to set up tables outdoors. Out of the main metropolitan area, the Sunset Whitney Club is a relaxed and versatile facility.

CAPACITY, FEES & DEPOSITS:

Room	Max. Guests	Charge
Sunset Room	200	$450
Whitney Room	120	400
Whitney Room & Patio	300	600
Gazebo & Lawn	200	150 *(with reception)*
Gazebo & Lawn	200	300 *(without reception)*

A deposit equal to the room charge is due when reservations are confirmed and is applied to the event total. The estimated cost is due 1 week prior to the event; the balance is payable at the end of the function. The room charge includes setup, cleanup, tables, chairs, linens, etc. for 4 hours of use. Extra hours can be arranged for $100/hour. Food service per person: buffets start at $10, luncheons at $8, dinners at $12 and hors d'oeuvres at $7. Tax and 15% gratuity are additional.

CANCELLATION POLICY: The deposit is refundable with 3 months' notice or if the space can be rebooked.

AVAILABILITY: Year-round, every day from 7am–midnight. Closed Christmas and Thanksgiving days.

SERVICES/AMENITIES:

Restaurant Services: yes
Catering: provided, no BYO
Kitchen Facilities: n/a
Tables & Chairs: provided
Linens, Silver, etc.: provided
Restrooms: wca
Cleanup: provided
Special Services: piano

Parking: large lots
Meeting Equipment: easel & screen
Overnight Accommodations: no
Telephone: pay phones
Outdoor Night Lighting: yes
Outdoor Cooking Facilities: BBQ
Dance Floor: yes

RESTRICTIONS:

Alcohol: provided, no BYO
Smoking: allowed
Music: amplified ok

Insurance: required
Wheelchair Access: yes
Other: decorations restricted, no confetti, open flames

Roseville

MAIDU
COMMUNITY CENTER

1550 Maidu Drive
Roseville, CA 95661
(916) 781-0690
Reserve for Events: 1–12 months in advance
Reserve for Meetings: 1–2 months in advance

This large, ultra-modern facility is the City of Roseville's brand new community center. Built to serve every segment of the community, it houses space for parties and meetings. The interior is fresh, airy and well designed. The lobby is impressive with a high, vaulted ceiling, and windows around the top let in lots of sunlight. A spacious patio with a gazebo in back is enclosed by a high brick fence that provides privacy and quiet. Surrounded by undeveloped park land, the center also enjoys a peaceful, natural environment.

CAPACITY, FEES & DEPOSITS:

Room	Seated	Reception	Cleaning Deposit	Security Deposit	Rental Fees/Hour
Reception Hall	280	450	$200	$200	$22–88
Meeting Rooms 1 & 2 Combined	130	150	100	100	12–39
Senior Meeting Room	50	70	50	50	5–19
Senior Activity Room	50	85	50	50	4–14

Rental fees vary depending on residential status plus a few other factors. A non-refundable security deposit, applied to the rental fee, is required when reservations are confirmed. The cleaning deposit and rental balance are due 2 weeks prior to the event. The cleaning deposit is usually returned after the event if the facility is left in clean condition.

CANCELLATION POLICY: The security deposit is only refunded if the space(s) can be rebooked.

AVAILABILITY: Year-round, Sun–Thurs, 6am–11pm; Fri–Sat, 6am–1am. Closed major holidays.

SERVICES/AMENITIES:

Restaurant Services: no
Catering: BYO
Kitchen Facilities: setup only
Tables & Chairs: provided
Linens, Silver, etc.: BYO

Overnight Accommodations: no
Telephone: pay phone
Outdoor Night Lighting: yes
Outdoor Cooking Facilities: BYO
Cleanup: caterer or renter

Restrooms: wca
Dance Floor: yes
Parking: large lot

RESTRICTIONS:
Alcohol: BYO
Smoking: outside only
Music: amplified ok

Other: PA system, podium, portable bar extra fee, tot lot
Meeting Equipment: no

Wheelchair Access: yes
Insurance: required
Other: decorations restricted, no open flames

R. J.'S VICTORIAN PALMS

315 Washington Blvd.
Roseville, CA 95678
(916) 782-3850
Reserve for Events: 1 week–6 months in advance
Reserve for Meetings: 1 day–6 months in advance

R. J.'s Victorian Palms is a white, plantation-style home built in 1909. Located on a tree-lined street in the historic district of Roseville, and surrounded by a seventy-year rose garden, the house is warm and inviting. Wide steps lead up to a lattice-enclosed porch, which is great for al fresco dining. Inside, hardwood floors, period light fixtures and built-in china cabinets, filled with antique tea cups and dishes, enhance a comfortable interior. If you're considering a large function, there are three connecting dining rooms, the largest of which has sizable bay windows with cushioned window seating. French doors open out to the latticed porch, making the entire dining area feel light and open. Other amenities include a ten foot oak bar, working fireplace and built-in stereo system. R. J.'s Victorian Palms will give you and your guests the flavor of a by-gone era.

CAPACITY:

Area	Standing	Seated
House	100	75
Porch	30	25
Garden Area	—	100

FEES & DEPOSITS: A $300 refundable cleaning/security deposit is required to secure your date. Half of the estimated food and beverage total is due when the contract is submitted; the event balance is payable 3 days prior to the event along with a certificate of insurance for alcohol. A final guest count is required 7 days in advance. A $50 cleaning fee is deducted from the deposit, which is normally returned 7 days after the event. Food service starts at $15/person for lunch, $20 for dinner. Beverages and tax are additional. Gratuity is not charged.

CANCELLATION POLICY: With 30 days' notice, the deposit will be refunded if the day can be rebooked. With less notice, the deposit is forfeited.

AVAILABILITY: Year-round, every day 7am–1am.

SERVICES/AMENITIES:

Restaurant Services: no
Catering: provided,no BYO
Kitchen Facilities: n/a
Tables & Chairs: provided
Linens, Silver, etc.: provided
Restrooms: wca
Dance Floor: CBA
Meeting Equipment: podium, screen

Parking: lot, on street
Overnight Accommodations: no
Telephone: house phone
Outdoor Night Lighting: yes
Outdoor Cooking Facilities: BBQ
Cleanup: provided
Other: event coordination

RESTRICTIONS:

Alcohol: BYO or CBA, liquor liability required
Smoking: outside only
Music: amplified ok

Wheelchair Access: yes
Insurance: alcohol liability required

ROSEVILLE OPERA HOUSE

Lincoln and Main
Roseville, CA 95678
(916) 773-0768
Reserve for Events: 2 months in advance
Reserve for Meetings: 1 week in advance

From the street, you might never know that this facility exists. You enter through a door on the side of an old Roseville building and walk upstairs to a large ballroom. Recently redecorated, the room is painted light pink with a cream colored ceiling and deep green trim. Drapes are artfully hung over the windows, adding softness to an otherwise unadorned space. Hardwood floors and a stage make the room adaptable to both special events and business functions—especially presentations.

CAPACITY: The Opera House can accommodate 250 seated guests or 320 for standing hors d'oeuvres.

FEES & DEPOSITS: A refundable $200 cleaning deposit is required when the date is confirmed. The rental fee for Saturday and Sunday is $450 for a 24-hour period. Hourly rates can be specified for Monday–Friday meetings. The rental balance is due 1 month prior to the event.

CANCELLATION POLICY: With 60 days' notice, the deposit is refunded.

AVAILABILITY: Year-round, every day.

SERVICES/AMENITIES:

Restaurant Services: no
Catering: BYO
Kitchen Facilities: minimal
Dance Floor: yes
Parking: adjacent lot
Overnight Accommodations: no

Tables & Chairs: provided
Linens, Silver, etc.: BYO
Restrooms: no wca
Outdoor Night Lighting: access only
Outdoor Cooking Facilities: no
Cleanup: renter or caterer

Telephone: no
Meeting Equipment: no

RESTRICTIONS:
Alcohol: BYO, any sale requires license
Smoking: not allowed
Music: amplified ok

Other: event coordination

Wheelchair Access: no
Insurance: certificate required
Other: no red wine or punch, no candles

Sacramento

AMBER HOUSE

1315 22nd Street
Sacramento, CA 95816
(916) 444-8085
Reserve for Events: 1 week–2 months in advance
Reserve for Meetings: 1 week in advance

Shaded by towering elm trees, Amber House is an elegant yet comfortable Craftsman-style inn just minutes from downtown Sacramento. The warm wood beamed ceilings, staircase, wainscotting and floors adds to the serenity of the interior. Antiques, oriental carpets and a brick fireplace make you feel right at home. Adjacent to the Amber House is a beautifully restored Mediterranean-style home featuring beveled and leaded glass, Grecian columns and elaborate wood moldings. Both provide an intimate setting for smaller functions and are especially good places for executive retreats when small business groups need to stay overnight. Amber House offers nicely appointed suites with marble tiled baths and jacuzzi tubs.

CAPACITY: The facility (both houses) accommodates up to 65 people.

MEETING ROOMS: There are 3 rooms that accommodate 5–25 people.

FEES & DEPOSITS: Rates start at $200 and vary with time required, guest count and services provided. A deposit of half the rental fee is required when reservations are confirmed. For meetings, beverage service is offered throughout the day. For overnight stays, please call for rates.

CANCELLATION POLICY: For special events, a full refund is given with 30 days' notice. For meetings, 7 days' notice is required.

AVAILABILITY: Every day, anytime.

SERVICES/AMENITIES:
Restaurant Services: no
Catering: BYO, licensed
Kitchen Facilities: adequate
Tables & Chairs: provided

Parking: on street, lot
Overnight Accommodations: 8 guestrooms
Telephone: guest phones
Outdoor Night Lighting: access only

Linens, Silver, etc.: caterer
Restrooms: no wca
Dance Floor: no
Other: full event coordination

RESTRICTIONS:
Alcohol: BYO
Smoking: outside only
Music: no amplified

Outdoor Cooking Facilities: no
Cleanup: caterer
Meeting Equipment: no

Wheelchair Access: no
Insurance: not required

AUNT ABIGAIL'S BED & BREAKFAST

2120 G Street
Sacramento, CA 95816
(800) 858-1568 or **(916) 441-5007**
Reserve for Events: 1 week–6 months in advance
Reserve for Meetings: 1–12 weeks in advance

The regulars who frequent Aunt Abigail's refer to it as their "home away from home." Built in 1912, this cube-style Colonial Revival structure retains many of the characteristics of the period. The dining room and living room, used for both business meetings and special events, have hardwood floors, oriental carpets and antique pieces throughout. The large fireplace, cheery light cream walls and lace curtains add warmth and charm and outside, the garden patio area is a quiet retreat for small gatherings. Situated on a tree-lined residential street, Aunt Abigail's provides a comfortable and restful getaway.

CAPACITY: The facility accommodates up to 35 guests.

MEETING ROOMS: The dining room can hold up to 20 people.

FEES & DEPOSITS: For meetings, the fee is $70 for the first hour and $25 for each additional hour with a 2-hour minimum. The maximum cost is $170 for a 7-hour day. Special event rental of the facility for 4 hours (11am–3pm) is $600; for 7 hours (1pm–8pm) including overnight booking the fee is $1,100. Half of the fee is due when reservations are confirmed; the balance 1 month prior to the event.

CANCELLATION POLICY: For special events, 1 month's notice is required for a full refund. With less notice, refunds apply only if the space is rebooked.

AVAILABILITY: Every day.

SERVICES/AMENITIES:
Restaurant Services: no
Catering: BYO, licensed
Kitchen Facilities: ample
Tables & Chairs: some provided
Linens, Silver, etc.: caterer
Restrooms: no wca

Parking: on and off street
Overnight Accommodations: 6 guestrooms
Telephone: guest phones
Outdoor Night Lighting: access only
Outdoor Cooking Facilities: no
Cleanup: caterer

Dance Floor: no

RESTRICTIONS:
Alcohol: BYO, no red wine
Smoking: outside only
Music: no amplified

Meeting Equipment: board and markers

Wheelchair Access: no
Insurance: not required

CALIFORNIA STATE RAILROAD MUSEUM

111 I Street
Old Sacramento, CA 95814
(916) 445-7387
Reserve for Events: 12 months in advance
Reserve for Meetings: up to 12 months in advance

For those of you who harbor a secret passion for trains, the Railroad Museum is nirvana. Home to 21 locomotives and cars, it is the finest train museum in North America. Lighting throughout is subdued, imbuing these magnificent, historical gems with a certain mystery. The largest locomotive here weighs over a million pounds while the oldest dates back to 1862. Many of the trains are displayed in the Roundhouse, a stark, vaulted structure that serves as a train "hangar." Events take place here, guests mingling among these monuments to railroad ingenuity. This is definitely one of the more unusual special event locations we've seen.

CAPACITY: The Museum accommodates 600 standing or 400 seated guests.

MEETING ROOMS: 2 theaters which seat up to 130 people, each, are available.

FEES & DEPOSITS: A refundable $250 cleaning deposit is due when reservations are confirmed. The basic rental fee is $1,250. If engines need to be moved, however, there is an added charge of $750 for the first one and $250 for the second. All fees are payable 30 days prior to the event.

CANCELLATION POLICY: With 2 weeks' notice, the deposit is refunded.

AVAILABILITY: Every day, 5pm–11pm except Thanksgiving and Christmas week.

SERVICES/AMENITIES:
Restaurant Services: no
Catering: BYO
Kitchen Facilities: no
Tables & Chairs: BYO
Linens, Silver, etc.: BYO
Restrooms: wca
Dance Floor: in Roundhouse

Parking: on street, lot
Overnight Accommodations: no
Telephone: pay phone
Outdoor Night Lighting: access only
Outdoor Cooking Facilities: no
Cleanup: renter or caterer
Meeting Equipment: no

RESTRICTIONS:
Alcohol: BYO, license required for sales
Smoking: outside only
Music: amplified ok

Wheelchair Access: yes
Insurance: liability required
Other: food restricted to Roundhouse

CAPITOL PLAZA HALLS

1025 Ninth Street, Suite 201
Sacramento, CA 95814
(916) 443-4483
Reserve for Events: 1 week–12 months in advance
Reserve for Meetings: 1 week–12 months in advance

When walking through this facility's undistinguished entrance, you wonder what it could possibly have to offer. A quick trip up the elevator, however, reveals an extraordinary pair of rooms which are perfect for parties and business functions. Over a hundred years old, both halls have 29-foot hand-painted ceilings restored by a local artist. The colors—teal green, pink, mauve, blue and gold leaf—are exquisite. Tall draped windows and chandeliers complete the feeling of elegance. Downstairs is another hall used for large events. It's more contemporary, with wood paneled walls and subdued lighting. Several smaller rooms, used primarily for business meetings, are also available. These halls are worth seeing even if you don't have your event here!

CAPACITY:

Room	Seated	Standing
Fraternity Hall	300	450
Temple Hall	300	450
Silver Room	300	500

For meetings up to 100 guests, the halls can be arranged to accommodate business activities in one half of the room, and dining or social activities in the other.

FEES & DEPOSITS: Weekend rates run $900–1,100. Weekday rates are negotiable. For events, a $300 deposit is due when reservations are confirmed and the balance is due 15 days prior to the event. Fees for meetings are payable on the day of the meeting.

CANCELLATION POLICY: The deposit will be refunded with 90 days' notice.

AVAILABILITY: Every day.

SERVICES/AMENITIES:

Restaurant Services: no
Catering: provided or BYO
Kitchen Facilities: minimal
Tables & Chairs: provided
Linens, Silver, etc.: provided for fee
Restrooms: wca
Dance Floor: yes
Meeting Equipment: full audio-visual

Parking: on street, valet
Overnight Accommodations: no
Telephone: pay phone
Outdoor Night Lighting: access only
Outdoor Cooking Facilities: no
Cleanup: provided
Special Services: event planning

RESTRICTIONS:

Alcohol: provided or BYO
Smoking: foyers or outside only
Music: amplified ok

Wheelchair Access: yes
Insurance: liability required
Other: decoration restrictions

DRIVER MANSION INN

2019 21st Street
Sacramento, CA 95818
(916) 455-5243 Sandi & Richard Kann
Reserve for Events: 3–12 months in advance
Reserve for Meetings: 1week–12 months in advance

Built in 1899, this colonial revival mansion is one of Sacramento's most significant Victorian residences. Set back on a grassy slope, the Inn appears regal and imposing as you walk up the steps to the entrance. Once inside, however, the warmth and airiness make you feel at home. The Garden Suite is spacious and lovely with hardwood floors, tall windows and lots of natural light. Oriental carpets, a working fireplace and antique fixtures add to the feeling of relaxed elegance. The dining room, with its dark peach walls, lace curtains and high ceilings is also a comfortable space for small get-togethers. For outdoor events, the Inn has a large garden patio shaded by an enormous picture-perfect oak tree. Located in a residential neighborhood, the Driver Mansion Inn provides guests with quiet and privacy.

CAPACITY: The facility can accommodate 100 guests.

MEETING ROOMS: 2 meeting rooms with a total capacity of 25 people.

FEES & DEPOSITS: A non-refundable deposit of $250–800, depending on the type of event, is required. Rental fees range from $250–2,000 depending on guest count, day of week, time of day and space(s) reserved.

AVAILABILITY: Year-round, every day.

SERVICES/AMENITIES:

Restaurant Services: no
Catering: provided
Kitchen Facilities: n/a
Tables & Chairs: provided
Linens, Silver, etc.: provided
Restrooms: no wca
Dance Floor: no

Parking: on street
Overnight Accommodations: 9 guestrooms
Telephone: guest phones
Outdoor Night Lighting: access only
Outdoor Cooking Facilities: BBQ
Cleanup: provided
Meeting Equipment: full range audio visual

RESTRICTIONS:

Alcohol: provided by caterer
Smoking: outside only
Music: amplified indoors only

Wheelchair Access: no
Insurance: not required

FAIRYTALE TOWN

1501 Sutterville Road
Sacramento, CA 95822
(916) 264-7061
Reserve for Events: 2–12 months in advance
Reserve for Meetings: 1–3 months in advance

King Arthur's Castle is a source of intrigue for most of the kids who wind their way through a maze to the mysterious castle core. What awaits them? A very special room where the birthday boy or girl can preside as King Arthur or Queen Guinevere for a day. A bona fide throne occupies the place of honor at the round table, and multicolored benches provide seating for the loyal subjects. And if the Castle leaves your child unenthralled, there's also Sherwood Forest where, as Robin Hood or Maid Marion, he or she can run wild with their band of merrry girls and boys. Fairytale Town provides everything you need to insure that your party will be a success: cake, ice cream, magic, juggling, storytelling, face painting and much more. Puppet shows performed in the Theater are a real favorite with children and their parents. The "Town" is also inhabited by live sheep, cows, ponies, goats, ducks, chicken and pigs. Not just for kids, this charming little park is also available to adults after closing. If you've still got a youthful imagination, it's a terrific place to play.

CAPACITY: For children's birthday parties during regular business hours, King Arthur's Castle and Sherwood Forest can hold 15 kids, 7 adults, max. After 6pm, the Town can hold up to 3,500 guests for a group function until dusk.

MEETING ROOMS: The Castle can accommodate 22; the Theater, 50–75 people.

FEES & DEPOSITS: A $100 refundable cleaning/security deposit is required when the application is submitted. The rental fee is $100/hour for a 2-hour minimum with the rental balance due 10 days prior to the event. There may be an additional deposit required if alcohol is included in your event. Call for birthday package prices and reservations, M–F, 1:30pm–4:30pm.

CANCELLATION POLICY: With 30 days' notice, the deposit is refunded.

AVAILABILITY: Year-round, every day. Closed when raining and on Christmas day. Birthday parties in the Castle can be held Monday–Saturday at 10:30am, 11:45am, 2:15pm and 3:30pm. Afterwards, children are free to play in the park until 5pm. Meetings can be scheduled weekdays, 10am–5pm.

SERVICES/AMENITIES:

Restaurant Services: no
Catering: provided or BYO
Kitchen Facilities: no
Tables & Chairs: BYO
Linens, Silver, etc.: BYO
Restrooms: wca
Dance Floor: grass area or BYO

Parking: large lot
Overnight Accommodations: no
Telephone: pay phone across street
Outdoor Night Lighting: yes
Outdoor Cooking Facilities: BBQ
Cleanup: renter or caterer
Meeting Equipment: CBA

RESTRICTIONS:

Alcohol: BYO, permit required

Smoking: outside only

Music: amplified within limits, permit required

Wheelchair Access: yes

Insurance: required w/alcohol

HYATT REGENCY SACRAMENTO
At Capitol Park

1209 L Street
Sacramento, CA 95814
(916) 443-1234
Reserve for Events: 3–6 months in advance
Reserve for Meetings: 1–12 weeks in advance

The Hyatt may be the busiest hotel in Sacramento. It has every kind of event space you can think of, including a terrace on the twelfth floor and access to the lovely park across the street. The lobby sets the tone—light, airy and soothing to the eye. Soft shades of grey, dusky pink, teal and mauve, touches of marble and an abundance of glass create a tasteful and distinctive environment. The Ballroom has an intricately patterned sixteen-foot ceiling and special lighting and mirrors which add sparkle. And for outdoor events, the hotel can arrange additional festivities among the trees on the Capitol grounds. For variety, elegance and all the amenities a cosmopolitan hotel can offer, the Hyatt is a superb choice.

CAPACITY:

Room	Seated	Reception
Golden State	100	100–150
Big Sur & Carmel	80	80
Trinity, Ventura, Santa Barbara & Tahoe	40–50	40–50
Busby Berkeley Lounge	60	200
Poolside Area	80	200
Regency Ballroom (has 6 sections)	1,075	1,650

FEES & DEPOSITS: A non-refundable deposit ranging from $200–1,000 is required, the rate dependent on room(s) reserved. The deposit is due when the contract is submitted. With no food service, meeting rooms rent for $200–2,000/day depending on group size and room(s) reserved. Per person rates: buffet brunches $15, luncheons $16, buffet luncheons $18, dinners $24, buffet dinners $28 and hors d'oeuvres start at $12/person. The estimated balance plus a final guest count are required 48 hours prior to the function. Tax and 17% gratuity are additional. If food and beverage service is provided, all or a portion of any room rental may be waived.

CANCELLATION POLICY: With 90 days' notice, the deposit will be refunded. With less notice, it will only be refunded if the space can be rebooked.

AVAILABILITY: Year-round, every day, anytime.

SERVICES/AMENITIES:

Restaurant Services: yes

Overnight Accommodations: 500 guestrooms

Catering: provided, no BYO
Kitchen Facilities: n/a
Tables & Chairs: provided
Linens, Silver, etc.: provided
Restrooms: wca
Parking: adjacent lots
Meeting Equipment: full audio-visual available

RESTRICTIONS:
Alcohol: provided, no BYO
Smoking: allowed
Music: amplified w/in limits

Telephone: pay phones
Outdoor Night Lighting: yes
Outdoor Cooking Facilities: yes
Cleanup: provided
Dance Floor: yes
Special Services: event coordination

Wheelchair Access: yes
Insurance: sometimes required

THE PENTHOUSE

2901 K Street
Sacramento, CA 95816
(916) 448-8520
Reserve for Events: 2–6 months in advance
Reserve for Meetings: 1 week–12 months in advance

The Penthouse, located on the top floor of the Sutter Square Galleria, is a striking, super-modern structure housing a collection of trendy shops. A relatively new facility, the Penthouse has already become a popular spot for special events. It's a large multi-function room that has been custom-designed down to the tables and chairs to provide maximum comfort and flexibility. Eye-soothing tones of mauve and teal green, and an immaculate and fresh appearance make this space very inviting. The management specializes in providing impeccable service, so for a special celebration in Sacramento, this is certainly a wonderful option.

CAPACITY: Suite A holds 150 seated or 200 standing; Suite B holds 80 seated or 100 standing. These rooms can be combined for a total 240 seated or 300 standing guests.

FEES & DEPOSITS:

	Meetings Half-Day	Meetings Full-Day	Saturday Events, 5 Hrs.	Sunday Events, 5 Hrs.
Suite A	$150	$300	$850	$550
Suite B	75	150	550	350
Suites A&B	225	450	1,200	800

Fees for weekday events vary with the number of guests and time frame requested. A holding deposit of $500 is required at the time of booking and will be subtracted from the room rental fee. A $400 refundable security deposit is due with the balance of fees 2 weeks prior to the event.

CANCELLATION POLICY: With 120 days' notice, the deposit will be refunded.

AVAILABILITY: Year-round, Friday 6pm–midnight; Saturday and Sunday, 11am–5pm and 6:30pm–

midnight. These time frames include some setup time.

SERVICES/AMENITIES:

Restaurant Services: 6 located in Galleria

Catering: provided, no BYO

Kitchen Facilities: adequate

Tables & Chairs: provided

Linens, Silver, etc.: provided

Restrooms: wca

Dance Floor: yes

Special Services: event planning

Parking: garage

Meeting Equipment: CBA

Overnight Accommodations: no

Telephone: pay phone

Outdoor Night Lighting: access only

Outdoor Cooking Facilities: no

Cleanup: provided

RESTRICTIONS:

Alcohol: provided or BYO, license required for sales

Smoking: outside only

Music: amplified ok

Wheelchair Access: yes

Insurance: not required

RADISSON HOTEL
Sacramento

500 Leisure Lane
Sacramento, CA 95815
(916) 922-2020 or **(800) 333-3333**
Reserve for Events: 3 months in advance
Reserve for Meetings: 3 months in advance

The Radisson Hotel underwent a thirty-month, forty million dollar renovation in 1989. Born as the Woodlake Inn in 1957, this sprawling complex has meeting, dining and lodging built around an eighteen-acre site. Remodeled in a contemporary, comfortable Mediterranean-style with tile roof, light stucco walls and Mexican pavers, it offers a multitude of choices for private parties and business functions. In the main building, the Grand Ballroom is the largest of the Radisson event spaces. Divisible into six separate rooms, it can expand or contract to fit your group size. Designed in a light apricot, the Ballroom has a stage, superb lighting and plenty of room for seated functions. Outdoors, the most notable feature of this site is a small lake, complete with a fountain that shoots fifty-foot sprays into the air. Bordering the lake is one of the Radisson's most sought-after spots, the Edgewater Deck. Warmed by the morning sun, the deck is a lovely place for a daytime reception, and in the evening, guests can enjoy cocktails and hors d'oeuvres under a starry sky. An outdoor patio called the Grove, is also available for parties, concerts and plays. And guests who want to have fun can rent paddleboats for a quick spin on the water. The Conference Plaza is not only well-designed for business functions, but is equally suitable for an outdoor reception. Seat your guests under umbrella-shaded tables, where they can appreciate the plaza's geometric design, with round fountain and rectangular lawns on all sides. If you need lots of flexibility or have an overly large gathering, the Radisson will come to the rescue.

CAPACITY:

Area	Seated	Reception
Grand Ballroom Total	1,350	1,800
Conference Plaza	280	500
Edgewater Deck	100	200

MEETING ROOMS: The Ballroom and Conference Plaza are available for meetings.

FEES & DEPOSITS: A $150–2,500 deposit depending on the space reserved, is required when reservations are confirmed. The deposit is applied to the total, and 2/3 of the estimated total is due 30 days prior to the event. The balance may also be due in advance of the event. Per person food service starts at $11.75 for luncheons, $15.75 for dinners, $23 for buffets and $11.75 and $15.75 for luncheon and dinner hors d'oeuvres, respectively.

CANCELLATION POLICY: With more than 30 days' notice, your deposit and fees are refunded. With 30 or less days' notice, refunds are given only if the space is rebooked.

AVAILABILITY: Year-round, every day, 6am–2am.

SERVICES/AMENITIES:

Restaurant Services: yes

Catering: provided, no BYO

Kitchen Facilities: n/a

Tables & Chairs: provided

Linens, Silver, etc.: provided

Restrooms: wca

Meeting Equipment: provided, extra fee

Other: event coordination, pianos, ice carvings

Parking: large complimentary lot

Overnight Accommodations: 320 guestrooms

Telephone: pay phone

Outdoor Night Lighting: yes

Outdoor Cooking Facilities: BBQ

Cleanup: provided

Dance Floor: yes

RESTRICTIONS:

Alcohol: provided, corkage $7.50/bottle

Smoking: allowed

Insurance: not required

Wheelchair Access: yes

Music: amplified ok

Other: decorations must be approved

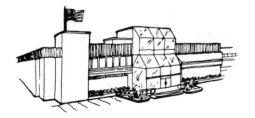

RANCHO ARROYO

9880 Jackson Road
Sacramento, CA 95827
(916) 364-7980
Reserve for Events: 1–12 months in advance
Reserve for Meetings: 2 weeks in advance

Rancho Arroyo Sports Complex literally has something for everyone. The Bar and Lounge area has a dance floor, suspended video screen and sound system. The Restaurant down the hall is spacious and has a glass wall overlooking the lagoon at the entrance of the facility. Rancho Arroyo may seem modest in size at first glance, but when you explore the place you're in for a surprise. In addition to all the "regular" event spaces, there are indoor tennis courts and an Olympic-size swimming pool where Olympic Gold Medalist Mark Spitz trained. When the courts are removed, this indoor area can accommodate 4,000 people! The only complex in the area with so much to offer, Rancho Arroyo is quite a unique facility for events.

MEETING ROOMS: 3 rooms with seated capacity of 65 guests each, all combined, they can hold up to 200.

CAPACITY, FEES & DEPOSITS:

Room	Seated	Reception	Fee/5 hours
VIP Room	25	—	$125
Restaurant	250	500	950
Poolside	500	1,000	1,500
Bar & Lounge	200	300	1,250
Indoor Tennis Courts	2,400	all 8 courts 6,000	all 8 courts 500/court
	300 each	750 each	500/court

A $75–250 refundable security deposit, the amount depending on which space(s) is reserved, is required when reservations are confirmed. The estimated total food and beverage balance is payable 48 hours prior to the event. Per person rates: seated luncheons $8–15, dinners $10–20, brunches $12–15, hors d'oeuvres $7–17 and buffets $13–20. Tax and a 17% gratuity are additional. Sometimes an additional security fee is required.

CANCELLATION POLICY: With 30 days' notice, the deposit will be refunded.

AVAILABILITY: Year-round, every day until 2am except some major holidays.

SERVICES/AMENITIES:

Restaurant Services: yes
Catering: provided, no BYO
Kitchen Facilities: n/a
Tables & Chairs: provided
Linens, Silver, etc.: provided
Dance Floor: yes
Parking: large lot
Meeting Equipment: yes

Overnight Accommodations: no
Telephone: pay phone
Outdoor Night Lighting: yes
Outdoor Cooking Facilities: yes
Restrooms: wca
Cleanup: provided
Special Services: event coordination, piano, bartenders

RESTRICTIONS:

Alcohol: provided, corkage $5/bottle
Smoking: designated areas
Music: amplified ok

Wheelchair Access: yes, elevators
Insurance: sometimes required
Other: decorations restricted

SACRAMENTO
GRAND BALLROOM

629 J Street
Sacramento, CA 95814
(916) 446-9491
Reserve for Events: 2–6 months in advance
Reserve for Meetings: 2 weeks–6 months in advance

The simple, unadorned lobby of this building does not prepare you for what comes next. Turn the corner and, voilá—you stand open-mouthed, gazing into the Grand Ballroom. And grand it is! After being submerged for years under carpets, wall separators and a bank facade, its soaring, forty-five-foot-high ceiling once again greets you in all its gold leaf splendor. The height and ornate detail take your breath away. High above, a multitude of plaster cast moldings have been painted, predominantly in gold, with dark teal highlights. Around the cornices are more detailed moldings painted in tans, creams and rich cocoa. Suspended from the ceiling are eight original light fixtures, all as enormous and detailed as the room. At the far end of the room, an elegant brass revolving door is ready to bring in guests and nearby, old-fashioned teller windows bring back memories of banking days past. The former "Paying" and "Receiving" windows, dressed in shiny brass and beveled glass, now function as the front of a spacious bar area. A light marble floor, ringed with a black marble border, is in keeping with the grand style. Several raised areas are perfect for buffet setups or band. For smaller parties or meetings, check out the Boardroom upstairs. Again, the ceiling here is outstanding, with intricate detailing in painted plaster. Gold leaf and trim highlight raised patterns. A white, hand-carved marble fireplace with large overhead mirror is the center focus of the Board Room. Dark, rich wood paneling and decorative wall friezes add warmth. This is a sensational room which must be seen to be appreciated. Downstairs is a women's restroom that is one of the best we've seen. Designed with the same refined quality as the Ballroom, the marble-clad women's room is gorgeous. For those interested in an elegant party in Sacramento, you're in luck. We're glad this neoclassic ballroom has been brought back to life.

CAPACITY: 500 seated guests; 700 for standing hors d'oeuvres.

MEETING ROOMS: The Ballroom accommodates to 500, the Boardroom 50–75.

FEES & DEPOSITS: A non-refundable $250 reservation fee and a $250 security deposit are required to secure your date. The rental fee balance is due 30 days prior to the event. Additional hours beyond the contracted time period will be billed at $75 per hour. Rental fees range from $500–1,500 depending on date, time and space(s) selected.

CANCELLATION POLICY: If notice of cancellation is given 60 or more days prior to the scheduled date, the security deposit will be refunded. If notice is given less than 60 days in advance, $500 will be retained.

AVAILABILITY: Year-round, every day from 8am to 1am.

SERVICES/AMENITIES:
Restaurant Services: no   *Parking:* public lots nearby, free on weekends

Catering: provided, no BYO
Kitchen Facilities: n/a
Tables & Chairs: provided
Linens, Silver, etc.: provided
Restrooms: wca
Meeting Equipment: sound system provided,
other equipment CBA, extra fee

RESTRICTIONS:
Alcohol: provided, if BYO $3.50/person bev. service
Smoking: outside only
Insurance: sometimes required

Overnight Accommodations: no
Telephone: pay phone
Outdoor Night Lighting: access only
Outdoor Cooking Facilities: no
Cleanup: provided
Dance Floor: yes
Other: full event coordination

Wheelchair Access: yes
Music: amplified ok
Other: no confetti or glitter

SACRAMENTO HISTORY MUSEUM

101 I Street
Old Sacramento, CA 95814
(916) 264-7057
Reserve for Events: 1–12 months in advance
Reserve for Meetings: 1 week in advance

The old fashioned brick facade of this museum belies its totally modern interior. A relatively new museum, it houses displays and information about much of Sacramento's local and regional history. The lobby is intriguing with its high reflective metal ceiling, slate floor and huge mural peopled by anonymous folks from the region's past. The museum has an open design—various galleries flow together and are visible to each other from different levels. All exhibits are accessible during your event. The museum's pride and joy is its Gold Gallery, containing $1,000,000 in Mother Lode gold chunks displayed in acrylic capsules. There's also an authentic reproduction of a miner's cabin, and plenty of Gold Rush artifacts. You can practice panning for gold with real gold pans, or try your luck with a gold panning videogame. A favorite pastime of visitors is to stand on a giant gold scale and see what their weight was worth in gold at the time of the Gold Rush and what it's worth today. Plans for late 1993 include the addition of a replica of a mine shaft. The museum's gold collection will be transferred from its current acrylic "home," and embedded in the mine shaft to give visitors a sense of what gold looked like in its natural setting. And if you want to combine a few history lessons with your event, docents are available. The History Museum is a fascinating place, certain to enhance any party.

CAPACITY: The facility accommodates 700 people.

MEETING ROOMS: The conference room holds 15–20 people.

FEES & DEPOSITS: Call for information regarding fees.

AVAILABILITY: For events, the museum is available Mon and Tues anytime, and Wed–Sun, 5pm to a negotiable hour. Meetings can be held anytime, 7 days a week.

SERVICES/AMENITIES:

Restaurant Services: no
Catering: preferred list or BYO w/approval
Kitchen Facilities: minimal
Tables & Chairs: some provided
Linens, Silver, etc.: BYO
Restrooms: wca
Dance Floor: CBA

Parking: on street, public garage
Overnight Accommodations: no
Telephone: pay phone
Outdoor Night Lighting: limited
Outdoor Cooking Facilities: no
Cleanup: caterer
Meeting Equipment: podium and microphone only

RESTRICTIONS:

Alcohol: BYO
Smoking: outside only
Music: amplified ok

Wheelchair Access: yes
Insurance: liability required

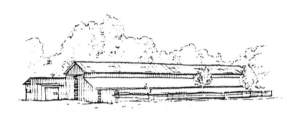

SACRAMENTO HORSEMEN'S ASSOCIATION

3200 Longview Drive
Sacramento, CA 95660
(916) 483-2845 or (916) 421-9060
Reserve for Events: 6 months in advance
Reserve for Meetings: 1 week–6 months in advance

Even if you're not a horse lover, the Sacramento Horsemen's Association Clubhouse may appeal to you. Here, you feel like you're in the country—not in urban Sacramento. As you drive in, you'll see a large red barn, corrals, horse paddocks and picnic areas. Located in Del Paso Park, on the other side of Haggin Oaks Municipal Golf Course, you can just make out the outline of fairways through a grove of stately, oak trees. For parties, the Clubhouse is the spot. It's not fancy, but it does have an informal charm. Inside, the Clubhouse decor is western-style rustic. The largest room has an open beam ceiling with knotty pine paneling. Adjacent is the bar area, with brick fireplace, and doors which open to a patio surrounded by lawn. The outdoor facilities back up onto a creek area with lots of large shade trees. Surprise your friends and arrive in a horse drawn carriage! Not for elegant, upscale functions—the Horsemen's Association Clubhouse is perfect for relaxed, unceremonious gatherings of friends.

CAPACITY: Inside, the facility can hold 175 guests; outside 200. The maximum capacity is 200 guests.

FEES & DEPOSITS: A refundable $100 cleaning/security deposit is required to hold your date. The rental fee, due 3 weeks prior to your function, varies; it runs about $450 per event.

CANCELLATION POLICY: If the space can be rebooked, the deposit will be returned.

AVAILABILITY: Year-round, daily 10am–midnight except Thurs–Fri, when the facility opens at 1pm.

SERVICES/AMENITIES:

Restaurant Services: no
Catering: BYO

Parking: large lot
Overnight Accommodations: no

Kitchen Facilities: fully equipped
Tables & Chairs: provided
Linens, Silver, etc.: BYO
Restrooms: wca
Meeting Equipment: BYO

RESTRICTIONS:
Alcohol: BYO
Smoking: outside only, no sales
Insurance: not required

Telephone: pay phone
Outdoor Night Lighting: yes
Outdoor Cooking Facilities: BBQs
Cleanup: caterer or renter
Dance Floor: yes

Wheelchair Access: yes
Music: amplified ok

A SHOT OF CLASS
and Bon Marche Ballroom

1020 11th Street
Sacramento, CA 95814
(916) 447-5340
Reserve for Events: 6–12 months in advance
Reserve for Meetings: 1–12 weeks in advance

A Shot of Class Restaurant is housed in a classic 1930s structure which used to be the Bon Marche Department Store. Fronting Cathedral Square, the building has planter boxes and a gray and white awning which extends far enough to shade the entry and several interior rooms. Yes, you can reserve the entire dining room for your private function. All is presented in a grand Art Deco motif. Twenty-three foot high walls are painted in a soft pink; large black urns, Erte-like sculpture and artwork on walls are also of 1930s vintage. Stylish linen-clad tables show off white linen napkins tucked vertically into wine glasses and a baby black grand piano is a permanent part of the dining experience. Popular for private dinners, the Alcove Room has a black lacquered screen that can totally or partially separate guests from the main dining room. Next door, in what was once the Better Women's Wear section of the old store, is the sizeable Bon Marche Ballroom with high ceiling, 1930s fixtures, art and soft colors. Here you'll find a dance floor, raised stage and plenty of space for a band. Adjacent to this is the Executive Room, a very small room with custom designed furnishings, perfect for dinners for up to twelve guests. The nicest thing about both the Restaurant and Ballroom is that A Shot of Class is the caterer as well as the event coordinator. A Shot of Class is multi-talented, extremely service oriented and very professional.

CAPACITY:	*Room*	*Seated*	*Standing Reception*
	Shot of Class Dining Room	250	400
	Alcove Room	60	75
	Bon Marche Ballroom	250	400
	Executive Room	12	—

FEES & DEPOSITS: A non-refundable $500 deposit, which is credited to the final bill, is required to secure your date. The room rental fee is $1/person per hour with a $400 minimum. A refundable security/cleaning fee is required. Food service is provided. Buffets start at $12/person and seated dinners at $13/person. Tax and a 15% service charge are additional. Half of the estimated total is due 2 weeks prior to the event; the final balance is due on the event day.

AVAILABILITY: Year-round, every day from 9am–1am.

SERVICES/AMENITIES:

Restaurant Services: yes
Catering: provided, no BYO
Kitchen Facilities: n/a
Tables & Chairs: provided
Linens, Silver, etc.: provided
Restrooms: wca
Meeting Equipment: CBA, extra fee
Other: event coordination, floral
   arrangements, ice carvings, cakes

Parking: nearby lot, valet CBA
Overnight Accommodations: no
Telephone: pay phone
Outdoor Night Lighting: access only
Outdoor Cooking Facilities: CBA
Cleanup: provided
Dance Floor: yes

RESTRICTIONS:

Alcohol: provided, no BYO
Smoking: allowed
Insurance: not required

Wheelchair Access: yes
Music: amplified ok

THE SPIRIT OF SACRAMENTO
and
THE MATTHEW McKINLEY

1207 Front St., #18
Sacramento, CA 95814
(800) 433-0263 or **(916) 552-2933**
Reserve for Events: 1–12 months in advance
Reserve for Meetings: 1–3 weeks in advance

Aptly named, the snappy red and white Spirit of Sacramento is hard to resist. Built in 1942, this paddlewheeler has graced the rivers of the west in a variety of roles—most notably as a "movie star" in the film *Blood Alley*. Today, she not only offers dining cruises, but is available for private and corporate parties. Have your event on one of two climate-controlled decks. The upper deck offers fabulous atrium seating—no matter where you sit, you're surrounded by the river and the sky. Photos of *Blood Alley* stars, John Wayne and Lauren Bacall, adorn the walls. White and burgundy linens add color and a touch of elegance. The second deck has an interior dining room with a river view from every table. The tongue-in-groove oak ceiling, red flock wallpaper and historical riverboat photos provide a glimpse of the golden days of riverboat travel. And for a treat, take a walk on the bow and let the sun and river breezes caress you as The Spirit gently wends its way up and down the Sacramento River. Newer than her sister ship, the Matthew McKinley is perfect for smaller get-togethers. The upper deck is open to the air, while the lower is fully enclosed. Rows of windows just above the water line bring the river almost to your table. If you're looking for an unusual place to hold a meeting or party, these two paddlewheelers can deliver an experience you and your guests will long remember.

CAPACITY: The Spirit of Sacramento can hold up to 350 seated or standing; the Matthew McKinley 150, maximum.

MEETING ROOMS: Meetings can be held on 2 decks of both boats. Special time and fee arrangements can be made.

FEES & DEPOSITS: A deposit of half the estimated total or rental fee is due 15 days after the reservation is made. The balance is payable 15 days prior to departure. Per person food rates run $6–12 for hors d'oeuvres, $15–20 for buffets and $22–24 for dinners. Bar, tax and a taxable 15% service charge are additional. Rental rates are as follows:

Vessel	Time	Weekday	Weekend
Spirit of Sacramento	3 hours	$3,450	$4,200
	4 hours	4,450	5,350
	ea. add. hour	975	1,100
Half of the Spirit of Sacramento	3 hours	1,950	2,375
	4 hours	2,500	3,000
	ea. add. hour	550	625
Matthew McKinley	3 hours	1,000	1,400
	4 hours	1,450	1,850
	ea. add. hour	350	400

CANCELLATION POLICY: The deposit is refundable with 60 days' notice.

AVAILABILITY: Year-round, daily, 24 hours a day.

SERVICES/AMENITIES:

Restaurant Services: no
Catering: provided
Kitchen Facilities: n/a
Tables & Chairs: provided
Linens, Silver, etc.: provided
Restrooms: Sp. of Sac is wca, MM is ltd. wca
Dance Floor: yes

Parking: on street, public garage
Overnight Accommodations: CBA special discount
Telephone: emergency only
Outdoor Night Lighting: yes
Outdoor Cooking Facilities: no
Cleanup: provided
Meeting Equipment: no

RESTRICTIONS:

Alcohol: provided, $7.50/corkage, W & C only
Smoking: outside decks only
Music: amplified ok, select from preferred list or by special permission only

Wheelchair Access: yes
Insurance: not required
Other: light decorations only, children must be supervised

STERLING HOTEL

1300 H Street
Sacramento, CA 95814
(800) 365-7660 or **(916) 448-1300**
Reserve for Events: 3 months in advance
Reserve for Meetings: 4 weeks in advance

The Sterling Hotel is one of the most charming hotels in Sacramento. Close to downtown, but on a tree-lined residential street, this white Victorian accommodates both business parties and special events. The elegant tone is set by dusky pink and cream walls, marble floors, high ceilings and striking light fixtures. You can bring your party into the intimate living room or in the completely private all-glass garden conservatory. Chanterelle, the hotel's four-star restaurant, caters all functions and can provide a contemporary space for small, private get-togethers. And, for business meetings, several spacious hotel suites are available.

CAPACITY: The living room can hold 48 seated or 110 standing; the Glass Garden 110 seated or 200 standing and the 4 Suites, 15 seated guests, each.

FEES & DEPOSITS: A non-refundable deposit of 75% of the rental cost is due when reservations are confirmed, with the balance due the day of the function. Daytime rental fees for the living room area are $775 for 5 hours. The Glass Garden rental fee is $995 for 5 hours. For small receptions, there is an additional charge of $275 for the first hour and $150 for each additional hour. Catering is done through Chanterelle Restaurant; the entire catering fee is due the day of the event.

AVAILABILITY: Year-round, every day.

SERVICES/AMENITIES:

Restaurant Services: yes
Catering: provided
Kitchen Facilities: n/a
Tables & Chairs: provided
Linens, Silver, etc.: provided
Restrooms: wca
Parking: on and off street, lot

Dance Floor: portable
Overnight Accommodations: 12 suites
Telephone: guest phones
Outdoor Night Lighting: access only
Outdoor Cooking Facilities: no
Cleanup: provided
Meeting Equipment: overhead & slide projector

RESTRICTIONS:

Alcohol: provided, corkage $5/bottle
Smoking: outside only
Music: some restrictions

Wheelchair Access: yes
Insurance: not required
Other: decorations restricted

TOWE FORD MUSEUM

2200 Front Street
Sacramento, CA 95818
(916) 442-6802   Kristin
Reserve for Events: 1–12 months in advance
Reserve for Meetings: 1 week–12 months in advance

This is not an ordinary place to hold an event! Essentially a car museum, this warehouse (located 1 mile south of Old Sacramento) is an automobile lover's paradise. While antique Fords are the car of choice here, many other vintage varieties are also on display. The building itself is spare—cement floor, utility lighting and a domed roof overhead are the only amenities. However, a special events area has been created with a stage and multi-level risers for seating guests. Have your party or reception here and experience the history and glamour of hundreds of gorgeous antique vehicles.

CAPACITY: The Museum can accommodate 300 seated or 500 standing for a reception.

MEETING ROOMS: The special events area can be used for meetings.

FEES & DEPOSITS: A refundable $200 cleaning deposit is required 1 month prior to the event. The rental fee is $600 for 6pm–midnight use of the building, payable in advance of the function. For day events, the fee is $6/person with a $200 minimum and a $600 maximum.

CANCELLATION POLICY: If the Museum is left in clean condition, the deposit is refunded.

AVAILABILITY: Year-round, every day from 6pm to midnight. Closed Christmas, Thanksgiving and New Year's days.

SERVICES/AMENITIES:

Restaurant Services: no
Catering: BYO
Kitchen Facilities: no
Tables & Chairs: provided
Linens, Silver, etc.: BYO
Restrooms: wca
Parking: large lot

Dance Floor: CBA, extra fee
Overnight Accommodations: no
Telephone: office phone
Outdoor Night Lighting: yes
Outdoor Cooking Facilities: BYO
Cleanup: renter or caterer
Meeting Equipment: podium, portable speaker, small screen

RESTRICTIONS:

Alcohol: BYO, any sales need permit
Smoking: outside only
Music: amplified ok

Wheelchair Access: yes
Insurance: certificate required

Yuba City

HARKEY HOUSE

212 C Street
Yuba City, CA 95991
(916) 674-1942   Lee Limonoff & Bob Jones
Reserve for Events: 2–4 months in advance
Reserve for Meetings: 2–4 weeks in advance

Harkey House is not only a bed and breakfast inn, but a delightful spot for small parties. The house is a creamy yellow, classical Italian Victorian over a hundred years old. In back, there is a wonderful brick patio with willow tree furniture and a covered trellis providing shade. A spa, pool and brick patio are added options. The Dining Room has a black and white tile floor, fireplace and high windows, providing light and privacy. The Living Room has a marble fireplace, comfortable seating and a unique piano that traveled all the way around the Cape. Each guestroom has a different theme and the entire house is fresh and inviting.

CAPACITY: The facility can accommodate 40 guests inside and 150 outdoors (total 190).

MEETING ROOMS: 4 meeting rooms that hold 6–36 guests.

FEES & DEPOSITS: A refundable security deposit of $125 and the rental fee are due 4 weeks prior to the event. The rental fee for use of either the inside or outdoor space is $200; rental of the entire facility costs $400.

CANCELLATION POLICY: A full refund will be given with 1 month's notice. With less than a month's notice the deposit will be refunded only if rebooked.

AVAILABILITY: Every day except Christmas.

SERVICES/AMENITIES:

Restaurant Services: no
Catering: BYO
Kitchen Facilities: adequate
Tables & Chairs: some provided
Linens, Silver, etc.: caterer
Restrooms: no wca
Dance Floor: outside patio

Parking: on street
Overnight Accommodations: 4 guestrooms
Telephone: guest phones
Outdoor Night Lighting: yes
Outdoor Cooking Facilities: BBQ
Cleanup: caterer
Meeting Equipment: VCR, easel

RESTRICTIONS:

Alcohol: BYO
Smoking: outside only
Music: amplified ok

Wheelchair Access: no
Insurance: not required

Ryde

GRAND ISLAND INN

14340 Highway 160
Ryde, CA 95680
(916) 776-1318
Reserve for Events: 1–12 months in advance
Reserve for Meetings: 1–12 months in advance

Now the Grand Island Inn, the historic Ryde Hotel was once owned by film star Lon Chaney's family. It was built as a classy gambling house to cater to the riverboat crowd coming from San Francisco and was a famous speakeasy and casino during prohibition. The four-story hotel, with pink stucco and navy blue canvas awnings, is designed in a classic California 1930s style. Inside it's all Art Deco with potted palms, small Egyptian statues, black lacquered ceiling fans and large Erte 30s-style posters. Available for private parties, the Inn provides distinctive spaces for any type of gathering. Functions can be held indoors or in the outdoor garden area.

CAPACITY: The inside capacity, main level, is 100 seated guests, 150 for a standing function; lower level (Cabaret) 250 seated, 350 standing. Combined with outdoor areas, the capacity is 700 guests, depending on the season.

MEETING ROOMS: The main level conference room can accommodate up to 40 guests. The lower level (Cabaret) can hold up to 200 seated for seminars; with classroom seating, 35–100 people.

FEES & DEPOSITS: A $200 deposit is required to hold your date; 90 days prior to the function, the deposit increases by $800.

Event rental fees: $50/hour for a 4-hour block; each additional hour is $100. Buffets or lunch/dinner entrees range from $13–20/person. Tax and 15% gratuity are added to the final total. Special executive retreat rates run $180/day.

CANCELLATION POLICY: With 90 days' notice, the deposit is fully refundable.

AVAILABILITY: Year-round, every day 8am–1am.

SERVICES/AMENITIES:

Restaurant Services: yes, seasonally
Catering: provided, no BYO
Kitchen Facilities: n/a
Tables & Chairs: provided
Linens, Silver, etc.: provided
Restrooms: limited wca
Dance Floor: yes
Meeting Equipment: CBA

Parking: large lot
Overnight Accommodations: 50 guestrooms
Telephone: pay phone
Outdoor Night Lighting: limited
Outdoor Cooking Facilities: CBA
Cleanup: provided
Other: swimming pool, recreation & docking facilities

RESTRICTIONS:
Alcohol: provided, corkage $5/bottle
Smoking: allowed
Music: amplified ok, DJ ok

Wheelchair Access: yes
Insurance: not required

Walnut Grove

GRAND ISLAND MANSION

13415 Grand Island Road
Walnut Grove, CA 95690
(916) 775-1705
Reserve for Events: 1–12 months in advance
Reserve for Meetings: 1–12 months in advance

On Grand Island, in the heart of California's lush Delta, lies an impressive, fifty-eight-room mansion. Surrounded by miles of orchards, the Grand Island Mansion has four stories, a terra cotta roof, spacious balconies with intricate iron railings and an entrance highlighted by enormous Corinthian columns. A cypress-lined circular driveway adds to the extraordinary setting. The estate faces a waterway and has its own yacht facility. Inside, the expertise of imported European craftsmen is seen everywhere: the white marble entrance hall, featuring a sweeping circular stairway, the ballroom with hardwood floors, beveled mirrored walls, sculptured fireplace, gold-gilded columns and crystal chandeliers. French doors lead to a brick courtyard surrounding a tiled swimming pool and spa. This place has it all: an eighteen-seat cinema, billiards room, a regulation bowling lane with new AMF automatic pinsetter and a charming old-fashioned soda fountain. Both a lovely garden and ballroom locations are available for special events.

MEETING ROOMS: The Grand Ballroom can hold 100–150 seated for a seminar; groups of 50–75 can be accommodated in any one of 3 main level meeting rooms.

CAPACITY: The inside capacity is 200 seated, buffet setup 500 guests, and combined with outdoor areas, 1,000 guests, depending on the season. There is a 100-guest minimum for an event. For meetings, smaller groups can be accommodated, minimum 50 guests.

FEES & DEPOSITS: A $200 deposit is required to secure your date; 90 days prior to the function, the deposit amount increases by $800. There are no rental fees if meal service is provided. Per person rates: luncheons range $19–25, dinners $22–26, buffets $22–25 and hors d'oeuvres start at $19.50. Tax and 15% gratuity are added to the final total. A $500 day use fee applies to meetings.

CANCELLATION POLICY: With 90 days' notice, the deposit is fully refundable.

AVAILABILITY: Year-round, daily.

SERVICES/AMENITIES:

Restaurant Services: no
Catering: provided, no BYO
Kitchen Facilities: n/a
Tables & Chairs: provided
Linens, Silver, etc.: provided
Restrooms: no wca
Dance Floor: yes

Parking: driveway, large lot
Overnight Accommodations: no
Telephone: house phone
Outdoor Night Lighting: yes
Outdoor Cooking Facilities: CBA
Cleanup: provided
Meeting Equipment: CBA

RESTRICTIONS:

Alcohol: provided, WBC only, corkage $5/bottle
Smoking: outside only
Music: amplified ok, DJ ok

Wheelchair Access: limited
Insurance: not required

Need a caterer, cake maker, florist? The Service Directory starting on page 614 features the best in the business.

Lodi

JAPANESE PAVILION AND GARDENS
Micke Grove Park

11793 Micke Grove Road
Lodi, CA 95240
(209) 953-8800 or **(209) 331-7400**
Reserve for Events: 6–12 months in advance
Reserve for Meetings: 1–3 weeks in advance

Sheltered by large pines, bamboo, azaleas and camellias, the Japanese Pavilion is an unexpected sight in Micke Grove Park. Located in a separate, fenced area within the park, it is evocative of the Far East. The Pavilion resembles a tastefully designed pagoda, with wood floors, simple wood detailing and decks plus a distinctive high pitched roof that slopes upward at the edges. Adjacent to the structure is a small pool with fountain and red footbridge. In the front, a generous expanse of lawn leads to several wide steps up to the Pavilion; in the back, a gentle ramp leads back into the garden. A popular location for events, the Pavilion has a special ambiance.

CAPACITY: The Pavilion and garden can be rented for 175 guests; inside seating is 50 guests and the garden alone can hold up to 175.

FEES & DEPOSITS: A $50–200 cleaning deposit for indoor use is required, $50–600 for outdoor use. The amount is based on guest count. The Pavilion and garden rental fee is $125 per 4-hour block and the garden alone rents for $65 per 2-hour block. Vehicle entry into the park is $2/car weekdays or $3/car on weekends; group passes can be purchased in advance. Fees and deposits are due within 2 weeks of making a reservation. The cleaning deposit is returned 20 days after the event. Note that there may be some restrictions regarding setup areas for food and alcohol.

CANCELLATION POLICY: With 21 days' notice, rental fees and cleaning deposit will be refunded. There's a cancellation fee of $25.

AVAILABILITY: Year-round, any time except for Christmas day.

SERVICES/AMENITIES:

Restaurant Services: no
Catering: BYO or CBA
Kitchen Facilities: no
Tables & Chairs: provided
Linens, Silver, etc.: BYO
Restrooms: wca nearby
Dance Floor: no dancing
Meeting Equipment: no

Parking: large lots
Overnight Accommodations: no
Telephone: pay phones
Outdoor Night Lighting: no
Outdoor Cooking Facilities: no
Cleanup: caterer or renter
Other: decorating CBA

RESTRICTIONS:

Alcohol: BYO, sales require permit
Smoking: outside only
Music: amplified ok, DJ ok

Wheelchair Access: yes
Insurance: not required

WINE AND ROSES COUNTRY INN

2505 West Turner Road
Lodi, CA 95242
(209) 334-6988
Reserve for Events: 2 weeks–3 months in advance
Reserve for Meetings: 1 week–2 months in advance

Secluded on a magnificent five-acre setting with towering trees, the Wine and Roses Country Inn is an outstanding destination for special events. Lush lawns and old-fashioned flower gardens surround the lovely, 90-year-old home that has been converted into a ten-room country inn. The Inn's courtyards and terrace are great for outdoor receptions and the inside is tastefully decorated in soft rose, rich burgundy with cream trim and windows with lace curtains. All meals are prepared with the finest and freshest of ingredients by the owner/chef, who is a graduate of the San Francisco Culinary Academy. The inn is family-owned and operated and the staff has expertise in coordinating all types of events. This is a very special place.

CAPACITY: The dining room can hold up to 65 seated and 90 standing guests. The sitting room holds up to 35 standing and the outside garden up to 200 guests.

MEETING ROOMS: The Executive Suite holds 18, the main dining room accommodates up to 30, and the Garden Pavilion holds 100.

FEES & DEPOSITS: For meetings, a $100 rental fee is due at the time of booking. Depending upon the size of the group, the rental fee may be waived. For special events, a non-refundable deposit of 50% of the rental fee is required to secure your date. The rental fee is $250–1,000, depending on guest count. The remainder of the rental fee is due 6 weeks prior to the event along with 50% of the estimated catering total; the balance is due the day of the function. Per person rates: continental breakfast $5, seated lunches start at $8, seated dinners $14–19, and buffets start at $13. Tax and service charges are additional.

CANCELLATION POLICY: If the Inn can be rebooked for a similar event, your deposit will be refunded less a $50 cancellation fee.

AVAILABILITY: Every day, anytime.

SERVICES/AMENITIES:

Restaurant Services: yes
Catering: provided, no BYO
Kitchen Facilities: n/a
Tables & Chairs: provided

Restrooms: wca
Dance Floor: courtyard or CBA, extra fee
Parking: large lot
Overnight Accommodations: 10 guestrooms

Linens, Silver, etc.: provided
Outdoor Night Lighting: yes
Outdoor Cooking Facilities: no
Cleanup: provided

RESTRICTIONS:
Alcohol: provided, corkage $5/bottle
Smoking: outside only
Music: amplified restricted

Telephone: house phone
Other: baby grand piano
Meeting Equipment: most provided
Special: event coordination

Wheelchair Access: yes
Insurance: sometimes required
Other: no balloons

Stockton

BOAT HOUSE

Oak Grove Regional Park
4520 West Eight Mile Road
Stockton, CA 95209
(209) 953-8800 or **(209) 331-7400**
Reserve for Events: 6–12 months in advance
Reserve for Meetings: 6–12 months in advance

This popular park, located between Interstate 5 and Highway 99, is an oasis on a hot summer's day. Lush green lawns, a meandering waterway, amphitheater, plus huge oaks and willows combine to create a wonderful destination for a private party. Large, colorful inflatables looking like tricycles on the water are available for rental. Of note is the Boat House, a simple wood structure with deck situated at the water's edge. With the adjacent barbecue and picnic tables, the Boat House can be used as an informal indoor/outdoor reception facility. For a small gathering of business associates, this is an ideal spot for a fun event.

CAPACITY: The Boat House can accommodate 32 seated or 50 standing guests.

FEES & DEPOSITS: The cleaning deposit is $50. The Boat House rental fee is $50 per 6-hour block and $20 for each additional hour. Vehicle entry into the park is $2/car weekdays or $3/car on weekends; group passes can be purchased in advance. Fees and deposits are due within 2 weeks of making a reservation. The cleaning deposit is returned 20 days after the event. Note that there may be some restrictions regarding alcohol.

CANCELLATION POLICY: With 21 days' notice, rental fees and cleaning deposit will be refunded. There's a cancellation fee of $25.

AVAILABILITY: Year-round, any day.

SERVICES/AMENITIES:
Restaurant Services: no
Catering: BYO or CBA

Restrooms: wca
Dance Floor: no

Kitchen Facilities: minimal
Tables & Chairs: provided
Linens, Silver, etc.: BYO
Outdoor Night Lighting: yes
Outdoor Cooking Facilities: BBQs

RESTRICTIONS:

Alcohol: BYO, sales require permit
Smoking: outside only
Music: amplified ok, DJ ok

Parking: large lots
Overnight Accommodations: no
Telephone: pay phones
Cleanup: caterer or renter
Meeting Equipment: no

Wheelchair Access: yes
Insurance: not required

Big Bend

RAINBOW LODGE

Hampshire Rocks Road
Big Bend, CA 95728
(916) 426-3661
Reserve for Events: 6–12 months in advance
Reserve for Meetings: 4 weeks–6 months in advance

Discover Rainbow Lodge. Here you can savor old Tahoe—where fireplaces were built of river rock, walls of granite and round, whole logs were used as posts and beams. This historic building, constructed in 1922, is located several miles west of Soda Springs on Donner Pass. It's a sturdy, handsome survivor of 1920s mountain architecture, now operating as a bed and breakfast. Parties are held in the Sierra Room, complete with stone walls, knotty pine ceiling and fireplace. The adjacent deck with umbrella-shaded tables overlooks the garden and gazebo. With oversized rustic furnishings and fixtures, the lobby is a comfortable place for people to unwind and socialize. Around the corner is a friendly bar, sprinkled with locals who come in to share tales. We really like the Rainbow. Treat your guests to one of the last authentic mountain lodges left in the Sierras.

CAPACITY: 120 seated guests; with outside spaces, 150 guests.

FEES & DEPOSITS: A $450 non-refundable rental fee is due when reservations are confirmed. Buffets run $14–25/person, seated meals $15–25/person. Half of the estimated food cost is payable 30 days prior to the event. The balance is due 7 days before the function along with a final guest count. Any remaining balance is due the day of the event. Tax and a 20% service charge on food are additional.

AVAILABILITY: Year-round, every day, anytime.

SERVICES/AMENITIES:

Restaurant Services: yes
Catering: provided, no BYO
Kitchen Facilities: n/a
Tables & Chairs: provided
Linens, Silver, etc.: provided
Restrooms: no wca
Meeting Equipment: easels
Other: event coordination and referrals

Parking: large lot
Overnight Accommodations: 30 guestrooms
Telephone: pay phone
Outdoor Night Lighting: yes
Outdoor Cooking Facilities: CBA
Cleanup: provided
Dance Floor: no

RESTRICTIONS:

Alcohol: provided, corkage $5/bottle
Smoking: allowed
Music: amplified ok

Wheelchair Access: yes
Insurance: not required

Norden

SUGAR BOWL RESORT

Sugar Bowl Ski Area
Norden, CA 95724
(916) 426-3651
Reserve for Events: 2 weeks in advance

Grab your shades and sun block! If you're looking for an informal setting for a mountain party, family get-together or rehearsal dinner, Sugar Bowl may be the answer. Located off Interstate 80 at Donner Summit, this ski resort offers a high altitude deck (6,900-foot elevation!) for group events. The deck is really large—a sun worshiper's dream! Backed on one side by the lodge and open on the other to snow-topped mountains and stream, it offers plenty of space for dining, dancing and sunning. The deck comes equipped with numerous picnic tables and giant barbecues. Guests can stay overnight and during the winter, ski like crazy during the day. At Sugar Bowl, blue sky, crisp mountain air and the smell of pine needles can make your special event come to life.

CAPACITY: 400 guests maximum.

FEES & DEPOSITS: A non-refundable facility fee is required when reservations are confirmed. The fee is $400 for parties of more than 100 guests; $200 for less than 100. Buffets run approximately $9–23/ person; seated service starts at $16. Half of the estimated event total is due 30 days in advance; the balance is payable the day of the function. Tax and a 15% gratuity are additional.

AVAILABILITY: Year-round, every day 7am–10pm.

SERVICES/AMENITIES:

Restaurant Services: yes
Catering: provided, no BYO
Kitchen Facilities: fully equipped
Tables & Chairs: provided
Linens, Silver, etc.: provided
Restrooms: wca limited
Meeting Equipment: no
Other: event coordination and referrals

Parking: ample
Overnight Accommodations: 29 guestrooms
Telephone: pay phone
Outdoor Night Lighting: limited
Outdoor Cooking Facilities: BBQs
Cleanup: provided or renter
Dance Floor: deck or lounge

RESTRICTIONS:

Alcohol: provided
Smoking: designated areas
Music: amplified ok

Wheelchair Access: no
Insurance: not required

South Lake Tahoe

TALLAC VISTA

1775 Sherman Way
South Lake Tahoe, CA 96151
(916) 541-4975 summer; **(916) 542-4166** winter
Reserve for Events: 1–3 months in advance
Reserve for Meetings: 1–3 months in advance

Situated on a high mountainside, within twelve acres of stately pines and massive boulders, Tallac Vista is a contemporary building, perfect for small, private functions. Owned and operated by the California Tahoe Conservancy, a state agency that implements acquisition and land management programs to protect the environment, it's named after Mt. Tallac, one of the highest peaks in the Sierra. On a calm day, you can see Mt. Tallac mirrored in the still, dark blue waters below. Park a small distance from the site and a private shuttle bus will take you to the building. It has panoramic views of the lake, the mountains and surrounding tall pines. Conference guests will appreciate large windows overlooking Lake Tahoe; outdoor lunch breaks can take place under the fragrant trees. The Tallac Vista building is light and open, with rustic beams and endless windows. Multi-level decks and verandas also have sweeping views. Isolated from traffic, this site is private, peaceful and quiet. Treat your guests to an evening reception, when incomparable sunsets on the lake create an extraordinarily beautiful ambiance.

CAPACITY: 75 guests, maximum.

MEETING ROOMS: The main room accommodates 75 people; 3 smaller areas, 25 people each and 3 outdoor decks, 75 people combined.

FEES & DEPOSITS: A non-refundable $75 deposit is required when reservations are confirmed. Rental fee is $175 per hour. The rental balance is due 2 weeks prior to the event. Corporate/government rates are available.

CANCELLATION POLICY: With less than 2 weeks' notice, service charges will apply.

AVAILABILITY: Year-round except January, February and March. Every day 9am–11pm.

SERVICES/AMENITIES:

Restaurant Services: no
Catering: BYO
Kitchen Facilities: no
Tables & Chairs: provided
Linens, Silver, etc.: BYO
Restrooms: wca
Meeting Equipment: TV, chalkboard

Parking: shuttle provided
Overnight Accommodations: no
Telephone: house phone
Outdoor Night Lighting: yes
Outdoor Cooking Facilities: no
Cleanup: caterer or renter
Dance Floor: no

RESTRICTIONS:
Alcohol: BYO
Smoking: not allowed
Music: amplified indoors only, restricted

Wheelchair Access: yes
Insurance: not required

Squaw Valley

RESORT AT SQUAW CREEK

Squaw Valley, CA 96146
(916) 583-6300
Reserve for Events: 1–12 months in advance
Reserve for Meetings: 1 week–12 months in advance

Wow! That's the simplest word we could come up with to describe how impressed we were by the year-round Resort at Squaw Creek. You've got to come for a visit—this splendid, multi-million dollar facility has to be seen to be fully appreciated. From its position slightly above the valley floor, views of the valley below and the surrounding mountains are phenomenal. For a corporate retreat, we can hardly think of a more suitable spot. It's got everything—conference suites, boardrooms, ballrooms, multiple sundecks and restaurants, three pools and a 250-foot cascading waterfall, footbridge and stream. Dressed for success, this facility is aesthetically decked out in glass, wood and granite. Tasteful furnishings, fixtures and artwork accent beautifully designed interior spaces. Outdoor decks and patios are likewise appointed with teak chairs and tables, huge umbrellas and distinctive paving underfoot. Not only does the resort offer top-notch spaces for meetings and events, but it also provides plenty of services to pamper guests. Have a sauna or a leisurely dip in the spa. An adjacent salon and massage room come fully staffed to rejuvenate tired meeting participants. No matter what your culinary tastes, the resort can arrange any menu to satisfy your needs. In-house restaurants include the elegant Glissandi, with world-class French cuisine in a deco setting, the more casual Cascades, with California regional food, Hardscramble Creek Bar & Grille, a chic bistro cafe and Bullwhackers, a high Sierra pub. Staying overnight? The resort's 405 guestrooms can accommodate corporate groups of almost any size. With great skiing and ice skating in winter, and golf, swimming, tennis and horseback riding in summer, you can turn your conference into a vacation getaway. Your staff will be eternally thankful for their introduction to and memories from the Resort at Squaw Creek.

CAPACITY:

Area	Seated	Standing	Area	Seated	Standing
Grand Sierra Ballroom	500	700	Glissandi Deck	75	100
Squaw Creek Ballroom	250	325	Bullwhackers Pub	80	120
Hardscramble Creek Bar & Grill	100	175	Cascades	240	—
Hardscramble Deck	250	325	Ice Skating Area*	250	325
Glissandi	80	120	*summer only*		

MEETING ROOMS: The resort has 33 meeting rooms including boardrooms and conference suites, 2 ballrooms that can be sectioned and eight other meeting areas. Groups as small as 8 or as large as 950 seated theatre-style can be accommodated.

FEES & DEPOSITS: A $500–1,000 deposit (depending on room size) is due when reservations are confirmed. There is no rental fee for meetings or events with food service, although there may be an additional charge if extra breakout rooms are required. Per person rates for luncheons are $15–30, buffets and dinners begin at $32. Sales tax and an 18% service charge are additional. The estimated event total is payable 3 days prior to the function.

CANCELLATION POLICY: With 2 months' notice, the deposit will be refunded if the space can be rebooked.

AVAILABILITY: Year-round, every day 6am–2am.

SERVICES/AMENITIES:

Restaurant Services: yes
Catering: provided, no BYO
Kitchen Facilities: n/a
Tables & Chairs: provided
Linens, Silver, etc.: provided
Restrooms: wca
Dance Floor: deck or indoors
Other: Conference Concierge & event coordination

Parking: valet
Overnight Accommodations: 405 guestrooms
Telephone: pay phones, guest phones
Outdoor Night Lighting: yes
Outdoor Cooking Facilities: BBQs
Cleanup: provided
Meeting Equipment: complete AV

RESTRICTIONS:

Alcohol: provided
Smoking: allowed
Music: amplified ok

Wheelchair Access: yes
Insurance: not required

Tahoe City

SUNNYSIDE
Restaurant and Lodge

1850 West Lake Blvd.
Tahoe City, CA 95730
(916) 583-7200
Reserve for Events: 6–12 months in advance
Reserve for Meetings: 1 day–3 months in advance

Recreated to resemble a classic 1920s mountain lodge, Sunnyside is constructed of wood siding, dormers, large timbers and stone. All is designed to evoke a romantic image of old Tahoe. The charm extends to the inside where hunting trophies frame a huge river rock fireplace, canoes hang from the ceiling and antique snow shoes tread across the walls. Light fixtures are craftsman-style brass, furnishings are rustic-chic "twig" and antique oak. Three dining rooms (two with wall-to-wall windows facing the Lake) are available for private parties. Each is tastefully appointed and painted in soft colors. For sun lovers, Sunnyside's spacious deck is spectacular. You can't get much closer than this to the Lake—it's right on the water's edge. Vivid green, blue and red umbrellas unfold to shade guests from bright rays. All details here, down to the deck's railings of lodgepole pine, are designed to maintain the flavor of a traditional Sierra lodge. Below the deck, colorful vessels await launch during summer months. In winter, snow capped roof and icicle drapes belie Sunnyside's cozy interior warmth. Have your special event on the sun-drenched deck or inside in the Lake Room. Popular for good reason, Sunnyside will impress your guests with a range of modern facilities presented with an ambiance of days gone by.

CAPACITY:

Room	Seated Guests	Room	Seated Guests
Lake Room	75–100	Emerald Room	50–75
Christ Craft	75	Deck	75

FEES & DEPOSITS: A refundable $500 deposit is due when reservations are confirmed. A room rental fee of $100 plus a cleanup and setup fee of $2/guest are also required. Buffets run approximately $15–25/person; seated dinners from $18–26/person. Tax and an 18% gratuity are additional. The balance is due the day of the event.

CANCELLATION POLICY: With 2 weeks' notice, the deposit will be refunded.

AVAILABILITY: Mid-September through mid-May, Monday–Saturday. Hours are 7am–5pm; evening hours can be extended to 11pm if the restaurant has been closed.

SERVICES/AMENITIES:

Restaurant Services: yes
Catering: provided, no BYO
Kitchen Facilities: n/a
Tables & Chairs: provided
Linens, Silver, etc.: provided
Restrooms: wca
Meeting Equipment: overhead projector, podium, easel

Parking: large lot
Overnight Accommodations: 28 guestrooms
Telephone: pay phone
Outdoor Night Lighting: yes
Outdoor Cooking Facilities: no
Cleanup: provided
Dance Floor: deck or indoors

RESTRICTIONS:

Alcohol: provided, corkage $5/bottle
Smoking: allowed
Music: amplified ok

Wheelchair Access: yes
Insurance: not required

Tahoma

EHRMAN MANSION

Sugar Pine Point State Park
Tahoma, CA 95733
(916) 525-7982
Reserve for Events: 6–12 months in advance

Experience the opulence of old Tahoe. The historic Ehrman mansion, completed in 1903, is one of the largest and most elegant estates on the Lake. In 1897, San Francisco businessman I. W. Hellman began buying property at Sugar Pine Point and by 1913 had acquired nearly two thousand acres. His grand summer home, called Pine Lodge, is considered one of the finest in the high Sierra. (It has since been renamed for his daughter, Florence Hellman Ehrman, who inherited the estate). This impressive brown-shingled home is multi-story, with stone foundation, fireplaces and walls. The inside is dark, with lots of woodwork and fancy beamed ceilings. Hollywood crews have been here—*Things Change* with Don Ameche and several segments of *The Young and the Restless* were filmed on the estate. The Mansion sits on a small rise, and as such, hors d'oeuvres receptions on the porch have great lake vistas through huge pines. Parties can be held on the estate lawns or in the nearby picnic area. Delight your friends and family with a period party by dressing up in turn-of-the-century costumes. The Ehrman Mansion is a one-of-a-kind event location.

CAPACITY: 150 guests, maximum.

FEES & DEPOSITS: The rental fee, damage deposit and certificate of insurance are required when the application is submitted. For events on the Mansion's porch, the fee is $200 with a $200 damage deposit. For outdoor functions, the fee is $100, with a $100 damage deposit, which includes park day use fees for the entire wedding party. With less than 15 guests, fees are waived. Parking for service vehicles needs approval.

CANCELLATION POLICY: With 48 hours' notice, the deposit will be refunded.

AVAILABILITY: June 15th–Labor Day, 1 event per day 5pm–9pm.

SERVICES/AMENITIES:

Restaurant Services: no

Catering: BYO

Kitchen Facilities: no

Tables & Chairs: BYO

Linens, Silver, etc.: BYO

Restrooms: wca

Dance Floor: no

Overnight Accommodations: no

Telephone: no

Outdoor Night Lighting: no

Outdoor Cooking Facilities: BBQ in picnic area

Cleanup: caterer or renter

Meeting Equipment: no

Parking: designated areas

RESTRICTIONS:
Alcohol: BYO, permit required
Smoking: outside only
Music: no amplified

Wheelchair Access: yes
Insurance: certificate required

Truckee

NORTHSTAR

Highway 267 at Northstar Drive
Truckee, CA 96160
(916) 587-0265
Reserve for Events: 3–12 months in advance
Reserve for Meetings: 1–12 months in advance

Although you may think Northstar is just a ski resort, think again. Here you'll find facilities that are well designed—plus comprehensive services that should appeal to anyone planning a special event. Designed as a self-contained village, Northstar can provide guests with winter and summer accommodations. Use the umbrella-dotted sun deck for an outdoor, mountain-air function. The deck sports a huge outdoor fireplace for informal barbecue feasts. Quiet and private, the wind through the trees and the birds provide the only sounds. If the weather is uncooperative, the indoor Alpine and Chaparral Rooms are great choices for an indoor party. Floor to ceiling windows allow light to flood in, affording glimpses of the deck and tall conifers beyond. The Alpine Room has a portable dance floor and bar. Dressed up with white linens and flowers, both rooms sparkle. As an added plus, Northstar's event staff will help coordinate all the essentials of your event. Chances are you never thought of Northstar as a business event location—now that you know, we urge you to take a closer look.

CAPACITY:

Area	Seated	Standing
Deck	200	300
Chaparral Room	150	300
Alpine Room	150	200

MEETING ROOMS: In addition to the Chaparral and Alpine Rooms, there are 4 other meeting areas that can accommodate 20–112 seated guests.

FEES & DEPOSITS: A deposit in the amount of one night's lodging per unit booked is due within 10 days of receipt of contract. The balance of the anticipated total is payable 45 days prior to the arrival date unless master billing is approved. Luncheon buffets and seated meals run approximately $10–22/ person. Northstar will customize any menu for your private party. Tax and a 17% service charge are additional.

CANCELLATION POLICY: If canceled within 30 days of the arrival date, the equivalent of one night's lodging is forfeited.

AVAILABILITY: Every day, anytime before November 15th and after April 1st.

SERVICES/AMENITIES:

Restaurant Services: yes

Catering: provided, no BYO

Kitchen Facilities: n/a

Tables & Chairs: provided

Linens, Silver, etc.: provided

Restrooms: wca

Meeting Equipment: TV, VCR, slide projector & screen

Other: event coordination & referrals

Parking: large lot

Overnight Accommodations: 225 condos

Telephone: pay phone

Outdoor Night Lighting: limited

Outdoor Cooking Facilities: BBQ

Cleanup: provided

Dance Floor: yes

RESTRICTIONS:

Alcohol: provided, champagne corkage $10/bottle

Wheelchair Access: yes

Smoking: allowed

Insurance: not required

Music: amplified ok

Need a caterer, cake maker, florist? The Service Directory starting on page 614 features the best in the business.

The Picnic Directory

ACTIVITIES

PICNIC FACILITIES	Maximum Capacity	Ballfields	Volleyball	Playground	Tennis	Hiking Trails	Biking Trails	Sailing/Boating	Basketball	Horseshoes	Bocci Ball	Horseback Riding	Archery	Fishing	Swimming
SAN FRANCISCO															
Golden Gate Park	25,000	•	•	•	•	•	•	•	•	•		•	•		
Stern Grove	300			•	•	•									
McLaren Park	5,000	•	•		•	•			•						
HALF MOON BAY AREA															
Half Moon Bay															
Cozzolino Park	200		•			•				•					
Francis State Beach	50					•	•							•	
Martin's Beach	300													•	•
Montara															
Montara Gardens	100														
San Gregorio															
Rancho San Gregorio	100	•	•			•					•				
NORTH BAY															
Angel Island	150		•			•	•						•		
Corte Madera															
Town Park	700	•		•	•				•						
Fairfax															
Deer Park Villa	500														
Lake Lagunitas	60					•	•				•			•	
Lagunitas															
Samuel P. Taylor Park	80					•	•								
Larkspur															
Piper Park	300	•	•	•	•	•			•	•				•	

AMENITIES									SERVICES									
Large BBQ Units	Small BBQ Units	Picnic Tables	Picnic Lawns	Amphitheatre / Stage	Lake / Body of Water	Creeks / Streams	Beach	Swimming Pool	Public Transportation	Sports Programs	Night Lighting	Restrooms	Water Available	Disabled Access	Parking / Entry Fee	Concessions	Boat Rentals	Misc. Rentals
•		•	•	•	•	•			•			•	•	•			•	•
•	•	•	•	•	•	•			•			•	•	•				
		•	•	•					•			•	•					
•		•		•		•					•	•	•	•				
	•	•			•		•		•			•	•	•	•			
		•			•		•					•	•	•	•	•		
		•		•					•		•	•	•	•				
•		•			•						•	•	•	•				
•	•	•			•							•	•	•		•		
	•	•	•		•				•			•	•	•				
		•										•	•	•				
•		•			•	•						•	•	•	•			
•		•				•						•	•	•				
•	•	•							•			•	•					

ACTIVITIES

PICNIC FACILITIES	Maximum Capacity	Ballfields	Volleyball	Playground	Tennis	Hiking Trails	Biking Trails	Sailing/Boating	Basketball	Horseshoes	Bocci Ball	Horseback Riding	Archery	Fishing	Swimming
Bootjack	50-65					•									
Boyle Park	150	•		•											
Cushing Memorial Theater	150					•									
Old Mill Park	100			•											
Outdoor Art Club	200														
Nicasio															
The Shadows	150		•			•	•			•	•			•	
Novato															
Hoog Park	60		•	•											
Miwok Park	200			•						•	•		•	•	
Pioneer Park	35			•	•				•						
Stafford Lake Park	1,000	•	•	•		•	•			•				•	
Point Reyes															
Pt. Reyes National Seashore	200–300					•									
Ross															
Marin Art & Garden Center	500														
San Anselmo															
Memorial Park	150	•	•	•	•				•	•					
San Rafael															
China Camp State Park	200														
Dominican College	1,000				•	•									
Falkirk Mansion	100														
Gerstle Park	140			•	•				•						
Freitas Memorial Park, Maria B.	50														
McInnis Park, John F.	100	•			•	•	•	•						•	
McNears Beach Park	200-300			•					•					•	•
Victor Jones Park	100	•		•											

	AMENITIES									SERVICES									
	Large BBQ Units	Small BBQ Units	Picnic Tables	Picnic Lawns	Amphitheatre / Stage	Lake / Body of Water	Creeks / Streams	Beach	Swimming Pool	Public Transportation	Sports Programs	Night Lighting	Restrooms	Water Available	Disabled Access	Parking / Entry Fee	Concessions	Boat Rentals	Misc. Rentals
	•	•	•							•			•	•					
	•		•	•		•				•			•		•				
					•					•			•	•	•				
	•		•	•	•					•									
			•		•					•		•	•	•	•				
	•		•		•			•				•	•	•	•				
	•		•	•								•	•	•	•				
	•		•	•		•				•		•	•	•	•				
	•		•	•								•	•	•					
	•		•	•		•							•	•	•	•			
		•	•				•						•	•	•		•		
										•		•	•	•	•				
	•	•	•	•						•	•		•	•	•				
				•	•					•			•	•	•				
				•						•			•	•	•				
	•	•	•	•									•						
		•	•	•									•						
	•	•	•	•		•				•		•	•	•	•		•		•
	•	•	•	•		•	•						•	•	•	•	•		
	•																		

ACTIVITIES

PICNIC FACILITIES	Maximum Capacity	Ballfields	Volleyball	Playground	Tennis	Hiking Trails	Biking Trails	Sailing/Boating	Basketball	Horseshoes	Bocci Ball	Horseback Riding	Archery	Fishing	Swimming
Sausalito															
Rodeo Beach Meeting & Conf. Center	60														
Stinson Beach															
Stinson Beach State Park	200		•										•	•	
Tiburon															
Paradise Beach Park	200							•	•				•	•	
PENINSULA															
Atherton															
Holbrook Palmer Park	250	•		•											
Belmont															
Twin Pines Park	100		•	•	•					•					
Burlingame															
Kohl Mansion	500		•	•	•				•					•	
Washington Park	100			•					•	•	•				
Los Altos															
Shoup Park	125			•	•										
Menlo Park															
Burgess Park	500-600	•	•	•	•				•					•	
Flood County Park	300	•	•	•	•					•					
Millbrae															
Central Park	100			•	•				•						
Green Hills Park	75			•						•	•				
Mountain View															
Rengstorff Park	200	•	•	•	•									•	
Cuesta Park	200		•	•	•					•	•				

	AMENITIES									SERVICES									
	Large BBQ Units	Small BBQ Units	Picnic Tables	Picnic Lawns	Amphitheatre / Stage	Lake / Body of Water	Creeks / Streams	Beach	Swimming Pool	Public Transportation	Sports Programs	Night Lighting	Restrooms	Water Available	Disabled Access	Parking / Entry Fee	Concessions	Boat Rentals	Misc. Rentals
			•				•						•	•	•				
		•	•	•		•	•			•			•	•	•	•			
	•	•	•	•		•	•						•	•	•	•			
			•	•						•		•	•	•	•				
	•	•	•	•	•	•				•			•	•	•				•
			•	•					•				•	•	•				
		•	•							•			•	•	•				
	•	•	•	•		•				•		•	•	•	•				
	•		•	•					•	•	•		•	•	•				
	•	•	•	•									•	•	•	•			
	•		•							•			•	•	•				
	•		•	•						•			•	•	•				
	•	•	•	•	•	•				•			•	•	•				•
	•	•	•	•						•	•	•	•	•	•				•

ACTIVITIES

PICNIC FACILITIES

PICNIC FACILITIES	Maximum Capacity	Ballfields	Volleyball	Playground	Tennis	Hiking Trails	Biking Trails	Sailing/Boating	Basketball	Horseshoes	Bocci Ball	Horseback Riding	Archery	Fishing	Swimming
Pacifica															
Frontierland Park	3,000		•	•		•				•					
Palo Alto															
Mitchell Park	99			•	•					•	•				
Rinconada Park	100			•	•					•				•	
Redwood City															
Red Morton Community Park	65	•		•	•				•	•	•			•	
San Bruno															
San Bruno City Park	200	•		•	•	•	•		•					•	
San Carlos															
Burton Park	50	•	•	•	•				•	•					
San Mateo															
Bayside/Joinville Park	200	•	•	•	•					•				•	
Beresford Park	150	•		•	•				•	•					
Central Park	300	•	•	•	•					•	•				
Coyote Point County Park	300		•	•				•	•				•	•	
Parkside Aquatic	200-250			•				•					•	•	
Shoreview Park	60	•	•	•	•				•						
South San Francisco															
Burri Burri Park	100	•		•					•	•					
Candlestick Pt. State Recreation Area	50					•	•						•		
Orange Memorial Park	100	•		•	•				•	•	•			•	
Westborough Park	70	•		•					•	•					
Woodside															
Huddart Park	450		•	•		•				•		•			
Skywood Chateau Restaurant	300					•	•		•						

AMENITIES   SERVICES

	Large BBQ Units	Small BBQ Units	Picnic Tables	Picnic Lawns	Amphitheatre / Stage	Lake / Body of Water	Creeks / Streams	Beach	Swimming Pool	Public Transportation	Sports Programs	Night Lighting	Restrooms	Water Available	Disabled Access	Parking / Entry Fee	Concessions	Boat Rentals	Misc. Rentals
	•	•	•	•	•					•		•	•	•	•				•
		•	•	•	•					•		•	•	•	•				
		•	•	•					•	•		•	•	•	•				
	•		•	•					•	•	•	•	•	•	•		•		
	•	•	•	•					•	•		•	•	•	•			•	
		•	•	•						•		•	•		•				
	•		•							•		•	•	•					•
			•							•		•	•						
	•	•	•	•	•	•				•		•	•	•			•		
	•		•	•		•		•				•	•	•		•	•		
	•		•	•		•	•	•				•	•	•			•	•	•
	•		•	•						•		•	•						
	•		•	•		•				•		•	•	•	•				
	•	•	•	•			•	•		•		•	•	•	•				•
	•					•				•		•	•	•	•				
	•		•	•		•				•		•	•	•	•				
	•		•	•		•							•	•	•	•	•		
	•		•									•	•	•	•				

ACTIVITIES

PICNIC FACILITIES	Maximum Capacity	Ballfields	Volleyball	Playground	Tennis	Hiking Trails	Biking Trails	Sailing/Boating	Basketball	Horseshoes	Bocci Ball	Horseback Riding	Archery	Fishing	Swimming
EAST BAY															
Alameda															
Crown Mememorial Beach	200					•	•	•						•	•
Antioch															
Contra Loma Regional Park	200					•	•	•				•		•	•
Berkeley															
Tilden Park	200		•	•		•	•					•		•	
Castro Valley															
Chouinard Vineyards	225														
Crow Canyon Park & Resort	3,000	•	•											•	
Cull Canyon Regional Rec. Area	150					•								•	•
Don Castro Regional Rec. Area	100					•								•	
Clayton															
Old Marsh Creek Springs	1,000	•	•	•					•					•	
Concord															
Baldwin Park	130	•		•					•						
Emeryville															
Emeryville Marina	30					•	•							•	
Fremont															
Ardenwood Historic Farm	1,200	•	•	•						•					
Coyote Hills Regional Park	75					•	•				•				
Hayward															
Garin/Dry Creek Regional Park	100					•	•			•		•	•		
Livermore															
Concannon Vineyard	500	•									•	•			

AMENITIES   SERVICES

	Large BBQ Units	Small BBQ Units	Picnic Tables	Picnic Lawns	Amphitheatre / Stage	Lake / Body of Water	Creeks / Streams	Beach	Swimming Pool		Public Transportation	Sports Programs	Night Lighting	Restrooms	Water Available	Disabled Access	Parking / Entry Fee	Concessions	Boat Rentals	Misc. Rentals
	•	•	•	•			•							•	•	•		•		•
	•		•	•		•	•							•	•	•				
	•		•		•	•								•	•	•		•		
			•										•	•		•		•		
	•		•					•						•	•	•		•		•
	•		•											•						
	•		•													•		•		
	•													•	•					
		•	•											•						•
	•	•	•	•										•	•	•				
	•	•	•													•		•		
	•		•			•							•	•						
	•		•	•									•	•						
		•										•	•					•		

ACTIVITIES

PICNIC FACILITIES	Maximum Capacity	Ballfields	Volleyball	Playground	Tennis	Hiking Trails	Biking Trails	Sailing/Boating	Basketball	Horseshoes	Bocci Ball	Horseback Riding	Archery	Fishing	Swimming
Del Valle Regional Park	500					•	•	•				•	•	•	
Fenestra Winery	50														
Livermore Valley Cellars	100														
Retzlaff Vineyards	150														
Wente Bros. Estate Winery	120														
Martinez															
Briones Regional Park	150					•						•			
Oakland															
de Fremery Park	50			•	•				•					•	
Dimond Park	100			•	•									•	
Joaquin Miller Park	250					•									
Montclair Park	200	•			•										
Redwood Regional Park	150			•		•	•				•				
Roberts Regional Recreation Area	300	•	•	•		•	•			•	•			•	
Temescal Regional Recreation Area	150			•		•							•	•	
Pinole															
Point Pinole Regional Shoreline	150		•	•		•	•			•		•			
Pleasanton															
Shadow Cliffs Reg. Recreation Area	200					•	•	•						•	•
Sunol Regional Wilderness	200					•	•					•			
Richmond															
Miller/Knox Regional Shoreline	200				•	•		•		•				•	
San Leandro															
Martin L. King Jr. Reg. Shoreline	200					•	•	•						•	
Lake Chabot Reg. Recreation Area	150		•			•	•	•		•				•	
San Ramon															
Little Hills Picnic Ranch	1,400	•	•	•		•			•	•				•	•

AMENITIES   SERVICES

	Large BBQ Units	Small BBQ Units	Picnic Tables	Picnic Lawns	Amphitheatre / Stage	Lake / Body of Water	Creeks / Streams	Beach	Swimming Pool	Public Transportation	Sports Programs	Night Lighting	Restrooms	Water Available	Disabled Access	Parking / Entry Fee	Concessions	Boat Rentals	Misc. Rentals
	•		•	•		•							•	•					
			•										•	•	•				
			•									•	•	•	•				
			•	•									•	•	•		•		
			•										•	•	•		•		
	•		•		•		•						•	•					
		•	•					•		•			•	•	•				
	•		•			•		•		•			•	•					
	•	•	•										•	•	•				
	•		•	•		•				•	•								
	•		•	•		•							•	•	•				
	•	•	•	•					•	•			•	•	•		•		
	•	•	•	•		•							•	•	•				
	•		•	•											•	•			
	•		•	•		•		•					•	•	•		•	•	
		•	•			•							•	•					
	•		•	•		•		•		•			•	•	•				
	•	•	•			•							•	•	•				
	•		•	•		•							•	•	•		•	•	
	•	•	•								•	•	•		•		•		•

ACTIVITIES

PICNIC FACILITIES	Maximum Capacity	Ballfields	Volleyball	Playground	Tennis	Hiking Trails	Biking Trails	Sailing/Boating	Basketball	Horseshoes	Bocci Ball	Horseback Riding	Archery	Fishing	Swimming
Walnut Creek															
Castle Rock Park	3,000	•	•	•		•			•	•			•		•
Turtle Rock Ranch	1,200	•	•	•						•				•	
SOUTH BAY															
Campbell															
Campbell Park	30			•		•	•			•					
John D. Morgan Park	300	•	•	•	•				•	•					
Cupertino															
Black Berry Farm	4,000	•	•	•						•	•			•	
Linda Vista Park	100	•		•											
Memorial Park	100	•		•	•										
Portal Park	75	•		•											
Gilroy															
Casa de Fruta	10,000	•	•	•		•	•		•	•				•	
Hecker Pass	7,000	•	•	•					•	•				•	
Los Gatos															
Lake Vasona Park	850		•	•		•	•	•		•			•		
Oak Meadow Park	1,220			•		•	•				•				
Milpitas															
Ed Levin Park	550	•	•		•	•	•	•		•		•		•	
Morgan Hill															
Guglielmo Winery	80								•						
San Jose															
Alum Rock Park	300		•	•		•				•		•			
Club Almaden	2,000		•	•						•					
Coyote-Hellyer Park	600-800		•	•		•	•			•				•	

	AMENITIES									SERVICES									
	Large BBQ Units	Small BBQ Units	Picnic Tables	Picnic Lawns	Amphitheatre / Stage	Lake / Body of Water	Creeks / Streams	Beach	Swimming Pool	Public Transportation	Sports Programs	Night Lighting	Restrooms	Water Available	Disabled Access	Parking / Entry Fee	Concessions	Boat Rentals	Misc. Rentals
	•	•	•					•			•	•	•				•		•
	•		•	•				•					•	•	•				
		•	•	•		•				•			•	•	•				
		•	•	•				•		•		•	•	•	•				
		•	•	•	•	•		•		•			•	•	•		•		•
		•	•									•	•	•	•				
		•	•	•															
		•	•									•	•	•	•				
	•		•	•	•	•		•				•	•	•	•				
	•		•	•	•	•		•			•	•	•	•			•		
	•	•	•	•			•	•					•	•	•	•		•	
	•	•	•	•	•			•		•			•	•	•	•			
	•	•	•			•							•	•	•	•			
	•		•	•						•		•	•	•					
	•		•	•				•					•	•	•	•			
	•		•	•				•		•		•	•	•					•
	•	•	•	•	•	•	•	•		•			•	•	•	•			

ACTIVITIES

PICNIC FACILITIES	Maximum Capacity	Ballfields	Volleyball	Playground	Tennis	Hiking Trails	Biking Trails	Sailing/Boating	Basketball	Horseshoes	Bocci Ball	Horseback Riding	Archery	Fishing	Swimming
Coyote Ranch	5000	•	•	•			•			•	•				
Emma Prusch Memorial Park	200														
Kelly Park	200-500														
Lake Cunningham Park	400-600			•	•			•	•		•			•	
PLC Tower	500		•	•					•	•	•			•	
Santa Clara															
Central Park	225	•		•	•				•					•	
Saratoga															
Cinnabar Winery	60					•	•				•				
Saratoga Springs	3,000		•	•		•			•	•			•	•	
Wildwood Park	200		•	•						•					
Sunnyvale															
Lakewood Park	425	•		•	•				•	•				•	
Las Palmas Park	150	•		•	•										
Serra Park	200	•		•	•										
Twin Creeks Sports Complex	20,000	•	•	•											
WINE COUNTRY, NAPA															
Calistoga															
Bothe-Napa Valley State Park	100					•				•				•	
Macedonia Park	500														
Old Faithful Geyser	120														
Sterling Vineyards	50														
Napa															
Enchanted Hills Camp	300	•		•		•		•	•	•				•	
Fuller Park	80			•						•					
Kennedy Park	120	•	•	•									•		

	Large BBQ Units	Small BBQ Units	Picnic Tables	Picnic Lawns	Amphitheatre / Stage	Lake / Body of Water	Creeks / Streams	Beach	Swimming Pool	Public Transportation	Sports Programs	Night Lighting	Restrooms	Water Available	Disabled Access	Parking / Entry Fee	Concessions	Boat Rentals	Misc. Rentals
	•		•	•	•							•	•	•	•				
		•	•	•	•						•		•	•	•	•			
	•		•	•	•	•				•			•	•	•	•			
		•	•			•					•		•	•	•	•	•	•	•
	•		•	•	•			•		•	•	•	•	•	•				•
	•	•	•	•	•	•				•		•	•	•	•				
			•	•								•	•	•	•				
	•		•		•	•		•				•	•	•	•		•		
	•	•	•	•	•	•							•	•	•				
	•		•	•					•		•		•	•	•				
	•	•	•	•						•	•		•	•	•				
	•	•	•	•		•				•			•	•	•				
	c	c	•	•	•					•	•	•	•	•	•		•		•
	•		•			•		•		•		•	•	•	•				
	•		•										•	•	•				
			•	•									•			•	•		
													•	•					
	•		•	•		•							•	•	•				
		•	•							•			•	•	•				
	•	•	•			•	•			•			•	•	•				

ACTIVITIES

PICNIC FACILITIES	Maximum Capacity	Ballfields	Volleyball	Playground	Tennis	Hiking Trails	Biking Trails	Sailing/Boating	Basketball	Horseshoes	Bocci Ball	Horseback Riding	Archery	Fishing	Swimming
Monticello Cellars	100														
Pine Ridge Winery	48				•										
Skyline Wilderness Park	100					•	•					•		•	
Rutherford															
Inglenook Winery	1,000														
Rutherford Hill Winery	70														
St. Helena															
Crane Park	80	•	•	•	•	•				•	•				
RustRidge Ranch and Winery	200														
St. Clement Vineyards	65														
V. Sattui Winery	150														
White Sulphur Springs	250		•			•			•	•					•
Yountville															
Lake Hennessey, Conn Dam	65		•	•				•		•				•	
Yountville City Park	100			•											
WINE COUNTRY, SONOMA															
Cloverdale															
City Park	600	•		•											
Yorty Creek at Lake Sonoma	200														•
Cotati															
Helen Putnam Park	100	•		•											
La Plaza Park	200			•											
Forestville															
Mark West Vineyards	150									•					
Geyserville															
Alexander Valley Fruit & Trading Co.	80		•												

| | AMENITIES | | | | | | | | | SERVICES | | | | | | | | | |
	Large BBQ Units	Small BBQ Units	Picnic Tables	Picnic Lawns	Amphitheatre / Stage	Lake / Body of Water	Creeks / Streams	Beach	Swimming Pool	Public Transportation	Sports Programs	Night Lighting	Restrooms	Water Available	Disabled Access	Parking / Entry Fee	Concessions	Boat Rentals	Misc. Rentals
	•		•	•									•	•	•				
	•		•	•	•							•	•	•	•				
	•		•			•							•	•					
				•									•	•	•				
			•										•	•					
	•		•	•									•	•	•		•		
	•		•	•									•	•	•				
													•	•	•				
	•		•	•									•	•	•		•		
	•		•	•		•						•	•	•					
	•		•	•	•								•						
	•		•	•									•	•					
	•		•	•						•			•	•	•				
		•	•		•		•						•	•					
			•	•						•	•		•	•					
			•	•						•			•	•					
	•		•	•		•							•	•	•				
	•		•	•									•	•					

ACTIVITIES

PICNIC FACILITIES	Maximum Capacity	Ballfields	Volleyball	Playground	Tennis	Hiking Trails	Biking Trails	Sailing/Boating	Basketball	Horseshoes	Bocci Ball	Horseback Riding	Archery	Fishing	Swimming
Trentadue Winery	300														
Warm Springs Dam, Lake Sonoma	200		•			•	•								
Glen Ellen															
Sonoma Valley Regional Park	40					•	•								
Guerneville															
Armstrong Redwoods State Reserve	150					•	•								
F. Korbel & Brothers	50														
Midway Beach	2,000		•							•			•	•	
Surrey Inn	700-900		•	•	•				•	•				•	
Healdsburg															
Alderbrook Winery	80														
Belvedere Winery	50														
Field Stone Winery	125														
Giorgi Park	75	•	•	•	•						•				
Rodney Strong Winery	550														
Villa Chanticleer	300			•		•				•					
Kenwood															
Morton's Warm Springs	2,400	•	•			•	•		•	•				•	
Oreste's Golden Bear	300														
Wine Country Wagons	60		•							•					
Pengrove															
Eagle Ridge Winery	150														
Petaluma															
Garden Valley Ranch	200														
Lucchesi Park	54		•	•	•	•							•		
Marin French Cheese Company	150														
McNear Park	200		•	•	•								•	•	

	Large BBQ Units	Small BBQ Units	Picnic Tables	Picnic Lawns	Amphitheatre / Stage	Lake / Body of Water	Creeks / Streams	Beach	Swimming Pool	Public Transportation	Sports Programs	Night Lighting	Restrooms	Water Available	Disabled Access	Parking / Entry Fee	Concessions	Boat Rentals	Misc. Rentals
			•	•						•			•	•	•				
	•		•	•		•							•	•	•				
		•	•	•		•				•			•	•	•				
	•	•	•		•								•	•	•				
			•							•			•	•	•				
			•	•	•	•	•						•	•	•		•	•	
	•		•	•					•	•		•	•	•	•				
			•	•									•	•	•				
			•	•									•	•	•				
	•		•	•									•	•	•				
		•	•										•	•	•				
	•		•	•						•			•	•	•				
	•		•	•									•	•	•				
	•		•	•		•			•		•	•	•	•	•	•	•		
	•		•			•							•	•	•				
	•		•	•		•							•						
	•		•	•						•			•	•	•				
			•			•				•			•	•	•				
	•		•	•		•				•	•		•	•	•				
	•		•	•		•							•	•	•		•		
	•		•	•		•		•	•		•	•		•	•	•		•	

ACTIVITIES

PICNIC FACILITIES

Picnic Facilities	Maximum Capacity	Ballfields	Volleyball	Playground	Tennis	Hiking Trails	Biking Trails	Sailing/Boating	Basketball	Horseshoes	Bocci Ball	Horseback Riding	Archery	Fishing	Swimming
Swim Center	300													•	
Rohnert Park															
Alicia Park	200	•		•	•				•					•	
Benecia Park	200	•												•	
Dorotea Park	200	•		•	•			•	•						
Santa Rosa															
Chateau DeBaun Winery	700	•	•												
Cloverleaf Ranch	500	•	•	•	•			•	•		•		•	•	
Cooper's Grove Ranch	200		•			•		•	•					•	
Doyle Park	200	•		•					•	•					
Finley Park	200		•	•	•				•						
Galvin Community Park	200	•			•								•		
Howarth Memorial Park	200	•		•	•	•	•				•		•		
Oak Hill Ranch	350	•	•			•			•		•			•	
Spring Lake Regional Park	150					•	•							•	•
Sebastopol															
Ragle Ranch Regional Park	150	•	•			•	•								
Sonoma															
Agua Caliente Springs	500		•											•	
Bartholomew Memorial Park	60														
Buena Vista Winery	150														
Maxwell Farms Regional Park	100	•	•	•	•	•	•								
Windsor															
Keiser Park	200	•		•				•							
Windsor Waterworks & Slides	1,500		•	•					•					•	

	AMENITIES									SERVICES									
	Large BBQ Units	Small BBQ Units	Picnic Tables	Picnic Lawns	Amphitheatre / Stage	Lake / Body of Water	Creeks / Streams	Beach	Swimming Pool	Public Transportation	Sports Programs	Night Lighting	Restrooms	Water Available	Disabled Access	Parking / Entry Fee	Concessions	Boat Rentals	Misc. Rentals
		•		•					•	•			•	•	•				
	•		•	•						•			•	•	•				
	•		•	•					•	•			•		•				
		•	•	•						•			•	•					
	•	•	•	•									•	•	•				
	•		•	•	•	•			•	•			•	•	•			•	•
	•		•			•	•		•					•					
	•	•	•	•			•			•			•	•	•				
	•		•	•						•			•	•	•				
	•		•	•			•						•	•	•				
	•	•	•	•		•				•		•	•	•	•	•	•		
	•		•	•	•				•				•	•	•				
	•	•	•	•		•	•	•					•	•	•	•	•	•	
	•		•			•				•	•		•		•				
	•	•	•	•	•	•			•	•			•	•	•		•		
			•	•		•							•	•	•				
			•			•							•	•	•				
		•	•			•				•			•	•		•			
	•	•	•		•					•	•		•	•					
		•	•	•		•				•			•	•	•		•		

ACTIVITIES

PICNIC FACILITIES	MAXIMUM CAPACITY	Ballfields	Volleyball	Playground	Tennis	Hiking Trails	Biking Trails	Sailing/Boating	Basketball	Horseshoes	Bocci Ball	Horseback Riding	Archery	Fishing	Swimming
SANTA CRUZ AREA															
Aptos															
Aptos Village Park	200			•											
Ben Lomond															
Highlands Park	500	•	•	•	•									•	
Felton															
Roaring Camp	2,000	•	•			•				•					
Santa Cruz															
Delaveaga Park	250	•	•	•		•				•		•			
Harvey West Park	3,000	•	•	•		•	•			•				•	
Harvey W. Park: Friendship Gardens	90	•	•	•		•	•			•				•	
Santa Cruz Beach Boardwalk Deck	1,500		•												
Watsonville															
Pinto Lake County Park	500	•				•							•		
MONTEREY PENINSULA															
Monterey															
El Estero Park	200	•		•									•		
Laguna Seca	10,000			•		•									
Pirate's Cove	2,000		•	•				•	•	•			•	•	
Monterey/Salinas															
Royal Oaks	900	•	•	•	•	•			•	•					
Toro County Park	2,000	•	•	•		•	•			•					

	Large BBQ Units	Small BBQ Units	Picnic Tables	Picnic Lawns	Amphitheatre / Stage	Lake / Body of Water	Creeks / Streams	Beach	Swimming Pool		Public Transportation	Sports Programs	Night Lighting	Restrooms	Water Available	Disabled Access	Parking / Entry Fee	Concessions	Boat Rentals	Misc. Rentals
			•	•		•					•		•	•	•	•				
	•	•	•	•		•					•			•	•	•	•			
	•		•											•	•	•	•	•		
	•		•			•					•			•	•	•	•			
	•		•					•			•			•	•	•		•		
	•		•					•			•			•	•	•		•		
	•		•		•		•				•	•		•	•	•		•		•
	•		•			•								•	•	•	•			
	•		•			•								•	•	•		•	•	
	•	•	•	•	•	•					•			•	•	•	•	•		
	•	•	•		•	•		•			•	•	•	•	•	•			•	•
	•	•	•	•										•	•	•	•			
	•	•	•	•										•	•	•	•			

SAN FRANCISCO

Golden Gate Park   415/666-7027, 415/666-7035

Between Stanyon and the Great Highway
and Fulton and Lincoln

(see entry in Event Locations section for more information)

Picnic Sites
*Lindley Meadow • Marx Meadow • Pioneer Log
Cabin • Sharon Meadow, Stowe Lake Area •
Speedway Meadow • 14th Avenue East • 19th
Avenue Playground • Additional Areas*

Golden Gate park is one of the largest man-made parks in the world with over 1,017 acres of lush landscaping. The park is home to the California Academy of Sciences, the Morrison Planetarium, The De Young Museum, the Japanese Tea Garden an arboretum, botanical gardens, and a wide variety of flower gardens. Some of the lesser-known attractions are a buffalo herd and two authentic windmills. Kids go bananas over the large children's playground, which features one of the oldest carrousels in the country. You can rent a boat on Stowe Lake, one of the park's numerous lakes, or hike or jog along miles of trails. All picnic sites are grassy areas surrounded by shade trees. Do a fund-raising race, or have a tennis tournament on some of the park's 21 tennis courts, followed by a grand picnic in one of the many meadows. Golden Gate Park truly has something for everyone.

- **RESERVE:** Up to 12 months in advance.
- **CAPACITY:**

Picnic Site	Capacity	Large BBQs	Small BBQs	Tables
Lindley Meadow	15,000	9	—	15
Marx Meadow	5,000	3	—	7
Pioneer Log Cabin	1,500	2	—	4
Sharon Meadow	20,000	3	—	7
Stowe Lake Area	100	3	—	12
Speedway Meadow	25,000	8	—	19
14th Avenue East	200	—	—	2
19th Avenue Playground	100	—	—	2
Additional Areas (12)	25–2,000	—	—	varies

- **FEES & DEPOSITS:** The use fee and a written request are due 5 working days after tentative reservations are made. Fees are $25 for groups up to 50, $50 for non-profits and groups over 50, $125–500 for company picnics. A damage/cleanup deposit is required from any group with over 100 people. For groups larger than 500, a certificate of liability may be required. If you plan to bring in your own tables, chairs, or other picnic equipment, you need to get approval from the reservation office.

- **RESTRICTIONS:** No vehicles permitted on grass; all debris must be bagged and removed from site; no food or beverages can be sold without a health permit. Pets must be on a leash. There is no tenting in the park without approval.

- **AVAILABILITY:** Year-round, 8am–sunset.

Stern Grove

415/666-7027, 415/666-7035

19th Ave. and Sloat
*(see Trocadero entry in Event Locations section for
more information)*

Picnic Sites
Circle 1 • Circle 2 • East Meadow

Stern Grove is a serene and majestic natural park surrounded by giant eucalyptus, redwood and fern trees. It's famous for the wide variety of concerts and cultural events performed on an outdoor stage Sundays throughout the summer. Circle 1 and Circle 2 are intimate, shady sites arranged in a campfire circle, and Circle 2 is adjacent to a pond.

- **RESERVE:** Up to 12 months in advance.
- **CAPACITY:**

Picnic Site	Capacity	Large BBQs	Small BBQs	Tables
Circle 1	25	—	1	1
Circle 2	25	—	1	1
East Meadow	250	2	—	8

- **FEES & DEPOSITS:** The use fee and a written request are due 5 working days after tentative reservations are made. Fees range from $50–125. A damage/cleanup deposit is required from any group with over 100 people. For groups larger than 500, a certificate of liability may be required. If you plan to bring in your own tables, chairs, or other picnic equipment you need to get approval from the reservation office.

- **RESTRICTIONS:** No vehicles permitted on grass; all debris must be bagged and removed from site; no food or beverages can be sold without a health permit. Pets must be on a leash. There is no tenting in the park without approval.

- **AVAILABILITY:** Year-round, 8am–sunset. Not available Sundays during the last 2 weeks of June through the 3rd Sunday of August due to concerts in the Grove.

McLaren Park

415/666-7027, 415/666-7035

Shelly Drive between Cambridge and Mansell

Picnic Sites
1 picnic site

What makes this park unique are its large grassy areas and lush rolling hills surrounded by trees. The park also has tennis courts and an amphitheater, as well as wide open turf areas for informal games and kite flying.

- **RESERVE:** Up to 12 months in advance.
- **CAPACITY:**

Picnic Site	Capacity	Large BBQs	Small BBQs	Tables
Area 1	5,000	—	6	10

■ **FEES & DEPOSITS:** The use fee and a written request are due 5 working days after tentative reservations are made. Fees range from $50–125. A damage/cleanup deposit is required from any group with over 100 people. For groups larger than 500, a certificate of liability may be required. If you plan to bring in your own tables, chairs, or other picnic equipment you need to get approval from the reservation office.

■ **RESTRICTIONS:** No vehicles permitted on grass; all debris must be bagged and removed from site; no food or beverages can be sold without a health permit. Pets must be on a leash. There is no tenting in the park without approval.

■ **AVAILABILITY:** Year-round, 8am–sunset.

HALF MOON BAY

Cozzolino Park   415/726-4383

12001 San Mateo Road off of Highway 92

Picnic Sites
1 picnic site

Part of the Cozzolino Ranch, the private picnic facilities here are set in a clearing of tall redwoods which provide partial shade. This is a pretty place, used for lots of family and company picnics. You can play volleyball, toss horseshoes or have a band and use the dance floor. When you rent the site, your group can have exclusive use of the picnic area, the bar and the barbecue pit. Restrooms are next to the group area.

- **RESERVE:** Up to 1 month in advance.
- **CAPACITY:**

Picnic Site	Capacity	Large BBQs	Small BBQs	Tables
Site 1	200	1	—	14

- **FEES & DEPOSITS:** The use fee is $150 plus a refundable $50 cleaning deposit. Fees are paid the same day as the event.
- **RESTRICTIONS:** No music after 9pm and no use of the creek.
- **AVAILABILITY:** Year-round, 8am–10pm, depending on the weather.

Francis State Beach   415/726-6203

Take 92 to Highway 1 south to Kelly Ave.
and turn right to the beach

Picnic Sites
Beach Picnic Site

Right on Half Moon Bay, Francis State Beach provides a large, sandy picnic area on the bluff above the beach. If you want to put your toes in the Pacific Ocean, a cement ramp leads down to the beach from the picnic area. Although it tends to be foggy much of the time here, picnickers still have terrific views of the ocean and can rent horses a mile and a half away. Note that restroom facilities are adjacent to the picnic site and that the Coastside Trail begins at Francis State Beach.

- **RESERVE:** First-come, first-served basis.
- **CAPACITY:**

Picnic Site	Capacity	Large BBQs	Small BBQs	Tables
Site 1	50	—	varies	varies

- **FEES & DEPOSITS:** Vehicle parking costs $4/car. Fees are paid upon park entry.
- **RESTRICTIONS:** Pets must be on leash, but not are not allowed on the beach.

■ **AVAILABILITY:** Year-round, 8am–sunset.

Martin's Beach   415/712-8020

Off Hwy 1, look for Martin's Beach sign, go to end of road   *Picnic Sites*
#16 Martin's Beach Road   *Beach Picnic Site*
Contact: Barbara Deeney

Just seven miles south of Half Moon Bay, you'll find Martin's Beach. This is a private beach facility located right on the Ocean. The group picnic area has fantastic views, and you can fish, stroll along the beach or build sandcastles. From April–September, the small deli store at Martin's Beach is open.

■ **RESERVE:** Up to 2 weeks in advance.
■ **CAPACITY:**

Picnic Site	Capacity	Large BBQs	Small BBQs	Tables
Site 1	300	—	BYO	15

■ **FEES & DEPOSITS:** Fees: $4/vehicle or $25/bus. For over 50 people, a $50 deposit is required along with a partial payment when reservations are made.
■ **RESTRICTIONS:** Pets must be on leash; clothing is required.
■ **AVAILABILITY:** Year-round, 6am–6pm. During winter, hours are 8am–4:30pm.

MONTARA

Montara Gardens   415/355-9750

---

496 Sixth Street between LeConte and Seventh Streets   *Picnic Sites*
Contact: Colleen   *2 patios*

Montara Gardens, originally the local Montara school, is in Montara, just six miles north of Half Moon Bay. This historic mission-style building and its gardens are available for private functions. The outdoor patios, surrounded by lush greenery, flowers and tall conifers, offer guests fleeting glimpses of the ocean beyond. Only six blocks from the beach, Montara Gardens has plenty of picnic tables, two gazebos and an indoor auditorium if the weather becomes inclement.

■ **RESERVE:** 1 month in advance.
■ **CAPACITY:**

Picnic Site	Capacity	Large BBQs	Small BBQs	Tables
2 patios	100	—	BYO	25

- **FEES & DEPOSITS:** Rental fees are paid when you make reservations. The use fee is $400 for 4 hours, every additional hour is $75. A $200 refundable deposit is also required.

- **RESTRICTIONS:** No amplified music is allowed outdoors; no hard alcohol or pets.

- **AVAILABILITY:** Year-round, 11am–7pm.

SAN GREGORIO

Rancho San Gregorio   415/747-0810

5086 La Honda Road, Hwy 84, 5 miles east of Hwy 1   *Picnic Sites*
Contact: Lee Raynor   *1 picnic site*

This is a private, tranquil bed and breakfast with barn and orchards. The picnic area is situated next to San Gregorio Creek, and has a shade canopy provided by large trees. Equipment for horseshoes, volleyball, badminton and croquet can be provided, and there's also a flat, grassy area for informal softball in the orchard. An 800 square foot barn is available for indoor dancing.

- **RESERVE:** Up to 6 months in advance.

- **CAPACITY:** 100 maximum (65 seated at tables)

Picnic Site	Capacity	Large BBQs	Small BBQs	Tables
Site 1	100	2	—	7

- **FEES & DEPOSITS:** For group picnics, reservations are required. Use fees are $50/hour, with a minimum of 4 hours. A $150 refundable damage deposit is required. Half of the estimated fee is due when reservations are confirmed; the balance is due 2 weeks prior to the event.

- **RESTRICTIONS:** Children must be supervised. No pets; smoking outdoors only. The house is off limits except for those who are staying overnight.

- **AVAILABILITY:** Year-round, from dawn to dusk.

ANGEL ISLAND

Angel Island State Park   800/444-7275 (Mistix)

Angel Island is located in the middle of SF Bay and   ***Picnic Sites***
must be reached by public ferry or private boat.   *Hill • Draw • Platform*

Located in San Francisco Bay, a short ferry ride from Tiburon, this 740-acre island features eucalyptus forests, trails suitable for jogging, hiking and bicycling, and several picturesque picnic areas. Two trails lead to the top of 781-foot Mount Livermore for spectacular views of San Francisco and the Bay.

- ■ RESERVE: 2 weeks in advance. You can also call the Ranger Station at 415/435-1915 for more information.
- ■ CAPACITY:

Picnic Site	Capacity	Large BBQs	Small BBQs	Tables
Hill	35–70	1	3	12
Draw	35–100	1	9	15
Platform	100–150	2	2	24

- ■ FEES & DEPOSITS: The use fee for Hill and Draw is $25 each; the Platform is $50. Fees are due on booking. There is also a Mistix reservation fee.
- ■ RESTRICTIONS: No pets, skates, skateboards, or amplified music. No wood fires.
- ■ AVAILABILITY: Year-round, 8am to sunset, although the last ferries depart the island at least 1 hour earlier.

CORTE MADERA

Town Park   415/927-5072

---

498 Tamalpais Drive, off Pixley   ***Picnic Sites***
Contact: Charlene Wolf, Recreation Department   *A, B, C, D, E, F and G*

Town Park provides extensive lawn areas with picnic tables and barbecues arranged mostly under trees. There are two children's playgrounds, softball field, tennis and basketball courts. A paved bicycle trail circles the park and a creek runs through it.

- ■ RESERVE: 6–8 weeks in advance.
- ■ CAPACITY: Areas A–G can be combined to accommodate 700 people.

Picnic Site	Capacity	Large BBQs	Small BBQs	Tables
Areas A–G	700	—	12	17

■ **FEES & DEPOSITS:** Up to 50 people, $75 plus a $46 cleaning deposit; 51–100 people, $125 plus $58; 101–200 people, $212 plus $115; 201–300 people, $363 plus $230; 301–500 people, $645 plus $600; 501–700 people, $1,290 plus $1,200. The softball field rents for $12/hour. The deposit is required to confirm the reservation; the fee balance is due 3 weeks before the event. Residents of Corte Madera are charged a lower rate. Call the Parks Department for details.

■ **RESTRICTIONS:** Groups serving alcohol must provide evidence of insurance. No glass containers, dogs or amplified music.

■ **AVAILABILITY:** Year-round during daylight hours.

FAIRFAX

Deer Park Villa   415/456-8084

367 Bolinas Road
Contact: Debbie Ghiringhelli
(see entry in Private Dining Room section for more information)

Picnic Sites
1 picnic site

The Villa is surrounded by four acres of redwoods, oaks and lush hydrangeas. The facility includes a front garden with outdoor dance area, bar, covered and heated patio, towering redwood trees and a small Japanese pagoda and footbridge. For group picnics, Deer Park Villa caters all events.

■ **RESERVE:** Up to 12 month in advance.

■ **CAPACITY:**

Picnic Site	Capacity	Large BBQs	Small BBQs	Tables
Redwood Grove	300	—	—	provided*

■ **FEES & DEPOSITS:** Deer Park Villa caters all group events. To reserve the Redwood Grove, a $2/person deposit is required. The deposit is applied toward catering costs which start at $14.75/person. *Tables and chairs will be provided as needed if your event is catered by Deer Park Villa.

■ **RESTRICTIONS:** No pets. Alcohol has to be purchased on site. Amplified music within guidelines.

■ **AVAILABILITY:** Year-round, during daylight hours.

Lake Lagunitas   415/924-4600, ext. 203

Sky Oaks Road at Bolinas-Fairfax Road   *Picnic Sites*
Contact: Hattie, Marin Municipal Water District (MMWD)   *1 picnic site*

There are hiking and bicycling trails surrounding this beautiful lake, as well as equestrian trails for horseback riders. Fishing is allowed with a California fishing license.

■ **RESERVE:** Up to 1 month in advance.

■ **CAPACITY:**

Picnic Site	Capacity	Large BBQs	Small BBQs	Tables
Site 1	60	1	—	6

■ **FEES & DEPOSITS:** Call MMWD for a permit, which must be returned with a $50 fee to confirm the reservation. The fee includes 5 parking passes; additional vehicles pay $3 each.

■ **RESTRICTIONS:** Alcohol is permitted, although kegs of beer are discouraged. No amplified music. Dogs on leashes are allowed.

■ **AVAILABILITY:** Year-round, during daylight hours.

LAGUNITAS

Samuel P. Taylor Park   800/444-7275 (Mistix)

8800 Sir Francis Drake Blvd.   *Picnic Sites*
                                                      1 picnic site

The Redwood Grove picnic site is a very peaceful area within the park. Nestled in a grove of second growth redwoods alongside a creek, this site is a shaded area with fire rings and a barbecue. The park has hiking and bicycling trails and a stream which runs through it.

■ **RESERVE:** 12 weeks in advance.

■ **CAPACITY:**

Picnic Site	Capacity	Large BBQs	Small BBQs	Tables
Site 1	80	2	—	10

■ **FEES & DEPOSITS:** There is a $100 fee plus the Mistix reservation charge.

■ **RESTRICTIONS:** No amplified music. Dogs must be on leash; owners are charged $1/dog.

■ **AVAILABILITY:** Year-round during daylight hours.

LARKSPUR

Piper Park   415/927-5110

---

250 Doherty Drive, off Magnolia   *Picnic Sites*
                                               1 picnic site

Inlets of the San Francisco Bay surround this 22-acre park, which features ballfields, volleyball, tennis, horseshoes and a children's playground. The picnic tables are in clusters, all in one major clearing. There are also hiking trails, and fishing along the edge of the water is allowed. A small dock is available at the end of the park, suitable for row boats or canoes.

- ■ **RESERVE:** Up to 2 months in advance. For June–September picnics, reserve by early March.
- ■ **CAPACITY:**

Picnic Site	Capacity	Large BBQs	Small BBQs	Tables
Site 1	300	—	5	24

- ■ **FEES & DEPOSITS:** The day-use fee for groups of 250–300 people is $425, plus a $100 refundable security deposit. Otherwise, the fee is $20 per table, plus a $25 deposit. Use of the softball field is $20 per hour; use of the volleyball court is $20 for the first hour, $10 each hour thereafter.

- ■ **RESTRICTIONS:** Alcohol is allowed for private consumption only. Amplified music is not allowed. The tennis courts are on a first-come, first-served basis and for use by residents only.

- ■ **AVAILABILITY:** Year-round during daylight hours.

MILL VALLEY

Bootjack   415/456-5218

On Mt. Tamalpais, on Panoramic Highway,   *Picnic Sites*
a quarter mile East of Pantoll   *1 picnic site*

Situated on the slopes of Mount Tamalpais, Bootjack has a lovely picnic area under native oak trees. Hiking trails lead up to the Mountain Theater and the East Peak, which have panoramic views of the Bay and East Bay hills.

- ■ **RESERVE:** Reserve at least 1 month in advance. You can also call the Ranger Station at 415/388-2070.
- ■ **CAPACITY:**

Picnic Site	Capacity	Large BBQs	Small BBQs	Tables
Site 1	50–65	4	1	15

■ **FEES & DEPOSITS:** Telephone reservations are accepted and a permit will be mailed out. Return the permit with 2 checks—a $25 rental fee and a $25 refundable security deposit to confirm the reservation. Parking costs $5/car.

■ **RESTRICTIONS:** Amplified music is not allowed.

■ **AVAILABILITY:** Year-round, 8am to sunset.

Boyle Park   415/383-1370

East Blithedale Avenue at East Drive   *Picnic Sites*
Contact: Stuart Kesler, Recreation Department   *1 picnic site*

Close to downtown Mill Valley, but in a quiet area with a seasonal creek running through it, Boyle Park offers tennis courts, ballfields, a children's playground, and a large lawn area with native oak trees around the perimeter.

■ **RESERVE:** 6–12 months in advance.

■ **CAPACITY:**

Picnic Site	*Capacity*	*Large BBQs*	*Small BBQs*	*Tables*
Site 1	150	1	—	10

■ **FEES & DEPOSITS:** A permit is required, obtainable by calling the Recreation Department. A $100 refundable security deposit is due within 1 week after receiving the permit. Use fees: $25 for up to 50 people; $50 for 51–100; $100 for 101–150. The rental fee for the ballfields is $10 per hour. A pass is needed to use the tennis courts.

■ **RESTRICTIONS:** The picnic area is open to only Mill Valley residents during the summer months. Amplified music is not allowed. Dogs must be on leash. Parking is very restricted and can be a problem on weekends.

■ **AVAILABILITY:** Year-round, during daylight hours.

Cushing Memorial Theater (Mountain Theater)   415/456-5218

Atop Mt. Tamalpais, on Ridge Crest Road, off Pantoll   *Picnic Sites*
                                                          1 picnic site

Set high on Mount Tamalpais, with views of the Bay and East Bay hills, the Mountain Theater is famous for its annual play, which is performed on six successive Sundays in May and June, drawing visitors from all around the Bay Area.

■ **RESERVE:** Up to 1 year in advance.

■ **CAPACITY:**

Picnic Site	*Capacity*	*Large BBQs*	*Small BBQs*	*Tables*
Theater	150	—	—	—

■ **FEES & DEPOSITS:** The reservation fee is $150, plus a $25 refundable security deposit. The fee and deposit are due (separate checks) with a completed permit application obtained by mail from the State Parks Department.

■ **RESTRICTIONS:** There are no picnic tables, although picnickers can take their food and sit in the theater, provided it isn't being used for a play. Barbecues are not permitted because of fire danger. No amplified music is allowed.

■ **AVAILABILITY:** Year-round, 8am to sunset.

Mill Valley Outdoor Art Club   415/383-2582

1 West Blithedale Avenue, off Throckmorton   *Picnic Sites*
Contact: Shirley   *1 picnic site*
(see entry in Event Locations section for more information)

Located in downtown Mill Valley, the Outdoor Art Club features a very picturesque, historic structure surrounded by a wide variety of flowers and trees. In front of the building is an attractive brick courtyard, framed by huge oaks. Catering is BYO. Dishes and tables are provided and arranged by the custodian according to your group's specifications.

■ **RESERVE:** 2–3 months in advance.

■ **CAPACITY:**

Picnic Site	Capacity	Large BBQs	Small BBQs	Tables
Site 1	200	—	—	6

■ **FEES & DEPOSITS:** The rental fee is $1,200, with half due when the reservation is made and the balance due 10 days before the event. There's also a $500 refundable security/cleaning deposit.

■ **RESTRICTIONS:** Parking can be a problem as the Club doesn't have a parking lot. Amplified music is not allowed.

■ **AVAILABILITY:** Year-round, 8am–1am on weekends. Weekday hours are negotiable.

Old Mill Park   415/383-1370

On Cascade at Throckmorton Ave.   *Picnic Sites*
Contact: Stuart Kesler, Recreation Department   *Redwood Ring • Large Picnic Area*

Old Mill Park is a lovely, historic park near downtown, and encompasses a large redwood grove. There is a historic mill above the creek, a children's playground and a natural amphitheater. T wo group picnic areas are available, one next to the playground and one next to the amphitheater.

■ **RESERVE:** 6–12 months in advance.

■ **CAPACITY:**

Picnic Site	Capacity	Large BBQs	Small BBQs	Tables
Redwood Ring	30	1	—	40
Large Picnic Area	100	—	—	12

■ **FEES & DEPOSITS:** A permit is required, obtainable by calling the Recreation Department. A $100 refundable security deposit is due within 1 week after receiving the permit. Use fees: $25 for up to 50 people; $50 for 51–100; $100 for 101–150.

■ **RESTRICTIONS:** During summer months, the picnic area is available to Mill Valley residents only. Amplified music is not allowed; dogs must be on leash. Parking is very restricted and can be a problem on weekends.

■ **AVAILABILITY:** Year-round, during daylight hours.

NICASIO

The Shadows   415/662-2012

1901 Nicasio Valley Road, Lucas Valley Road
Contact: Joseph Destein
(see entry in Event Locations section for more information)

Picnic Sites
1 picnic site

The Shadows is a private enclave set amidst towering redwoods, close to hiking and bicycling trails. Its a woodsy and intimate spot for small social and business groups looking for something different. A cultural and educational retreat, it's perfect for group picnics. It features a swimming pool, putting green, volleyball court, horseshoes and bocci ball. A golf course is nearby.

■ **RESERVE:** 2 months in advance.

■ **CAPACITY:**

Picnic Site	Capacity	Large BBQs	Small BBQs	Tables
Site 1	150	1	—	8

■ **FEES & DEPOSITS:** The fee is $500/day, payable when reservations are made.

■ **RESTRICTIONS:** No pets allowed.

■ **AVAILABILITY:** Year-round, Monday–Thursday only, 9am–11pm.

NOVATO

Hoog Park   415/897-4323

---

558 Marin Oaks Drive at Montura Way

Picnic Sites
1 picnic site

This is a sunny, three-acre neighborhood park featuring children's play structures and two volleyball courts. Most of the park has lush, rolling lawns. A small stand of trees shades a handfull of picnic tables.

- ■ **RESERVE:** Up to 3 months in advance.
- ■ **CAPACITY:**

Picnic Site	*Capacity*	*Large BBQs*	*Small BBQs*	*Tables*
Site 1	60	2	—	10

- ■ **FEES & DEPOSITS:** Use fees are $11/hour for Novato residents, $13/hour for non-residents. The total fee is due 30 days prior to the event.
- ■ **RESTRICTIONS:** Alcohol may be consumed only in reserved areas.
- ■ **AVAILABILITY:** Year-round, from dawn to 10pm.

Miwok Park   415/897-4323

2200 Novato Blvd., San Miguel Way

Picnic Sites
1 picnic site

The Museum of the American Indian, open Tuesday–Saturday, 10am–4pm, Sunday 12–4pm, is located in Miwok Park. There is a children's playground, horseshoes, and bocci ball. Fishing is allowed in the creek.

- ■ **RESERVE:** Up to 3 months in advance.
- ■ **CAPACITY:**

Picnic Site	*Capacity*	*Large BBQs*	*Small BBQs*	*Tables*
Site 1	200	2	—	30

- ■ **FEES & DEPOSITS:** Use fees are $11/hour for Novato residents, $13/hour for non-residents. The total fee is due 30 days prior to the event.
- ■ **RESTRICTIONS:** Alcohol may be consumed only in reserved areas.
- ■ **AVAILABILITY:** Year-round, from dawn to 10pm.

Pioneer Park   415/897-4323

1007 Simmons Lane, Novato Blvd.   *Picnic Sites*
                                              1 picnic site

Pioneer Park has tennis and basketball courts and a children's playground. Of interest is an old cemetery located on park grounds.

- ■ **RESERVE:** Up to 3 months in advance.
- ■ **CAPACITY:**

Picnic Site	Capacity	Large BBQs	Small BBQs	Tables
Site 1	35	1	—	5

- ■ **FEES & DEPOSITS:** Use fees $11/hour for Novato residents; $13/hour for non-residents. The total fee is due 30 days prior to the event.
- ■ **RESTRICTIONS:** Alcohol may be consumed only in the reserved area.
- ■ **AVAILABILITY:** Year-round, from dawn to 10pm.

Stafford Lake Park   415/499-6387

Novato Blvd., San Marin Drive   *Picnic Sites*
Contact: Veronica, Marin County Parks Department   *Area 1, 2, 3 and 4*

This very popular 139-acre park on the shores of lovely Stafford Lake includes a large lawn area with a softball field, volleyball court, horseshoes and a children's playground. Fishing and amplified music are allowed. There are hiking and bicycling trails criss-crossing the park.

- ■ **RESERVE:** Suggested 3–6 months in advance. Reservations are accepted up to 1 year in advance.
- ■ **CAPACITY:** Several group areas may be combined to hold up to 1,000+.

Picnic Site	Capacity	Large BBQs	Small BBQs	Tables
Area 1	500	1	—	20
Area 2	500	1	—	20
Area 3	100	1	—	10
Area 4	100	1	—	10

- ■ **FEES & DEPOSITS:** The small sites cost $50 per day; the large sites $300. Reservations are made by phone. A permit will be mailed and must be returned within 10 days with the total fee. Entrance fees are $1/car between October 26 and April 1. During the summer, the weekday entrance fee is $3/car; weekends $5/car.
- ■ **RESTRICTIONS:** No pets allowed.
- ■ **AVAILABILITY:** Year-round. Summer hours are 7am–8pm; winter hours, 9am–5pm.

POINT REYES

Point Reyes National Seashore	415/663-8525 Ranger's Office

On Bear Valley Road, off Highway 1 at Olema

Picnic Sites
Drakes Beach • Bear Valley • Beach

Point Reyes National Seashore occupies 65,000 acres of wilderness, featuring spectacular views and more than 70 miles of trails which run through meadows and pastures, across cliffs and over high ridges. There is also beach access at a few locations. The park headquarters are located in Bear Valley, the trail head for many of the trails. There is also a horse ranch adjacent to the park headquarters building.

- ■ **RESERVE:** Reservations not accepted, but groups must notify the Ranger's Office in advance when they will be arriving.
- ■ **CAPACITY:**

Picnic Site	Capacity	Large BBQs	Small BBQs	Tables
Drakes Beach	50	—	6	6
Bear Valley	100	—	10	10
Beach	200–300	—	—	—

- ■ **FEES & DEPOSITS:** None required.
- ■ **RESTRICTIONS:** No amplified music. No dogs.
- ■ **AVAILABILITY:** Year-round during daylight hours.

ROSS

Marin Art and Garden Center	415/454-1301

30 Sir Francis Drake Blvd.
(see entry in Event Locations section for more information)

Picnic Sites
1 picnic site

The Art and Garden Center is well-known for its ten acres of beautiful grounds in the heart of prestigious Ross. Just off Sir Francis Drake Blvd., this facility is not only a favorite among Marin residents because of its park-like setting, and but it attracts groups from all over the Bay Area.

- ■ **RESERVE:** 9–12 months in advance.

- **CAPACITY:**

Picnic Site	Capacity	Large BBQs	Small BBQs	Tables
Site 1	500	—	BYO	BYO

- **FEES & DEPOSITS:** A non-refundable deposit is required and must be paid in advance to secure your date. The amount depends on the type of function. Rental fees: $850 for up to 300 guests; $1,000 for up to 400; and $1,200 for up to 500 guests.

- **RESTRICTIONS:** Caterer must be licensed; amplified music is not allowed.

- **AVAILABILITY:** Year-round, during daylight hours and only on weekends.

SAN ANSELMO

Memorial Park   415/258-4640

1000 Sir Francis Drake Blvd. at San Francisco Blvd.   *Picnic Sites*
Contact: Sharon Vogel   *1 picnic site*

Memorial park is a sunny expanse of lawn dotted with young trees. The group picnic site has two large barbecue pits and is adjacent to a fully enclosed children's playground. The park also features three baseball diamonds, horseshoe pits and basketball, volleyball and tennis courts.

- **RESERVE:** 6 weeks in advance.

- **CAPACITY:**

Picnic Site	Capacity	Large BBQs	Small BBQs	Tables
Site 1	150	2	3	16

- **FEES & DEPOSITS:** A permit is required, obtainable by mail. The permit must be returned with the fee: $50 a day for up to 50 people; $75 for 51–75 people; $100 for 76–100 people; $150 for 101–150 people. Sports equipment for volleyball, basketball, soccer and baseball (including frisbees) is available for a $100 deposit.

- **RESTRICTIONS:** No alcohol. Amplified music requires prior approval by the police department.

- **AVAILABILITY:** Year-round during daylight hours.

SAN RAFAEL

China Camp State Park   **415/456-0766** Ranger Station

Exit Highway 101 at North San Pedro Road

Picnic Sites
1 picnic site

China Camp contains what's left of the last and largest of the Bay's shrimping villages. Chinese fishermen netted shrimp here, dried them and shipped them back to China during the 1880s. The park is located on San Pablo Bay and has terrific views of the East Bay hills. There's also a museum focusing on the history of China Camp. The cool but calm Bay waters are good for swimming and there's a pebbly, narrow beach for sunbathing. Volleyball and horseshoes are available and fishing is allowed from the pier.

■ **RESERVE:** 6 weeks in advance, beginning in January for that year.

■ **CAPACITY:** 200

Picnic Site	*Capacity*	*Large BBQs*	*Small BBQs*	*Tables*
Site 1	200	2	—	25

■ **FEES & DEPOSITS:** Up to 50 people, $75 plus a $50 refundable security deposit; 51–100 people, $125 plus a $100 deposit; 101–200 people, $225 plus a $150 deposit. There's also a $3–5/car parking fee.

■ **RESTRICTIONS:** There is no running water and only chemical toilets. Groups of 100 can use one of the large barbecues; groups of 200 can use both. Amplified music is not allowed.

■ **AVAILABILITY:** Year-round, 8am to sunset.

Dominican College   **415/485-3228**

---

50 Acacia Ave., in the historic section of San Rafael
Contact: Maureen McKinney
(see entry in Event Locations section for more information)

Picnic Sites
Forest Meadows • Anne Hathaway Garden

The grounds of this century-old college are situated in a quiet residential area of San Rafael, on an 80-acre wooded campus. Of note is the grand, three-story Victorian structure that's the centerpiece of Dominican College. There are two separate areas for picnics and other outdoor events. Forest Meadows is suitable for large groups and the Anne Hathaway Gardens is a lovely setting for smaller gatherings, with a lawn ringed by roses and annuals. There are tennis courts and hiking trails near Forest Meadows.

■ **RESERVE:** Up to 12 months in advance.

■ **CAPACITY:**

Picnic Site	Capacity	Large BBQs	Small BBQs	Tables
Forest Meadows	1,000	—	BYO	BYO
Anne Hathaway Garden	100	—	BYO	BYO

■ **FEES & DEPOSITS:** Forest Meadows costs $500/day; Anne Hathaway Gardens $220. The tennis courts can be rented for $85/day.

■ **RESTRICTIONS:** Groups must supply everything they need, including tables, barbecues, etc.

■ **AVAILABILITY:** Year-round during daylight hours.

Falkirk Mansion   415/485-3328

1408 Mission Street
(see entry in Event Locations section for more information)

Picnic Sites
1 picnic site

Magnificent oaks and colorful blooming magnolias frame the historic Falkirk Mansion, a lovely Queen Anne Victorian built in 1888, presiding over eleven acres in the heart of San Rafael. The Mansion is surrounded by decks, verandas, and sloping lawns which are great for informal gatherings.

■ **RESERVE:** 6–8 months in advance.

■ **CAPACITY:** 100

Picnic Site	Capacity	Large BBQs	Small BBQs	Tables
Site 1	100	—	—	—

■ **FEES & DEPOSITS:** From April 16 to October 14, the rental fee is $690 for up to 6 hours, $165/hour for any time exceeding 6 hours. From October 15 to April 15, the fee is $540 for up to 6 hours, $135/ hour overtime. Half the rental fee is due when you make reservations; the balance is due 45 days prior to the event.

■ **RESTRICTIONS:** No barbecues or outdoor heaters. Caterers must be selected from an approved list. The facility allows only a few serving tables to be set up outside. Groups can use the decks and verandas or lay out blankets on the lawn for picnics.

■ **AVAILABILITY:** Year-round, until 11pm.

Maria B. Freitas Memorial Park   415/485-3333

Exit Freitas Parkway off 101, Montecillo Road
and Nova Albion

Picnic Sites
Gazebo • Plateau

Often referred to as the "Water Park", Maria B. Freitas Memorial Park features a large wading pool for children. Above the pool is a plateau with expansive lawns, lighted tennis courts, and two reservable picnic sites on grass.

- **RESERVE:** 3–6 months in advance, beginning in January for that year.
- **CAPACITY:**

Picnic Site	Capacity	Large BBQs	Small BBQs	Tables
Gazebo	20-25	—	—	2
Plateau	50	—	3	5

- **FEES & DEPOSITS:** The use fee is $20–40 a day. A permit is required, obtainable from the San Rafael Community Center, 618 B Street. The fee is due with the completed permit.
- **RESTRICTIONS:** No amplified music. Proof of insurance is needed to serve alcohol.
- **AVAILABILITY:** Year-round, during daylight hours.

Gerstle Park   415/485-3333

San Rafael Ave. off of D Street or Clark Street
Contact: Karen

Picnic Sites
Grove • Arbor • Areas 1, 2 & 3

Towering redwoods shade most of this very pretty, older park. A thick redwood grove, a wisteria arbor, and three shaded, grassy areas are all available for picnics. The park also has flower gardens, a playground, basketball and tennis courts.

- **RESERVE:** 3–6 months in advance, beginning in January for that year.
- **CAPACITY:** Areas 1–3 can be combined for groups up to 140 people.

Picnic Site	Capacity	Large BBQs	Small BBQs	Tables
Grove	200	1	—	20
Arbor	15–20	—	—	2
Area 1	20	—	1	2
Area 2	75–100	1	—	5
Area 3	20	—	1	3

- **FEES & DEPOSITS:** The group use fee is $20–70/day. A permit is required, obtainable from the San Rafael Community Center, 618 B Street. Fees are due with the completed permit.
- **RESTRICTIONS:** No amplified music. Proof of insurance is needed to serve alcohol.
- **AVAILABILITY:** Year-round, during daylight hours.

John F. McInnis Park   415/499-6387

300 Smith Ranch Road, exit from Highway 101   *Picnic Sites*
Contact: Veronica, Marin County Parks Department   *1 picnic site*

This 441-acre facility, Marin County's newest park, features softball fields, tennis courts, soccer fields, a canoe launching dock, golf driving range, golf course and scale model car track. Jogging trails, a nature trail and bicycling paths wind through the park.

- ■ **RESERVE:** 2 weeks in advance.
- ■ **CAPACITY:**

Picnic Site	Capacity	Large BBQs	Small BBQs	Tables
Site 1	50–100	1	2	10

- ■ **FEES & DEPOSITS:** The use fee is $75 for large groups. No other fees are required.
- ■ **RESTRICTIONS:** No pets.
- ■ **AVAILABILITY:** Year-round, 8am–10pm during summer months

McNears Beach Park   415/499-6387

Hwy 101 to Central San Rafael exit, east on 2nd St.   *Picnic Sites*
which becomes San Pedro Rd. Go 4–5 miles, turn right   *Arbor Area • Area 1 • Area 2 • Area 3*
onto Cantera Way
Contact: Veronica, Marin County Parks Department

This is Marin County's most popular park. Located on San Pedro Bay, it features a swimming pool, tennis courts, lawn areas and a sandy beach. A concession stand and fishing pier are also available.

- ■ **RESERVE:** 3 months in advance.
- ■ **CAPACITY:**

Picnic Site	Capacity	Large BBQs	Small BBQs	Tables
Arbor Area	200	1	1	20
Area 1	75–150	—	2	10
Area 2	75–150	—	2	10
Area 3	75–150	—	2	10

- ■ **FEES & DEPOSITS:** The reservation fee is $75/day from late October to early April. During the summer months the fee is $75 weekdays, $150 on weekends. There's also a $1 entrance fee for cars from late October to early April, $3 on summer weekdays, $5 on summer weekends. There's an additional fee for use of the swimming pool: $4/adult, $3/teenager and $2/child.
- ■ **RESTRICTIONS:** No pets. The concession stand and pool are only open between Memorial Day and Labor Day.
- ■ **AVAILABILITY:** Year-round. Summer hours are 8am–8pm; winter hours, 8am-5pm.

Victor Jones Park   415/485-3333

Robinhood and Maplewood Drives   *Picnic Sites*
Contact: Karen   *1 picnic site*

This three–acre neighborhood park includes a ballfield, basketball and shuffleboard courts plus a children's playground. A shaded group picnic site has tables and a barbecue.

- ■ **RESERVE:** 3–6 months in advance, beginning in January for that year.
- ■ **CAPACITY:** 100

Picnic Site	Capacity	Large BBQs	Small BBQs	Tables
Site 1	100	1	—	8

- ■ **FEES & DEPOSITS:** The fee is $20–40/day. A permit is required, obtainable from the San Rafael Community Center, 618 B Street. The fee is due with the completed permit.
- ■ **RESTRICTIONS:** No amplified music. Proof of insurance is needed to serve alcohol.
- ■ **AVAILABILITY:** Year-round, during daylight hours.

SAUSALITO

Rodeo Beach Meeting & Conference Center   415/332-820

Take 101 to Alexander Exit, double back left under Hwy 101   *Picnic Sites*
to uphill right turn (Conzelman Rd) and follow signs to   *Conference Center • Beach Picnic Area*
beach & Fort Cronkhite. The Center is on Bunker Road. This
is the closest building to the beach at the end of the road,
building 1054.

Operated by the Pacific Energy and Resources Center, the Rodeo Beach facility offers meeting and conference space and is ideal for group retreats. The relaxed, historic park setting overlooks the Pacific Ocean, just twenty minutes from downtown San Francisco. Groups can use the building for get-togethers and can take advantage of a warming kitchen (which allows groups to cater their own functions either indoors or outdoors), restrooms and running water. Exterior spaces and the beach are available for picnics.

- ■ **RESERVE:** 2 months in advance.
- ■ **CAPACITY:** 40 indoors, 60 outdoors.

Picnic Site	Capacity	Large BBQs	Small BBQs	Tables
Site 1	60	—	—	2+

- **FEES & DEPOSITS:** A $150 security deposit is required to secure a date. Use fees for the ground floor of the building are $175/day or $125/day for non-profits.
- **RESTRICTIONS:** No hard liquor or amplified music.
- **AVAILABILITY:** Year-round, during daylight hours. This facility is within the Golden Gate National Recreation Area and is subject to GGNRA regulations.

STINSON BEACH

Stinson Beach State Park   **415/868-0942** Ranger Station

The entry is near Highway 1 and Panoramic Highway.   *Picnic Sites*
Several Group Picnic Areas

Looking for a wide-open picnic area on a beach? Stinson Beach is one of the most popular beaches in the Bay Area, and is only a short walk from this 51-acre State park. Lifeguard stations on the beach provide volleyball nets.

- **RESERVE:** First-come, first-served.
- **CAPACITY:**

Picnic Site	*Capacity*	*Large BBQs*	*Small BBQs*	*Tables*
Site 1	200	—	30	30

- **FEES & DEPOSITS:** none
- **RESTRICTIONS:** No amplified music.
- **AVAILABILITY:** Year-round. Summer hours are 9am–10pm; fall hours, 9am–8pm; winter and spring hours, 9am-6pm.

TIBURON

Paradise Beach Park   415/499-6387

East shore of Tiburon Peninsula
Contact: Veronica, Marin County Parks Department

Picnic Sites
Areas 1, 2, 3, 4 and 5

This is a beautiful nineteen-acre park overlooking San Pablo Bay. Its large lawn area, horseshoe pit, sandy beach and fishing pier make it a popular picnic venue.

- **RESERVE:** 3 months in advance.
- **CAPACITY:**

Picnic Site	Capacity	Large BBQs	Small BBQs	Tables
Area 1 & 2	200 ea	1 ea	2 ea	10 ea
Area 3–5	100 ea	1 ea	2 ea	8 ea

- **FEES & DEPOSITS:** The reservation fee is $150 for Areas 1 and 2; $50–75 for Areas 3, 4, or 5. Fees must be paid within 10 days of making the reservation. Entrance fees are $5/car on summer weekends, $3 on summer weekdays, $1 every day between late October and early April.

- **RESTRICTIONS:** No pets or amplified music.

- **AVAILABILITY:** Year-round. Summer hours are 7am–8pm; winter hours are 8am–5pm.

Need a caterer, cake maker, florist? The Service Directory starting on page 614 features the best in the business.

ATHERTON

Holbrook Palmer Park	415/688-6534

150 Watkins Ave. between Middlefield Road and El Camino
(*see entry in Event Locations section for more information*)

Picnic Sites
3 picnic sites

Holbrook Palmer Park is what remains of an old estate, complete with historic buildings, mature oak trees and an 1870 water tower. The Park has 22 acres of open space in exclusive, residential Atherton. For group picnics, there are two large lawn areas with large trees around their perimeter, and a third by the children's play area. Tables can be provided or you can bring your own tables or barbecues. The Jennings Pavilion is a modern structure with plenty of room indoors and a patio which can hold even more.

- **RESERVE:** Up to 12 months in advance.
- **CAPACITY:**

Picnic Site	Capacity	Large BBQs	Small BBQs	Tables
Site 1	250	1	—	1
Jennings Pavilion	250	—	—	provided

- **FEES & DEPOSITS:** For 10–30 people, a $10/day use permit is required. For large group functions, a $250 refundable deposit is required and all fees are due 1 month prior to the event. Fees for use of the site including use of Jennings Pavilion: 1–100 guests, $1,000; 101–200, $1,500; and 201–250 guests, $1,900. Fees include tables, chairs and setup.

- **RESTRICTIONS:** No amplified music outside, no bar or sales of alcohol. Amplified music is only allowed indoors.

- **AVAILABILITY:** Year-round, 8am–5pm.

BELMONT

Twin Pines Park	415/595-7441

At the intersection of 1225 Ralston Ave. and Sixth Ave.

Picnic Sites
1 picnic site

Twin Pines is an older park with nice landscaping and mature trees encircling the group picnic site. The picnic area is rustic, with a very large barbecue pit. During wet months, there's a creek which flows through one portion of the park. Younger picnickers will enjoy the new play area adjacent to the group picnic area. Restrooms are within walking distance.

■ **RESERVE:** The group picnic site is for Belmont residents only. Reservations can be made 4 months in advance.

■ **CAPACITY:**

Picnic Site	Capacity	Large BBQs	Small BBQs	Tables
Site 1	100	1	—	10

■ **FEES & DEPOSITS:** There is a $2 reservation filing fee. Volleyball and horseshoe equipment is available for rent.

■ **RESTRICTIONS:** Sale of alcohol requires a permit. No amplified music; dogs must be on leash.

■ **AVAILABILITY:** Year-round, sunrise to sunset.

BURLINGAME

Kohl Mansion   415/591-7422

2750 Adeline Drive
Contact: Pat Nelson
(see entry in Event Locations section for more information)

Picnic Sites
1 picnic site

This is a prestigious, historic estate site, nestled in the hills of Burlingame. Well-known for hosting elegant weddings and corporate events, the Kohl Mansion also has outdoor facilities for group picnics. Set on a large parcel, the stately rose-brick manor overlooks three tennis courts, an Olympic-sized swimming pool and rose garden. Group functions can be held under tents or on the lawns or terraces.

■ **RESERVE:** Recommended up to 12 months in advance for Saturdays and Sundays during summer months.

■ **CAPACITY:**

Picnic Site	Capacity	Large BBQs	Small BBQs	Tables
Site 1	350–400	—	—	provided*

■ **FEES & DEPOSITS:** Use fees include use of the grounds, swimming pool, tennis courts, courtyard and garden, but not use of Kohl Mansion's interior. Fees include security personnel and a tour of the Mansion. Site fees: up to 100 guests, $3,000; 101–150 guests, $3,500; 151–250, $4,000; 251–400, $4,500. *Tables and chairs can be provided for only 150 guests.

■ **RESTRICTIONS:** No baseball is allowed on lawns. Caterers must be licensed if food is served on site. No amplified music is allowed.

■ **AVAILABILITY:** Year-round, 8am–10pm on weekends. Daily, June 15–August 15, 8am–10pm.

Washington Park   415/344-6386

850 Burlingame Ave., east of the Burlingame
railroad station

Picnic Sites
1 picnic site

Open to residents only, Washington Park offers guests a large, group picnic area. This three-acre park is well-maintained, with mature trees, a rose garden nearby and a children's play area.

- ■ **RESERVE:** 3–6 months in advance for weekend use. Weekdays are on a first-come, first-served basis.
- ■ **CAPACITY:**

Picnic Site	*Capacity*	*Large BBQs*	*Small BBQs*	*Tables*
Site 1	100	—	5	8

- ■ **FEES & DEPOSITS:** The group area is for residents or businesses with a Burlingame address. Reservations are required. A $75 use fee plus a refundable $75 security deposit are due when you make reservations.

- ■ **RESTRICTIONS:** The following are not allowed: animals, alcohol, bicycles, amplified music or chairs on lawns.

- ■ **AVAILABILITY:** The picnic sites may be reserved on weekends only, March 1–October 1, 9am–dusk. Weekdays, on a first-come, first-served basis.

LOS ALTOS

Shoup Park   415/941-0950 ext. 300

400 University Ave. across from Main St. on the
other side of Foothill Expressway

Picnic Sites
1 picnic site

Here, you feel like you're really out in the woods. Shoup Park provides a beautiful setting, with tall redwood trees, lush landscaping and lots of privacy. It's very peaceful and quiet.

- ■ **RESERVE:** Reservations can be made 2 months in advance.
- ■ **CAPACITY:**

Picnic Site	*Capacity*	*Large BBQs*	*Small BBQs*	*Tables*
Site 1	125	2	—	10

- ■ **FEES & DEPOSITS:** A use permit and refundable deposit are required. The deposit for residents is $350, non-residents $500. Use fees are: $91 for resident half-day use, non-residents $148. For full-day use, residents $130, non-residents, $223. An alcohol permit is also required.

- ■ **RESTRICTIONS:** No amplified music or structured sports activities allowed. Alcohol consumption with permit only.

■ **AVAILABILITY:** Year-round, 9am–9pm.

MENLO PARK

Burgess Park   415/858-3484

Burgess Dr. at Alma   *Picnic Sites*
                                                  Areas 1–5

Burgess Park is designed for activities. Adjacent to the community center and other civic buildings, it has athletic fields, an outdoor volleyball court, swimming pool, children's wading pool, parcourse and community theater. Group picnic areas are situated under a grove of oak trees, and three can be reserved in combination for large functions.

■ **RESERVE:** Reservations can be made 6 months in advance.

■ **CAPACITY:** The group sites can hold 500 people if Areas 2–4 are combined.

Picnic Site	Capacity	Large BBQs	Small BBQs	Tables
Area 1–4	25–50 ea	1 ea	—	3 ea
Area 5	25–50	—	—	3 ea

■ **FEES & DEPOSITS:** The use fees are: 300 people, $150 non-resident, $75 residents; 100 people, $50 non-residents, $25 residents. For groups over 100 people, a $100 security deposit is required. Full payment is due when the use permit is submitted. There's an additional fee for use of athletic fields, call for current prices.

■ **RESTRICTIONS:** Beer and wine only. All animals must be on leash. Amplified music is not allowed and electrical usage cannot exceed 30 watts. No vehicles are permitted on the fields.

■ **AVAILABILITY:** Year-round, sunrise to sunset.

Flood County Park   415/363-4021

Bay Road at Marsh Road   *Picnic Sites*
                                                  1 picnic site

Flood Park is an urban park covering 25 acres which has a remarkable grove of heritage oaks. Group picnic sites are scattered throughout this relatively flat, open space. Active picnickers will enjoy three volleyball courts, baseball field, softball field, horseshoe pits and award-winning playground, specially designed to accommodate handicapped users

■ **RESERVE:** Reservations can be made 12 months in advance. Reserve early for spring and summer months.

■ **CAPACITY:** Group areas can be combined to accommodate 500–600 people.

Picnic Site	Capacity	Large BBQs	Small BBQs	Tables
Oak	200–300	8	—	24
Pine	175–200	1	2	22
Bay	60–100	1	2	8
Redwood	60–100	—	2	8
Maple	100	1	2	12
Madrone	50	1	2	5
Fir	50	—	2	6

■ **FEES & DEPOSITS:** A use permit is required for groups. Fees for 101–150 people, $113; 151–200, $150; over 200 people, $188. Fees must be paid 14 days after reservations have been made. April–October vehicle parking costs $4/car.

■ **RESTRICTIONS:** Beer and wine only. No pets or amplified music.

■ **AVAILABILITY:** Year-round, daily sunrise to sunset.

MILLBRAE

Central Park   415/259-2360

477 Lincoln Circle at Palm Street
Contact: Karla McElroy or John Espinoza

Picnic Sites
1 picnic site

The group picnic area is adjacent to the recreation center where there's a large, brick barbecue available to picnickers. Tennis courts, large, open lawns and two playgrounds with new play equipment are nearby. Amplified music is allowed.

■ **RESERVE:** On a first-come, first-served basis.

■ **CAPACITY:**

Picnic Site	Capacity	Large BBQs	Small BBQs	Tables
Site 1	100	1	—	20

■ **FEES & DEPOSITS:** No use fees are required unless you rent the picnic area in conjunction with the assembly room.

■ **RESTRICTIONS:** No alcohol. Animals must be on leash.

■ **AVAILABILITY:** Year-round, sunrise to sunset.

Green Hills Park   415/259-2360

Corner of Ludeman Lane and Magnolia Ave.
Contact: Karla McElroy or John Espinoza

Picnic Sites
1 picnic site

Large, mature trees shade the group picnic area at Green Hills Park. There are rolling, green lawns and nicely landscaped areas for free play. A small totlot and bocci ball court are nearby. Amplified music is allowed.

- ■ **RESERVE:** First-come, first-served basis.
- ■ **CAPACITY:**

Picnic Site	Capacity	Large BBQs	Small BBQs	Tables
Site 1	75	—	3	6

- ■ **FEES & DEPOSITS:** No fees are required.
- ■ **RESTRICTIONS:** No alcohol. Pets must be on leash.
- ■ **AVAILABILITY:** Year-round, sunrise to sunset.

MOUNTAIN VIEW

Rengstorff Park   415/903-6331

201 South Rengstorff Ave. off the Central Expressway

Picnic Sites
Red • Orange • Blue • Green

Picnic tables are arranged under shade trees and surrounded by lawns. Volleyball and tennis courts and two softball diamonds can be used by groups.

- ■ **RESERVE:** Reservations are taken for group use May–October and may be made by Mountain View residents or companies with Mountain View addresses up to 3 months in advance. Reservations must be made in person.
- ■ **CAPACITY:** If all four sites are combined, up to 200 people.

Picnic Site	Capacity	Large BBQs	Small BBQs	Tables
4 Areas	50 ea	1 ea	—	6 ea

- ■ **FEES & DEPOSITS:** No permit is required. For the group picnic area, the use fee is $35 which is paid when reservations are made.
- ■ **RESTRICTIONS:** No amplified music, portable barbecues or tables. Dogs must be on leash. Alcohol consumption restricted to beer and wine.
- ■ **AVAILABILITY:** Year-round, weekdays 9am to sunset, weekends 8am to sunset.

Cuesta Park   415/903-6331

685 Cuesta Drive at Grant Road

Picnic Sites
Red • Orange • Blue • Green

This is a pretty, 29-acre park, with rolling hills, lots of trees and large, open lawn areas great for frisbee throwing or picnic games. Picnic areas are semi-private. Volleyball, bocci ball, horseshoes and a children's play area are nearby. Cuesta Park also has a very nice tennis center.

■ **RESERVE:** Reservations are taken for group use May–October and may be made by Mountain View residents or companies with Mountain View addresses up to 3 months in advance. Reservations must be made in person.

■ **CAPACITY:** If all four sites are combined, up to 200 people.

Picnic Site	*Capacity*	*Large BBQs*	*Small BBQs*	*Tables*
4 Areas	50 ea	1 ea	—	6–9 ea

■ **FEES & DEPOSITS:** No permit is required. For the group picnic area, the use fee is $35 which is paid when reservations are made.

■ **RESTRICTIONS:** No amplified music, portable barbecues or tables. Dogs must be on leash. Alcohol consumption restricted to beer and wine.

■ **AVAILABILITY:** Year-round, weekdays 9am to sunset, weekends 8am to sunset.

PACIFICA

Frontierland Park   415/738-7380

Yosemite Drive and Oddstad Blvd.

Picnic Sites
1 large picnic site

It's not foggy here! When the rest of Pacifica is socked-in, Frontierland Park is in the sun. This is a relatively new park with large, open lawn areas nestled against the hills which are perfect for organized games. There's a large playground, parcourse and jogging track around the perimeter of the park. From this venue, you can see all of Pacifica below and the ocean at a distance.

■ **RESERVE:** There is 1 large group picnic area that can be reserved 3–4 months in advance for peak summer season.

■ **CAPACITY:** Up to 3,000 if you reserve the entire park. The large picnic area is reservable, the other 5 sites are on a first-come, first-served basis.

Picnic Site	*Capacity*	*Large BBQs*	*Small BBQs*	*Tables*
Site 1	350	1	15	20

■ **FEES & DEPOSITS:** Use fee is $25/day plus a $25 refundable deposit for the keys to the barbecues. Sports equipment requires a $100 refundable deposit. Fees must be made Monday–Friday, prior to the event.

■ **RESTRICTIONS:** No amplified music, softball or baseball. Glass is not permitted and no additional barbecues can be brought in.

■ **AVAILABILITY:** Year-round, dawn to dusk.

PALO ALTO

Mitchell Park   415/493-7674

600 East Meadow Drive near Middlefield Rd.

Picnic Sites
Pine Grove • The Arbor • East Meadow •
Redwood

Equipped with tennis courts, two children's play areas, bocci ball and shuffle board court, Mitchell Park aims to please. This is a fifteen-acre park with large, open grass areas, and picnic sites surrounded by trees. Leafy canopies make the group picnic areas comfortable on warm days. There is a children's wading pool, available during summer months.

■ **RESERVE:** Group picnic sites can be reserved by Palo Alto residents or companies with Palo Alto addresses up to 12 months in advance.

■ **CAPACITY:**

Picnic Site	Capacity	Large BBQs	Small BBQs	Tables
Redwood, Arbor, East Meadow	99 ea	—	4 ea	4 ea
Pine Grove	99	—	4	8

■ **FEES & DEPOSITS:** Group picnic area reservations can be made by Palo Alto residents only. Fees for 16–49 people, $20/day; 50–74, $25/day; 75–90, $30/day and 91–100, $35/day. An additional $25 cleaning/damage deposit is required. Payment of all fees is required when the application is submitted in person.

■ **RESTRICTIONS:** No amplified music or additional barbecues. Dogs must be on leash. Alcohol consumption requires a liquor liability insurance certificate which must be received 1 week in advance of the event and costs $100.

■ **AVAILABILITY:** Year-round, sunrise to 10:30pm.

Rinconada Park   415/493-7674

777 Embarcadero near Middlefield Rd.

Picnic Sites
The Sequoia

This fifteen-acre park which has a lovely redwood tree grove. Rinconada's picnic area, located in a clearing surrounded by tall redwoods, is pretty and quiet. There are horseshoes, tennis courts, a children's wading and large lap pool (for summer use), and playgrounds for kids and tots. A special treat for kids is the junior museum and children's library adjacent to the picnic area.

■ **RESERVE:** Sequoia picnic site can be reserved by Palo Alto residents or companies with Palo Alto addresses up to 12 months in advance.

■ **CAPACITY:**

Picnic Site	Capacity	Large BBQs	Small BBQs	Tables
Sequoia	100	—	4	4

■ **FEES & DEPOSITS:** Group picnic area reservations can be made by Palo Alto residents only. Fees for 16–49 people, $20/day; 50–74, $25/day; 75–90, $30/day and 91–100, $35/day. An additional $25 cleaning/damage deposit is required. Payment of all fees is required when the application is submitted in person.

■ **RESTRICTIONS:** No amplified music or additional barbecues. Dogs must be on leash. Alcohol consumption requires a liquor liability insurance certificate which must be received 1 week in advance of the event and costs $100.

■ **AVAILABILITY:** Year-round, sunrise to 10:30pm.

REDWOOD CITY

Red Morton Community Park   415/780-7250

1400 Roosevelt Ave. near Valota Road

Picnic Sites
1 picnic site

Red Morton Park is a beautiful public open space that has large lawn areas for picnics or volleyball. Visitors can play horseshoes and bocci ball. The main picnic area is covered, and there are additional picnic tables near the children's play equipment. A rose garden, lighted tennis court and swimming pool (for summer use) are additional amenities.

■ **RESERVE:** First-come, first-served basis.

■ **CAPACITY:**

Picnic Site	Capacity	Large BBQs	Small BBQs	Tables
Site 1	60–65	1	—	10

■ **FEES & DEPOSITS:** No permit or fees are required.

■ **RESTRICTIONS:** The following are not allowed: dogs, alcohol or glass containers. Amplified music requires a permit.

■ **AVAILABILITY:** Year-round, 6am–10:30pm.

SAN BRUNO

San Bruno City Park   415/877-8868

Crystal Springs Road at Oak Ave. and Donner

Picnic Sites
Area 1 • Area 2 • Beckner Shelter • Area 4

San Bruno Park encompasses 31-acres and includes four picnic areas, four tennis courts, playground equipment for both tots and older kids, baseball diamond and pool for summer use. This is a lovely park with paved paths, parcourse and open spaces that are great for informal games, such as volleyball. It's also connected to the Junipero Serra County Park, so there are plenty of hiking trails nearby.

■ **RESERVE:** Reservations can be made 12 months in advance.

■ **CAPACITY:**

Picnic Site	Capacity	Large BBQs	Small BBQs	Tables
Area 1	75	1	—	8
Area 2	50	—	2	6
Beckner Shelter	200	1	—	8
Area 4	75	1	—	8

■ **FEES & DEPOSITS:** Area 1, 2 and 4 use fees for residents, $30; non-residents $60. For Beckner Shelter, use fee for residents $100; non-residents $200. All fees are due when reservations are made.

■ **RESTRICTIONS:** Swimming is for residents of San Bruno only. No additional barbecues, amplified music or pets.

■ **AVAILABILITY:** Year-round, dawn to dusk.

SAN CARLOS

Burton Park   415/802-4382

1017 Cedar Street at Brittan Ave.   *Picnic Sites*
                                             Playground • Les Mundell Grove

This popular neighborhood park in the center of town covers a square block. It has three lighted tennis courts, outdoor basketball courts, both softball and hardball diamonds, a children's playground and an enclosed totlot. The on-site recreation center provides indoor activity rooms. Although this is a city park in the middle of town, there are shaded lawns and lots of trees that give you a feeling of the non-urban outdoors.

■ **RESERVE:** San Carlos residents or businesses only for group picnic reservations, which must be made in person up to 3 months in advance. In the Playground picnic area, 2 tables are reservable, 4 are on a first-come, first-served basis; in Les Mundell Grove 3 tables are reservable.

■ **CAPACITY:**

Picnic Site	Capacity	Large BBQs	Small BBQs	Tables
Playground	25–50	—	5	2–6
Les Mundell Grove	25–50	—	3	3

■ **FEES & DEPOSITS:** For group picnics, reservations are required. The Playground use fee is $10/day, Les Mundell Grove, $15/day. Fees are paid when reservations are made.

■ **RESTRICTIONS:** The following are not allowed: alcohol, dogs, skateboards or amplified music.

■ **AVAILABILITY:** Year-round, from 8am to sunset.

SAN MATEO

Bayside/Joinville Park   415/377-4734

2111 Kehoe Ave. and Roberta St.   *Picnic Sites*
Contact: Reservations Coordinator   *1 picnic site*

Developed in 1988, this new park features a swimming pool, multi-purpose field and lighted tennis courts. It's adjacent to Marina Lagoon and San Francisco Bay, with views of the water. Of note is an island near the shore which is the nesting habitat of Foresters Terns. Group picnic areas are adjacent to the multi-purpose field.

- **RESERVE:** Reservations may be made 12 months in advance.
- **CAPACITY:**

Picnic Site	Capacity	Large BBQs	Small BBQs	Tables
Site 1	200	4	—	18

- **FEES & DEPOSITS:** A permit is required, obtainable by calling the Recreation Department. Use fees are per table groupings: 1–5 tables, $20/day, 6–10 tables, $40/day and over 11 tables, $60/day. Fees are paid in full when the permit application is filled out. An alcohol permit costs $5–10, depending on group size.
- **RESTRICTIONS:** Alcohol permit is required; no amplified music. Dogs must be on leash.
- **AVAILABILITY:** Year-round, 8am–8pm.

Beresford Park   415/377-4734

2720 Alameda de las Pulgas
Contact: Reservations Coordinator

Picnic Sites
Beresford 1, 2 and 3 • Shelter

Beresford is an eighteen-acre park which was recently renovated in 1988. It has tennis courts and a large children's play area with group picnicking areas conveniently located around the play area. A picnic shelter, multi-purpose field, basketball court, horseshoe pits and softball field are also available. A creek and a grove of tall eucalyptus are additional amenities.

- **RESERVE:** San Mateo residents or businesses/organizations with a San Mateo address, only. Reservations may be made 12 months in advance.
- **CAPACITY:**

Picnic Site	Capacity	Large BBQs	Small BBQs	Tables
Shelter	150	1	—	10
Areas 1	40	1	—	3
Area 2	60	2	—	4
Area 3	40	1	—	3

- **FEES & DEPOSITS:** The use fee is $75/day for the shelter with overhang, $25/day for each of the other 3 areas. Fees must be paid in full in person. Alcohol permits cost $5–10 depending on group size. A restroom key deposit is $10.
- **RESTRICTIONS:** Alcohol requires permit.
- **AVAILABILITY:** Year-round, dawn to dusk.

Central Park   415/377-4734

5th Street and El Camino   *Picnic Sites*
Contact: Reservations Coordinator   *various picnic sites*

One of the oldest and most historic parks in San Mateo, Central Park is fully equipped to handle a diverse crowd. There's a Japanese Tea Garden with fish pond, miniature train ($1/ride), tennis courts and expansive lawns shaded by large, mature trees. There are sizable group picnic areas and a children's play area. Tennis courts and a ballfield are also available.

- **RESERVE:** Reservations may be made 12 months in advance.
- **CAPACITY:** 300 total, dispersed over various group picnic areas.

Picnic Site	Capacity	Large BBQs	Small BBQs	Tables
Group Areas	300	1	3	22

- **FEES & DEPOSITS:** Use permits are obtained at Shoreview Park. Use fees are per table grouping: 1–5 tables, $25/day, 6–10 tables, $50/day and over 11 tables, $75/day. Fees are paid in full when the permit application is filled out. Rental of the softball field is $8/hour plus a $2 application fee.
- **RESTRICTIONS:** The following are not allowed: alcohol without a permit, amplified music, or additional tables. There's restricted auto access. Dogs must be on leash.
- **AVAILABILITY:** Year-round, 8am–8pm.

Coyote Point County Park   415/363-4021

1701 Coyote Point Drive, exit 101   *Picnic Sites*
                                                 Eucalyptus Area • Beach Area

Coyote Point County Park includes a city-owned golf course, marina and beach. There's even an environmental museum which shows educational exhibits of local animals and their habitats. The Beach Area picnic site is surrounded by lawns and is near the beach. Here you can experience refreshing sea breezes, great Bay views, and do a little windsurfing. The Eucalyptus Area is in a shaded eucalyptus grove, overlooking the marina. Each area has four picnic sites and you can reserve one or more of them. Note that one site in each of the two areas is wheelchair accessible and can accommodate 16 people in wheelchairs. Coyote Point also has bike trail that links up to a regional trail along the San Mateo County shoreline.

- **RESERVE:** Reservations may be made 12 months in advance.
- **CAPACITY:** The maximum capacity if you reserve all 4 sites in an area is 300.

Picnic Site	Capacity	Large BBQs	Small BBQs	Tables
Eucalyptus (4 sites)	60–80 ea	2 ea	—	8 ea
Beach Area (4 sites)	60–80 ea	2 ea	—	8 ea

- **FEES & DEPOSITS:** A permit for groups is required. For 1–50 people the fee is $38; 51–80, $60; 81–

100, $75; 101–150 people, $113; 151–200 people, $150; over 200 people, $188. Vehicle parking costs $4/car. Fees must be paid 14 days prior to the event.

- **RESTRICTIONS:** No pets, amplified music or hard alcohol.
- **AVAILABILITY:** Year-round, daily sunrise to sunset.

Parkside Aquatic   415/377-4734

Roberta and Seal Streets
Contact: Reservations Coordinator

Picnic Sites
1 picnic site

This is a picturesque, linear park dotted with mature palm trees. Parkside Aquatic has a launch ramp and beach with play equipment. Paddle boats, sailboats, and swimming areas are available, too. Group picnic areas are surrounded by lawn. Some have windscreens and most have individual barbecues.

- **RESERVE:** First-come, first-served basis.
- **CAPACITY:**

Picnic Site	Capacity	Large BBQs	Small BBQs	Tables
Site 1	200–250	6	—	10

- **FEES & DEPOSITS:** No fees are required.
- **RESTRICTIONS:** No alcohol or amplified music allowed. Dogs must be on leash.
- **AVAILABILITY:** Year-round, 8am–8pm.

Shoreview Park   415/377-4734

950 Oceanview Ave. between Norfolk and Cottage Grove
Contact: Reservations Coordinator

Picnic Sites
1 picnic site

Shoreview is an older park with sizable trees. It's an attractive open space and very popular for group picnics. There's a sheltered picnic area with an adjacent play area and lawn for volleyball. Tennis courts and a softball field are nearby.

- **RESERVE:** Reservations may be made 12 months in advance.
- **CAPACITY:**

Picnic Site	Capacity	Large BBQs	Small BBQs	Tables
Site 1	60	2	—	4

- **FEES & DEPOSITS:** A use permit for group picnics is required. The fee is $25/day. An alcohol permit costs $5 for groups up to 50, $10 for groups over 50 people. From November–May 1, there's a $10 fee for the restroom key.

- ■ **RESTRICTIONS:** No amplified music or auto access. Alcohol is by permit. Dogs must be on leash.
- ■ **AVAILABILITY:** Year-round, 8am–8pm.

SOUTH SAN FRANCISCO

Burri Burri Park   415/877-8560

200 Arroyo Drive above El Camino

Picnic Sites
4 picnic sites

This park is well-shaded by large trees and has two tennis courts, basketball court and baseball field. There is a large playground for kids aged ten and over, plus a totlot for the younger set. The park is wheelchair accessible.

- ■ **RESERVE:** Up to 12 months in advance.
- ■ **CAPACITY:** You can reserve any 2 areas up to a maximum capacity of 100.

Picnic Site	*Capacity*	*Large BBQs*	*Small BBQs*	*Tables*
Area 1	70	—	3	6
Area 2	20	—	2	2
Area 3	30	—	3	3
Area 4	30	—	2	3

- ■ **FEES & DEPOSITS:** Use fees for residents, $35/day; non-residents, $40/day.
- ■ **RESTRICTIONS:** Pets must be on a leash. No portable barbecues or campfire stoves.
- ■ **AVAILABILITY:** Year-round, 8am–sunset. Restrooms are open 10am–5pm, additional hours require an extra fee.

Candlestick Point State Recreation Area   415/557-4069

Hunter's Point Expressway across from
Candlestick Stadium

Picnic Sites
Jack Rabbit • Pelican • Plover • Wind Harp Hill

Situated on 45 acres bordering the San Francisco Bay, the park has bike and hiking trails, a jogging parcourse, open expanses of lawns and landscaped areas. Visitors can windsurf on the Bay or fish from the park's two fishing piers.

- ■ **RESERVE:** Up to 8 weeks in advance.

■ **CAPACITY:** You can increase the capacity of each site by bringing your own tables and chairs.

Picnic Site	Capacity	Large BBQs	Small BBQs	Tables
Jack Rabbit	100	2	—	6
Pelican	100	2	—	5
Plover	100	2	—	8
Wind Harp Hill	100	1	—	7

■ **FEES & DEPOSITS:** Use fees must be paid 7 days in advance. The cost to reserve a group area is $40. If a 49er game is being played, there is an additional fee per car to park vehicles.

■ **RESTRICTIONS:** Dogs must be on leash.

■ **AVAILABILITY:** Year-round, 8am–sunset.

Orange Memorial Park   415/877-8560

Orange Ave. and Memorial Drive

Picnic Sites
Pine Shelter • Birch Grove

Pine Shelter is a covered and enclosed picnic area surrounded by pine trees. There is a large play area adjacent to the site. Birch Grove is a smaller picnic area with a large open area for games. The park has an Olympic-size pool, baseball diamond, soccer field and tennis courts (by reservation).

■ **RESERVE:** Up to 12 months in advance.

■ **CAPACITY:**

Picnic Site	Capacity	Large BBQs	Small BBQs	Tables
Pine Shelter	100	—	3	10
Birch Grove	100	1	—	4

■ **FEES & DEPOSITS:** Use fees for residents, $55; non-residents $60. It costs an additional $8/hour to reserve before 10am or after 5pm. Ballfields must be reserved for group use. Fees are payable when reservations are made.

■ **RESTRICTIONS:** Wine and beer only. No amplified music or portable barbecues. Pets must be on leash.

■ **AVAILABILITY:** Year-round. Birch Grove is available 8am–sunset; Pine Shelter, 10am–5pm (additional hours can be arranged for a fee).

Westborough Park   415/877-8560

2380 Galway Drive at Westborough Blvd.

Picnic Sites
1 picnic site

Westborough Park has a sheltered picnic area with a lawns near the entry and a baseball diamond towards the back of the park. A play area is conveniently located next to the picnic tables. Two tennis courts and a basketball court are nearby.

- **RESERVE:** Up to 12 months in advance.
- **CAPACITY:**

Picnic Site	Capacity	Large BBQs	Small BBQs	Tables
Site 1	70	—	2	6

- **FEES & DEPOSITS:** Use fees must be paid in advance. The cost to reserve a group area ranges from $40–45. It costs an additional $8/hour to reserve before 10am or after 5pm.
- **RESTRICTIONS:** Wine and beer only. No amplified music or portable barbecues. Pets must be on leash.
- **AVAILABILITY:** Year-round, 8am–sunset.

WOODSIDE

Huddart Park   415/363-4021

1100 King's Mountain Rd. Take Woodside Road west, off Hwy 280, through town of Woodside, turn right on Kings Mountain, go 3 miles uphill.

Picnic Sites
Zwierlein • Redwood • Oak • East Meadow •
West Meadow • Shelter Buildings

Lush and woodsy, this county park in the Woodside hills is one of San Mateo's largest. Huddart has some very private, secluded group picnic areas. Facilities include three shelter buildings, which provide partial cover for group picnics, sites with barbecue pits, lots of nature trails for hiking or horseback riding and a playground for children. Redwood groves offer shelter for picnic areas, some of which are in clearings. Others picnic spots are scattered amongst day use areas.

- **RESERVE:** Reservations are required for all group areas and shelter buildings. You can make reservations way in advance, which is advisable since this popular park books up early.
- **CAPACITY:** East and West Meadows can be combined to hold 450 people.

Picnic Site	Capacity	Large BBQs	Small BBQs	Tables
Zwierlein	500	2	—	30
Redwood	250	2	—	8
Oak	200	2	—	6
East Meadow	300	2	—	16
West Meadow	150	2	—	6
3 Shelter Bldgs.	125 ea	—	—	—

■ **FEES & DEPOSITS:** For day group picnic area use, the fees are: $100/day for each shelter, Zwierlein, $75–375; Redwood Area, $38–188; Oak Area, $38–150; East Meadow, $38–225; West Meadow, $38–113. The fees range depending on number of users. A $4/car entry fee is required. Use fees are due 2 weeks from the day you make a reservation, and once payment is received, a permit is mailed. If you cancel, refunds are only possible 30 days prior to the picnic.

■ **RESTRICTIONS:** Cutting and gathering of wood, pets, amplified music and hard alcohol are prohibited. No ground fires or portable barbecues.

■ **AVAILABILITY:** Year-round, 8am-8pm or until dusk.

Skywood Chateau Restaurant   415/851-7444

17311 Skyline Blvd. at Hwy 84 & 35
Contact: Mr. Bisher

Picnic Sites
1 picnic site

Skywood Chateau provides lots of picnic tables on a sun-drenched, two-level deck, and full-service catering for events. Atop Skyline Boulevard, the restaurant overlooks a beautiful redwood tree setting with panoramic views of the Bay.

■ **RESERVE:** Up to 6 months in advance.

■ **CAPACITY:**

Picnic Site	Capacity	Large BBQs	Small BBQs	Tables
Deck	300	provided	—	provided

■ **FEES & DEPOSITS:** Fees are based on group size and menu selected. Call for rates.

■ **RESTRICTIONS:** No pets or outside catering allowed .

■ **AVAILABILITY:** Year-round, 8am–2am.

ALAMEDA

Crown Memorial Beach Regional Shoreline   510/636-1684

Take the Alameda Tube from Oakland on Webster St.; turn right on Central Ave., then left on McKay.

Picnic Sites
Neptune • Crolls Garden • Mariner's Lagoon • Seawind • Dune • Sand Castle

A two-and-a-half-mile stretch of shoreline, the Robert W. Crown Memorial State Beach, affords a view of the Bay to San Francisco. An important urban nature site, it hosts many outdoor activities and is widely recognized as an excellent wildlife viewing area. A visitor's center provides information about the Bay's natural resources and inhabitants.

■ **RESERVE:** EBRPD recommends phone reservations be made at least 3 weeks in advance; by mail, at least four.

■ **CAPACITY:** 6 picnic sites accommodate 50–200 people.

Picnic Site	Capacity	Large BBQs	Small BBQs	Tables
Neptune	150	2	—	11
Crolls Garden	100	2	—	9
Mariner's Lagoon	50	1	—	5
Seawind	200	2	—	13
Dune	50	2	—	7
Sand Castle	50	2	—	6

■ **FEES & DEPOSITS:** Reservations for any of these sites may be made through the East Bay Regional Park District's reservation office.

■ **RESTRICTIONS:** Alcoholic beverages are prohibited on the beach, and are allowed only in the following designated picnic areas (beer & wine permit required): Neptune, Crolls Garden, Mariner's Lagoon, and Seawind. Lawn areas near all picnic sites are non-reservable, and EBRPD asks that they be shared with all park visitors. As with all EBRPD parks, sound amplification is not permitted.

■ **AVAILABILITY:** Year-round, daily.

Prices and policies do change. Call each facility and confirm everything you read in Perfect Places.

ANTIOCH

Contra Loma Regional Park   510/636-1684

Take the "A" Street/Lone Tree Way exit from
Highway 4; travel south through Antioch on
Lone Tree Way; take a right on Blue Rock Road,
then another right on Frederickson Lane, which
leads into the park.

Picnic Sites
Cattail Cove • Lupine Rocks • Meadow Lark
• Locust Grove • Redwing • Loma Island •
Mustard Hill

This 776-acre park contains an 80-acre reservoir open year-round for fishing, boating, boardsailing and swimming. During the summer months, lifeguards watch the swim area and sailboards may be rented. Nearby picnic areas, which are wheelchair accessible, offer shade and green lawns. Trails connect Contra Loma to neighboring Black Diamond Mines Regional Preserve.

■ **RESERVE:** EBRPD recommends phone reservations be made at least 3 weeks in advance; by mail, at least 4.

■ **CAPACITY:** 7 picnic sites accommodate 50–200 people.

Picnic Site	Capacity	Large BBQs	Small BBQs	Tables
Cattail Cove	150	1	—	10
Lupine Rocks	50	1	—	5
Meadow Lark	50	1	—	6
Locust Grove	200	2	—	13
Redwing	50	1	—	5
Loma Island	150	2	—	15
Mustard Hill	150	2	—	10

■ **FEES & DEPOSITS:** Reservations for any of these sites may be made through the East Bay Regional Park District's reservation office. Sailboard lessons may be purchased during the summer, and there is a nominal fee for using one's own sailboard.

■ **RESTRICTIONS:** Lawn areas near all picnic sites are non-reservable, and EBRPD asks that they be shared with all park visitors. Though private boaters may launch their own vessels, only electric motors are permitted (no gasoline engines). Fisherpersons 16 years of age or older must have a State Fishing License and a daily District Fishing Permit. As with all EBRPD parks, sound amplification is not permitted.

■ **AVAILABILITY:** Year-round, daily.

BERKELEY

Tilden Park   510/636-1684

Along the ridegline of the Berkeley/Oakland Hills.

Picnic Sites
Willows • Laurel • Padre • Island • Carousel
• Buckeye • Alders • Meadow • Lakeview •
Mineral Springs • Quarry

First opened to the public in 1936, Tilden has long been a favorite nature site among Bay Area residents. It has something for everyone. Among its features are Lake Anza's sandy beach swim area, an eighteen-hole golf course, merry-go-round, pony ride, botanic garden, and miniature steam passenger train. Wildcat Creek, rugged natureways, large meadows and playfields adorn Tilden's various picnic locations. Ask about areas especially well-suited for children's parties. Parking and restroom facilities are available near each picnic site.

■ **RESERVE:** EBRPD recommends phone reservations be made at least 3 weeks in advance; by mail, at least 4.

■ **CAPACITY:** 13 picnic sites accommodate 35–200 people.

Picnic Site	Capacity	Large BBQs	Small BBQs	Tables
Willows	100	1	—	8
Laurel	150	1	—	12
Padre	150	1	—	10
Island	100	1	—	7
Carousel	50	1	—	4
Buckeye	50	1	—	5
Alders	50	1	—	5
Meadow	50	1	—	5
Lakeview	50	1	—	6
Mineral Springs	200	3	—	12
Quarry	35	1	—	6

■ **FEES & DEPOSITS:** Reservations for any of these sites may be made through the East Bay Regional Park District's reservation office.

■ **RESTRICTIONS:** Lawn areas or playing fields near most picnic sites are non-reservable. EBRPD asks that they be shared with all park visitors. Though private boaters may launch their own vessels, only electric motors are permitted (no gasoline engines). Fisherpersons 16 years of age or older must have a State Fishing License and a daily District Fishing Permit. As with all EBRPD parks, sound amplification is not permitted.

■ **AVAILABILITY:** Year-round, daily.

CASTRO VALLEY

Chouinard Vineyards   510/582-9900

33853 Palomares Canyon Road

Picnic Sites
1 picnic site

Separate from the cluster of other wineries in the Livermore area, Chouinard Vineyard's 110-acres are found in a serene, heavily wooded canyon between two ranges of hills. The picnic site itself lies beneath large oak, maple and redwood trees. No barbecue pits, but catering is available (or BYO). It is handicap-accessible. Cabernet and Sauvignon Blanc vineyards surround the winery itself, a restored redwood barn. Inquire about evening music events during summertime.

- **RESERVE:** Advance reservation required only for large groups.
- **CAPACITY:**

Picnic Site	Capacity	Large BBQs	Small BBQs	Tables
Area 1	225	—	—	25

- **FEES & DEPOSITS:** The picnic area is available for use by Chouinard customers.
- **RESTRICTIONS:** Purchase of wines at Chouinard Vineyards is not mandatory, but suggested. No pets.
- **AVAILABILITY:** Year-round, daily. Tasting room open on weekends, noon–5pm.

Crow Canyon Park & Resort   510/582-1630

8000 Crow Canyon Road

Picnic Sites
8 picnic sites

Nicknamed the "Park of 1,000 Trees," this privately-owned park operates year-round. Crow Canyon's 40 acres offer eight picnic sites, and many activities. A heated swimming pool (with lifeguard), ballfields, and volleyball courts are among the amenities to be enjoyed here, while flowerbeds, patios and grape arbors with wisteria add to its visual ambiance. Catering is also available, as well as numerous children's activities. The owners of Crow Canyon have taken measures to make this park accessible to disabled persons.

- **RESERVE:** Timeframe varies depending on time of year and individual requirements. Summer is busy.

■ **CAPACITY:** 8 picnic sites accommodate up to 3,000.

Picnic Site	*Capacity*	*Large BBQs*	*Small BBQs*	*Tables*
Area 1–7	varies	1 ea	—	varies
Area 8	varies	3	—	varies

■ **FEES & DEPOSITS:** Reservation fee varies with type of package desired. A company on a budget will find Crow Canyon eager to design an affordable event.

■ **RESTRICTIONS:** Flush toilets are located next to swimming area and in the middle of the park, but not at picnic sites. However, for those who cannot walk to them, portable toilets may be requested at specific sites.

■ **AVAILABILITY:** Year-round, daily.

Cull Canyon Regional Recreation Area   **510/636-1684**

Off Crow Canyon Road take Cull Canyon Road; the park is on Heyer Ave., to the left after the stoplight.

Picnic Sites
Creekview • Maple • Footbridge

The exceptional swim complex at Cull Canyon and a sandy beach with lifeguards on duty, draw many water lovers during warm weather months. The park also offers hiking and a nineteen-acre reservoir for those who like to fish. Restroom facilities are located near all picnic areas.

■ **RESERVE:** EBRPD recommends phone reservations be made at least 3 weeks in advance; by mail, at least 4.

■ **CAPACITY:**

Picnic Site	*Capacity*	*Large BBQs*	*Small BBQs*	*Tables*
Creekview	100	2	—	8
Maple	150	2	—	12
Footbridge	150	2	—	11

■ **FEES & DEPOSITS:** Reservations for any of these sites may be made through the East Bay Regional Park District's reservation office. There is a swimming fee. Fishing permits may be purchased at the concessions stand.

■ **RESTRICTIONS:** Lawn areas or playing fields near picnic sites are non-reservable. EBRPD asks that they be shared with all park visitors. Fisherpersons 16 years of age or older must have a California Fishing License and an EBRPD Fishing Access Permit. As with all EBRPD parks, sound amplification is not permitted.

■ **AVAILABILITY:** Year-round, daily.

Don Castro Regional Recreation Area   510/636-1684

From Highway 580 eastbound, exit at Center Street (Castro Valley) and travel south; turn left on Kelly Street, then left again on Woodroe to the park entrance.

Picnic Sites
Bass Cove • Ridge Top

The shallow waters of the Don Castro swim lagoon are particularly attractive to children who like to wade, while the adjacent lake is used for boating and swimming. Hikers might find an array of wildlife along the water's edge or inland. Fishing is also popular in this periodically-stocked lake.

- **RESERVE:** EBRPD recommends phone reservations be made at least 3 weeks in advance; by mail, 4.
- **CAPACITY:**

Picnic Site	Capacity	Large BBQs	Small BBQs	Tables
Bass Cove	50	1	—	5
Ridge Top	100	1	—	7

- **FEES & DEPOSITS:** Reservations for either of these sites may be made through the East Bay Regional Park District's reservation office. There is a swimming fee. Fishing permits may be purchased at the concessions stand.

- **RESTRICTIONS:** Lawn areas located near the picnic sites are non-reservable. EBRPD asks that they be shared with all park visitors. State Fish and Game regulations apply here. Fisherpersons 16 years of age or older are required to have a California Fishing License and a District Fishing Permit. As with all EBRPD parks, sound amplification is not permitted.

- **AVAILABILITY:** Year-round, daily.

CLAYTON

Old Marsh Creek Springs   510/672-7007

12510 Marsh Creek Road

Picnic Sites
7 picnic sites

This private park, totalling fifteen acres with a natural creek, offers shady, picturesque environments for picnicking. Smaller groups may choose one of seven locations, each with its own barbecue grill. A larger function might do well to rent the front lawn area, complete with white gazebo (other gazebos are scattered about the park). There is a reception building with restroom facilities. Activities offered at Old Marsh Creek Springs include horseshoes, baseball, volleyball and swimming (no lifeguard). There is also a special area for tots.

■ **CAPACITY:** Groups as large as 1,000 may be served using several (or all) areas at once.

Picnic Site	Capacity	Large BBQs	Small BBQs	Tables
Areas 1–7	150 ea	1 ea	—	provided
Lawn Area	400	1	—	provided

■ **FEES & DEPOSITS:** Payment is required in advance; no refunds. The reservation fee varies with the type of group package desired.

■ **RESTRICTIONS:** No hard liquor is allowed inside the facility.

■ **AVAILABILITY:** Year-round, daily.

CONCORD

Baldwin Park   510/671-3083

2750 Parkside Circle

Picnic Sites
Site 1 • Site 2

Baldwin Park, a quiet, eighteen-acre setting, has two reservable sites among its shade trees. Site 1, near a softball field, overlooks the park area and is surrounded by a grassy field. There are basketball courts at Baldwin, and a totlot for small children. Site 2 is has an informal lawn with a gravel base.

■ **RESERVE:** Reservations must be made in person. For information and availability, call the above number.

■ **CAPACITY:**

Picnic Site	Capacity	Large BBQs	Small BBQs	Tables
Site 1	130	—	1	8
Site 2	60	—	1	6

■ **FEES & DEPOSITS:** Reservation fees vary depending on site desired and client's resident/nonresident status. Alcohol cannot be served at picnics without an alcohol permit, which may be purchased for $10. A "Picnic Pak," containing sports equipment, may be rented for a nominal fee and a refundable deposit.

■ **RESTRICTIONS:** An alcohol permit ($10) is required for liquor consumption in the park.

■ **AVAILABILITY:** Year-round, daily.

EMERYVILLE

Emeryville Marina

510/596-4340 Marina Office

Westward end of Powell Street

Picnic Sites
2 picnic sites

This linear marina hugs the Bay and wows visitors with panoramic views of San Francisco and Marin. Access to the mudflats, a well-known site for local art and sculpture seen from the freeway, may be made from here. For the picnicker who wants to keep his/her shoes clean and dry, there are plenty of other attractions at two picnic areas. Bring your own barbecue and enjoy sea breezes while cooking up a storm. Walking and biking trails, expansive lawns, and lovely vistas make this a wonderful spot for a leisurely stroll. Colorful boats of all kinds are docked nearby at the Emeryville Marina. Fishing, of course, is another activity at the Marina's pier.

- **RESERVE:** Group reservations are required.
- **CAPACITY:** Each site seats about 30.

Picnic Site	Capacity	Large BBQs	Small BBQs	Tables
Site 1	30	—	1	3
Site 2	30	—	1	3

- **FEES & DEPOSITS:** Reservations may be made through the Emeryville Marina Office.
- **RESTRICTIONS:** No alcohol is allowed. Contact the Marina Office regarding permits, information and assistance.
- **AVAILABILITY:** Year-round, daily.

FREMONT

Ardenwood Historic Preserve

510/462-1400

34600 Ardenwood Blvd.
(see entry in Event Locations for more information)

Picnic Sites
Whistle Stop • Orchard View • Walnut Grove • Crabapple Corner

Ardenwood Historic Farm is an East Bay Regional Park District facility operated in the public interest by The Picnic People, Inc. As Its name suggests, Ardenwood envokes a sense of farmlife as it may have been a century ago. This is a full-service park, offering many sports facilities and children's activities, as well as specialized rides, tours, displays and shops devoted to the historic aspects of the park. Picnic People will customize a package that's right for your group, from providing professional on-site catering to supervised activities for all age groups.

- **RESERVE:** Advance reservations required.
- **CAPACITY:** 4 picnic sites accommodate 75–1,200 people.

Picnic Site	Capacity	Large BBQs	Small BBQs	Tables
Whistle Stop	300	varies	varies	33
Orchard View	200	varies	varies	22
Walnut Grove	150	varies	varies	16
Crabapple Corner	100	varies	varies	11

- **FEES & DEPOSITS:** Fees vary depending on group size, picnic site, and extras. Ask about weekend rates and exclusive/half-exclusive use. Special discounts during May, June and October, as well as holiday weekends. Groups must purchase beverages on site.

- **RESTRICTIONS:** The park specifies: "As Ardenwood is an historic experience, certain 'modern day' activities are not allowed, such as balloons, frisbees, bicycles, radios and motorized toys. Other historical limitations may apply." Use of an outside caterer is not allowed, although you may BYO food and cook it yourself. Alcoholic beverage service regulations are strictly enforced.

- **AVAILABILITY:** Year-round, daily.

Coyote Hills Regional Park   510/636-1684

From Highway 84 in Fremont, exit at Newark Blvd; travel north until Newark becomes Ardenwood Blvd.; turn left onto Commerce (which eventually becomes Patterson Ranch Road) which leads into the park.

Picnic Sites
Hoot Hollow

Since 1968, Coyote Hills Regional Park has been able to offer its 1,039 acres to Bay Area residents and visitors. Historic Native American sites enhance the beauty of this venerable natureway. A wildlife sanctuary, the park is home to a large variety of animal inhabitants who dwell in the grassy hills, freshwater marshes and seasonal wetlands. Coyote Hills is widely recognized as an excellent wildlife viewing area and hiking trails afford a closer look. There's one picnic area in the park, adjacent to a lawn area, parking and restroom facilities.

- **RESERVE:** EBRPD recommends phone reservations be made at least 3 weeks in advance; by mail, at least 4.
- **CAPACITY:**

Picnic Site	Capacity	Large BBQs	Small BBQs	Tables
Hoot Hollow	75	2	—	9

- **FEES & DEPOSITS:** Reservations for any of these sites may be made through the East Bay Regional Park District's reservation office. There's a fee for parking.
- **RESTRICTIONS:** As with all EBRPD parks, sound amplification is not permitted.
- **AVAILABILITY:** Year-round, daily.

HAYWARD

Garin/Dry Creek Regional Park   510/636-1684

From Highway I-880 in Hayward, take Industrial
Blvd. to Mission Blvd.; a right on Mission, then left
on Garin Ave. will lead you to the park.

Picnic Sites
Cattlemen's • Buttonwood • Ranchside • Pioneer

Garin/Dry Creek Regional Park features Jordan Pond, where fishing for big-mouth bass, bluegill and
sunfish is a major attraction. Horseshoes, biking, hiking and horseback riding are perfect accompa-
niments to a picnic in one of four developed sites. A Visitor Center displays historic elements of the
Hayward area.

■ **RESERVE:** EBRPD recommends phone reservations be made at least 3 weeks in advance; by mail, at
least 4.

■ **CAPACITY:**

Picnic Site	Capacity	Large BBQs	Small BBQs	Tables
Cattlemen's	100	2	—	7
Buttonwood	100	2	—	7
Ranchside	100	2	—	7
Pioneer	50	1	—	5

■ **FEES & DEPOSITS:** Reservations may be made through the East Bay Regional Park District's
reservation office. There's a parking fee per car.

■ **RESTRICTIONS:** Lawn areas or playing fields near picnic sites are non-reservable. EBRPD asks that
they be shared with all park visitors. As with all EBRPD parks, sound amplification is not permitted.

■ **AVAILABILITY:** Year-round, daily.

LIVERMORE

Concannon Vineyard   510/447-3760

4590 Tesla Road
(see entry in Event Locations section for more information)

Picnic Sites
*Indoor Area • Grape Arbor • Three Smaller
Areas • La Pergola*

Concannon Vineyards is a large facility that offers a variety of areas for picnics, from manicured lawns
and arbor-covered trellises to large, open fields. It gives the wine-loving picnicker a taste of one of
Livermore's many vineyards. Boxed lunches may be purchased here, and outdoor lighting is
available for nighttime events. Also among Concannon's attractions: weekend horse & carriage rides

and winery tours. Picnic sites are accessible to the disabled.

- **RESERVE:** Reservations must be made in advance; crowds vary with season.
- **CAPACITY:** 6 sites accommodate 50–500 people.

Picnic Site	Capacity	Large BBQs	Small BBQs	Tables
Indoor Area (Tasting Rm)	80	—	—	—
Grape Arbor	250	—	—	—
3 Smaller Areas	50–100 ea	—	—	—
La Pergola	500	—	—	—

- **FEES & DEPOSITS:** Reservation fees vary, depending on the event package chosen.
- **RESTRICTIONS:** Smoking permitted outside only. No BYO beverages; picnickers are encouraged to make a wine purchase. (Concannon offers soda in addition to their wine selection.)
- **AVAILABILITY:** Year-round, daily. Regular hours for tasting Mon–Sat, 10am–4:30pm; Sun, noon–4:30pm. Weekend winery tours are available.

Del Valle Regional Park   510/636-1684

About 9 miles south of Livermore.

Picnic Sites
Oak Point • Cedar Mt. View • Lichen Bark • School House Flats • Gray Pine • Eagles View • Fiesta Grande • Arroyo Mocho • Agua Vista • Tokes • Beach View

Among EBRPD's most richly–endowed parks, Del Valle has something to please any picnicking group. A five-mile lake, surrounded on all sides by a nature expanse totaling 4,500 acres, the park has a lot to offer the hiker, camper, swimmer (two beaches, lifeguard on duty during specified hours), fisherperson, sailor, biker, horseback rider or all–around outdoor-lover.

- **RESERVE:** EBRPD recommends phone reservations be made at least 3 weeks in advance; by mail, at least 4. For camping information, call 510/562-2267
- **CAPACITY:**

Picnic Site	Capacity	Large BBQs	Small BBQs	Tables
Oak Point	300	2	—	11
Cedar Mt. View	50	1	—	4
Lichen Bark	300	2	—	11
School House Flats	300	2	—	11
Gray Pine	50	1	—	4
Eagles View	150	4	—	11
Fiesta Grande	500	4	—	28
Arroyo Mocho	150	2	—	11
Agua Vista	150	1	—	10
Tokes	50	1	—	5
Beach View	50	1	—	4

■ **FEES & DEPOSITS:** Reservations for any of these sites may be made through the East Bay Regional Park District's reservation office. There's a fee for parking, boat launching and camping.

■ **RESTRICTIONS:** All picnic sites are walk-in only; no vehicles may enter these areas. Lawn areas near picnic sites are non-reservable. EBRPD asks that they be shared with all park visitors. A California State Fishing Permit and a daily Fishing Permit are required. As with all EBRPD parks, sound amplification is not permitted.

■ **AVAILABILITY:** Year-round, daily.

Fenestra Winery   510/862-2292

---

83 East Vallecitos Road

Picnic Sites
1 picnic site

This small husband-and-wife-owned vineyard built in 1889, offers quaint hospitality, a rural setting and a winery committed to quality. The setting is informal and charming. The winery itself lies on the side of a hill. Guests park above and walk down to the winery. The picnic area is small, but all are welcome to enjoy the limited number of outdoor tables. There are no barbecue pits here—they are considered a fire hazard during dry months.

■ **RESERVE:** Large groups are asked to call ahead.

■ **CAPACITY:**

Picnic Site	*Capacity*	*Large BBQs*	*Small BBQs*	*Tables*
Area 1	50	—	—	6

■ **FEES & DEPOSITS:** The picnic area can be reserved for customers only.

■ **RESTRICTIONS:** Smoking is not permitted at Fenestra. No BYO beverages— picnickers are encouraged to make a wine purchase.

■ **AVAILABILITY:** Year-round, daily. Fenestra is open for wine tasting and sales only on Saturdays and Sundays, noon–5pm.

Livermore Valley Cellars   510/447-1751

1508 Wetmore Road

Picnic Sites
1 picnic site

As with all the vineyards we surveyed in the East Bay, the wine is described as the main attraction. The owner of Livermore Valley Cellars takes particular pride in the fact that no chemicals are used in the production of the wines here, and also ascribes the distinctive flavor of LVC wines to the excellent water quality used in winemaking. As for the picnic site itself, it's located on 33 acres of land which is characterized by a couple of little knolls surrounded by an expanse of shady Chinese Elms. Gentle breezes are refreshing on a warm day.

- **RESERVE:** The picnic site is only reservable if you've got a large group.
- **CAPACITY:**

Picnic Site	Capacity	Large BBQs	Small BBQs	Tables
Area 1	100	—	BYO	13

- **FEES & DEPOSITS:** The picnic area can be reserved for customers only. There's no charge for use of facilities. A caterer is available to serve meals ranging from $8–12/person (cleanup provided). Soft drinks are available.

- **RESTRICTIONS:** No BYO beverages—picnickers are encouraged to make a wine purchase. Please note that only dry, white wines are sold at this vineyard.

- **AVAILABILITY:** Year-round. Wine tastings are daily, 11:30am–5pm.

Retzlaff Vineyards   510/447-8941

1356 South Livermore Ave.

Picnic Sites
1 picnic site

Retzlaff is a serene, bucolic winery setting with a long, rectangular lawn framed by hundred-year-old California pepper trees. The area is very private, lovely and pleasant. Round picnic tables with umbrellas are available. There are no barbecue grills on site, but you can negotiate bringing your own. Retzlaff can also cater a more formal picnic or luncheon. The area is accessible to wheelchairs.

- **RESERVE:** Group functions require reservations.
- **CAPACITY:**

Picnic Site	Capacity	Large BBQs	Small BBQs	Tables
Area 1	150	—	BYO	5*

- **FEES & DEPOSITS:** Catering services are available; there is a nominal fee for potluck meals. *Retzlaff will provide additional tables and chairs, as needed, if an event is catered here.

- **RESTRICTIONS:** No BYO beverages—all alcoholic beverages must be purchased from Retzlaff.

- **AVAILABILITY:** Year-round, daily. Tastings Mon–Fri noon–2pm, Sat & Sun noon–5pm.

Wente Bros. Estate Winery   510/447-3603

5565 Tesla Road.

Picnic Sites
1 picnic site

(see entry in Event Locations section for more information)

A patio and large Mulberry trees create the scene for an informal picnic at Wente Bros. The year-round picnic area enjoys partial shade, and lights can be set up for evening events. A caterer may be hired through their facility. And, of course, Wente wines are available for tasting and purchase.

- **RESERVE:** Reserve as far in advance as possible for events during warm months.
- **CAPACITY:** Maximum 120 people. An additional 70 may be seated inside the tasting room.

Picnic Site	Capacity	Large BBQs	Small BBQs	Tables
Area 1	120	—	—	5

- **FEES & DEPOSITS:** For groups of 26–75 people, there is a $1/person fee; over 75, the charge goes up. Any group over 25 persons is required to pay for Wente food service, which ranges from $10 (for a boxed lunch) to $25/person.
- **RESTRICTIONS:** No BYO beverages—picnickers are encouraged to make a wine purchase.
- **AVAILABILITY:** Year-round, daily. Tastings Mon–Sat, 10am–5pm; Sun, 11am–5pm.

MARTINEZ

Briones Regional Park   510/636-1684

From Highway 24, exit at Orinda Village; travel north on Camino Pablo Road, which will turn into San Pablo Dam Road; turn right onto Bear Creek Road (at the traffic light); park entrance is on right.

Picnic Sites
Newt Hollow • Oak Grove

Two creeks (Bear Creek and Grayson Creek) run through the rugged landscape of Briones Regional Park. With 5,706 acres of natural terrain, hiking is a popular activity here. Picnickers can also enjoy archery or kite flying in an informal setting. Newt Hollow has an open stage area, making this a popular site for wedding receptions and group events. A word of advice: bring lots of liquids and shade devices during summer months. It can get very hot here and there are no swimming facilities.

- **RESERVE:** EBRPD recommends phone reservations be made at least 3 weeks in advance; by mail, at least 4.
- **CAPACITY:**

Picnic Site	Capacity	Large BBQs	Small BBQs	Tables
Newt Hollow	150	1	—	13
Oak Grove	50	1	—	5

- **FEES & DEPOSITS:** Reservations for either of these sites may be made through the East Bay Regional Park District's reservation office. There's a fee for parking and dogs.
- **RESTRICTIONS:** As with all EBRPD parks, sound amplification is not permitted.
- **AVAILABILITY:** Year-round, daily.

OAKLAND

---

de Fremery Park   510/832-0360

Adeline and 16th Street

Picnic Sites
3 picnic sites

DeFremery Park, characterized by large Magnolias and well-kept lawns, offers a swimming pool, basketball and tennis courts (no need to reserve), and playground equipment. A historic, Victorian building serves as the recreation center. There is also a social hall with bathroom facilities inside (in addition to several outdoor ones). The park is flat with cement walkways winding throughout, lending itself easily to wheelchairs. Each picnic area has tables and a barbecue pit.

- **RESERVE:** Reservations are not necessarily needed. If, on a given day, no one has reserved a site in advance, it is available on a first-come, first-served basis. The park is well-used during the summer.
- **CAPACITY:**

Picnic Site	*Capacity*	*Large BBQs*	*Small BBQs*	*Tables*
Site 1	20	—	1	2
Site 2	30	—	1	3
Site 3	50	—	1	5

- **FEES & DEPOSITS:** Reservations fees vary depending on group size.
- **RESTRICTIONS:** As with all EBRPD parks, sound amplification is not permitted.
- **AVAILABILITY:** Year-round, daily.

Dimond Park   510/531-7055

3860 Hanly Road at Lymand Road

Picnic Sites
Redwood Grove • Sequoia • Church Area

Among Dimond Park's amenities are tennis courts, swimming pool, hiking trail and a creek. Each of the three picnic sites has distinct characteristics. Redwood is named after the grove of large trees which keep it shady; Sequoia enjoys more sun and features a circle of tables around a tree at its center; and the Church Area is named for benches and tables which are arranged in rows like pews.

- **RESERVE:** Suggested lead time is 3–4 weeks, sometimes more.
- **CAPACITY:**

Picnic Site	*Capacity*	*Large BBQs*	*Small BBQs*	*Tables*
Redwood Grove	100	2	—	varies
Sequoia	100	2	—	varies
Church Area	100	—	—	varies

■ **FEES & DEPOSITS:** Reservations for any of these sites may be made through the East Bay Regional Park District's reservation office.

■ **RESTRICTIONS:** Handicap accessibility is questionable at all 3 sites. There is no barbecue pit at the Church Area, nor may you BYO. Park curfew is 10pm–7am. No alcohol is allowed. As with all EBRPD parks, sound amplification is not permitted.

■ **AVAILABILITY:** Year-round, daily.

Joaquin Miller Park   510/238-3186

From Highway 13 in Oakland, take Lincoln Ave. exit east (this is Joaquin Miller Blvd.); take Robinson Drive left–entrance into the park.

Picnic Sites
Baywood • Craib A • Craib B • Fernwood • Fire Circle • Greenwood • Horseshoe • Pinewood • Redwood Glen • Moses Monument

One of Oakland's more than 100 reservable parks, Joaquin Miller Park offers nine sites, each with tables, barbecue pits and water. Bathroom facilities are near each picnic site. Picnickers may bring sports equipment to take advantage of lawn areas throughout the park. Craib A and B are most accessible to the disabled.

■ **CAPACITY:**

Picnic Site	Capacity	Large BBQs	Small BBQs	Tables
Baywood	250	varies	varies	18
Craib A	80	varies	varies	8
Craib B	40	varies	varies	4
Fernwood	90	varies	varies	7
Fire Circle	120	varies	varies	7
Greenwood	75	varies	varies	9
Horseshoe	80	varies	varies	9
Pinewood	60	varies	varies	7
Redwood Glen	120	varies	varies	8
Moses Monument	40	—	—	4

■ **FEES & DEPOSITS:** Reservations may be made by phone or in person. Fees vary depending on site reserved and number of people. A deposit is required. All sites that have not been reserved will be available to the public on a first-come, first-served basis.

■ **RESTRICTIONS:** No hard liquor is allowed. Beer and wine in picnic areas only. Sports meadow areas are non-reservable and are for use by all park visitors. No musical activity without prior written approval.

■ **AVAILABILITY:** Year-round, daily.

Montclair Park   510/339-8919

6300 Moraga Ave. at Thornhill Drive

Picnic Sites
East Picnic Area • Central Picnic Area

Formerly a railroad easement, Montclair Park was built in the 1930s by the Works Progress Administration (WPA). The park encompasses seven acres, and has a duck pond, children's area, "Western Town" (a miniature 'town' for children, built by volunteer parents circa 1950), softball diamond which can be reserved, volleyball/basketball courts and tennis courts. The East Picnic Area is sunny and has a big weeping willow. The Central Picnic Area is larger and half in shade. There is a low wall surrounding this site, suitable for seating an additional 100 people.

■ **CAPACITY:** Additional low-wall seating in the Central Picnic Area brings the total to 200.

Picnic Site	*Capacity*	*Large BBQs*	*Small BBQs*	*Tables*
East Picnic Area	50	2	—	6
Central Picnic Area	100	4	—	6

■ **FEES & DEPOSITS:** A fee is required for an all-day reservation, plus a refundable deposit.

■ **RESTRICTIONS:** Flat and grassy, the East Picnic Area is the only area accessible to handicapped. Steps and gravel at Central Picnic Area present problems for wheelchairs.

■ **AVAILABILITY:** Year-round, daily.

Redwood Regional Park   510/636-1684

From Highway 580 in Oakland, exit at 35th Ave. and travel east; 35th Ave. turns into Redwood Road when it passes over Highway 13; continuing up Redwood Road, the park entrance is three miles beyond the intersection at Skyline Blvd., on the left.

Picnic Sites
Wayside • Quail • Owl

Where commercial logging mills once functioned during the mid-1800s, now redwood trees stand over a hundred feet tall. Redwood Creek is home to a (recently identified) unique species of rainbow trout; consequently, fishing is prohibited. A children's play area is located about 200 yards from the Owl Picnic Area.

■ **RESERVE:** EBRPD recommends phone reservations be made at least 3 weeks in advance; by mail, at least 4.

■ **CAPACITY:**

Picnic Site	*Capacity*	*Large BBQs*	*Small BBQs*	*Tables*
Wayside	150	2	—	9
Quail	50	2	—	6
Owl	150	2	—	9

■ **FEES & DEPOSITS:** Reservations for any of these sites may be made through the East Bay Regional Park District's reservation office. There is a seasonal parking fee.

■ **RESTRICTIONS:** Lawn areas near all picnic sites are non-reservable, and EBRPD asks that they be shared with all park visitors. As with all EBRPD parks, sound amplification is not permitted.

■ **AVAILABILITY:** Year-round, daily.

Roberts Regional Recreation Area   510/636-1684

Take Highway 13 to Joaquin Miller Road; go east up the hill and turn left on Skyline Blvd. Roberts is one mile up the road, on the right.

Picnic Sites
Sycamore • Diablo Vista • Manzanita • Huckelberry • Madrone • Bay Vista • Redwood Bowl

Roberts Regional Recreation Area was opened to the public in 1953. There was an immediate and enthusiastic response to its 100 acres. A popular picnic site for families and groups, the park is characterized by fragrant redwoods and lush greenery. The sports facilities (swimming pool, playfields, archery range, volleyball court and a children's area) enhance any group function.

■ **RESERVE:** EBRPD recommends phone reservations be made at least 3 weeks in advance; by mail, at least 4.

■ **CAPACITY:**

Picnic Site	Capacity	Large BBQs	Small BBQs	Tables
Sycamore	50	1	—	5
Diablo Vista	150	2	—	15
Manzanita	300	2	—	9
Huckleberry	100	1	—	7
Madrone	50	1	—	5
Bay Vista	300	3	—	12
Redwood Bowl	50	3	1	13

■ **FEES & DEPOSITS:** Reservations for any of these sites may be made through the East Bay Regional Park District's reservation office. The volleyball court may be used on a first-come, first-served basis. Call for archery range information (510/531-9853). There's a fee for parking and swimming.

■ **RESTRICTIONS:** Lawn areas near all picnic sites are non-reservable, and EBRPD asks that they be shared with all park visitors. Pets are prohibited at the swimming pool, bathing beach and nature areas. Alcoholic beverages are prohibited near swimming areas or within 50 feet of paved roads or parking areas; beer and wine permitted elsewhere. As with all EBRPD parks, sound amplification is not permitted.

■ **AVAILABILITY:** Year-round, daily.

Temescal Regional Recreation Area   510/636-1684

Next to Highway 24/13 interchange in Oakland.

Picnic Sites
North Temescal • Parkview • Streamside
• Big Rock

Native Californians once lived along the shores of Lake Temescal, which was, before being dammed, only a creek. One of EBRPD's three original parks, Temescal Regional Recreation Area has been open to the public since 1936 and is one of the East Bay's most popular parks. It offers nature lovers 48 acres of lush greenway, including a thirteen-acre lake. Picnic enthusiasts also enjoy swimming, fishing, hiking and other outdoor activities.

■ **RESERVE:** EBRPD recommends phone reservations be made at least 3 weeks in advance; by mail, at least 4.

■ **CAPACITY:**

Picnic Site	Capacity	Large BBQs	Small BBQs	Tables
North Temescal	150	3	—	9
Parkview	75	2	—	6
Streamside	75	1	1	5
Big Rock	50	1	—	4

■ **FEES & DEPOSITS:** Reservations for any of these sites may be made through the East Bay Regional Park District's reservation office. There is a seasonal parking fee.

■ **RESTRICTIONS:** Lawn areas near all picnic sites are non-reservable, and EBRPD asks that they be shared with all park visitors. As with all EBRPD parks, sound amplification is not permitted.

■ **AVAILABILITY:** Year-round, daily.

PINOLE

Point Pinole Regional Shoreline   510/636-1684

Take Hilltop Dr. exit from I–80; turn right on San Pablo Ave. and left on Atlas Rd., which will veer left and become Giant Hwy; the park is on the right.

Picnic Sites
Giant Cluster • The Palms

Eucalyptus groves dominate Point Pinole, while panoramic Bay views are the compelling shoreline attraction. Settle in one spot for an informal picnic among the trees or venture out into the Park's 2,147 acres. You can hike, bike or bring your horse to explore a myriad of trails that criss-cross Point Pinole. Volleyball, horseshoe pits and a children's play area offer entertainment for picnickers of any age. There is also a 1,225-foot fishing pier.

- **RESERVE:** EBRPD recommends phone reservations be made at least 3 weeks in advance; by mail, at least 4.

- **CAPACITY:**

Picnic Site	Capacity	Large BBQs	Small BBQs	Tables
Giant Cluster	150	2	—	10
The Palms	50	2	—	6

- **FEES & DEPOSITS:** Reservations for any of these sites may be made through the East Bay Regional Park District's reservation office. There is a seasonal parking fee and a shuttle fee from the main parking lot.

- **RESTRICTIONS:** Lawn areas near all picnic sites are non-reservable, and EBRPD asks that they be shared with all park visitors. As with all EBRPD parks, sound amplification is not permitted.

- **AVAILABILITY:** Year-round, daily.

PLEASANTON

Shadow Cliffs Regional Recreation Area   510/636-1684

From Highway 580 in Pleasanton, exit at Santa Rita Road and continue south; take a left on Valley, then left again on Stanley; Shadow Cliffs is on the right.

Picnic Sites
Seven Limbs • Fiesta • Lakeside • North Beach • Marina View

Water lovers will be delighted with the four-flume waterslide, located at Shadow Cliff's 90-acre lake. Fishing is a popular sport here year-round since the lake is stocked regularly. While visiting the park for a picnic, enjoy a visit to the sandy beach, conquer a hiking trail or take out the binoculars for a closer look at the wide variety of birds.

- **RESERVE:** EBRPD recommends phone reservations be made at least 3 weeks in advance; by mail, at least 4.

- **CAPACITY:** 5 picnic sites accommodate 50–200 people.

Picnic Site	Capacity	Large BBQs	Small BBQs	Tables
Seven Limbs	100	2	—	9
Fiesta	100	2	—	9
Lakeside	200	4	—	11
North Beach	50	1	—	6
Marina View	50	1	—	6

- **FEES & DEPOSITS:** Reservations for any of these sites may be made through the East Bay Regional Park District's reservation office. Fisherpersons 16 years of age or older must have a State Fishing License with stamps and an EBRPD One-Day Fishing Access Permit. Senior Fishing Access Permits, good for a year after date of purchase, are available to seniors 62 and older. A Beer & Wine Permit is issued with each reservation. There is a parking fee.

■ **RESTRICTIONS:** Lawn areas near all picnic sites are non-reservable, and EBRPD asks that they be shared with all park visitors. As with all EBRPD parks, sound amplification is not permitted.

■ **AVAILABILITY:** Year-round, daily.

Sunol Regional Wilderness   510/636-1684

From Oakland, travel east on Highway 680; follow signs for Tracy to Highway 680 junction; drive south on 680; take the Calaveras Road/Highway 84 exit (a bit south of Sunol); a left on Calaveras Road to Geary Road will lead into the park.

Picnic Sites
Leyden Flats • Alameda Grove

Majestic trees of wide-ranging variety, and fields of colorful spring wildflowers provide a gorgeous background setting for a wonderful picnic at Sunol Regional Wilderness. Rock climbers will love the challenge of the massives (large rocks) at Indian Joe Cave Rocks. Bird watching along Alameda Creek (the county's largest creek) is a favorite pastime. (The visitor center sells identification kits and guides for birds and wildflowers.) Other wildlife creatures may be easily spotted year-round.

■ **RESERVE:** EBRPD recommends phone reservations be made at least 3 weeks in advance; by mail, at least 4.

■ **CAPACITY:**

Picnic Site	Capacity	Large BBQs	Small BBQs	Tables
Leyden Flats	50	—	—	6
Alameda Grove	200	—	7	16

■ **FEES & DEPOSITS:** Reservations for either of these sites may be made through the East Bay Regional Park District's reservation office.

■ **RESTRICTIONS:** Lawn areas near the picnic sites are non-reservable, and EBRPD asks that they be shared with all park visitors. Due to summer fire hazards, the park may close on short notice at any time, while other fire restrictions may be enforced. As with all EBRPD parks, sound amplification is not permitted.

■ **AVAILABILITY:** Year-round, daily.

Prices and policies do change. Call each facility and confirm everything you read in Perfect Places.

RICHMOND

Miller/Knox Regional Shoreline   510/636-1684

Take Highway 580 toward the Richmond/San Rafael Bridge; exit at Cutting Blvd., then turn left on West Cutting to Gerrard; take another left onto Gerrard (through the tunnel, where it turns into Dornan Drive) to the park.

Picnic Sites
Big Meadow • Hills View • Lagoon View • Marsh Hawk • Sea Gull • Killdeer • Pintail • Canvasback • Pickleweed

Miller/Knox Park, with its 260 acres of rolling hills and shoreline, offers spectacular panoramas of the Bay Area's hills and bridges, Mt. Tamalpais, and of course, San Francisco. Take advantage of Keller Beach while visiting the park, or enjoy the bicycle and hiking paths. Strong winds from the water make for great kite flying. Or just bring your binoculars for some rewarding bird-watching.

■ **RESERVE:** EBRPD recommends phone reservations be made at least 3 weeks in advance; by mail, at least 4.

■ **CAPACITY:** 9 picnic sites accommodate 50–200 people.

Picnic Site	Capacity	Large BBQs	Small BBQs	Tables
Big Meadow	100	2	—	9
Hills View	75	2	—	7
Lagoon View	50	2	—	5
Marsh Hawk	100	2	—	7
Sea Gull	200	3	—	13
Killdeer	150	2	—	11
Pintail	200	2	—	13
Canvasback	100	2	—	8
Pickleweed	50	1	—	4

■ **FEES & DEPOSITS:** Reservations for any of these sites may be made through the East Bay Regional Park District's reservation office .

■ **RESTRICTIONS:** Lawn areas near all picnic sites are non-reservable, and EBRPD asks that they be shared with all park visitors. The following sites only offer disabled-access toilets: Big Meadow, Hills View, and Lagoon View. As with all EBRPD parks, sound amplification is not permitted.

■ **AVAILABILITY:** Year-round, daily.

SAN LEANDRO

Lake Chabot Regional Recreation Area   510/636-1684

From Highway 580 in San Leandro, exit east at 150th Ave. Fairmont Drive (which becomes Lake Chabot Road); travel south; entrance is on the left.

Picnic Sites
Elderberry • Heron • Mallard • Turtle • Willow • Cove

Picnic among rolling hills and grassy meadows while your group enjoys volleyball, horseshoes or just relaxing out in the sun. Originally built as a primary water source for the East Bay, Lake Chabot's reservoir now serves as an emergency back-up water supply. Purity measures prohibit any kind of swimming in the lake. Fishing, on the other hand, is a popular sport here. Boats for recreation or sport may be rented for a fee (no private boats allowed).

■ **RESERVE:** EBRPD recommends phone reservations be made at least 3 weeks in advance; by mail, at least 4.

■ **CAPACITY:**

Picnic Site	Capacity	Large BBQs	Small BBQs	Tables
Elderberry	150	1	—	12
Heron	75	2	—	7
Mallard	50	1	—	6
Turtle	100	2	—	9
Willow	150	2	—	11
Cove	200	2	—	15

■ **FEES & DEPOSITS:** Reservations for any of these sites may be made through the East Bay Regional Park District's reservation office. Rent horseshoes, with a refundable deposit, at the Marina concession. There is a parking fee.

■ **RESTRICTIONS:** Lawn areas near all picnic sites, volleyball courts, and horseshoe pits are non-reservable, and EBRPD asks that they be shared with all park visitors. Handicapped-accessible restrooms are located near the concession stand. As with all EBRPD parks, sound amplification is not permitted.

■ **AVAILABILITY:** Year-round, daily.

Martin Luther King Jr. Regional Shoreline Park   510/636-1684

Take Highway I-880 to the Hegenberger Road exit; travel west to Doolittle Drive, where you will turn right; the park is on your right, just past Swan Way.

Picnic Sites
Pelican • Blue Heron • Rail • Tern • Buffle head • Egret • Kingfisher • Plover

Formerly called the San Leandro Bay Regional Shoreline, this 1,200-acre shoreline park offers miles of trails and lawn expanses, along with many outdoor activities. Bird watchers will be delighted year-round by the great variety of birds at the Arrowhead Marsh Area. Restrooms or chemical toilets are found by each picnic area.

■ **RESERVE:** EBRPD recommends phone reservations be made at least 3 weeks in advance; by mail, at least 4.

■ **CAPACITY:** 8 picnic sites accommodate 35–150 people.

Picnic Site	Capacity	Large BBQs	Small BBQs	Tables
Pelican	150	2	—	9
Blue Heron	150	1	—	9
Rail	150	1	—	9
Tern	150	2	—	11
Bufflehead	35	—	2	4
Egret	50	—	2	6
Kingfisher	35	—	2	4
Plover	50	—	2	5

■ **FEES & DEPOSITS:** Reservations for any of these sites may be made through the East Bay Regional Park District's reservation office. Lawn areas near all picnic sites are non-reservable, and EBRPD asks that they be shared with all park visitors.

■ **RESTRICTIONS:** State Fish and Game rules apply here. Fisherpersons 16 years of age or older must have a State Fishing License. As with all EBRPD parks, sound amplification is not permitted.

■ **AVAILABILITY:** Year-round, daily.

SAN RAMON

Little Hills Picnic Ranch   510/462-1400

18013 Bollinger Canyon Road

Picnic Sites
High Falutin' Hill • Lowlander's Holler • Moonshine Heaven • Buckeye Flat • Lookout Ridge • Wildcat Canyon • Johnson's Gulch

Little Hills is an East Bay Regional Park District facility operated in the public interest by The Picnic People, Inc. Select a package customized for your group, then leave the event planning to the park staff. A full-service facility, Little Hills offers all kinds of supervised sports activities, nature tours and children's entertainment plus evening events during the summer. Professional catering is provided (you must have at least partial catering). Ask about their summer evening events (80-person minimum), with exclusive park use.

■ **RESERVE:** Advance reservations required.

■ **CAPACITY:** Picnic sites can be combined to accommodate up to 1,400 people.

Picnic Site	Capacity	Large BBQs	Small BBQs	Tables
High Falutin' Hill	300	varies	varies	33
Lowlander's Holler	200	varies	varies	22
Moonshine Heaven	200	varies	varies	22
Buckeye Flat	150	varies	varies	16
Lookout Ridge	100	varies	varies	11
Wildcat Canyon	75	varies	varies	8
Johnson's Gulch	50	varies	varies	6

■ **FEES & DEPOSITS:** Fees vary depending on group size, picnic site, and extras. Ask about weekend rates and exclusive/half-exclusive use. Groups must purchase beverages on site from Little Hills.

■ **RESTRICTIONS:** Archery on weekends only. Use of an outside caterer is not allowed. No outside band or D.J. allowed. Alcoholic beverage service regulations are strictly enforced.

■ **AVAILABILITY:** Year-round, daily.

WALNUT CREEK

Castle Rock Park   510/462-1400

1700 Castle Rock Road

Picnic Sites
Eddybrook Hollow • Ford's Well • High Steppin' Hill • Pool Oak Terrace • Castle Tree • Castle View • Shady Glen

Castle Rock is an East Bay Regional Park District facility operated in the public interest by The Picnic People, Inc. It is a fully-equipped park for all types of events, located in a wooded, country setting. You can customize a group package that best suits your group's needs, choosing from a wide array of sports activities, menus and picnic sites. You can combine sites to accommodate larger groups.

■ **RESERVE:** Advance reservations required.

■ **CAPACITY:** Picnic sites can be combined to accommodate up to 3,000 people.

Picnic Site	Capacity	Large BBQs	Small BBQs	Tables
Eddybrook Hollow	500	varies	varies	58
Ford's Well	450	varies	varies	46
High Steppin' Hill	350	varies	varies	36
Pool Oak Terrace	250	varies	varies	25
Castle Tree	150	varies	varies	17
Castle View	100	varies	varies	12
Shady Glen	75	varies	varies	8

■ **FEES & DEPOSITS:** Fees vary depending on group size, picnic site, and extras. Weekend rates and corporate mid-week rates are available. Special discounted dates are available in May, June, October and during holiday weekends. In-house catering is required for exclusive and half-exclusive use. Groups are required to purchase beverages through Castle Rock Park.

■ **RESTRICTIONS:** Archery on weekends only. Use of an outside caterer is not allowed. Alcoholic beverage service regulations are strictly enforced.

■ **AVAILABILITY:** Park hours 10:30am–5pm. Weekend hours until 5:30pm.

Turtle Rock Ranch   510/837-2517

On Mt. Diablo. Take Hwy. 680-24 N., exit Ygnacio
Valley Rd., go 2 mi. to Walnut Ave, right, then right on
Oak Grove, left on Northgate through the Mt. Diablo Park
entrance, 6 mi. up Mt. Diablo to the ranch.
(see entry in Event Locations section for more information)

Picnic Sites
Areas A, B, C, D and E

Turtle Rock Ranch is a privately owned facility, located just ten miles from downtown Walnut Creek on the slopes of Mt. Diablo. It offers entertainment packages, catering and supervised activities for groups. Gather next to the swimming pool on the spacious, trellis-covered patio, or sunbathe on the adjoining lawns. Swimming, softball, volleyball, pingpong, game coordinators and special children's events are included in the reservation fee.

■ **RESERVE:** 1 week to 12 months in advance.

■ **CAPACITY:** 60–1,200 people. Areas can be combined.

Picnic Site	*Capacity*	*Large BBQs*	*Small BBQs*	*Tables*
Areas A–E	1,200	provided	—	provided

■ **FEES & DEPOSITS:** The use fee is $850 for weekday events, $380–3,100 for weekend picnics (the fee is dependent on the area reserved). Half of the food, beverage and optional entertainment cost is required 5 days prior to the event, and the balance is payable on the day of the event. Food runs $7.50–11.50/person and beverages run $3–3.50/person. Entertainment packages run $200–3,500. There is no charge for children under 5 years.

■ **RESTRICTIONS:** No pets. You cannot bring in your own food or beverages. Smoking outside only. Insurance may be required.

■ **AVAILABILITY:** May 15–October 15, every day from 8am–9pm.

Need a caterer, cake maker, florist? The Service Directory starting on page 614 features the best in the business.

CAMPBELL

Campbell Park   408/866-2105

Gilman and Campbell Ave. between Dell Ave. and
the San Tomas Expressway

Picnic Sites
2 picnic areas

This 80-acre, woodsy park features the Los Gatos Creek Trail. Alongside the trail are a parcourse, fish ponds, large lawn areas, and one reservable picnic site with covered tables and a barbecue. There are also two small playgrounds and three horseshoe pits. Outside caterers are permitted.

- ■ **RESERVE:** You can reserve up to 3 months in advance.
- ■ **CAPACITY:**

Picnic Site	Capacity	Large BBQs	Small BBQs	Tables
Site 1	30	—	1	2

- ■ **FEES & DEPOSITS:** No permit is required, however an application must be filled out for group use. Fee for residents, $25; non-residents, $50. For over 75 people, a $50 refundable deposit is required. All fees are paid when the application is submitted.
- ■ **RESTRICTIONS:** Beer and wine consumption only in picnic areas. No animals or vehicles on park grounds.
- ■ **AVAILABILITY:** Year-round, 7am to dusk.

John D. Morgan Park   408/866-2105

---

540 West Rincon Ave. between Budd Ave. and
the San Tomas Expressway

Picnic Sites
Section A, B & C

This is a very pretty park. A tree-lined path winds throughout the grounds which include extensive lawns, two playgrounds, hardball and softball diamonds, a soccer field, horseshoe pits and tennis and basketball courts. The picnic areas are surrounded by grass and trees.

- ■ **RESERVE:** You can reserve up to 3 months in advance, but no less than 2 weeks in advance.
- ■ **CAPACITY:**

Picnic Site	Capacity	Large BBQs	Small BBQs	Tables
Section A	100	—	3	4
Section B	300	2	—	15
Section C	100	—	3	5

- ■ **FEES & DEPOSITS:** No permit is required, however an application must be filled out for group use. Fee for residents, $25; non-residents, $50. For over 75 people, a $50 refundable deposit is required. Athletic fields may be reserved for an additional fee. All fees are paid when the application is submitted.

■ **RESTRICTIONS:** Beer and wine consumption only in picnic areas. No animals or vehicles on park grounds.

■ **AVAILABILITY:** Year-round, 7am to dusk.

CUPERTINO

Blackberry Farm   408/252-0465

21975 San Fernando Ave. at Byrne

Picnic Sites
Pine Grove • Fallen Oak • Captain Stevens •
Hillside • Oak Grove • Sycamore • Additional
Picnic Areas 1–8

This historic park was the site of a farm built in 1850, and some of the original buildings still stand. Picnickers will love holding an old-fashioned picnic here because it has that "Little House of the Prairie" feeling. The picnic areas are shaded by huge oaks and sycamore trees, and all have tables and barbecues. The park also has a running stream, wading pool and two large pools with lifeguards.

■ **RESERVE:** Reservations can be made up to a year in advance.

■ **CAPACITY:** Single areas accommodate 50–1,200 people. If you combine areas, the entire facility can hold 4,000.

Picnic Site	Capacity	Large BBQs	Small BBQs	Tables
Pine Grove	100–300	1	—	40
Fallen Oak	50–450	2	—	56
Captain Stevens	200–400	1	—	50
Oak Grove	500–1,200	2	—	150
Sycamore	400–1,200	2	—	150
Additional Areas (8)	50–200 ea	1 lg or sm BBQ ea		10–25 ea

■ **FEES & DEPOSITS:** Use fees vary depending on group size and areas selected. A deposit is required, and a contract and full payment are due 14 days after reservations are made. Full catering services are available starting at $7/person.

■ **RESTRICTIONS:** No amplified music or pets. No outside caterers permitted.

■ **AVAILABILITY:** May through September from 10am–sunset. Closed Mondays. In September, open Saturdays and Sundays only.

Linda Vista Park   408/865-1384

At the end of Linda Vista Drive   *Picnic Sites*
                                               1 picnic area

Linda Vista is a rural, eleven-acre park with two playgrounds and a large, open lawn area. The picnic site is on a partially shaded bluff overlooking the surrounding countryside.

- **RESERVE:** Residents can reserve up to 90 days in advance, non-residents up to 30 days. Reservations must be made in person.
- **CAPACITY:**

Picnic Site	Capacity	Large BBQs	Small BBQs	Tables
Site 1	100	1	—	14

- **FEES & DEPOSITS:** A use permit is required for groups. Use fees for residents $25, non-residents $40. Full payment is required when you apply for a permit. There's an additional cost for use of athletic fields.
- **RESTRICTIONS:** No amplified music or cars on paved paths. Pets must be on leash. Beer and wine consumption with meals only.
- **AVAILABILITY:** Year-round, 10am to 1 hour after sunset.

Memorial Park   408/865-1384

Mary Street and Stevens Creek Blvd.   *Picnic Sites*
                                               1 picnic site

Set among Memorial Park's 27 acres are large lawns, a duckpond, fountain and picturesque gazebo. Two playgrounds, an amphitheater, tennis courts and a softball field are additional attractions. Only one of the many picnic sites is reservable, but all the sites have tables and barbecues.

- **RESERVE:** Residents can reserve up to 90 days in advance, non-residents up to 30 days. Reservations must be made in person.
- **CAPACITY:**

Picnic Site	Capacity	Large BBQs	Small BBQs	Tables
Site 1	100	1	2	16

- **FEES & DEPOSITS:** A use permit is required for groups. Use fee for residents $25, non-residents $40. The fee for electricity at the site is $16.50. Full payment is required when you apply for a permit. There's an additional cost for use of athletic fields.
- **RESTRICTIONS:** No amplified music or cars on paved paths. Pets must be on leash. Beer and wine consumption with meals only.
- **AVAILABILITY:** Year-round, 10am to dusk.

Portal Park   408/865-1384

Portal Avenue

Picnic Sitess
1 picnic area

Portal Park is a small, traditional neighborhood park. The well-maintained lawns are shaded by large, mature trees, and the picnic area is adjacent to a children's playground.

- **RESERVE:** Residents can reserve up to 90 days in advance, non-residents up to 30 days.
- **CAPACITY:**

Picnic Site	Capacity	Large BBQs	Small BBQs	Tables
Site 1	75	1	2	9

- **FEES & DEPOSITS:** A use permit is required for groups. Use fee for residents $25, non-residents $40. Full payment is required when you apply for a permit. There's an additional cost for use of athletic fields.
- **RESTRICTIONS:** No amplified music or cars on paved paths. Pets must be on leash. Beer and wine consumption with meals only.
- **AVAILABILITY:** Year-round, 10am to 1 hour after sunset.

GILROY

Casa de Fruta   408/842-9316

10031 Pacheco Pass Highway

Picnic Sites
Buckeye Bend • Bamboo Grove • The Meadows •
Cone Oak • Serene Sycamore • Floral Hill •
Mulberry Glen • Laurel • Lawn

Picnickers will be surprised at what this facility has to offer. Casa de Fruta is an interesting mix of 24-hour restaurant, a country store and deli, a fruit stand, a candy factory and a sweet shop with ice cream and pies. Groups can take advantage of a petting zoo, train rides, wine and cheese tasting, a country stage, a baseball field, walking trails, a playground, creek, swimming pool and pony rides. This pleasant country setting is perfect for large, corporate functions. Shaded picnic sites are sizable, with views of the surrounding foothills.

- **RESERVE:** Reservations can be made up to 6 months in advance.
- **CAPACITY:** Minimum 25 guests. Areas can be combined, and the entire facility can hold up to 10,000.

Picnic Site	Capacity	Large BBQs	Small BBQs	Tables
Floral Hill	100	provided*	3–4	provided
All other 7 sites	500 ea	provided*	3–4	provided

* *Each site has enough picnic tables to accommodate its capacity. Extra tables can be provided as needed, and large barbecues are provided for a fee.*

■ **FEES & DEPOSITS:** Use fees range from $17–20/person for food and beverages and use of site. Without in-house catering, the use fee is $3/person. Outside caterers cannot be used, however BYO is allowed. A $50 deposit is required to secure your date.

■ **RESTRICTIONS:** No pets.

■ **AVAILABILITY:** Year-round, daily 9am–7pm, weather permitting.

Hecker Pass   408/842-2121

3050 Hecker Pass Rd. From San Jose, take 101 south to Masten exit, go left on Santa Teresa, right on Hecker Pass Hwy, go 2 miles, entry is on left.
(see entry in Event Locations section for more information)

Picnic Sites
12 picnic sites

Because Hecker Pass has its own plant nursery, this exceptionally well-maintained private facility is beautifully landscaped with a wide variety of trees, shrubs and colorful flowers. There's a large pool, bordered by grass and palm trees, and over six acres of open turf, great for softball or other activities. All of the group picnic areas are shaded by trees or trellises. For more excitement, the recreation complex delights children with a carrousel, Fish Ride, Tub-of-Fun ride, family roller coaster, train and stagecoach.

■ **RESERVE:** 6–12 months in advance.

■ **CAPACITY:** If you rent the entire facility, it can accommodate up to 7,000 people.

Picnic Site	*Capacity*	*Large BBQs*	*Small BBQs*	*Tables*
Sites 1–12	50–1,500	provided	provided	provided

■ **FEES & DEPOSITS:** A $5/person deposit is required; half the estimated cost is due 60 days prior to the event, the balance is billed. Catering is provided starting at $23/adult, $18.50/child (age 4–13 years). Children's supervised activities and entertainment are included in the catering fee, featuring face painting, puppet shows, story-telling and a children's treasure hunt. Adult activities can be arranged by request.

■ **RESTRICTIONS:** No outside alcohol or catering. No pets.

■ **AVAILABILITY:** Mid-April through mid-October, 11am–5pm, daily. Other times by special arrangement.

LOS GATOS

Lake Vasona Park   408/358-3751

Blossom Hill road between Highway 17
and University

Picnic Sites
Lakeview • Peppertree • Pond 1 • Pond 2 •
Gateway Pavilion • Blossom Valley • The Circle
• Raintree

Lovely Lake Vasona, surrounded by lawns and trees, is the centerpiece of this huge, 164-acre city park, The shaded picnic areas are situated on lawns and for more active picnickers, paddle boat rentals are available for an on-the-water experience. For bicyclists and roller skaters, there is a paved pathway that forms a U around the lake.

- **RESERVE:** Reservations can be made up to 12 months in advance.

- **CAPACITY:** The entire park can accommodate 850. There are 117 small barbecues on a first-come, first-served basis.

Picnic Site	Capacity	Large BBQs	Small BBQs	Tables
Lakeview	100	1	—	13
Peppertree	100	1	—	18
Pond 1	100	1	—	14
Pond 2	100	1	—	12
Gateway Pavilion	100	1	—	10
Blossom Valley	100	1	—	10
The Circle	150	1	—	20
Raintree	100	1	—	8

- **FEES & DEPOSITS:** A permit for group use is required. Fees range from $55–83/day and a $100 cleaning deposit is also required. Vehicle parking costs $3/car. All fees must be paid 14 days after reservations have been made.

- **RESTRICTIONS:** No amplified music. Beer and wine consumption only.

- **AVAILABILITY:** Year-round, daily 8am–dusk.

Oak Meadow Park   408/354-6809

Blossom Hill Road at University

Picnic Sites
Areas 1, 2, 3 & 4

Although it's an urban park, Oak Meadow is completely enclosed by trees. The park features a large turf area, creek, carousel, playground, volleyball courts and the Billy Jones Wildcat Railroad. Two of the picnic areas are sunny, open fields, while the other two are more rustic, set among shade trees. Both have tables and large barbecue pits.

- **RESERVE:** Reservations can be made starting January 1 for that year.
- **CAPACITY:** Areas 1 & 2 and areas 3 & 4 may be combined.

Picnic Site	Capacity	Large BBQs	Small BBQs	Tables
All 4 areas	50 ea	1 ea*	—	5 ea

* *Area 1 & 2 share a large BBQ*

- **FEES & DEPOSITS:** A use permit is required for group use. Use fees are $30 for one area, $55 for 2 areas. Payment is required 14 days after reservations are made. Vehicle parking costs $3/car for non-residents. If you bring your own caterer, there is an additional $35 fee.
- **RESTRICTIONS:** No amplified music. Beer and wine consumption only, no baseball on weekends.
- **AVAILABILITY:** Year-round, daily 8am–dusk.

MILPITAS

Ed Levin Park   408/358-3751

3100 Calaveras Road at Downing Road

Picnic Sites
Sandy Wool • Elm • Spring Valley • Oak Knoll

Ed Levin Park sits in the east foothills of South San Jose. This 3,000-acre park offers hang gliding, an equestrian trail, a golf course, and two lakes for fishing and boating, all in a pleasant, natural setting. The picnic sites are open fields partially shaded by oak trees.

- **RESERVE:** Reservations can be made 12 months in advance.
- **CAPACITY:** Sites can be combined to accommodate 550. In addition to the reservable areas below, there are 18 additional barbecues and 176 tables available on a first-come, first-served basis.

Picnic Site	Capacity	Large BBQs	Small BBQs	Tables
Sandy Wool	150	1	—	38
Elm	200	1	—	49
Spring Valley	100	1	—	49
Oak Knoll	100	1	—	8

- **FEES & DEPOSITS:** An application for group use is required. Use fees range from $55–110. Parking is $3/car. Fees are paid when reservations are made.
- **RESTRICTIONS:** No vehicles are allowed on the park grounds; beer and wine consumption only. Dogs must be on leash. No amplified music. No power boating and no swimming.
- **AVAILABILITY:** Year-round, 8am–dusk.

MORGAN HILL

Guglielmo Winery   408/779-2145

1480 East Main Ave.

Picnic Sitess
1 picnic area

Guglielmo is a family-run winery with a tasting room and an attractive grapevine-covered patio. The picnic site is a large lawn overlooking the vineyards with views of the surrounding mountains.

- **RESERVE:** Reservations can be made 1 month in advance.
- **CAPACITY:**

Picnic Site	Capacity	Large BBQs	Small BBQs	Tables
Site 1	80	1	—	6

- **FEES & DEPOSITS:** The use fee for 4 hours is $250. A $100 deposit is due when reservations are confirmed, the balance is due the day of the event.
- **RESTRICTIONS:** Wine must be purchased on-site; beer CBA. No pets.
- **AVAILABILITY:** May–September, 10am–6pm.

SAN JOSE

Alum Rock Park   408/277-5561

Alum Rock Ave. at Penitencia Creek Road

Picnic Sites
Buckeye • Rustic Land • Ramada • Chaparral • Sycamore • Log Cabin

Here, picnickers will find a rustic, woodsy park with hiking trails, a youth science institute, natural wildlife trails, volleyball courts, horseshoe pits, totlots and a visitors center with small animals. Alum Rock's picnic sites are set amongst trees and have barbecues and tables. For active groups, there's a lawn area available for unstructured games.

- **RESERVE:** Reservations can be made up to 6 months in advance.
- **CAPACITY:** Picnic areas cannot be combined to accommodate larger groups.

Picnic Site	Capacity	Large BBQs	Small BBQs	Tables
Buckeye	30	—	varies	varies
Rustic Land	300	—	varies	varies

Ramada	30	—	varies	varies
Chaparral	120	1	varies	varies
Sycamore	75	—	varies	varies
Log Cabin	150	1	varies	varies

■ **FEES & DEPOSITS:** A permit for group use is required. Fees are based on area selected and group size, ranging from $35–85/area. Vehicle parking costs $3/car. All fees are paid when you confirm reservations. Reservations must be made in person

■ **RESTRICTIONS:** No amplified music or pets. Beer and wine only. There may be fire restrictions during summer months. If the fire danger is severe the park may be temporarily closed.

■ **AVAILABILITY:** Year-round, 8am to a half hour after sunset.

Club Almaden   408/268-4239

21350 Almaden Road

Picnic Sites
Water Tower • Main Area • The Glade

Nestled in a valley, Club Almaden's six acres of emerald green lawns and beautiful gardens provide a delightful setting for a company picnic. The centerpiece is a large, 1854 home overlooking the grounds and babbling brook. Each picnic site is set on a soft surface of granite or rock filings, and offers a fantastic view of the Santa Cruz mountains.

■ **RESERVE:** Reservations can be made 6 months in advance.

■ **CAPACITY:** By combining formal picnic areas and additional common space, the entire facility can accommodate 2,000.

Picnic Site	*Capacity*	*Large BBQs*	*Small BBQs*	*Tables*
Water Tower	250	provided	provided	provided
Main Area	550	provided	provided	provided
The Glade	150	provided	provided	provided

■ **FEES & DEPOSITS:** Group picnic packages range from $21.50/person to $23.50/person and include admission, food, beverages, entertainment and parking. One third of the total event cost is required to secure your date. Half the balance is due 2 weeks prior, and the remainder is due the day of the event.

■ **RESTRICTIONS:** You must use the on-site caterer. No amplified music or pets.

■ **AVAILABILITY:** Year-round, Monday–Saturday, 11am–5pm; Sunday, noon–6pm. Evening picnics are available by special arrangement.

Coyote-Hellyer Park   408/358-3751

985 Hellyer Ave. near Highway 101

Picnic Sites
Sylvandale 1 & 2 • Shadowbluff • San Juan Batista • Cottonwood • La Raza

Coyote-Hellyer is a large park facility near Highway 101. With 223 acres of manicured lawns, a lake stocked with trout and clusters of mature trees, it offers groups a variety of picnicking experiences. In addition to seven group picnic areas, it has an Olympic training velodrome, nature museum and a twelve mile bike path.

- **RESERVE:** Reservations can be made up to 12 months in advance.
- **CAPACITY:** In addition to the reservable group tables below, there are 67 picnic tables available on a first-come, first-served basis.

Picnic Site	*Capacity*	*Large BBQs*	*Small BBQs*	*Tables*
Sylvandale 1	100	1	—	12
Sylvandale 2	100	1	—	12
Shadowbluff	65	1	—	13
San Juan Batista	65	1	—	9
Cottonwood	300	1	—	26
La Raza	300	1	—	14
Velodrome	150	1	—	12

- **FEES & DEPOSITS:** A permit for group use is required. Fees range from $39–165/day and a $100 cleaning deposit is also required. All fees must be paid 14 days after reservations have been made.
- **RESTRICTIONS:** Amplified music is limited. Beer and wine consumption only.
- **AVAILABILITY:** Year-round, daily 8am–dusk.

Coyote Ranch   408/463-0661

Monterey Highway at Metcalf

Picnic Sites
Pepper Tree • Elm • Arbor • Oak

At Coyote Ranch, you don't have to lift a finger. This is a private picnic facility that takes care of all the details, including food service and beverages. Group picnics include hosted games, clowns, pony rides, horse-drawn hayrides, bands, stage shows and a lot more. Volleyball, softball and horseshoes are also available. Slightly rustic in appearance, Coyote Ranch has acres of lawn and plenty of shaded areas. Guests can relax under the many oak and pepper trees that dot the grounds.

- **RESERVE:** Reservations can be made 1–18 months in advance.
- **CAPACITY:** The facility can accommodate up to 5,000 people if you rent the entire ranch. BBQs and picnic tables are provided as needed.

Picnic Site	Capacity	Large BBQs	Small BBQs	Tables
Pepper Tree	1,000	varies	—	varies
Elm	800	varies	—	varies
Arbor	600	varies	—	varies
Oak	225	varies	—	varies

■ **FEES & DEPOSITS:** Group picnic packages are provided. A minimum fee or guest count is required. Call for rates.

■ **RESTRICTIONS:** No pets. Beverages must be arranged through the Ranch.

■ **AVAILABILITY:** April–November: Saturdays, 10am–5pm; Sundays, 11am–5:30pm; Sat & Sun evenings, 7:15pm–midnight.

Emma Prusch Memorial Park   408/926-5555

647 South King Road at Story Road   *Picnic Sites*
                                                 Area 1 • Area 2

Now a public park, Emma Prusch was once a working farm. A remnant from the past, the park contains an 1890s farm house and antique farm equipment. A barn houses larger animals and there's a yard for smaller ones such as chickens and pigs. Of note is a fruit orchard adjacent to the picnic area bearing 120 rare varieties of fruit. An urban farm, Emma Prusch offers visitors a chance to get their fingers dirty working in several community gardens. There are also five acres of open turf for kite flying, volleyball and other informal games.

■ **RESERVE:** Reservations can be made up to 3 months in advance.

■ **CAPACITY:**

Picnic Site	Capacity	Large BBQs	Small BBQs	Tables
Area 1	200	1	2	29
Area 2	80	1	—	10

■ **FEES & DEPOSITS:** Use fees for groups up to 35 people is $35. From 36–75 people, $60; 76 people or more, $85. Parking is free. The fee must be paid when reservations are confirmed.

■ **RESTRICTIONS:** A permit is required for amplified music; pets must be on leash.

■ **AVAILABILITY:** Year-round, 8:30am–sunset.

Prices and policies do change. Call each facility and confirm everything you read in Perfect Places.

Kelley Park   408/277-5561

1300 Senter Road at Story Road

Picnic Sites
Alder Circle • Manuel Briar • Arbor • Twin Oaks • Family Circle

One of this city's oldest parks, Kelley Park is known for its Japanese Friendship Garden, complete with coy ponds, and its large, historical museum complex. A living recreation of old San Jose with historically significant buildings and exhibits, the San Jose Historical Museum offers groups a glimpse of the homes and businesses that once graced the streets of early San Jose. Smaller picnickers will be thrilled with the Happy Hollow Toddler Park Zoo, which is also a part of Kelly Park. Five group areas offer guests shade on warm, summer days.

- **RESERVE:** Reservations must be made in person and can be made up to 6 months in advance.
- **CAPACITY:**

Picnic Site	Capacity	Large BBQs	Small BBQs	Tables
Alder Circle	35	—	varies	varies
Manuel Briar	75	—	varies	varies
Arbor	100	—	varies	varies
Twin Oaks	120	—	varies	varies
Family Circle	200	1	varies	varies

- **FEES & DEPOSITS:** An application for group use is required. Fees will depend on site selected and group size. Vehicle parking costs $3/car. All fees are paid when reservations are made.
- **RESTRICTIONS:** No amplified music or pets. Beer and wine consumption only.
- **AVAILABILITY:** Year-round, 8am until 1 hour after sunset.

Lake Cunningham Park   408/277-5561

Between Tully Road and White Road near the Capitol Expressway

Picnic Sites
Silver Creek • Ruby Creek • Alder Leaf • Cypress Pavilion

Adjacent to Raging Waters, lake Cunningham offers picnic groups an opportunity to fish and rent paddleboats. There's also a large lawn for organized activities, a parcourse, play area and horseshoe pits.

- **RESERVE:** Reservations must be made in person and can be made up to 6 months in advance.
- **CAPACITY:**

Picnic Site	Capacity	Large BBQs	Small BBQs	Tables
Silver Creek	75	—	varies	varies
Ruby Creek	75	—	varies	varies

Alder Leaf	200	—	varies	varies
Cypress Pavilion	400	1	varies	varies

■ **FEES & DEPOSITS:** A permit is required for group use. Except for the Cypress Pavilion, fees range from $60–85/day per group area. The Cypress Pavilion costs $275 plus a $250 security deposit. Vehicle parking costs $1/car. All fees are paid when reservations are made.

■ **RESTRICTIONS:** No pets or amplified music except by permit in the Cypress Pavilion. Beer and wine only. No swimming.

■ **AVAILABILITY:** Year-round, 8am to a half hour after sunset.

PLC Tower   408/578-8059

2887 McLaughlin Ave. near the intersection of
Capitol Expressway and 101

Picnic Sites
1 picnic area

Ensconced in a residential area, PLC Tower is hidden from view by a white fence, making it an unusually secluded spot for an urban park. This private facility provides all the services any group could want, from five theme packages to customized menus. For swimmers, there's a large swimming pool, and for others, PLC has horseshoe pits, volleyball and large, open turf areas for organized games. Kids will especially like the play areas near group picnic sites.

■ **RESERVE:** Reservations can be made up to 4 months in advance.

■ **CAPACITY:**

Picnic Site	*Capacity*	*Large BBQs*	*Small BBQs*	*Tables*
Site 1	500	2	—	40

■ **FEES & DEPOSITS:** Fees will depend on package selected and group size. There are also theme packages available. A refundable $250 security deposit is required. For rental of the site only, June–September, without a group package, the fee is $1,600, 10am–4pm or $650 from 5pm–10pm. Sunday use fee for 6 hours is $1,200.

■ **RESTRICTIONS:** No glass bottles or pets.

■ **AVAILABILITY:** Year-round, 10am–10pm.

Need a caterer, cake maker, florist? The Service Directory starting on page 614 features the best in the business.

SANTA CLARA

Central Park   408/984-3223

---

969 Kiely Blvd. between Homestead and Benton

Picnic Sites
Pavilion • Arbor

Central Park offers groups a variety of options. This 52-acre facility houses the main Santa Clara Library, an international swim center, softball field, tennis courts, lawn bowling and a small parcourse. For group functions, the wisteria-covered Pavilion and Arbor offer picnickers refuge from the sun on hot days.

- **RESERVE:** Group reservations can be made in person by residents or by a company with a Santa Clara address up to 4 months in advance.
- **CAPACITY:** The Pavilion can be sectioned into thirds (each third holding 50) and can hold up to 175.

Picnic Site	Capacity	Large BBQs	Small BBQs	Tables
Pavilion	175	2	5	21
Arbor	225	3	—	28

- **FEES & DEPOSITS:** The use fee is $25 per each section of the Pavilion, plus a refundable $50 deposit. Payment is made when the application is completed in person. Call for Arbor rates.
- **RESTRICTIONS:** If your group is going to consume beer or wine, a reservation is required. Caterers must be approved by the City of Santa Clara. Dogs must be on leash and amplified music requires a permit.
- **AVAILABILITY:** Year-round, 8am–8:30pm in summer months, 8am–7pm in winter.

SARATOGA

Cinnabar Winery   408/741-5858

23000 Congress Springs Road between Pierce and Sanborn

Picnic Sites
1 picnic area

Set high up in the Santa Cruz Mountains and surrounded by vineyards, this small winery offers a group picnic area with two adjacent wisteria-covered trellises. Visitors have great views of the skyline and adjacent mountains while sampling Cinnabar wares. Tastings and tours are available.

- **RESERVE:** Group reservations can be made up to 4 weeks in advance.

■ **CAPACITY:**

Picnic Site	Capacity	Large BBQs	Small BBQs	Tables
Site 1	60	—	—	3

■ **FEES & DEPOSITS:** The use fee is $500 for 25–49 people; $1,000 for 50–70 people. 25% of the anticipated event total is required as a deposit plus a $500 security deposit. The balance is due by the end of the event.

■ **RESTRICTIONS:** Wine must be purchased on-site. No amplified music. Limited parking.

■ **AVAILABILITY:** Year-round, 8am–dusk, every day.

Saratoga Springs   408/867-3016

22801 Big Basin Way

Picnic Sites
Longbridge • Cathedral Grove • Creeks Bend •
Hilltop • Redwood Grove • Saratoga Cove •
Booker

Offering a shady, lush and woodsy setting, Saratoga Springs is a private facility which provides full service picnics for large groups, everything from food and theme parties to supervised activities. Specializing in old-fashioned, family-style picnics, Saratoga Springs has seven different group areas with all the amenities. Towering redwoods and several creeks create a secluded, rustic environment, yet visitors can still enjoy modern amenities and activities such as sunbathing around the swimming pool.

■ **RESERVE:** Group reservations can be made up to 5 months in advance.

■ **CAPACITY:** Groups can rent the entire facility, which holds up to 3,000, maximum.

Picnic Site	Capacity	Large BBQs	Small BBQs	Tables
Longbridge	800	4	—	100+
Cathedral	300	2	—	30
Creeks Bend	300	2	1	30
Hilltop	100	1	—	10
Saratoga Cove	100	1	—	10
Booker	100	1	1	10
Redwood Grove	125	2	—	13

■ **FEES & DEPOSITS:** Fees depend on which areas are reserved and group size. Package rates include food, beverages and special picnic services such as supervised face painting, children's carnival or picnic games. A $500–1,000 deposit is required when reservations are confirmed; the balance is due the day of the event. Call for specific rates.

■ **RESTRICTIONS:** Beverages must be purchased on site, BYO can be arranged. No pets allowed.

■ **AVAILABILITY:** April through October, 10am–5pm and 6:30pm–midnight.

Wildwood Park   408/867-3438

20764 Fourth Street at Big Basin Way

Picnic Sites
1 picnic site

Close to downtown Saratoga, Wildwood Park is a hidden jewel-of-a-park in a lovely residential area. This four-acre facility has emerald green lawns which are perfect for volleyball and informal games. Horseshoe pits, a stage and a children's play area offer other activities. Saratoga Creek flows adjacent to the park, providing a riparian environment for native trees including huge sycamores.

■ **RESERVE:** Group reservations can be made up to 12 months in advance.

■ **CAPACITY:**

Picnic Site	Capacity	Large BBQs	Small BBQs	Tables
Site 1	200	2	2	16

■ **FEES & DEPOSITS:** A permit is required. The use fee for residents is $50 for 25–50 people; $75 for 51–200 people. The non-resident use fee is $75 for 15–50 people; $125 for 51–200 people. A $100 refundable security deposit is required for group use, payable when the application for use is submitted.

■ **RESTRICTIONS:** Beer and wine only. Dogs must be on leash. No parking is permitted inside the park.

■ **AVAILABILITY:** Year-round, sunup to sunset.

SUNNYVALE

Lakewood Park   408/730-7350

834 Lakechime Drive at Lakehaven

Picnic Sites
Group Areas 1, 2 & 3

Lakewood is a large city park, with athletic fields, basketball and tennis courts, horseshoe pit and play area. Picnickers have three shaded group picnic areas, surrounded by lawns, and sixteen acres for fun and games.

■ **RESERVE:** Reservations are taken for May–October, only. The rest of the year is on a first-come, first-served basis. Residents can reserve up to 6 months in advance, non-residents 3 months in advance.

■ **CAPACITY:** You can combine areas, totalling 425 people.

Picnic Site	Capacity	Large BBQs	Small BBQs	Tables
Group Area 1	75	1	—	7
Group Area 2	100	1	—	10
Group Area 3	230	1	—	23

- **FEES & DEPOSITS:** A use permit is required for group use. Residents $18/area, non-residents $45/area. Payment must be made when booking the picnic site. To reserve athletic fields, and extra fee is required.

- **RESTRICTIONS:** No amplified music or portable barbecues. Dogs must be on leash. Wine and beer consumption only.

- **AVAILABILITY:** Year-round, 8am–dusk.

Las Palmas Park   408/730-7350

---

850 Russet Drive at Spinosa   *Picnic Sites*
                                               Group Areas 1, 2 & 3

Called Las Palmas because of the multiple palm trees that grace the site, this relatively new public park is located in a residential area of Sunnyvale. Expanses of lawns for informal games and three group picnic areas surround a pond which is filled with water during non-drought years.

- **RESERVE:** Reservations are taken for May–October, only. The rest of the year is on a first-come, first-served basis. Residents can reserve up to 6 months in advance, non-residents 3 months in advance.

- **CAPACITY:** Combined areas can hold up to 150 people.

Picnic Site	Capacity	Large BBQs	Small BBQs	Tables
Group Area 1	40	—	3	5
Group Area 2	20	1	6	9
Group Area 3	90	1	2	6

- **FEES & DEPOSITS:** A use permit is required for group use. Residents $18/area, non-residents $45/area. Payment must be made when booking the picnic site. To reserve athletic fields, and extra fee is required.

- **RESTRICTIONS:** No amplified music or portable barbecues. Dogs must be on leash except in dog run area. Wine and beer consumption only.

- **AVAILABILITY:** Year-round, 8am–dusk.

Serra Park   408/730-7350

---

739 The Dalles at Hollenbeck   *Picnic Sites*
                                               Group Areas 1, 2, 3 & 4

Serra Park has four, shaded group picnic sites, surrounded by open lawn areas for informal activities. Lighted tennis courts, children's play area and barbecues are additional amenities, as is a seasonal creek which courses through the park during wet months.

- **RESERVE:** Residents can reserve up to 6 months in advance, non-residents 3 months in advance.

■ **CAPACITY:** Combined, the group areas can hold up to 200 people.

Picnic Site	Capacity	Large BBQs	Small BBQs	Tables
Group Area 1	40	1	1	4
Group Area 2	20	1	—	2
Group Area 3	50	1	1	5
Group Area 4	90	1	3	10

■ **FEES & DEPOSITS:** A use permit is required for group use. Residents $18/area, non-residents $45/area. Payment must be made when booking the picnic site. To reserve athletic fields, and extra fee is required.

■ **RESTRICTIONS:** No amplified music or portable barbecues. Dogs must be on leash. Wine and beer consumption only.

■ **AVAILABILITY:** Year-round, 8am–dusk.

Twin Creeks Sports Complex   408/734-0888

---

969 Caribbean Drive at Highway 237

Picnic Sites
1 large area

Twin Creeks is a sizable, private facility with indoor and outdoor spaces which can accommodate both group and corporate picnics. Picnickers will love the ten baseball diamonds with batting cages—and if your group doesn't play baseball, other athletic games can be played on these fields. Two sand volleyball courts and a totlot are also available.

■ **RESERVE:** Reservations are recommended 1 month in advance for spring and summer months, 1 week in advance for other times during the year.

■ **CAPACITY:** 20,000 in total; smaller groups can be accommodated.

Picnic Site	Capacity	Large BBQs	Small BBQs	Tables
Site 1	20,000	provided	provided	provided

■ **FEES & DEPOSITS:** Payment in full is required prior to the event. Most events are catered by an in-house caterer and each menu is customized. The use fee depends on group size, menu selected and use of services. An insurance binder is also required.

■ **RESTRICTIONS:** Catering is provided unless you choose the "buy-out" clause in the agreement. Alcohol is provided, no BYO.

■ **AVAILABILITY:** Year-round, 9:30am–3:30pm weekdays only.

CALISTOGA

Bothe-Napa Valley State Park

707/942-4575   Park Ranger

3801 St. Helena Highway North, off Highway 29

Picnic Sites
1 picnic site

Bothe-Napa is a 1,916-acre park with ten miles of hiking trails, mostly through a cool, wooded canyon. A mile and a quarter trail leads to the Old Bale Mill, a restored water-powered flour mill. The group picnic area is covered and there's a double sink and electrical outlets. The adjacent swimming pool is open on weekends starting Memorial Day weekend, and every day from mid-June through Labor Day.

- **RESERVE:** Up to 6 months in advance.
- **CAPACITY:**

Picnic Site	Capacity	Large BBQs	Small BBQs	Tables
Site 1	100	1	—	10

- **FEES & DEPOSITS:** Reservations are accepted by telephone and will be held for up to 10 days. Payment must be received within that period or the reservation is canceled. For groups of up to 60, the fee is $66 plus a non-refundable $6 reservation fee. The fee balance is refundable if groups cancel up to 2 weeks prior to the event. Groups over 60 require approval of the park supervisor and pay an additional $1/person. Use of the pool is $3 for adults and $1 for children under 17.

- **RESTRICTIONS:** Amplified music is allowed only by special arrangement, and will increase the use fee. $1 million in liability insurance may be required. Night lighting is available by special arrangement.

- **AVAILABILITY:** Year-round, 8am to sunset.

Macedonia Park

415/731-7687

---

645 Lomell Road, Silverado Trail
Contact: Basil Tonas

Picnic Sites
1 picnic site

Featuring a quiet, wooded setting for outdoor events, this private park has a large group picnic area. The site is an open, grassy space with a familiar, cozy feeling, bordered on one side by an attractive vineyard. Visitors can also walk to a Greek Orthodox Church located on a hilltop within the grounds.

- **RESERVE:** 3–6 months in advance.
- **CAPACITY:**

Picnic Site	Capacity	Large BBQs	Small BBQs	Tables
Site 1	500	1+	—	70

- **FEES & DEPOSITS:** For groups of 500, the use fee is $400. This amount is negotiable for smaller groups.
- **RESTRICTIONS:** none

■ **AVAILABILITY:** Year-round, during daylight hours.

Old Faithful Geyser   707/942-6463

1299 Tubbs Lane, between Highways 128 and 29   *Picnic Sites*
                                                   1 picnic site

Old Faithful Geyser of California is one of only three Old Faithful geysers in the world. Guests to this 22-acre park will be thrilled because the picnic area surrounds the geyser, which usually erupts every forty minutes. Another attraction is the exotic animal zoo, which is contained within the facility.

■ **RESERVE:** First-come, first-served.

■ **CAPACITY:**

Picnic Site	*Capacity*	*Large BBQs*	*Small BBQs*	*Tables*
Site 1	120	—	—	20

■ **FEES & DEPOSITS:** The fee is $4 for adults; $2 for children aged 6–11; no charge for children under 6; $3.50 for seniors over 60. Groups of 20 or more receive a 20% discount. Bus groups receive free admission for the driver and a guide.

■ **RESTRICTIONS:** Alcohol is allowed. Barbecues may be brought in by special arrangement; however, on very windy days, park authorities may not allow them to be used.

■ **AVAILABILITY:** Year-round, 9am–6pm during the summer; 9am–5pm during the winter.

Sterling Vineyards   707/942-3358

1111 Dunaweal Lane, St. Helena Highway   *Picnic Sites*
Contact: Ford LeStrange   *1 picnic site*

Reached by an aerial tram ride up a steep 300-foot knoll, Sterling Vineyards appears from the distance like a white castle on a mountaintop. Constructed in 1969 as a state-of-the-art winery, Sterling has architecture reminiscent of an old Mediterranean monastery, with white walls, clean straight lines and rounded belfries. Of note is the self-guided tour through the winery, with passages and overlooks that allow guests to view the entire winemaking process without a guide. Guests park below and take the tram up for group functions. Catered picnics are held on the terrace.

■ **RESERVE:** 4 months in advance.

■ **CAPACITY:**

Picnic Site	*Capacity*	*Large BBQs*	*Small BBQs*	*Tables*
Terrace	50	provided	—	provided

■ **FEES & DEPOSITS:** There is a $9–11 use fee/person. This includes the tram ride up to the winery from the parking lots and a guided tour of the facility and wine tasting. Catering is can be arranged through an approved list of caterers, and averages $20/person for a buffet lunch, including wine service.

■ **RESTRICTIONS:** Only Sterling wines may be consumed on the premises, no other alcohol is allowed.

■ **AVAILABILITY:** Year-round, 10:30am–4:30pm.

NAPA

Enchanted Hills Camp   415/431-1481 or 707/224-4023

3410 Mt. Veeder Road
Contact: Kathy Abrahamson, Lighthouse for the Blind

Picnic Sites
1 picnic site

Situated on the slopes of Mount Veeder above the Napa Valley, this 311-acre camp has a swimming pool, lake with rowboats, baseball field, basketball court, outdoor bowling, horseshoes, hiking trails and a sensory playground. All facilities, except the swimming pool, are included with day-use rental.

■ **RESERVE:** 3 months in advance.

■ **CAPACITY:**

Picnic Site	*Capacity*	*Large BBQs*	*Small BBQs*	*Tables*
Site 1	300	1	—	7

■ **FEES & DEPOSITS:** Less than 50 people, $500 per day; 50–100 people, $800; more than 100 people, $1,000. Groups must provide a Red Cross certified lifeguard to use the pool. The fee for pool use is $100/day.

■ **RESTRICTIONS:** Alcohol and music are allowed. Groups must obtain $500,000 liability insurance coverage naming the Lighthouse for the Blind and Visually Impaired as additional insured.

■ **AVAILABILITY:** September through May. The swimming pool is open May–September.

Fuller Park   707/257-9529   Pks and Rec Depart.

At the corner of Jefferson and Laurel Streets.

Picnic Sites
The Oaks • The Cedars • Sequoia Area

Located in downtown Napa, this is a traditional neighborhood park. The picnic areas are grassy with large shade trees throughout, and the park also provides a children's playground and horseshoe pits.

■ **RESERVE:** At least 2 weeks in advance.

■ **CAPACITY:** 3 sites accommodating 40–80 people.

Picnic Site	*Capacity*	*Large BBQs*	*Small BBQs*	*Tables*
The Oaks	80	—	1	8
The Cedars	80	—	1	8
Sequoia Area	40	—	1	4

■ **FEES & DEPOSITS:** The reservation fee is $30, plus $55 for non-Napa residents. There is also a $50 refundable security deposit. The security deposit is due immediately on booking with the fee balance due 30 days before the event.

- **RESTRICTIONS:** Alcohol is not permitted. Music is allowed within reasonable sound limits.
- **AVAILABILITY:** Year-round, from sunup to sundown.

Kennedy Park   **707/257-9529** Parks & Rec Depart.

Napa-Vallejo Highway, by Napa Valley College   *Picnic Sites*
                                                Pines • Redwood • Mulberry 1 & 2

What's nice about this 340-acre park is that it's on the Napa River and has that out-in-the-middle-of-nowhere feeling. It's adjacent to a golf course and includes a boat ramp, children's playground, duck pond, sand volleyball courts, softball field and hiking trails. The picnic sites are secluded, well shaded grassy areas. Fishing is allowed with a California fishing license.

- **RESERVE:** At least 2 weeks in advance.
- **CAPACITY:** 4 sites accommodating 60–120 people.

Picnic Site	Capacity	Large BBQs	Small BBQs	Tables
Pines	80	1	—	8
Redwood	80	1	—	8
Mulberry 1	120	1	—	12
Mulberry 2	60	—	1	6

- **FEES & DEPOSITS:** The reservation fee is $30 for Pines, Redwood and Mulberry 2, $55 for Mulberry 1, plus $55 for all sites for non-Napa residents. There is also a $50–75 refundable security deposit for events which don't include alcohol. This increases to a flat $200 deposit for events including alcohol. The security deposit is due immediately on booking with the fee balance due 30 days in advance of the event.
- **RESTRICTIONS:** Music is allowed within reasonable sound limits.
- **AVAILABILITY:** Year-round, from sunup to sundown.

Monticello Cellars   **707/253-2802**

4242 Big Ranch Road, off Oak Knoll   *Picnic Sites*
Contact: Chris or Linde   *1 picnic site*

Monticello Cellars has a private, secluded garden encircled by a lattice enclosure called "The Grove". Picnickers will like the shade trees that surround the perimeter and the rose garden which is located at one end of the garden. Guests can sample different varietals in the tasting room or stroll around the site. A centerpiece of this winery is the Jefferson House, which was designed after Tom Jefferson's home, Monticello.

- **RESERVE:** 1 month in advance.

- **CAPACITY:**

Picnic Site	*Capacity*	*Large BBQs*	*Small BBQs*	*Tables*
Site 1	100	1	—	10

- **FEES & DEPOSITS:** There is a $5/person use charge, which includes a tour, wine tasting and use of the reserved picnic area. Catering can be arranged.

- **RESTRICTIONS:** Monticello prefers that only their wines are consumed on the premises. No other form of alcohol is allowed. Music may require prior approval.

- **AVAILABILITY:** Year-round, 10am–4:30pm.

Pine Ridge Winery   707/253-7500

5901 Silverado Trail, Yountville Crossroads
Contact: Carla Johnson, Events Manager

Picnic Sites
1 picnic site

The picnic area at Pine Ridge is nestled among pine trees surrounded by lawns, and offers a fantastic view of the vineyards. The winery also features a barbecue, outdoor stage, hiking path, swing sets, cave tours and wine tasting.

- **RESERVE:** Up to 2 months in advance.

- **CAPACITY:**

Picnic Site	*Capacity*	*Large BBQs*	*Small BBQs*	*Tables*
Site 1	48	1	—	8

- **FEES & DEPOSITS:** The facility use fee is $2.50/person, which includes a tour of the caves and barrel tasting. Catering can be arranged, costs ranging up to $30/person, depending on the menu selected. A 25% deposit is due on booking, with the balance due the day of the event.

- **RESTRICTIONS:** Non-amplified music is allowed by arrangement.

- **AVAILABILITY:** The tasting room is open 11am–5pm, but hours for evening picnics can be arranged.

Skyline Wilderness Park   707/252-0481

2201 East Imola Avenue, 4th Street

Picnic Sites
1 picnic site

Here you'll find more than thirty-five miles of hiking, bicycling and equestrian trails. Fishing for bass and bluegill is allowed in Lake Marie, which is surrounded by 850 acres of parkland. There are spectacular views of San Francisco from the park's ridges on clear days.

- **RESERVE:** Available on a first-come, first-served basis.

- **CAPACITY:**

Picnic Site	*Capacity*	*Large BBQs*	*Small BBQs*	*Tables*
Site 1	100	1	—	20

- **FEES & DEPOSITS:** There is a $4 vehicle entry fee into the park. Mountain bikes or horses pulled in a trailer are an additional $1 (for two horses or two bicycles).

- **RESTRICTIONS:** Alcohol and music are allowed within reason.
- **AVAILABILITY:** Year-round. Winter hours are 8am–5pm; summer hours 8am–8pm.

RUTHERFORD

Inglenook Winery   707/967-3362

1991 St. Helena Highway, Rutherford Cross Road
Contact: Ramona Giusti, Events Coordinator

Picnic Sites
1 picnic site

This is an ideal place for groups that would like a more formal, catered event. The impressive, ivy-covered winery buildings are over a hundred years old and are surrounded by expansive, tree-shaded lawns and a large gravel courtyard. The use fee includes a historical tour and wine tasting.

- **RESERVE:** 6 months in advance.
- **CAPACITY:**

Picnic Site	Capacity	Large BBQs	Small BBQs	Tables
Site 1	1,000	—	—	provided

- **FEES & DEPOSITS:** The facility use fee is $20/person. This includes tables, chairs, wine glasses, flowers, wait service and a half bottle of wine. Catering, from an approved list, is an additional $18-20/person. 25% deposit is due on booking; the balance will be invoiced after the event.
- **RESTRICTIONS:** Only Inglenook wines may be consumed on the premises.
- **AVAILABILITY:** April to November. Luncheons are scheduled 11:30am–2pm; dinners starting at 6pm.

Rutherford Hill Winery   707/963-7194

200 Rutherford Hill Road, off Silverado Trail

Picnic Sites
3 picnic sites

Rutherford Hill has a pleasant and peaceful picnic area with three groups sites under native oak trees. The group areas are off to one side of the winery building and can be reserved for exclusive use. There is also a large tasting room and tours can be arranged.

- **RESERVE:** 1 month in advance.
- **CAPACITY:**

Picnic Site	Capacity	Large BBQs	Small BBQs	Tables
Area 1	60	—	—	6
Area 2	70	—	—	7
Area 3	50	—	—	5

■ **FEES & DEPOSITS:** There is a facility use fee of $5/person, which includes a tour and tasting. $10/person includes wine for the picnic. Catering is also available for $22–28/person, depending on the menu chosen. Half the total charges are due as a deposit to confirm the reservation, with the balance due on arrival.

■ **RESTRICTIONS:** Only Rutherford Hill wine may be consumed on the premises, no other alcohol is allowed.

■ **AVAILABILITY:** Year-round, 10am–4:30pm.

ST. HELENA

Crane Park   707/963-5706

Crane & Grayson Avenues   *Picnic Sites*
Contact: Kathleen Carrick, Recreation Director   *2 picnic sites*

Surrounded by vineyards, this ten-acre park features two group picnic areas, ballfields, volleyball, tennis, horseshoes, bocci ball and a children's playground. There are also hiking trails.

■ **RESERVE:** Up to 12 months in advance.

■ **CAPACITY:**

Picnic Site	Capacity	Large BBQs	Small BBQs	Tables
Site 1	80	1	—	8
Site 2	80	1	—	8

■ **FEES & DEPOSITS:** The reservation fee for up to 50 people is $50; 51–100 is $100; over 100 is $150. There is also a $50 refundable cleaning deposit.

■ **RESTRICTIONS:** No music or piñatas.

■ **AVAILABILITY:** Year-round, 6am–10pm.

RustRidge Ranch and Winery   707/965-9353

Hwy 29 to Hwy 128, turn off at Rutherford. Past Lake   *Picnic Sites*
Hennessey, at the Y, turn left on to Chiles & Pope Valley   *1 picnic site*
Rd.; continue 3-1/2 miles to Lower Chiles Valley Rd,
turn right to 2910 Lower Chiles Valley Road

Converted from a thoroughbred horse ranch to vineyards in 1974, this 442-acre facility still raises thoroughbred race horses, as well as producing several varietal wines. Located in the foothills of Napa in the picturesque Chiles Valley, RustRidge is situated at the summit of a narrow valley, with views of rolling vineyards and pastures below. This winery/bed and breakfast is named for the rust hue that colors the ridge of the local hills at sunset.

- **RESERVE:** 2 months in advance.
- **CAPACITY:**

Picnic Site	Capacity	Large BBQs	Small BBQs	Tables
Site 1	200	1	—	20

- **FEES & DEPOSITS:** The use fee is $5–10 per person depending on the type of event. Payment in full is required on the day of the event.
- **RESTRICTIONS:** The winery prefers that only their wines be consumed on the premises. Other types of alcohol by arrangement. There is only 1 restroom, so large groups will need to rent portables.
- **AVAILABILITY:** Year-round, 10am–4pm. Extended hours can be arranged.

St. Clement Vineyards   707/963-7221

2867 St. Helena Highway
Contact: Jennifer Lamb

Picnic Sites
1 picnic site

St. Clement is a landmark building. Painted a lemon yellow and perched atop a knoll above Highway 29, it's hard to miss. Three acres of winery grounds surround this Victorian home, the interior of which has been converted into a lovely tasting room. There are several areas adjacent to the building where catered group picnics can be held. A private tour and tasting can also be arranged.

- **RESERVE:** At least 1 week in advance.
- **CAPACITY:**

Picnic Site	Capacity	Large BBQs	Small BBQs	Tables
Site 1	65	—	—	provided

- **FEES & DEPOSITS:** There is a $30/person use fee, which includes round tables, linens, chairs, and flowers. The winery will provide a list of approved caterers, or groups can arrange their own. However, the winery requires that the food must be in keeping with the wines served, and caterers not on the approved list must meet with the winery staff in advance. A private tour and tasting is $5/person.
- **RESTRICTIONS:** Only St. Clement wines can be consumed on the premises.
- **AVAILABILITY:** May–September, 10am–4pm.

V. Sattui Winery   707/963-7774

1111 White Lane, off Highway 29
Contact: Robert O'Malley
(see entry in Event Locations section for more information)

Picnic Sites
1 picnic site

V. Sattui is a family-owned winery that started over a hundred years ago, and it's still operated by the 4th generation of the founding family. Set further back on the site is a massive stone building reminiscent of California's early wineries. It's surrounded by two acres of tree-shaded picnic grounds and thirty-five acres of vineyards. The tasting room and gourmet deli are in front, right off Highway 29, and are ringed by lush green lawns, oak trees and beautiful roses. Picnic tables are scattered about for informal picnicking. Although food and beverages are sold through the deli, wines can be purchased only at the winery.

■ **RESERVE:** 2 weeks in advance. Reservations are accepted for group picnics on weekdays only from March to October, and every day from November to February. Otherwise, the very popular picnic area is available on a first-come, first-served basis.

■ **CAPACITY:**

Picnic Site	Capacity	Large BBQs	Small BBQs	Tables
Site 1	150	1	—	12*

■ **FEES & DEPOSITS:** Catered, European-style buffet lunch picnics are available, $15–20/person. This includes a selection of domestic and imported cheeses, meats, fruit, salads, fresh-baked French bread and wine. The winery also conducts a private tour of the facility and wine tasting which is included in the use fee. *Additional tables are provided as needed for large groups.

■ **RESTRICTIONS:** Only V. Sattui wines may be consumed on the premises. Music is allowed within reasonable sound limits.

■ **AVAILABILITY:** November to February, 9am–5pm. March to October, 9am–6pm.

White Sulphur Springs   707/963-8588

3100 White Sulphur Springs Road, follow Spring   *Picnic Sites*
Street from downtown   *1 picnic site*
Contact: Betty or Buzz Foote

Not far from downtown St. Helena in a secluded canyon, is California's first and oldest resort. Established in 1852, White Sulphur Springs is composed of eight white cottages, an inn, small hotel and lodge. A creek meanders through the site and there are actually warm sulphur pools available to guests. Further up the canyon, are rustic wood picnic tables and chairs, wrought-iron benches and barbecues plus a log foot-bridge to Indian Meadow, another picnic area. The Resort can accommodate a variety of outdoor activities including volleyball, basketball, horseshoes, badminton, croquet and hiking a trek to year-round waterfalls is a treat.

■ **RESERVE:** 2 months in advance.

■ **CAPACITY:**

Picnic Site	Capacity	Large BBQs	Small BBQs	Tables
Site 1	250	1	—	30

■ **FEES & DEPOSITS:** Rental fees for use of the picnic area are $6/person, Sunday through Thursday, $12/person, Friday and Saturday. Catering is BYO or picnic lunches are available, from $8/person and barbecues from $13. A 50% deposit is required at booking. The balance is due on arrival. Fees and deposits are non-refundable.

■ **RESTRICTIONS:** The restrooms are not wheelchair accessible.

■ **AVAILABILITY:** March–November, 10am–10pm.

YOUNTVILLE

Lake Hennessey, Conn Dam Picnic Area   707/257-9529

1000 Sage Canyon Road, off Silverado Trail
City of Napa Parks and Recreation Department

Picnic Sites
1 picnic site

Located right on Lake Hennessey, this shaded, rustic picnic area is adjacent to volleyball, horseshoe pits and a small playground.

- **RESERVE:** 2 weeks in advance.
- **CAPACITY:**

Picnic Site	*Capacity*	*Large BBQs*	*Small BBQs*	*Tables*
Site 1	65	1	—	8

- **FEES & DEPOSITS:** No fees are required. Fishing is allowed on the lake with a valid California Fishing License and there is a $1 one-day fee for a fishing permit.
- **RESTRICTIONS:** none
- **AVAILABILITY:** Memorial Day–Labor Day, weekends and holidays only.

Yountville City Park   707/944-8851   City of Yountville

Corner of Washington and Lincoln, off Madison

Picnic Sites
1 picnic site

The main elements of this park are a huge lawn area and large children's playground with all new equipment.

- **RESERVE:** First-come, first-served.
- **CAPACITY:**

Picnic Site	*Capacity*	*Large BBQs*	*Small BBQs*	*Tables*
Site 1	100	1	—	8

- **FEES & DEPOSITS:** No fees are required.
- **RESTRICTIONS:** No alcohol sales are permitted. A permit is required for amplified music, obtainable at no charge from City Hall.
- **AVAILABILITY:** Year-round, during daylight hours.

CLOVERDALE

City Park   707/894-2521

482 West 2nd Street, off Jefferson   *Picnic Sites*
Contact: Diana Edwards, Cloverdale City Hall *1 picnic site*

City Park is a well-maintained, old-fashioned park with expansive lawn areas and huge, oak shade trees. Facilities include a large barbecue pit, stage area, horseshoe pits, softball field and children's playground.

- ■ **RESERVE:** 3 months in advance during the summer months.
- ■ **CAPACITY:**

Picnic Site	*Capacity*	*Large BBQs*	*Small BBQs*	*Tables*
Site 1	600	1	—	50

- ■ **FEES & DEPOSITS:** Groups must complete a reservation form, which can be obtained by calling or visiting City Hall. Use fees for the group picnic area are being updated now, call for details.
- ■ **RESTRICTIONS:** No alcohol sales are permitted. Amplified music requires approval by the chief of police.
- ■ **AVAILABILITY:** Year-round, 9am–10pm.

Yorty Creek at Lake Sonoma   707/433-9483

Hot Springs Road, at Highway 101   *Picnic Sites*
Contact: Gloria Malone   *1 picnic site*

Yorty Creek meanders into the north end of Lake Sonoma. The group picnic area borders a pleasant beach for swimming and launching small boats, and features covered eating areas, complete with running water.

- ■ **RESERVE:** Available on a first-come, first-served basis.
- ■ **CAPACITY:**

Picnic Site	*Capacity*	*Large BBQs*	*Small BBQs*	*Tables*
Site 1	200	—	1	12

- ■ **FEES & DEPOSITS:** No fees are required.
- ■ **RESTRICTIONS:** Dogs must be on leash. Amplified music is not allowed.
- ■ **AVAILABILITY:** Year-round, from dawn to dusk.

COTATI

Helen Putnam Park   707/792-4600

Myrtle Avenue, corner of Park & Myrtle
Contact: Sarah Anna

Picnic Sites
1 picnic site

Perfect for sports-minded picnickers, Helen Putnam's six acres make up a quiet, out-of-the-way neighborhood open space. The group picnic site is a large, partially shaded lawn area adjacent to soccer and softball fields, and a children's playground.

- **RESERVE:** Available on a first-come, first-served basis.
- **CAPACITY:** The park can accommodate groups of 100, although there is very limited picnic table seating available.

Picnic Site	Capacity	Large BBQs	Small BBQs	Tables
Site 1	100	—	—	5

- **FEES & DEPOSITS:** There is no charge to use the picnic area.
- **RESTRICTIONS:** Alcohol is not permitted.
- **AVAILABILITY:** Year-round during daylight hours.

La Plaza Park   707/792-4600

Corner of Old Redwood Highway and West Sierra
Contact: Sarah Anna

Picnic Sites
1 picnic site

Located in downtown Cotati, La Plaza Park is actually four neighboring open spaces bisected by city streets. One of the four sections is the group picnic area which has a large lawn shaded by tall trees. The site also features a bandstand and a children's playground.

- **RESERVE:** At least 1 month in advance.
- **CAPACITY:** The park can accommodate 200 people, although there is very limited picnic table seating.

Picnic Site	Capacity	Large BBQs	Small BBQs	Tables
Site 1	200	—	—	5

- **FEES & DEPOSITS:** Groups must contact City Hall and pay a $60 refundable cleaning deposit plus $15 for use of the bandstand and electricity. Groups must also provide a certificate of liability insurance for $1 million.
- **RESTRICTIONS:** Alcohol is not permitted.
- **AVAILABILITY:** Year-round, during daylight hours.

FORESTVILLE

Mark West Vineyards   707/544-4813

7010 Trenton-Healdsburg Road near River Road
Contact: Eunice

Picnic Sites
1 picnic site

Mark West Vineyards offers lovely grounds with gorgeous views of surrounding vineyards. There are many trees and an open lawn area for casual get-togethers. Tours of the vineyard, on foot or by horse and carriage, can be arranged. Visitors who request it, can see the Vineyard's carnivorous plant greenhouse.

- **RESERVE:** 2 months in advance.
- **CAPACITY:** The facility can accommodate groups up to 150 people.

Picnic Site	Capacity	Large BBQs	Small BBQs	Tables
Site 1	150	1	—	16

- **FEES & DEPOSITS:** Catering is BYO or can be arranged. The use fee for bringing your own food is negotiable. For catered picnics, the cost is $15–20/person. All fees are due 2 weeks in advance of the event.
- **RESTRICTIONS:** Mark West is a bonded winery. Wine can be purchased from the tasting room; no other alcohol is permitted.
- **AVAILABILITY:** Year-round, 10am–5pm.

GEYSERVILLE

Alexander Valley Fruit & Trading Co.   800/433-1944

5110 Highway 128 at Alexander Valley Road
Contact: Laurie, Dae or Steve

Picnic Sites
1 picnic site

Quiet and secluded, Alexander Valley Fruit & Trading Co. is a mix of winery, gourmet shop and tasting room. Surrounded by vineyards in a rural area, it is off the beaten path. This family-owned facility feels comfortable and homey. You can sample different food products and wines in the Tasting Room, and outdoor vineyard walks with the winemaker can be arranged. The group picnic lawn sits atop a hill with vineyard views, and is partially shaded by persimmon and walnut trees.

- **RESERVE:** At least 1–6 months in advance.

■ **CAPACITY:**

Picnic Site	Capacity	Large BBQs	Small BBQs	Tables
Site 1	80	1	—	12

■ **FEES & DEPOSITS:** For groups providing their own catering, there is a $5 fee per person. Catering can be arranged through the facility for $15–20/person, depending on the menu chosen. Half of the charges are due when the reservation is confirmed, with the balance due on the day of the picnic.

■ **RESTRICTIONS:** none

■ **AVAILABILITY:** Year-round, 10am–5pm.

Trentadue Winery   707/433-3104

19170 Geyserville Avenue, off Independence
Lane exit from Highway 101
Contact: Susan Foster

Picnic Sites
1 picnic site

Trentadue is located in the heart of the serene and exquisite Alexander Valley, twenty minutes from Santa Rosa. Framed by acres of vineyards, this family-owned winery provides a bucolic outdoor setting for informal get-togethers. A majestic weeping willow and latticed vine-covered arbors provide shade during summer months and an expansive lawn is ringed by blooming flowers, redwoods and maples. The picnic area has a large grassy area where a variety of games can be arranged, a stage area and space for dancing. Private tours of the winery can be arranged and kitchen facilities are available for catered events or for groups bringing in their own food. Barbecues are not available, but groups can BYO.

■ **RESERVE:** 2 months in advance.

■ **CAPACITY:**

Picnic Site	Capacity	Large BBQs	Small BBQs	Tables
Site 1	300	—	—	9

■ **FEES & DEPOSITS:** There is a flexible fee structure for groups using picnic tables. Call the winery for details. For groups renting the facility for a more elaborate event, there is a $150 minimum rental fee. In addition, there is a $13/person fee for 100–300 people for the Chardonnay Special Events Plan (linen tablecloths and wine glasses provided), or $15/person fee for the Champagne Special Events Plan (linen tablecloths, napkins, china, silverware, cups, saucers and wine glasses provided).

■ **RESTRICTIONS:** This is a bonded winery: only Trentadue wines may be consumed on the premises. No other alcohol is allowed.

■ **AVAILABILITY:** Year-round, 8am–9pm. The tasting room is open daily.

Warm Springs Dam, Lake Sonoma   707/433-9483

3333 Skaggs Springs Road near Dry Creek Road,
west off Highway 101

Picnic Sites
Day Use 1 • Day Use 2 • Day Use 3

Famous for its fish hatchery, Warm Springs draws visitors from all over the Bay Area and the Wine Country. There's a Visitor Center which offers a remarkable look at how hatcheries work, and really interesting tours of the facility are enjoyed by children and adults, alike. Outdoors, two of the facility's picnic areas are covered; the third is in a grove of trees. Nearby, there are forty miles of hiking trails and a bicycle loop trail.

■ **RESERVE:** For summer months (April 1 to September 30), suggested timeframe 30–60 days in advance by mail. During winter months (October 1 to March 31), reservations will be taken by phone.

■ **CAPACITY:**

Picnic Site	Capacity	Large BBQs	Small BBQs	Tables
Day Use 1	200	1	—	10
Day Use 2	200	1	—	10
Day Use 3	200	1	—	10

■ **FEES & DEPOSITS:** Applications are sent by mail, and must be returned with a $25/day use fee. Only cashier's checks or money orders are accepted. Reservations are confirmed on a first-come, first-served basis once the completed application and fee are received. There is no fee for the winter months.

■ **RESTRICTIONS:** Amplified music is not allowed. Dogs must be on leash.

■ **AVAILABILITY:** Year-round, from dawn to dusk. The Visitor Center is open Thursdays through Mondays, 9:30am–5pm.

GLEN ELLEN

Sonoma Valley Regional Park   707/527-2041

13630 Sonoma Highway, Hwy 12

Picnic Sites
1 picnic site

This rural regional park is entirely oak woodland, and features hiking and bicycling trails and an attractive lawn area. The picnic site is set on a hillside, well shaded by huge oak trees and adjacent to a grassy field large enough to be used for most athletic activities.

■ **RESERVE:** Reservations are accepted from January 1 for that year and early reservations are suggested for summer months.

■ **CAPACITY:**

Picnic Site	Capacity	Large BBQs	Small BBQs	Tables
Site 1	40	—	1	15

■ **FEES & DEPOSITS:** Permits are required for groups, and fees are based on group size. The fees are: $15 for 25–50 people; $20 for 51–100 people; $25 for 101–150 people. There is also a refundable cleaning deposit required for groups over 50. For 50–100 people it is $50; for 101–150 people it is $75. For groups of over 150 people, the fee is $30 and the cleaning deposit is $100. There is also a $1 fee/car, and groups are required to carry liability insurance of $1 million.

■ **RESTRICTIONS:** Alcohol is allowed at present but that may change. Amplified music is not allowed.

■ **AVAILABILITY:** Year-round, from dawn to dusk.

GUERNEVILLE

Armstrong Redwoods State Reserve   707/869-2015

17000 Armstrong Woods, off Highway 116

Picnic Sites
1 picnic site

This 728-acre reserve features a magnificent ancient redwood grove, including the tallest and oldest trees remaining in this part of California. The Parson Jones tree is 310 feet tall; the Colonel Armstrong tree is 1,400 years old. There are acres of hiking trails, including the Discovery Trail—a braille trail for the visually impaired. There is also a large outdoor amphitheater.

■ **RESERVE:** Up to 1 year in advance. The group picnic area is also available on a first-come, first-served basis, if it hasn't been reserved.

■ **CAPACITY:**

Picnic Site	*Capacity*	*Large BBQs*	*Small BBQs*	*Tables*
Site 1	150	1	1	15

■ **FEES & DEPOSITS:** The use fee is $165, payable with a permit application. An application can be obtained by writing or calling the park.

■ **RESTRICTIONS:** Amplified music is not allowed.

■ **AVAILABILITY:** Year-round, from 8am to 1 hour past sunset.

F. Korbel & Brothers   707/887-2294

13250 River Road, near Odd Fellows Road
Contact: Barbara Newman

Picnic Sites
Redwood Deck • Redwood Grove

Groups will be delighted with Korbel's two picnic areas. One is a shady, redwood deck bordered by tall trees along the perimeter, with wonderful views of the vineyards. The other is a sun-dappled clearing amid towering redwoods. Korbel has a tasting room where groups can sample and purchase sparkling wines and champagnes. Deli food is also available.

- **RESERVE:** Available on a first-come, first-served basis. Reservations are not accepted.
- **CAPACITY:** The facility can accommodate a total of 50 people.

Picnic Site	Capacity	Large BBQs	Small BBQs	Tables
Redwood Deck	24	—	—	6
Redwood Grove	30	—	—	7

- **FEES & DEPOSITS:** There's no charge to use the picnic facilities. Group tours of the winery are available by reservation and payment of a $50 refundable deposit.
- **RESTRICTIONS:** Barbecues are not permitted. Groups can bring in alcohol or purchase wine and champagne in the tasting room. Music is sometimes allowed by special arrangement.
- **AVAILABILITY:** Year-round, 9am–5pm.

Midway Beach   707/869-0501

15045 River Road, between Rio Nido and
 Guerneville
Contact: Susie or Carol

Picnic Sites
1 picnic site

Midway Beach will make you feel like you're in another world. This is a secluded two and a half acre park and beach located on the tree-laden banks of the Russian River. Midway Beach's group picnic area is a large lawn set 200 feet back from the river, with attractive views of the surrounding countryside. The park also offers good swimming areas, a snack bar, two pro sand volleyball courts and seasonal salmon fishing. You may bring your own barbecues.

- **RESERVE:** 1 month in advance.
- **CAPACITY:**

Picnic Site	Capacity	Large BBQs	Small BBQs	Tables
Site 1	2,000	—	—	6

- **FEES & DEPOSITS:** There is no charge for groups.
- **RESTRICTIONS:** Dogs must be on leash and under owner's control; 5MPH speed limit; no glass containers (alcohol is allowed).
- **AVAILABILITY:** May to October, 6:30am–10pm.

Surrey Inn   707/869-2002

16590 River Road near downtown Guerneville
Contact: Dawn
(see entry in Event Locations section for more information)

Picnic Sites
1 picnic site

Less than two blocks from the center of town, this Russian River resort offers terrific facilities for outdoor functions. Totally private and enclosed by tall redwoods, the Surrey Inn is a three-and-a-half-acre enclave featuring a pool, pool house with changing rooms and lawns. For more active guests, there are tennis courts, basketball, horseshoes and volleyball. Play equipment for restless youngsters is also provided.

- **RESERVE:** 2–3 months in advance.
- **CAPACITY:** Outdoor spaces can accommodate up to 1,000 people.

Picnic Site	Capacity	Large BBQs	Small BBQs	Tables
Site 1	700–1,000	1	—	—

- **FEES & DEPOSITS:** A non-refundable $500 security deposit is required. The rental fee is $500 for up to 100 guests, $2,000 for 500, and $4000 for 1,500 people if indoor spaces are reserved.
- **RESTRICTIONS:** No loud, amplified music. Liability insurance is required.
- **AVAILABILITY:** Year-round, 6am–2am.

HEALDSBURG

Alderbrook Winery   707/433-9154

2306 Magnolia Drive
Contact: Kathy Mooney

Picnic Sites
1 picnic site

A 63-acre ranch was purchased in 1981 and transformed into Alderbrook Winery. Surrounded by fifty-five acres of estate vineyards, the Winery has a relatively new, but old-fashioned-looking gray building with broad verandas and railings, painted in contrasting white. Wide porches have great views of the surrounding vineyards and hillsides, and one side faces a magnificent line of Lombardy Poplar trees that turn colors in the fall. Several picnic tables are available on the porches and others are next to the building. The tasting room is open daily.

- **RESERVE:** 1 month in advance.
- **CAPACITY:**

Picnic Site	Capacity	Large BBQs	Small BBQs	Tables
Site 1	80	—	—	10

- **FEES & DEPOSITS:** There is a flexible fee structure depending on the event and the number of guests.
- **RESTRICTIONS:** Beer or hard liquor cannot be brought onto the premises and Alderbrook prefers that groups purchase their wines here.
- **AVAILABILITY:** Year-round, 10am–5pm.

Belvedere Winery   707/433-8236

4035 Westside Road, central Healdsburg exit off
Highway 101
Contact: LaVonne Holmes

Picnic Sites
1 picnic site

Belvedere features a lovely lawn area and flower garden with picnic tables nestled in the redwoods, as well as a large redwood deck with additional tables and chairs and expansive views of the surrounding hills. The tasting room is also open daily. Catering is available by arrangement with Belvedere's in-house chef.

- **RESERVE:** 2 weeks in advance.
- **CAPACITY:**

Picnic Site	Capacity	Large BBQs	Small BBQs	Tables
Site 1	50	—	—	7

- **FEES & DEPOSITS:** There is a flexible fee structure depending on the size of the group and length of time they reserve the picnic area. The minimum charge is $2.50/person.
- **RESTRICTIONS:** The winery requests that only Belvedere wines be consumed on the premises. Music is allowed within reasonable sound limits.
- **AVAILABILITY:** Year-round, 10am–4:30pm.

Field Stone Winery   707/433-7266

10075 Highway, Chalk Hill Road
Contact: Roger Hull

Picnic Sites
Back Area • Front Area

Field Stone Winery has two beautiful picnic areas under native oak trees, with views of the surrounding vineyards and hills. There are two large barbecue pits in the front picnic area and groups may bring their own barbecues for use in the back area.

- **RESERVE:** At least 6 months in advance for summer weekends.
- **CAPACITY:**

Picnic Site	Capacity	Large BBQs	Small BBQs	Tables
Back Area	125	—	—	20
Front Area	50	1	—	8

- **FEES & DEPOSITS:** The basic charge is $3/person and the winery will provide tablecloths and wine glasses. If large groups would like to reserve the whole winery for a weekend day, there is a minimum charge of $1,000.
- **RESTRICTIONS:** Field Stone is bonded only for wine, which can be purchased at discount in the tasting room. Beer or other alcohol is not permitted. Music is allowed within reasonable sound limits.

■ **AVAILABILITY:** Year-round, 10am until dark. The tasting room, featuring award-winning estate bottled wines, is open 10am–5pm.

Giorgi Park   707/431-3301

University and Piper Streets   *Picnic Sites*
Contact: Lori Moore, Parks & Recreation Department   *1 picnic site*

Giorgi Park is a neighborhood open space surrounded by large, shady oak trees. The park has ballfields, horseshoe pits, and tennis, volleyball and bocci ball courts. A large playground is being constructed and will be available by the summer of 1993.

■ **RESERVE:** 60 days ahead for the summer months.

■ **CAPACITY:**

Picnic Site	Capacity	Large BBQs	Small BBQs	Tables
Site 1	75	—	5	10

■ **FEES & DEPOSITS:** No fees or permits are required unless a group wants exclusive use of the facility. For that, a permit will be required, which is arranged through the Parks and Recreation Department. The permit fee for Healdsburg residents is $50; for non-residents it's $200.

■ **RESTRICTIONS:** Alcohol is not permitted and no amplified music is allowed.

■ **AVAILABILITY:** The park is open year-round, daily.

Rodney Strong Vineyards   707/431-1533

11455 Old Redwood Highway, at Eastside Road   *Picnic Sites*
Contact: Bill Holland or Susan Grand   *1 picnic site*

Rodney Strong features an attractive picnic area in a nice winery setting. Picnics are held on a large lawn partially shaded by olive trees and surrounded by the vineyards. The tasting room is open daily.

■ **RESERVE:** 3 months in advance.

■ **CAPACITY:**

Picnic Site	Capacity	Large BBQs	Small BBQs	Tables
Site 1	550	1	—	6*

■ **FEES & DEPOSITS:** The charge to rent the picnic area is $100/ hour. Catering costs vary depending on the caterer and menu chosen. *Tables and chairs, in addition to the picnic tables, can be rented at an extra cost. Half of the deposit is required when reservations are made; the balance is due the day of the event.

■ **RESTRICTIONS:** Only Rodney Strong wines can be consumed on the grounds. Catering must be arranged from an approved list provided by the winery.

■ **AVAILABILITY:** Year-round, 10am–5pm.

Villa Chanticleer   707/431-3301

1248 North Fitch Mountain Road   *Picnic Sites*
(see entry in Event Locations section for more information)   *1 picnic site*

This unique seventeen-acre facility is nestled in the hills above Healdsburg. Originally established in 1910 as an exclusive vacation resort, it's now owned by the City of Healdsburg and has been remodeled for public use. The redwood tree picnic setting is pleasant, quiet and cool. There is an outdoor area for food preparation, with counters and sink plus a playground. Adjacent to the Villa are hiking trails.

■ **RESERVE:** This is a popular site. Reserve 6–12 months ahead for the summer months.

■ **CAPACITY:**

Picnic Site	*Capacity*	*Large BBQs*	*Small BBQs*	*Tables*
Site 1	250–300	2	—	30

■ **FEES & DEPOSITS:** There is no fee for weekday use by local non-profit organizations; non-profits are charged $25 for weekend use. The use fees for groups are $50 for Healdsburg residents; $200 for non-residents. A use permit is required, arranged through the Parks & Recreation Department.

■ **RESTRICTIONS:** Alcohol is allowed for an additional $50 fee. Smoking is allowed outside; amplified music is not permitted.

■ **AVAILABILITY:** Year-round, 8am to sundown.

KENWOOD

Morton's Warm Springs   707/833-5511

1651 Warm Springs Road, Highway 12   *Picnic Sites*
                                                 11 picnic sites

Morton's Warm Spring's twenty acres includes two swimming pools with lifeguards on duty and a children's wading pool, changing rooms, lockers and showers. Fresh mineral water is pumped daily into the pools. The facility also has two volleyball courts, regulation softball field with batting cage, basketball court, ping-pong tables, video game arcade, and horseshoe pits. Nearby hiking, bicycling and jogging trails are abundant.

■ **RESERVE:** At least 6 months in advance for weekends.

■ **CAPACITY:** 11 group picnic areas for 50–700 people. The facility, all areas combined, can accommodate up to 2,400 people.

Picnic Site	Capacity	Large BBQs	Small BBQs	Tables
Area 1 Upper Lawn	50–80	—	—	8
Oak Upper	90–125	2	—	15
Oak Lower	90–125	2	—	15
Lower Lawn	50–80	1	—	10
Creekside	50–75	2	—	10
North Creekside	75–125	2	—	10
Back Area 1	75–100	1	—	12
Back Area 2	50–80	1	—	10
Back Area 3	200–400	2	—	45
Back Area 4	350–700	2	—	80
Back Area 5	75–100	1	—	12

■ **FEES & DEPOSITS:** The fee structure is based upon the number of people guaranteed on the reservation contract: 50–199 people, $3.75 each; 200–499 people, $3.50 each; 500+ guests, $3.25 each. Any additional guests will be charged at the group rate and no-shows will not be refunded or credited. A 60% deposit is required with the contract and the balance is due prior to the group's departure. The entire resort can also be reserved exclusively for $5,000. Catering can be arranged. Groups using a caterer other than Morton's, are charged an additional 50 cents/person for labor/maintenance costs. In case of cancellation, written notice must be received at least 45 days prior to the reserved date or the deposit will be forfeit, unless the group reschedules or the reserved area can be rebooked.

■ **RESTRICTIONS:** Glass bottles are not permitted.

■ **AVAILABILITY:** May and September, open weekends and holidays. June, July and August, open every day except Monday. Resort hours are 10am–7:30pm weekends and holidays, 10:30am–6pm weekdays.

Oreste's Golden Bear   707/833-2327

1717 Adobe Canyon Road, off Highway 12
Contact: George Grant or Adrian

Picnic Sites
1 picnic site

Located just off Highway 12, Oreste's is nestled on the slope of Hood Mountain and is approached from a lovely sun-dappled country road. This is where mineral springs, a pond and cascading Sonoma Creek made the original "Golden Bear" rustic lodge a popular place in the 1920s for hunters and fishermen. This is a pretty and private creekside setting within 35 acres of park-like grounds. The site offers a huge 40-foot stone barbecue and shaded terraces which hug the edge of rocky Sonoma Creek. During summer months the creek is dammed to form pools, next to which guests can enjoy a catered picnic.

■ **RESERVE:** Up to 1 year in advance for weekend events.

■ **CAPACITY:**

Picnic Site	Capacity	Large BBQs	Small BBQs	Tables
Creekside Terrace	300	1	—	35*

■ **FEES & DEPOSITS:** Catering is provided at $19.50–30.00/ person, and includes BBQ, salad, dessert, and coffee. Wine is $10/carafe, and beer is $2–2.50/glass. *Tables and chairs are provided as needed.

■ **RESTRICTIONS:** Amplified music is not allowed. Disabled access is restricted to the outdoor patio area.

■ **AVAILABILITY:** Oreste's is closed January 1–February 14. Otherwise, it's open 9am–4:30pm.

Wine Country Wagons   707/833-2724

---

510 Kenilworth Road, off Warm Springs Road and Mervyn   *Picnic Sites*
Contact: Pat Alexander   *1 picnic site*

The special feature of Wine Country Wagons is a two and a half hour horse-and-wagon ride with stops at three wineries for tasting, followed by a five-course catered picnic in a beautiful meadow. The picnic area has a huge maple tree at its center, and is surrounded by maples and California pepper trees which provide a wonderful, leafy canopy overhead. A stream runs through the meadow. Music can be arranged or groups can bring their own. Electricity is available. Volleyball and horseshoes can be arranged.

■ **RESERVE:** At least 1 month in advance.

■ **CAPACITY:**

Picnic Site	Capacity	Large BBQs	Small BBQs	Tables
Site 1	60	1	—	10

■ **FEES & DEPOSITS:** The charge is $50/person. A 50% deposit is required to hold the date; the balance is due on arrival. Glasses and corkscrews are provided.

■ **RESTRICTIONS:** Alcohol is not provided with the picnic, although wine can be purchased during the winery tours.

■ **AVAILABILITY:** May–October. The wagon ride starts at 10am and the picnic is usually over by 2:30pm.

PENNGROVE

Eagle Ridge Winery   **707/664-9463**

---

111 Goodwin Avenue. Take the Penngrove exit off Hwy
101, left on Goodwin Ave. which is at the intersection
of Ely Road and Petaluma Blvd.
Contact: Sue Phillippi

Picnic Sites
1 picnic site

The historic winery building at Eagle Ridge was the location of the first commercial creamery in
Sonoma and is a registered County Landmark. Situated on a hill overlooking the beautiful Petaluma
Valley, it commands a spectacular view of the Sonoma Mountains. Eagle Ridge is a small, family-
operated winery, specializing in fine premium wines. It has lots of picnic tables, a lawn area, barbecue,
large grape arbor and a redwood deck which extends into the vineyard. There is ample parking and
access for handicapped and seniors.

- ■ **RESERVE:** 6 months in advance.
- ■ **CAPACITY:**

Picnic Site	*Capacity*	*Large BBQs*	*Small BBQs*	*Tables*
Site 1	150	1	—	10

- ■ **FEES & DEPOSITS:** There is a $50/hour charge during the winery's business hours (11am–4pm); $75
per hour before and after. A $100 deposit is requested when reservations are made.

- ■ **RESTRICTIONS:** Only Eagle Ridge wines may be consumed on winery grounds. Non-alcoholic
beverages may be brought in. Amplified music is not allowed.

- ■ **AVAILABILITY:** Year-round, 9am–8pm. The winery's tasting room is open daily, 11am–4pm.

PETALUMA

Garden Valley Ranch   **707/795-0919**

---

498 Pepper Road, off Stoneypoint Road
Contact: Bob Galyean
(see entry in Event Locations section for more information)

Picnic Sites
1 picnic site

Located three miles north of Petaluma, this is the perfect location for lovers of roses, gardening or
horticulture. The seven-acre ranch contains some 4,000 rose bushes cultivated for the sale of the
blooms, and a one-acre garden where fragrant plants are grown for potpourri blends. Several
Victorian-style structures, a manicured lawn and adjacent gardens are available for large functions.

■ **RESERVE:** 6–12 months in advance.

■ **CAPACITY:**

Picnic Site	Capacity	Large BBQs	Small BBQs	Tables
Site 1	200	—	—	25

■ **FEES & DEPOSITS:** Half the use fee is due when reservations are made. The balance and a $400 refundable security deposit are due 2 weeks prior to the event. Rental rates for 4 hours are: $750 for 50 people, $1,350 for up to 200 people. Time needed for setup and cleanup is provided at no charge. Tables, umbrellas, and chairs are available for an extra charge.

■ **RESTRICTIONS:** Catering and alcohol is BYO. Barbecues are not available, but can be brought in.

■ **AVAILABILITY:** May to October, 10am–8pm.

Lucchesi Park   707/778-4380

---

320 North McDowell Blvd.

Picnic Sites
1 picnic site

Lucchesi Park's 31-acres offer picnickers volleyball, basketball, lighted tennis courts and a soccer field. There's also a lake stocked with fish and a children's playground. The group picnic area features a large barbecue pit, tables and lawn area. Restrooms, water, and electricity are available. There is disabled access and the park can be reached by public transportation.

■ **RESERVE:** 6–12 months in advance for the summer months.

■ **CAPACITY:**

Picnic Site	Capacity	Large BBQs	Small BBQs	Tables
Site 1	54	1	—	8

■ **FEES & DEPOSITS:** A permit is required to reserve the group picnic area. The Parks Department prefers that applicants obtain permits in person, although they will mail out the application if there is a large distance involved. The completed permit must be accompanied by a $100 refundable deposit.

■ **RESTRICTIONS:** A $500,000 liability insurance policy is required with the City of Petaluma as an additional insured. No glass containers. Amplified music is allowed until 10pm within reasonable volume limits.

■ **AVAILABILITY:** Year-round, from dawn to dusk.

Marin French Cheese Company   707/762-6001

7500 Red Hill Road, on the Petaluma-Point Reyes Road, one mile South of Novato Blvd.
Contact: Jim or Julie

Picnic Sites
Front Area • Rear Area

Well known for its Rouge et Noir and Camembert cheeses, the Marin French Cheese Company has been has been at this location for 128 years. In addition to a well-stocked deli with beverages and different foods, it offers two picnic sites (restricted to non-profit groups, clubs and customers) in a pleasant country setting. The front area has an open lawn equipped with barbecue. The rear area is a grassy field surrounded by trees. Volleyball nets are available, and the Cheese Company offers hourly tours from 10am–4pm.

■ **RESERVE:** Reservations are accepted from January 1 for that year. This is a popular spot, so early reservations are recommended.

■ **CAPACITY:**

Picnic Site	Capacity	Large BBQs	Small BBQs	Tables
Front Area	50	1	—	10
Rear Area	100–150	2	—	25

■ **FEES & DEPOSITS:** No use fee is required. Groups using the large barbecue need to complete a picnic reservation form.

■ **RESTRICTIONS:** The group area is only available to non-profits, clubs and customers. Wines and food can be purchased in the Cheese Company store. Music is allowed within reasonable sound limits.

■ **AVAILABILITY:** Year-round, 9am–5pm. The Cheese Company offers tours every hour 10am–4pm.

McNear Park   707/778-4380

F & 11th Street

Picnic Sites
1 picnic site

McNear Park is a seven and a half acre park with baseball and soccer fields, and lighted softball field and tennis courts. There is also a playground, fishing, and limited walking trails. The group picnic area has a large barbecue pit, tables, and lawn areas. Restrooms, water and electricity are available. There is disabled access, and the park can be reached by public transportation.

■ **RESERVE:** 6–12 months ahead for the summer months.

■ **CAPACITY:**

Picnic Site	Capacity	Large BBQs	Small BBQs	Tables
Site 1	200	1	—	25

■ **FEES & DEPOSITS:** A permit is required to reserve the group picnic area. The Parks Department prefers that applicants obtain permits in person, although they will mail out the application if there is a large distance involved. The permit must be accompanied by a $100 refundable deposit.

■ **RESTRICTIONS:** The Parks Department requires a $500,000 liability insurance policy, naming the City of Petaluma as an additional insured. Alcohol is permitted, no glass containers, and amplified music until 10pm.

■ **AVAILABILITY:** Year-round, from dawn to dusk.

Swim Center   707/778-4380

900 East Washington Street, Highway 101   *Picnic Sites*
Contact: Christine, Parks & Recreation Department   *1 picnic site*

Conveniently located right off of Highway 101, the Swim Center has a 50–meter outdoor swimming pool and a pleasant picnic area. The picnic site is a poolside lawn, partially shaded by large magnolia trees.

- ■ **RESERVE:** At least 2 weeks in advance. 3 months in advance is recommended.
- ■ **CAPACITY:**

Picnic Site	*Capacity*	*Large BBQs*	*Small BBQs*	*Tables*
Site 1	300	—	1	—

- ■ **FEES & DEPOSITS:** A $100 deposit is required to confirm the reservation, plus a $50/hour (or more) use fee depending on the size of the group and number of lifeguards required.
- ■ **RESTRICTIONS:** A $1 million liability insurance policy is required.
- ■ **AVAILABILITY:** From Memorial Day through Labor Day.

ROHNERT PARK

Alicia Park   707/584-7357

300 Arlen Drive, off Commerce Blvd.   *Picnic Sites*
City of Rohnert Park Recreation Department   *1 picnic site*

This is a five-acre neighborhood park with ballfields, horseshoe pits, a playground and two lighted tennis courts. There are also swimming and wading pools (with outdoor showers) open from Memorial Day weekend through Labor Day. The picnic site is a lawn area with several tables and a barbecue and is reservable by Rohnert Park residents only.

- ■ **RESERVE:** At least 1 month in advance for weekends. Reservations are accepted starting March 1 for the year.
- ■ **CAPACITY:**

Picnic Site	*Capacity*	*Large BBQs*	*Small BBQs*	*Tables*
Site 1	200	1	—	10

- ■ **FEES & DEPOSITS:** There is no charge to reserve the group picnic area. Reservations must be made in person at the Recreation Department, 5401 Snyder Lane, 8:30am–4:30pm, Monday–Friday.
- ■ **RESTRICTIONS:** Open to Rohnert Park residents only. Alcohol is allowed, no glass bottles, and liability insurance is required for groups of over 100 if serving alcohol. A permit is required for music.
- ■ **AVAILABILITY:** Year-round, sunup to sundown.

Benecia Park   707/584-7357

7469 Bernice, Southwest Blvd. and Burton Avenue

Picnic Sites
1 picnic site

Active picnickers will appreciate this is a six-acre park. It has two softball fields, and a swimming pool with three meter diving board and showers. The pool is open from Memorial Day weekend through Labor Day. The picnic site is an open, lawn area with tables and a barbecue, reservable by Rohnert Park residents only.

- **RESERVE:** At least 1 month in advance for weekends. Reservations are accepted starting March 1 for the year.
- **CAPACITY:**

Picnic Site	*Capacity*	*Large BBQs*	*Small BBQs*	*Tables*
Site 1	200	1	—	11

- **FEES & DEPOSITS:** There is no charge to reserve the group picnic area. Reservations must be made in person at the Recreation Department, 5401 Snyder Lane, 8:30am–4:30pm, Monday–Friday.
- **RESTRICTIONS:** Open to Rohnert Park residents only. Alcohol is allowed, no glass bottles, and liability insurance is required for groups of over 100 if serving alcohol. A permit is required for music.
- **AVAILABILITY:** Year-round, sunup to sundown.

Dorotea Park   707/584-7357

895 Santa Dorotea Circle, off Country Club Drive

Picnic Sites
1 picnic site

This is a six-acre park with a baseball field, night-lighted basketball court, two night-lighted tennis courts and practice backboard, horseshoe pits and a children's playground. The group picnic site is a grassy area with several tables and two barbecues, reservable by Rohnert Park residents only.

- **RESERVE:** At least 1 month in advance for weekends. Reservations are accepted starting March 1 for the year.
- **CAPACITY:**

Picnic Site	*Capacity*	*Large BBQs*	*Small BBQs*	*Tables*
Site 1	200	—	2	7

- **FEES & DEPOSITS:** There is no charge to reserve the group picnic area. Reservations must be made in person at the Recreation Department, 5401 Snyder Lane, 8:30am–4:30pm, Monday–Friday.
- **RESTRICTIONS:** Open to Rohnert Park residents only. Alcohol is allowed, no glass bottles, and liability insurance is required for groups of over 100 if serving alcohol. A permit is required for music.
- **AVAILABILITY:** Year-round, sunup to sundown.

SANTA ROSA

Chateau DeBaun Winery	707/571-7500

5007 Fulton Road	*Picnic Sites*
Contact: John Burton	*1 picnic site*
(see entry in Event Locations section for more information)	

Chateau DeBaun is an impressive French chateau-style winery, surrounded by acres of vineyards and walnut trees. The winery has a spacious courtyard patio, framed by roses, which faces orchards. The winery will set up a private tasting in the Meadow for picnic groups and can help arrange catering.

- **RESERVE:** 1 month in advance.
- **CAPACITY:**

Picnic Site	*Capacity*	*Large BBQs*	*Small BBQs*	*Tables*
Site 1	700	1	1	14

- **FEES & DEPOSITS:** There is a flexible fee structure depending on the event.
- **RESTRICTIONS:** Alcohol is negotiable. Music is allowed.
- **AVAILABILITY:** Year-round, from 11am to 1 hour before sundown.

Cloverleaf Ranch	707/545-5906

3890 Old Redwood Highway at	*Picnic Sites*
Mendocino/Old Redwood Highway	*1 picnic site*

Imagine having your next company picnic in a Western ghost town, complete with buildings, stagecoach and wagons. This 200-acre ranch has that and more: a lake, swimming pool, tennis and volleyball courts, softball field and horseshoes. Kayaking, canoeing and fishing are allowed on the lake and swimming is allowed in both the lake and pool. The facility provides sports equipment, and guided horseback rides can be arranged along nearby trails. Catering is BYO or the facility will provide a list preferred caterers.

- **RESERVE:** 6 months in advance.
- **CAPACITY:**

Picnic Site	*Capacity*	*Large BBQs*	*Small BBQs*	*Tables*
Site 1	500	1	—	40

- **FEES & DEPOSITS:** Up to 100 people, use fees are $12/person; 101–200, $10/person; over 200, $8/person. A $250 deposit is due when you make reservations; the balance is due the day of the event. Trail rides cost $18/person.
- **RESTRICTIONS:** Beer and wine are allowed. Other alcohol requires a special license. Groups must

provide a certificate of insurance for $1 million, naming the facility as an additional insured.

■ **AVAILABILITY:** March to mid-June and September to the end of November; specific hours by arrangement.

Coopers Grove Ranch   707/571-1928

5763 Sonoma Mountain Road, off Presley
Contact: Madeline Turner

Picnic Sites
1 picnic site

Set on 75 acres of rolling hills, this ranch offers panoramic views of the surrounding countryside. Picnics can be held on open lawns or in secluded redwood groves. The ranch also offers a swimming pool, pond (with rowboat) and creeks, flower gardens, hiking trails and a volleyball court.

■ **RESERVE:** 6 months in advance.

■ **CAPACITY:**

Picnic Site	Capacity	Large BBQs	Small BBQs	Tables
Site 1	200	—	3	4

■ **FEES & DEPOSITS:** The use fee for picnic areas is $400–600, depending on the number of people in the group. A 50% deposit is required when booking, with the balance due on arrival.

■ **RESTRICTIONS:** There are only 2 small barbecues and 4 picnic tables available—additional barbecues and tables have to be brought in. Groups need to rent portable restrooms, as none are available for outdoor events. Smoking is not allowed.

■ **AVAILABILITY:** Year-round, hours by arrangement.

Doyle Park   707/524-5115

Sonoma Avenue

Picnic Sites
1 picnic site

Although located in downtown Santa Rosa, Doyle Park still manages to offer picnickers a secluded feeling. This open space has large trees and a seasonal creek. Active groups will like the ballfields, basketball courts, horseshoes and a children's playground.

■ **RESERVE:** Santa Rosa residents may reserve 1 year in advance; non-residents 90 days.

■ **CAPACITY:**

Picnic Site	Capacity	Large BBQs	Small BBQs	Tables
Site 1	200	1	1	20

■ **FEES & DEPOSITS:** A permit is required to rent the group picnic area. Call the Parks Department first to check availability, then go to the Community Center at 415 Steele Lane to fill out a permit. An $11 non-refundable processing fee is due with the completed permit. A $50 refundable deposit is due for corporate picnics, and with music, an additional $50 deposit is required.

■ **RESTRICTIONS:** Alcohol is allowed, no glass containers. Amplified music is allowed within reason.

■ **AVAILABILITY:** The park is open year-round, 6am–9pm, April through October; 6am–6pm, November through March.

Finley Park   707/524-5115

Stonypoint Road

Picnic Sites
1 picnic site

This new 27-acre park is mostly open space, with lots of large lawns that can accommodate group picnics. Activities include a playground, horseshoes, volleyball and tennis courts.

■ **RESERVE:** Santa Rosa residents may reserve 1 year in advance; non-residents 90 days.

■ **CAPACITY:**

Picnic Site	*Capacity*	*Large BBQs*	*Small BBQs*	*Tables*
Site 1	150–200	1	—	20

■ **FEES & DEPOSITS:** A permit is required to rent the group picnic areas. Call the Parks Department first to check availability, then go to the Community Center at 415 Steele Lane to fill out a permit. An $11 non-refundable processing fee is due with the completed permit. A $50 refundable deposit is due for corporate picnics, and with music, an additional $50 deposit is required.

■ **RESTRICTIONS:** Alcohol is allowed, no glass containers. Amplified music is allowed within reason.

■ **AVAILABILITY:** The park is open year-round, 6am–9pm, April through October; 6am–6pm, November through March.

Galvin Community Park   707/524-5115

Yulupa Avenue (cross streets)

Picnic Sites
1 picnic site

This is a beautiful eighteen-acre park with twelve lighted tennis courts, softball fields, and two fly casting ponds. The group picnic area includes three separate pavilions, each accommodating fifty people. The Parks Department will reserve the entire group area for groups of 100 or more.

■ **RESERVE:** Santa Rosa residents may reserve 1 year in advance; non-residents 90 days.

■ **CAPACITY:** *Picnic Site*	*Capacity*	*Large BBQs*	*Small BBQs*	*Tables*
Site 1	150–200	1	—	20

■ **FEES & DEPOSITS:** A permit is required to rent the group picnic areas. Call the Parks Department first to check availability, then go to the Community Center at 415 Steele Lane to fill out a permit. An $11 non-refundable processing fee is due with the completed permit. A $50 refundable deposit is due for corporate picnics, and with music, an additional $50 deposit is required.

- **RESTRICTIONS:** Alcohol is allowed, no glass containers. Amplified music is allowed within reason.

- **AVAILABILITY:** The park is open year-round, 6am–9pm, April through October; 6am–6pm, November through March.

Howarth Memorial Park   707/524-5115

Summerfield Road

Picnic Sites
1 picnic site

Howarth has it all. This popular park has a group picnic site situated under trees and surrounded by lawn. There are lighted tennis courts, ballfields, pony rides, hiking and biking trails and a playground. A petting zoo and lake are additional amenities. Picnickers can also fish or rent boats.

- **RESERVE:** Santa Rosa residents may reserve 1 year in advance; non-residents 90 days.

- **CAPACITY:**

Picnic Site	*Capacity*	*Large BBQs*	*Small BBQs*	*Tables*
Site 1	200	1	1	20

- **FEES & DEPOSITS:** A permit is required to rent the group picnic areas. Call the parks Department first to check availability, then go to the Community Center at 415 Steele Lane to fill out a permit. An $11 non-refundable processing fee is due with the completed permit. A $50 refundable deposit is due for corporate picnics, and with music, an additional $50 deposit is required.

- **RESTRICTIONS:** Alcohol is allowed, no glass containers. Amplified music is allowed within reason.

- **AVAILABILITY:** The park is open year-round, 6am–9pm, April through October; 6am–6pm, November through March.

Oak Hill Ranch   707/528-6498

3485 Porter Creek Road

Picnic Sites
1 picnic site

Eight miles off Highway 101 at the River Road
exit and four miles from Calistoga.
Contact: Penny Swerengin

Oak Hill Ranch sits on 400 acres in the mountains between Santa Rosa and Calistoga. The large picnic area is enhanced by a swimming pool, showers, sand volleyball court, archery, and a billiard room. There is a commercial kitchen available for groups bringing in outside caterers. Catering is available from the Ranch, and Oak Hill will provide white linens and fresh flowers for the tables. Ice and large coolers are also provided to groups renting the picnic facility.

- **RESERVE:** Reserve by January for the summer months. This is a popular spot.
- **CAPACITY:**

Picnic Site	Capacity	Large BBQs	Small BBQs	Tables
Site 1	350	1	—	25

- **FEES & DEPOSITS:** The day use fee for the first 50 people in any size group, is $10/person. For 51–100 people the fee is $8/person; for over 100 people the fee is $7/person. Catering is available at $10–15/person depending on the menu chosen. Groups wishing to use the stage area pay a $300 refundable damage deposit. Full payment is required 1 week before the event.

- **RESTRICTIONS:** none

- **AVAILABILITY:** Year-round, 8am–5pm; longer hours by arrangement.

Spring Lake Regional Park   707/539-8092

5390 Montgomery Drive
End of Newanga Avenue

Picnic Sites
Upper Jack Rabbit • Lower Jack Rabbit • Oak Knolls

Spring Lake is a 72-acre lake with a three-acre, fully staffed swimming lagoon featuring a concession stand and boat rentals. The surrounding 329-acre park consists of rolling oak woodlands which support a bike path and miles of hiking trails. Spring Lake's three picnic areas are quiet, wooded spaces with limited views of the lake.

- **RESERVE:** 12 months in advance for a minimum of 20 people at Upper Jack Rabbit; 25 minimum at Lower Jack Rabbit and Oak Knolls.
- **CAPACITY:**

Picnic Site	Capacity	Large BBQs	Small BBQs	Tables
Upper Jack Rabbit	65–75	—	1	8
Lower Jack Rabbit	150	1	—	20
Oak Knolls	120	1	—	15

- **FEES & DEPOSITS:** A permit is required to reserve the group picnic areas. You can ask for a permit application by mail. Return the completed application with a deposit of $15 for groups under 50 people; $20 for groups of 50–150 people. The reservation deposit is non-refundable and a refundable cleaning and security deposit may be required. There is a $3 entrance fee/vehicle.

- **RESTRICTIONS:** Amplified music is not allowed. Dogs must be on a 6-foot leash.

- **AVAILABILITY:** Year-round, from sunrise to sunset.

SEBASTOPOL

Ragle Ranch Regional Park   707/527-2041

500 Ragle Road, Covert Road and Highway 12

Picnic Sites
Gazebo • Volleyball Area • Large Picnic Area

Since there is no community park nearby, Ragle Ranch is a popular site for local sports activities. This regional open space has a nature study area and a peace garden. The area near the park's entry consists of soccer and baseball fields and volleyball courts, next to which is a small picnic area. Beyond the athletic fields, is the main group picnic area, situated on lawns and shaded by large oaks. The gazebo area has nice views.

■ **RESERVE:** Reservations are accepted from January 1 for that year. This is a popular park so reserve early for the summer months.

■ **CAPACITY:** The facility can accommodate 150 people, maximum.

Picnic Site	Capacity	Large BBQs	Small BBQs	Tables
Gazebo	50	1	—	6
Volleyball Area	50	—	1	5
Large Group Area	150	1	—	20

■ **FEES & DEPOSITS:** Permits are required for groups, and use fees are based on group size. Use fees: $15 for 25–50 people; $20 for 51–100 people; $25 for 101–150. There is also a refundable cleaning deposit required for groups of over 50. For 50–100 people it is $50; for 101–150 people it is $75. For groups of over 150 people, the fee is $30 and the cleaning deposit is $100. There is also a $1 fee/car, and groups are required to carry liability insurance of $1 million.

■ **RESTRICTIONS:** Alcohol is allowed at present, but that may change. Amplified music is not allowed.

■ **AVAILABILITY:** Year-round, from dawn to dusk.

SONOMA

Agua Caliente Springs   707/996-6822

17350 Vailetti Drive, Highway 12
Contact: Nino Vailetti

Picnic Sites
1 picnic site

Located in the countryside a few miles from Sonoma, the main feature at Agua Caliente is the natural mineral water, which fills three swimming pools and a jacuzzi. (The water in the pools is changed daily.) There is also a large, partially shaded lawn with tables and barbecue, available for poolside picnics.

- ■ **RESERVE:** 1 month in advance.
- ■ **CAPACITY:**

Picnic Site	Capacity	Large BBQs	Small BBQs	Tables
Site 1	500	1	1	100

- ■ **FEES & DEPOSITS:** $7/person for up to 50 people; $6.75/person for 51–100 people; $6/person for over 100 people. A $100 deposit is required to hold the reservation.
- ■ **RESTRICTIONS:** Music is allowed within reasonable volume limits.
- ■ **AVAILABILITY:** April 1–September 30, 10am–6:30pm.

Bartholomew Memorial Park   707/938-2244

19013 Old Winery Road, Lovall Valley

Picnic Sites
1 picnic site

Groups of fifty or more can have exclusive use of Bartholomew Park. Docent-led tours of the restored villa are available. Buena Vista Winery, which has a very pleasant tasting room, is close by.

- ■ **RESERVE:** 2 weeks in advance.
- ■ **CAPACITY:**

Picnic Site	Capacity	Large BBQs	Small BBQs	Tables
Site 1	60	—	—	10

- ■ **FEES & DEPOSITS:** No use fee is required.
- ■ **RESTRICTIONS:** Music is prohibited. Barbecues are not permitted on the premises because of the fire danger.
- ■ **AVAILABILITY:** Year-round on Wednesdays, Saturdays and Sundays only, 10am–4pm.

Buena Vista Winery   707/938-1266

18000 Old Winery Road, Lovall Valley
Contact: Patti Poole or James Patrick, Events
Coordinator
(see entry in Event Locations section for more information)

Picnic Sites
1 picnic site

This winery is generally acknowledged as the birthplace of premium wines in California. The Old Winery building, built in 1857, is a striking two-story stone structure located in a cool clearing of eucalyptus, redwoods and lush greenery. In front of the building is a large paved courtyard, dotted with huge, old wine kegs. Dappled sunlight from the tall canopy of trees provides a comfortable and relaxing atmosphere for outdoor picnics. The winery will provide a preferred list of musicians and

DJs. They will also provide a list of preferred caterers, although groups can bring their own food.

- ■ **RESERVE:** 1–6 months in advance depending on the season and group size.
- ■ **CAPACITY:**

Picnic Site	Capacity	Large BBQs	Small BBQs	Tables
Site 1	150	—	—	100

- ■ **FEES & DEPOSITS:** The cost is $5–7/person, and includes a tour and private tasting. Groups will also receive a discount card allowing them a 15% discount on wine purchases.
- ■ **RESTRICTIONS:** No outside alcohol can be brought in; groups can buy Buena Vista wines on the premises. There are no barbecue grills on winery grounds.
- ■ **AVAILABILITY:** The winery is open 10am–5pm, year-round. Picnics can be scheduled during those hours and evenings after 6:30pm by arrangement.

Maxwell Farms Regional Park   707/539-8092

Highway 12 & El Verano, (cross streets)

Picnic Sites
1 picnic site

Maxwell Farms offers a large, grassy picnic site with neat rows of trees and an adjacent playground. The park also has several large soccer and baseball fields and an expansive green lawn.

- ■ **RESERVE:** Up to 1 year in advance for the summer months.
- ■ **CAPACITY:**

Picnic Site	Capacity	Large BBQs	Small BBQs	Tables
Site 1	100	—	1	8

- ■ **FEES & DEPOSITS:** Use applications are by mail or phone. The fee is due with the completed application: $15 for up to 50 people; $20 for 51–100. There is also a $1 entry fee/vehicle. A use permit and cleaning deposit is required for bands.
- ■ **RESTRICTIONS:** There is no parking immediately adjacent to the group picnic area and disabled access is restricted.
- ■ **AVAILABILITY:** Year-round, sunrise to sunset.

WINDSOR

Keiser Park   707/838-1000

7000 Windsor River Road, one block east of Starr Road

Picnic Sites
1 picnic site

This is a 20-acre park with a beautiful native oak grove where picnics can be held on native grasses among the trees. The park also includes an outdoor stage, an athletic field and a playground.

- **RESERVE:** 2 months in advance.
- **CAPACITY:**

Picnic Site	Capacity	Large BBQs	Small BBQs	Tables
Site 1	200	1	1	20

- **FEES & DEPOSITS:** A permit is required. Call and request an application. Once that is returned, the use fees will be determined and a deposit will be requested. The permit is issued once the deposit is received. Fees are based on group size and whether you have a non-profit or for-profit organization. Non-profits pay $20 for 51–100 people. The fee increases in $5 increments to $35 for groups of up to 200. For-profits pay $20 for 51–100 people, up to $55 for 200. A cleaning/damage deposit is also required, which ranges $50–250 depending on group size.

- **RESTRICTIONS:** General liability insurance is required in the amount of $1 million, naming the Town of Windsor as an additional insured. Alcohol is prohibited in the park.

- **AVAILABILITY:** Year-round, 7am to dusk.

Windsor Waterworks & Slides   707/838-7760

8225 Conde Lane, Highway 101
Contact: Edie

Picnic Sites
several picnic sites

This facility offers several group picnic sites surrounding their waterslides. Some of the areas are lawns with tall shade trees, others have tables and barbecues. In addition to the four waterslides, swimming pool and toddler pool, the waterworks offers volleyball, horseshoes and a playground.

- **RESERVE:** 2 months in advance.
- **CAPACITY:**

Picnic Site	Capacity	Large BBQs	Small BBQs	Tables
Group Areas	1,500	1	1	200

- **FEES & DEPOSITS:** For groups under 200, use fees for the entire facility, including water slides, is $10.25/person for adults, $9.95 for children ages 2–12 (minimum height required 48".) Fees for use of the picnic areas and swimming pools are $3.95/adults, $2.95/children ages 2–12. Call for group rates .

- **RESTRICTIONS:** Alcohol is allowed, no glass containers or live music.

- **AVAILABILITY:** May to September, 10am–7pm.

APTOS

Aptos Village Park	408/462-8333

100 Aptos Creek Road off of Soquel Ave.

Picnic Sites
1 picnic site

This is a lovely, small public park which has an emerald, green lawn surrounded by a low white fence. It's set in a bowl, encircled by tall redwoods and pines. There's a small clubhouse in the park plus a gazebo and children's playground. Quiet and peaceful, Aptos Village Park is a favorite for local group picnics.

- **RESERVE:** You can reserve up to 2 weeks in advance, but 45 days' notice is preferable.
- **CAPACITY:**

Picnic Site	Capacity	Large BBQs	Small BBQs	Tables
Site 1	200	1	—	12

- **FEES & DEPOSITS:** A use permit is required. The fee is $62/hour or $405 for 8 hours.
- **RESTRICTIONS:** Beer and wine consumption only in picnic areas. No animals or vehicles on park grounds.
- **AVAILABILITY:** Year-round, daily 10am–dusk.

BEN LOMOND

Highlands House and Park	408/462-8333

8500 Highway 9
(see entry in Event Locations section for more information)

Picnic Sites
Site A • Site B

The Highlands House, built in the 1930s as a residence, is now the centerpiece of Highlands Park. The two-story white house and grounds sit quite a way below Highway 9, ensuring quiet and a sense of privacy. The setting is lovely with expansive lawns, huge magnolia and pine trees, well-maintained landscaping and a small pool.

- **RESERVE:** Reservations can be made 45 days in advance.
- **CAPACITY:** The house and grounds combined, up to 500 people.

Picnic Site	Capacity	Large BBQs	Small BBQs	Tables
Site A	100	1	—	8
Site B	100	1	—	8

- **FEES & DEPOSITS:** A use permit is required and a $50–100 deposit for an alcohol permit. Use fees range from $62–89, depending on group size, residency or nonprofit status. There's a parking fee from May–October of $2/car and the pool can be rented for $22.50/hour. All fees are made when finalizing reservations.

- **RESTRICTIONS:** No amplified music. Dogs must be on leash. Alcohol requires a permit.

- **AVAILABILITY:** Year-round, 9am–dusk.

FELTON

Roaring Camp   408/335-4484

The intersection of Graham Hill Road and
Roaring Camp Road.
Contact: Jeanette
(see entry in Event Locations section for more information)

Picnic Sites
8 separate picnic areas

Deep in the heart of the Santa Cruz Mountains is one of America's last steam-powered, daily-operated passenger railroads. This narrow gauge steam train runs through forests of giant redwoods and over steep grades and switchbacks to Bear Mountain. Large group picnics are their specialty and can include chuckwagon barbecues, famous moonlight train parties and square dancing. For the sports-minded, there are horseshoe pits, volleyball and softball fields.

- **RESERVE:** Reservations can be made 2 weeks–6 months in advance.

- **CAPACITY:** 2,000 people can be accommodated in 8 separate picnic areas. The minimum for group rental is 25 people.

Picnic Site	Capacity	Large BBQs	Small BBQs	Tables
8 areas combined	up to 2,000	3	—	50*

- **FEES & DEPOSITS:** Vehicle parking costs $3/car. Use fees for the group picnic areas are: 75 people, $100; 150 people, $200; and 250 people, $350. Functions can be catered in-house, and final prices will depend on picnic packages selected. If you select a package event, parking will be included in the price. *Tables and chairs will be provided as needed if you host a catered event here.

- **RESTRICTIONS:** Dogs must be on leash. No amplified music.

- **AVAILABILITY:** Year-round, daily dawn–dusk.

SANTA CRUZ

Delaveaga Park   408/429-3663

Branciforte Drive at Highway 1

Picnic Sites
Lone Tree • Cathedral Grove • Twisted Tree •
Three Willows • Forty Thieves

This is an enormous park, encompassing over 550 acres. There are five group picnic areas, with parking and restrooms nearby. Delaveaga also has a golf course, driving and archery ranges and three children's play areas. A creek runs through the site during rainy months.

- **RESERVE:** Reservations can be made 12 months in advance.
- **CAPACITY:**

Picnic Site	Capacity	Large BBQs	Small BBQs	Tables
Lone Tree	180	2	—	18
Cathedral Grove	225	2	—	22
Twisted Tree	225	2	—	25
Three Willows	250	2	—	25
Forty Thieves	100	1	—	10

- **FEES & DEPOSITS:** A use permit is required. For exclusive use of the park, the use fee is $700/day with a $250 deposit. All day use fees for residents: Lone Tree $135, Cathedral Grove $95, Twisted Tree $55, Three Willows $95 and Forty Thieves $ 95. Non-resident use fee is an additional $10/day.
- **RESTRICTIONS:** Alcohol is only allowed in group picnic areas. A sound permit is required for amplified music; dogs must be on leash.
- **AVAILABILITY:** Year-round, daily 9am–9pm.

Harvey West Park   408/429-3663

314 Evergreen Street at intersection
of Highways 1, 9 and 17

Picnic Sites
Evergreen • Oak • Buckeye • Wagnor Grove

Harvey West Park is fully equipped to handle group functions. Featuring a swimming pool, football stadium, soccer field, railroad train with antique steam engine and a museum, it has something for everyone. There are gardens surrounded by tall redwoods and four large picnic areas for groups, most with parking and restrooms nearby.

- **RESERVE:** Reservations can be made 12 months in advance.
- **CAPACITY:** If you rent the entire park, up to 3,000 people.

Picnic Site	Capacity	Large BBQs	Small BBQs	Tables
Evergreen	300	3	—	30

Oak	108	1	—	10
Buckeye	50	1	—	5
Wagnor Grove	100	2	—	10

■ **FEES & DEPOSITS:** A use permit is required. For exclusive use of the park, the use fee is $1,250/day with a $250 deposit. All-day use fees for residents: Evergreen $135, Oak $95, Buckeye $55 and Wagnor Grove $95. Non-resident use fee is an additional $10/day.

■ **RESTRICTIONS:** Alcohol is only allowed in group picnic areas. A sound permit is required for amplified music; dogs must be on leash.

■ **AVAILABILITY:** Year-round, daily 9am–9pm.

Harvey West Park: Friendship Gardens   408/429-3663

Harvey West Blvd.

Picnic Sites
Friendship • Upper Glen • Herb Garden •
Bay • Overlook

Five group picnic areas are available, of which four are handicap accessible. Picnickers will find large lawn areas, barbecues and nice vistas.

■ **RESERVE:** Reservations can be made 12 months in advance.

■ **CAPACITY:**

Picnic Site	Capacity	Large BBQs	Small BBQs	Tables
Friendship	90	2	—	9
Upper Glen	90	2	—	9
Herb Garden	24	1	—	2
Bay	30	1	—	2
Overlook	24	1	—	2

■ **FEES & DEPOSITS:** A use permit is required. All-day use fees for residents: Friendship $75, Upper Garden $95, Herb Garden $45, Bay $45 and Overlook $45. Non-resident use fee is an additional $10/day.

■ **RESTRICTIONS:** Alcohol is only allowed in group picnic areas. No amplified music; dogs must be on leash.

■ **AVAILABILITY:** Year-round, daily 9am–9pm.

Santa Cruz Beach Boardwalk Beach Deck   408/423-5590

400 Beach Street at Cliff Street

Picnic Sites
Beach Deck

California's only seaside amusement park offers old-fashioned beach barbecues. From both the upper and lower beach deck, you can smell salt air and feel ocean breezes. Barbecues are set up on the upper deck where food is served. Picnickers move to the lower deck to eat, which offers umbrella-shaded tables and is built right on the beach. During the picnic, groups can sample the Boardwalk's many rides or just relax on the beach. There is shopping galore, restaurants and miniature golf in addition to beach volleyball and sunbathing.

- **RESERVE:** Reservations can be made 12 months in advance. Saturdays are very popular.
- **CAPACITY:** 1,500 on the Beach Deck. Other areas are available for groups over 1,500 people.

Picnic Site	Capacity	Large BBQs	Small BBQs	Tables
Beach Deck	1,500	provided	—	provided

- **FEES & DEPOSITS:** A minimum $1,000 deposit is required when reservations are made. Use fees include food service and range from $23–25/person depending on menu selection. The fee also includes non-alcoholic beverages (beer and wine are available) and unlimited Boardwalk rides. A discounted parking fee is additional.
- **RESTRICTIONS:** No alcohol on the beach, no outside caterers and no pets.
- **AVAILABILITY:** Daily, April–October; call for specific timeframes.

WATSONVILLE

Pinto Lake County Park   408/462-8333

---

757 Green Valley Road

Picnic Sites
Site A • Site B

Pinto Lake Park is a scenic delight and an exceptional bird watching area. Surrounded by Santa Cruz foothills, this is a 183-acre park with open terrain sloping gently down to Pinto Lake, a lovely, natural lake. For group picnics, there are lawn areas and two covered picnic pavilions with large barbecues and individual restrooms. Picnickers will enjoy the fishing pier, athletic fields and miles of hiking trails nearby.

- **RESERVE:** Reservations can be made 45 days in advance. Call Mon–Fri, noon–4pm.
- **CAPACITY:** Each picnic area holds 100 people. If you also rent the athletic fields, up to 500 people.

Picnic Site	Capacity	Large BBQs	Small BBQs	Tables
Sites A & B	100 ea	1 ea	—	10 ea

- **FEES & DEPOSITS:** A use permit is required and a $50–100 deposit for an alcohol permit. Use fees for a 6-hour minimum range from $62–105, depending on group size. There's a parking fee of $2/car. All fees are made when finalizing reservations.
- **RESTRICTIONS:** Dogs must be on leash. No camping allowed.
- **AVAILABILITY:** Year-round, daily 10am–dusk.

MONTEREY

El Estero Park   408/646-3866

At the intersection of Del Monte and
Camino Aguajito Streets

Picnic Sites
1 picnic site

Big eucalyptus trees encircle El Estero's picnic area which has tables and a huge barbecue pit, plus great views of the lake. Picnickers can play volleyball or frisbee on adjacent lawns. Lake Estero is very pretty, and there's a boating concession with paddle boats and canoes for the adventurous and a new fishing pier. This park is close to Fisherman's Wharf and to the huge stretch of lawn that leads to the beach at Monterey Bay Park. For pedestrians, joggers or bicyclists, note that the linkage with the regional trails system is close by. And for kids, the Dennis the Menace park is also adjacent (daily, 10am–dusk), with lots of Dennis the Menace-inspired playthings to absorb the energy of youthful picnickers.

- **RESERVE:** Reservations must be made in person. For summer dates, reserve early—this is a popular spot. If you'd like to rent the ballfield, call 408/646-3880.
- **CAPACITY:**

Picnic Site	Capacity	Large BBQs	Small BBQs	Tables
Site 1	200	1	—	25

- **FEES & DEPOSITS:** A use permit is required but no use fees.
- **RESTRICTIONS:** No amplified music or alcoholic beverages without permit. Dogs must be on leash.
- **AVAILABILITY:** Year-round, daily 6am–10pm. The snack bar is open weekends, year-round, and during the summer, Tue–Sun 11am–5pm.

Laguna Seca   408/755-4899

1025 Salinas Road (Monterey Highway 68)

Picnic Sites
Island • Trackview • Media Center •
Formula One

Home of one of California's favorite race tracks, Laguna Seca is a great spot for very large group picnics before, during or after the races. This is a popular venue for corporate annual picnics because it has the largest group picnic sites in the county. From a two-person intimate picnic on a five-acre island to a 20,000 person company social, Laguna Seca can accommodate everyone. Picnickers can watch the races from three of the four group areas and cook up a storm on huge, brick barbecues. For those less interested in car racing, there's a rifle and pistol range within driving distance plus campgrounds and lake with hiking trails nearby.

■ **RESERVE:** You can reserve up to 12 months in advance.

■ **CAPACITY:**

Picnic Site	Capacity	Large BBQs	Small BBQs	Tables
Island	500–10,000	1	—	700+
Trackview	1,000	1	—	60
Media Center	200	1	—	20
Formula One	50	1	—	5–10

■ **FEES & DEPOSITS:** No permit is required. Vehicle parking is $4/car. Use fees for group areas are: Trackview $150/day, Formula One $35/day, Island $150/day and Media Center $50/day. Payment is due when reservations are confirmed.

■ **RESTRICTIONS:** No alcohol sales. Dogs must be on leash and amplified music requires a permit.

■ **AVAILABILITY:** Year-round, 8am–5:30pm except for Christmas.

Pirate's Cove   408/372-1807

285 Figueroa Street near DelMonte

Picnic Sites
1 picnic site

This is a private picnic facility right on the beach. Pirate's Cove is run by Adventures-by-the-Sea, a professional events organization which provides supervised activities along with theme parties, menus, corporate team building and initiative development programs such as ocean kyaking. Bike tours and rentals are available.

■ **RESERVE:** Reservations can be made 12 months in advance.

■ **CAPACITY:** Indoors in a historic building, 449 people; outdoors 2,000.

Picnic Site	Capacity	Large BBQs	Small BBQs	Tables
Site 1	2,000	2*	2*	12*

■ **FEES & DEPOSITS:** Fees are based on the package selected, group size and menu. Call for details. 90% of the fee is required 30 days in advance of the event. *Tables, chairs and barbecues well be provided as needed for catered events.

■ **RESTRICTIONS:** No outside caterers; all food is provided in-house.

■ **AVAILABILITY:** Year-round, daily 9am–midnight.

MONTEREY/SALINAS

Royal Oaks   408/755-4899

537 Maher Road at Echo Valley Road

Picnic Sites
Acorn • Shady Oak • Live Oak • Hidden Oak

Established in 1966, Royal Oaks is Monterey County's oldest regional park. Just twelve miles from downtown Salinas, this 122-acre park is set in a small valley studded with Coast Live Oaks. It has multiple group areas and large lawns, most surrounded by large oaks and other mature trees, which provide plenty of shade on warm days. Horseshoes, basketball courts, tennis courts, a baseball diamond and children's play area are easily accessible.

■ **RESERVE:** Reservations can be made up to 12 months in advance.

■ **CAPACITY:** If you combine group picnic sites, the total is 900 maximum. Other individual picnic areas are first-come, first-served.

Picnic Site	Capacity	Large BBQs	Small BBQs	Tables
Acorn	200	1	—	22
Live Oak	200	1	—	22
Hidden Oak	200	1	—	22
Shady Oak	300	1	—	25

■ **FEES & DEPOSITS:** No permit is required. The use fee for Live Oak, Hidden Oak and Acorn is $39/day each; Shady Oak $49/day. If you combine areas, just add each area's fees together. Fees must be paid in full when making reservations. There is a $4/car entry fee.

■ **RESTRICTIONS:** A permit is required for amplified music. Alcohol may not be sold. Dogs must be on leash.

■ **AVAILABILITY:** Year-round, daily 8am–5:30pm. Closed Christmas.

Toro County Park   408/755-4899

501 Salinas Road (Monterey Highway 68)
Take Portola Dr. exit off Hwy 68

Picnic Sites
Badger Flats • Sycamore • Quail Meadows •
Buckeye • Oak Grove

Only six miles from downtown Salinas, this 4,756-acre county park is a haven for visitors as well as deer, coyote and a rare mountain lion. Toro's pastoral setting offers five group picnic sites with tables and grills, conveniently located near restrooms and lawn activity areas. Picnickers have access to over twenty miles of riding and hiking trails and spectacular views of the Salinas Valley from higher ground. For outdoor enthusiasts, there is an equestrian staging area, two softball fields, playgrounds, horseshoe pits and volleyball courts.

■ **RESERVE:** Reservations can be made 12 months in advance.

■ **CAPACITY:** 1,500 total if you combine group areas. There are additional sites on a first-come, first-served basis.

Picnic Site	Capacity	Large BBQs	Small BBQs	Tables
Badger Flats	200	1	—	22–25
Sycamore	200	1	—	22–25
Quail Meadows	500	1	—	50–60
Buckeye	500	1	—	50–60
Oak Grove	150	1	—	19–20

■ **FEES & DEPOSITS:** No use permit is required. Vehicle parking costs $4/car. Use fees are $39/day for the group sites that can hold 200 people; $59/day for the sites that can hold up to 500 people. Fees are paid when reservations are confirmed.

■ **RESTRICTIONS:** A permit is required for amplified music. No alcohol sales. Dogs must be on leash.

■ **AVAILABILITY:** Year-round, daily 8am–5:30pm except Christmas.

Need a caterer, cake maker, florist? The Service Directory starting on page 614 features the best in the business.

Perfect Places
Service Directory

The professionals listed in **Perfect Places** *are special.*

They are unequivocally the best in the business—the people I'd recommend to my friends and business associates without hesitation. I personally endorse each individual or company represented in *Perfect Places,* so when you call them, you can feel as confident as I do about their abilities.

How did I find them?

Actually, they found me. Since I don't "advertise" my service directory, they either discovered it by reading one of my guidebooks or heard about it via word-of-mouth. Because they know I only accept the industry's top performers, the really good service providers love our screening process.

I turned away ad dollars! I must be crazy, right?

Not really. It's my way of guaranteeing that you get to choose from only the finest service providers in Northern California—including some who claim they never advertise. Those candidates who received consistent, rave reviews made it into this book. Everyone else was (nicely) turned down.

Getting into Perfect Places *is tough.*

Because I *endorse* the vendors in this publication, I want to feel absolutely sure each one is top-notch. Since one-time satisfied customers are not the best qualified to evaluate my potential advertisers, we require a list of 10–30 *trade* references from each candidate. These are professionals in the events field who have worked with them over time, and are able to assess their level of expertise.

We call every single reference and ask about the professionalism, technical competency and service orientation of the advertisers in question. Each interview takes from 15 to 60 minutes. When you talk to that many people, you get a clear picture of who's doing a superb job and who isn't.

I've done the legwork so you won't have to worry.

I've spent an enormous amount of time putting the highest caliber service providers at your fingertips. If you call the companies and individuals listed in my directory, you'll eliminate a time-consuming search. And, because I've thoroughly checked the reputation of each, you won't have to worry. It's an honor to represent these professionals in *Perfect Places* and a real pleasure to bring the best services in Northern California to your attention.

Full Service Catering

DIFFERENT
BEAUTIFUL
THE BEST

415 - 552 - 8550

Valet Service

**Floral and decorative planning
for all occasions**

**Specializing in Romantic and
European design**

Bouquet preservation

Meeting all your individual needs

Karen Baba

415) 349-7111

By Appointment

Beverage Catering

BARTENDERS UNLIMITED

*distinguished
beverage
catering*

HOSTED AND NO-HOST BAR SERVICES
FOR ALL SPECIAL OCCASIONS.
PLEASE CALL FOR COMPLIMENTARY CONSULTATION.
415 454 3731

est 1979

*serving
all of
California*

Index

DID YOU BORROW THIS BOOK?

If you want your very own copy, order one
directly from Hopscotch Press!

And, if you'd like a copy of *HERE COMES THE GUIDE,*
our 480-page wedding and reception
location guidebook, you can order one, too.
In fact, if you purchase both, we'll make you
a special offer of $5.00 OFF!

☐ _____ YES! I want to receive a copy of *PERFECT PLACES!*

Copies @ $24.00 each
(Includes tax, shipping & handling;
for more than 1 book, add $1.)   Total $_____

☐ _____YES! I want a copy of *HERE COMES THE GUIDE!*

Copies @ $24.00 each
(Includes tax, shipping & handling;
for more than 1 book, add $1.)   Total $_____

☐ _____YES! I want to receive both *HERE COMES THE GUIDE* and
PARTY PLACES!

Both for $40.00 (that's $5.00 off the total, and
includes tax, shipping & handling)   Total $_____

Mail my copies to:

Name_____

Address_____

City, State, Zip_____

Or just call us at 510/525-3379 and order your books over the phone!

HOPSCOTCH PRESS 1563 Solano Avenue, Suite 135 • Berkeley, CA 94707

About the Author

Lynn Broadwell is a marketing professional
for the events industry. Her companies,
Lynn Broadwell & Associates and Hopscotch Press,
provide consulting services, publications and products
which are designed to meet the needs of
both the public and the event professional.
She has been featured in articles, on radio and TV
throughout Northern California.

Hopscotch Press publishes *Perfect Places*
and *Here Comes The Guide.*

Lynn is a graduate of UC Berkeley,
with an undergraduate degree in
landscape architecture and
a masters degree in business.
She lives in the Berkeley Hills with her
husband, Doug, and son, Matthew.